Power and Privilege

A Theory of Social Stratification

Power and Privilege

A Theory of Social Stratification

Gerhard E. Lenski

The University of North Carolina Press
Chapel Hill and London

Library of Congress Cataloging in Publication Data

Lenski, Gerhard Emmanuel, 1924–
  Power and privilege.

  Originally published: New York: McGraw-Hill, 1966.
  Bibliography: p.
  Includes index.
  1. Social classes. 2. Power (Social sciences)
3. Income distribution. I. Title.
HT609.L44   1984   305.5'12   83-26049
ISBN 0-8078-4119-6 (pbk.)

04   9 8 7 6

TO JEAN

Preface to the Paperback Edition

MUCH HAS HAPPENED in sociology and in the other social sciences since *Power and Privilege* was written twenty years ago. Mountains of new data have been assembled and analyzed, more sophisticated techniques of quantitative analysis have been introduced, and theoretical perspectives have changed. Because of these and other developments, it is only fitting on the occasion of the publication of this new paperback edition to ask how the theory presented in *Power and Privilege* has fared in the light of the changes that have occurred.

As author of the volume, I cannot claim to be an unbiased observer. Nor can I claim to be familiar with all of the relevant work of the last two decades. So far as I can judge, however, both the general theory presented in chapters 2, 3, 4, and 13 and the various special theories presented in chapters 5 through 12 have stood the test of time well up to this point. While there are materials I would add and details I would alter if I were starting afresh today, I have not seen anything that persuades me that the basic theory is unsound. The model of relations among constants and variables shown on page 439 still seems to me to be essentially correct, and the same is true of the special theories derived from this more general theory.

Although this may seem an act of self-congratulation, I believe it is rather a consequence of the synthesizing methodology that I employed in the development of the theory (see pages 17 to 22). By building on a foundation laid by others, and by combining inductive and deductive logic in the construction of the theory, I minimized the risks and avoided many of the usual hazards.

Concerning the central question that confronts every theory of social stratification (i.e., who gets what and why?), the most important development of the last twenty years has been the greatly increased accessibility of data on the socialist societies of eastern Europe. These societies are singularly important because they have been the testing ground for many of the important ideas developed by Karl Marx and his followers. For more than half a century, a Marxist elite has enjoyed unchallenged control of the institutional structures of Soviet society and has carried out a series of massive social experiments designed to destroy historic patterns of social inequality and to build in their stead a more egalitarian, socialist society. Similar experiments have been conducted in the satellite societies of eastern Europe that came under Soviet control following World War II. No serious student of social stratification can afford to ignore these experiments or fail to ponder their results.

Unfortunately, Marxist elites were highly secretive about such matters for many years and made it almost impossible to obtain even the most basic kinds of information about life in their societies. Soon after the Revolution, the teaching of sociology and the conduct of sociological research were outlawed. During the long period of Stalin's reign, the situation steadily deteriorated and reliable information became increasingly difficult to obtain (Inkeles, 1950). As late as the 1950s, the best source of information on daily life in Soviet society was the reports of escapees who had fled (cf., Inkeles and Bauer, 1959).

Following Stalin's death in 1953, the situation slowly began to improve. Restraints on novelists were gradually relaxed, and by 1956 sociologists in Poland, such as Stanislaw Ossowski, who had been under house arrest, were again allowed to teach, write, and do research. By the time I was writing *Power and Privilege* in the years from 1962 to 1965, the flow of relevant materials had begun to quicken. Novels, such as Vladimir Dudintsev, *Not By Bread Alone* (1957), Alexander Solzhenitsyn, *One Day in the Life of Ivan Denisovich* (1963), and Fedor Abramov, *The New Life* (1963), were providing far more intimate details on Soviet life than had previously been available, and books and articles by Polish sociologists (e.g., Stephan Nowak, Michal Pohoski, Adam Sarapata, and Wlodzimierz Wesolowski) were providing the first systematic, quantitative data on stratification in a Soviet-style society.

Since the early 1960s, the trickle of information on stratification in the socialist societies of eastern Europe has turned into a flood. During the late 1960s and throughout the 1970s, Polish sociology enjoyed a period of increasing freedom, and Polish sociologists used this opportunity well. In countless surveys and other studies, they explored mobility patterns, attitudes toward social inequality, attitudes toward elites, beliefs concerning social equity, and dozens of other subjects. During this period they were joined in these endeavors by Yugoslav and Hungarian sociologists, and, for a brief period, by Czech sociologists as well.

Thanks to their efforts, and those of journalists and novelists, we know far more today about the outcome of the great social experiments undertaken by Marxist elites than was known twenty years ago. More than that, the passage of another twenty years since the establishment of Marxist control in these societies has provided us with a far better opportunity to judge the effects of Marxist innovations on a population whose earliest socialization was in societies free from the influences of the older capitalist and/or feudal order.

Probably the most important lesson to be learned from these experiments is that human nature is not nearly as malleable, nor as free from inherent tendencies to promote self-interest, as Marx and many other social theorists since the Enlightenment have imagined. Efforts to create "the new socialist man," who puts the needs of society ahead of his own personal needs and desires, have been singularly disappointing. Moral incentives have proven no match for material incentives, and Marxist elites have been compelled—or have chosen—to create an occupational system of stratification that is remarkably similar in many ways to that found in non-Marxist industrial societies.

This is a system in which, as in other systems, the holders of power enjoy innumerable privileges denied to others (Matthews, 1978). It is also a system in which, as one of Poland's leading sociologists has put it,

> the workers are still hired labor. The socialist revolution does not change the relation of the worker to the machine, nor does it change his position within the factory. . . . His relation to the machine and to the organizational system of work requires his subordination to the foreman and the management of the factory. He receives wages according to the quantity and quality of work performed, and he must obey the principles and regulations of work discipline. (Szczepanski, 1970, p. 125)

According to one recent study of occupational prestige, there is a correlation of 0.79 between the Soviet and American systems (Treiman, 1977, table 4.1). Ironically, this is a slightly stronger correlation than that observed between the Soviet and Polish systems.

These are not isolated examples. Other work by Polish sociologists tells of the existence of a dual labor market system that is remarkably similar to one that American sociologists have recently found in this country. As one of Poland's leading students of stratification explains it,

> The development of new, productive, and important sectors of the economy (e.g., heavy and chemical industries) is usually linked to higher wages in these sectors. Therefore, the electrician employed in a textile or foodstuffs factory will earn even less than the electrician employed in a foundry or refinery, even

though their qualifications, as well as the complexity of their work, are identical. (Wesolowski, 1979, p. 126)

Or, finally, it might be noted that a recent study of the causes of income variations in Polish society indicated that the variance was better explained by the sex of workers than by any other single factor (Pohoski, 1978; see also Swafford, 1978, on women's earnings in Soviet society). Little wonder, then, that specialists on the socialist societies of eastern Europe are increasingly coming to the conclusion that these societies are best understood as a variant form of industrial society rather than as some new and unique form in their own right (Jones, 1983).

All this is not to suggest that the massive social experiments undertaken by Marxist elites in eastern Europe have accomplished nothing. As I have written elsewhere (Lenski, 1978), Marxist elites appear to have succeeded in reducing the level of *economic* inequality below that found in non-Marxist industrial societies. But the price they have paid for this appears to have been a much greater degree of *political* inequality. It seems as though substantial limitations on economic inequality can only be achieved and sustained by politically repressive means. Looking back at both the discussion of socialist societies in chapters 10 through 12 and the statement of the general theory in chapters 2, 3, 4, and 13, I find little that I would change on the basis of what has been learned since the mid-1960s concerning the revolutionary socialist societies of eastern Europe.

The one change of theoretical importance that I would make would be the addition of a discussion of the ways in which capitalism, socialism, and communism coexist in modern industrial societies and how variations in the mix of these three elements account for many of the differences among industrial societies. As I have argued elsewhere (Lenski, 1984), the guiding principle in capitalist subsystems is "to each according to his property." In socialist subsystems, the principle is "to each according to his work," and in communist subsystems, "to each according to his need." All three of these principles are operative in American society today. Capital gains, dividends, rents, interest, and entrepreneurial profits are distributed on the basis of ownership of property. Wages, salaries, and commissions are distributed as rewards for work performed. Welfare payments, food stamps, home heating payments, unemployment compensation, disability payments, medicaid, and the income transfer components of social security and medicare, as well as free public education, access to public parks, museums, and other public facilities are provided on the basis of need. Judging from recent governmental data, it appears that approximately 20 percent of the national income in the United States is distributed as rewards for ownership of property, 70 percent as rewards for work, and 10 percent in response to need.

In most of the socialist societies of eastern Europe, there is very little private *ownership* of the means of production, but a small minority of the population exercises effective *control* of such property and often uses that control for its own private benefit. In fact, some western Marxist critics of these societies have accused them of practicing "state capitalism" (Cliff, 1974; Sweezy and Bettelheim, 1971). In any case, this is one of the reasons why the systems of stratification in the societies of eastern Europe do not differ more than they do from those in the so-called "capitalist" societies of the West. By acknowledging explicitly the coexistence of these several principles of distribution in *all* modern industrial societies, I believe we would come closer to explaining the seeming paradox posed by the similarities between the two subsets of industrial societies.

Variations among industrial societies, with respect to the relative strength of the capitalist, socialist, and communist subsystems, are comparable in many ways to the variations among agrarian societies with respect to the relative strength of rulers and governing classes (see pages 231 to 242 below). In both instances, the variations define what appears to be the most important variable dimension of the distributive systems in an important set of societies.

For those who desire a more detailed and current view of stratification in the eastern European societies, there are now a number of excellent books on the subject. These include Mervyn Matthews, *Class and Society in Soviet Russia* (1972), and *Privilege in the Soviet Union: A Study of Elite Life-Styles Under Communism* (1978); Walter Connor, *Socialism, Politics, and Equality: Hierarchy and Change in Eastern Europe and the USSR* (1979); and David Lane, *The End of Social Inequality?: Class, Status and Power Under State Socialism* (1982). In a more popular vein, there is Hedrick Smith, *The Russians* (1976). For the perspectives and insights of eastern Europeans themselves, there are such varied sources as Andrei Amalrik, *Involuntary Journey to Siberia* (1970); Roy Medvedev, *Let History Judge: The Origins and Consequences of Stalinism* (1972); and Wlodzimierz Wesolowski, *Classes, Strata and Power* (1979).

If I were rewriting *Power and Privilege* today, I would add a chapter on the less developed countries of the Third World. This chapter would have two foci: (1) the place of those societies in the global system of stratification, and (2) the system of inequality within the societies themselves.

One of the more important developments in sociological theory in the last twenty years has been the formulation of world-system theory by Immanuel Wallerstein (1974, 1980). Building on foundations laid by Marx, Lenin, and various Latin American proponents of dependency theory, Wallerstein has formulated a theory of societal development that sees the underdevelopment and poverty of the Third World as a necessary consequence of the development and wealth of the First World. In effect, he sees the various nations of the world as participants in a global system of stratification.

According to Wallerstein, a Euro-centered world economy began to take shape in the late fifteenth and early sixteenth centuries, and over the years it has gradually spread until the entire world is now caught up in a single economic system that is governed by the competitive principles of capitalism. In this system, a minority of nations in Europe, North America, Japan, and Australia control most of the critical resources and therefore enjoy most of the benefits. At the opposite extreme, there is a larger number of nations in Africa, Latin America, and much of Asia that control few resources and are exploited by the first set of nations. Between these extremes, there is a third set of nations, especially in east Asia, but in other areas as well, that are more favorably situated than the second set, but much less favorably situated than the first. These three sets of societies are referred to by Wallerstein and others as the core, the periphery, and the semiperiphery, respectively. Their roles and statuses in the world system of stratification correspond to the roles and statuses of the bourgeoisie, the proletariat, and the petite bourgeoisie or new middle class in societal systems of stratification.

No observer of the modern world can fail to acknowledge the existence of the modern world economy and the system of stratification to which it has given rise. On the other hand, as Wallerstein himself has noted, the Euro-centered world economy of the last 500 years is not the first in human history. However, he argues (Wallerstein, 1974, p. 16) that it is the first world economy that has not evolved into a political empire.

While not denying the unique qualities of the modern world system, I would stress, more than Wallerstein does, the fact that inequality among societies has been a basic fact of human life for more than five thousand years. Ever since the first societies made the shift from hunting and gathering to horticulture as their primary means of subsistence, the potential for societal inequality has been present. Moreover, it did not take long before the possibility was transformed into a reality and some societies began to embark on military, political, and economic programs that advanced their own interests at the expense of their neighbors. In short, it seems to me that the ultimate source of the inequality among societies has been technological advance rather than the relatively recent capitalist mode of production.

To some, this may seem an unimportant distinction, but I disagree. It suggests that even if the modern capitalist world economy were destroyed through a global socialist revolution, as Wallerstein hopes will happen, it would be too much to expect that this would bring to an end the era of societal inequality. As we have already seen in the struggles between Russia and China, China and Vietnam, Vietnam and Kampuchea, and in the relations of dominance between Russia and its satellites or Vietnam and its satellites, there is no reason to expect that equality and justice will prevail in relations among socialist societies any more than it prevails within them. Thus, a successful global socialist revolution would change the nature of the system of intersocietal inequality that now exists, but we should not expect that it would bring intersocietal inequality to an end.

If I were analyzing the global system of inequality, I would also want to shift the emphasis in the explanation of the current system. If I understand

Wallerstein and his followers (e.g., Chase-Dunn, 1975; Rubinson, 1976) correctly, they suppose that the status of nations in the modern world system is determined entirely, or at least primarily, by the operation of the capitalist world economy. I would argue that other factors are also involved and are even more important. Recent research (Lenski and Nolan, 1984) has shown, for example, that the technological and economic heritage of modern societies explains more of the variance in societal development and in recent rates of economic growth than is explained by the status of societies in the world economy. Third World nations that practiced plow agriculture prior to contact with modern industrial societies have been far more successful developmentally than societies that practiced hoe and digging-stick horticulture prior to contact.

This is hardly surprising in the light of the theory developed in *Power and Privilege* and expanded later in various editions of *Human Societies* (1970, 1974, 1978, 1982). Plow agriculture is far more productive than horticulture. This has made possible a much larger economic surplus in agrarian societies, and this, in turn, made possible a greatly increased division of labor, greater dependence on monetary systems and a cash economy, greater development of literacy, the growth of the state and state bureaucracies, and other developments well before the first contact with industrial societies. Consequently, modern Third World societies with a tradition of plow agriculture have brought far greater social and cultural resources into the twentieth century than have Third World societies with a horticultural tradition.

It is also no coincidence that these two sets of societies are geographically differentiated (Lenski and Nolan, 1984). In the temperate regions of the world, most horticultural societies were replaced by agrarian societies long ago. In most tropical and semitropical areas, however, this change was not possible prior to the development of modern industrial technology. As William McNeill (1976) has shown, societies in tropical and semitropical areas have been severely handicapped by unusually large and diverse populations of micropredators (i.e., bacteria and viruses) that sap the vitality of human populations and kill off horses and oxen, on which the practice of plow agriculture depends. In addition, tropical and semitropical societies have been handicapped by poorer soils and more serious problems of weed control (Farmer, 1968; Meggers, 1954; Watters, 1960) and in much of the Old World by the absence of navigable rivers and larger waterways, such as the Mediterranean and North seas, that so facilitated the growth of international trade and commerce prior to the invention of modern means of transportation.

Recent research (Nolan, 1983) also indicates that variations in demographic patterns also contribute enormously to variations in rates of societal economic growth—a principle that the post-Maoist leadership of China has also come to recognize in recent years. In brief, it seems to me that Immanuel Wallerstein and other advocates of world system theory have attempted to explain too much on the basis of the capitalist world economy.

Without minimizing its importance, one can see clearly the influence of other factors, several of which appear to be even more important than the modern world economy.

Turning to the systems of inequality that exist *within* Third World societies, there are a number of points that merit attention. To begin with, there is the coexistence of preindustrial and industrial systems of stratification: parts of the populations of these societies occupy statuses whose power, privilege, and prestige are based on resources of the older social order, while other parts occupy statuses whose value is determined by resources derived from the new, industrial order. This often leads to conflict within these societies as each segment of the population strives to protect or advance its own special interests.

Because I have discussed this subject elsewhere (Lenski, 1970; Lenski and Lenski, 1982), there is no need to repeat the details here. Suffice it to say that there are a number of important differences between the systems of stratification in industrializing horticultural and industrializing agrarian societies, reflections of their differing histories. For example, the tribal mode of social organization has survived to the present day in most industrializing horticultural societies. In these societies, tribal membership is still an important social resource and, therefore, the basis of major political struggles. In fact, tribal groups are often the primary basis of party divisions in these societies and their struggles for control of the machinery of government, and the resources it controls are often the central fact of political life (see, for example, the recent histories of Nigeria, Kenya, Uganda, and Zimbabwe, among others). In contrast, tribal groups are either nonexistent in industrializing agrarian societies or are marginal in their political life (see, for example, China, Iran, Vietnam, or Mexico).

Revolutionary movements led by Marxist elites have enjoyed considerable success in most Third World societies, despite the fact that this is not at all what Marx anticipated in his analysis of the trends of history in the nineteenth century. According to the conventional wisdom of our own day, these movements are the responses of oppressed peasant masses to the exploitation of tiny privileged minorities. Although it is obvious that this motivation has been crucial to the success of these movements, at least in industrializing agrarian societies, there is much more to the story. For example, there is nothing new about exploitation in these societies, especially in those with an agrarian past. Nor is there anything new about peasant revolts. This will be clear to anyone who reads chapters 8 and 9 of this volume. The problem, therefore, needs to be restated: it is not enough to ask why there is unrest and revolutionary ferment in so many of these societies. We need, instead, to ask why these revolutionary movements are so much more successful today than in the past.

By rephrasing the question in this way, we gain a number of important insights into the current situation. We discover, for example, that much of the success of these revolutionary movements has been due to their ability to mobilize individuals who are making, or have made, the transition from the older social order to the newer. Much of the leadership of these movements has come from university students and university-educated professionals whose education has sensitized them to the trends of the modern world, its values, and the opportunities it affords. They have become critical of the older elites and impatient with their reluctance to yield control, even when these older elites are their fathers and kinsmen. Thus, what seems to many First World observers to be a simple struggle between a wealthy and oppressive elite and the impoverished masses is usually more complex. Usually, much of the revolutionary elite is recruited from among the sons and daughters of the old elite, and, above all, from the new educational elite. Thus, the struggle is also a contest between generations and between individuals dependent on an older, traditional social order and its resources and other individuals dependent on a newer, industrial-based social order and its resources. For highly educated members of the younger generation, especially those whose prospects through the usual channels seem unpromising, revolutionary movements offer the tantalizing promise of a short-cut to power. To ignore these aspects of the dynamics of stratification in Third World nations is to oversimplify an extraordinarily complex and interesting process that could teach us much about the forces that are ultimately responsible for systems of social inequality.

One of the more striking developments of interest to students of stratification in the last twenty years has been the rise of the new women's movement and its spread from this country to others. The current phase of the movement seems to have gotten its start in 1963 with the publication of Betty Friedan's book, *The Feminine Mystique*. This book set in motion for the first time in nearly half a century a sustained process of agitation for greater rights for women. Three years after the publication of Friedan's book, in 1966, the National Organization for Women (NOW) was established.

Since then, the women's movement has grown tremendously in numbers and influence, especially among the better educated. This growth has led, among other developments, to a tremendous increase in research and writing about women and their place in society. The writing includes a growing number of volumes that focus on the system of sexual stratification and examine it in the same kind of comparative and theoretical framework developed in *Power and Privilege*. Those who wish to explore this subject in greater depth than was possible in the present volume and to familiarize themselves with the findings of the new research on the subject have a number of resources to which they can turn. These include Rae Lesser Blumberg, *Stratification: Socioeconomic and Sexual Inequality* (1978) and Charlotte O'Kelley, *Women and Men in Society* (1980), both of which provide broad and comprehensive summaries of modern research on all of the major types of societies from hunting and gathering to industrial. They also provide valuable discussions of the system of sexual stratification in socialist societies.

For more detailed treatments of the status of women in Soviet society there are now a number of sources including Gail Lapidus, *Women in Soviet Society* (1978) and William Mandel, *Soviet Women* (1975). For a more detailed examination of sexual stratification in American society, set in a comparative framework, there is Joan Huber and Glenna Spitze, *Sex Stratification: Children, Housework, and Jobs* (1983), and for more detailed discussions of the status of women in preindustrial societies, one may now read Ester Boserup, *Women's Role in Economic Development* (1970); Ernestine Friedl, *Women and Men: An Anthropological View* (1975); and Martin K. Whyte, *The Status of Women in Preindustrial Societies* (1978).

At the time when *Power and Privilege* was written, gender stratification was ignored by students of stratification. The prevailing view, as expressed by functionalist writers, asserted that the family was the basic unit in systems of stratification and the status of women was derived from the status of the male head of household on whom they were dependent (i.e., their father or husband). The chief alternative to this was Marxian theory, which focused on economically defined classes as the basic unit in systems of stratification. Like functionalist theory, it largely ignored the role of sexual inequality in the distribution of power, privilege, and prestige.

By shifting the focus of attention to the resources on which claims to rewards are based, *Power and Privilege* provided a theoretical framework that drew attention to gender distinctions (and also to age distinctions) as one of the bases of social inequality. Thus, the index contains such varied entries as "sex status and rewards," "sex-based class system," "women, occupational handicaps," "women, variations in status," and "women's status." In effect, the theory anticipated the newer mode of thinking about the relationship of sex differentiation to social stratification. More than that, it anticipated the current emphasis on variations in women's role in the economy as a (or the) major determinant of variations in their status in society (e.g., Friedl; Blumberg). It was not successful, however, in anticipating the subsequent revival of the women's movement and its varied achievements.

Another major development in the study of social stratification in the last twenty years has been a significant shift away from the study of social mobility to the study of the attainment process initiated by Peter Blau and Otis Dudley Duncan (1967). During the 1970s, sociological journals were filled with studies that replicated and extended Blau and Duncan's original work. The aim of this research has been to measure the relative strength of the variables influencing the educational, occupational, and income statuses of individuals and groups of individuals.

Blau and Duncan's paradigm was responsible for a subtle, but important, shift in the formulation of the problem in this area of research. Where the older mobility studies focused primarily on societal rates of mobility and the reasons for variations and changes in these rates, the newer status attainment studies have focused on the achievements of individuals and sets of individuals within societies and the factors responsible. Stimulated by the work of William Sewell and others at the University of Wisconsin (e.g., Sewell, Haller, and Portes, 1969; Sewell, Haller, and Ohlendorf, 1970), much of the research has focused on the social psychological processes involved in status attainment.

Although it is clear that our understanding of the social psychological processes that influence the attainments of individuals has been substantially advanced by this line of research and also that quantitative values can now be placed on many of the determinants of the attainments of various populations (e.g., American males, American females, British males, British females, etc.), it is less clear how this line of research has advanced our understanding of the societal processes that shape the social environments in which individuals and groups of individuals compete for resources and rewards. Probably the most important contribution of the status attainment studies to macrosociology has been their demonstration of the limited degree to which the status advantages of one generation are transmitted to the next in modern industrial societies. This is, of course, no small contribution, since it clarifies one of the important characteristics of these societies that stratification theory must explain.

More recently, because of concern with the limitations of the explanatory value of the attainment paradigm on the macrosocial level, a number of researchers have struck out in new directions. Drawing on the work of economists (e.g., Averitt, 1968), who developed the idea of a dual economy, some (e.g., Bibb and Form, 1977; Beck, Horan, and Tolbert, 1978) have shown that there are important differences in the earnings of workers depending on the industrial sector in which they are employed. Workers in heavy industries that are usually oligopolistic, because of the enormous capitalization required, tend to receive higher wages than similar workers in more highly competitive light industries.

Some of those engaged in this research (e.g., Beck, Horan, and Tolbert) have interpreted their findings as a response to the workings of a capitalist economy, but there is reason to question this conclusion. As noted previously, eastern European sociologists (e.g., Wesolowski, 1979) report remarkably similar patterns in socialist societies. The common denominator involved in the two societies seems, rather, to be the greater bargaining power of workers in the more productive and critical sectors of the economies of industrial societies. It stretches the limits of credulity to suggest that it is merely coincidence that so many of the same sectors tend to be advantaged (or disadvantaged) in both "capitalist" America and "socialist" Poland.

Looking back at the revised model of the general theory of stratification in the final chapter of *Power and Privilege* (see page 439) I find surprisingly little that I would change in the light of the research and theoretical discussions of the last twenty years. I would certainly retain the principle that the characteristics of distributive systems are shaped by the interaction of constants with variables, and I find it disappointing that the role of constants is still generally ignored in sociology despite the tremendous advances that have been made in the field of genetics in particular and in the biological sciences in general. One would have supposed that the old eighteenth-century belief in the infinite malleability of human nature would be dead by now.

With respect to the variables, there are some minor changes I would make, but the basic structure of relationships shown in the figure on page 439 still seems sound. Above all, it still appears that the level of technology available to a society and the economic, political, and demographic consequences of the implementations of that technology is, by far, the most powerful single determinant, or set of determinants, of the characteristics of systems of stratification.

One change that I would make if I were redrawing the diagram today would be the addition of an arrow indicating the influence of environmental conditions on the level of technological development of societies. For reasons indicated earlier, it is now clear to me that Betty Meggers (1954), William McNeill (1976), and others have been correct in their assertions that environmental factors can constrain, and sometimes even prevent altogether, indigenous technological advance beyond a certain point.

I would also want to add an arrow indicating the existence of feedback from political systems to economic systems. The experience of Soviet-style societies demonstrates clearly that this type of feedback not only exists, but is important.

Finally, if I were redrawing the figure on page 439, I would insert an arrow from societal type to ideology. The dominant ideologies in societies, as Marx and Engels recognized more than a century ago, are not accidents of history or cultural sports. They are, instead, products of the social system in which they emerge and, more especially, of the technoeconomic system. Capitalism and communism, in the forms we know them today, are products of technologically advanced societies and could never have become the dominant ideologies of simpler societies. Both address problems and respond to opportunities that only emerge in technologically advanced societies. In contrast, animism and ancestor worship are ideologies that reflect the limitations of the information available to members of simpler societies that lack the technology and technologically-based science of modern industrial societies.

At the same time, however, it should be noted that the influence of ideologies on the distributive process is usually more indirect than I have shown it in the figure on page 439. Variations in ideology are important primarily because of the influence they have on political elites. This, in turn, can have effects on the economies of societies, thanks to the feedback mechanisms noted above. In brief, ideologies are more closely linked to societal type than my model indicated.

Developments of the last twenty years leave me more convinced than ever of the need of macrosociologists to develop special theories that are grounded in a more general theory, as I proposed in *Power and Privilege*. It is not satisfactory to move directly from general theory to analyses of individual societies and subsocietal systems as functionalists and others have attempted to do for many years. Nor is it satisfactory to employ a succession of *ad hoc* special theories (e.g., theories of totalitarian societies, Islamic societies, less developed societies, urban societies) that are not grounded in any general theory and that are constructed solely for the purpose of dealing with some limited problem. Karl Marx, Herbert Spencer, and many other nineteenth-century scholars had a better grasp of the requirements of science in this regard than most contemporary theorists. One can only hope that in the years ahead, a growing number of macrosociologists will come to see that general theories are no substitute for specific theories, just as specific theories are no substitute for general theories.

Before concluding the preface to this new edition of *Power and Privilege*, I should mention that the work that went into the writing of this book led me to a growing and continuing interest in comparative and historical macrosociology. Any who are interested in where this interest led may examine the most recent edition of *Human Societies* (Lenski and Lenski, 1982) or other of my subsequent work. Currently, I am working on a monograph, tentatively entitled, "Ecological-Evolutionary Theory: Principles and Applications," in which I attempt to spell out the principles of ecological-evolutionary theory in greater detail than has been possible in *Human Societies* and also to show how the theory can be applied to a highly diversified set of problems and made to yield insights that have not always been evident, even to specialists.

Gerhard Lenski
November, 1983

References

Abramov, Fedor: *The New Life: A Day on a Collective Farm*, translated by George Reavey (New York: Grove Press, 1963).

Amalrik, Andrei: *Involuntary Journey to Siberia*, translated by Mariya Harari and Max Hayward (New York: Harcourt, Brace, Jovanovich, 1970).

Averitt, Robert: *The Dual Economy: The Dynamics of American Industry Structure* (New York: Horton, 1968).

Beck, E. M., Patrick Horan, and Charles Tolbert: "Stratification in a Dual Economy: A Sectoral Model of Earnings Determination," *American Sociological Review*, 43 (1978), pp. 704–720.

Bibb, Robert, and William H. Form: "The Effects of Industrial, Occupational, and Sex Stratification on Wages in Blue-Collar Markets," *Social Forces*, 55 (1977), pp. 974–996.

Blau, Peter, and Otis Dudley Duncan: *The American Occupational Structure* (New York: Wiley, 1967).

Blumberg, Rae Lesser: *Stratification: Socioeconomic and Sexual Inequality* (Dubuque, Iowa: William C. Brown, 1978).

Boserup, Ester: *Women's Role in Economic Development* (New York: St. Martin's Press, 1970).

Chase-Dunn, Christopher: "The Effects of International Economic Dependence on Development and Inequality: A Cross-National Study," *American Sociological Review*, 40 (1975), pp. 720–738.

Cliff, Tony: *State Capitalism in Russia* (London: Pluto Press, 1974).

Connor, Walter: *Socialism, Politics, and Equality: Hierarchy and Change in Eastern Europe and the USSR* (New York: Columbia University Press, 1979).

Dudintsev, Vladimir: *Not By Bread Alone* (New York: Dutton, 1957).

Farmer, B. H.: "Agriculture: Comparative Technology," *International Encyclopedia of the Social Sciences*, vol. I, pp. 202–208.

Friedan, Betty: *The Feminine Mystique* (New York: Norton, 1963).

Friedl, Ernestine: *Women and Men: An Anthropologist's View* (New York: Holt, Rinehart, and Winston, 1975).

Huber, Joan, and Glenna Spitze: *Sex Stratification: Children, Housework, and Jobs* (New York: Academic Press, 1983).

Inkeles, Alex: "Social Stratification and Mobility in the Soviet Union: 1940–1950," *American Sociological Review*, 15 (1950), pp. 465–479.

————, and Raymond Bauer: *The Soviet Citizen* (Cambridge, Mass.: Harvard University Press, 1959).

Jones, T. Anthony: "Models of Socialist Development," *International Journal of Comparative Sociology*, 24 (1983), pp. 86–99.

Lane, David: *The End of Social Inequality?: Class, Status, and Power Under State Socialism* (London: Allen & Unwin, 1982).

Lapidus, Gail: *Women in Soviet Society: Equality, Development and Social Change* (Berkeley: University of California Press, 1978).

Lenski, Gerhard: *Human Societies* (New York: McGraw-Hill, 1970).

————: "Marxist Experiments in Destratification," *Social Forces*, 57 (1978), pp. 364–383.

————: "Income Stratification in the United States: Toward a Revised Model of the System," *Research in Social Stratification and Mobility*, 3 (1984), forthcoming.

————, and Jean Lenski: *Human Societies* (New York: McGraw-Hill, 1974, 1978, 1982).

————, and Patrick Nolan: "Trajectories of Development: A Test of Ecological-Evolutionary Theory," *Social Forces* (1984, forthcoming).

Mandel, William: *Soviet Women* (Garden City, N.Y.: Doubleday Anchor, 1975).

McNeill, William H.: *Plagues and People* (Garden City, N.Y.: Doubleday, 1976).

Matthews, Mervyn: *Class and Society in Soviet Russia* (New York: Walker, 1972).

————: *Privilege in the Soviet Union: A Study of Elite Life-Styles Under Communism* (London: Allen & Unwin, 1978).

Medvedev, Roy: *Let History Judge: The Origins and Consequences of Stalinism*, translated by Colleen Taylor (New York: Knopf, 1971).

Meggers, Betty: "Environmental Limitations on the Development of Culture," *American Anthropologist*, 56 (1954), pp. 801–824.

Nolan, Patrick D.: "Status in the World Economy and National Structure and Development: An Examination of Developmentalist and Dependency Theories," *International Journal of Comparative Sociology*, 24 (1983), pp. 109–120.

Nowak, Stefan: "Changes of Social Structure in Social Consciousness," *Polish Sociological Bulletin*, 10 (1964), pp. 34–53.

O'Kelley, Charlotte: *Women and Men in Society* (New York: Van Nostrand, 1980).

Pohoski, Michal: "Interrelations Between the Social Mobility of Individuals and Groups in the Process of Economic Growth in Poland," *Polish Sociological Bulletin*, 2 (1964), pp. 17–33.

———: personal communication, 1978.

Rubinson, Richard: "The World Economy and the Distribution of Income Within States: A Cross-National Study," *American Sociological Review*, 41 (1976), pp. 638–659.

Sarapata, Adam: "Iustum Pretium," *Polish Sociological Bulletin*, 7 (1963), pp. 41–56.

———, and Wlodzimierz Wesolowski: "The Evaluations of Occupations by Warsaw Inhabitants," *American Journal of Sociology*, 66 (1961), pp. 581–591.

Sewell, William, Archibald Haller, and Alejandro Portes: "The Educational and Early Occupational Status Attainment Process," *American Sociological Review*, 34 (1969), pp. 82–92.

Sewell, William, Archibald Haller, and George Ohlendorf: "The Educational and Early Occupational Achievement Process: Replication and Revision," *American Sociological Review*, 35 (1970), pp. 1014–1027.

Smith, Hedrick: *The Russians* (New York: Quadrangle, 1976).

Solzhenitsyn, Alexander: *One Day in the Life of Ivan Denisovich*, translated by Max Hayward and Ronald Hingley (New York: Bantam, 1963).

Swafford, Michael: "Sex Differences in Soviet Earnings," *American Sociological Review*, 43 (1978), pp. 657–673.

Sweezy, Paul, and Charles Bettelheim: *On the Transition to Socialism* (New York: Monthly Review Press, 1971).

Szczepanski, Jan: *Polish Society* (New York: Random House, 1970).

Treiman, Donald J.: *Occupational Prestige in Comparative Perspective* (New York: Academic Press, 1977).

Wallerstein, Immanuel: *The Modern World-System*, vol. I (New York: Academic Press, 1974).

———: *The Modern World System*, vol. II (New York: Academic Press, 1980).

Watters, R. F.: "The Nature of Shifting Cultivation: A Review of Recent Research," *Pacific Viewpoints*, 1 (1960), pp. 59–99.

Wesolowski, Wlodzimierz: *Classes, Strata and Power*, translated by George Kolankiewicz (London: Routledge & Kegan Paul, 1979, original edition, 1966).

———: "Strata and Strata Interest in Socialist Society," in Celia Heller (ed.), *Structured Social Inequality* (New York: Macmillan, 1969), pp. 465–477.

Whyte, Martin K.: *The Status of Women in Preindustrial Societies* (Princeton, N.J.: Princeton University Press, 1978).

Preface

DURING THE LAST fourteen years, while teaching a course and seminar on social stratification, I found myself confronted each year anew with the task of bringing together in a meaningful way the diverse and often contradictory contributions of the various theorists who have written on this subject. This was no simple matter, as the names of Marx, Spencer, Gumplowicz, Sumner, Veblen, Mosca, Pareto, Michels, Sorokin, Parsons, Davis, Dahrendorf, and Mills indicate.

At first it seemed that nothing could be done other than to present the works of the various writers in chronological sequence, treating each as more or less unique. Gradually, however, the possibility of a more comprehensive and meaningful organization of the materials became evident. Eventually I came to see that theories as contradictory as those of Marx and Mosca, or of Dahrendorf and Parsons, can be understood within a single, unified framework. This becomes possible once one views the development of thought in the field from the perspective of Hegel's dialectic, with its intriguing insight that ideas generate opposing ideas, and that the resulting struggle between them generates a synthesis which incorporates elements of both within a new and distinctive context.

Applying the Hegelian dialectic to the past, one easily discovers a meaningful pattern in the otherwise confusing history of stratification theory. Since ancient times, the basic controversies have been between two schools of thought, one made up of the proponents of a conservative thesis that social inequality is both inevitable and just, the other of proponents of a radical antithesis that it is neither.

But the dialectical view of stratification theory is more than a useful device for summarizing the work of the past. It also sensitizes one to current trends and developments, and provides a basis for anticipating future ones. Above all, it sensitizes one to the recent emergence of a third theoretical position which, in Hegelian terms, can only be described as a synthesis.

One of the chief aims of this volume has been to create a greater awareness of this development, which I believe is widely sensed but seldom verbalized. Such awareness is prerequisite to more rapid progress in stratification theory and research.

A second, and no less basic, aim of this volume is to describe and advance the synthesis. In particular, I have sought to refine and sharpen the statement of the synthesis by relating its basic propositions to the broadest possible range of ethnographic, historical, and sociological data, in the belief that the inductive method is no less important in theory building than the deductive.

I am not so naïve as to suppose that what follows represents the synthesis toward which stratification theory is moving. However, I am certain that such a synthesis *is* emerging, and that I have identified its basic outlines with some accuracy. I am encouraged in my belief by several recent publications, notably those of Ossowski and van den Berghe, which indicate that others are arriving, independently, at a similar point of view.

In order to develop a systematic body of theory, and not merely a collection of conceptual categories, I begin the statement of the synthesis with certain basic postulates about the nature of man and society (Chapter 2). These serve as the basis for a series of general propositions about the dynamics of the distributive process and the structures they generate (Chapters 3 and 4). These, in turn, serve as the foundation for a series of more specific propositions about the distributive systems of five basic types of societies (Chapters 5 to 12).

This ordering of materials may suggest a largely deductive approach on the part of the author, with certain postulates and propositions being accepted uncritically, followed by a search for evidence to support them. Actually, nothing could be further from the truth. The theory was developed by means of both induction and deduction, and when it did not fit the facts, it was modified. When the process began some years ago, the theory was much closer to the functionalists' position than it is at present; exposure to an ever wider range of comparative materials forced a shift which, unfortunately, is not visible in this volume.

Some may question the heavy reliance on the inductive approach since it is currently fashionable in certain sociological circles to equate theory building with a purely deductive approach. Happily, this fashion seems to be dying as its essential sterility becomes more and more evident and as the theoretical importance of induction is more clearly recognized.

From the methodological standpoint, the data used in testing the theory are far from ideal. Systematic, quantitative data would be much better. However, this would take a large, well-financed team of scholars a decade or more, and even then it is doubtful whether accurate measures of all the variables could be obtained for anything resembling a representative sample of societies. Suffice it to say that the present data were not gathered with an eye to proving preconceived hypotheses. Rather, every effort was made to read the relevant literature as widely as possible to determine the degree to which deductive hypotheses were supported. In presenting findings, I have tried to keep the quantitative model in mind, and therefore have striven to identify and report not only the central tendencies, but also the ranges, deviations, and, where present, skewing tendencies. Needless to say, I look forward to the day when more precise techniques can be introduced.

This book differs from most of the current volumes in this area in several ways that deserve at least brief note. First, it is focused on the *causes* of stratification rather than its consequences. The latter have received far more attention, probably because they are more readily amenable to study by means of the currently popular survey research method. Without denying the importance of the latter, I believe the study of causes is even more important and deserving of investigation.

Second, as its title indicates, this volume is focused on *power* and *privilege* rather than prestige. The reasons for this will become clearer later (see especially Chapters 2 and 3).

Finally, I have taken the liberty of redefining the field. I equate social stratification with *the distributive process in human societies—the process by which scarce values are distributed.* Though superficially unorthodox, I believe this definition reflects the central concern of major stratification theorists far more accurately than most current definitions, which identify the field with the study of social classes or strata. These are merely the structural units which sometimes emerge as a result of the workings of the distributive process, but the process itself is the basic phenomenon.

Before concluding, I must express my appreciation to certain persons and organizations. Above all, I am indebted to the many scholars upon whose work I have drawn for stimulation, and whose ideas and research I have so often incorporated into this volume. As far as possible, I have attempted to credit their contributions in footnotes and bibliography, but I realize that one can never fully acknowledge the extent of his indebtedness in this way.

The many students who participated in my stratification seminar during the last twelve years have also made a substantial contribution. More than anyone else, they made me dissatisfied with a simple eclectic or historical approach to stratification theory.

I owe a very special debt of gratitude to the Social Science Research Council and its Executive Associate, Dr. Elbridge Sibley, for support which freed me from my normal academic responsibilities for a number of months. I am also indebted to the Institute for Research in Social Science of the University of North Carolina for secretarial assistance, and to both that university and the University of Michigan for intellectual stimulation and the opportunity to do the necessary research.

Various scholars have been good enough to read all or part of the manuscript and offer suggestions and criticisms. These include Robert Bellah, Peter Carstens, John Gulick, John Honigmann, Richard Simpson, and Gideon Sjoberg. I have benefited greatly from their comments, many of which led to important revisions.

Finally, I owe an immense debt to my wife, to whom this book is gratefully dedicated, and without whose constant support and encouragement it would never have been written. In addition, I am especially grateful for her careful and invaluable editing of the manuscript.

GERHARD E. LENSKI

Contents

1/The Problem: Who Gets What and Why?

"Curiouser and curiouser!" cried Alice.
Lewis Carroll

SOON AFTER PRESIDENT KENNEDY'S ELECTION in the fall of 1960, Americans were again reminded of one of the curious features of their national life. When the President selected Robert S. McNamara for the post of Secretary of Defense, the press reported the substantial financial sacrifice the nominee would be forced to make. While still only a vice-president of the Ford Motor Company, McNamara received salary and other compensation in excess of $400,000 a year.[1] With his promotion to the presidency of the company (just prior to his appointment as Secretary of Defense) he was certain to make substantially more. By contrast, as Secretary of Defense for the nation he received a salary of only $25,000, or roughly 5 per cent of what he would have received as president of the Ford Motor Company.

[1] This figure was cited both by *Time* and *U.S. News and World Report* in their issues of December 26, 1960.

Few Americans seem to have been greatly surprised by these facts, and fewer still were shocked or disturbed. Like the natives of Lewis Carroll's remarkable Wonderland, they saw nothing strange or incongruous in their surroundings.

Yet if one reflects on this matter, one cannot help being impressed by its curious quality. The same man with the same skills and talents moves to a post of far greater importance, and undoubtedly a more trying one, and finds his compensation reduced 95 per cent. In his new position, where he bears much of the burden of the defense of the nation, he receives a salary no greater than that of thousands of minor executives in industry.

If this were but an isolated instance, we might regard it as an interesting oddity, a curious exception to the rule, and think no more about it. But such is not the case. Even a superficial examination of American life reveals innumerable instances in which the rewards men receive bear little or no relation to the value of the services they render or the sacrifices they make in their performance. Many substantial fortunes have been built in a few short years by speculation in stocks and real estate, often with borrowed funds, but the public record reveals no instance in which a great fortune was ever established by a lifetime of skilled and conscientious labor in the foundries, shops, or mills of this country. Entertainers who reach the top in their field often receive several hundred thousand dollars a year. By contrast, the top pay for public school teachers, regardless of ability, is not greatly in excess of $10,000 a year. Playboys like John Jacob Astor III live lives of ease and indolence, while the vast majority of those who do the work which makes this way of life possible struggle to make ends meet.

What is the explanation of this situation which, like Wonderland, grows curiouser and curiouser the more we examine it? What principles govern the distribution of rewards in our society and in others? What determines the magnitude of the rewards each man receives?

These questions have long been argued and debated. In modern times they have become the heart and core of a special field of study within sociology known as "social stratification." This label has been unfortunate for it encourages a seriously oversimplified view of modern social structure. Even worse, it fosters an excessive concern with questions of structure at the expense of more basic problems concerning the processes which generate these structures.

This field might better be identified as the study of the "distributive process." Virtually all the major theorists in the field, regardless of their theoretical and ideological biases, have sought to answer one basic question: *Who gets what and why?* [2] This is the question which underlies all the discussions of classes and strata and their structural relationships, though in some recent empirical research it seems to have been almost forgotten.

The chief aim of this book is to answer this basic question and the host of secondary questions to which it gives rise. Since this is not the first attempt to do this, we shall begin by reviewing the various theories already propounded to see what light they shed on the problem. In doing this, we shall attempt to see whether there is not some basic pattern to the development of thought in this field—a pattern which, once identified, can provide a foundation for our entire inquiry.

Early Pre-Christian Views

Where and when men first began to reflect on the nature of the distributive process and the causes of inequality is anybody's guess. The fact of inequality is almost surely as old as the human species. No known society has ever had a completely egalitarian social system. From primitive Stone Age communities to complex industrial societies, inequality has always been present, though its forms and degree vary considerably.

In the simplest societies in the world today, the fact of inequality is taken for granted, as are other familiar features of existence. Undoubtedly this was true in prehistoric societies. The belief that conditions need not be as they are is characteristic of socially and technologically more advanced societies.

Some of the earliest records of thought on this subject are found in the writings of the early Hebrew prophets who lived approximately 800 years before Christ. In the writings of such men as Amos, Micah, and Isaiah we find repeated denunciations of the rich and powerful members of society. They were concerned not merely with the use of wealth and power, but, more significantly, with the means by which they had been acquired. A good example of this was Micah's vigorous indictment of the leading citizens of his day:

[2] Some years ago Harold Lasswell suggested that *politics* was the study of "who gets what, when, how." While politics and the distributive problem are so closely interrelated that one can never completely separate them, it is a serious mistake to equate them. Lasswell, himself, has come to recognize this, as indicated in his more recent book, coauthored with Abraham Kaplan, *Power and Society: A Framework for Political Inquiry* (New Haven, Conn.: Yale University Press, 1950). In their discussion of class, caste, status, and skill groups, they write, "It is a description of the social structure which answers the question 'who gets what, when, and how' " (pp. 67–68). They then go on to say, "It follows from the definition that the social structure is analyzable into relationships among classes." In short, it seems that Lasswell no longer equates politics with the distributive process.

> Hear this, you heads of the house of Jacob
> and rulers of the house of Israel,
> who abhor justice
> and pervert all equity,
> who build Zion with blood
> and Jerusalem with wrong . . .
> Woe to those who devise wickedness
> and work evil upon their beds!
> When the morning dawns they perform it,
> because it is in the power of their hand.
> They covet fields and seize them;
> and houses, and take them away;
> they oppress a man and his house,
> a man and his inheritance.
> Therefore thus says the Lord:
> Behold, against this family I am devising evil. . . .[3]

Elsewhere the prophet describes the rich men of Israel as "full of violence," the princes and judges as asking for bribes, and the merchants as using a "bag of deceitful weights." All these practices are described as contrary to the will of the Lord, and as perversions which will lead to the nation's destruction.

In India, also, men gave thought to the basis of social inequality long before the Christian era. However, the dominant point of view was very different from that expressed by Micah, though here, too, the matter was viewed in a religious perspective. In the introduction to *The Laws of Manu,* compiled by Hindu priests about 200 B.C., we find an account of the creation of the world. In contrast to the Biblical account, it states that social inequalities were divinely ordained for the good of the world. In words ascribed to Manu, the great lawgiver:

> For the sake of the prosperity of the worlds, he [the Lord, the divine Self-existent] caused the Brahmana, the Kshatriya, the Vaisya, the Sudra to proceed [in turn] from his mouth, his arms, his thighs, and his feet. . . . But in order to protect this universe, He, the most resplendent one, assigned separate [duties and] occupations to those who sprang from his mouth, arms, thighs, and feet.
> To Brahmana he assigned teaching and studying [the Veda], sacrificing for their own benefit and for others, giving and accepting [of alms]. The Kshatriya he commanded to protect the people . . . The Vaisya to tend cattle . . . One occupation only the Lord prescribed to the Sudra, to serve meekly even these [other] three castes.[4]

[3] Excerpts from the second and third chapters of Micah, according to the Revised Standard Version Bible (New York: Nelson, 1953), copyrighted 1946 and 1952, by permission.
[4] *The Laws of Manu,* translated by G. Bühler, in the series, *Sacred Books of the East,* edited by Max Müller (Oxford: Clarendon Press, 1886), vol. 25, excerpts from pp. 13–14 and 24, by permission. Similar accounts may be found elsewhere in Hindu writings.

In these strikingly divergent views of Micah and the priestly compilers of *The Laws of Manu*, we find the essential elements of two points of view concerning social inequality which have dominated men's thinking from ancient times to the present. One is essentially supportive of the *status quo*, viewing the existing distribution of rewards as just, equitable, and frequently also inevitable. The other is highly critical, denouncing the distributive system as basically unjust and unnecessary.

In the pages which follow, I shall refer to the first of these viewpoints as the "conservative thesis" and the second as the "radical antithesis." These terms seem fitting since historically the major controversies over social inequality have been essentially dialogues between proponents of these two schools of thought. One may question the wisdom of labeling the conservative position the thesis and the radical the antithesis, since this suggests that one predates the other. Actually, logic and what evidence there is suggest that neither viewpoint is significantly older than the other. Apparently both have developed side by side with each expression of either point of view stimulating the development of the other.

Over the centuries these two views of inequality have been stated again and again by scholars and laymen alike. Though the form of the argument changes somewhat, the essential elements remain, as social inequality is condemned as unjust, unwarranted, and unnecessary, and defended as just, equitable, and essential. Neither view has ever achieved a monopoly over the minds of men in any society. In ancient Israel it is clear that large numbers of the prophets' contemporaries did not agree with them. A substantial proportion of the people continued to think of the monarchy as a divinely ordained institution, and probably had no difficulty in extending this view to other institutions which fostered inequality. In India the thesis of the orthodox Brahmin priests was under continuing attack for centuries from heretical religious movements such as Jainism and Buddhism, both of which contained distinct egalitarian tendencies.

The Greek philosophers of the classical period provide us with our first glimpses of the dialectic in action. In his famous work on politics, Aristotle deliberately sought to refute the radical proposals of men such as Plato and Phaleas of Chalcedon, both of whom advocated the communal ownership of property. Although Aristotle did not defend all aspects of the existing social order as ideal or even as just, he was a vigorous supporter of the basic institutions undergirding the system of social inequality. He defended not only the institution of private property, but also the institution of slavery. In speaking of the latter, Aristotle asserted:

> It is clear that some men are by nature free, and others slaves, and that
> for these latter slavery is both expedient and right.[5]

While he did not deny that some men who should be free have been
enslaved by force and violence, this had no bearing on the justice and
propriety of the institution itself.

Phaleas and Plato, by contrast, did not hesitate to attack the basic
institutional structure of society. Phaleas advocated the redistribution of
land on an egalitarian basis. Plato's proposals were even more radical,
especially in *The Republic*. Here he advocated the communal ownership
of *all* forms of property, and the establishment of a ruling class which
would have even wives and children in common. This class would be
selected on the basis of moral virtue, intellect, and love of knowledge. The
central thesis of *The Republic* is summed up in one short passage:

> Until philosophers are kings, or the kings and princes of this world have
> the spirit and power of philosophy, and political greatness and wisdom
> meet in one, and those commoner natures who pursue either to the exclu-
> sion of the other are compelled to stand aside, cities will never have rest
> from their evils. . . .[6]

Plato serves as a useful reminder that egalitarianism is not an essential feature of the radical antithesis. Some radicals, like Phaleas, have
been egalitarians; perhaps the majority have been. Others, like Plato,
have not objected to social inequality per se, but rather to the specific
institutional bases on which the existing system of inequality rested. In
Plato's Republic, equality would extend only to material possessions and
presumably also to opportunity for advancement (though on this latter
point, Plato's treatment tends to be self-contradictory).[7] Honor and
power would be reserved for the ruling class of guardians.[8] Basically,
Plato exemplifies the elitist position within the radical camp. Radical
elitists, like egalitarians, are critical of the existing system of allocating
rewards but, unlike the egalitarians, find nothing objectionable in social

[5] Aristotle, *Politics*, translated by Benjamin Jowett (New York: Modern Library,
1943), p. 60.
[6] Plato, *The Republic*, translated by Benjamin Jowett (New York: Modern Library,
n.d.), p. 203, quoted by permission of the Oxford University Press.
[7] At times he speaks of "degrading the offspring of the guardians when inferior, and
. . . elevating into the rank of guardians the offspring of the lower classes, when
naturally superior," but in his description of the educational system of the Republic
he seems to envisage a special educational system limited to the children of the
guardians, with the completion of this system a prerequisite for admission to the ranks
of the guardians. Hence it is not clear how the children of the lower classes in his
Republic would have equal opportunity to become guardians, unless one imagines
their superior potential visible in infancy.
[8] Plato argues that the guardians can be trained not to value power except as a means
to the end of serving the entire community.

inequality per se. In general, this elitist branch of the radical tradition has attracted scholars and intellectuals; egalitarianism, by contrast, has had a greater appeal for the masses of common people, the workers, farmers, and peasants.

Christian Views from Paul to Winstanley

It is not our purpose here to trace each and every expression of thesis and antithesis from ancient times to the present. This would require an entire book in itself and would provide only a limited understanding of the problem of who gets what and why. Instead, our aim is to direct attention to a few of the more important expressions of these two points of view so as to provide the necessary background for the analysis which follows.

In its earliest phases, Christianity represented an interesting mixture of both radical and conservative elements, undoubtedly a reflection of the fact that social inequality per se was not of major concern to Jesus and his early followers. Nevertheless, their teachings and actions are by no means wholly irrelevant.

The goals which Jesus set before men, and his criticisms of the popular goals of his day, reflect a clear rejection of the latter. The communism of the early Church in Jerusalem clearly constituted an implicit criticism of the inequalities present in society. So, too, does the letter of James, thought by many to be a brother of Jesus and the first bishop of the Church in Jerusalem. In it he criticizes the early Christians for showing greater deference to the "man with gold rings and fine clothing" than to the poor man in shabby clothing.

But in the writings of St. Paul, who was destined to have such a profound influence on later Christian thought, a much more conservative spirit is evident. In at least four different places in his letters to the early churches he specifically enjoined slaves to obey their masters on the grounds that this is a legitimate expectation of their masters and presumably one sanctioned by God.[9] St. Peter expressed the same thought in one of his letters. The frequency of these statements suggests that primitive Christianity tended to foster radical notions among many of the converts from the depressed classes of the Roman world—notions which Paul and Peter felt obliged to combat. Both men, like Aristotle, regarded slavery as a part of the natural order and compared the obedience which slaves owe to their masters to the obedience which children owe their

[9] Eph. 6:5; Col. 3:22; I Tim. 6:1; and Titus 2:9.

parents. Both linked their injunctions to obedience with parallel injunctions to those in authority to show respect to their subordinates and treat them in a kind and fatherly way.

As the Church gained in power and influence, the more radical tendencies in Christianity gradually lost ground, at least among church leaders. The conservative viewpoint came in time to be regarded as virtually a matter of doctrine, and as such was developed and elaborated to a high degree.

The conservative thesis achieved one of its most perfect expressions in the work of John of Salisbury, an English bishop of the twelfth century. In the *Polycraticus*, he developed in great detail the organismic analogy, first suggested centuries before in the works of Aristotle and the priestly compilers of *The Laws of Manu*. However, John developed this line of thought more fully than earlier writers and made it the foundation of his entire social philosophy.

According to John, society is like the human body. The prince is the head, and the judges and governors of provinces are the eyes, ears, and tongue. The senate is the heart, and those who wait on the prince are the sides. Soldiers and officials are the hands, while the tax collectors and other financial officers are the stomach and intestines. The common people are the feet. The clergy are the soul.

John argued that the prince is subject only to God and those who represent Him on earth—the clergy. All others must obey and serve the prince, especially the common people who, because they are the feet of society,

> always cleave to the soil and need the more especially the care and foresight of the head, since while they walk upon the earth doing service with their bodies, they meet the more often with stones of stumbling. . . .[10]

John, like all conservative intellectuals, saw society as a system of parts which, though differentiated in function, are united by ties of mutual dependence. The principle of *noblesse oblige* was also important. In his chapter entitled, "Of Those Who Are the Feet of the Commonwealth," he concluded that the commonwealth will be sound and flourishing only when,

> the higher members shield the lower, and the lower respond faithfully and fully in like measure to the just demands of their superiors, so that each and all are as it were members one of another by a sort of reciprocity, and

[10] John of Salisbury, *The Statesman's Book*, translated by John Dickinson (New York: Knopf, 1927), p. 65, by permission. For a startlingly similar view, see David Malo's discussion of the traditional Hawaiian theory of government, *Hawaiian Antiquities*, translated from the Hawaiian by N. B. Emerson in 1898 (written about 1840), Bernice P. Bishop Museum, Special Publication No. 2, 1951, p. 187.

each regards his own interest as best served by that which he knows to be most advantageous for the others.[11]

In brief, far from being a hindrance to the well-being of society, social inequality is a necessary prerequisite. This has been a central affirmation of proponents of the conservative thesis from the earliest times to the present and the organismic analogy has always proven one of the most effective vehicles for communicating it to the widest possible audience.

But if the leaders and scholars of the medieval Church were convinced of the virtues of social inequality, all of the common people were not. From the twelfth century on, a succession of religious movements flourished which criticized wealth and commended poverty. Some, like the Franciscan movement, concentrated more on the latter theme and were incorporated into the structure of the Church without too much difficulty. Others, like the Waldensian movement, which criticized the wealth and power of the Church, became persecuted heretical sects. But both evoked support because of their marked egalitarian tendencies and both relied heavily on the radical elements in Scripture.

This succession of radical Christian movements which began during the Middle Ages continued long after the Reformation and did not finally die out until the Marxist movement in the nineteenth century gave radicalism a new direction and a new hope. In many of these movements there was only a limited development of ideology; in others, talented leaders gave clear and vigorous expression to the radical antithesis in its egalitarian form.

Prominent among the latter was the Englishman, Gerrard Winstanley, seventeenth-century leader of the Leveller sect known as the Diggers (because of their practice of cultivating, without consent, lands of the wealthy which were lying idle). Winstanley's views on social inequality were diametrically opposed to those of John of Salisbury, as the following excerpts from his writings reveal:

> In the beginning of time the great creator Reason made the earth to be a common treasury, to preserve beasts, birds, fishes, and man, the lord that was to govern this creation; for man had domination given to him over the beasts, birds, and fishes. But not one word was spoken in the beginning that one branch of mankind should rule over another. . . .[12]

Elsewhere he wrote:

> I tell you Jesus Christ, who is that powerful spirit of love, is the head Leveller. . . .[13]

---

[11] Ibid., p. 244.
[12] Gerrard Winstanley *Selections from His Works*, edited by Leonard Hamilton (London: Cresset Press, 1944), p. 37, by permission.
[13] Ibid., p. 97.

How then had social inequality come about? Winstanley had no doubts about that:

> So selfish imaginations taking possession of the five senses . . . and working with covetousness, did set up one man to teach and rule over another. And thereby the spirit was killed, and man was brought into bondage and became a greater slave to such of his own kind than the beasts of the field were to him.[14]

Force was also involved. Repeatedly throughout his writings he argued that social inequality in England had its origin in the Norman Conquest by William the Conqueror, who forcibly expropriated the lands of the English and distributed them among his officers and men. Winstanley argued that their descendants still controlled the wealth of England and "the power of the sword was and is [still] the seal of their title" to their estates.

Winstanley was especially critical of the legal system and developed a theme which was destined to be repeated later by other proponents of the radical antithesis:

> For what are all those binding and restraining laws that have been made from one age to another since that Conquest, and are still upheld by fury over the people? I say, what are they, but the cords, bands, manacles, and yokes that enslaved English, like Newgate prisoners, wears [sic] upon their hands and legs as they walk the streets; by which those Norman oppressors and these their successors from age to age have enslaved the poor people, killed their younger brother, and would not suffer Jacob to arise? [15]

Early Modern Views from Locke to Mosca

Since the English revolution of 1648, the forces of radical egalitarianism have made tremendous advances both politically and intellectually. On the political front, two major revolutions have been successfully fought in the name of egalitarianism, and a massive international political movement, socialism, has been organized, profoundly affecting the life of most of the nations of the world. In fact, roughly half of the people in the world today live in nations in which Socialist or Communist Parties hold power.

On the intellectual front, the changes have not been quite so dramatic. Nevertheless, in the period since 1648 the radical antithesis has achieved a degree of intellectual sophistication, maturity, and respect-

[14] *Ibid.*, p. 37.
[15] *Ibid.*, p. 40.

ability comparable to that achieved earlier by the conservative thesis. A big step in this direction was taken in the seventeenth and eighteenth centuries by Locke and Rousseau, who popularized the theory that sovereignty ultimately resides in the people as a whole, not the king. Their writings laid the foundation for the modern understanding of natural rights and did much to undermine the older theory of the divine right of kings. Though Locke and Rousseau were not the first to propound the theory that the powers of governments derive from the consent of the governed, it was not until the eighteenth century that this theory came to be the basis for successful political action.

If the major egalitarian movements of the eighteenth century were directed at the destruction of *legal* inequality, those of the nineteenth and twentieth centuries have been aimed at the eradication of *economic* inequality. In this era socialism ceased to be merely a form of idle speculation for philosophers given to utopian fantasies and became a political movement embracing millions of people. The radical antithesis came of age intellectually with the writing of *The Communist Manifesto* by Karl Marx and Friedrich Engels in 1848. Here was presented in brief form a penetrating analysis of the causes of social inequality combined with a political program of action designed to speed the birth of a new and more equitable social order. In later writings Marx and Engels enlarged upon and modified to some degree the ideas set forth in the *Manifesto* but their basic tenets changed little.

As is well known, the basic postulate of their theory of distribution is that the nature of distributive systems is essentially a function of productive systems. In the earliest and simplest societies communism was inevitable since the economy did not lend itself to the private ownership of the means of production. Later, as agriculture became established, the means of production fell into private hands leading to the division of society into classes. As the productive system changed in other ways, the distributive system responded and, since productive systems continually change, societies passed through a series of evolutionary stages, soon to culminate in the establishment of a new era of equality and freedom, when private ownership of the means of production is finally eliminated.

Another of Marx's basic postulates is that social evolution and economic progress occur as a result of the operation of a modified Hegelian dialectic in which the basic units are classes. Thus classes are the vital forces in history and their struggles the necessary prerequisites to all progress.

A third postulate in Marxian theory, and one of the most important is that of determinism. For Marx the main course of history was inevitable.

The most that men could do was speed or slow the course of its move-ment; they could not reverse it or alter its direction. This element, when viewed in combination with certain of Marx's more accurate specific predictions, has made his theory sometimes appear to be not merely true, but Truth.[16]

Many of the specific elements of Marxian theory were borrowed from earlier sources, as Marx himself admitted.[17] For example, the principle that rewards should be distributed "to each according to his needs," is almost a direct quotation from Acts of the Apostles in which the practice of the early Christian community in Jerusalem is described.[18] Similarly, the important Marxian thesis that laws are nothing but instruments of oppression used by the ruling class to exploit the masses is no more than a restatement of Winstanley's view. In some instances Marx even bor-rowed from the conservatives, as in his concept of the inevitability of inequality under present conditions. However, while many individual ele-ments were borrowed, the theory *as a whole* represented a unique and unusually persuasive statement of the radical antithesis.

The power of Marxian theory is not merely a function of the political strength of the Marxian movement, as some imagine. It is capable of commanding respect in its own right, as evidenced by the large number of scholars and intellectuals who have borrowed from it in greater or lesser degree despite their lack of sympathy for the political movements which act in Marx's name.

While the radical view of social inequality has made great progress in modern times, the conservative view has also found able proponents. Probably the most important of these was Adam Smith, author of *The Wealth of Nations* and founder of modern economics. Smith's great con-tribution to knowledge lay in his analysis of markets and formulation of the laws which govern their operation. His great contribution to con-servative thought lay in his development of the concept of "the invisible hand," whereby "the private interests and passions of men" are led in the direction "which is most agreeable to the interests of the whole society." According to Smith, a free and unrestrained market system motivates men to engage in precisely those activities which their fellows most desire, by pricing products directly in proportion to the demand and inversely in

[16] This tendency has been fostered also by the ambiguity and even by the internal contradictions in much of Marx's writings. These permit a constant reinterpretation when events fail to conform to predicted patterns, a practice the value of which can hardly be exaggerated.

[17] See, for example, Marx's letter to Joseph Weydemeyer, quoted in part by Lewis Feuer (ed.), *Karl Marx and Friedrich Engels: Basic Writings on Politics and Philos-ophy* (Garden City, N.Y.: Doubleday Anchor, 1959), p. 457.

[18] See Acts, 4:35.

proportion to the supply. Though no one plans for the common good, and every man pursues his own private interests in a selfish fashion, the good of the whole is obtained. Men produce what is desired and profit from it. Thus when market systems are allowed to function without political interference, it is as though an invisible hand guided and directed the actions of men in those ways which are most beneficial to them and to their fellows.

In the following century the rise of Darwinian theory provided a striking new argument for conservative theorists. The Social Darwinians argued, by analogy, that individual men are sifted and sorted like plant and animal species. Because of this process of selection, those with greater natural talents fare better than their less talented fellows. The former rise to positions of prominence in society; the latter form the working masses.

This view was set forth vigorously early in the twentieth century by William Graham Sumner in his widely read book, *Folkways*.[19] Sumner described the class system of society as being essentially a measure of the social worth of men, which in turn was basically a measure of native ability. He was prepared to concede that there would be some inequities in any system of stratification because of chance or luck. However, these would always be of minor importance.

Because he saw class systems as resting on the foundation of genetic differences, Sumner argued that classes are not true social groups. Rather they are heuristic categories which the social scientist creates for analytical purposes. In the empirical world there are no real divisions between the classes, since with respect to both ability and rewards men are ranked in a continuous series from top to bottom, with only minute differences between each man and those just above and below him.

While Social Darwinians like Sumner were developing their important reformulation of the conservative thesis, an Italian scholar, Gaetano Mosca, was developing yet another. In his important volume, *Elementi di scienza politica*, published in English as *The Ruling Class*, Mosca reacted vigorously against the theories of socialism which were becoming increasingly popular. His argument is summed up in two basic postulates:

Human societies can never function without political organization.
Political organization necessarily involves inequalities in power.

Given these postulates, Mosca concluded that there will always be two classes of people—"a class that rules and a class that is ruled." Further-

[19] See also his pamphlet, *What Social Classes Owe to Each Other* (New York: Harper & Row, 1903).

more, since most men are self-seeking, the ruling class will also be a privileged class from the economic standpoint.

According to Mosca, the ruling class is always a minority of the population. It maintains itself in several ways. In the first place, it is always highly organized and thus enjoys a great advantage in its relations with the unorganized majority. Second, to some degree most ruling classes drain off the potential leadership of the inferior classes by accepting the most talented members of these classes into their own ranks. Third, through the use of what Mosca calls "political formulas," or theories justifying social inequality, the masses are led to accept their lot as rightful and, usually, as inevitable. Finally, sheer habit leads the great majority of those in the lower classes to go about their daily work without even questioning the justice or inevitability of their position in society. In short, even though the ruling class is only a minority, and in large societies a rather small one, many factors undergird and stabilize its position of advantage.

In one of the most interesting and insightful parts of Mosca's work he attacked Marxian theory as hopelessly utopian and unrealistic in its vision of a classless society. Writing more than two decades before the Russian Revolution, Mosca predicted that if the Communists ever came to power, and if they destroyed the private ownership of the means of production, their Communist or collectivist societies would still require officials, and these would come to form a new ruling class.[20]

Functionalists and Conflict Theorists

Since World War I the social sciences have undergone many changes. Above all, they have become very research-oriented and the research techniques of today bear little resemblance to those of the pre-World War I era. Nevertheless, it is important not to lose sight of the elements of continuity with the past.

This element of continuity is especially evident in modern theories of social inequality. Most of these theories stem directly from either the conservative or radical tradition. This is a source of both strength and weakness. It is a source of strength because it incorporates and preserves many valid insights of the past. It is a source of weakness because it preserves the tendency to make social analysis subservient to moral judgments and political interests and because it often leads to formulations of hypotheses which do not lend themselves to empirical proof or disproof.

[20] Gaetano Mosca, *The Ruling Class*, translated by Hannah Kahn (New York: McGraw-Hill, 1939), especially pp. 281–286.

Most modern theories of inequality fall into one or the other of two major categories. Those which stem from the conservative tradition are usually referred to as "functionalist" theories. Those which have their roots in the radical tradition are commonly labeled "conflict" theories.

Among the leading functionalist theorists of the present day, at least two have spelled out their views on inequality and stratification in some detail. These are Talcott Parsons and his former student, Kingsley Davis. Both approach the problem of inequality from the perspective of society at large, seeing it as a necessary feature of any properly functioning human society. Davis summed up the functionalist approach in a single sentence when he wrote:

> Social inequality is thus an unconsciously evolved device by which socie-
> ties insure that the most important positions are conscientiously filled by
> the most qualified persons.[21]

This is the essence of the functionalist position: stratification arises basically out of the needs of societies, not out of the needs or desires of individuals.

Neither Parsons nor Davis says that all of the characteristics of any given system of stratification arise in response to societal needs. Both concede that other factors operate in the real world to modify systems of inequality to some degree. However, judging from their failure to pursue this aspect of the problem, neither considers such factors to be of major importance.

Davis argues that systems of stratification arise in response to two specific needs common to every human society. First, there is the need to instill in the abler members the motivation to occupy important and difficult positions which require greater than average ability. Second, society must motivate such men, once they are in these positions, to perform the duties attached to them. Hence, it must provide them with greater rewards.

Davis cites two factors as the major determinants of the magnitude of the rewards attached to positions: (1) their functional importance for the society and (2) the relative scarcity of qualified personnel. Positions which are extremely important and which suffer from a shortage of qualified personnel receive the highest rewards. Those which are unimportant and for which there is an abundance of qualified personnel receive minimal rewards. Since all positions can never be of equal importance, nor all men equally qualified for the more responsible positions, inequality is inevitable. Not only is it inevitable, it is necessarily beneficial to everyone,

[21] Kingsley Davis, *Human Society* (New York: Macmillan, 1949), p. 367.

since the survival and well-being of every individual is contingent on the survival and well-being of society.

Parsons' approach to the subject differs more in form than in substance. He starts from the assumption that in every human society there are certain shared values. Since values arise out of the needs of society and since the basic needs of all societies are more or less similar, these values tend to be similar the world over. What differs from one society to the next is the relative ranking of these values. One society may value efficiency more highly than stability, while another may reverse the order, but every society is obliged to value both efficiency and stability to some degree.

The system of stratification in any society is essentially an expression of the value system of that society. The rewards which men and positions enjoy are a function of the degree to which their qualities, performances, and possessions measure up to the standards set by their society. Since men necessarily differ in these respects, inequality is inevitable.[22]

By contrast with the functionalists, conflict theorists approach the problem of social inequality from the standpoint of the various individuals and subgroups within society.[23] *Their* needs and desires, rather than the needs of society as a whole, provide the basic postulates for this school of theorists. The difference between the two schools can be seen most clearly in their members' approach to the phenomenon of power. In reviewing C. Wright Mills's book, *The Power Elite*, Parsons charged:

> The essential point is that, to Mills, power is not a facility for the performance of function in and on behalf of the society as a system, but is interpreted exclusively as a facility for getting what one group, the holders of power, wants by preventing another group, the "outs" from getting what it wants.[24]

Conflict theorists, as their name suggests, see social inequality as arising out of the struggle for valued goods and services in short supply. Where the functionalists emphasize the common interests shared by the members of a society, conflict theorists emphasize the interests which

[22] For the chief statement of Parsons' views on stratification, see "A Revised Analytical Approach to the Theory of Social Stratification," in Reinhard Bendix and S. M. Lipset, *Class, Status and Power: A Reader in Social Stratification* (New York: Free Press, 1953), pp. 92–128.

[23] Labels can sometimes be misleading when applied to groups of scholars, and this one is no exception. I do not include under the heading of conflict theorists writers such as Lewis Coser, author of *The Functions of Social Conflict* (New York: Free Press, 1956). Though this volume is focused on conflict, its basic purpose is to show how conflict serves society as a whole. In short, the underlying theoretical orientation is functionalist.

[24] Talcott Parsons, "The Distribution of Power in American Society," *World Politics*, 10 (October, 1957), p. 139.

divide. Where functionalists stress the common advantages which accrue from social relationships, conflict theorists emphasize the element of domination and exploitation. Where functionalists emphasize consensus as the basis of social unity, conflict theorists emphasize coercion. Where functionalists see human societies as social systems, conflict theorists see them as stages on which struggles for power and privilege take place.

This is not to say that all conflict theorists totally deny the validity of the functionalists' approach. One, Ralf Dahrendorf, even concedes that society is basically "Janus-headed," and that functionalists and conflict theorists are simply studying two aspects of the same reality. He, however, like Davis, Parsons, Mills, and other theorists of these two schools, is content to limit his own analysis to one facet of reality, ignoring the crucial question of how the two are tied together.

The Emerging Synthesis

Yet must the matter be left there? Can there not be a synthesis of the valid insights of both the conservative and radical traditions, of modern functionalism and conflict theory, and the development of a single integrated theory of social inequality?

The central thesis of this volume is that this is not only possible, but the process is already under way. A third approach to the subject of social inequality is already becoming evident, an approach which slowly but surely is laying the foundation of what in Hegelian terms would be called the "synthesis." Like the Hegelian synthesis it integrates the valid insights of thesis and antithesis by approaching the problem on a different level. Whereas both thesis and antithesis are essentially *normative* theories of inequality, i.e., primarily concerned with moral evaluation and the question of justice, the synthesis is essentially *analytical*, i.e., concerned with empirical relationships and their causes. Whereas both thesis and antithesis rely on logic and isolated illustrations as methods of validating propositions, the synthesis relies on the systematic mobilization of empirical data. In short, *the synthesis is largely the result of the modern application of the scientific method to the study of the age-old problem of human inequality.*

A definite movement toward the synthesis is evident even in the writings of the functionalists and conflict theorists mentioned above. In the writings of most of these men the moralistic element is clearly subordinated to the analytical and, although they rely heavily on logic and isolated illustration, it is clear that they concede the superiority of systematic evidence in determining the validity of general statements. Functionalists and conflict theorists are linked to the older conservative and radical traditions chiefly by virtue of their choice of basic postulates. Functionalists rely chiefly on postulates borrowed from the conservative tradition and thus are led to a view of inequality which emphasizes its necessary and socially beneficial aspects. Conflict theorists, by contrast, build on postulates drawn from the radical tradition and hence arrive at a very different view of society. While recognizing these links between modern social theorists and the older philosophical traditions, it is equally important to recognize the differences which set them apart. Scholars such as Davis, Parsons, Dahrendorf, and even Mills in his earlier years, have already taken a substantial step in the direction of the synthesis.

There are others, however, who have gone even further, and these scholars deserve special attention since their work represents the closest approximation yet to the emerging synthesis. One of the pioneers in this movement was the great German scholar, Max Weber. Though he never developed a systematic theory of stratification, he often dealt with various aspects of the distributive process. In his treatment of the subject the analytical approach was clearly dominant, and he incorporated in his work valid insights from both historic traditions.[25] The same can be said of his distinguished Italian contemporary, Vilfredo Pareto.[26]

Another pioneer in the synthesizing movement has been Pitirim Sorokin. His early work, *Social Mobility,* is probably the first extensive and systematic treatment of social stratification in which the synthetic perspective is dominant.[27] Here one can see a judicious combination and blending of elements out of both traditions. This manifests itself especially in the utilization of a multidimensional view of stratification, a common tendency in synthetic work, one evident also in the work of Weber.[28]

In the last decade, an important new stage has been achieved in the emergence and development of the synthesis. For the first time in history, some scholars have come to view the problem clearly and consciously in dialectical terms. The first to achieve this was the able Polish sociologist, Stanislaw Ossowski. In his book, *Class Structure in the Social Consciousness,* published initially in 1957, the year following the Polish and Hun-

[25] Among those writings translated into English, see especially Max Weber, *The Theory of Social and Economic Organization,* translated by A. M. Henderson and Talcott Parsons (New York: Free Press, 1947), especially parts 3–5, or *From Max Weber: Essays in Sociology,* translated by H. H. Gerth and C. Wright Mills (Fair Lawn, N.J.: Oxford University Press, 1946), especially parts 7 and 14–17.
[26] *The Mind and Society,* translated by A. Bongiorno and Arthur Livingston and edited by Livingston (New York: Harcourt, Brace & World, 1935), especially vols. III and IV.
[27] New York: Harper & Row, 1927.
[28] For a more recent statement of Sorokin's views on stratification see *Society, Culture and Personality* (New York: Harper & Row, 1947), chaps. 14 and 15.

garian uprisings, Ossowski again confronted the issues dividing Marxists and functionalists in their views and interpretations of class structure.[29] However, unlike those who have dealt with this problem before, Ossowski did not ask, "Which view is correct?" Rather, he sought to demonstrate that *both views are fundamentally correct.* He argued that this is possible because human societies are far more complex than either theoretical system has ever acknowledged and both have presented only a partial view, or one which emphasizes certain aspects of reality to the neglect of others. For example, he declared that there are certain facts consistent with both Soviet and American claims that their own societies are classless societies, just as there are others which support their charges that the other's is a class-stratified society. Similarly, he shows how the same society can be analyzed as a two-class society in Marxian terms and as a three- or more class society in functionalist terms.

More recently a young Belgian-American sociologist, Pierre van den Berghe, published a paper along similar lines. In it he sought to show that Marxian and functionalist theory, "the two major approaches which have dominated much of social science, present partial but complementary views of reality." [30] To do this, he examined four important areas of convergence and overlap, showing that even on points of apparent disagreement synthesis can be achieved. While his treatment of the problem was much less detailed than Ossowski's, and much less focused on the subject of stratification, it shares the same point of view.

It is interesting to note that neither Ossowski nor van den Berghe seem to have been aware of the work of the other, and the present writer became aware of their work only in the closing stages of the preparation of this volume. Each reacted independently to the same basic stimuli and the nature of the response seems to have been shaped largely by the nature of these stimuli. This suggests that the synthetic view of social stratification is not so much the product of the efforts or insights of any single individual or group of individuals as it is a spontaneous working out of a complex sociointellectual process and the reflection of basic trends and developments in the work of many widely scattered scholars.

Until recently movement toward the synthesis has been more by drift than by design. A basic aim of this book is to speed the process by calling attention to the dialectical pattern in the development of thought

[29] Translated by Sheila Patterson (New York: Free Press, 1963). See also Ossowski's paper, "Old Notions and New Problems: Interpretations of Social Structure in Modern Society," *Transactions of the Third World Congress of Sociology* (London: International Sociological Association, 1956), vol. 3, pp. 18–25.
[30] "Dialectic and Functionalism: Toward a Theoretical Synthesis," *American Sociological Review*, 28 (1963), pp. 695–705.

in the field, and by outlining the basic nature of the synthesis toward which we seem to be moving. To do this, elements have been drawn from both of the older theoretical traditions together with others which are found in neither.

The process of synthesis takes different forms in different fields of inquiry, but there are certain common tendencies which deserve recognition. Above all, the process of synthesis normally involves *the reformulation of problems and concepts*. Many of the impasses into which proponents of thesis and antithesis have got have developed because both parties have asked the same wrong question or utilized the same faulty concepts. Too often we fail to recognize that the questions we ask and the concepts we use have assumptions built into them—assumptions which often prove to be faulty when subjected to critical scrutiny, and which therefore preclude any adequate solution of the problem at issue. Just as there may be no true answer to the question, "When did you stop beating your wife?" there may be none to the question, "Will totalitarianism or democracy prevail in the future?" Each contains hidden assumptions which force answers into a limited range of categories, none of which may represent a reasonable approximation of the truth. Similarly, as Ossowski has shown, the traditional concepts we use often prejudice the mode of our thought.[31] As the limitations of traditional concepts and questions come to be recognized, and as new and better concepts and questions are formulated, a process of synthesis occurs spontaneously. This process can be speeded up, however, by a conscious recognition of the nature of the problem and by deliberate efforts to search out inadequate concepts and questions.

There are two ways of reformulating problems and concepts that have proven of such general utility that they deserve special recognition. The first is the technique of *transforming categorical concepts into variable concepts*. Categorical concepts, by their very nature, force one to think in limiting "either-or" terms. For example, either a caste system is present in a society or it is not. When categorical concepts are transformed into variable concepts, one is no longer faced with the task of choosing between what are often two (or three or more) faulty views. Instead, he is invited to ask *to what degree* a given phenomenon is present. Thus, we cease to ask whether a caste system exists in American society, and ask instead to what degree it is present.

The second technique involves *breaking down compound concepts into their constituent elements*. Many of the traditional concepts used to describe systems of stratification subsume a variety of loosely related

[31] *Op. cit.*, chap. 11.

variables. The concept "vertical mobility" is a good example of this. Recent research has made sociologists increasingly aware of the need to differentiate between inter- and intragenerational mobility, and between occupational, educational, and other forms of mobility. Generalizations which may apply to one of these types of mobility may be utterly false if applied to vertical mobility generally. As is evident, the shift from categorical to variable concepts, together with the breaking down of compound concepts, encourages the asking of more fruitful questions, and this in turn usually leads to increasing agreement in areas of controversy. In the chapters which follow, a deliberate effort has been made to reformulate many traditional problems and concepts in these ways.

In every field of study there are three basic questions which must be answered. First, what is the *nature* of the phenomenon in question? Second, what are the *causes* of its uniformities and variations? Third, what are the *consequences* of its existence or action? The present volume is concerned chiefly with the first two problems. The third is discussed only when the element of feedback is present, i.e., when the consequences of a given pattern of distribution affect the distributive pattern itself. The decision to limit the analysis in this way was based chiefly on the recognition of the complexity of the first two problems and the desire to do justice to them, and secondarily on the belief that the third problem has been more thoroughly investigated and involves fewer difficulties.

There is one other "peculiarity" of this volume which deserves comment. In recent decades many American sociologists have come to equate theory building with the use of purely deductive logic.[32] This is a serious error since successful theory building requires *both inductive and deductive logic*. To limit oneself to pure deductive reasoning in a field such as sociology is impossible, at least if one desires to be relevant; to attempt it and to claim it is only to deceive oneself and others and to inhibit the normal development of theory.

In the early stages of this volume the primary emphasis is on deductive logic. Later, as the analysis shifts from the most general level to the level involving a specific type of society, the emphasis shifts increasingly to inductive logic. At this later stage one could pretend that all the generalizations presented were derived by a rigorous and inexorable logic from the basic premises set forth in the earlier chapters, but this would be untrue. Despite the shift in emphasis, there is a remarkable compatibility between these two sets of generalizations—so much so, in fact, that

---

[32] This seems to be due in large measure to the influence of Talcott Parsons. There is a subtle irony here since the deductive element in Parsons' work has never been very prominent or rewarding but, despite this, the image remains.

together they form a reasonably well integrated body of theory. To expect more at this stage is to be utopian.

Basic Issues

Before concluding this chapter, it is important to review and summarize the basic issues which have emerged out of the historic controversy between conservatives and radicals. Any truly synthetic theory must address itself to these issues. Hence, this summary will serve not only as the conclusion to this historical review but also as the point of departure and foundation for all that follows.

In summarizing a controversy as extensive and protracted as this one has been, some degree of oversimplification is inevitable. Conservatives have not always agreed among themselves, nor have radicals. The only belief common to all conservatives has been their belief that the existing system of distribution was basically just; the only belief common to all radicals has been their belief that it was basically unjust. On other matters there has been no single conservative or radical position to which each and every adherent subscribed. Nevertheless, given the basic assumption about the justice or injustice of the system, other views tend to follow, with the result that most conservatives have lined up on one side of the key issues and most radicals on the other. It is these dominant tendencies with which we are concerned here.

One of the most basic issues dividing radicals and conservatives over the centuries has been that concerning the nature of man himself. Historically, conservatives have been distrustful of man's basic nature and have emphasized the need for restraining social institutions. By contrast, radicals have been distrustful of these restraining institutions and have taken an optimistic view of man's nature. This difference can be seen quite clearly in the French Revolution, where the conservatives put their trust in the monarchy and the Church and the radicals in man himself, emancipated from the restraints of these "corrupting" institutions.

A second basic issue has been that concerning the nature of society. As noted before, conservatives have traditionally viewed society as a social system with various needs of its own which must be met if the needs and desires of its constituent members are to be met. Radicals, by contrast, have tended to view society more as the setting within which various struggles take place; it is significant chiefly because its peculiar properties affect the outcome of the struggles.

Third, radicals and conservatives have also differed on the question of the degree to which systems of inequality are maintained by coercion.

Radicals have generally emphasized coercion as the chief factor undergirding and maintaining private property, slavery, and other institutions which give rise to unequal rights and privileges. Conservatives, on the other hand, have argued that coercion plays only a minor role and inequality arises as a necessary consequence of consensus (i.e., because of values which are shared widely throughout society, even by the less privileged elements) and/or innate differences among men.

Fourth, proponents of the two traditions have differed concerning the degree to which inequality in society generates conflict. Radicals have seen this as one of the chief consequences of inequality; conservatives have generally minimized it.

Fifth, a genuine disagreement exists concerning the means by which rights and privileges are acquired. Radicals have laid great emphasis on force, fraud, and inheritance as the chief avenues. Conservatives, by contrast, have stressed more justifiable methods such as hard work, delegation by others, and so forth.

Sixth, conservatives have always regarded inequality as inevitable. Radicals, or at least those in the egalitarian tradition, have taken the opposite view, though in the case of Marxian theory they concede its inevitability at certain stages of societal development.

Seventh, a major disagreement has always existed with respect to the nature of the state and of law. Radicals have commonly regarded both as instruments of oppression employed by the ruling classes for their own benefit. Conservatives have seen them as organs of the total society, acting basically to promote the common good.

Eighth, and finally, conservatives have tended to regard the concept of class as essentially a heuristic device calling attention to aggregations of people with certain common characteristics. Radicals, however, have been much more inclined to view classes as social groups with distinctive interests which inevitably bring them into conflict with other groups with opposed interests. Perhaps we might summarize much of the foregoing by saying that conservatives have tended to be realists with respect to the concept "society" and nominalists with respect to the concept "class," while radicals have generally taken the opposite position.

These, then, are the basic issues. In the chapters which follow we shall return to them repeatedly since the synthesis must either take a position with respect to each of them or reformulate them. It may not be inappropriate to say at this point that we shall adopt the latter course as often as the former.

2/Man and Society

Man is the only animal that blushes.
Or needs to.
Mark Twain

ONE OF THE BASIC FACTS of human existence is the curious intermingling of good and evil in the affairs of men. On some occasions men have displayed the greatest acts of self-sacrifice and heroism. At other times they have engaged in the most appalling acts of cruelty and selfishness. This strange dualism has provided an endless source of material for poets and playwrights since the days of Homer.

Social philosophers and social scientists have found that they, too, must reckon with this aspect of human life, but for them it represents a problem rather than a resource. For how does one explain such varied behavior in a single species, and often in a single individual?

Historically, most efforts to answer this question have led to the conclusion that human behavior springs from two opposing sources, one of good, the other of evil. God is the source of good and the devil the source of evil. Or, nature is the source of good and society the source of evil. Or, reason is the source of good and the passions the source of evil. In short, the good we observe in men springs from one source, the evil from another.

The classical solution has found favor with both radical and conservative theorists. They differ, however, when they identify the sources. As noted in the last chapter, radicals tend to identify society as the source of evil. Man is basically good, they argue, and the evil we observe in his actions reflects the influence of corrupting institutions. In contrast, conservatives have generally maintained that evil has its origin in the egoistic drives of the individual and that the function of society is to restrain and redirect these harmful tendencies in ways which serve the common good.

Of course, these generalizations oversimplify matters to some degree; the lines are not always drawn so clearly.[1] Nevertheless, this fundamental difference between the conservative and radical views of man and society underlies many of the differences in their theories of distribution. By making this distinction explicit, it becomes easier to identify one of the major sources of controversy between these two intellectual traditions and thus clarify one of the major tasks confronting proponents of the synthetic view.

The chief objective of this chapter is to set forth certain postulates about the nature of man and society which form the foundation for the emerging synthesis. Some are drawn from the conservative tradition, some from the radical, and some from neither. No attempt will be made to give a total view of either man or society. Rather, attention will be concentrated on those aspects of both which are most relevant to the theory of distribution.

The Nature of Man

The starting point in every sociological discussion of the nature of man is the deceptively simple assertion that *man is a social being obliged by nature to live with others as a member of society.* On this proposition at least, radicals and conservatives agree, and this serves as the *first postulate* in our general theory.

To say that man is a social being is not to deny that a few individuals withdraw from society and live as hermits. The human race could not

---

[1] For example, Marxist theory is a radical theory critical of social institutions only so long as Marxists are out of power. Once they gain power, as in Russia and China, the profoundly conservative elements in this theory come to the fore. The drastic shift in ideological orientation required of Communists in the era following the 1917 Revolution was undoubtedly one reason for the frequent purges of Old Bolsheviks.

survive on this basis. however, since its chief weapon in the struggle for existence has always been culture, and culture is uniquely a social product. Social life is essential not only for the survival of the species but also for the maximum satisfaction of human needs and desires. Through cooperative activity men can satisfy many needs and desires which could never be met otherwise and can satisfy most other needs much more efficiently, i.e., with greater return for less effort or other investment.

To say that man is a social being is also to say that the society into which he is born shapes his character and personality in ways over which he has no control and of which he is often unaware. Peter Berger expressed this well when he wrote:

> Society not only controls our movements, but shapes our identity, our thought and our emotions. The structures of society become the structures of our own consciousness. Society does not stop at the surface of our skins. Society penetrates us as much as it envelops us.[2]

If our first postulate is relatively noncontroversial, the same cannot be said of the second. It takes us directly into the realm of one of the bitterest disputes between radicals and conservatives—the dispute concerning the origin of evil. As noted in the last chapter, the radical view of man and society steadily gained in popularity and intellectual respectability after the English revolution of the seventeenth century. In an era of European growth and expansion, this optimistic view, which postulated society as the source of evil, found increasing acceptance, especially among intellectuals. Since the rise of Nazism and the outbreak of World War II, however, the trend has been halted and, for the first time in roughly three centuries, the pendulum seems to be moving in the opposite direction. On every hand the evidence mounts that the evil in men's actions is rooted more deeply than radical theorists had supposed. Neither the French Revolution nor the Russian produced the utopias that were promised despite revolutionary institutional change. Though the patterns of men's lives have been changed greatly by the social and technological revolutions of modern times, egoism, selfishness, and cruelty continue to loom large.

Paralleling the argument from modern history is that from contemporary psychology, where current theory and research undermine our faith in the natural goodness of man no less than do political events. Recent research reveals the human infant as an extremely self-centered creature, motivated solely by his own needs and desires. If we rid ourselves of the romantic aura which surrounds babies in our society, we discover

[2] Peter Berger, *Invitation to Sociology* (Garden City, N.Y.: Doubleday Anchor, 1963), p. 121.

that they are totally involved in reducing the various tensions created by their biological nature and the environment. Their early actions are simply trial-and-error probings to discover methods of reducing or relieving these tensions.

In time, of course, the normal child learns to take the wishes of others into account. But this does not mean that he is any less motivated to maximize his own satisfactions. Rather, it means that he has learned that the attainment of his own goals is inextricably linked with the interests of others. For example, a boy who acquires a taste for baseball soon finds that he can satisfy this taste only by cooperating with others who share his enthusiasm. Because he cooperates with them and obeys the rules of the game we should not assume that he is no longer seeking to maximize his own satisfactions. On the contrary, we can be sure he is!

Children's games afford far more insights into the nature of social organization than is usually recognized. In particular, they demonstrate the process by which institutions with their elements of cooperation and morality and their concepts of right and justice can emerge from the actions of an originally unorganized aggregation of individuals each selfishly seeking to maximize his own personal satisfactions. To achieve this maximization individuals are forced to work (and play) together, but they find that this can be rewarding only if the activity takes place within the framework of a system of rules which, above all else, protects the cooperative activity itself. This can only be done if certain basic rights are guaranteed to all of the essential participants; e.g., each boy is guaranteed his turn at bat. This may seem to entail some sacrifice on the part of the stronger or abler participants, but really it does not, since the only alternative is the cessation of the cooperative activity and all its benefits. Thus, for them, as for the other participants, adherence to the rules can be accounted for merely as a form of *enlightened self-interest.*

Many years ago William Graham Sumner coined the phrase "antagonistic cooperation" to call attention to this paradoxical feature of human life.[3] As he pointed out, men are "brought into association and held there by compulsion"—the compulsion of self-interest. He declared that "it is quite as wrong to assume mutual good-will as the basis of human cooperation as it would be to suppose its existence between the bee and the

---

[3] See *Folkways* (Boston: Ginn, 1906), p. 32. The quotations which follow are from Sumner and Albert Keller, *The Science of Society* (New Haven, Conn.: Yale University Press, 1927), vol. I, pp. 28–29. For another good discussion of this subject, see Bronislaw Malinowski, *Crime and Custom in Savage Society* (New York: Harcourt, Brace & World, 1926), especially chap. 5. For a good recent discussion of this same essential problem, see Dennis Wrong, "The Oversocialized View of Man," *American Sociological Review,* 26 (1961), pp. 183–193.

clover or the rhinoceros and the tick bird." In his opinion, "most cooperation has in it . . . suppressed antagonisms that are overborne by practical
advantage." While he may have overstated the case somewhat, it is especially applicable in the case of those forms of social organization which
are so large and complex that they embrace total strangers.

If one is fond of paradox and irony, one might go further and argue
that cooperation itself is one of the basic sources of conflict in human life.
If man were a solitary species, with each individual living apart from all
the rest except for mating, as is the case with certain animals, there would
be far less conflict among men. If each produced only for himself and
there were no division of labor and exchange of goods, one of the major
sources of human strife would be eliminated. By contrast, when men join
forces in a cooperative enterprise, whether it be a family or total society,
both the opportunity and the motivation for conflict are greatly increased.
This is an aspect of the social scene which most conservative theorists
have neglected.

We cannot argue, however, that simple self-interest, enlightened or
otherwise, is the only motivating force in human affairs. When we take an
objective view, we recognize that the problem is more complicated than
this. Self-sacrifice *is* an observable reality no less than self-seeking: parents *do* sacrifice for their children and soldiers for their buddies.

From the moral standpoint, these forms of action are highly com-
mendable. Nevertheless, as some of the more insightful observers of the
human scene have pointed out, such actions involve a strong element of
self-seeking. Jesus pointed this out to his followers at one point where he
said, "If you love only those who love you, what credit is that to you?
Even tax collectors do that." Many actions appear as sacrifices only when
the larger context is ignored. Seen in context, such actions appear as parts
of a mutually beneficial system of exchanged favors.

Whatever else is true of this kind of sacrificial action, it is not disinterested. Such actions are seldom taken on behalf of strangers, nor do
we expect it. Rather, they presuppose the existence of highly valued and
rewarding interpersonal ties between the parties involved. For lack of a
better term, we might call this pattern of action "partisan self-sacrifice"
and the interests served by it "partisan group interests" to differentiate it
from the disinterested pattern of self-sacrifice involved in truly altruistic
action.

There is one other aspect of this matter deserving note. Groups which
generate sacrificial action by their members in their relations with one
another typically foster a very different pattern of action in relations with
outsiders. In fact, it sometimes seems that the stronger the sacrificial tend-

encies in *intragroup* relations, the weaker such tendencies in *intergroup* relations. This means that our *judgments about the frequency and importance of sacrificial action in human life are a function of the social level on which we focus*. If we make the family or some other primary group the object of our analysis, we are far more likely to be impressed by the evidences of self-sacrifice than if we examine a large and complex nation. When we view human action in this broader perspective, as we shall in this volume, we soon discover that these groups which generate so much sacrificial action in their internal relations are often capable of the most ruthless pursuit of their partisan group interests when dealing with outsiders, even though the latter are members of the same society.[4]

Closely related to this is the self-sacrificing action of the "true believer," to use Eric Hoffer's apt phrase—the fanatically dedicated member of a social movement which has "found the cure for the ills of mankind" and is prepared to force its adoption on a "stupidly" resisting world. Though the true believer is convinced that he is sacrificing himself for the good of his fellow men, others recognize the important psychic benefits he derives from his participation in such a movement. Self-sacrifice in this case is self-deception; the actions of the true believer seldom serve the needs of others as others see them.

Another questionable form of self-sacrifice is the practice of *noblesse oblige*. The well-to-do in some societies accept certain obligations, such as charity, almsgiving and public service, which yield no obvious returns for themselves. Again, however, the element of self-interest intrudes. For the very wealthy, philanthropy costs relatively little but usually yields substantial dividends. It is one of the few trustworthy routes to honor and prestige, and for those who have everything else, this can be important (see the discussion of the principle of marginal utility on page 36 of this chapter). Also, as the Lynds demonstrated in their famous study of Middletown, philanthropy can be made to pay handsome political and economic dividends.[5] This is not to say that all charitable actions are prompted by self-interest but only that the element of self-interest is not incompatible with philanthropy. A more serious question which must be directed at charitable action concerns its relative importance in the total economy. Charitable donations usually represent only a small fraction of all expendi-

---

[4] For an extreme instance of this, see Edward Banfield, *The Moral Basis of a Backward Society* (New York: Free Press, 1958), which provides a vivid description of a southern Italian village in which extremely intense family ties go hand in hand with the most callous disregard for other members of the community.
[5] Robert Lynd and Helen Lynd, *Middletown in Transition* (New York: Harcourt, Brace & World, 1937), chap. 3. A similar pattern can be found in many other parts of the world, as will become evident in later chapters. See especially chaps. 6 and 7.

tures; like icing on a cake, their visibility is no measure of their substance.

Lest it seem that all human action is motivated solely by self-interest,
it must be affirmed that some is clearly motivated by a genuine concern
for others, with no overtones of self-interest. Clearly there are forces in
human experience which are capable of evoking the response of *unselfish
or altruistic love*.[6] However, since in most persons this pattern of response
has only a limited development, altruistic action is most likely to occur in
the minor events of daily life where little is at stake. Apparently many
men develop a genuine desire to be generous and kind in their dealings
with others but find it "impossible" to act in this way when much is at
stake. Thus altruistic action is concentrated on the level of lesser events
and decisions, and is infrequent on the level of major social decisions. In
fact, it appears that one can state as a generalization that *the frequency
of altruistic action varies inversely with the magnitude of the values involved*.

This is not to say that men are immoral when major values are at
stake. Rather, it points to the need to differentiate between two kinds of
morality, *pragmatic morality* and *ideal morality*. Pragmatic morality is the
basis of all popular moral codes, and is based on the recognition that men
need one another, and therefore condemns many kinds of harmful actions,
especially those which threaten to undermine the social order. Ideal
morality, by contrast, has never been accepted as the basis of any popular
moral code, since it not only condemns harmful actions but requires that
men love others as they love themselves and without regard to possible
rewards.

This does not mean that altruism, or unselfish love, is of little or no
importance. It is extremely important from both the psychological and
moral standpoints, and human existence would be much poorer and
harsher if it were absent. It is not, however, a major determinant of the
distribution of power and privilege.

Thus, when one surveys the human scene, one is forced to conclude
that *when men are confronted with important decisions where they are
obliged to choose between their own, or their group's, interests and the
interests of others, they nearly always choose the former*—though often
seeking to hide this fact from themselves and others. This is the *second
postulate* in our theory. As is evident, it leans far in the direction of the
conservative position with its skeptical view of the innate goodness of
man.

[6] Certain religious ideologies, in combination with the personal experience and recognition of undeserved love, seem to be the chief sources of this.

Before leaving this controversial postulate, it may be well to point out that the exchange system and the division of labor in all the more complex societies serve as veils which largely hide this ugly truth. In complex societies men seldom see the consequences of their own economic and political actions. Rather, they observe the workings of the impersonal market system, which favors some and penalizes others. Success or failure thus appears to result from impersonal forces, or forces so complex that the influence of any single individual becomes negligible. This helps to foster the myth that man is by nature good and kind.

The *third postulate* in our theory pertains to the objects of men's strivings. Some, such as the air we breathe, are readily available to all, but most are not. *Most are in short supply*—that is, the demand for them exceeds the available supply.

This is a normal feature of the world of nature. Though we often speak of nature's bounty, the fact remains that all living things have a reproductive capacity which, in view of the limited supply of food and other resources, makes it inevitable that large numbers will die well before the end of their normal life span and most of the others live close to the margin of subsistence.

To some extent man has been able to free himself from these difficulties. Thousands of years ago he learned to increase his food supply and, more recently, he has learned to control reproduction. Yet while man enjoys certain advantages when compared with other living things, he also suffers from certain disadvantages. Unlike the various plants and animals, *man has an insatiable appetite for goods and services*. No matter how much he produces and consumes, he always desires more. This is true chiefly because the goods and services he consumes have a *status value* as well as a utilitarian value. If automobiles were simply a means of transportation, a society able to control its reproduction could eventually satisfy this demand. However, automobiles are also status symbols; hence there is no limit to the demand for their improvement and for the goods and services utilized in their production. The very nature of status striving makes it inevitable that the demand will exceed the supply: those of lower status constantly strive to equal those of higher status and those of higher status always seek to preserve the difference. Given these conditions, satiation is impossible no matter how much man increases production or restricts population increase.

If our first three postulates are correct, that is, if man is a social being, and if most of his important actions are motivated by self-interest or partisan group interest, and if many or most of the objects of his striving are in short supply, then it follows logically that *a struggle for re-*

wards will be present in every human society. This struggle need not always assume violent forms. On the contrary, it can be carried on within the framework of some system of rules. However, the absence of violence does not mean that the struggle is any less real or serious for the parties involved.

Before concluding this portion of our discussion, two further postulates should be entered into the record. The first of these, and fourth in our series, is that *men are unequally endowed by nature with the attributes necessary to carry on these struggles.* Some are born with serious physical handicaps which severely limit their chances. Others are handicapped in less obvious ways, such as by poor physical coordination, mild brain damage, lack of stamina, or even ugliness.

These inequalities in natural endowment are not the primary source of social inequality. But they are important enough to provide some foundation for the ancient conservative thesis that nature is the source of social inequality.

Fifth, and finally, for the present, we postulate that *man tends to be a creature of habit and powerfully influenced by the social counterpart of habit, namely, custom.* William James once called habit "the enormous flywheel of society" and this still seems a fair characterization since habit, like the flywheel, brings the powerful factor of inertia into play in human affairs. The same is true of custom. From the standpoint of the distributive process both habit and custom are tremendously important since they tend to stabilize existing systems of distribution by causing men to accept and take for granted even those distributive arrangements which work to their disadvantage and are not essential. Thus such arrangements prove far more durable and stable than one would expect and persist far longer than a careful analysis of the pattern itself would otherwise indicate.

The Nature of Society

Building on this view of man, it is now possible to turn to the more difficult problem of the nature of human societies. As indicated in the last chapter, here, too, there is a basic conflict between the views of conservatives and radicals and between their intellectual heirs, contemporary functionalists and conflict theorists.

In the conservative tradition human societies have been repeatedly compared to biological organisms. Like organisms, (1) they are systems made up of specialized and interdependent parts, (2) the whole normally outlives the various parts which are continuously being replaced, and (3) the whole has needs which must be met if it is to survive and thrive, and it is the function of the parts to satisfy these needs through their specialized activities. In short, societies, like organisms, are systems in which the survival and well-being of the whole is achieved through the mutual cooperation of the parts. Through such cooperation the good of the whole is obtained and, as a consequence, the good of all the parts.

It is no coincidence that one of the major statements of modern functionalist theory is entitled *The Social System.*[7] Functionalist theory is usually *systemic* theory, positing the systemic character of human societies at the outset and then seeking to explain the action of the parts in terms of the needs and requirements of the whole.

Conflict theory, in contrast, is usually *antisystemic* in character. It emphasizes the conflicts and struggles which constantly threaten to destroy the fabric of society. It is much less concerned with the total society and its needs than with the subunits within societies, the classes, parties, factions, and interest groups, which are forever contending for the advantage. As we noted in Chapter 1, radical theorists tend to view human societies as settings within which the conflicts of life are acted out. They are important chiefly because their characteristics, e.g., their level of economic development, affect the outcome of the struggles. The struggles and the struggling factions, not society, are the central object of concern.

Both of these views strike a responsive chord in any open-minded student of society. Both clearly contain an element of truth. Cooperation is certainly a pervasive feature of all human life and so, too, is conflict. Some patterns of human action make sense only when interpreted in the light of the needs of society as a whole, while others make sense only when interpreted in the light of individual needs and desires. To the degree that any theory denies the importance of either the social or the antisocial elements in human societies, it ignores an important aspect of life and becomes an unreliable interpreter of the human scene.

In order to integrate and synthesize the valid insights of both these traditions, it is necessary to reexamine with some care the concept of "systems," which is so important to conservative theorists. This is a concept which social theory cannot ignore; but neither can it be accepted uncritically as is usually done today.

Basically the concept refers to an organization of interdependent parts possessing a unitary character. Sociologists have borrowed it from other disciplines, such as astronomy, physics, and biology, in an endeavor

[7] Talcott Parsons, *The Social System* (New York: The Free Press, 1951).

to combat the extreme individualism and psychological reductionism of so much of popular thought, especially in the United States. As a weapon in this struggle it has been extremely effective; as a tool in social analysis its record is less impressive.

The greatest source of difficulty is that this concept is normally conceived of in *categorical* terms. Either something is a system or it is not. There is no middle ground. If an aggregation of people are interdependent to any appreciable degree, modern functionalists feel justified in analyzing their way of life in systemic terms. Building on this foundation they then proceed to develop their elaborate analyses, which strain to find social utility in every established pattern of action.

This usage ignores two important facts. First, *systems vary greatly in the degree of the interdependence and integration of their parts.* The constituent parts of human societies enjoy a measure of independence and autonomy which far exceeds that of the parts of most biological organisms or mechanical systems. To ignore this is to invite confusion. Second, *there is no such thing as a perfect human social system in which the actions of the parts are completely subordinated to the needs of the whole.* This is a theoretical construct which has no counterpart or even remote approximation in the real world.[8]

These facts have important implications for social theory. In the first place, if there is no such thing as a perfect social system, we should stop spinning theories which postulate their existence and direct our energies toward the building of theories which explicitly assume that all human organizations are *imperfect systems.* Second, social theorists (and researchers too) should stop trying to find *social* utility in all the varied behavior patterns of men; they should recognize that many established patterns of action are thoroughly antisocial and contribute nothing to the general good. Third, we should expect to find *both* cooperation and conflict as continuous and normal features of human life and should stop viewing conflict as a pathological or abnormal condition, as is often done in contemporary functionalist theory. Fourth, we should devote more attention to the causes and consequences of variations in the degree of group integration. Finally, we must learn to think of distributive systems as reflecting *simultaneously* system needs and unit needs, with each often subverting the other.

[8] Hobbes saw this clearly as his comparison of man with the bees and ants indicates. Of the latter he wrote, "among these creatures the common good differs not from the private; and being by nature inclined to the private, they procure thereby the common benefit. But man, whose joy consists in comparing himself with other men, can relish nothing but what is eminent." Thomas Hobbes, *Leviathan* (New York: Liberal Arts, 1958), chap. 17.

Societal Interests and Individual Interests: Their Relationship

This last point deserves special attention since conservative theorists so often deny that there is any basic conflict between the interests of the group and the interests of the individual, asserting that what is good for society is good for the individual, and vice versa. The classic effort in modern times is Adam Smith's famous treatise, *The Wealth of Nations*. The father of modern economics developed a very impressive case for the thesis that, through the alchemy of the market, the single-minded pursuit of self-interest by each of the members of society redounds to the benefit of society as a whole. A century later the Social Darwinians developed a similar thesis. They maintained that as a result of the operation of the laws of natural selection, only the fittest survived, so that once again the pursuit of self-interest redounded to the benefit of society as a whole.

While it is surely true that the destinies of an individual and his society are linked, there is no simple 1-to-1 relationship between them. This can be illustrated in a number of ways. When a society prospers, some of its members may even experience financial disaster. Conversely, when the economy of a society declines, some of its members may benefit greatly, as shown by the stock market crash of 1929.

Logically, it is not possible for the interests of society to be compatible with the interests of all its members if the interests of these members are themselves incompatible to any appreciable degree. Yet, as we have seen, this is precisely the case. Under such conditions, the most that is possible is that the interests of society are consistent with the interests of *some* of its members. As we shall see later, there is good reason to believe that in many societies throughout history the interests of only a small minority of the members were significantly identified with the interests of the total society.

The conflict between societal interests and individual interests can be shown in yet another way. From the standpoint of society as a whole, it is desirable that the key positions be filled by the best qualified men. From the standpoint of the individual motivated by self-interest, it is usually desirable that he fill one of these positions himself. In most instances, the interests of the individual will be subversive of the interests of the society and vice versa.

Conservative theorists have often argued that occupancy of the key positions in a society is evidence of superior ability and therefore that the actions of the occupants benefit all. However, critics reply, "Superior ability at what? Picking one's parents? Force? Deceit?" Unhappily, these have often been major factors in the acquisition of key positions. The circularity in the logic of the conservative defense is of such a nature as to render it meaningless.

Individual Interests: Their Nature

Up to this point we have frequently referred to societal interests and individual interests, but without ever stating precisely what either is. On first consideration, it may seem that the nature of these interests is so obvious that no discussion is needed. When one reflects on these matters, however, certain difficulties are encountered, especially with respect to the concept of societal interests.

One of the great temptations in this area is to play God and identify these interests with what one feels they ought to be, or what they "really" are. This is, in effect, the practice of the Marxists and other ideologues who know what is good for an individual or a society even better than the persons involved. Such an approach may be fruitful politically, but not scientifically.

If we reject this deductive approach, we are forced back on induction. Two alternatives present themselves: (1) inductions based on *statements* made by the individual or group; (2) inductions based on *inferences from the actions* of the individual or group. Of these two, the latter seems wiser for two reasons. First, both individuals and groups often have reasons for misrepresenting their true interests: dissimulation is often profitable. Second, since the work of Freud, we cannot ignore the role of the subconscious in human behavior. Men's actions are often motivated by desires and goals of which they are only dimly aware. For both reasons it is wiser to base our judgments of the interests which prompt men's actions on what they do rather than on what they say.

The goals or interests of individuals are sufficiently familiar so that an elaborate review of them is unnecessary. However, two complications should be mentioned. First, it is essential to recognize that all men do not share the same goals and even those who do, do not always rank them the same. Three men may value wine, women, and song, but while one values wine most, the second prefers women, and the third song. Such differences are of considerable importance since men are constantly faced with the necessity of choosing among desirable ends.

The economists' concept of "marginal utility" points up the other complication. With respect to many goals, the value varies inversely with the quantity already in hand. Most men are prepared to sacrifice more for their first pair of shoes than for their second, and more for the second than for their tenth. The same is true of most other goods and services: more value is attached to the first units than to later.

These complications make the task of establishing meaningful propositions about the goals toward which men strive difficult, but not impossible. To begin with, it is clear that the great majority of men have always accorded *survival* the highest priority. Though there have been exceptions, such as religious and political martyrs and heroic warriors, most men have not shared their values. The dominant philosophy has been stated in the simple rhyme:

He who fights and runs away
May live to fight another day.

Death ends all hopes, dreams, and ambitions centered in this world. Even those whose goals are centered in the next world usually cling tenaciously to life in this.

The fact that survival is usually given the highest priority has far-reaching implications for the social life of man. First of all, *it causes might or force to be the most effective deterrent and also the supreme sanction in human affairs*. It is no coincidence that violence is the last court of appeal in human conflicts. As will become evident in later chapters, this is a matter of great importance for our theory of distribution.

Because most men value survival so highly, anything which facilitates survival is also valued highly. Practically, this means that food and other goods and services which provide *sustenance* are highly valued, especially since they are normally in short supply.

After survival, it is more difficult to say which is man's most important goal. Probably the two chief contenders are *health* and *status, or prestige*. Little needs to be said concerning health since the value men attach to it is evident in every society. Everywhere men are prepared to pay dearly for the sake of health and freely admit it.

Status, or prestige, is a different matter. Men often deny that they are greatly concerned with it. In our own society, for example, few people will admit to others, or even to themselves, that they value status highly. When we examine their actions, however, the concern for status quickly becomes evident. It influences almost every kind of decision from the choice of a car to the choice of a spouse. Fear of the loss of status, or honor, is one of the few motives that can make men lay down their lives on the field of battle. Robert Lowie, a leading anthropologist of the last generation, was not far wide of the mark when he wrote that primitive man is not a miser, sage, or beast of prey, but rather a peacock. The same might be said of civilized man. The classic documentation of this can be found in Thorstein Veblen's insightful volume, *The Theory of the Leisure Class*.

Modern social psychology helps us understand the great importance men attach to prestige or status. Self-respect is a necessary element in every healthy, properly functioning personality. Where self-respect is destroyed, motivation is undermined. Beginning with Charles Horton Cooley, social psychologists have shown that self-respect is in large measure a function of the respect accorded by others. In other words, the image we form of ourselves is largely a reflection of the image others form of us. Hence, our psychological health and well-being are greatly dependent on our status in the groups we value.

This does not mean that emotional health depends on election to high office or anything of the sort. For most persons, the respect of family and associates is sufficient. However, the same psychological process which causes men to need this limited degree of respect also creates a demand for more. The desire for status gives rise to an insatiable appetite. Few men receive so much honor and respect that they will not seek more when the opportunity presents itself. Thus it is that so many decisions in daily life, and especially the more important, reflect the element of status striving.

Creature comfort is another basic goal. However, it does not compare with survival, health, and status. Often it is difficult to distinguish between men's concern for status and for comfort, with the result that we overestimate the value attached to the latter. For example, the purchase of a car commonly reflects a concern for both. Despite much talk about the utilitarian features of automobiles, however, manufacturers have not found an extensive market for a strictly utilitarian vehicle. The same is true of countless other products whose demand is shaped by both status and utility. Robert Lowie's comparison of man to the peacock has more truth in it than we normally admit.

Two other widely shared goals are the desire for *salvation* in the next world and *affection* in this. For the most part, these goals do not generate any serious social struggles. Like the air we breathe, salvation is available to all who seek it, in most of the major faiths. Affection is not so readily available but, since it is something produced and distributed by primary groups, the struggles for it do not normally assume significance at the societal level.

Men's concern with salvation, together with their fear and love of God, do influence our analysis in another way though. Where men recognize the existence of a system of supernatural sanctions, their actions may be deflected from the course they would follow if this element were not in the picture. How great the deflection is depends both on the nature of the religious system and the seriousness with which it is taken by its adherents. Many religions provide strong supernatural sanction for the existing system of power and privilege, and their chief effect is likely to be a reinforcement of the *status quo*. Certain others, however, notably Judaism and Christianity, provide a basis for an ethical criticism of the existing order and hence sometimes encourage attacks on the *status quo*. Religions which contain a strong ethical component may also function to dull somewhat the sharp cutting edge of self-interest. They may make men of power a bit slower to press their advantage to the point where others are seriously harmed or destroyed. This humanizing role of certain religions can easily be exaggerated, but it can also be overlooked; in the social sciences the latter tendency has been the more common.

All of the goals mentioned thus far are valued in their own right. There are other goals, however, which are sought largely or entirely for their *instrumental* value—that is, because they facilitate the attainment of the goals already mentioned. The classic example is *money*. In and of itself money has little power to satisfy normal human desires, but as a medium of exchange, it can be used to attain creature comforts, improved health, status, and even survival itself. For this reason, money is the object of intense competition in every society where it is found. Because it is a medium of exchange, it can serve equally well men with very different goals. It is as useful to the man who puts status ahead of comfort as to the man who reverses the order. Hence the struggle for money (and also other goals of instrumental value) is at least as intense as the struggle for status, survival, comfort, and other basic goals.

Other forms of wealth occupy a more ambiguous position since they may be sought for their own sake or merely for their instrumental value. It is clear, however, that the intensity of the struggle for wealth is greatly increased because of its instrumental value, which usually increases the number of competitors greatly.

Organizational office and other institutionalized roles with established rights and prerogatives are also widely sought because of their instrumental value. Status and income are attributes of most responsible positions, and in the case of major offices in important organizations, great honor and high income are normally assured. In addition, those in positions of responsibility usually have large numbers of persons prepared to do their bidding, at least within the bounds defined by the authority of their office. Hence, offices, like money, are eagerly sought because they facilitate the attainment of so many goals. By winning high office in the realm of politics, economics, education, or religion, an individual can satisfy many, if not most, of his desires. In the case of women, the role of *wife* is of crucial importance in most societies since it is the basis for many, if not most, of their rights and privileges. Because the magnitude of these rights is so often dependent on the magnitude of the husband's resources, there is usually an active competition for the role of wife of any man of means or promise.

Education, or *training,* constitutes another goal men usually seek more for its instrumental than for its intrinsic value. While there have always been some who valued knowledge for its own sake, most men have sought it chiefly because they thought it useful. With the increasing bureaucratization of the world of work, it seems likely that formal education will become even more eagerly sought in the future.

To attain these goals, individuals are obliged to utilize, as best they can, the various resources with which they are endowed by nature and society. These include possessions and such personal attributes as energy, intelligence, beauty, and physical coordination. Each individual uses these in an effort to achieve those things he values most. In the process, his initial resources are used to obtain instrumental rewards such as education, money, and position, and these in turn are used as resources to obtain or preserve the ultimate satisfactions such as status, comfort, health, and life itself.

This "exchange" process constitutes one of the most important aspects of every distributive system and should be a matter of major concern to students of the distributive process and of stratification.[9] However, unlike the classical economists, we cannot limit our concern to those exchanges which are conducted in accord with the established rules of business practice. We must concern ourselves with both the legal and illegal, the ethical and the unethical, the peaceable and the violent. Were we to limit ourselves to those exchanges which are legal, ethical, and peaceable, we should arrive at a quite misleading answer to the question of who gets what and why. Far too many of the most crucial exchanges—those which establish basic patterns for thousands or millions of subsequent exchanges —fall outside the realm of the legal, the ethical, and the peaceable. In fact, as will become evident in later chapters, the most important exchanges (when judged from the standpoint of their effect on subsequent exchanges) are often the most violent, unethical, and illegal. This is why the classical economists have managed to shed so little light on the ques-

[9] For two recent and noteworthy contributions in this area, see George C. Homans, *Social Behavior* (New York: Harcourt, Brace & World, 1961), and Peter Blau, *Exchange and Power in Society* (New York: Wiley, 1964).

tion of who gets what and why, despite the fact that they have written voluminously on the subject of distribution. Unhappily, the scope of their inquiry has been much too narrow.

Societal Interests: Their Nature

Societal interests are much more difficult to define than individual interests. This is because human societies are such imperfect systems. Their members frequently work at cross-purposes with one another, and the actions of the whole are often harmful to the parts.

A similar situation exists in the case of individuals, but it is less serious since organisms are more perfect systems. Drug addicts, for example, seek drugs even though rationally they want to stop and even though the continued use of the drug is harmful to their nervous system and other parts of the body. Yet in such instances, we do not hesitate to list drugs as one of the primary goals of the individual.

If the same principle is applied to human societies, we are obliged to define as the goals of a given society *those ends toward which the more or less coordinated efforts of the whole are directed—without regard to the harm they may do to many individual members, even the majority.* This means, in effect, that in those societies controlled by a dominant class which has the power to determine the direction of the coordinated efforts of the society, *the goals of the society are the goals of this class.*

Though this conclusion may be disturbing to those with democratic convictions, it seems the only defensible one. Furthermore, it has the virtue of clarifying certain otherwise perplexing problems. For example, it explains why members of politically dominant classes have always found it so much easier than other members of society to "recognize" the "convergence of the interests of the individual and the interests of society." [10] This approach also helps clarify the relation between societal and individual interests. It makes clear that the interests of the individual and his society are not necessarily the same. Whether they are depends largely on the nature of the society and the individual's position in it.

At the risk of oversimplification, one may say that the coordinated actions of societies are directed largely toward one or the other of two basic goals. First and foremost, they are directed toward *the maintenance of the political status quo within the group.* Since perfect stability or equi-

---

[10] For example, a recent president of General Motors and Secretary of Defense asserted that "what is good for General Motors is good for the country, and vice versa." Similarly, the United States Chamber of Commerce has long argued that what is good for business is good for the country.

librium is impossible, this goal might better be described as *the minimization of the rate of internal political change*. This manifests itself in various ways, but particularly in the development of the machinery of state and other agencies and instruments of social control, in the great concern for law and order which every society's leaders express, and in the cultivation of political ideologies which justify the *status quo*. It is also seen in the universal concern of societies and their leaders with defense against foreign aggression.

The second basic goal of societies is *the maximization of production and the resources on which production depends*. Sometimes this has been sought by efforts to promote technological advance; more often it has been through war and conquest.

Neither of these two basic goals receives priority in every society. In some, efforts to minimize political change seem to take preference over efforts to maximize production, while in others the reverse is true. In general it appears that *the goal of maximizing production has priority in relatively unstratified societies and that the goal of minimizing political change has priority in societies in which power and privilege are monopolized by a few.* In societies in which neither of these conditions exists, the two goals seem to be given roughly equal priority.

Other goals might be named, but they are little more than variants or extensions of these two. This suggests one final conclusion about societies: *societies, like individuals, are basically self-seeking units*.[11] In fact, the history of intersocietal relations suggests that the self-seeking element in societies is, if anything, more pronounced than in individuals.

[11] Seen in a broadly comparative perspective, this is an attribute which they share with all forms of life. Much might be gained if more attention than is currently fashionable were paid to the biological bases of human life, and if man and society were viewed as parts, admittedly distinctive, of the world of nature.

3/The Dynamics of Distributive Systems

*Not being able to make that which is just strong,
man has made that which is strong just.*

Pascal

IN ANALYSES of social stratification, it is a temptation to turn immediately to the interesting and much debated structural problems, such as those concerning the nature, number, and composition of classes. While such questions must inevitably be a part of any adequate treatment of the subject, they are secondary in importance to questions about the processes which give rise to the structures. Moreover, to attempt to deal with the structural problems without prior attention to these processes, as is sometimes done, is to put the cart before the horse and create confusion. For these reasons, the present chapter will be concerned chiefly with problems of dynamics, reserving most structural problems for the next chapter.

Two Laws of Distribution

When one seeks to build a theory of distribution on the postulates about the nature of man and society set forth in the last chapter, one soon discovers that these lead to a curious, but important, *dualism*. If those postulates are sound, one would predict that almost all the products of men's labors will be distributed on the basis of two seemingly contradictory principles, *need* and *power*.

In our discussion of the nature of man, it was postulated that where important decisions are involved, most human action is motivated either by self-interest or by partisan group interests. This suggests that power alone governs the distribution of rewards. This cannot be the case, however, since we also postulated that most of these essentially selfish interests can be satisfied only by the establishment of cooperative relations with others. Cooperation is absolutely essential both for survival and for the efficient attainment of most other goals. In other words, men's selfish interests compel them to remain members of society and to share in the division of labor.

If these two postulates are correct, then it follows that *men will share the product of their labors to the extent required to insure the survival and continued productivity of those others whose actions are necessary or beneficial to themselves.* This might well be called the first law of distribution, since the survival of mankind as a species depends on compliance with it.

This first law, however, does not cover the entire problem. It says nothing about how any *surplus*, i.e., goods and services over and above the minimum required to keep producers alive and productive, which men may be able to produce will be distributed. This leads to what may be called the second law of distribution. If we assume that in important decisions human action is motivated almost entirely by self-interest or partisan group interests, and if we assume that many of the things men most desire are in short supply, then, as noted before, this surplus will inevitably give rise to conflicts and struggles aimed at its control. If, following Weber, we define power as the probability of persons or groups carrying out their will even when opposed by others,[1] then it follows that *power will determine the distribution of nearly all of the surplus possessed by a society.* The qualification "nearly all" takes account of the

[1] See Max Weber, *The Theory of Social and Economic Organization*, translated by A. M. Henderson and Talcott Parsons (New York: Free Press, 1947), p. 152, or Max Weber, *From Max Weber: Essays in Sociology*, translated by H. H. Gerth and C. Wright Mills (Fair Lawn, N.J.: Oxford University Press, 1946), p. 180.

very limited influence of altruistic action which our earlier analysis of the nature of man leads us to expect.

This second law points the way to another very important relationship, that between our two chief variables, power and privilege. If privilege is defined as possession or control of a portion of the surplus 13 produced by a society, then it follows that *privilege is largely a function of power, and to a very limited degree, a function of altruism.* This means that to explain most of the distribution of privilege in a society, we have but to determine the distribution of power.

To state the matter this way suggests that the task of explaining the distribution of privilege is simple. Unfortunately, this is not the case since there are many forms of power and they spring from many sources. Nevertheless, the establishment of this key relationship reduces the problem to more manageable proportions, since it concentrates attention on one key variable, power. Thus if we can establish the pattern of its distribution in a given society, we have largely established the pattern for the distribution of privilege, and if we can discover the causes of a given distribution of power we have also discovered the causes of the distribution of privilege linked with it.

To put the matter this way is to invite the question of how the third basic element in every distributive system, *prestige,* is related to power and privilege. It would be nice if one could say that prestige is a simple function of privilege, but unfortunately this does not seem to be the case. Without going into a complex analysis of the matter at this point, the best that can be said is that empirical evidence strongly suggests that *prestige is largely, though not solely, a function of power and privilege, at least in those societies where there is a substantial surplus.*[2] If this is true, it follows that even though the subject of prestige is not often mentioned in this volume, its pattern of distribution and its causes can largely be deduced from discussion of the distribution of power and privilege and their causes in those societies where there is an appreciable surplus.

Graphically, the relationship between these three variables, as set forth in the propositions above, can be depicted in this way:

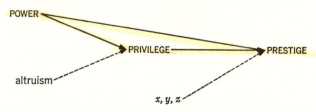

[2] For evidence supporting this generalization, see p. 430. I have not attempted to establish this generalization by deductive logic since this would be a major under-

The solid lines indicate major sources of influence, the dashed lines secondary sources.

To make this diagram complete, one other dashed line should probably be added, indicating some feedback from prestige to power. Thus a more accurate representation of the relationships would look like this:

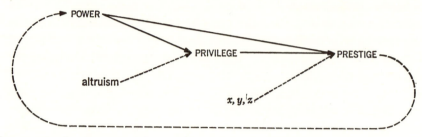

Power is the key variable in the triad from the causal and explanatory standpoint. Hence, it is with this variable that we shall be primarily concerned in the analysis which follows.

The Variable Aspects of Distributive Systems

As the statement of the two laws indicates, the second law does not have any effect on the distributive process until the conditions specified in the first have been satisfied. Until the necessities of life have been made available to enough productive, mutually interdependent members of the group, there is no surplus to be fought over and distributed on the basis of power. Thus, as a first hypothesis we would be led to predict that *in the simplest societies, or those which are technologically most primitive, the goods and services available will be distributed wholly, or largely, on the basis of need.*

As the productivity of societies increases, the possibility of producing a surplus steadily increases, though it should be noted that the existence of a surplus is not a function of technological advance alone. Even though we cannot say that the surplus available to a society increases proportionately with advances in the level of technology, such advances increase the probability that there will be a surplus and also that there will be a sizable surplus. Hence, as a second hypothesis we are led to predict that *with technological advance, an increasing proportion of the goods and services available to a society will be distributed on the basis of power.*

taking requiring the introduction of new postulates and would divert the analysis from its primary task. For the same reason I have not attempted to deal with prestige in other parts of this volume except incidentally.

In view of the dualistic basis of the distributive process, and the variations to which this must necessarily give rise, it would be unwise to attempt to develop a single general theory of distribution or stratification to cover all societies. Rather, we will gain far more if we follow the example of the economists in their analyses of the behavior of markets. As they discovered years ago, it is impossible to create a single general theory of market behavior except of the most limited nature. In order to deal effectively with most of the more complex aspects of market behavior, it is necessary to take account of the existence of different kinds of markets. This has led to the distinction between theories of perfect and imperfect competition. The latter can be further subdivided into theories of oligopoly, monopoly, monopsony, and so forth. In other words, on closer inspection the theory of market behavior turns out to consist of a small number of general principles which constitute the general theory of markets, and a whole series of more limited principles applicable only under specific conditions.

The same approach is required in stratification theory, if our analysis up to this point is sound. If the first two laws of distribution and the two hypotheses based on them are valid, then *the nature of distributive systems will vary greatly, depending on the degree of technological advance in the societies involved.* The variations should be every bit as great as those which differentiate markets where perfect competition prevails from those where imperfect competition holds sway.

For this reason, the major part of this volume will be devoted to a series of analyses of distributive systems in specific types of societies, with the types defined in technological terms. The handful of universally applicable principles of distribution can be dealt with quite briefly and with reasonable adequacy in this chapter and the next.

While the foregoing is reason enough to base our special theories on societal types defined in technological terms, there is one other great advantage derived from this approach. Past research has made it clear that technology is never an isolated variable in sociocultural systems. On the contrary, it tends to be linked fairly closely with a whole series of other variables which evidently stand in a dependent relationship to it.[3] This is especially true of many social organizational variables which are linked with distributive systems and tend to define their limits of possible

[3] See, for example, L. T. Hobhouse, G C. Wheeler, and M. Ginsberg, *The Material Culture and Social Institutions of the Simpler Peoples* (London: Chapman & Hall, 1930) and Alvin W. Gouldner and Richard A. Petersen, *Notes on Technology and the Moral Order* (Indianapolis: Bobbs-Merrill, 1962) for broadly comparative studies, or Ralph Linton, *The Tanala: A Hill Tribe of Madagascar* (Chicago: Field Museum of Natural History, 1933) for an excellent case study.

variation, e.g., nature and extent of division of labor, maximum community size, etc. Hence, *by classifying societies on the basis of technology, we are, in effect, simultaneously controlling, wholly or in part, many other relevant variables*. The value of this will become evident beginning in Chapter 5.

To say that many other characteristics of human societies vary with technology is not to say that all do. Clearly some do not, and others do so only to a limited degree. Wilbert Moore has suggested that supernatural beliefs and aesthetic forms are not so closely correlated with technology as most forms of social organization.[4] The same may also be true of certain basic aspects of family life. However, while these exceptions deserve recognition and careful consideration, they do not vitiate the basic principle involved.

It should also be noted that classifying societies on the basis of the nature of their technology does not imply that all those in a single category have *identical* distributive systems any more than that all oligopolistic markets function the same way. Obviously there are variations within each societal type just as within each type of market, and an effort will be made to identify and account for the more important of them. However, these may be thought of as *second-order variations,* which are best dealt with after the first-order variations have been established and the internal uniformities associated with them clearly delineated.

In dealing with these second-order variations we shall sometimes have to rely on inductive logic to establish both causal and descriptive generalizations. However, this will not always be the case. Sometimes deductive logic can be employed. For example, if the size of a society's surplus affects the nature of its distributive system, and if the size of the surplus depends to some degree on the nature of the physical environment, then we should predict that *differences in the physical environment will lead to secondary differences in distributive systems*. More specifically, the richer the environment, the larger the surplus and the greater the importance of power in the distributive process.

There are also reasons for predicting that the influence of environmental differences will be greater in primitive societies than in those which are technologically more advanced. To begin with, technological advance makes possible the geographical expansion of societies, and the larger the territory occupied by a society, the less the probability that the total environment will be extremely favorable or unfavorable and the

---

[4] Wilbert E. Moore, *Social Change* (Englewood Cliffs, N.J.: Prentice-Hall, 1963), pp. 72–76.

greater the probability that it will include a mixture of favorable and unfavorable land. Hence, environmental variation should be less among the larger, technologically advanced societies than among the smaller, more primitive. In addition, technological advance frequently means the development of alternative solutions to the various problems of production. Technologically advanced societies, therefore, should be less hampered by environmental limitations than primitive societies are, and thus *environmental variation should have less effect on the level of productivity in advanced societies than in primitive.*

Another important source of secondary variation has been identified by Stanislaw Andrzejewski in his important but neglected book, *Military Organization and Society.*[5] As he has shown, both deductive logic and empirical data indicate that *the degree of inequality in societies of a given level of technological development tends to vary inversely with what he calls "the military participation ratio,"* that is *the proportion of the adult male population utilized in military operations.* Where most adult males are utilized for such purposes, the degree of inequality tends to be less than in those in which military needs are supplied by a small force of military specialists. Thus, this factor can also be used to explain some of the secondary variations which are found among societies of the same technological type.

A third source of secondary variations which can be anticipated is the technological variation which exists even among societies classified in the same category. No two societies are identical from the technological standpoint, and their classification into technological types is based on similarities (or identity) with respect to certain fundamental characteristics and ignores secondary differences. If primary differences in technology cause major differences in distributive systems, *one would expect these secondary differences in technology to generate lesser differences in distributive systems.* Thus, one would expect considerable differences between a society in the first stages of industrialization and one which is highly industrialized, just as one would expect differences between a hunting and gathering society with no alternative mode of food production and one which has some rudimentary forms of horticulture to supplement its diet.

Finally, as will become evident later in this chapter, *one can expect secondary variations associated with the stage a society occupies in what I shall call "the political cycle"* (see page 59 of this chapter). In effect, this is a measure of the degree to which the prevailing distributive system

[5] (London: Routledge, 1954), especially chap. 2.

is accepted as legitimate. While this is linked somewhat with the level of technological development of societies, it is no simple function of this variable and hence exercises a substantially independent influence.

Force and Its Transformation

Of the two principles which govern the distributive process, need and power, the first is relatively simple and poses few problems of great importance or difficulty. Unhappily, the same cannot be said of the second. Of all the concepts used by sociologists, few are the source of more confusion and misunderstanding than power. Hence it is necessary to spell out in some detail the nature of this concept and how it functions in the distributive process.

As a starting point, it may be well to return briefly to one of the postulates introduced in the last chapter. There it was assumed that survival is the chief goal of the great majority of men. If this is so, then it follows that *the ability to take life is the most effective form of power.* In other words, more men will respond more readily to the threat of the use of *force* than to any other. In effect, it constitutes the final court of appeals in human affairs; there is no appeal from force in a given situation except the exercise of superior force. Hence force stands in the same relationship to other forms of power as trumps to the other suits in the game of bridge, and those who can exercise the greatest force are like those who control trumps.

This fact has been recognized by countless observers of the human scene in every age. As Pascal put it, "Not being able to make that which is just strong, man has made that which is strong just." Cicero made the same point when he said, "Laws are dumb in the midst of arms," and Hobbes asserted that "Covenants without the sword are but words, and of no strength to secure a man at all."

This principle is also recognized by the leaders of nations, the practical men of affairs. Every sovereign state restricts, and where possible prohibits, the independent exercise of force by its subjects. States may be tolerant of many things, but never of the growth of independent military organizations within their territories. The reason is obvious: any government which cannot suppress each and every forceful challenge to its authority is overthrown. Force is the foundation of sovereignty.

On this point there is no dispute between conservatives and radicals. Their arguments are concerned only with the ends served by the state's use of force. Conservatives insist that might is employed only as the handmaiden of right, to restrain and rebuke those who put self-interest above the common good, while radicals maintain that the state employs might to suppress right, in defense of selfish interests.

If force is the foundation of political sovereignty, it is also the foundation of the distributive system in every society where there is a surplus to be divided. Where coercive power is weak, challenges inevitably occur, and the system is eventually destroyed and replaced by another based more firmly on force. Men struggling over control of the surplus of a society will not accept defeat so long as there is a higher court of appeals to which they may take their case with some likelihood of success and profit to themselves.

The principle involved here is essentially the same as the principle of escalation with which modern military men are so concerned. Small wars based on small weapons inevitably grow into more deadly wars utilizing more deadly weapons if, by advancing the level of conflict, one of the parties anticipates turning defeat into victory. Similarly, in the case of conflicts within societies, the parties involved are always motivated to take the issue to the final court of appeals so long as there is the likelihood of benefiting by it. While men wll not resort to armed revolution for trivial gains, when control over the entire surplus of a society is involved, the prospect is more enticing. The attractiveness varies directly with the weakness of the current regime.

Nevertheless, as Edmund Burke, the famed English conservative, recognized, "The use of force alone is but temporary. It may subdue for a moment; but it does not remove the necessity of subduing again: and a nation is not governed, which is perpetually to be conquered." Though force is the most effective instrument for seizing power in a society, and though it always remains the foundation of any system of inequality, it is not the most effective instrument for retaining and exploiting a position of power and deriving the maximum benefits from it. Therefore, regardless of the objectives of a new regime, once organized opposition has been destroyed it is to its advantage to make increasing use of other techniques and instruments of control, and to allow force to recede into the background to be used only when other techniques fail.

If the new elite has materialistic goals and is concerned solely with self-aggrandizement, it soon discovers that the rule of might is both inefficient and costly. So long as it relies on force, much of the profit is consumed by the costs of coercion. If the population obeys only out of fear of physical violence, a large portion of the time, energy, and wealth of the elite are invariably consumed in the effort to keep it under control and separate the producers from the product of their labors. Even worse, honor, which normally ranks high in the scale of human values, is denied to those who rule by force alone.[6]

If materialistic elites have strong motives for shifting from the rule of might to the rule of right, ideologically motivated elites have even stronger. If the visions and ideals which led them to undertake the terrible risks and hardships of revolution are ever to be fulfilled, the voluntary cooperation of the population is essential, and this cannot be obtained by force. Force is, at best, the means to an end. That end, the establishment of a new social order, can never be fully attained until most members of society freely accept it as their own. The purpose of the revolution is to destroy the old elite and their institutions, which prevent the fulfillment of this dream. Once they are destroyed, an ideological elite strives to rule by persuasion. Thus *those who seize power by force find it advantageous to legitimize their rule once effective organized opposition is eliminated.* Force can no longer continue to play the role it did. It can no longer function as the private resource of a special segment of the population. Rather it must be transformed into a public resource used in the defense of law and order.

This may seem to be the equivalent of saying that those who have at great risk to themselves displaced the old elite must now give up all they have won. Actually, however, this is not at all necessary since, with a limited exercise of intelligence, force can be transformed into authority, and might into right.

There are various means by which this transformation can be effected. To begin with, by virtue of its coercive power, a new elite is in a good position to rewrite the law of the land as it sees fit. This affords them a unique opportunity, since by its very nature law is identified with justice and the rule of right. Since legal statutes are stated in general and impersonal terms, they appear to support abstract principles of justice rather than the special interests of particular men or classes of men. The fact that laws exist prior to the events to which they are applied suggests an objective impartiality which also contributes to their acceptance. Yet laws can always be written in such a way that they favor some particular segment of society. Anatole France saw this clearly when he wrote, "The law in its majestic equality forbids the rich as well as the poor to sleep under bridges, to beg in the street, and to steal bread." Edwin Sutherland provided detailed documentation of the presence of such bias, as have a host

---

[6] For a good discussion of the limitations of rule by force, see Robert Dahl and Charles Lindblom, *Politics, Economics, and Welfare* (New York: Harper & Row, 1953), pp. 107–109. See also Karl A. Wittfogel, *Oriental Despotism: A Comparative Study of Total Power* (New Haven, Conn.: Yale University Press, 1957), chap. 4.

of others.[7] In short, laws may be written in such a way that they protect the interests of the elite while being couched in very general, universalistic terms.

Often a new elite finds that it does not even need to change the laws to accomplish its ends. Typically the old laws were written to serve the interests of the holders of certain key offices, and once these offices have been seized, the new elite can use them as resources to build their fortunes or attain other goals.

Institutions which shape public opinion serve as a second instrument for legitimizing the position of new elites. Through the use of a combination of inducements and threats, educational and religious institutions, together with the mass media and other molders of public opinion, can usually be transformed into instruments of propaganda for the new regime. A determined and intelligent elite working through them can usually surround itself with an aura of legitimacy within a few months or years.

The concept of "propaganda," or the manipulation of consensus, is an integral element in the synthetic theory of stratification. A recognition of this phenomenon and the special role it plays in the distributive process enables us to avoid the impasse which has driven Dahrendorf and others to despair of ever reconciling the conservative and radical traditions. Consensus and coercion are more closely related than those who preach the Janus-headed character of society would have us believe. *Coercive power can often be used to create a new consensus.*

There is probably no better example of this than the Soviet Union. Here a small minority seized control of the machinery of state in 1917 and used the coercive powers of the state to transform the educational system of the nation and the mass media into one gigantic instrument of propaganda. Within a single generation the vast majority of Russians were converted to a sincere and genuine support of most of the basic elements of the Communist Party's program.[8]

In the short run, propaganda may be used to support a great variety

[7] Edwin Sutherland, *White Collar Crime* (New York: Holt, 1949). For a very different kind of documentation of the partiality of laws, see Philip Stern, *The Great Treasury Raid* (New York: Random House, 1964) or any of the many excellent books on political lobbying by vested interests and the benefits derived therefrom.
[8] For documentation of this sweeping generalization, see Alex Inkeles and Raymond Bauer, *The Soviet Citizen* (Cambridge, Mass.: Harvard University Press, 1959). On the basis of interviews with hundreds of displaced persons from the Soviet Union immediately after World War II, these writers concluded that there was only limited questioning of the wisdom of state socialism, centralized planning, and the other major elements of Soviet domestic policy. The chief criticisms were directed at the means employed by the Party in achieving its ends—especially the use of terror. This same conclusion has been reached by most other experts on the Soviet Union.

of programs and policies adopted by an elite. In the long run, however, its basic aim is the dissemination of an ideology which provides a moral justification for the regime's exercise of power. Gaetano Mosca put it this way:

> Ruling classes do not justify their power exclusively by *de facto* possession of it, but try to find a moral and legal basis for it, representing it as the logical and necessary consequence of doctrines and beliefs that are generally recognized and accepted.[9]

Most of the theories of political sovereignty debated by philosophers have been intellectualized versions of some popular ideology. This can be seen in the now discredited belief in the divine right of kings. In our own day, the belief in popular sovereignty serves the same justifying function. A basic element in our current American ideology is the thesis expressed by Lincoln that ours is a "government of the people, by the people, for the people." Another basic element is incorporated in Francis Scott Key's oft-sung phrase, "the land of the free." It is difficult to exaggerate the contribution of these beliefs to the political stability of our present political system and of the distributive system based on it.

Finally, the transformation of the rule of might into the rule of right is greatly facilitated by the pressures of daily life, which severely limit the political activities of the vast majority of mankind. Though the majority may become politically active in a significant way for a brief time in a revolutionary era, the necessity of securing a livelihood quickly drives most from the political arena. For better or worse, few men have the financial resources which enable them to set aside their usual economic activities for long. As a result, the affairs of state in any civilized society, and in many that are not, are directed by a small minority. The majority are largely apolitical. Even in popular democracies the vast majority do no more than cast a ballot at infrequent intervals. The formulation of public policy and the various other tasks required by the system are left in the hands of a tiny minority. This greatly facilitates the task of a new regime as it seeks to make the transition from the rule of might to the rule of right.

The Rule of Right

On first consideration it may seem that the rule of right is merely the rule of might in a new guise, and therefore no real change can be expected in the distributive process. Such a view is as unwarranted as that which

[9] Gaetano Mosca, *The Ruling Class*, translated by Hannah Kahn (New York: McGraw-Hill, 1939), p. 70.

denies the role might continues to play in support of vested interests, even under the rule of right. The fact is that, as the basis of power is shifted from might to right, certain subtle but important changes occur which have far-reaching consequences.

To begin with, if the powers of the regime are to be accepted as rightful and legitimate they must be exercised in some degree, at least, in accord with the conceptions of justice and morality held by the majority —conceptions which spring from their self-interest and partisan group interests. Thus, even though the laws promulgated by a new elite may be heavily slanted to favor themselves, there are limits beyond which this cannot be carried if they wish to gain the benefits of the rule of right.

Second, after the shift to the rule of law, the interests of any single member of the elite can no longer safely be equated with the interests of the elite as a whole. For example, if a member of the new elite enters into a contractual arrangement with some member of the nonelite, and this turns out badly for him, it is to his interest to ignore the law and break the contract. However, this is not to the interest of the other members of the elite since most contractual arrangements work to their benefit. Therefore, it is to their interest to enforce the law in support of the claims of the nonelite to preserve respect for the law with all the benefits this provides them.

Vilfredo Pareto, the great Italian scholar who has contributed so much to our understanding of these problems, has pointed out a third change associated with the shift from the rule of might to the rule of right. As he observed, those who have won power by force will, under the rule of right, gradually be replaced by a new kind of person and in time these persons will form a new kind of elite. To describe the nature of this change, Pareto wrote of the passing of governmental power from "the lions" to "the foxes." [10] The lions are skilled in the use of force, the foxes in the use of cunning. In other words, the shift from the rule of might means that new skills become essential, and therefore there is a high probability that many of the elite will be displaced because they lack these skills. This displacement is greatly facilitated by the fact that the interests of the elite as a class are no longer identical with the interests of each individual member, which means that individually they become vulnerable. Even those who hang on are forced to change, so that in time the nature of the elite as a class is substantially altered, provided it is not destroyed first by a new leonine revolution or coup. Though this change means increased reliance on intelligence and less on force, as Pareto's

[10] See Vilfredo Pareto, *The Mind and Society,* translated by A. Bongiorno and Arthur Livingstone and edited by Livingstone (New York: Harcourt, Brace & World, 1935), vol. III, especially paragraphs 2170–2278.

choice of the term "fox" and his emphasis on "cunning" indicate, the shift to the rule of right is not the beginning of the millennium when lambs can lie down safely with lions—or foxes. Nor is it the end of the era in which self-interest and partisan group interests dominate human action.

As Pareto's analysis suggests, the rule of the foxes means not merely the rise and fall of individuals, but also changes in the power position of whole classes. Specifically, it means some decline in the position of the military and a corresponding rise by the commercial class and the class of professional politicians, both of which are traditionally skilled in the use of cunning. To a lesser degree, it means some improvement in the status of most of the nonmanual classes engaged in peaceful, civilian pursuits.

Fourth, and finally, the transition from the rule of might to the rule of right usually means greater decentralization of power. Under the rule of might, all power tends to be concentrated in the hands of an inner circle of the dominant elite and their agents. Independent centers of power are viewed as a threat and hence are destroyed or taken over. Under the rule of right, however, this is not the case. So long as they remain subject to the law, diverse centers of power can develop and compete side by side. This development is not inevitable, but it can, and probably will, happen once the elite no longer has to fear for the survival of the new regime. As many observers have noted, the degree of unity within a group tends to be a function of the degree to which the members perceive their existence as threatened by others.

In view of these changes, it becomes clear that shifts from the rule of might to the rule of right and vice versa constitute one of the more important sources of variation within societal types defined in technological terms. In other words, even among societies at the same level of technological development, we must expect differences along the lines indicated above, reflecting differences in their position on the might-right continuum.

The Varieties of Institutionalized Power

As the foregoing makes clear, *with the shift from the rule of might to the rule of right, power continues to be the determinant of privilege, but the forms of power change.* Force is replaced by institutionalized forms of power as the most useful resource in the struggle between individuals and groups for prestige and privilege, though force still remains in the picture as the ultimate guarantee of these more genteel forms.

Institutionalized power differs from force in a number of ways which deserve note. To begin with, it is a socially acceptable form of power, which means that those who exercise it are less likely to be challenged and more likely to obtain popular support than are those who use force. Second, institutionalized power tends to be much more impersonal. Individuals claim the benefits of institutionalized power not because of their personal qualities or accomplishments, which might easily be challenged, but simply because they occupy a certain role or office or own a certain piece of property. To be sure, it is often assumed that those who enjoy the benefits of institutionalized power are entitled to them by virtue of superior accomplishments or personal qualities, but this is not the crucial issue and the beneficiary does not have to demonstrate these things. It is enough just to be the occupant of the role or office or the owner of the property. Institutionalized power insures that the benefits flow automatically to such persons without regard to their personal qualities or accomplishments. This is, of course, the chief reason why those who gain power by force strive to convert force into institutionalized power.

Institutionalized power takes many forms, but it always involves the possession of certain enforceable rights which increase one's capacity to carry out one's own will even in the face of opposition. It would be impossible to identify and discuss all these many forms here, but it is important to identify some of the more basic and show their varied nature.[11]

One of the basic distinctions within the category of institutionalized power is that between *authority* and *influence*. Authority is the enforceable right to command others. Influence, by contrast, is much more subtle. It is the ability to manipulate the social situation of others, or their perception of it, by the exercise of one's resources and rights, thereby increasing the pressures on others to act in accordance with one's own wishes.[12] Though these two forms of institutionalized power are quite distinct on the analytical level, they are often hopelessly intertwined on the empirical.

Institutionalized power varies not only in the mode of its action but also in terms of the foundations on which it rests. Here one can speak of

[11] There have been numerous attempts to classify the various forms of power, but none have been completely successful. For three of the better efforts, see Herbert Goldhamer and Edward Shils, "Types of Power and Status," *American Journal of Sociology*, 45 (1939), pp. 171–182; Harold Lasswell and Abraham Kaplan, *Power and Society: A Framework for Political Inquiry* (New Haven, Conn.: Yale University Press, 1950), chap. 5; and Robert Bierstedt, "An Analysis of Social Power," *American Sociological Review*, 15 (1950), pp. 730–738.

[12] In many sociological writings the relationship between power and influence is extremely confusing. Sometimes they are treated as synonymous, other times as two distinct phenomena with no area of overlap. Influence should be treated as one special type of power. This approach is consistent both with good English usage and with the insights of some of the abler social theorists. For example, *Webster's Collegiate Dictionary* (5th ed.) defines influence as "the act or the power of producing an effect *without apparent force or direct authority*" (emphasis added).

a distinction between *the power of position* and *the power of property*. The power of position means *the power which rightfully belongs to the incumbent of any social role or organizational office possessing authority or influence*. This can be seen in the case of officers of state who enjoy great authority and influence so long as they continue to occupy their post, but who lose it when they are replaced. While this is one of the more impressive examples of the power of position, the same basic phenomenon can be seen in the case of the incumbents of a host of lesser roles. One must include under this heading not merely positions in political organizations, but also those in economic, religious, educational, and military organizations, together with age and sex roles, roles in kin groups, roles in racial and ethnic groups, and every other kind of role or office with authority or influence.

A second foundation on which institutionalized power commonly rests is the *private ownership of property*. Though property and position have often been closely linked, the connection is neither necessary nor inevitable. The ownership of property is frequently dissociated from occupancy of a particular office or role. Since property is, by definition, something in short supply and hence of value, the owner of property controls a resource which can be used to influence the actions of others. The more he owns, the greater is his capacity to influence, and thus the greater his power. In some instances, as in the ownership of slaves or of a political office which has been purchased,[13] the power of property can take the form of authority. It also takes the form of authority to the extent that the owner is entitled to proscribe certain actions by others—that is, order them *not* to do certain things, such as trespass on his land.

Before concluding this brief introduction to institutionalized power, it may be well to take note of Simmel's observation that where the rule of law or right prevails, there is always a two-way flow of influence (and sometimes, one might add, of authority as well) between the more powerful and the less powerful.[14] This point is easily forgotten, since the very concept "power" suggests a one-directional flow. To say that there is a two-way flow does not mean that the flow is equally strong in both directions, but it does mean that one should not ignore the secondary flow or the factors responsible for it and the consequences of it.[15]

[13] On the purchase of offices, see pp. 224–225.
[14] Georg Simmel, *The Sociology of Georg Simmel,* edited and translated by Kurt Wolff (New York: Free Press, 1950), part 3.
[15] More recently the same point was made by Robert Dahl and Charles Lindblom in their book *Politics, Economics and Welfare,* part 4, where they point to the existence of four sociopolitical systems, two of which, price systems and polyarchical systems, involve some measure of influence by the less powerful over the more powerful.

Political Cycles

As a reading of history makes clear, there has usually been a more or less cyclical alternation in human societies between periods in which the rule of might held sway and others in which the rule of right was dominant to greater or lesser degree. These political "cycles," as I shall call them, each span the existence of a given political regime.[16] Each cycle begins with the forcible seizure of power by a new elite and involves an initial phase of violence during which organized resistance is either destroyed or suppressed. The next phase is one in which the regime strives to reduce its dependence on naked force and to increase its legitimate authority. During this phase the trend toward constitutionalism, or the rule of right, may be halted or even reversed if the power of the elite is seriously challenged by forces either at home or abroad. However, unless there is a steady succession of such challenges, the long term trend involves a reduction in the active role of force and coercion and an increase in the role of persuasion and incentive until finally the cycle comes to an end when the regime is overthrown by its successor or some foreign conqueror.

To introduce the concept of cycles into our theory is not to imply that history repeats itself or that one cycle is exactly like another. Obviously cycles differ in a number of significant ways.

To begin with, cycles do not have any uniform duration. Some are very brief, as in the case of the cycle which began in Russia with the February Revolution of 1917 and ended with the October Revolution in the same year. Others extend over centuries, as in the case of the present British cycle, which dates back to the middle of the seventeenth century.

Short cycles differ considerably from those of longer duration. Because they are so brief, the process of legitimation, or constitutionalism, hardly gets started, and a new era of violence may be instituted before the last has really ended.

Even where cycles are of comparable duration, other factors inevitably influence the progress of constitutionalism, either hindering or promoting its growth. For example, the nature of the struggles which initiate the cycle can be quite important. Other things being equal, constitutionalism develops more quickly after a prolonged and bitter war to free the nation from foreign tyranny than after a revolution which sets brother

---

[16] I shall use the term "regime" to refer to the members of a particular political elite who come to power by force and to all their successors who come to power by legitimate means. Thus a regime governs from the time of its victory in one revolution until its defeat or overthrow in a subsequent war or revolution.

against brother. The nature of the preceding regime or regimes is also likely to have some effect. Societies which have never developed a tradition of constitutional government move more slowly in this direction than those which have such a tradition. Also, it is logical to predict that the traditions of constitutionalism develop more quickly after a brief and limited palace revolution than after a prolonged and far-reaching social revolution.

The economic situation of a nation is also likely to affect the degree to which constitutionalism develops. One would predict that a high level of productivity and a rapid advance in the level of productivity would each be conducive to the development of constitutional government. Both provide increased opportunities for men to satisfy their desires without recourse to violence.

Taking all of the foregoing together, it may be predicted that *constitutional government will be most highly developed where (1) the political cycle is of long duration, (2) the present regime was established during a war of national independence, (3) constitutional government flourished before the present cycle began, (4) there have been few, if any, serious threats to the existing regime, (5) a high level of productivity prevails, and (6) there is a period of rapid economic development.* In short, the full flowering of constitutional government depends upon a peculiar combination of circumstances which have not occurred often in human history.

Other important differences in political cycles are linked with the nature of the elite which overthrew the old regime and dominated the first phase of the new cycle. Sometimes plunder and self-aggrandizement are their sole concern; these may be called "materialistic" elites. Trujillo's regime in the Dominican Republic and the Saudi dynasty in Arabia are classic examples from recent history.

In some instances, however, elites are motivated by ideals and visions of a more equitable social order. These may be called "ideological" elites.[17] The Communist regimes which won control in Russia, Yugoslavia, and China in recent decades are examples of this type of elite.

Frequently there is some mixing of these two elements, and sometimes this mixture is highly complex. For example, a frank and honest appraisal of the American Revolution indicates that both elements were present. While some of the Founding Fathers were chiefly concerned with the attainment of the noble ideals set forth in the Declaration of Independence and the Preamble to the Constitution, others were more con-

---

[17] Pareto makes a similar distinction, though without using these labels (paragraph 2268)

cerned with avoiding the payment of taxes to the British crown. The fact that materialistic and ideological elements are sometimes intermingled suggests that we must think of this distinction in variable, rather than categorical, terms.

When one materialistic elite succeeds another, only minor changes are likely in the distributive system. One gang of rascals replaces another in those public offices which provide the best opportunities for plunder. These are often called "palace revolutions," since all that is involved is a turnover in personnel in the elite positions. Sometimes, if such an elite is especially vigorous and inventive, these changes in personnel may be accompanied by changes in the formal structure of government. A republic may give way to a monarchy, or vice versa. Such changes may be motivated by a desire either to make the government a more efficient instrument of plunder or to simulate social reforms and thus for a time to silence potential critics.

When ideological elements are dominant in a successful elite, much more substantial changes can be expected in both the political and the distributive systems. Along with sweeping changes in personnel, there are usually pervasive and meaningful changes in the structure of government (and often other basic institutions as well). The term "social revolution" is often employed to emphasize the difference between this type of revolution and "palace revolutions." The labels are not important, but the differences to which they direct attention are: palace revolutions affect only the few, while social revolutions affect everyone—even the Dr. Zhivagos who strive mightily to ignore them.

While the differences between political cycles should never be minimized, neither should the underlying similarities. In every society there is a natural tendency for those who seize power by force to strive to rule by constitutional means, so far as circumstances permit. Yet in the end every regime is destroyed by force or the threat of it. This is the basic theme on which there are a thousand variations.

Cyclical theories have never had a great appeal for Americans, who, because of their peculiar national experience, have inclined to more optimistic theories of history. For those chiefly familiar with American history, supplemented somewhat by an acquaintance with British history, it has been easy to interpret human history as a whole, including the political component, as one more or less consistent movement from the crude, the primitive, and the tyrannical, to the efficient, the productive, and the democratic. Unfortunately, when we broaden our horizons to take account of Cuba, Paraguay, Bolivia, Argentina, Brazil, Peru, Hungary, Yugoslavia, France, Poland, Germany, Russia, Syria, Iran, India, Vietnam, China, and indeed most of the rest of the world, our faith in the progressive character of political history is badly shaken. For who would dare assert that there has been any progressive trend of long duration leading to an increase in either constitutional or democratic government in these nations?

Progressive theories of political development are likely to find wide acceptance only in those societies fortunate enough to enjoy an unusually long cycle during which the legitimation process can come to full flower. Britain and the United States have been unusually fortunate in this regard, with the former enjoying a cycle now three centuries old and the latter one which will soon be two centuries old. By contrast, in just the last half century both Poland and Cuba have each experienced the violent overthrow of no less than four regimes and the initiation of four new political cycles. Unhappily, the experiences of these nations are more nearly typical than those of Britain and the United States. This is probably the major reason why American theory in the field of stratification seems so strange and irrelevant to many foreign observers. It is adapted to a very special set of conditions which have no counterpart in most societies.

The Middle Classes and the Institutionalization of Power

As historians and students of politics have long recognized, revolutions are the work of small minorities. Hence, when the revolution is over, the new elite is obliged to employ the services of others to achieve their objectives. Only in this way can they hope to bring the surplus of the society effectively under their control and effect its transformation into the kinds of goods and services they desire.

Fortunately for the new elite, their position of power provides them with the necessary resources for securing the help they need. The portion of the economic surplus they already control can be used to hire an army of technicians and specialists who can bring still more of the surplus under control. This can then be used to hire others to transform the raw materials into fine homes, beautiful clothes, works of art, public monuments, personal services, and the thousand and one things that men of power and privilege desire, or, in the case of an ideological elite, to staff the institutions which will transform society.

This process leads to the creation, extension, or perpetuation of a middle stratum of technicians and specialists working in the service of the elite. These include public officials, craftsmen, artists, servants, merchants, soldiers, priests, and scholars. The chief task of the officials is to locate the economic surplus and separate it from its producers. As Shaw's Caesar put it when challenged to explain his great interest in Egyptian taxes, "My friend, taxes are the chief business of a conqueror of the world." Craftsmen and artists are necessary to transform the surplus into the kinds of goods and services desired by the elite. Merchants facilitate the movement of goods to the places where they are wanted by those with the means to purchase them. Personal servants provide the innumerable services which men of rank cannot provide for themselves. Priests and scholars contribute to the maintenance of public order and, when they fail, the military can take over. In short, a complex apparatus is brought into being, the primary function of which is to insure the elite's continued control over the economic surplus and its transformation into the varied kinds of goods and services the elite·desires.

As should be evident, those in the employ of the elite are rewarded in proportion to the value of their services to the elite, and the scarcity of the supply of replacements. Contrary to such functionalist theorists as Kingsley Davis and Wilbert Moore, these roles are not rewarded in proportion to their contribution to the common good.[18] It is the needs of the elite, not the needs of the total society, which determine the demand curve for such services. *The distribution of rewards in a society is a function of the distribution of power, not of system needs.* This is inevitable in such imperfect systems as human societies.

When a political cycle survives for an appreciable period of time, the nature of the middle classes and their relation to the political elite gradually changes. In eras of constitutional rule there is a tendency for these classes to arrogate to themselves certain of the powers and privileges of the elite. This is not difficult since it is their normal function to act on behalf of the elite. Powers delegated often become powers lost; once lost they are not easily recovered. Thus it appears that *the greater the degree of constitutionalism in a society, the less the middle classes function merely as agents of the elite and the greater their personal independence, autonomy, and security.* This is an important development and we shall have frequent occasion to refer to it in later pages. However, it should not be allowed to obscure the more basic relation between the middle classes and the elite which continues even in an era of constitutionalism.

Reactions

Up to this point we have viewed the struggles for power and privilege chiefly from the standpoint of the elite, noting how, by various means, they bring the surplus of society under their control. This is only half the story, however, since in sociology, as in physics, *actions produce reactions.*

[18] Kingsley Davis and Wilbert Moore, "Some Principles of Stratification," *American Sociological Review,* 10 (1945), pp. 242–249.

Thus the exercise of power and privilege by elites invariably produces reactions by other members of society. These are no less important than the actions which produce them, hence they will be our primary concern for the remainder of the chapter.

These reactions are extremely varied, and one of the major tasks of stratification theory is to determine how the different segments of the population react, and with what consequences. The goal is to predict as accurately as possible the nature, frequency, and consequences of re-actions to elite rule. In our examination of these reactions we shall begin with those which are the least threatening to the current elite and proceed by stages to the discussion of revolutionary movements, which pose the greatest threat.

Of all the many reactions to the exercise of power and privilege in societies, the one most valued by the elites themselves is that of *competition among nonelites for positions in their employ.* In order to attract the best qualified men to these important middle stratum positions, elites make them more desirable than other nonelite positions. In the case of certain key positions, the inducements are substantial. A vigorous compe-tition naturally develops for these positions, and members of the elite are only too happy to encourage it since they are the chief beneficiaries. What-ever expenses they incur can easily be recouped many times over when these positions are filled by capable, zealous, and loyal men.

Every system of power and privilege also sets in motion a deadly *struggle for survival among the offspring of the common people,* except in those societies which are able to control reproduction or in which there is a temporary shortage of population such as may be created by major plagues, famines, or other disasters. Unhappily, mankind has always been able to produce more offspring than society can maintain, especially when the economic surplus is skimmed off by a privileged elite. Usually there has not been land enough for every farmer's son to farm, nor farmers enough for every farmer's daughter to marry. Hence some of the common people of almost every generation have been reduced to the status of beggars, criminals, and prostitutes. Such persons have usually had short lives, since at this level the competition for survival is intense.[19] From the stand-

[19] It would be a mistake to suppose that conditions would have been very different if there had been no elite to appropriate the economic surplus. Without the elite, there would have been no economic surplus, since population growth would have kept pace with gains in productivity—at least prior to the development of modern methods of birth control. Strange as it may seem, until modern times there was an economic sur-plus in societies chiefly because the ambitions of the elite kept the growth of popula-tion in check.

Taking a long-run view of this problem, it is clear that the exploitative character of elites and their expropriation of the economic surplus were necessary prerequisites

point of the elite, the struggles which developed among the common people have been a matter of little concern, since human fecundity always insured an ample supply of qualified producers. In fact, these struggles probably served the interests of the elite by diverting attention from their own exploitative role, thus affording them a considerable measure of security against popular protest and revolution.

A third reaction to the exercise of power and privilege is one which usually annoys elites but represents no serious threat to their security or status. This is the response of *petty thievery* by those in subordinate positions. Wherever household servants are employed, petty thievery is almost taken for granted. In many societies it is common practice for craftsmen to keep part of the materials with which they work for their own private use, and peasants often hide a portion of their harvest from tax collectors or from landlords with whom they have sharecropping arrangements. Such practices are irritating to elites, but because the losses are small and involve many isolated incidents, it is usually not worth their while to do much about them. Occasionally, when some flagrant violation is detected, the offender may be punished severely in the hope of intimidating others, but this procedure rarely stops the practice.

A fourth type of reaction to the exercise of power and privilege manifests itself in the *efforts of members of the middle classes to gain control over powers, privileges, and resources traditionally reserved to the elite*. Most elites, when they come to power, limit control over key resources to their own number. For example, in many societies the ownership of land has been the privilege of a noble elite. Similarly, the franchise was limited at first to the wealthy.

This situation causes great insecurity for members of the middle classes, since their position of modest power and privilege is so largely dependent on the continuing goodwill of their superiors. If they lose favor, they have no resources to fall back on. Hence, there is a natural desire to gain control of some resources which would free them from this dependence. Not only does this hold the promise of greater security for the future, it also insures greater power and privilege in the present.

Certain members of the middle classes have not only the motives, but also the means to implement them. This is especially true of officials

to social progress. Had there been no exploitative elites, there would have been no economic surplus to support the technicians, inventors, artists, philosophers, prophets, and other cultural innovators who brought modern civilization into being. If one values modern civilization, or any important aspect of it, he has the age-old phenomenon of exploitation to thank for it. This is no justification for all aspects of these systems of exploitation, since much of the economic surplus was used in culturally unproductive ways, but it does serve as yet another reminder of the complexity of the human condition.

serving an elite which is anxious to withdraw from the tiresome tasks of managing its own affairs to cultivate the art of leisure. As with petty thievery, such action is so subtle in character that an elite is often oblivious to its existence until it is too late to do anything about it.

This particular pattern of reaction to the exercise of power and privilege is especially important because it plays such an important role in the development of constitutional government. Those who respond this way are men of cunning rather than men of force, to use Pareto's terms. Because of this, they find a complex system of law well suited to their purposes, and they strive by every means at their disposal to increase the law's importance and power.

A fifth type of reaction to power and privilege manifests itself in *crimes of violence directed against members of the elite and their agents.* More often it is against the latter since, as the working arm of the elite, they come into more frequent contact with the lower classes, who are the chief offenders. These crimes are always taken very seriously. The severity of the punishments undoubtedly reflects a recognition of the existence of widespread, latent hostility toward the holders of power and the realization that anything less than prompt and severe punishment may encourage more widespread violence. Furthermore, when crimes of this sort occur, the interests of the elite and the middle classes coincide and all the holders of power line up on the same side, thus making for a very unequal contest.

Up to this point, the reactions with which we have been concerned have all involved the uncoordinated actions of individuals. Sometimes, however, the exercise of power and privilege in a society leads to *collective* reactions by large numbers of the common people. For the moment we shall be concerned only with the nonviolent cases.

This type of action is possible only under two conditions. Either there must be a constitutional regime in power which recognizes the right of the common people to organize in defense of their own interests, or the ruling elite must be hard pressed by foreign foes and badly in need of the military service of the common people. A good example of the latter may be seen in the early successes of the Roman plebeians in their struggles with the patricians in the fifth century B.C. It is probably no coincidence that this type of reaction has become so much more common in the last century in the western world. Ever since the French Revolution drastically changed the techniques of warfare by introducing conscription and the mass army, elites have been much more dependent on the common people. This may well have been one of the major reasons for the extension of the franchise in the last century and for the growing acceptance by elites of labor unions, workingmen's political parties, and all the other organizations designed to promote and protect the interests of the common people.

A final form which the reaction to power and privilege often takes involves the clergy. Earlier they were listed among the members of the middle classes which act as agents of the ruling elite. Actually, this is not completely accurate, since the clergy enjoy a basis of power partly independent of the ruling elite. Unlike the other specialists and technicians who make up the middle classes, the clergy perform services which the masses value. Furthermore, they are also agents of a higher power than the elite and because of this even the elite usually respect and fear them to some degree. Hence, they are in a unique position to make demands on the economic surplus. In fact, according to archaeologists, the demands the priests made in the name of the gods they served were probably the basis for the formation of the first economic surplus in the ancient Middle East.[20]

Throughout history there has been *a continuing struggle between the political and religious elites in most nations.* In these struggles the chief weapon of the religious elite has been their influence over political ideologies. By themselves they can often block the coveted path to legitimation and therefore can often fight the political elite on fairly even terms.

Sometimes the political elite has emerged victorious, sometimes the religious. Usually, however, the result has been a compromise involving an alliance of church and state. In exchange for the ideological support of the priests, the political elite protect them against religious competition. Such an arrangement usually works to the common advantage of both parties.

The net effect of these many and varied reactions to the exercise of power and privilege by political elites is the strengthening of the tendency toward constitutional government. Constitutional government is, in essence, government which is based more on consent than on force. To obtain this consent, some concessions are required.

In effect, constitutional government rests on the foundation of an exchange which serves the interests both of the elite and of the other segments of the population. The elite forswear the use of violence except under more or less specified conditions, hence introducing an element of predictability and order into the life situation of the others. In exchange they receive the consent of others to their rule, which includes the tacit support of their use of force when it is in keeping with the dictates of the

[20] See V. Gordon Childe, *Man Makes Himself* (London: Watts, 1936), especially the latter part of chap. 6 and all of chap. 7.

law. In a sense, there is something approximating a social contract, but since it is between unequals, it differs from the idealized versions described by earlier writers.

Thus the views of both conservatives and radicals contain an element of truth. Government does indeed rest on the foundation of consent, as the conservatives have maintained, but it also rests on the foundation of force, as the radicals have asserted. In short, both positions are true, but neither is the whole truth.

The Downfall of Regimes

Despite the best efforts of political elites, no regime survives forever. From the standpoint of the study of distributive systems, the forces which bring about the downfall of regimes are no less important than those which stabilize and strengthen them.

Though many factors contribute to the downfall of political regimes, there are only two means by which they are actually overthrown, *war* and *revolution*. It is on these which we must focus.

From the standpoint of any theory of distribution, war is simply a special form of the ubiquitous and continuous struggle for control of the economic surplus. What makes it distinctive is that it involves a struggle between two established elites rather than between elite and nonelite elements of the same society. Every established elite has at its disposal armed forces to protect or advance its interests. The chief deterrent to war has usually been the absence of profitable opportunity. No elite ever embarked on a war of conquest unless the probable gains outweighed the probable costs. As a result, wars have been less likely when there has been a reasonable balance of power between nations than when one nation enjoyed a definite advantage.

Pareto suggested that one of the factors which may upset the balance of power, and hence precipitate wars and revolutions, is the overreliance of constitutional governments on cunning. In other words, they strive to replace military might with skill in diplomacy and similar techniques, and in the end bring about their own destruction. While Pareto may have overstated the case, there is reason for believing that constitutional regimes have this tendency.

On the other hand, constitutional regimes are less likely to initiate aggressive action. Those who have come to power by the exercise of cunning, or intelligence, are less inclined to use force except as a last resort, unless the risks are obviously slight (as in Britain's wars with African tribes during the period of colonial expansion).

Finally, since the fruits of war usually go only to the elite, one would predict that the larger the percentage of the population involved in the decision of whether or not to fight, the less the probability of aggressive action. Thus the likelihood of a democratic nation starting a war of aggression is less than that of a nondemocratic state. One should not assume, however, that this factor is decisive, since even in a democracy an elite can sometimes stir the populace to militance through the skillful use of propaganda.

When an elite is victorious in war, it has three options so far as its treatment of the conquered elite is concerned. First, it may destroy the latter and assume its powers directly. Second, it may incorporate the conquered elite in its own system of power in a subordinate position. Third, it may replace it with a new elite of its own choosing, one which would comply with its demands in future years and permit much of the surplus of its own society to be drained off by tribute, trade, or other means. A conquered elite survives as an elite only if the second alternative is adopted. Otherwise the old regime comes to an end and with it the political cycle, with all that this implies.

War poses fewer problems than successful revolutions, since in the case of war, both parties possess the necessary means. In the case of revolution, the situation is more complicated. A successful revolution requires at least three ingredients: (1) men, (2) organization, and (3) resources. But where can these be found apart from elites themselves?

In every state there is always one group which possesses the necessary resources. This is none other than the organization entrusted with the defense of the state and the existing regime: *the military establishment*. It is no coincidence that in the course of history the great majority of revolutions have been carried out by military men. Others may be hostile and others may be greedy and ambitious, but they lack the means to implement their desires. The military always has the *means* at its disposal: it only requires the *motivation*. Since the means are the rarer of the two, revolutions originating in the armed forces of a nation are vastly more common than ones originating elsewhere. Furthermore, they are far more likely to be successful. In fact, they rarely fail unless the military is divided against itself.

Machiavelli recognized this danger and in *The Art of War* advised that "war . . . ought not to be followed as a business by any but princes or governors of commonwealths; and if they are wise men they will not suffer any of their subjects or citizens to make that their only profession." The British aristocracy also recognized the danger, and for this reason long maintained the purchase system whereby top positions in the military were reserved for men of wealth, who had a vested interest in the preservation of the status quo. As Lord Palmerston put it a century ago:

> If the connection between the Army and the higher class of society were dissolved, then the Army would present a dangerous and unconstitutional appearance. It was only when the Army was unconnected with those whose property gave them an interest in the country, and was commanded by unprincipled military adventurers, that it ever became formidable to the liberties of the nation.[21]

Judging by the startled reactions with which so many Americans greeted the various "colonels' revolts" in Asia and the Middle East after World War II, these principles are poorly understood in this country. As noted previously, training in American history is poor preparation for understanding the political life of most of the rest of the world.

Many, if not most, of the revolutions led by military men have been simply palace revolution.[22] For this reason, the majority of sociologists have shown little interest in them, thinking them of minor importance.

This lack of interest in palace revolutions is largely a reflection of the influence of Marx and Engels. Their work, both scholarly and political, has oriented modern social science to a one-sided concern with social revolutions. However, if our analysis of the nature of political cycles is correct, palace revolutions can also be extremely important. *Where they are a recurrent phenomenon, they seriously hinder the development of constitutionalism.* For those who value the freedom of the individual from tyranny and despotism, this is no minor matter.

While military men are usually the leaders of palace revolutions, *intellectuals* are likely to be the leaders of social revolutions. They alone can supply the one crucial ingredient without which social revolutions are impossible—a new ideology to challenge and destroy the existing one. Ideologies are the stock in trade of intellectuals. They are the opinion leaders with respect to important philosophical questions. Intellectuals may be engaged in any type of employment, but they are concentrated in teaching, preaching, and the arts.

Intellectuals are easily alienated by systems of power and privilege. They are like ministers without portfolio, experts without the power to translate their ideas into public policy. Hence there is a natural basis for alienation. Enlightened elites, therefore, usually find it wise to flatter

---

[21] Quoted by Cecil Woodham-Smith, *The Reason Why* (New York: McGraw-Hill, 1953), chap. 2. This volume provides a fascinating discussion of the operation of the purchase system in nineteenth-century England and some of the events which led to its eventual elimination. Quoted by permission.

[22] There have been some exceptions, however, as the careers of Atatürk and Nasser testify.

them with attention and honors, thus securing their gratitude and support.

Such tactics have usually worked quite well. Most intellectuals have stoutly defended the conservative position, thus making a major contribution to the defense of power and privilege. By their skill with symbols they have successfully proven to the common people the inevitability, as well as the countless advantages, of the *status quo*.

Sometimes, however, elites become careless, or certain intellectuals have refused to respond to their blandishments. By themselves, rebellious intellectuals are no threat to a political elite. They lack the numbers and resources necessary to bring about a successful revolution. However, working in conjunction with others, they can provide the catalytic agent, the counterideology, which is necessary for every successful social revolution.

Another segment of the population of most societies which is attracted with great frequency to social revolutions is that made up of *ethnic, racial, and religious minorities.* These groups usually hold special grievances against the dominant majority and thus are more receptive to counterideologies. Unlike the lower class members of the dominant group, there is no common cultural tie to provide a basis for identification with the elite.

Such groups can usually supply numbers to revolutionary causes, and organization as well. Above all, they can sometimes provide financial resources, which are often so difficult for revolutionary movements to acquire. While minority status groups are usually excluded from the higher social and political levels of society, as we noted earlier, they sometimes make substantial economic advances. The economic success of the Jews in Europe, the Hindus in Africa, the Japanese in Hawaii, and the Jains in India are but a few examples. The wealthy members of such groups have often been among the major financial backers of social revolutions.

No social revolution can succeed, however, so long as the army stands firmly behind the existing regime. Lenin saw this clearly when he wrote, "No great revolution has happened or can happen without the disorganization of the army." Katharine Chorley came to a similar conclusion in her book, *Armies and the Art of Revolution*, which is probably the best study available on the role of the armed forces in revolutions.[23] In her opinion no revolution of the masses can be successful unless the military forces of the old regime are either subverted or neutralized. So long as the military stand firmly behind the regime, it not only can survive but

[23] (London: Faber, 1943).

can crush any rebellion directed against it. History shows few exceptions to this.

Thus, we are again driven back to a recognition of the crucial role played by specialists in force, both in the preservation and destruction of political regimes. Although a few revolutions have succeeded without support from the armed forces, these have usually occurred at the time the army was badly demoralized and disintegrating, e.g., the Russian Revolution of 1917. Having postulated that force is the final court of appeals in human conflicts, these facts should not surprise us.

4/The Structure of Distributive Systems

The greatest and the best of our race have necessarily
been nurtured in the bracing school of poverty
—the only school capable of producing
the supremely great, the genius.
Andrew Carnegie

AS THE LAST CHAPTER DEMONSTRATES, it is never entirely possible to separate analyses of social dynamics from analyses of social structure. Even though we were concerned chiefly with the dynamics of distributive systems, structural considerations frequently intruded. In the present chapter the situation is reversed and our chief concern will be with structural matters, but again the separation will be far from perfect. The simple fact is that both structure and dynamics are abstractions from the same reality and hence can never be completely divorced from one another. Thus, even though the primary concern of this chapter is with the structural aspects of distributive systems, it will be necessary to devote considerable attention to problems of dynamics.

Since the study of structure is the study of relationships among parts, it is necessary to begin this examination of the structure of distributive systems by establishing the nature of these parts. This is a fairly simple matter since there are only three types of units with which we shall be concerned, *individuals, classes,* and *class systems.* Each of these represents a different level of organization within distributive systems. Individuals are the basic level and, as such, constitute the units within classes. The latter, in turn, are the units within class systems.[1] To complete the picture, the several class systems of a society (and normally there are several) are the units within distributive systems.

The nature of the first of these kinds of units is self-evident and requires no further discussion. The other two, however, have been used in so many ways that they have become sources of considerable confusion. Hence, it is to them that we now turn.

Classes

The confusion surrounding this term is largely a result of the complexity of the reality it represents and of the tendency of scholars to oversimplify. As our analysis of the last chapter indicated, stratification is a multidimensional phenomenon. Human populations are stratified in various ways, and each of these alternative modes of stratification provides a basis for a different conception of class. Thus, although one may legitimately analyze the population of a given community in terms of prestige classes, this does not exhaust the subject of stratification. The same population can also be analyzed in terms of power classes or privilege classes. Analytically each of these is quite distinct, though empirically there is a substantial measure of overlap as our earlier analysis indicated.

The difficulty is further increased since even these three modes of classification are not unidimensional. As shown in the last chapter, power takes many forms and these cannot always be reduced to a meaningful common denominator. An individual may have large property holdings without occupying a correspondingly important and powerful office and vice versa. Similarly, an individual may occupy an important and powerful role in one institutional system but not in others.

In view of this, it is clear that the term "class" should not be defined too narrowly. More can be gained by defining the term broadly and then distinguishing carefully between different kinds of classes. Therefore, we might best define a class as *an aggregation of persons in a society who*

---

[1] As will be noted later, the concept "class" may actually apply to several adjacent levels of organization, as when we speak of subclasses within classes. However, this does not alter the basic fact that classes are a level of organization standing between individuals and class systems.

stand in a similar position with respect to some form of power, privilege, or prestige.

This is *not* to say that all types of classes are equally important for theoretical and analytical purposes. On the contrary, if our goal is to answer the question of "who gets what and why?" and if our analysis of the last two chapters has any validity at all, *power* classes must be our chief concern. The distribution of privilege and prestige seem largely determined by the distribution of power, at least in those societies in which a significant surplus is produced.

In the last chapter we also saw that power manifests itself in two basic forms, force and institutionalized power. The latter, in turn, can be subdivided into the power of position and the power of property. Building on this, a power class may be defined as *an aggregation of persons in a society who stand in a similar position with respect to force or some specific form of institutionalized power.* For example, the concept "power class" may be applied to such varied aggregations as factory workers, wealthy landowners, or the members of a military junta which rules by force. Though the bases of their power differ, each constitutes an aggregation of persons who occupy a similar position with respect to some specific form of power.

Since the term "power class" is awkward, and since the concept is required so often in the analysis which follows, I shall usually dispense with the qualifying adjective and simply speak of "class." Unless otherwise indicated, "class" will hereafter refer to groupings defined in terms of power.

Though the definition of class seems relatively simple and straightforward, there are certain ideas implicit in it which are not completely obvious and require examination before moving on to other matters. To begin with, though the classes with which we shall be concerned are defined *in terms* of power, this does not mean that they all *have* power. On the contrary, some have virtually no power, as in the case of the expendables in agrarian societies (see Chapter 9).

Second, given this definition, a single individual may well be a member of half a dozen power classes. This is inevitable whenever the various forms of power are less than perfectly correlated with one another. To illustrate, in contemporary American society a single individual may be a member of the middle class with respect to property holdings, a member of the working class by virtue of his job in a factory, and a member of the Negro "caste." Each of the major roles he occupies, as well as his status in the property hierarchy, influences his chances of obtaining the things he seeks in life, and thus each places him in a specific class.

Since these resources are so imperfectly correlated, he cannot be located in any single class. In this connection, it may be appropriate to note that this tendency seems to become progressively more pronounced as one moves from technologically primitive to technologically advanced societies. In other words, *the necessity of multidimensional analyses seems greatest in modern industrial societies.*

Third, though the definition does not say so explicitly, *the members of every power class share certain common interests with one another, and these shared interests constitute a potential basis for hostility toward other classes.* This follows as a logical corollary of the fact that what unites the members of a class is their common possession, control, or utilization of something which affects their chances of fulfilling their wishes and desires. Given our earlier assumptions about the nature of man, it follows that all members of a given class have a vested interest in protecting or increasing the value of their common resource and in reducing the value of competitive resources which constitute the bases of other classes.

This is not to say that the members of a class always have a conscious awareness of their common interest, much less that they act collectively on the basis of it. Nor are they always consciously or overtly hostile to members of other classes. These are possibilities which may be realized, but there is nothing inevitable about them.[2]

One final feature of the definition deserving note is the somewhat vague and annoying phrase, "a similar position." The critical reader will ask how much similiarity is required and will find, unhappily, that there is no definite answer. Whether we like it or not, this kind of phrasing is forced on us by the nature of the reality we seek to analyze. In most cases human populations simply are not stratified into a limited number of clearly differentiated, highly discrete categories. Rather, they tend to be strung out along continua which lack breaks that can be utilized as class boundaries. Furthermore, if we were to insist that members of classes stand in *identical* positions with respect to the distribution of things of value, we should have thousands, possibly millions, of classes in many societies, most with but a handful of members, and some with only one.

To avoid this, we are forced to use less restrictive criteria, but this forces us to use less *precise* ones. In general, students of stratification have found it more advantageous to employ a smaller number of larger and more inclusive classes. Thus, there are frequent references to broad categories such as peasants, merchants, workers, professionals, and so forth.

[2] In other words, the present definition is on the same level as Marx's definition of *Klass an sich*, not his definition of *Klass für sich*.

The use of such categories is not meant to deny the existence of internal variation within these classes. Obviously each class can be subdivided into more homogeneous subcategories or subclasses, e.g., prosperous peasants and poor peasants or rich merchants and poor merchants. The extent to which this is done depends largely on the nature of the study. In a highly specialized study with a narrow scope, much more attention is likely to be given to these subclasses than can be given in a broadly comparative study such as the present one.

Castes, Estates, Status Groups, and Elites

In much of the writing on social stratification, reference is made to certain other kinds of collectivities beside classes. Four, in particular, figure prominently in this literature—"castes," "estates," "status groups," and "elites." How is each of these terms related to class?

Caste, like class, has been defined in a variety of ways. Underlying all or nearly all the definitions, however, is the idea of a group whose membership is rigidly hereditary. When caste and class are used as contrasting terms, castes are thought of as groups out of which and into which mobility is virtually impossible. As a matter of fact, much of the membership of classes is also hereditary and conversely some mobility is possible where castes are involved. A more precise statement of the relationship would be that *upward* mobility by individuals is socially legitimate where classes are involved, but not in the case of castes.[3]

Actually, however, there is no need to treat caste and class as separate phenomena. In the interest of conceptual parsimony one can quite legitimately define caste as a special kind of class—at least when class is defined as broadly as it has been here. Thus we may say that *a class is a caste to the degree that upward mobility into or out of it is forbidden by the mores.*

A second type of collectivity often referred to by writers on stratification is the estate. The term comes from medieval European history (though it has a wider relevance) and refers to *a legally defined segment of the population of a society which has distinctive rights and duties established by law.*[4]

[3] Downward mobility is usually permitted in caste systems as a penalty for violation of certain caste mores. For a good early discussion of the relation between castes and other classes, see Charles Horton Cooley, *Social Organization* (New York: Scribner, 1909).
[4] See, for example, Egon Bergel, *Social Stratification* (New York: McGraw-Hill, 1962), p. 68.

Again, there is no necessary contradiction between the definitions of estate and class. Thus we may say that *a class is an estate to the degree that its existence, rights, and privileges are established by law.*

The third concept, "status groups," has been introduced into discussions of stratification by the translators of the writings of Max Weber. In many of his writings, Weber used the noun *Stände* and the adjective *ständisch.* Sometimes he used the noun to refer to medieval European estates, but other times he used both the noun and adjective to refer what might be called "estate-like" phenomena, such as occupational groups, the First Families of Virginia, ethnic groups, and even Indian castes. The common denominator underlying all of these, in Weber's view, was the honor or prestige of the group, a collective attribute which automatically applies to all members. Thus status groups, or *Stände,* differ from classes which are, in his usage, based on economic power. He also adds that status groups are normally communities which develop distinctive subcultures, while classes more often tend to be mere aggregations or social categories. Finally, status groups are much more likely to be hereditary groupings.[5]

While it is clear that these groupings which Weber's translators call status groups fall within our definition of classes, it is not so clear just how they fit into our framework. Some of his status groups seem to be essentially prestige classes, e.g., the First Families of Virginia. Others, however, are also power classes. In the latter case, the common denominator which unites them and sets them apart from other classes is their *endogamous, hereditary,* and *communal* character. While all classes have these characteristics to some extent, status groups have them to a marked degree.[6] It is in the sense that I shall use the term later in this volume applying it chiefly to racial, ethnic, and religious groups.

The fourth, and final, term requiring comment is the somewhat elusive term "elite." Unlike the other three, elites cannot be regarded merely as a special kind of class. On the contrary, sometimes they are less than a class while at other times they are more. In the former case, one may refer to the most powerful (or most priviliged or prestigeful) segment of a class as the elite *of that class.* In the latter case, one may refer to two or more classes as constituting the political elite *of a society.* As yet another alternative, one may speak of a single class as constituting the political elite of a society. In short, the term has come to mean merely *the highest ranking segment of any given social unit, whether a class or*

[5] See Max Weber, *From Max Weber: Essays in Sociology,* translated by H. H. Gerth and C. Wright Mills (Fair Lawn, N.J.: Oxford University Press, 1946), pp. 186–194, for his most systematic treatment of the concept.

[6] Castes, therefore, may be regarded as the extreme type of class or status group since the hereditary, endogamous, and communal traits are maximized in them.

total society, ranked by whatever criterion one chooses.[7] In the present volume, the criterion invoked will be *power*, unless otherwise indicated.

The boundaries of elites, like the boundaries of classes, are usually imprecise—and for the same reason. In both instances we are confronted with data which are distributed in what is essentially a continuous series, largely lacking in meaningful breaks or gaps. Under the circumstances, social analysts have little choice but to introduce arbitrary boundaries of their own creation, just as economists do when confronted with income distributions.

In view of the foregoing, it seems clear that the single concept of "class" can be used to cover all the collective aspects of systems of stratification. This does not mean, however, that all kinds of classes are alike in all respects. Some are based on power, others on privilege, and still others on prestige. Some of those based on power are based on the power of position, some on the power of property. Some are based on one kind of position, others on another. Some are self-conscious communal groups, others are mere social categories. Some are almost entirely hereditary, others are not. Some are legal entities, most are not. These are all variable properties of classes and one of the important, but often neglected, tasks of stratification theory and research is to clarify these variable features and identify the forces responsible for them.

Class Systems

Of the three levels of organization within the structure of distributive systems, that of class systems is the one most often overlooked. The reason for this is not hard to find. If one takes a unidimensional view of social stratification, as has been customary, there is but one class system in any given society, and hence "the class system" and "the distributive system" are synonymous.

However, once the multidimensional character of distributive systems is recognized, this is no longer possible. Once we recognize that power rests on various foundations and that these are not always reducible to some single common denominator, we are forced to think in terms of a series of class hierarchies or class systems. These constitute a level of organization intermediate between a single class and the total distributive system.

For purposes of formal definition, a class system may be said to be

[7] For a similar view of the subject, see Vilfredo Pareto, *The Mind and Society*, translated by A. Bongiorno and Arthur Livingston and edited by Livingston (New York: Harcourt, Brace & World, 1935), vol. III, paragraph 2027ff.

a hierarchy of classes ranked in terms of some single criterion. As indicated previously, each class system in a society contains within it all the members of that society. Thus every member of American society holds simultaneous membership in some class within the occupational, property, racial-ethnic, educational, age, and sexual class systems.

Figure 1 may help to clarify the nature of class systems by showing graphically their relation to the other three levels of organization, the individual, the class, and the distributive system as a whole. This figure depicts the distribution of power in a fictional Latin American society. In this society there are four important sources of power: (1) political activity, (2) wealth, (3) work, or occupational activity, and (4) ethnicity. These are not of equal importance, as indicated by the varying weights ranging from 2 to 10 shown in the column headings. Within each class system there are a series of classes varying in number from three (in the ethnic class system) to seven (in the occupational class system). The

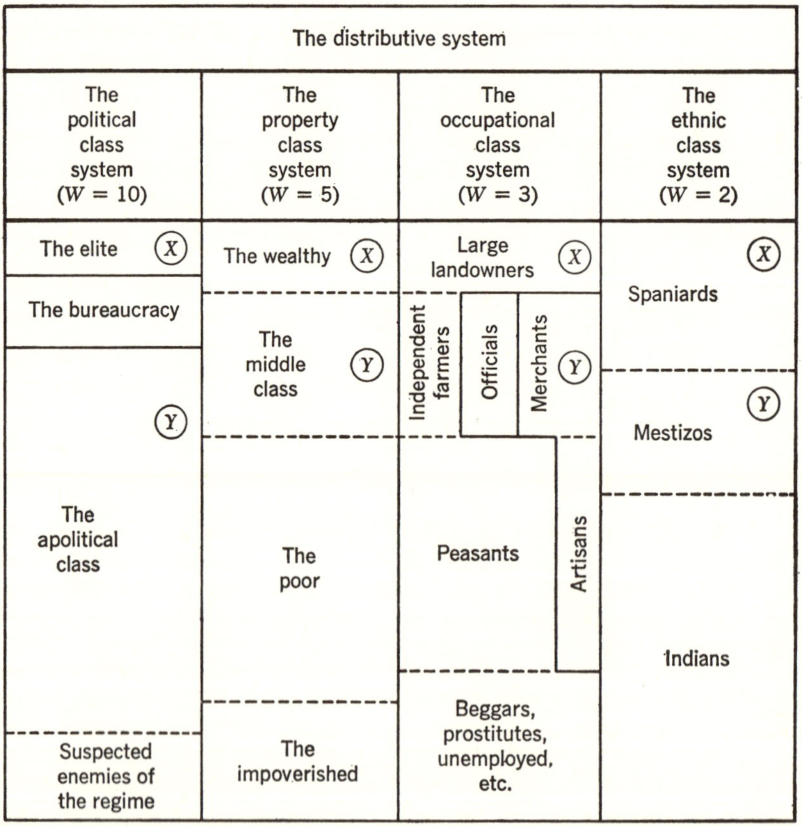

The distributive system			
The political class system ($W = 10$)	The property class system ($W = 5$)	The occupational class system ($W = 3$)	The ethnic class system ($W = 2$)
The elite (X)	The wealthy (X)	Large landowners (X)	(X)
The bureaucracy	The middle class (Y)	Independent farmers / Officials / Merchants (Y)	Spaniards
(Y)			Mestizos (Y)
The apolitical class	The poor	Peasants — Artisans	Indians
Suspected enemies of the regime	The impoverished	Beggars, prostitutes, unemployed, etc.	

Figure 1 Graphic representation of the structure of the power dimensions of the distributive system of a *fictional* society.

boundaries between the classes vary in sharpness, with some being fairly well defined (those marked with a solid line), while others represent little more than arbitrary points on what is essentially a continuum (those marked by a dashed line). The circled figures ⓧ and ⓨ represent two individuals. The former is a wealthy landowner of Spanish descent who is also a member of the political elite; the latter is a middle-class mestizo with a small business who is politically inactive but tending to support the existing regime. Where the rule of might prevails, as in this fictional society, the statuses of individuals in the several class systems tend to be quite consistent; as constitutionalism develops, inconsistent statuses become more common for reasons indicated in the last chapter.

One of the great advantages of a conscious recognition of class systems as a distinct level of organization is that we are led to see that the struggle for power and privilege involves not only struggles between individuals and classes, it also involves *struggles between class systems, and thus between different principles of distribution.* For example, in recent decades, we have witnessed in the United States and elsewhere vigorous efforts to increase the importance of the educational class system, often in conjunction with efforts to reduce the importance of the racial-ethnic and sexual class systems. In totalitarian nations repeated efforts have been made to increase the importance of the political class system at the expense of other kinds of class systems, especially the property class system. Under such conditions, the relation of individuals to The Party tends to become the key to power and privilege while other resources become secondary. In some instances changes in the relative importance of class systems occur without deliberate efforts and simply reflect the influence of changing social or technological conditions. An understanding of such shifts is also important for an adequate understanding of the distributive process as a whole.

Class systems differ from one another in a number of ways which deserve recognition. As Figure 1 indicates, they differ in both *importance* and *complexity.* Some have far more influence than others on the chances of men's obtaining the goals they seek. Similarly, some involve more complex structures than others; e.g., compare the occupational and ethnic class systems in Figure 1.

Two other variable features of class systems are their *span* and *shape.*[8] Span refers to the range of variation found within a class system. The shape of a system refers to the patterning of the distribution of cases.

[8] These terms are from Bernard Barber, *Social Stratification: A Comparative Analysis of Structure and Process* (New York: Harcourt, Brace & World, 1957), pp. 87-93. His use of these terms is virtually identical with Sorokin's earlier usage of the terms height and profile. See Pitirim Sorokin, *Social Mobility* (New York: Harper & Row, 1947), part I.

When charted graphically this may result in a pyramidal structure with the great majority of individuals concentrated on the lower levels, or it may result in some more or less skewed variant of a normal curve with the majority of individuals in the middle levels, or still other patterns. As Sorokin has pointed out, men are able to change the shape of some class systems more readily than others. He suggests, for example, that we can control the shape of political class systems more easily than those of property class systems.[9]

Fifth, class systems vary with respect to the *degree of mobility* which is possible within them. In some, as in the case of sexual and racial class systems, the positions of individuals are virtually fixed. In others, movement is possible in widely varying degrees.[10]

Sixth, class systems differ in terms of the *degree of hostility* which prevails between classes. In a few instances, class warfare of the type envisioned by Marx has prevailed, at least for a period of time. At the other extreme, there has often been a virtual absence of hostility. There is good reason for supposing that class hostility is inversely related to opportunities for mobility, though available evidence suggests that the relationship is far from perfect.

Finally, class systems differ in *the degree of institutionalization.* In some systems the rights and duties of the several classes are firmly embedded in custom and undergirded by a universally accepted ideology which serves to legitimize inequalities. In extreme cases, custom has become translated into law. At the other extreme, certain class systems have been based almost entirely on the ability of the favored class to control others by naked force.

One of the important tasks confronting students of stratification in the next several decades will be to establish the factors responsible for variations in each of these dimensions. To date only a beginning has been made, largely because attention has been directed elsewhere.

Citizenship: A Potentially Unique Resource

Before turning our attention from the structural units which make up distributive systems to the systems themselves, it is necessary to consider

[9] *Ibid.,* p. 92–93.
[10] Various writers have argued that it is impossible to develop a single measure of the degree of vertical mobility in a population since the *volume of movement* and the *distance of movement* cannot be reduced to a single common denominator. While granting the practical difficulties involved in getting an adequate measure of social distance, one can argue that there is nothing impossible about this. On the contrary, the physical sciences long ago resolved such problems by developing combined measures such as foot-pounds.

briefly the relevance of *citizenship* for our analysis. As T. H. Marshall, the British sociologist, made clear more than a decade ago, citizenship can be thought of as a resource much like other kinds of positions and property, since it, too, guarantees certain rights to individuals and hence is a basis of power.[11] Unlike other resources, however, it does not always divide the population into "haves" and "have-nots"—at least not in the more advanced industrial nations of the modern world.

In an earlier period the rights of citizenship were reserved for the few and citizenship, like other resources, did divide men into classes. Sometimes citizenship divided the members of societies into citizens and noncitizens, other times into first- and second-class citizens. This traditional pattern can be seen in the early history of this country, when the population was divided into enfranchised citizens, unenfranchised freemen, and slaves. Each stood in a different relation to the state, with enfranchised citizens in the most favored position and slaves in the least.

Today slavery has disappeared in advanced industrial societies and the right of franchise has been extended to include nearly all adults. As a result, citizenship tends to be a resource which all share alike.

Since citizenship is shared by all, one might suppose that it no longer has any special relevance for the student of stratification. This is not the case, however. Citizenship continues to figure prominently in the distributive process. Those who lack other kinds of resources, together with those who, for ideological reasons, believe in social equality, have combined to fight for the enhancement of the value of citizenship at the expense of those resources which generate inequality. This struggle is evident in recent controversies involving the issue of property rights versus human rights. Those who advocate the primacy of human rights over property rights typically advocate the enlargement of the rights of citizenship at the expense of the traditional rights of property. Their opponents take the opposite position. Thus the struggle becomes not merely a struggle between classes, but also a struggle between class systems and thus between differing principles of stratification.

Historically oriented students of stratification will recognize that the modern era is not completely unique in this, since in preindustrial societies the less powerful classes often fought the more powerful classes in the same way, and not without some success. At the very least, they often succeeded in establishing certain uniform legal rights, including the right to a public trial based on an established body of law. Sometimes they were even able to establish the right of all men to protection from extortionary

[11] T. H. Marshall, *Citizenship and Social Class* (London: Cambridge University Press, 1950).

and irregular taxation and other abuses. To be sure, men of property and position usually fought to prevent such rights from being established and to undermine them if they were. Usually they were successful in these efforts. Only in the more advanced industrial societies of the modern era, however, is citizenship simultaneously a resource of *major* importance and one shared by all.

In many ways this centuries-old effort to enhance the value of common citizenship can be viewed as an attempt to reestablish the ascendancy of *need* over *power* as the dominant principle of distribution. As noted in the last chapter, in those societies which are technologically most primitive, need, rather than power, is the chief determinant of "who gets what." With technological advance and the growing capacity to produce a surplus, power became the chief determinant. Today, an organized effort is being made to restore the importance of need. Ironically, however, it appears that this reversal can occur only if the advocates of need can mobilize more power than the advocates of power.[12] This is because advanced industrial societies, unlike primitive hunting and gathering societies, have a surplus and thus their distributive pattern is not dictated by economic necessity. Thus one is led to the conclusion that if need should ever be restored to the position of dominance, it would not rest on the same foundation as that on which it rested in technologically primitive societies.

Distributive Systems

Having completed our examination of the various kinds of units which form the structure of distributive systems, we are now in a position to consider these systems *as totalities*. It should be remembered that we have focused on the *power* dimensions and largely ignored privilege and prestige. However, if our earlier analysis was correct, this should cause no serious difficulties or errors, since the distributive patterns of the other two basic rewards are largely extensions of the patterns of power.

Viewed in their totality, distributive systems resemble a system of wheels within wheels. The complexity of these systems varies considerably and seems to be largely a function of the societies' level of technology.

---

[12] There is a paradox involved here which should be noted. In modern industrial democracies, a class of less powerful individuals can become *collectively* more powerful than a class of more powerful individuals. This is because there is a difference between the power of the individual and the power of his class. A class of powerful individuals is not necessarily more powerful than a class of less powerful individuals if the latter are much more numerous and are able to organize effectively.

As one might expect, distributive systems, like other units of social organization, have properties which can serve as bases of comparison. Unfortunately, however, precise measurement of these properties is usually impossible. Furthermore, the nature of most distributive systems precludes the use of simple, unidimensional measures, thus compounding the difficulties.

Nowhere are these difficulties more evident than in efforts to compare distributive systems on the basis of their *degree of inequality*. To begin with, precise, quantitative data of the kinds we require are lacking for most societies. In addition, all the various forms of power cannot be reduced to a single common denominator, and thus no single measure can fully express the extent of inequality in most societies.

Nevertheless, *meaningful* comparisons are possible. Fortunately, the differences in inequality among distributive systems are so great in many cases that it is possible to make rough comparisons which can be defended (compare, for example, the degree of inequality in hunting and gathering societies reported in Chapter 5 with that in agrarian societies in Chapters 8 and 9). Furthermore, there is sufficient consistency between most of the major class systems in most societies (i.e., marked status inconsistency is sufficiently uncommon) so that the use of summary measures can be meaningful—especially if qualifications are added to take account of those class systems which are not closely linked with the rest.

On the basis of the postulates set forth in the last two chapters, one would predict that *the degree of inequality in distributive systems will vary directly with the size of a society's surplus.* Some modification of this general pattern could develop, however, when conditions permit persons who individually lack power to combine and organize, and thus to develop a collective counterbalance to those with greater individual power. Such developments seem most probable in democratic nations with an egalitarian or socialist ideology.

A second important property of distributive systems is their *rate of vertical mobility*. Here, too, the same methodological problems arise. Here, too, however, the possibility of rough but meaningful comparisons seems possible, especially if appropriate qualifications are made for significant variations between class systems and between inter- and intra-generational mobility.[13] Unfortunately, our theory provides us with no basis for predicting systematic variations in the rates of vertical mobility.

[13] See footnote 10 above for a brief discussion of the feasibility of handling *volume of movement* and *distance of movement* in a single measure.

On an *ad hoc* basis, however, one might predict that they will tend to *vary directly with the rate of technological and social change*. Such change should lead to changes in the bases of power and, in a period of flux, traditional means of transmitting and retaining power should prove somewhat less effective than in periods of relative stability.

The degree of class hostility is a third variable feature of distributive systems. The same methodological problems and possibilities that apply to the first two variables apply here as well. Here, too, there is no basis for predicting systematic variations, but again an *ad hoc* hypothesis suggests itself. If, as suggested earlier, the lack of opportunities for upward mobility is one of the sources of class hostility, one would predict that *the degree of class hostility will tend to vary inversely with the rate of upward mobility*. Since the rate of upward mobility is assumed to be only one among several factors contributing to class hostility, we should not expect a strong relationship.

There are other properties of distributive systems which might also be used as bases for comparison, as for example, the degree of their complexity, institutionalization, and so forth. However, the three stated above seem the most important, and it is with these that we shall be chiefly concerned in the chapters which follow.

Reactions to Status Inconsistency

Before concluding this chapter, it is necessary to turn back again briefly to a problem of dynamics which has been brought into focus by our examination of structural matters. When one takes a multidimensional view of distributive systems he soon finds himself confronted with another interesting problem involving men's reactions to the unequal distribution of power and privilege (see Chapter 3, page 63, for the earlier discussion). This is the question of *men's reactions to the phenomenon of status inconsistency*.

The recognition of this problem is largely a modern development, because unidimensional views of stratification had such a strong hold on men's minds until recently that the very existence of the problem passed almost unnoticed. Even the few who did note it, such as Cooley and Sorokin, gave it scant attention.

More recently, however, a body of theory and research has developed which suggests that pronounced status inconsistencies of certain kinds tend to be a source of stress and give rise to distinctive reactions which are not predictable simply from a knowledge of the rank of the individual in each of the respective status systems.[14] This theory is based on the postulate that individuals strive to maximize their satisfactions, even, if necessary, at the expense of others. This means that an individual with inconsistent statuses or ranks has a natural tendency to think of himself in terms of that status or rank which is highest, and to expect others to do the same. Meanwhile others, who come in contact with him have a vested interest in doing just the opposite, that is, in treating him in terms of his lowest status or rank.

One can see how this works, and the consequences of it, by imagining the interaction of a Negro doctor and a white laborer in a situation where neither the racial nor occupational status system alone is relevant. The former, motivated by self-interest, will strive to establish the relation on the basis of occupation (or perhaps education or wealth), while the latter, similarly motivated, will strive to establish the relationship on the basis of race. Since each regards his own point of view as right and proper, and since neither is likely to view the problem in a detached, analytical fashion, one, or both, are likely to be frustrated, and probably angered, by the experience.

The practice of "one-upmanship," as this pattern of action has sometimes been called, is so common in everyday life that most who indulge in it hardly give it any thought. The net effect, however, is to create considerable stress for many persons of inconsistent status. As a result, such persons are likely to find social interaction outside the bounds of the primary group (where others tend to be like themselves) somewhat less rewarding than does the average person.

This is important for a general theory of stratification if such experiences lead individuals to react against the existing social order and the political system which undergirds it. Thus far there is some limited evidence that this kind of reaction does occur, and that persons of incon-

---

[14] Unfortunately, there is still no good summary of the relevant literature on this subject and no definitive treatment. Among others, the following have given special attention to the stress hypothesis: George Homans, "Status among Clerical Workers," *Human Organization*, 12 (1953), pp. 5–10; Gerhard Lenski, "Status Crystallization: A Non-vertical Dimension of Social Status," and "Social Participation and Status Crystallization," *American Sociological Review*, 19 and 21 (1954 and 1956), pp. 405–413 and 458–464; Irving Goffman, "Status Consistency and Preference for Change in Power Distribution," *ibid.*, 22 (1957), pp. 275–281; A. Zaleznik et al., *The Motivation, Productivity, and Satisfaction of Workers* (Cambridge, Mass.: Harvard University Press, 1958); Elton Jackson, "Status Consistency and Symptoms of Stress," *American Sociological Review*, 27 (1962), pp. 469–480. Methodological problems have been a source of difficulty in this area, but two recent papers point the way to their resolution. These are Lenski, "Comment," *Public Opinion Quarterly*, 28 (1964), pp. 326–330, and Elton Jackson and Peter Burke, "Status and Symptoms of Stress: Additive and Interaction Effects," *American Sociological Review*, 30 (1965), pp. 556–564.

sistent status are more likely to support liberal and radical movements designed to alter the political *status quo* than are persons of consistent status. The classic case of this has been the strong support which successful Jewish merchants and professional men have given such movements in every part of the world. Similar examples can be found among economically successful members of other ethnic, racial, and religious minorities. In fact, political sociologists have shown that such individuals are much less likely to support established conservative parties than are persons in the same occupational class who are members of the majority group. Thus, voting studies show that with class position held constant, Catholics are more likely than Protestants to support liberal or socialist parties in Protestant nations, while Protestants are more likely to support such parties in Catholic nations.[15]

This inconsistency reaction is not nearly so important from the quantitative standpoint as it seems to be from the *qualitative*. The great majority of the supporters of liberal and radical movements will probably always be persons of consistently low status. Such movements also require *leaders* and *resources*, however, and persons of consistently low status are not likely to have either the training or the skills necessary to lead such movements successfully, nor are they likely to have money to spare. By contrast, persons of inconsistent status are frequently in a position to supply one or both of these necessary ingredients, thus greatly increasing the probability of the success of such movements. As a result, their importance may well be out of all proportions to their numbers.

In this connection it is interesting to note that for all their concern with revolutionary movements, Marx and Engels never really developed an adequate explanation for the source of their leadership. They simply asserted that certain members of the *bourgeoisie* would rise above their class perspective and, seeing the true and inevitable course of history, throw in their lot with the proletariat. Neither Marx nor Engels ever explained how this was possible. The present theory offers one possible explanation for this otherwise puzzling aspect of revolutionary movements.

Retrospect and Prospect

Having completed the general theoretical introduction, we are now ready to turn to the task of testing its relevance in various types of societies. The remainder of the book, however, will be not only a test of the general

[15] See, for example, S. M. Lipset, *Political Man* (Garden City, N.Y.: Doubleday, 1959), pp. 247–248.

theory, but also an attempt to develop a series of more specialized theories of stratification or distribution, each applicable to a specific type of society.

Before turning to this second stage of our analysis, it may be well to review briefly the central elements of the general theory and the nature of their interrelations. This can be done quite simply with the aid of the diagram in Figure 2.[16]

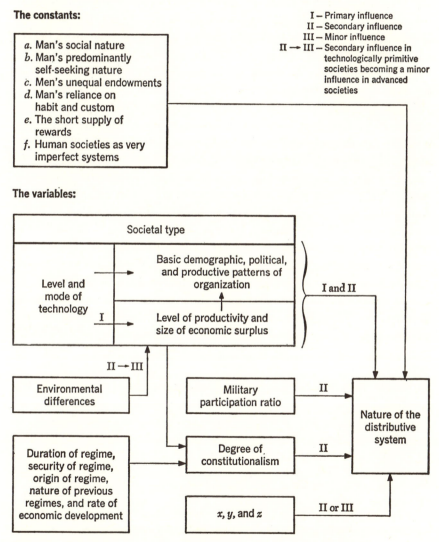

The constants:

a. Man's social nature
b. Man's predominantly self-seeking nature
c. Men's unequal endowments
d. Man's reliance on habit and custom
e. The short supply of rewards
f. Human societies as very imperfect systems

I — Primary influence
II — Secondary influence
III — Minor influence
II → III — Secondary influence in technologically primitive societies becoming a minor influence in advanced societies

The variables:

Societal type

Level and mode of technology   I

Basic demographic, political, and productive patterns of organization

Level of productivity and size of economic surplus

I and II

II → III

Environmental differences

Military participation ratio   II

Duration of regime, security of regime, origin of regime, nature of previous regimes, and rate of economic development

Degree of constitutionalism   II

x, y, and z II or III

Nature of the distributive system

Figure 2 Diagramatic summary of the general theory of stratification.

[16] I am very grateful to Donald Ploch, a recent member of my stratification seminar, for the suggestion that I summarize the theory diagrammatically.

As this figure makes clear, the theory is designed to explain the nature of distributive systems. It seeks to do this in terms of the combined influence of certain constant and variable features of the human situation. The arrows indicate the hypothesized direction of the flow of causal influence, and the Roman numerals their hypothesized importance.

This figure serves as a reminder that this theory predicts that *variations in technology* will be the most important single determinant of variations in distributive systems. In part this is because of the influence of technology on the level of productivity and the size of the economic surplus; in part it is because of the direct and indirect influence of technology on basic demographic, political, and productive patterns of organization. The theory also leads us to predict secondary variations in distributive systems as a consequence of secondary variations in technology, or those which occur among societies of the same societal type.

Though this theory predicts that variations in technology are the most important single determinant of variations in distribution, it does not hypothesize that they are the only determinant. Three others are specifically singled out: (1) *environmental differences*, (2) *variations in the military participation ratio*, (3) *variations in the degree of constitutionalism*. In addition, since this is not a closed theory, it is assumed that other factors also exercise an influence. These are indicated by the symbols x, y, and z. One of the important concerns in the analysis which follows will be the identification of these factors and the determination of the magnitude of their influence. Some will prove of importance only in societies of a single type, and perhaps only with reference to a single, minor aspect of distributive systems. Others, however, may prove to be much more important, and it is with these that we shall be especially concerned.

Given the nature of this theory, the organization of materials for the remainder of the volume is clear. Since it is predicted that technological variation is the primary determinant of variations among distributive systems, societies should be classified in technological terms, and this scheme of classification should be used to order the presentation of data. If the theory is sound, this method of presentation should prove frutiful; if not, it should prove a source of considerable confusion.

The system of classifying societies used in the following chapters reflects the influence of dozens of anthropologists and archaeologists who have wrestled with this problem. Lewis Henry Morgan, the pioneer American anthropologist, distinguished between three basic societal types, savage, barbarian, and civilized.[17] The first two were further subdivided

[17] Lewis Henry Morgan, *Ancient Society* (New York: Holt, 1877), pp. 9–10.

into upper, middle, and lower levels, the criteria differentiating the several levels being technological in nature.

Though Morgan's scheme is no longer used, most of the more recent efforts to develop a societal typology based on technological criteria reflect its influence. It is seen in the work of such widely separated scholars as the British sociologist Hobhouse, the British archaeologist Childe, the American anthropologist Goldschmidt, and the American sociologist Duncan.[18] The system of classification used in this volume stems directly from that of Goldschmidt.

Goldschmidt identifies six basic societal types which he sees as related to one another in the manner described in Figure 3. The higher the position, the more advanced the type is technologically. The arrows indicate the probable evolutionary sequence according to Goldschmidt. Thus, though herding societies are technologically less advanced than agricultural-state societies, he hypothesizes that the former evolved from the latter. It may be relevant to note here that Goldschmidt's two hunting and gathering types correspond closely to Morgan's savage societies, his herding and horticultural types to Morgan's barbarian, and his agricultural-state and industrial types to Morgan's civilized.

The differences between Goldschmidt's scheme and that used in this volume can be seen by comparing Figures 3 and 4. First, Goldschmidt's nomadic and settled hunting and gathering societies are treated as a single type on the grounds that the differences between them are due chiefly to environmental factors rather than technological; i.e., when hunting and gathering peoples are not nomadic, it is because their environment is fertile enough to sustain a sedentary human population. Second, the horticultural type is divided into two categories, a simple and an advanced. This was not planned in advance, but a careful reading of the ethnographic literature made it inescapable. Goldschmidt himself anticipated the need for this step when he wrote, "Our horticultural category is the broadest and internally the most varied of the lot, and closer examination may ultimately provide sensible and useful subdivisions." [19] Third, it has been necessary to make certain additions to Goldschmidt's typology. Fishing societies are largely subsumed under the "settled hunting and gathering" rubric in his scheme, while maritime societies are presumably included under the "agricultural-state society" rubric. The need for these

[18] See L. T. Hobhouse, G. C. Wheeler, and M. Ginsberg, *The Material Culture and Social Institutions of the Simpler Peoples* (London: Chapman & Hall, 1930); V. Gordon Childe, *Man Makes Himself* (London: Watts, 1939); Walter Goldschmidt, *Man's Way: A Preface to the Understanding of Human Society* (New York: Holt, 1959), especially chap. 6; and O. D. Duncan, "Social Organization and the Ecosystem," in Robert E. Faris, *Handbook of Modern Sociology* (Chicago: Rand McNally, 1964), pp. 48–61.

[19] Goldschmidt, *op. cit.*, p. 194.

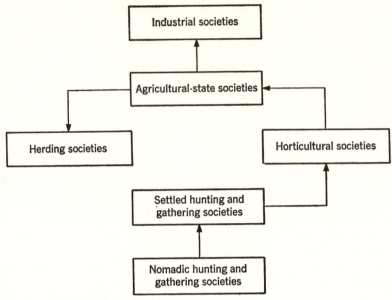

Figure 3   Goldschmidt's societal typology.

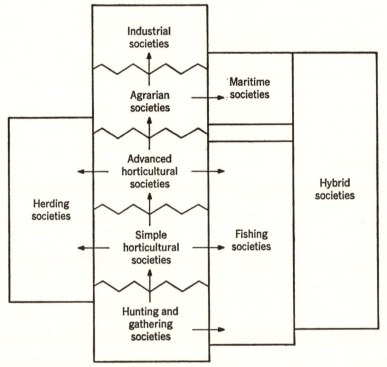

Figure 4   Societal typology for *Power and Privilege*.

distinctions will be explained in Chapters 5 and 8 respectively. Finally, the system of classification used in this volume makes allowance for a variety of *hybrid* types—societies which involve curious and often complex intermixtures of technology. Such societies arise as a result of the diffusion of technology from more advanced societies to less advanced. Thus, many of the Plains Indians in this country in the nineteenth century fit none of the traditional types. Rather, they were hunting and gathering or simple horticultural societies with certain important elements of agrarian technology grafted on, e.g., the horse and the gun. These elements, though few in number, altered the character of these societies so greatly that it is impossible to treat them as hunting and gathering or simple horticultural societies. Similarly, contemporary Indian society (in Asia) can be viewed as a hybrid type involving a complex intermixture of technological elements from agrarian and industrial societies. To lump such societies with "pure" types can only lead to confusion.

The present typology is predicated on the assumption that there is an underlying continuum, in terms of which all societies can be ranked. This continuum is a measure of a society's *overall technological efficiency*, i.e., the value of a society's gross product in international markets divided by the human energy expended in its production. Unfortunately, this concept is not easily operationalized, and we are forced to rely on simpler and more obvious criteria for classificatory purposes. This is the reason for classifying societies in terms of their basic techniques of subsistence. Such data are readily available and seem highly correlated with overall technological efficiency.

The chief disadvantage of this method of classification is that it introduces a certain area of overlap between adjacent societal types. For example, for operational purposes agrarian societies are differentiated from advanced horticultural on the grounds that the latter lack the plow. Sometimes, however, the most advanced horticultural societies have made other advances which result in slightly greater *overall* efficiency than exists in certain of the least advanced agrarian societies. (This is the reason for the jagged lines between certain societal types in Figure 4.) Fortunately, the extent of such overlap is not great.

Finally, it should be noted that the present study deals with only five of the eight basic types identified in Figure 4 and with none of the hybrid types. The selection of these five was determined chiefly by their crucial importance in human history and because collectively they cover the total range of variation in technological efficiency. The limitations of time and space precluded extending the analysis to the other types, but one hopes that this can be done in the not too distant future.

5/Hunting and Gathering Societies

When Adam delved and Eve span
Who was then the gentleman?
John Ball

HUNTING AND GATHERING SOCIETIES are the most primitive of all human societies with respect to technology in general and mode of production in particular. Nevertheless, throughout most of human history this was the only type of society known to man. It is only in the last ten thousand years that men have advanced to the point where they have been able to control and enlarge their food supply through the cultivation of plants and the domestication of animals.

Fortunately for modern social scientists, these advances have been slow to spread and the older way of life survived into the modern era in certain of the more inaccessible and infertile areas of the world. Hence it has been possible for trained observers to study the ways of life of peoples whose productive systems are radically different from our own. Among such groups are the aborigines of Australia, the Tasmanians, the Semang and Sakai of Malaya, the Kubu of Sumatra, the Punan of Borneo, the Vedda of Ceylon, the Andaman Islanders, the Pygmies and Bushmen of Africa, a number of South American Indian tribes in the Amazon basin, the Gran Chaco, and Patagonia, certain of the Indian tribes of North America in the region from the Great Plains to the Pacific Coast, and some of the Eskimos. It is on these peoples that we shall depend for empirical data to test our hypotheses about the influence of productive systems on the distributive process, and also for additional insights into the distinctive characteristics of distributive systems at this level of economic development.

Two types of societies which might seem to fit under the heading of hunting and gathering societies will be excluded. The first are societies in which *fishing* constitutes a major source of subsistence. While fishing might be regarded as simply a variant form of hunting, there is good reason for treating this as a doubtful hypothesis to be explored rather than as an assumption on which to build. Available evidence indicates that the yields from fishing are both greater and less variable than those from hunting, thus raising the level of productivity and otherwise altering the nature of societies.[1] Hence, this chapter will not attempt to deal with groups such as the Kwakiutl, Haida, Tlingit, and other fishing tribes of the Northwest Coast of North America, or the Guato, Mura, Yaruro, and other "aquatic nomads" of the rivers of South America.[2]

The second category to be excluded are those societies which did not come to the attention of Western observers until they had been substantially transformed by contact with European civilization and the introduction of technological traits which are completely alien to traditional hunting and gathering societies. Included here are the Plains Indians of the United States whose cultures were transformed by the influence of the horse and the gun (and sometimes the fur trade as well) long before the first direct contacts with Europeans. This category also includes the Plains Indians of southeastern South America who incorporated the horse and cattle into their cultures prior to direct contact with Europeans. For a time anthropologists were inclined to minimize the influence of these elements on native cultures, but more recent work strongly indicates that they exercised a revolutionary effect.[3] Most modern anthropologists be-

[1] For discussions of the difference fishing can make see Gordon Hewes, "The Rubric 'Fishing and Fisheries,'" *American Anthropologist*, 50 (1948), pp. 238–246; Julian Steward, *Theory of Culture Change* (Urbana, Ill.: University of Illinois Press, 1955), chap. 10; or John Honigmann, *The World of Man* (New York: Harper & Row, 1959), pp. 308–311.
[2] For a good introduction to the Northwest Coast Indians, see Philip Drucker, *Indians of the Northwest Coast* (New York: McGraw-Hill, 1955); for the fishing tribes of South America, see Julian H. Steward and Louis Faron, *Native Peoples of South America* (New York: McGraw-Hill, 1959), pp. 437–444.
[3] For the earlier view, see Clark Wissler, "The Influence of the Horse in the Development of Plains Culture," *American Anthropologist*, 16 (1914), pp. 1–25. For the more

lieve that the horse and gun led to greatly increased mobility, warfare, numbers, wealth, and inequality, all of which represented marked departures from the usual pattern in hunting and gathering societies. In some instances the introduction of the horse and gun even led societies on the horticultural level of development to "revert" to hunting as their chief means of subsistence, further complicating the problems of analysis. For all these reasons these theoretically "contaminated" or "hybrid" societies have been excluded from the present analysis.

Common Features of Hunting and Gathering Societies

Although hunting and gathering societies differ in a number of ways, they share a great many important characteristics simply because of their common means of subsistence. Were it not for these many associated characteristics it would be much more difficult to develop a special theory of stratification for these societies.[4]

To begin with, where techniques of food production are primitive and inefficient (in the sense of product value per unit of energy expended), other elements of technology are also primitive. These include techniques of providing shelter, making clothes (if these are used), making tools and weapons, transportation, etc. For example, the tools and weapons in these societies are invariably made of wood, stone, bone, and other materials taken directly from nature, since the techniques of metal working are unknown.[5]

---

recent view, see A. L. Kroeber, "Native Culture of the Southwest," University of California Publications, *American Archaeology and Ethnology*, 23 (1928), pp. 375–398; Bernard Mishkin, *Rank and Warfare among the Plains Indians*, Monographs of the American Ethnological Society, 3 (1940), especially chaps. 2 and 6; Oscar Lewis, *The Effects of White Contact upon Blackfoot Culture*, Monographs of the American Ethnological Society, 6 (1942); John C. Ewers, "The Horse in Blackfoot Indian Culture, with Comparative Material from Other Western Tribes," (Washington, D.C.: Smithsonian Institution, Bureau of American Ethnology), Bulletin 159 (1955). On the South American Indians, see Steward and Faron, *op cit.*, pp. 384 and 408–413.

[4] See the essay by C. Daryll Forde, "Primitive Economics," in Harry Shapiro (ed.), *Man, Culture, and Society* (Fair Lawn, N.J.: Oxford Galaxy, 1960) for a good discussion of the many consequences of reliance on a primitive technology. Unfortunately, Forde fails to differentiate between the various types and levels of primitive technologies, thus creating some unnecessary confusion. His discussion lumps together hunting and gathering societies with many fishing, pastoral, and horticultural societies. See also Steward and Faron, chap. 13, for a good summary description of the common characteristics of the hunting and gathering tribes of South America, and Honigmann, pp. 303–308 for a more general discussion.

[5] Of course, through trade, members of hunting and gathering societies have often been able to obtain metal tools and weapons from their more advanced neighbors. This has only been possible, however, in the last five or six thousand years (or since techniques of metal working were first invented). Throughout most of human history, hunting and gathering societies were completely dependent on tools of wood and stone.

There is, of course, a marked circularity or interaction among all the various elements in what might be called the hunting and gathering syndrome. For example, primitive techniques of food production hamper the development of tools and weapons by making occupational specialization impossible, while the primitive character of tools and weapons makes advances in methods of food production difficult. Though I shall not attempt to point out all of the combinations and permutations of the various elements in the hunting and gathering syndrome, the reader should keep in mind that most of these elements reinforce each other, thereby strengthening the system as a whole and rendering change and progress difficult. Once these interrelationships are recognized, one ceases to wonder why our prehistoric ancestors remained so long at this level and begins, instead, to wonder how they ever escaped it.

Because of the primitive character of their technology and tools, the members of hunting and gathering societies live close to the subsistence level for much of the year. There is, of course, variation in this respect, as in others discussed here, and a few of the most advanced hunting and gathering societies resemble the simplest horticultural societies in having a small economic surplus. In the typical hunting and gathering society, however, there is no sustained economic surplus, and life is often an alternation of periods of feast and famine, or abundance and shortage, with the latter usually more frequent.[6] Because most of these societies lack techniques and facilities for preserving and storing most types of food for any extended period of time, life is lived largely on a day to day basis.[7] This means that when conditions are favorable and food abundant, the members commonly gorge themselves, and then go hungry a few days or weeks later when food is again scarce. An early missionary among the Indians of Lower California reported that "twenty-four pounds of meat in twenty-four hours is not deemed an extraordinary ration for a single person" after a successful hunt; more recently an anthropologist among

[6] Allan Holmberg reports that two of the most frequent expressions one hears in a Siriono camp are, "My stomach is very empty," and "Give me some food." See *Nomads on the Long Bow: The Siriono of Eastern Bolivia,* Smithsonian Institution, Institute of Social Anthropology, Publication No. 10 (1950), p. 30. See also Honigmann's statement that "such people [i.e., hunters and gatherers] are often hungry but, unlike some agricultural people, their hunger is less one for specific nutrients than for food itself" (p. 306).

[7] Holmberg reports meat does not keep for more than three days among the Siriono (*ibid.,* p. 34). Less typical are the Paiutes, who stored certain products for weeks or months, and the Kung Bushmen, who dried meat and were able to keep it for some time. See C. Daryll Forde, *Habitat, Economy and Society* (London: Methuen, 1934), p. 36, on the Paiutes; and Lorna Marshall, "The Kung Bushmen of the Kalahari Desert," in James L. Gibbs (ed.), *Peoples of Africa* (New York: Holt, 1965), p. 255, on the Kung Bushmen.

the Siriono of eastern Bolivia reported seeing men eat as much as thirty pounds of meat in a day.[8]

Another feature of hunting and gathering societies is that they are invariably small. If societies are defined as socially autonomous populations, then each local band or community constitutes a separate society. Larger and more complex systems of social organization are virtually impossible at this level of development.[9] Two separate studies have found that the average population of hunting, gathering, and fishing communities numbers about fifty.[10] The largest hunting and gathering societies seem to have numbered not more than a few hundred, and even this modest size was possible only because of unusually favorable environmental conditions.[11]

Another important characteristic of hunting and gathering groups is that they are usually nomadic or seminomadic. A sample of more than seventy hunting and gathering societies from the Human Relations Area Files indicates that only about 10 per cent were able to maintain a settled village life.[12] The reasons for this are not hard to find: within a short time the food-gathering techniques employed by hunters and gatherers normally reduce the supply of edible plants and animals in a given area below the level required to maintain the human population and the group is compelled to move on.[13] Often a group follows some more or less regular pattern of movement from place to place, so that in time it returns to the point from which it started.

The nomadic character of this way of life combines with the limited

[8] Jacob Baegert, S. J., *Account of the Aboriginal Inhabitants of the California Peninsula,* translated and arranged by Charles Rau, *Smithsonian Institution: Annual Reports for 1863 and 1864,* reprinted in Carleton S. Coon (ed.), *A Reader in General Anthropology* (New York: Holt, 1948), p. 72; Holmberg, p. 36.
[9] See p. 101 below for a further discussion of this matter.
[10] George Peter Murdock, *Social Structure* (New York: Macmillan, 1949), p. 81; and Julian Steward, "The Economic and Social Basis of Primitive Bands," in *Essays in Anthropology Presented to A. L. Kroeber* (Berkeley, Calif.: University of California Press, 1936), p. 333. See also Steward's more recent statement that patrilineal bands average fifty individuals and seldom exceed a hundred (*Theory of Culture Change,* Urbana, Ill.: University of Illinois Press, 1955, p. 125).
[11] A. L. Kroeber, *Handbook of American Indians of California,* Smithsonian Institution, Bureau of American Ethnology, Bulletin 78 (1925), pp. 491 and 689–690 on the Yokuts and Cupeño Indians.
[12] Calculated from George Peter Murdock, "World Ethnographic Sample," *American Anthropologist,* 59 (1957), pp. 664–687.
[13] See, for example, Colin Turnbull, "The Mbuti Pygmies of the Congo," in Gibbs, pp. 286–287. He writes, "After about a month, as a rule, the fruits of the forest have been gathered all around the vicinity of the camp, and the game has been scared away to a greater distance than is comfortable for daily hunting. As the economy relies on day-to-day quest, the simplest thing is for the camp to move. . . ." Though the figure of a month is lower than reports from most other groups, the basic pattern is the same.

productivity to prevent any substantial accumulation of capital. Lacking beasts of burden and mechanical means of transportation, these people are severely limited in what they can accumulate and their possessions are few. One observer found it possible to list all the possessions of one tribe in a single sentence:

> Their whole furniture, if that expression can be applied at all, consists of a bow and arrows, a flint instead of a knife, a bone or pointed piece of wood for digging roots, a turtle-shell serving as basket and cradle, a large gut or bladder for fetching water and transporting it during their excursions, and a bag made like a fishing net from the fibres of aloe, or the skin of a wild cat, in which they preserve and carry their provisions, sandals, and perhaps other insignificant things which they happen to possess.[14]

While this is an extreme case, the possessions of even the most affluent hunting and gathering societies are not much more numerous.[15] Furthermore, the possessions of the members of such societies are largely items needed for subsistence activities.

Since community and society are normally one and the same at this level of technological development, each community tends to be a self-sufficient entity and *communal* specialization is limited. Where the rudiments of communal specialization and intercommunity trade are found, they are usually a function of environmental peculiarities. For example, among the Andaman Islanders there is a certain degree of commerce carried on between the coastal dwellers and those who live in the forests, reflecting the availability of different resources. Even in this type of situation, however, only a small percentage of the total product is traded between communities. Most of the goods and services enjoyed by the members of the local group are produced by the group itself.

Specialization at the *individual* level is also severely limited in hunting and gathering societies, particularly with respect to economic and political activities. As every introductory textbook notes, specialization in these areas normally occurs only along age and sex lines. Perhaps a more meaningful way of describing the situation would be to say that the crucially important role of adult male is still largely unspecialized or undifferentiated with respect to economic and political activities.

One of the few exceptions to this is the singling out of some individual to perform certain leadership functions. Even this, however, is not a uni-

---

[14] Baegert, p. 67.
[15] For a comparable summary description of the possessions of the Yahgan of Patagonia, a shellfish-gathering group, see the Rev. Thomas Bridges, in Coon, p. 108. See, also, Marshall, pp. 256–257, on the Kung Bushmen.

versal pattern.[16] Owing to the limited productivity of the group, the leader or headman, can rarely be spared from the routine tasks of production. Hence, the role is usually no more than a part-time specialty. For example, Schapera writes of the headmen of the Bushmen and the Bergdama, "Their official duties . . . seldom take up the whole or even the greater part of their normal daily life, and may indeed require less frequent attention; and when not engaged on public business they follow the same occupations as all other people." [17]

In some of these groups there are a few other part-time specialties, such as the "food-master" among the Bergdama, whose special responsibilities include the making of decisions as to which wild foods can safely be eaten and the delivery of official messages between communities. This, however, is an infrequent type of specialization. Much more common is the role of shaman or medicine man. This role is found in the great majority of hunting and gathering societies, though the forms it takes are variable. Sometimes it is combined with that of headman, more often it is separate. Sometimes the shaman may be a woman, but usually the role is reserved for men. Sometimes this role is divided into various subspecialties, though in most cases the shaman is a general practitioner. Despite these variations, however, one universal feature seems to be that this role, like that of headman, is always a *part-time* specialty and the shaman, too, spends most of his time in the same basic activities as other adult males.

The same factors which inhibit the development of specialization at the individual level also inhibit the development of specialized subgroups and institutions within the society. The entire population (or at least, all of the adult males) tends to function as a unit in most basic activities. The chief exceptions are in the areas of marriage and reproduction, and of ritual and sociability. Hence families and sodalities are the only important subgroups within the populations of hunting and gathering communities.[18] Specialized work groups of an enduring character or specialized military or political groups are absent. Governments, standing armies, political parties, and business enterprises of an exclusive or specialized character are all unknown in hunting and gathering societies. The household and

[16] Julian Steward reports some cases of small bands without chiefs, *Basin-Plateau Aboriginal Socio-political Groups,* Smithsonian Institution, Bureau of American Ethnology, Bulletin 120 (1938), p. 247. See also Colin Turnbull, "The Lesson of the Pygmies," *Scientific American,* 208 (January, 1963), pp. 31 and 35, or "The Mbuti," pp. 302–305, where he reports that the Pygmy bands have no headmen, except those appointed by outsiders, and these headmen have no powers to speak of.

[17] I. Schapera, *Government and Politics in Tribal Societies* (London: Watts, 1956), p. 93. See also Holmberg's description of the Siriono chief, quoted on p. 107 below.

[18] For a brief discussion of sodalities, see Elman Service, *Primitive Social Organization: An Evolutionary Perspective* (New York: Random House, 1962), pp. 73–76. See also Steward, *Theory,* pp. 138–139.

the local band, then, are the two basic units of social organization and most of the activities of the members are organized in terms of one or the other. Hunting and gathering societies are unique in this respect.

Especially significant in this connection is the absence of effective political organization beyond the local level noted earlier. While occasionally the headman of one local group gains a measure of influence over other local groups, this is quite uncommon and, furthermore, his influence is invariably tenuous. The relationships which he establishes rarely outlive him. It is hardly an exaggeration to say that among hunting and gathering peoples, each local community is politically autonomous.

Variable Features of Hunting and Gathering Societies

While these societies have many characteristics in common, there are certain variable features which, though of secondary concern for our analysis, it would be unwise to ignore.[19] Many of these differences are the direct result of differences in the physical environment. Each hunting and gathering society is obliged to obtain most of its necessities from its own limited territory and hence is obliged to adjust to the peculiarities of this area. As a consequence, there are inevitably differences between groups located in the tropics and those in temperate zones or the Arctic, between groups inland and those on coastal waters, between groups located in deserts and those in areas with ample rainfall. These differences are much greater than those between industrial societies in equally varied climes, since the latter are not so dependent on the immediate environment. Moreover, industrial societies are able to modify the environment itself to some extent, something which is not possible for hunting and gathering societies.

Hunting and gathering societies also differ in other ways which seem to have little or no relationship to variations in habitat. For example, they vary greatly in the degree to which they have developed beliefs about the supernatural. In some societies, these beliefs are highly developed; in others, only the barest rudiments are found.[20] Where they are found, beliefs vary considerably in form and content. Similarly, variations are found with respect to patterns of family organization. In some hunting and gathering societies, monogamy is the rule, in others, polygyny is practiced. Polygyny may be either sororal or nonsororal, widespread or

[19] For good summary discussions of such differences see either Forde, *Habitat*, chap. 18, or Steward, *Theory*, pp. 137–142 and compare chaps. 6–8.
[20] For a good short review of religious variation among the hunters and gatherers of South America, see Steward and Faron, pp. 389–391 and the relevant sections of chap. 14.

occasional. Marital residence may be patrilocal, matrilocal, bilocal, uxori-patrilocal, or, in a few cases, uxoribilocal or uxorineolocal.[21] There is some reason for thinking that the patrilocal pattern is the "normal" pattern in the more primitive hunting and gathering societies prior to contact with more advanced societies, but this is still an imperfectly tested hypothesis.[22] In any case, it seems clear that there is considerable variation in marriage and kinship practices from one hunting and gathering society to another.

Last, but not least, these societies differ to some extent in the degree of their technological development. Some are so primitive that they have not yet mastered the techniques of making fire.[23] At the other extreme, some have mastered the rudiments of horticulture and plant small gardens to supplement their basic food supply.[24] Though other differences might also be cited, these should be sufficient to make it clear that while hunting and gathering societies have much in common, they are by no means identical.

Common Features of Distributive Systems

Of all the various characteristics shared by hunting and gathering societies, the one of key importance for students of stratification is the absence of any appreciable economic surplus. According to the first and second laws of distribution set forth in Chapter 3, men are free to monopolize or expropriate only that portion of the product of the group which is not required to sustain the producers. If this is true, and if hunting and gathering societies are incapable of producing any appreciable economic surplus, then our theory leads us to predict that there will be relative equality in these societies, at least with respect to the distribution of goods and services.

The facts support this prediction. If any single feature of the life of hunting and gathering societies has impressed itself upon observers, it is the relative equality of the members. In fact, many untrained observers

[21] See Murdock, "World Ethnographic Sample," *American Anthropologist*, 59 (1957), pp. 664–687, for evidence on all these points. For example, his codes indicate that limited polygyny is the most common form of marriage among the sixty-four hunting and gathering societies for which data are available, but is practiced by only 31 per cent of the total. Similarly, with respect to residence, the patrilocal pattern is the most common, but practiced by only 37 per cent.
[22] See, especially, Service, chap. 3. Steward takes a somewhat similar view in *Theory*, chaps. 7 and 8, but the differences between his view and that of Service are probably more important than the similarities.
[23] See, for example, Colin Turnbull, *The Forest People* (New York: Simon and Schuster, 1961), p. 58, on the Pygmies of the Congo.
[24] See Steward and Faron, p. 392, or Murdock, "World Ethnographic Sample," for examples of this.

have reported perfect equality in certain of these societies. While the more careful observations of trained observers force us to reject these extreme claims, the fact remains that the distributive process in hunting and gathering societies is radically different from that in industrial societies such as our own, or the agrarian societies from which industrial societies have so recently emerged.

The Andaman Islanders provide a good illustration of a relatively pure and uncontaminated hunting and gathering society, and one which has not developed even the more rudimentary forms of horticulture. In writing of their economic life, Radcliffe-Brown reports that "it approaches to a sort of communism." [25] Land, the basic resource of the group, is communally owned, thus insuring equal access to the necessities of life. While the produce of the land and all portable property are privately owned, the Andamanese have customs which offset the usual effects of private ownership. For example, though all food is private property, "everyone who has food is expected . . . to give to those who have none." The result is that "practically all of the food obtained is evenly distributed through the whole camp, the only inequality being that the younger men do not fare so well as their elders." In the case of other forms of privately owned property, an egalitarian distribution is assured by the Andamanese custom of exchanging presents. This practice, when combined with the tradition of according honor to persons who are generous with their possessions, insures near equality in the distribution of goods. In such a society a man stands to gain more by sharing than by hoarding.[26]

While no one hunting and gathering society is completely representative of all, a person familiar with the distribution of goods in Andamanese society is not likely to be greatly surprised by what he finds in most of the others. In those societies, too, one finds a close approximation to equality in the distribution of goods. This is usually achieved, as among the Andamenese, by the communal ownership of land and by some type of institutionalized redistributive process.[27] Often there is some limited

[25] A. R. Radcliffe-Brown, *The Andaman Islanders* (New York: Free Press, 1948, originally published 1922), pp. 43ff.

[26] As Forde points out, he gains not only honor but also security by his generosity, since those who receive from him recognize a moral obligation to repay later if he should ask it. See "Primitive Economics," p. 337.

[27] In some hunting and gathering societies, even the concept of communally owned land is lacking. Anyone may seek food anywhere, and the local group does not deny access to outsiders. See, for example, Steward, *Socio-political Groups*, pp. 254ff. On the other hand, there are some societies in which the redistributive process does not seem to be firmly established and hence there is frequent hoarding. The Siriono are noteworthy in this respect (see Holmberg, pp. 36 and 61–62), though the manner of hoarding and the reported attitudes of the people strongly suggest that the principle of sharing is not absent even in this very uncooperative group. Thus there is some variation, but it is limited.

inequality, with certain segments of the population faring a bit better than others. In the case of the Andamanese the old men enjoy some advantage over the younger. Among the Siriono, the senior wife in a polygynous family and her children are reported to fare somewhat better than the junior wife and hers. In some societies men fare better than women. These differences, however, represent little more than secondary variations on the basic theme of substantial equality.

The one significant exception occurs in the case of those societies which practice the elimination of the unproductive members of the group. In many of these societies, those who are helpless because of old age, injury, or illness are denied the necessities of life and in some instances are put to death by their fellow tribesmen. For example, the Rev. Thomas Bridges wrote that the Yahgan occasionally hastened the end of their relatives by strangulation, but he was careful to point out that "this was kindly meant and there were good reasons for it." [28] It was done only when the individual was completely helpless and only with the consent of all except the victim, who was normally incapable of responding at this point. A much more common practice has been to abandon such persons at the time of breaking camp. In many hunting and gathering societies, infanticide has been practiced also, thereby eliminating children who are born defective or who otherwise appear to threaten the security of the group. These practices seem always based on the simple logic that the limited resources of the group cannot long support unproductive individuals. Hence, those who have no reasonable prospect of becoming self-supporting members of the group have no legitimate claim on what others produce. This is a very specific exception to the more general rule of equal, or near equal, access to the necessities of life, and furthermore does not apply in all hunting and gathering societies.

The distribution of prestige is a very different matter from the distribution of goods. Here there is no problem of short supply, and inequality does not threaten the group's chances of survival. As a consequence, the unequal distribution of honor tends to be the rule rather than the exception in hunting and gathering societies, just as our theory would lead us to expect.[29] However, for reasons which will become evident shortly, the degree of prestige inequality falls far short of that with which members of more advanced societies are familiar.

Once again we may turn to Andamanese society as one which is reasonably typical, at least in the more basic aspects of the matter. Radcliffe-

[28] Bridges, in Coon, p. 97.
[29] This expectation is based on our assumptions that it is man's nature to strive to maximize his status in the eyes of others and that men are unequally endowed by nature to compete for the rewards society has to offer.

Brown, the leading authority on these people, reports that honor and respect are accorded to three kinds of people: (1) older people, (2) people endowed with supernatural powers, and (3) people with certain valued personal qualities, notably, "skill in hunting and warfare, generosity and kindness, and freedom from bad temper." Though it is not completely clear from Radcliffe-Brown's account, there is some indication that men are more likely than women to be highly honored.

Such inequality might properly be called "functional inequality." [30] In other words, the benefits and honors enjoyed by the few represent *a return for services rendered to the many under conditions free from any form of social coercion or man-made shortage*. This can be seen most clearly in the case of an individual who is honored for his skill in hunting and for his generosity. The less able members of the group reward such a person with prestige and influence in exchange for a share in the game he kills. By this spontaneous and uncoerced exchange, those who are generously endowed by nature with talent and energy are stimulated to produce more, and those who are not have greater assurance of obtaining the necessities of life. The alternative would be deprivation, suffering, and possible death for the less able, and, for the more able, surfeit of food and loss of prestige and the respect of others. Thus, *potentially disastrous inequalities in subsistence are transformed into inequalities in prestige and influence, a much safer and more satisfying arrangement.*

One may question whether *all* the inequality in honor and influence in Andamanese and similar societies results in genuine gains for the less favored. For example, are the services of most primitive medicine men of real value to others? This leads into an area of possible disagreement. One observer may feel that the peace of mind a skillful shaman creates for his patients justifies the prestige he receives, while another may not. In this situation it may be wiser to rely on the natives' judgment of the matter and differentiate between functional and nonfunctional inequality on the basis of the relative freedom of the individuals involved. If the exchange is free of man-made coercive elements, then it is reasonable to view such inequality as is generated as functional. If one takes this approach, it is clear that most of the inequality evident in primitive hunting and gathering groups is of just this type.

In hunting and gathering societies, prestige usually goes hand in hand with political influence. The reasons for this are not hard to find. Government by coercion is an impossibility in these societies. The leader

---

[30] This label is suggested by R. H. Tawney's distinction between "the functional society" and "the acquisitive society," in his book, *The Acquisitive Society* (New York: Harcourt, Brace & World, 1920).

of the group is not supported by a force of specialists in violence who are dependent on his favor and therefore motivated to follow his orders. All men are trained and equipped for fighting and the same weapons and training are available to all. The only differences among them are those inherent in the physical constitutions and personalities of the individuals and, while a single man who is unusually well endowed by nature may be the equal, or even the master, of two less favorably endowed men, he is not likely to be able to coerce or defend himself against three who join forces against him. Furthermore, dissatisfied followers may always desert their leader and attach themselves to another band.[31] It follows, therefore, that government must be by persuasion. This means that in any situation in which there is no one obviously correct course of action, effective leadership is possible only if a majority of the population is predisposed to follow the direction of certain individuals and to reject that of others. In short, the limited political development of these societies creates a situation in which honor and respect are necessary prerequisites to political influence.[32]

The same conditions which make honor and respect necessary qualifications for political influence also serve to limit the extent of political inequality possible. The extremes of political domination and subordination are impossible in a society where men must govern by persuasion. This is manifested in various ways, one of the most important being the practice of government by council. This practice is so widespread that Gunnar Landtman, the Finnish sociologist, was led to conclude from his study of stratification in primitive societies that "among the most primitive races tribal authority is exercised almost universally in the democratic form of a general council, while governments representing the monarchic principle are almost entirely absent among peoples usually relegated to the lowest group." [33] While Landtman exaggerates somewhat the prevalence of this mode of government, the fact remains that most ethnographic reports from hunting and gathering societies contain some reference to groups of this type and often indicate that they are of considerable importance.

[31] See, for example, Schapera, p. 193.
[32] Julian Steward provides a good illustration of this in the case of the Northern Paiutes, of whom he writes, "The chief was succeeded by his son, provided he were intelligent, good, and persuasive. Otherwise a brother or some other member of his family, or even an unrelated person *who was assured of popular support,* succeeded him." Of the Shoshoni he writes, "A chief's authority was consequently of uncertain scope and duration and depended largely upon his *persuasiveness.*" See *Socio-political Groups,* pp. 56 and 251 (emphasis added).
[33] Gunnar Landtman, *The Origin of the Inequality of the Social Classes* (London: Routledge, 1938), pp. 309–310.

Even in those groups which are governed by a headman, his powers are usually quite limited. To begin with, they seldom extend beyond the bounds of his own band and when they do, they are extremely tenuous. More serious limitations arise from the fact that the headman has virtually no tenure or authority. Time and again we read, as in the case of the Northern Maidu Indians of California, that the headman "held his place only so long as he gave satisfaction." [34] If the people were dissatisfied, he was quickly replaced. In the case of the Arunta of Australia we are told that the headman ". . . has, *ex officio*, a position which, if he be a man of personal ability, *but only in that case*, enables him to wield considerable power. . . ." [35] Radcliffe-Brown makes the same point in writing of the Andamanese headman, of whom he says, "Of authority the leading men have little or none, but of influence they have a good deal," at least when they are popular with their people.[36]

One of the best descriptions of the position of a "typical" headman in a hunting and gathering society has been written by Allan Holmberg, an American anthropologist who lived among the Siriono of eastern Bolivia. He writes:

> Presiding over every band of Siriono is a chief, who is at least nominally the highest official of the group. Although his authority theoretically extends throughout the band, in actual practice its exercise depends almost entirely upon his personal qualities as a leader. In any case, there is no obligation to obey the orders of a chief, no punishment for nonfulfillment. Indeed, little attention is paid to what is said by a chief unless he is a member of one's immediate family. To maintain his prestige a chief must fulfill, in a superior fashion, those obligations required of everyone else.
>
> The prerogatives of chieftainship are few. . . . The principal privilege of a chief, if it could be called such, is that it is his right to occupy, with his immediate family, the center of the [communal] house. Like any other man he must make his bows and arrows, his tools; he must hunt, fish, collect, and plant gardens. He makes suggestions as to migrations, hunting trips, *etc.*, but these are not always followed by his tribesmen. As a mark of status, however, a chief always possesses more than one wife.
>
> While chiefs complain a great deal that other members of the band do not satisfy their obligations to them, little heed is paid to their requests. I was told, for instance, both by Indians and by whites who had contact with them, that the chief was entitled to a share of every catch of game that was made. While I was living at Tibaera, I had an excellent chance to check this matter empirically, and I found that this was not, as said, usually the case, but rarely so. The more general rule was to avoid giving the chief anything, if possible. . . .

[34] Roland Dixon, "The Northern Maidu," in Coon, p. 272.
[35] Baldwin Spencer and F. J. Gillen, *The Arunta: A Study of a Stone Age People* (London: Macmillan, 1927), vol. I, p. 10 (emphasis added).
[36] Radcliffe-Brown, p. 47.

In general, however, chiefs fare better than other members of the band. Their requests more frequently bear fruit than those of others because chiefs are the best hunters and are thus in a better position than most to reciprocate for any favors done them.[37]

As the foregoing indicates, personal qualities are tremendously important in Siriono society, and the same is true of all other hunting and gathering societies. If a headman is a better man than the others in his group he will fare better than they, but not otherwise. As Holmberg states, headmen generally fare better than others only because they "are the best hunters."

In some hunting and gathering societies, however, the position of headman offers certain special advantages, though only for a man of ability. Spencer and Gillen report that the headman's position could provide the basis for considerable power among the Arunta, though they stress that this was true only for an able man. In the case of the Bergdama of southwest Africa it is reported that the headman "is treated with universal respect, being specified as a 'great man' by adults and 'grandfather' by children; he usually has the most wives (sometimes three or more); he has the pick of all wild animal skins for clothing himself and his family, and only his wives wear necklaces or girdles of ostrich eggshell beads; and he receives special portions of all game killed in the chase, and tribute from men finding honey or growing tobacco." [38] The Bergdama headmen are more fortunate than most; the typical pattern probably lies between the Siriono and Bergdama patterns. Even in the Bergdama case, however, it may be seen that the perquisites of office are not very great, but then it would be surprising if they were, in view of the limited productivity of these groups.

The same general patterns may be observed in the case of the shaman, a role also associated with prestige, influence, and special perquisites. In fact, this role sometimes brings greater rewards than that of headman. For example, in the case of the Northern Maidu it is reported that the shamans are "as a rule obeyed much more than the chief." Furthermore, "the chief was chosen largely through the aid of the shaman who was supposed to reveal to the old men the choice of the spirits." [39] Among the Northern Maidu this office was not inherited, though in other societies it sometimes is. However, inherited or not, the benefits of the role go only to those who can prove their rights to them. Shamans are constantly on trial and those who are unable to demonstrate their com-

[37] Holmberg, pp. 59–60. Quoted by permission.
[38] Schapera, p. 117.
[39] Dixon, pp. 282 and 272, respectively.

petence and power are not likely to benefit greatly. In addition to the usual tests of their powers in the case of illness and other crises, some societies provide institutionalized tests which pit shaman against shaman to see whose powers are the greatest. For example, the Northern Maidu held an annual dance to which all shamans were invited. At this dance each attempted to overcome the others by means of magic. The dance continued until only one man was left standing and he was declared the foremost shaman of all. Undoubtedly those who were eliminated in the early stages suffered a serious loss of status and with it most of the benefits of their position.[40]

The perquisites of the shamans have been substantial in many societies. Radcliffe-Brown reports that once an Andamanese shaman has established his reputation, "he not only receives the respect of others but also makes a considerable personal profit." [41] Father Baegert reports that successful shamans among the Indians of Lower California were able "to obtain their food without the trouble of gathering it in the fields, for the silly people provided them with the best they could find, in order to keep them in good humor and to enjoy their favor." [42] Such advantages, however, are always contingent on performance, and ethnographic reports make it clear that success is dependent on distinctive personality traits which the majority lack.

Much of the foregoing may be summarized by saying that *in primitive hunting and gathering societies, power, privilege, and prestige are largely a function of personal skills and ability.* Inheritance only provides opportunity; to be of value to the individual, confirming actions based on personal qualities are required. Where these are lacking, the possession of an office is of little benefit. In this respect hunting and gathering societies differ greatly from more advanced societies.

The reason for this is that these societies lack certain things which facilitate the transmission of advantage from one generation to the next. To begin with, they possess little wealth, and wealth is one of the best means for passing advantages from father to son. Given sufficient wealth, children of limited ability can hire talented men to manage their affairs, and thus continue to enjoy both power and privilege. This simply is not possible in societies where a man's possessions are so meager. Second, these societies have no hereditary roles with established prerogatives which accrue to the incumbent *regardless of ability*. The limited resources of hunting and gathering societies preclude such luxuries; every office-

[40] For a good description of this contest, see *ibid.*, pp. 283–284.
[41] Radcliffe-Brown, p. 177.
[42] Baegert, p. 79.

holder must, of necessity, continuously validate his right to the office and its associated prerogatives. Finally, these societies are too small to develop differentiated class-based subcultures such as those found in more advanced societies. In the latter, there are marked differences in the way of life from one class to another and children born into the upper classes, and therefore socialized in families sharing a distinctive culture, enjoy a special advantage over children raised in lower strata. In hunting and gathering societies opportunities for differential socialization are very limited and the children of headmen and shamans normally grow up in close association with other children.

All this indicates that the rate of *intergenerational* mobility is very high in hunting and gathering societies. There is little to prevent the talented son of an untalented father from rising to a position of leadership. While he may be denied the office of headman or shaman in a society where these positions are inherited, he can usually become a more powerful figure than the official headman if his abilities warrant it. Ethnographic accounts contain a number of reports of figurehead chiefs who deferred to other, abler, men.[43]

The rate of *intragenerational* mobility is also high in these societies. Age makes a great difference in the advantages which an individual enjoys, though the specific nature of the relationship varies from one society to another. In many groups, perhaps most, the aged are highly honored and enjoy considerable influence. This is well illustrated by the Australian aborigines, whose societies are often described as gerontocracies. In these societies the position of the individual steadily improves with advancing age. In other societies, such as the Eskimo, the Siriono, and the Indians of Lower California, aging is associated with declining advantages and the middle or early adult years are the best years of life.

This difference seems to be a function of variations in environment and technology. In less difficult environments and in societies where technology has advanced somewhat, the aged can be supported and may, in fact, be an asset to the group by virtue of the knowledge and wisdom they have accumulated through a lifetime of experience. The Tiwi of northern Australia provide a good example of this. In this island tribe, older women are much more highly valued than young, simply because they are more efficient food gatherers.[44] In the case of the Arunta, Spencer and Gillen indicate that the older men are influential because they are usually "more learned in ancient lore or more skilled in matters of magic." However, if

[43] For example, Spencer and Gillen report that the headman of an Arunta band is not always the most important member of the council (vol. I, pp. 9–10).
[44] C. W. M. Hart and Arnold R. Pilling, *The Tiwi of Northern Australia* (New York: Holt, 1960), p. 35, etc.

these qualities are lacking in the elderly, younger people are more highly regarded.[45] In short, it is not old age per se, but rather the special qualities that accompany it which lead to special power and influence.

Sex, like age, is a factor in the distributive process in these societies, though its importance is variable. Women invariably occupy a position inferior to men, though in some societies the differential is not great. Women are almost always excluded from the role of headman and usually are ineligible to become shamans or participate in council meetings. To what extent such inequality can be called functional is difficult to say, but it would be a mistake to suppose that the superior position of the men is simply a reflection of their greater physical strength. By virtue of their unique role in childbearing and child nurture, women appear unable to become skilled hunters or warriors.[46] In a society in which the welfare of the group is intimately connected with, and dependent on, the skills of hunters and warriors, it is inevitable that nonparticipants in the critical functions of hunting and fighting will not enjoy the same measure of honor and influence as participants. On the other hand, women do not suffer so far as the distribution of food is concerned; in fact, given the absence of any significant surplus, it seems likely that women approach equality with men in this area.

Though, as a group, women enjoy less prestige and influence than men, all women are not equal. Usually the status of a married woman reflects the status of her husband. For example, Holmberg writes, "to be married to a man who is a good hunter and to have several children are the most important status marks of a woman." [47] Radcliffe-Brown reports that among the Andamanese "the wife of a leading man generally exercises the same sort of influence over the woman as her husband does over the men." [48] Howitt reports a similar pattern among the Kulin of Australia.[49] In a few instances there are reports that certain women enjoyed more influence than some of the men. In writing of the Kurnai, another Australian tribe, Howitt states that some women had considerable influence by

[45] Spencer and Gillen, vol. I, p. 12.
[46] Edwin Thompson Denig reports the dramatic tale of a Crow Indian woman who became an outstanding warrior and chief, but it is significant that she never married a man, and never assumed womanly responsibilities except in her early years. In later years she "married" four "wives" who performed the necessary women's tasks in her household. This case strongly suggests that no individual, however talented, is able to fill successfully the roles of both wife-mother and hunter-warrior. See *Five Indian Tribes of the Upper Missouri* (Norman, Okla.: University of Oklahoma Press, 1961), pp. 195–200.
[47] Holmberg, p. 58.
[48] Radcliffe-Brown, p. 47.
[49] A. W. Howitt, *The Native Tribes of South-East Australia* (London: Macmillan, 1904), p. 308.

virtue of their age and ability, and adds that "such women were consulted by the men, and had great weight and authority in the tribe." [50]

One final factor which influences the life chances of individuals in hunting and gathering societies is their family connections. As we have already noted, the roles of headman and shaman are often hereditary, thus providing some with opportunities for special advantages by the simple accident of birth. In addition, there are occasional reports that the brothers or other close relatives of important men share their benefits to some extent. However, this seems to be a very secondary factor in the total picture, since all the evidence indicates that nothing can compensate for personal incompetence in these societies, and little can block a man of demonstrated abilities either in hunting and fighting or in magic. Holmberg's description of the situation among the Siriono is typical. He writes:

> Within the band, those people who are most closely related to the chief probably enjoy the greatest number of privileges, but I was unable to confirm this as an outstanding feature of Siriono society. It is probably true, to be sure, that the brother of a chief enjoys more privileges than a distantly related cousin. But in a society like the Siriono, where the food supply is both scarce and insecure, a person's status necessarily depends more on his ability as a provider of food than on any other single factor. This was clearly brought home to me time and time again while I was at Tibaera.[51]

Thus, we return to the point from which we started: *the central fact of life for all hunting and gathering societies is the absence of any appreciable economic surplus.* The distributive system of every such society is influenced by this. While some variation is possible, as we have seen, it is so limited that there is a pronounced similarity among the distributive systems of every society at this level. Though it would be a mistake to ignore the differences, it would be a more serious mistake to exaggerate them.

Variable Features of Distributive Systems and Their Causes

Turning to the variable features of the distributive systems of hunting and gathering societies, it is important to keep in mind that these variations cover only a small part of the total range possible in human societies. Marked forms of inequality, such as are regularly found in agrarian and industrial societies, are completely absent in hunting and gathering societies.

[50] *Ibid.,* p. 316.
[51] Holmberg, p. 58. Quoted by permission.

The most significant variations in the distributive systems of hunting and gathering societies are as follows:

1. Variations in the pattern of leadership or government, ranging from the absence of any office above the family head (rare) to the presence of a headman or chief with limited influence over several local bands (very uncommon), the usual pattern being a headman with limited influence over his own band
2. Variations in the influence of shamans or medicine men, ranging from the absence of such persons (rare or uncommon) to the situation in which such individuals are the most influential members of the group (frequent), the most common pattern apparently being one in which such individuals occupy a position of influence and prestige equal or nearly equal to that of the headman of the band
3. Variations in pattern of landownership, ranging from the private ownership of land by families (very rare) to the absence of any concept of landownership (infrequent), the usual pattern being communal ownership by local bands
4. Variations in the importance of redistributive techniques ranging from the situation in which they are not very important (rare or uncommon) to one in which they are a major feature of the economy (most common)

On theoretical grounds there are a number of possible explanations for such differences. These include:

Differences in the physical environment
Differences in the social situation or environment
Differences in the level of technology
Cultural diffusion
Differing influences of great men
Differences in traditions
Chance

One of the best discussions of this problem is contained in Julian Steward's important ecological study of the Western Shoshoni Indians of Nevada and nearby areas, and their Ute and Paiute neighbors.[52] By comparing the social organization of several local bands which share a common cultural tradition but live in differing physical environments, Steward is able to make some estimate of the extent to which variations in social

[52] Steward, *Socio-political Groups*. See also his earlier paper, "The Economic and Social Basis of Primitive Bands," pp. 331–350, and Forde, *Habitat*, chap. 18.

organization are a function of *variations in the physical environment*, and to what extent the explanation must be sought elsewhere.

His analysis strongly indicates that certain differences involving the distributive process are a function of environmental differences. For example, the Paiute Indians of Owens Valley practiced the communal ownership of land while the others did not. Steward maintains that this was because their land was more fertile and provided sufficient plant and animal life to sustain a stable human population. In contrast, the territory occupied by the Western Shoshoni, Utes, and other Paiutes was much less fertile and, even more important, notoriously erratic in its yield. An area producing an abundance one year might produce almost nothing the next. This uncertain situation compelled those groups to go wherever the quest for food might lead, and precluded any system of landownership.[53]

Steward's analysis also indicates that the presence or absence of the role of headman is linked with environmental variations. He found this role absent only in rather small bands. Since the size of the band is greatly influenced by the fertility of the immediate area, it seems that this difference, too, can be linked with environmental variation.

Steward also attributes certain differences in the powers of headmen to the *social situation of the group*. Specifically, he attributes the temporary development of interband leadership in the nineteenth century to the struggle with white settlers. Faced with this crisis, the Indians of this area responded by delegating a measure of interband authority to certain leaders which they had not previously done.[54] Serrano reports a similar pattern among the Charrua of South America, and Gunnar Landtman came to the conclusion on the basis of his broadly comparative study of primitive peoples that war or intertribal conflict has been one of the major factors strengthening the authority of leaders and promoting social inequality.[55]

Finally, Steward indicates that certain variations in the life of the Basin-Plateau tribes were due to *cultural diffusion*. For example, he explains the presence of the special office of "chief's speaker" in certain bands as a borrowed element. The same, he feels, was true of the requirement in some bands that headmen experience visions.[56]

Steward does not discuss the influence of variations in *level of tech-*

[53] Steward, *Socio-political Groups*, especially pp. 255–256.
[54] *Ibid.*, pp. 246–251.
[55] See Antonio Serrano, "The Charrua," in Julian Steward (ed.), *Handbook of South American Indians* (Washington, D.C.: Smithsonian Institution, Bureau of American Ethnology, 1946), vol. I, p. 194, and Landtman, p. 320 in particular, and chaps. 7 and 16 in general.
[56] Steward, *Social-political Groups*, p. 252.

nology among the tribes he studied, presumably because they were minimal. However, a more broadly comparative examination indicates, as our theory would lead us to expect, that such variations have a similar effect to those produced by variations in environmental conditions. Thus, in societies which practice a rudimentary horticulture, populations tend to be larger, settlements more permanent, and leadership roles more sharply defined.[57] One suspects that there may also be increased rewards for the occupants of these roles.

During the last generation, the hypothesis that *great men* are capable of influencing culture and social organization has been anathema to most sociologists and anthropologists.[58] In the main their rejection of this hypothesis has been sound, since the influence of great men was obviously overrated in an earlier period. Furthermore, this hypothesis too often led to the psychologizing of social analysis.

Today, however, the great-man theorists have been driven from the field and it is possible to reexamine the problem somewhat more dispassionately. Sidney Hook, the philosopher, has provided an excellent beginning in his provocative book, *The Hero in History.*[59] Hook believes the social determinists of the last hundred years have thrown out the baby with the bath water in their eagerness to get rid of exaggerated hero worship. He bases his conclusion on an analysis of several specific historical events, including the Russian Revolution.

Ethnographic evidence from hunting and gathering societies supports Hook. For example, Howitt describes a famous chief of the Dieri tribe in Australia who was able, simply by virtue of his unique personal powers, to influence tribes as much as a hundred miles distant, an extraordinary achievement.[60] In addition, he exercised various powers over his own people which were not customary. For example, he separated married couples when they could not agree, and gave away in marriage young women who were not related to him. At the other extreme, there have been numerous headmen who lacked the personal qualities necessary to insure the enjoyment of the traditional prerogatives of their office. Such differences in distributive systems can be explained only if one takes into account the personal characteristics of leading men.

Many social determinists and environmentalists have also been reluc-

[57] See, for example, Steward and Faron's discussion of the various Ge-speaking peoples in the eastern Brazilian highlands (pp. 362–372).
[58] For one of the most vigorous attacks on the great-man hypothesis, see Leslie White, *The Science of Culture* (New York: Grove Press, 1949), chap. 9.
[59] Sidney Hook, *The Hero in History: A Study in Limitation and Possibility* (Boston: Beacon Press, 1955, original edition 1943).
[60] Howitt, pp. 297–299.

tant to give *tradition,* or *the cultural heritage of a group,* its due. Patterns of action once established are not quickly erased and, despite the arguments of functionalists such as Malinowski, there is an element of inertia in the life of human groups which is not easily or quickly overcome.[61] Patterns of action which become habitual and which do not cause obvious difficulties are often retained simply because the mastery of new behavior patterns is an inconvenience and hence resisted by most people, and especially by older people, who learn more slowly but usually occupy the seats of power.

To say that men respond to their group's traditions is simply to say that no generation begins with a *tabula rasa* or blank slate. In the highly impressionable early years of life, each individual is exposed to the culture of his group and internalizes much of it so that it becomes difficult to destroy. Both culture and personality work to preserve many elements from the past in ways of which people are largely oblivious, e.g., in various aspects of language. Thus it is reasonable to hypothesize that some of the differences between distributive systems of societies currently at the same level of economic development and in comparable environmental settings (both social and physical), and with comparable technology and leadership may be reflections of differences in their pasts. This seems especially likely considering the strongly conservative character of primitive men, which anthropologists have so often noted.

Finally, it seems probable that *chance* is also a factor contributing to variations in distributive systems. Even Friedrich Engels, one of the fathers of modern social determinism, did not deny its influence. In fact, he developed a definition of chance, or historical accidents, which he described as those "things and events whose inner connection is so remote or so impossible of proof that we can regard it as non-existent, or negligible." [62] Only those who still believe in the possibility of complete knowledge, the dream of certain nineteenth-century scientists, can omit chance, so defined, from their theories.

[61] See Bronislaw Malinowski, *A Scientific Theory of Culture* (Chapel Hill, N.C.: University of North Carolina Press, 1944), chap. 3, for a vigorous attack on the concept of "survivals." Unfortunately, as in the rejection of the great-man theory cited earlier, there is a mixture of sense and nonsense here, due to an element of semantic legerdemain. For an alternative approach, see Gerhard Lenski, *The Religious Factor* (Garden City, N.Y.: Doubleday, 1961), pp. 304–308.

[62] In Lewis Feuer (ed.), *Karl Marx and Friedrich Engels: Basic Writings on Politics and Philosophy* (Garden City, N.Y.: Doubleday Anchor, 1959), p. 398.

6/Simple Horticultural Societies

*The chores of life exact energy from the talented
which should be devoted to higher things . . .
It is not for ourselves we ask.
It is for the good of society.*
Michael Young

TEN THOUSAND YEARS AGO primitive men first learned
how to cultivate, or raise for themselves, certain of the
plants on which they depended for food. This important discovery laid the foundation for the eventual
emergence of the first horticultural societies some centuries or millennia later. This form of social organization spread both by diffusion and independent invention to large parts of the world, though subsequently
it was superseded in many areas by still more advanced forms of social organization.

As their name implies, horticultural societies are
societies built upon the foundation of a gardening
economy. In this respect they differ both from the
more primitive hunting and gathering societies, in
which the cultivation of plants is either absent or of
secondary importance, and from the more advanced

117

agricultural societies, which employ more efficient techniques of cultivation and farm on a larger scale.[1] Perhaps the best single criterion for differentiating between horticulture and agriculture is that the latter employs the plow as the basic tool in cultivation while the former depends on the more primitive hoe or the still more primitive digging stick.

Horticultural societies once flourished throughout most of Europe, the Middle East, and South and East Asia before they were replaced by, or evolved into, agricultural societies. In more recent times they have flourished in much of North and South America, sub-Saharan Africa, and certain of the islands of the Pacific.

As noted in Chapter 4, the societies which practice horticulture are extremely varied and it is necessary to differentiate between the more and less advanced. This can best be done in terms of the following criteria:

1. Is the digging stick or the hoe the basic tool in cultivation?
2. Are terracing and irrigation (other than by natural flooding) practiced?
3. Are techniques of fertilization (other than by burning over the land in clearing or by natural flooding) practiced?
4. Is metallurgy practiced and are metal tools of cultivation manufactured?

Simple horticultural societies are those which rely on the digging stick and practice none of these advanced techniques. *Advanced horticultural societies* rely on the hoe and practice one or more of the advanced techniques.[2]

In modern times simple horticulturalists have been found chiefly in North and South America and certain of the larger islands of the Pacific, notably New Guinea.[3] Hence it is with these groups that we shall be concerned in this chapter. Though simple horticultural societies once flourished in many other areas, our knowledge of those societies is restricted to scattered material artifacts, and these afford only limited insights into the working of their distributive systems.

[1] The word "horticulture" comes from the Latin words *horti* and *cultura,* meaning the cultivation of a garden, whereas "agriculture" come from *agri* and *cultura,* meaning the cultivation of a field.
[2] For a dramatic illustration of what the introduction of just one of these factors can do to a society, see Ralph Linton's description [*The Tanala: A Hill Tribe of Madagascar* (Chicago: Field Museum of Natural History, 1933)] of the transformation of Tanala society as a result of the introduction of irrigation.
[3] African horticulturalists are omitted because they used hoes and practiced metallurgy. Most of the horticulturalists from Mexico to Peru are omitted because they used hoes and practiced irrigation, and often terracing and fertilization. These groups will be examined in the next chapter.

Common Features of Simple Horticultural Societies

Simple horticultural societies strongly resemble hunting and gathering societies, especially when the latter are in very favorable environments. In such things as community size, per capita productivity, degree of social inequality, and so forth, there appears to be considerable overlap. As Goldschmidt points out, this is largely a function of environmental variation: the size of communities, level of productivity, and degree of inequality in hunting and gathering societies in very fertile settings tend to be somewhat greater than in simple horticultural societies in unfavorable settings.[4] Under *comparable* conditions, however, simple horticultural societies are normally larger, more productive, and less egalitarian. We also find that *on the average* simple horticultural societies are more highly developed in all these ways, and the upper limit of their range is significantly higher.

This can be illustrated by comparing population data for the two types of societies. In the case of hunting and gathering societies, it will be recalled, the society and the community were identical and communities averaged no more than fifty persons. In simple horticultural societies, by contrast, societies often contain more than one community and the average size of communities is greater.

At the present time it is still impossible to say whether the multicommunity or single community society is the more common among simple horticulturalists. Both occur with considerable frequency. The Hasinai of Texas provide a good example of a multicommunity society, consisting of a very durable and stable federation of nine villages.[5] Early Spanish writers reported that the Cayuvava of eastern Bolivia were governed by a single chief who controlled seven villages, some with as many as 2,000 inhabitants.[6] Other sources report similar structures among such scattered groups as the Kapauku and Garia of New Guinea, the Jivaro, Paressí, and Xaray of South America, the Yuma of the American Southwest, the Iroquois of the Northeast, and various tribes of the South-

[4] Walter Goldschmidt, *Man's Way: A Preface to the Understanding of Human Society* (New York: Holt, 1959), p. 149.

[5] John Swanton, *Source Material on the History and Ethnology of the Caddo Indians,* Smithsonian Institution, Bureau of American Ethnology, Bulletin 132 (1942), especially pp. 107–173.

[6] Julian Steward and Louis Faron, *Native Peoples of South America* (New York: McGraw-Hill, 1959), p. 350; or Julian Steward (ed.), *Handbook of South American Indians,* Smithsonian Institution, Bureau of American Ethnology, Bulletin 143 (1946), vol. III, p. 427.

east.[7] Usually these societies contained only a handful of villages, seldom more than ten. Sometimes, too, intercommunity ties were unstable and impermanent or loose knit and not of great importance. Nevertheless, they constitute a substantial advance compared with the organizational patterns of hunting and gathering societies.

Though it is impossible to state exactly the average size of simple horticultural communities, it appears that it is probably between one and two hundred, or two to four times the average in hunting and gathering societies.[8] The upper limit is somewhat easier to identify and is approximately 3,000 persons, or at least five times the figure for hunting and gathing communities.[9]

Given the greater size of horticultural communities and the multi-community character of many simple horticultural societies, it is clear that the average size of simple horticultural societies is greater than that of hunting and gathering societies, though it is still impossible to say just what the ratio is. A conservative estimate might place it at about 5 to 1. With respect to the *upper limit,* however, the contrast is more pronounced. In the case of the Iroquois, for example, the population may have approached 16,000 at one time, or at least twenty-five times the maximum

---

[7] See Leopold Pospisil, "Kapauku Paupuan Political Structure," in F. Ray (ed.), *Systems of Political Control and Bureaucracy in Human Societies,* Proceedings of the 1958 meetings of the American Ethnological Society, p. 9; C. G. Seligmann, *The Melanesians of British New Guinea* (London: Cambridge University Press, 1910), pp. 58–59 on the Garia; M. W. Stirling, *Historical and Ethnographical Material on the Jivaro Indians,* Smithsonian Institution, Bureau of American Ethnology, Bulletin 117 (1938), pp. 38–41 on the Jivaro; Steward and Faron, p. 350 on the Xaray and p. 258 on the Paressí; C. Daryll Forde, *Habitat, Economy and Society* (London: Methuen, 1934), pp. 251 and 257 on the Yuma and the tribes of the American Southeast; and George Peter Murdock, *Our Primitive Contemporaries* (New York: Macmillan, 1934), pp. 304ff. on the Iroquois.

[8] This is my own estimate, based on a reading of both ethnographic and archaeological materials. See, for example, V. Gordon Childe, who reports that Neolithic villages in Europe comprised eight to fifty houses, suggesting populations from 30 to 300 [in "The New Stone Age," in Harry Shapiro (ed.), *Man, Culture and Society* (Fair Lawn, N.J.: Oxford Galaxy, 1960), p. 105], or H. Ian Hogbin who reports that the average size of villages in New Guinea is 200 [in *Transformation Scene: The Changing Culture of a New Guinea Village* (London: Routledge, 1951), p. 30]. See also Steward and Faron who indicate that the simple horticulturalists in South America had population densities five times that of hunters and gatherers (compare their statements on pp. 298 and 383).

[9] This figure is reported by both Murdock, with reference to the Iroquois, and Steward and Faron, with reference to various peoples in the tropical forest of South America (see Murdock, *Contemporaries,* p. 297 and Steward and Faron, p. 299). Other instances of simple horticultural communities with populations of one to two thousand are fairly common. See, for example, Leo Simmons, *Sun Chief* (New Haven, Conn.: Yale University Press, 1942), p. 10, or Fred Eggan, *Social Organization of the Western Pueblos* (Chicago: University of Chicago Press, 1950), p. 176 on the Indians of the American Southwest.

number found in any single hunting and gathering society.[10] Though this was probably a very exceptional case, it indicates the organizational and demographic potential of these societies.

The greater size of simple horticultural societies clearly reflects the greater productivity of their economies. Although much of this increase in productivity is consumed by population increase, a part of it takes the form of an economic surplus. This manifests itself most clearly in the new "leisure" which members of these societies enjoy. Unlike the members of hunting and gathering societies, they are not compelled to spend most of their working hours in the search for food and other necessities of life, but are able to use more of their time in other ways.

One of the uses to which this new "leisure" has been put is the *production of various kinds of nonessential goods.* A good example can be found in the construction of houses and other types of buildings. The structures of most simple horticultural peoples are far superior to those of hunters and gatherers. For example, so primitive a group of horticulturalists as the Boro of South America are reported to build communal houses which are 60 to 70 feet on each side and 30 or more feet in height.[11] The Iroquois built structures which were from 50 to 150 feet in length and in one instance reached 300 feet.[12] The Kiwai Papuans probably hold the record, having constructed one building which proved to be 519 feet long.[13] Nothing comparable to these structures can be found among hunting and gathering peoples.[14]

In many instances the new "leisure" which a horticultural economy makes possible has been devoted to *ceremonial activities.* One cannot review the ethnographic literature on simple horticultural societies without being impressed by the frequent references to ceremonial activities and the great amount of time given to them in many of these societies. The classic case of this occurs among the Zuñi Indians of New Mexico, whose way of life has been so vividly described by Ruth Benedict in *Patterns of Culture.* The Zuñi devote a tremendous amount of time and energy to these activities, which constitute the focal point of the life of the group.

[10] Murdock, *Contemporaries,* p. 319.
[11] Forde, *Habitat,* pp. 133–134.
[12] Murdock, p. 297.
[13] Gunnar Landtman, *The Kiwai Papuans of British New Guinea* (London: Macmillan, 1927), p. 5.
[14] It is significant to note that archaeologist V. Gordon Childe reports similar differences between the early Neolithic horticulturalists and their hunting and gathering predecessors. In fact, the Danubians, a simple horticultural people of Central Europe, constructed communal longhouses quite similar to those built several thousand years later by the Iroquois. See Childe, "The New Stone Age," in Shapiro, p. 104.

Although the Zuñi (and other Pueblo Indians) are extreme in this respect, ceremonial activities play an important part in the life of most simple horticultural societies. Often these are organized around a number of secret societies or clubs and a calendar of festival occasions, as in the case of the Iroquois. Frequently special buildings are erected for these purposes, something which rarely happens in hunting and gathering societies.[15] In the case of groups with fewer resources, such as the Mountain Arapesh of New Guinea, the frequency and elaboration of ceremonial activities are more limited but are still an important and prominent feature of the life of the group.

Warfare is still another use to which the new "leisure" has been put. This is not to say that warfare is unknown in hunting and gathering societies, but rather that it tends to be a very occasional activity. In some simple horticultural societies, however, warfare is elevated to the point where it becomes a way of life, with food production and other industrial pursuits relegated to a secondary place, at least in the lives of the men. The Jivaro Indians of the upper Amazon are a classic example of this. As early as the seventeenth century, one Spanish Jesuit wrote that their "ruling passion, the object of their rejoicings, of their pleasures, and of their greatest felicity, is war." More recently an American ethnologist wrote of the Jivaro's "never-ending cycle of blood-revenge feuds which may vary in extent all the way from an individual murder by a single man from ambush to desperate struggles of extermination in which several hundreds may be involved." [16] The focal point of all these activities appears to be the tsantsa ceremony, in which the heads of captured enemies are shrunken and preserved. Though the Jivaro are an extreme case, they reflect a widespread tendency among simple horticulturalists. Warfare is clearly much more frequent and much more important among these people than among hunters and gatherers.[17]

In this connection it is important to note that references to the taking of captives are far more frequent in studies of simple horticultural societies than in studies of hunting and gathering groups. One finds this practice in both North and South America and also in New Guinea.[18] Male captives are commonly tortured and slain and often eaten afterwards (cannibalism seems more common in this type of society than any

[15] For examples of how elaborate and impressive these buildings can be, see the photographs of Papuan clubhouses in Seligmann, *op. cit.*
[16] Both quotations are from Stirling, pp. 43 and 42.
[17] Again archaeological evidence points in the same direction. See Childe, "The New Stone Age," p. 107.
[18] On South America, see Steward and Faron, pp. 304–305; on North America, see Murdock on the Iroquois in *Contemporaries*, pp. 309–311; on New Guinea, see Seligmann, pp. 318-319 on the Mekeo.

other).[19] Occasionally, however, they are adopted into the tribe, and in time usually come to enjoy all the rights and privileges of full-fledged members of the group. By contrast, women captives are more likely to be made "slaves" and forced to marry and work for their captors.[20]

One of the most important consequences of the adoption of horticulture is a reduction in the frequency with which communities must move about. Though communities are seldom of a fixed or permanent nature in simple horticultural societies, still they are much less nomadic on the average than hunting and gathering bands. The latter are usually obliged to migrate at least once a year. By contrast, communities in simple horticultural societies tend to remain at the same place for a number of years. For example, the Boro of South America move only every several years, and the Iroquois are reported to have remained in the same village for ten to twelve years.[21] In a few instances, notably in the American Southwest, truly permanent settlements were possible, thanks to natural irrigation or flooding which constantly brought new, fertile topsoil to the fields to replace exhausted soil.[22]

It is difficult to exaggerate the importance of this development. So long as people must constantly be on the move, it is hard for them to accumulate material possessions, particularly when everything must be carried on their backs. When the frequency of such moves is substantially reduced, it is much easier to accumulate possessions of every kind. These include not only objects of utilitarian value such as tools, weapons, clothes, pottery, baskets, and so forth, but also a substantial array of other objects like masks and other equipment used in ceremonial gatherings, status symbols such as skulls and other trophies, and artistic creations such as musical instruments. In short, the members of simple horticultural societies own both more and more varied possessions than the members of hunting and gathering societies.

Compared with hunting and gathering societies, simple horticultural societies generally display a much higher level of specialization at both the individual and communal levels. At the individual level, this

---

[19] Elman Service in *Primitive Social Organization: An Evolutionary Perspective* (New York: Random House, 1962), says that "terrorization, or psychological warfare, seems to be at its highest development in tribal society" (p. 115). He feels that this is due to the inevitably inconclusive nature of tribal warfare which precludes decisive engagements or the effective conquest of one group by another.

[20] The practice of "slavery" in simple horticultural societies will be examined in greater detail later in the chapter. See page 130.

[21] For the Boro, see Forde, *Habitat,* p. 135, and for the Iroquois, see Murdock, *Contemporaries,* p. 295.

[22] Forde, *Habitat,* p. 230. Many New Guinea villages also seem to remain for long periods in a single area. See, for example, Seligmann, p. 228, who refers to traditions indicating that one village had been in the same area for five generations.

manifests itself in a marked increase in specialized economic, political, and religious roles in most of these societies. Elaborate religious ceremonials sometimes require a great number of priestly specialists. Generally these are only part-time specialties but in some instances, as among the Zuñi, the major priestly offices are full-time vocations and their occupants are freed from the task of providing their own livelihood.[23]

Political offices are also more numerous and more likely to be full-time positions than in hunting and gathering societies. One of the most significant developments in this connection is the creation in many of these societies of a staff of subordinates whose primary responsibility is to assist the headman or chief and do his bidding. This undergirds his authority and reduces somewhat his dependence on persuasion. Such arrangements are found in varying degrees of elaboration, though even in the most extreme cases chiefly staffs remain quite modest in size, at least when compared with more advanced societies.

The Trumaí Indians of South America provide a good example of minimal development along this line. In this tiny group, two individuals were designated as subchiefs. Their sole responsibility seems to have been to act in the place of the chief, or village headman, when he was away from the village.[24] The Roro of New Guinea are more nearly typical. Among them the chief's first assistant was clearly identified as war chief as well as enforcer of the chief's orders.[25] His second assistant, usually a man of wealth and influence, had the responsibility "to be near his chief and prepared to render assistance in all ceremonies in the clubhouse, and generally to save him trouble and see that things go smoothly." [26]

Even in the realm of economic activity specialization is evident. In the case of the Iroquois there was a rudimentary form of specialization, with the old men and others incapable of hunting and fighting devoting themselves to the manufacture of weapons and tools.[27] A more highly developed pattern is evident among the Kiwai Papuans, where specialization is not limited to the aged or infirm. Recognizing that all men are not equally skilled in the production of all things, they leave the production of items requiring considerable skill to "the experts." This applies to the manufacture of canoes, drums, harpoon shafts, artistic work, and scarification. Those who have special skills in these areas tend to become part-

[23] See Irving Goldman, "The Zuni Indians of New Mexico," in Margaret Mead (ed.), *Cooperation and Competition among Primtive Peoples,* rev. ed. (Boston: Beacon Press, 1961), p. 332.

[24] Robert Murphy and Buell Quain, *The Trumaí Indians of Central Brazil,* Monographs of the American Ethnological Society, 24 (1955), p. 54.

[25] Seligmann, p. 218.

[26] *Ibid.*

[27] Murdock, *Contemporaries,* p. 301.

time specialists.[28] Similar developments are reported in some other simple horticultural societies.[29]

At the communal level, too, there is evidence of greater specialization among simple horticulturalists than among hunters and gatherers. This usually manifests itself in increased trade and commerce between villages or even between societies. Landtman provides a good illustration of the degree to which specialization and trade are sometimes developed at this level. He reports that the Kiwai islanders trade canoes, sago, garden produce, bows, arrows, mats, belts, women's grass petticoats, and feathers; their neighbors, the Mawata people, trade coconuts, certain shells, fish, dugong and turtle meat, and objects made of cassowary and dugong bones; the Torres Straits islanders, stones axes, stone clubs, harpoon shafts, all kinds of shells, and dugong and turtle produce; and the bushmen of the interior, various kinds of birds' feathers, cassowary bones, bows, arrows, and garden produce.[30]

V. Gordon Childe reports evidence of similar, though probably less extensive, trade among simple horticultural communities in Neolithic Europe. For example, he mentions that Mediterranean shells have been found in Neolithic villages and graves throughout the Danube basin and even in the valleys of the Oder, Elbe, and Rhine. Also, there seems to have been a lively trade in choice rocks and rock artifacts, but Childe says that "neither miners, axe-grinders, nor hucksters are likely to have been 'full-time specialists.'" Though clearly there are variations in the degree of economic specialization and trade in simple horticultural societies, many, if not most, seem to specialize to some extent in the production of commodities the raw materials for which are abundant in their own territory but in short supply elsewhere.

Finally, specialization also manifests itself in the formation of numerous organizations, apart from the family and kin group. These usually take the form of secret societies and social clubs for men, with their primary functions generally being either religious or social in character. They also frequently serve to express—or perhaps facilitate—male dominance. As noted earlier, these organizations lead to the creation of a considerable number of specialized roles and offices, some of which assume tremendous political significance and hence have far-reaching consequences for the distributive process.[31]

[28] Landtman, *The Kiwai*, p. 168.
[29] See, for example, Murdock, *Contemporaries*, p. 335 on the Hopi Indians of the American Southwest.
[30] Landtman, *The Kiwai*, pp. 213–214.
[31] For a good description of such groups among horticulturalists in South America, see Robert Lowie, "Social and Political Organization of the Tropical Forest and Marginal Tribes," in Steward, *Handbook*, vol. V, pp. 335–339.

Common Features of Distributive Systems

If the first and second laws of distribution are valid, and if the foregoing analysis of the nature of simple horticultural societies is reasonably accurate, then inequalities in power and privilege should be more marked in these societies than in hunting and gathering societies. This is, in fact, the case: one of the striking differences which emerges from any comparison of these two types of societies is that social inequalities are more pronounced in the horticultural. This is not to deny the existence of some overlap between them, a point which will be considered in the next section of this chapter. However, on the average there is a definite difference between the two categories, and *many* simple horticultural societies exhibit a degree of inequality unmatched in *any* hunting and gathering society.

The extreme which political inequality could occasionally attain in simple horticultural societies is suggested by the Hasinai Indians of Texas.[32] Fray Casañas, the first missionary to work among these people, has given us the following picture of this facet of their life.

> In each tribe [i.e., village] there is a *caddi*. He is like a governor ruling and commanding his people. The office of *caddi* also descends through the direct line of blood relationship. Each *caddi* rules within the section of country occupied by his tribe, no matter whether it be large or small. If large, they have certain officials named *canahas*. Of these, there are seven or eight to aid in governing. If the tribe is small, there are only three or four. It is their duty to relieve the *caddi* and to publish his orders by reporting that the *caddi* commands this or that. They frighten the people by declaring that, if they do not obey orders, they will be whipped and otherwise punished. These *canahas*, in turn, have their subordinates called *chaya*. They do everything the *canahas* tell them to do. They have still other officials whom they call *tammas*. These are the officers who promptly execute orders. They whip all the idlers with rods, beating them on the

[32] Though the Hasinai possessed the horse, their culture was not dominated by the horse complex to anything like the degree characteristic of the true Plains Indians. John Swanton, who has written the definitive monograph on the Caddo Indians of whom the Hasinai were a part, has written: "The Hasinai were prevented from becoming fully fledged Plains Indians by their devotion to agriculture and the pressures of more northern tribes. . . . All of the Caddo originally possessed a woodlands culture, and we may say that in reality they never became anything other than woodland people, though part of them took on for a while a Plains veneer." (*Op. cit.*, p. 198.) Thus, while the political pattern described in the text above may reflect the influence of the horse to some extent, this influence was probably limited. This conclusion is reinforced by evidence from certain South American tribes, such as the Manasí or Bauré, which are referred to in the text which follows.

legs and over the stomach. . . . The peace and harmony among the officials described is so great that during the year and three months we have
been among them we have not seen any quarrels—either great or small.
But the insolent and lazy are punished.[33]

Over the local *caddices* was still another official known as the *xinesí*,
whom Casañas described as "like a petty king over them." Other statements indicate that he was also the high priest of the tribe. This official,
unlike the *caddices*, was freed from the obligation of providing his own
livelihood.

The Indians of South America provide a number of other examples
of chiefly power and privilege. For example, the chiefs of the Manasí had
a staff of subordinates to enforce their commands and lived in a huge
house built by their subjects. They also had two large fields tilled by their
subjects for their benefit, and received the first fruits of the crops of the
villagers and a share of all game and fish.[34] In the case of the Bauré, another group in the same general area, the chiefs also enjoyed great power
and could even impose a death sentence. Like the Manasí chiefs, they
were freed from common labor and were supplied by their subjects with
all their material needs.[35] These groups are especially interesting since
both are neighbors of the Siriono described in the last chapter, thus affording a comparison with some measure of control over environmental conditions.

In New Guinea and elsewhere a second type of inequality is often
encountered, that based on *wealth*. The Kuma, a tribe of the interior
highlands, provide a good example of this. The Australian anthropologist
Reay states, " 'Big men' are found among the Kuma, of the kind commonly
encountered in New Guinea. They are wealthy and polygamous." [36] Status

[33] From "Descriptions of the Tejas or Asinai Indians: 1691–1722," translated by
Mattie Austin Hatcher, *Southwestern Historical Quarterly*, 30 (1927), pp. 216-217.
Quoted by permission.
[34] Alfred Métraux, *Native Tribes of Eastern Bolivia and Western Matto Grosso*, Smithsonian Institution, Bureau of American Ethnology, Bulletin 134 (1942), pp. 128–131.
Steward and Faron classify the Manasí, Bauré, Mojo, Paressí, and Xaray as chiefdoms
and link them with the more advanced chiefdoms of the Circum-Caribbean area. From
the technological standpoint, however, they were less advanced, since they farmed
without irrigation or terracing (p. 253). In fact, Steward and Faron state that "in
horticulture, housing, village composition, and certain sociopolitical and religious features, these Indians resembled the Amazonian peoples" (p. 252). In short, though they
stand near the boundary between simple and advanced horticultural societies, they
seem more properly classified with the former.
[35] Métraux, *Native Tribes*, p. 69.
[36] Marie Reay, *The Kuma* (Melbourne: Melbourne University Press, 1959), p. 114.
See also Landtman's discussion of the Kiwai for a very similar picture, *The Kiwai*, p.
168, or Pospisil on the Kaupauku, p. 11.

and reputation are the major goals men seek and these depend chiefly on a man's wealth as measured in terms of wives, pigs, plumes, and shell ornaments.[37] Wives are the crucial form of wealth, since they are the one productive form of wealth that is in short supply. The ideal of every Kuma man is to have ten wives, but Reay reports that at the time of her study she knew of none who had more than six. Even this, however, meant marked disparities in wealth and status within the tribe. In one clan there were eighty-seven men old enough to marry. Of these, one had four wives, five had three, twelve had two, fifty had one, and nineteen were unmarried.[38] This was the basis of a very real system of stratification. There was even a term of opprobrium applied to the men who had no prospects of ever marrying because of personal unattractiveness. They were known as "knock-about men" (there were five of them in the clan Reay studied) and were treated as pariahs, being excluded from the ceremonial dances which were major events in Kuma life.[39]

A third form of inequality found in most simple horticultural societies is based on *religion and magic*. Just as in hunting and gathering societies, certain individuals are recognized as having special powers. The chief difference is that these powers are likely to yield more substantial material benefits in simple horticultural societies than in hunting and gathering groups, where prestige tends to be the primary reward. The Jivaro of South America provide a good example of the material benefits which can accrue to shamans in simple horticultural societies. In this group the shaman is likely to be the wealthiest man in his village, his wealth being the return he extracts for his services.[40] Among the Manasí, the priests apparently ranked directly below the chief and, like him, were wholly or largely supplied with the material necessities of life.[41] Similar reports come from numerous other groups.

In many simple horticultural societies, magical skills or religious powers are the most valuable resource of all. For example, among the Guaraní of Paraguay it is reported that though each community had a chief, "the actual power was often in the hands of a shaman." [42] Further west, some of the backward and very isolated tribes of the mountainous Montaña are said to have had no political authority above the family head, except when fighting, and that the shamans often assumed leader-

---

[37] Reay, pp. 97–98.
[38] *Ibid.*, pp. 84–85. In another study from New Guinea, it is reported that no man had as many as five wives and more than half the married men had only one. See F. E. Williams, *Papuans of the Trans-Fly* (Oxford: Clarendon Press, 1936), p. 149.
[39] *Ibid.*, pp. 47–48 and 161.
[40] Stirling, pp. 115–121.
[41] Métraux, p. 130.
[42] Alfred Métraux, "The Guaraní," in Steward, *Handbook*, vol. III, p. 85.

ship.[43] One tribe, the Quijo, regularly made them chiefs. This pattern of shamanistic dominance was not limited to South America, as the case of the Zuñi illustrates.[44]

Another fairly common pattern is that in which the chief assumed religious functions. Examples of this can be found among such varied groups as the Paressí, Mojo, Chiriguano, and Guaraní, to cite but a few.[45] As Robert Lowie has put it, a "chief's influence is definitely enhanced when he combines religious with secular functions." [46] In short, despite variations in detail, *religious or magical powers are one of the primary sources of social inequality in many, and probably most, simple horticultural societies.*

A fourth important form of inequality found in many simple horticultural societies is that based on *military prowess*. Once again, a comparison with hunting and gathering societies indicates points of similarity and points of difference. In both types of societies men who are brave and skillful in the use of weapons are honored. The difference appears when one examines the way in which bravery and skill with weapons are used. In the more primitive hunting and gathering societies *hunting* is the major component of the adult male role and is much more important than fighting. With the development of horticulture, the importance of hunting declines considerably, and in many cases military pursuits fill the vacuum by providing men with new opportunities for demonstrating prowess. As noted previously, warfare often is one way men use their new "leisure." Thus the military element is much more pronounced in simple horticultural societies than in hunting and gathering groups. A second difference between the two is also linked with the new "leisure." Because of the reduced demands on men's time in many of these societies, it becomes possible to institutionalize the celebration of the warrior role. This manifests itself in the development of specialized warrior societies and warrior ceremonies, all of which tend to consolidate and validate claims to prestige based on military prowess and insure a satisfying recognition and reward for the warrior heroes.

In some simple horticultural societies, military prowess is a prerequisite to the chieftainship, as in the case of the Chiquito Indians of South America.[47] More often, however, men of military ability are appointed to the office of war chief, an office sometimes subordinate to that

---

[43] Julian Steward, "The Tribes of the Montaña and Bolivian East Andes," *ibid.*, p. 528.
[44] See, for example, Goldman, p. 313.
[45] See Steward, *Handbook*, vol. III, pp. 85, 355, 419, and 478.
[46] "Social and Political Organization," in Steward, *Handbook*, vol. V, p. 345.
[47] Métraux, *Native Tribes*, p. 125.

of civil chief and other times equal to it. This pattern is found in areas as widely separated as New Guinea and the American Southwest.[48] As the title suggests, the war chief functions as the leader of the group in military campaigns. In addition, he frequently has important civil functions, and is often second in command in such matters.

The exercise of military prowess has sometimes given rise to *slavery*, a fifth form of inequality. As noted earlier, male captives are usually killed or adopted, but women are often taken as prizes of war and put to work as members of their captor's household. They become, in effect, their captor's property. Nevertheless, it is somewhat misleading to call them slaves. For one thing, their status is not greatly different from that of the other women in the household. Furthermore, their children are normally free and hence full-fledged members of the tribe. Thus, their situation is intermediate between that of free persons and true slaves of the type encountered in more advanced societies. One might refer to this pattern as protoslavery or incipient slavery in order to call attention to the important differences which set it apart from the more familiar pattern, involving an hereditary class of persons of both sexes, typically in a very degraded status.[49]

A sixth, and final, form of inequality in simple horticultural societies is that based on *skill in oratory*. For example, it is reported that "oratory and arms are the two outstanding paths to fame and distinction among the Iroquois." [50] While this is not typical of all societies at this level, a surprising number honor in some way the "Rhetoric Thumpers," as the Kuma of New Guinea aptly call them. In many instances, as among the Kuma, the chief's assistant is chosen for his skill in oratory and functions as the chief's spokesman. Among the Guaraní of South America, "an eloquent man distinguished in warfare might become chief." [51]

Since the rewards which orators receive in simple horticultural societies are freely accorded them and not based on the possession of coer-

---

[48] See, for example, Seligmann, chaps. 19 and 29 and Eggan, p. 108 or Swanton, pp. 171 and 191.

[49] Steward and Faron discuss this practice, which seems to have been especially common among South American tribes. See especially pp. 253, 256, and 302–303. As they note, after the arrival of the Spanish there was apparently a tendency for some of these tribes to raid neighboring tribes simply to obtain captives which could be sold to the Spanish. Because of their heavy involvement in the slave trade, these raiders found it necessary to keep male slaves of their own to perform the various economic functions they themselves had previously performed, thus leading to the creation of something approaching a true slave class. While the evidence on this subject is far from satisfactory, it appears that this was not a spontaneous and indigenous development, but purely a response to the peculiar conditions created by Spanish colonization.

[50] Murdock, *Contemporaries*, p. 305.

[51] Métraux, "Guaraní," p. 85.

cive powers, it is fair to ask what services they render which lead others to honor and reward them. Apparently there are a number of kinds of service, though usually not all in the same society. Some orators are entertainers, some are inspirational leaders, some are idea men, some are historians, and some simply are used to dignify, or give "tone," to important occasions. Men value all these functions and therefore reward those who are most skillful in performing them.

As the foregoing indicates, simple horticulturalists have not been slow to seize the opportunities for power and privilege afforded them by the modest economic surpluses of their societies. Any comparison between their societies and those of hunting and gathering peoples makes it clear that inequalities in power and privilege are nearly always more pronounced in the former.

Not only are the inequalities greater, they are also more institutionalized, a development made possible by the increase in "leisure" and the greater opportunities for specialization. In hunting and gathering societies, very few social positions have been formalized to the point where they merit the title of "office." Usually they are no more than informal roles with certain more or less distinctive functions. In horticultural societies, by contrast, many positions have been formalized to the point where they have a title and a definite set of responsibilities and privileges.

This development is extremely important since it complicates the relationship between the personal attributes of an individual and his status. No longer is the latter a simple function of the former; *now status is a complex function of both his personal attributes and his office or offices.* Now it becomes possible for an individual to enjoy a reward to which his personal attributes alone would not entitle him.

The Hasinai of Texas provide a good illustration of this new development. When one of their chiefs died before his son and heir reached maturity, the son was still acknowledged as chief. During his minority the other officials formed a council and ruled in his stead, but stepped aside when he came of age.[52] Under such conditions personal ability counted for little and the accident of birth for everything. This individual did not have to prove his superior abilities as a leader of his people—they acknowledged it long before any demonstration of such abilities was possible. This is a new possibility which develops in human societies as soon as the vital functions of societies come to be linked with institutionalized offices.

As the illustration of the Hasinai chief indicates, discrepancies between ability and status are most likely to occur when offices come to be transmitted as "property" from one generation to the next. Under these

[52] Swanton, p. 171.

conditions the correlations between ability and status, and between performance and reward, are likely to be much lower than when an office is
made available to all in free and open competition. Even in the latter case,
however, some discrepancy is likely to develop when individuals are
given extended or indefinite tenures in office. In short, *the development
of offices in society represents an important early step in the direction of
stabilizing, solidifying, and institutionalizing systems of social inequality.*

Certain definite advantages accrue to society as a whole as a consequence of this development. The alternative would seem to be anarchy
in any complex society. The chief disadvantage, as noted above, is the
growing gap between performance and reward which institutionalization
fosters. If one could plot the net benefit to societies on a graph, he would
probably find it to be curvilinear, with the high point occurring somewhere in the middle ranges of institutionalization.

In theory, a considerable number of key offices in simple horticultural societies are transmitted as "property" from one generation to the
next, as in the case of the Hasinai chieftainship. In fact, however, careful
inspection indicates that certain controls operate to prevent abuses. For
example, though the Jivaro Indians customarily pass the office of chief
from father to son, the heir of one of the most powerful chiefs of modern
times was obliged to relinquish the office because he was sickly.[53] In the
case of the Kuma it is reported that the leadership of subsubclans (the
highest political office in the group) was supposed to pass from father to
son, but when a careful check was made it was found that in 36 per cent
of the cases investigated, someone else occupied the position.[54]

The tendency to make such exceptions seems to reflect the tenuous
quality of the institutional and organizational structure of the societies in
question. It is significant that the Hasinai, who had a well-developed
political system, with numerous officials providing support for the chiefs,
were able to tolerate an incompetent individual in this office, whereas the
Jivaro, the Boro, and the Kuma, who lack this, find it necessary to ignore
the rules of succession when this threatens to put an unqualified individual in office. Most simple horticultural societies resemble the latter more
than they do the Hasinai, so far as political development is concerned.
Thus they are inclined either to ignore the rules of succession from time
to time or, as in some cases, to define them in such a way that there is no

[53] Stirling, pp. 40–41.
[54] Reay, p. 114. Similar patterns can be found in many other groups. For example,
Lowie says that "in many tribes [in South America] substitutes serve if the customary
successor is deemed unfit." See "Social and Political Organization," in Steward, *Handbook*, vol. V, p. 346.

automatic succession.[55] Furthermore, many limit the tenure of chiefs to the years in which they are vigorous and capable, and make provision for them to step aside when they become too old to fulfill the requirements of their office.[56] Others make tenure conditional on good behavior.[57]

On the basis of such evidence, it appears that simple horticultural societies occupy a position intermediate between that of hunting and gathering societies on the one hand and advanced horticultural and agrarian societies on the other. As in the latter, the functions of leadership have come to be institutionalized and localized in formal offices and the elements of authority and coercion are evident; as in the former, power and privilege are not normally regarded as "property" which can be retained indefinitely or transmitted within families without regard to the qualifications of the possessor.

Another significant feature of the distributive process of virtually all simple horticultural societies is the relative importance of the individual's personal skills. Though not so crucial as in hunting and gathering societies, they are still much more important than in most more advanced societies. Most simple horticultural societies provide numerous opportunities for well-qualified men to advance themselves. For example, any male Hasinai had the opportunity to win the honorific title of *amayxoya*, or "great man," and have this attached to his name. All that was required was distinction in battle.[58] Hence this honor was not in short supply. The only limitation on achievement was set by the character and constitution of the individual.

The Kuma of New Guinea provide an even more fascinating example of the same principle. In this group, in which power and privilege were limited to a minority of wealthy polygynists, a careful study revealed that success was partly a function of age. Thus while only a third of the adult males might be regarded as influential men at any one time, three-fifths of the men eventually attained positions of leadership.[59]

On the basis of available evidence, it appears that high rates of both inter- and intragenerational mobility are common in most simple horticultural societies. Success is not limited to a fortunate few born into

[55] Among the Iroquois, only members of certain extended families could become sachems, but the choice of the particular individual was left to the family. See Murdock, *Contemporaries*, p. 306. A similar situation prevailed among the Mekeo of New Guinea (Seligmann, p. 346).

[56] For example, the Manasí had the chief yield to his son when the son came of age. However, the son first had to validate his right to the office by leading a war party. See Métraux, *Native Tribes*, pp. 128–129.

[57] See, for example, the Iroquois, Murdock, *Contemporaries*, p. 307.

[58] Stirling, p. 170.

[59] Reay, p. 116.

favored families, though compared with hunting and gathering societies a shift in this direction is evident. As we have already seen, there is some inheritance of office. In other cases, as among the Kuma, it is important to be born into a prosperous subclan, since those born into poorer ones have more difficulty finding the means to purchase a wife. In still other cases, as among the Araona of South America, it was important to be part of a large family and to have numerous relatives if one aspired to the chieftainship, with the result that competition for this office was somewhat restricted.[60] However, despite these occasional limitations, conditions are far more fluid and opportunities for getting ahead far more numerous in simple horticultural societies than in those which are technologically more advanced.

In simple horticultural societies, as in hunting and gathering societies, there are no gross inequalities in material possessions. The reasons for this are twofold. First, *most material necessities are readily available to all.* In most of these societies plenty of land is available and anyone willing to work can supply his own needs. (This abundance of land may well be a by-product of the chronic state of warfare which is so common among these societies, and the high mortality rates which result.)

A second factor which seems to promote equality in material goods is *the relative absence of capital goods.* As a result, the demand for goods is much more limited than in more advanced societies, since the marginal utility of consumer goods declines more rapidly than the marginal utility of capital goods. The one thing always in short supply in simple horticultural societies is *prestige.*[61] Under the circumstances, those who accumulate an appreciable surplus of material goods are very likely to *give it away* since by so doing they can acquire the one thing they do not have enough of, prestige. Thus it is not surprising to find in ethnographic reports frequent references to the liberality of chiefs, shamans, and others who were in a position to accumulate an abundance of goods.[62]

To persons raised in technologically advanced societies, especially those with a capitalist tradition, the practice of giving away one's wealth as freely as is done in many of these societies seems singularly illogical and an indication of either an amazing concern for others or an obvious lack of common sense. Actually it is neither. Instead, it represents a shrewd and well-calculated pursuit of self-interest designed to maximize an individual's return on his investment of time, energy, and other resources.

[60] Métraux, *Native Tribes,* p. 39. See also the Kapauku of New Guinea (Pospisil, p. 18).
[61] In some of these societies one might add wives to this.
[62] In Kuma society, for example, reputation and status are achieved by dispensing wealth—except for wives—with a lavish hand. Reay states, "Just as a prosperous clan enhances its reputation by presenting food to others, so a prosperous person enhances his reputation by disposing of his valuables."

To understand the logic of this system, there are several points which must be clearly recognized. First, women are the one really crucial form of capital goods in this type of society.[63] Second, in these societies there is a norm of reciprocity which makes it incumbent on individuals to repay all gifts with other gifts of equal value. Third, the principle of marginal utility is applicable here as elsewhere. Finally, status is as highly valued among these people as among us, and the desire for it just as insatiable.

Given these conditions, a "potlatch" pattern [64] is almost inevitable.[65] Men have only a limited capacity for the consumption of plumes, shell ornaments, and even pigs. Beyond a certain point, the individual finds that he stands to gain more by giving them away than by keeping them, since in so doing he both enhances his reputation and puts those who cannot repay under moral obligation to him.[66] Wives, however, are another matter. Being a very scarce and immensely valuable form of capital, they are hoarded and accumulated just as capital is in our own society. Thus the successful man, the "big man," is the individual who is able to accumulate capital, thereby insuring himself a steady stream of consumer items which can be exchanged for prestige and influence. In this way the skillful entrepreneur obtains for himself not only the material necessities of life, but also the more intangible rewards which looms so large in the eyes of those whose material needs are satisfied.

Thus it becomes clear that such actions, though technically "giveaways," are in reality *exchanges*. Those rich in goods trade their material surplus for deference or prestige, of which an unlimited supply is available. *The net effect of such actions is greatly to reduce inequality with respect to material possessions while substantially increasing it in the areas of prestige and influence.*

Before concluding this section a brief examination is necessary of the role of age and sex in the distributive process. On the whole, the situation in simple horticultural societies does not seem very different from that in hunting and gathering societies. Generally men enjoy a somewhat higher status than women, though there are variations in this respect, with societies ranging from near equality in a few cases to pronounced male dominance in others. The male advantage is more marked in some areas of life

[63] Pigs are also an important type of capital goods, but they are only productive when tended by women; otherwise they would run wild and be of no value to any single individual even though they breed prolifically. Also, they are not nearly in such short supply.

[64] This term refers to the famous ceremonies of the Indians of the Northwest Coast, at which the high point was the lavish distribution of gifts.

[65] To say that a "potlatch" pattern is "almost inevitable" does not mean that the pattern need be developed everywhere to the same degree as on the Northwest Coast.

[66] In writing of the Kapauku of New Guinea, Pospisil makes the point that a man's debtors are among his most reliable followers, and that giving to those who cannot repay is one of the surest paths to influence and honor (p. 21).

than others. For example, it is more pronounced with respect to political and military activities than with respect to material possessions. Even in the former areas, however, considerable evidence indicates that it is easy to exaggerate the degree to which women are subordinated in primitive life. For example, there are scattered reports of women chiefs, and in the case of the Iroquois the power of electing sachems was vested almost entirely in the hands of women.[67] As in hunting and gathering societies, the status of a woman is usually closely linked with that of the man on whom she is dependent.[68]

With respect to *age*, increasing years are usually an asset in simple horticultural societies, at least up to the point where senility sets in. There are various reasons why this is so, but one is almost certainly the psychological influence of early childhood experiences. During the highly impressionable years of childhood, individuals come to associate authority and prestige with the older generation. So long as an older person remains physically and mentally vigorous, these childhood impressions are likely to survive, with the result that the younger person continues to grant deference long after the older one has lost his capacity to exact it. Furthermore, the older generation often has the advantage of organization: challenges to its authority usually come from single individuals, but tend to be met by a united front of elders. Since organization is one of the major bases of power, they are usually able to resist quite effectively. Finally, members of the older generation are generally the keepers of tradition, and in societies which place high value on tradition, this is an important source of strength.

Variable Features of Distributive Systems

Simple horticultural societies are no more carbon copies of one another than are hunting and gathering societies or any of the other major types. One need only compare the peaceful Zuñi of New Mexico with the warlike Jivaro of South America to realize how great the differences can be. As with hunting and gathering societies, however, the differences in pat-

[67] For examples of women chiefs, see Seligmann, pp. 346–347, Swanton, pp. 172–173, or Métraux on the Chiriguano in Steward, *Handbook,* vol. III, p. 479; for a discussion of the role of Iroquois women, see Murdock, *Contemporaries,* pp. 306–307.
[68] For two valuable discussions of the role of women in primitive societies, see Forde, *Habitat,* pp. 408–410 and Lowie, *Social Organization* (New York: Holt, 1948), pp. 263–266. Both point up the complexity of the relative status of women and the difficulties involved in any attempt to generalize about their status, even within a single society. As both point out, the treatment women receive, the character and extent of their labor, their legal status, and the degree of public prominence must all be considered, and their status in one respect is not necessarily comparable to their status in another.

terns of distribution cover only a limited portion of the total range of variation observable in human societies.

Many of these differences should already be apparent as a result of the preceding analysis. They can be summarized under four basic headings: (1) differences in degree of inequality, (2) differences in type of inequality, (3) differences in the sources of inequality, and (4) differences in degree of vertical mobility.

With respect to *degree of inequality*, the range of variation is not great, though it appears somewhat greater than in hunting and gathering societies. This is chiefly because the upper limit of the range is extended somewhat further toward the pole of inequality. The lower limits for the two types of societies do not appear very different. Among simple horticultural societies at this lower extreme, such as the Boro or Trumaí of the Amazon region, inequality seems to be almost entirely due to differences in personal or biological characteristics. Society adds little to these differences in any way, and hence inequality is minimal.[69] At the other extreme there are societies, such as the Hasinai of Texas, the Kuma of New Guinea, or the Bauré of South America, with a level of inequality unmatched in any true hunting and gathering society.

There is a second important difference between hunting and gathering and simple horticultural societies with respect to degree of inequality. If we think in terms of the frequency distribution curves for the two types of societies, the ethnographic literature suggests that both are skewed, but in opposite directions. Whereas the curve for hunting and gathering societies seems strongly skewed in the direction of minimal inequality, the curve for simple horticultural societies seems slightly skewed in the opposite direction. Thus the overlap is not as great as a comparison of their ranges, or limits, might suggest.

As inequality becomes more marked, it tends to become more variable in *type*. As the discussion earlier in this chapter indicates, there is quite a difference between the systems of stratification in Hasinai and Kuma societies. In the former, political inequality, or differences in degree of political authority, are much more pronounced than differences in wealth; in the latter, this relationship is reversed. There are also differences in the value attached to religious and magical powers, military prowess, and skills in oratory. For example, the Pueblo Indians honor religious distinction much more than military distinction. The Jivaro reward both. Such differences are common.

[69] In some of these societies, for example, the chiefs were obliged to work like commoners. See, for example, Steward, *Handbook*, vol. I, p. 489, on the Canella, or vol. V, p. 342 and vol. III, p. 478, on the Chiriguano.

Third, there are differences in the *sources of inequality*. In some societies inequality is due almost entirely to differences which are biological in origin. This is especially true of those simple horticultural societies with minimal inequality. In other societies, social factors play a much larger role. Sometimes these social factors serve merely to magnify the effect of the biological factors. At other times, however, they tend to displace the biological factors. This is especially likely to occur when the social factors are *inheritable,* as in the case of private property or offices which pass from father to son.

Finally, as the preceding suggests, there are differences in the *degree of vertical mobility*. All the available evidence indicates that this is greatest in those societies where the inheritance of key resources such as wealth and office are minimal. The appearance of these factors serves to stabilize patterns of inequality and to make it easier for those who enjoy power, privilege, and prestige to retain them and pass them on to their children.[70]

As the foregoing makes clear, all four variable features are highly interrelated. Among simple horticultural societies a low degree of inequality tends to be linked with (1) minimal variation in the types of inequality, (2) maximal importance of biological factors as sources of inequality, and (3) maximal mobility. By contrast, a high degree of inequality is linked with (1) maximal variation in types of inequality, (2) minimal importance of biological factors, and (3) minimal mobility. These relationships are obviously not accidental.

These differences among peoples of the same societal type give rise to many interesting questions concerning causes which have, as yet, been hardly examined. For the present it appears that the best we can do is hypothesize that the same factors cited in the analysis of variations among hunting and gathering societies (see page 113) are also operative among simple horticultural societies. This is clearly an area meriting careful study in the future.

A Critical Development

One of the most important developments associated with the emergence of horticultural societies is the strengthening of the position of political leaders. As noted in the last chapter, the prerogatives of headmen are few in hunting and gathering societies, and these men are obliged to govern

[70] See, for example, Reay's discussion of this subject as it applies to the Kuma. The systems of private property and polygyny in this tribe had the effect of keeping boys raised in poor subclans poor and those raised in prosperous clans prosperous. Obviously, a similar pattern exists wherever lucrative offices are hereditary, as tends to be true of the Manasí and Mojo.

by persuasion. Authority is almost totally absent, hence tyranny is virtually impossible.

In most simple horticultural societies the prerogatives of leaders are substantially greater. Often they wear special insignia or clothing, setting them apart.[71] In addition, they are often shown special deference, as in the case of the Manasí chiefs, whose people address them only in a very formal manner and in whose presence the young people are not permitted to sit, or as in the case of the Atsahuaka chief, in whose presence the people speak in whispers.[72] In a great many cases the chiefs of simple horticultural societies have special privileges. For example, Jivaro chiefs are entitled to first choice among women captives, Chiquito chiefs are permitted to practice polygamy, and Boro chiefs are given larger and more convenient garden plots.[73] Quite commonly these chiefs are exempted from manual labor and have their material necessities supplied by their people.[74] In a number of instances they receive the equivalent of taxes, or a share in the product of the labors of others.[75] Finally, in many instances they can declare war and lay military obligations on others, and in a few instances they can even terminate wars which are in progress.[76]

Obviously, no single chief has all these prerogatives, but some enjoy a number of them. While a few of these rights are found in some hunting and gathering societies, most are not. Most represent new elements of chiefly authority. As a consequence, one finds the first traces of real tyranny in these societies. The cases in which this is reported are not numerous, but they are sufficient to indicate the beginnings of a development destined to have far-reaching consequences in more advanced societies.

One of the clearest evidences of this incipient tyranny is found in an Australian anthropologist's discussion of the political situation in the tribes on the northeast coast of New Guinea. This writer, H. Ian Hogbin, states:

> . . . most headmen appear to have used their powers with fairness and discretion. One or two, however, are said to have become filled with their own importance and behaved as though they were masters of their people.

[71] See, for example, the Boro as reported by Seligmann, pp. 220–221 the Kuma as reported by Reay, p. 114, or the Chiriguano as reported by Métraux in Steward, *Handbook*, vol. III, p. 479.

[72] See Métraux, *Native Tribes*, pp. 129 and 53, respectively.

[73] For the Jivaro, see Stirling, p. 56; for the Chiquito, see Métraux, *Native Tribes*, p. 125; for the Boro, see Forde, *Habitat*, p. 135.

[74] See, for example, the Hopi (Murdock, *Contemporaries*, p. 336), the Manasí, the Bauré, and the Paressí (Métraux, *Native Tribes*, pp. 129, 69, and 165, respectively).

[75] See, for example, the Manasí and the Paressí (Métraux, *ibid.*).

[76] See, for example, the description of the powers of the Hasinai war chief according to an early Catholic missionary (Stirling, p. 191). For an example of peacemaking powers, see Seligmann, p. 58.

Yomsa', for example, committed adultery a number of times, was always demanding pigs, and carried out sorcery against all who opposed him.[77]

He then goes on to say that such headmen were usually removed from the scene sooner or later. For instance, Yomsa' was enticed to a lonely part of the beach by some of his own relatives and there stabbed in the throat. This proved to be an ideal solution to the problem; the necessity for blood revenge was eliminated because one of Yomsa's own kinsmen wielded the knife. Hogbin reports that in another community with a similar problem the whole village joined in the assassination.

These cases are interesting because they indicate that in simple horticultural societies a very limited degree of tyranny is possible, but that the means are not yet available for the tyrant to protect himself against the reaction which inevitably develops if he presses his interests too far. For one thing, he lacks a staff of dependent specialists whose interests are linked with his. Furthermore, the general democracy in weapons and the universal experience in their use combine to put him at a disadvantage against an aroused opposition (though sometimes chiefs have special magical powers which can be used for private advantage [78]). Finally, those he exploits are in constant contact and communication with one another so that he does not enjoy any organizational advantage such as tyrants in more complex societies enjoy when dealing with their opponents. All these factors combine to limit the opportunities for the development of tyrannical government in simple horticultural societies. However, it is in societies at this level of development that the first halting steps are taken.[79]

One other factor which contributes significantly to the beginning of tyranny is the way in which certain societies handle the redistributive problem. In some societies this is done in a decentralized, nonpolitical fashion; in others, a centralized, political solution is adopted. In the former instance, those who are able to produce a surplus of consumer goods simply hold a feast and distribute the surplus to their guests directly. In

---

[77] Hogbin, pp. 144–145. Quoted by permission.

[78] In this connection it is important to realize that sorcery actually can be highly effective in primitive societies, owing to the almost universal belief in the efficacy of magic. The anthropological record makes it very clear that many primitives have been killed by sorcery alone.

[79] There are a number of other indications of this tendency in ethnographic reports. For example, Swanton reports that the Caddo chiefs frequently followed the practice of calling the old men of the village together for consultation before taking action, but then proceeded to do what they, the chiefs, thought best (p. 172). In the case of the Takanan of South America we are told that the common people were obliged to work hard for their chiefs (Métraux, *Native Tribes,* p. 40). The Bauré apparently found it necessary to develop the practice of having certain of the older men remind the chiefs of their duty when they seemed inclined to abuse their authority (*ibid.,* p. 69).

other societies, however, the chief functions as a middle man, and goods are brought to him for redistribution.[80] This technique affords a unique opportunity for one individual to exercise an inordinate degree of control over the life of his society, provided there is an appreciable surplus. If there is, the chief is in a position to withdraw some of it for his own use, though he would probably have to justify his action by cultivating the belief that this was, somehow, for the benefit of the group as a whole. If the surplus is very small, as is the case in virtually all simple horticultural societies, he is probably unable to do more than free himself and his immediate family from the burdens of food production and other menial labor. When the surplus becomes larger, however, it becomes possible for the chief to free others from subsistence activities and put them to work at tasks of his choosing. Given our earlier assumptions about the nature of man, we should predict that such persons will usually be given tasks which benefit the chief first and foremost, and only incidentally, if at all, the other members of the tribe. Since the enlargement of the surplus is a development which comes to full flower only in advanced horticultural societies, the testing of this prediction must be postponed until the next chapter.

[80] See, for example, the Koita of New Guinea (Seligmann, p. 54).

7/Advanced Horticultural Societies

The king should not eat with his brothers
lest they poison him.
Zulu proverb

WHERE AND WHEN the first advanced horticultural societies appeared are questions which still remain unanswered. On the basis of available evidence it appears that they had their beginnings in the Middle East more than 6,000 years ago.[1] For our purposes, however, this is far less important than the subsequent spread of this type of society through diffusion or independent invention to all of the five major continents.

[1] Archaeological research clearly indicates the practice of irrigation in the al' Ubiad period in Mesopotamia, which dates back to the end of the fifth millennium B.C. See, for example, V. Gordon Childe, *New Light on the Most Ancient East*, rev. ed. (London: Routledge, 1952); or *Social Evolution* (London: Watts, 1951); or Robert Braidwood, "The Agricultural Revolution," *Scientific American*, 203 (1960). See also William F. Albright, *The Archaeology of Palestine* (London: Penguin, 1956), chap. 4, or *From the Stone Age to Christianity*, 2d ed. (Garden City: Doubleday Anchor, 1957), pp. 137–146 on the Chalcolithic Age, which may have begun as early as the middle of the fifth millennium B.C.

Though advanced horticultural societies were superseded by agrarian societies long ago in many parts of the world, in a few areas they survived into the modern era, thus affording opportunities for direct observation of their daily life by persons able to record what they saw. In some instances these observers have even been trained anthropologists or enthnographers. This has been true chiefly in the advanced horticultural societies of sub-Saharan Africa. In the case of those in the New World, in the region from Peru to Mexico, reports by *trained* observers are lacking, since these societies were effectively destroyed at the time of the Spanish Conquest four centuries ago. Nevertheless, there is considerable documentary evidence from early Spanish explorers, missionaries, and officials which makes clear at least the basic characteristics of most of these societies.

As a consequence, our analysis of stratification in advanced horticultural societies must be based chiefly on those found in sub-Saharan Africa and, to avoid the complications of too extensive diffusion, those which are non-Islamic.[2] To a lesser degree we can also draw on evidence from South and Central America and from the archaeological record, though such sources will be used chiefly for the purpose of checking generalizations suggested by the African evidence.

These limitations are not so serious as they might at first seem. For one thing, there are a very large number of advanced horticultural societies in Africa and they are scattered over a wide variety of environmental settings. Thus, we are not forced to limit our inquiry to a handful of societies in a highly homogeneous environment. Furthermore, in recent decades the volume of research on these societies has increased greatly and the quality has also improved. The resources available, therefore, seem adequate for our purposes, even though they are not as extensive as one might desire.

Common Features of Advanced Horticultural Societies

When one compares the advanced horticultural societies of sub-Saharan Africa with the simple horticultural societies of North and South America or New Guinea, one quickly discovers a host of striking and important

[2] Usually I shall omit the areas in the northern portion of the western Sudan, which have been subject to substantial Islamic influences for approximately a thousand years, as well as those in the eastern Sudan and Horn areas, where the influence of Middle Eastern peoples and pastoral tribes has been very strong. Thus I hope to minimize the influence of direct and pervasive diffusion from more advanced societies, though I realize that the influence of diffusion cannot be completely eliminated in any part of horticultural Africa.

differences. These begin in the realm of technology and extend into almost every other sphere of life.

As we have already noted, the basic instrument of cultivation in simple horticultural societies is the digging stick. Among the Boro, for example, "the same tool serves as spade, hoe and rake."[3] By contrast, African horticulturalists almost without exception employ *metal hoes* of various designs. As the English anthropologist Forde puts it, such hoes "are far superior to the digging sticks of [simple horticulturalists] and, wielded by men, they turn up the soil to a much greater depth."[4] This is of great importance in societies which do not employ fertilizers and hence quickly deplete the nutrients in the surface soil.

Metal can also be used in a variety of other tools to increase their efficiency. This is especially true of tools such as axes and knives, which quickly lose their cutting edge when made of stone. Metal also increases the efficiency and deadliness of weapons.

The advanced horticultural societies of Africa have enjoyed other advantages over simple horticultural societies. By virtue of their relative proximity to the great centers of civilization, African horticulturalists were able to acquire a great number of edible plants which had their origins in far distant places. For example, bananas, taro, and yams, which constituted the staple crops along most of the West African coast when the first Portuguese explorers arrived, apparently were imports from Southeast Asia, having been introduced in East Africa over a thousand years ago.[5] According to one authority, "Africans grow approximately nine-tenths of all the cultivated plant varieties known to man."[6] Of course, some of this is due to recent European influence, and furthermore only a part of the total is available in any given society. Nevertheless, the advanced horticultural societies of Africa generally have a much wider variety of cultivated plants at their disposal than have the simple horticultural societies of the Americas or New Guinea.

Diversity is a great asset in any society for two reasons. First, it permits the utilization of a wider range of soils or land areas, since different crops require different conditions. Second, it permits a more sustained use of a given piece of land, since it facilitates crop rotation (whether consciously or unconsciously practiced). In either case, food production is increased.

In the New World, the technological superiority of the advanced

---

[3] C. Daryll Forde, *Habitat, Economy and Society* (London: Methuen, 1934), p. 136.
[4] *Ibid.*, p. 154.
[5] See George Peter Murdock, *Africa: Its Peoples and Their Cultural History* (New York: McGraw-Hill, 1959), pp. 222ff.
[6] *Ibid.*, p. 21.

horticultural societies is again clearly evident, especially in the case of the Incas. The greatest achievements of the Incas in the area of food production were probably those associated with irrigation and terracing. In order to make the best possible use of their water supply, they built huge systems of canals and ditches that served not only entire valleys, but in some cases carried water to several adjoining valleys. One canal was 75 miles long, and one aqueduct linked with it consisted of an earthwork four-fifths of a mile long and 50 feet high. In addition, these people terraced mountainsides thousands of feet high and made trips off the coast to obtain guano to fertilize their fields.[7]

The technological superiority of the advanced horticulturalists can also be seen in the tools they used. The Incas, for example, used both the *taclla* and *lampa*. The former was a protoplow, about 6 feet in length with both a footrest and shoulder rest for greater leverage; its point was frequently made of bronze.[8] The *lampa*, or hoe, resembled an old-fashioned adze more than a modern hoe; it was used for breaking up clods, weeding, and general cultivation and it, too, had a bronze blade.

In the Circum-Caribbean area and in Mexico, techniques of food production were not as highly developed as in Peru, but even there one finds irrigation, terracing, and fertilization.[9] The greatest achievement in this area was probably the *chinampa*, or floating garden, a system of horticulture developed by the Aztecs.

It is very easy for members of modern industrial societies to underestimate the importance of developments such as these. Careful study makes it clear that the shift from hunting and gathering to horticulture, and the advances in horticultural technology, made possible revolutionary changes in human societies. One of the best indications of this comes from an agricultural survey of the Yucatán, the home of the Maya, undertaken some years ago by the Carnegie Institution. This study indicated that the average Maya corn farmer, using traditional techniques, could raise enough corn with forty-eight days' labor to supply his family for an entire year.[10] Even if it takes another forty-eight days' labor to supply his family's other essential needs, it is clear that the Mayan farmer has a consid-

---

[7] See Julian Steward and Louis Faron, *Native Peoples of South America* (New York: McGraw-Hill, 1959), pp. 87–88. For a more detailed description, see John H. Rowe, "Inca Culture at the Time of the Spanish Conquest," in Julian Steward (ed.), *Handbook of South American Indians*, Smithsonian Institution, Bureau of American Ethnology, Bulletin 143 (1946), vol. II, especially pp. 210–233.

[8] For pictures of this tool, see Steward, *Handbook*, vol. II, p. 213.

[9] See, for example, Steward and Faron, pp. 180–184 or Victor von Hagen, *The Ancient Sun Kingdoms of the Americas* (Cleveland: World Publishing, 1961), pp. 61, 68–69, 81–86, 128–129, and 246–252.

[10] Sylvanus G. Morley, *The Ancient Maya* (Stanford, Calif.: Stanford University Press, 1946), pp. 154–155.

erable amount of free time which he can devote to other kinds of activities. As one student of the Maya has pointed out, it was just this surplus time which made possible the building of the famous Mayan pyramids, temples, palaces, colonnades, ball courts, dance platforms, courts, plazas, and causeways.[11] He could have added that this surplus time also made possible the expansion of the state and the high incidence of warfare found in advanced horticultural societies the world over.

As might be expected, these technological advances also had *demographic consequences*. Above all, they made possible the enlargement of societies both by geographical extension and by increased density. As seen in the last chapter, the populations of simple horticultural societies seldom rise much above 15,000 and usually fall far short of this. In advanced horticultural societies the upper limit is raised at least two hundredfold. The Inca Empire, for example, is estimated to have had a population of about 4,000,000 at the time the Spaniards arrived, and the Maya are thought to have numbered 3,000,000 in the ninth century.[12] Even a less advanced group, the Chibcha of what is now Colombia, is estimated to have numbered 300,000 at the time of the Conquest.[13] In Africa no horticultural society seems to have reached the size of Incan and Mayan societies in the precolonial era, but many apparently numbered 100,000 or more and a few may even have passed the million mark.[14]

In part this growth potential is simply a reflection of advances in agricultural technology which make possible substantial increases in population density. Densities of 100 or more per square mile are found in many advanced horticultural societies, and in the case of the Ibo of Nigeria, 1931 census figures reveal an overall density of 260 per square mile, with figures for certain areas even higher.[15]

In the main, however, the size of advanced horticultural societies is a reflection of an important new development in human affairs which is seen clearly for the first time at this level of economic development, namely,

[11] *Ibid.*, pp. 155–156.
[12] See Steward and Faron, p. 121 on the Inca, and von Hagen, p. 221 on the Maya.
[13] Steward and Faron, p. 212.
[14] See Murdock, "World Ethnographic Sample," *American Anthropologist*, 59 (1957), pp. 675–677, which records numerous peoples in the sample as having "political integration in large independent units averaging at least 100,000 in population" (see col. 15). One of the largest societies was that of the Ganda, which in the nineteenth century was reported to number from 500,000 to 1,000,000. See Margaret Chave Fallers, *The Eastern Lacustrine Bantu* (London: International African Institute, 1960), p. 52.
[15] For figures on the Ibo, see K. M. Buchanan and J. C. Pugh, *Land and People in Nigeria* (London: University of London Press, 1955), p. 60. Some years ago L. Dudley Stamp of the University of London calculated that southern Nigeria could maintain a population of 144 persons per square mile, indefinitely and without damage to the soil, using slash-and-burn cultivation and hoe culture. See "Land Utilization and Soil Erosion in Nigeria," *Geographical Review*, 28 (1938), pp. 32–45.

empire building. In simple horticultural and hunting and gathering societies empire building seems to be impossible. To begin with, the resources of these societies are insufficient to build the necessary military and political machines. In addition, the surplus produced by potential victims is too meager to justify the effort. Conflicts between these societies, therefore, are limited to raiding and plundering.

With the emergence of advanced horticultural societies, it becomes both possible and profitable for ambitious and warlike peoples to establish relatively permanent control over other groups. The economic surplus is sufficiently great to sustain the necessary military and political machine and to justify the necessary expenditure of effort. As a consequence of this process of empire building, peoples of diverse cultural traditions are often brought within the framework of a single political system.

There are numerous indications that most of the larger societies in sub-Saharan Africa today developed in this way. For example, in writing of the Yoruba of Nigeria, one of the most populous groups in that part of the world, Forde states, "there is little doubt that the Yoruba state was built up by a process of military expansion, and that many of the Yoruba-speaking peoples of today are the descendants of subject groups who have adopted the speech and customs of their conquerors." [16] A similar situation prevailed in the New World. The Incas seem to have been a very small and insignificant group a century before the Spanish Conquest. During that century, however, they conquered a great number of other peoples, who were speedily absorbed culturally as well as politically.[17] Thus, on both continents, conquest and empire building were important factors in societal growth and expansion.

As these examples indicate, political organization reached a fairly high level of development in many parts of horticultural Africa and America before contacts were made with Europeans. States covering thousands of square miles were governed by strong central authorities. In a number of instances, dynasties were established which lasted for several centuries.[18] In writing of these states, one leading anthropologist maintained that "in the thoroughness of their political institutions and in the skill with which social institutions were utilized to lend stability to the political structure, they far exceeded anything in Europe prior to the six-

[16] Forde, *Habitat*, p. 164.
[17] For a summary of these developments, see Rowe, in Steward, *Handbook*, vol. II, pp. 203–209; Steward and Faron, pp. 112–188 and 133; von Hagen, pp. 404–429 and 576–579; and Joseph Bram, *An Analysis of Inca Militarism*, Monographs of the American Ethnological Society, 4 (1941).
[18] See, for example, John Roscoe, *The Baganda* (London: Macmillan, 1911), p. 214.

teenth century." [19] Although this is clearly an exaggeration, it can at least be said that they compared favorably with their European counterparts of the early Middle Ages.

Not all the horticultural societies in Africa engaged in empire building, by any means. Those that did not, however, often fell victim to those that did. Hence it appears that prior to European contact and domination, the majority of the population of horticultural Africa below the Sahara were either members or subjects of expansionist states. Nevertheless, some escaped this fate, so that it would be a mistake to suppose that all advanced horticultural societies are of this type. This is one of the important variable features of advanced horticultural societies.

When alien peoples are conquered and absorbed by advanced horticultural societies, their identity is not invariably lost or destroyed. On the contrary, they often take their place as a distinctive subunit within the dominant society. This transition is often accomplished quite easily and naturally, especially in those societies which maintain distinctions on the grounds of descent. In such societies a newly conquered group, or one which requests annexation (a not uncommon practice), is likely to become simply another clan or descent group, frequently retaining its own internal organization. This has clearly happened in the case of the Azande of east central Africa and the Ndebele of Southern Rhodesia.[20] In many other African societies, clans or other descent groups are reported to be concentrated in certain localities, which strongly suggests that before the days of empire building they were autonomous local groups.[21]

In the New World the evidence is less clear, chiefly because of the early disintegration of the advanced horticultural societies. Nevertheless, there is good reason to believe that most of the lesser "clans" in both Inca and Aztec society were the descendants of once independent peoples.[22]

[19] Ralph Linton, *The Tree of Culture* (New York: Vintage Books, 1959), p. 170.
[20] For the Azande, see P. T. W. Baxter and Audrey Butt, *The Azande and Related Peoples* (London: International African Institute, 1953), p. 11; for the Ndebele, see A. J. B. Hughes and J. van Velsen, *The Ndebele* (London: International African Institute, 1954), pp. 71–72. Among the latter, these descent groups, known as "tribes," have grown so large that their functions have been transferred to subunits formed within them, though the larger groups are still identifiable by their common names and strongly influence the status of individuals.
[21] See, for example, Hilda Kuper, *The Swazi* (London: International African Institute, 1952), p. 20, or Melville Herskovits' comments on the Dahomean sibs, in *Dahomey: An Ancient West African Kingdom* (Locust Valley, N.Y.: Augustin, 1938), chap. 10. These are but two of many such examples. See also Linton's comments on the relation of clans and state in Buganda, which suggest a similar origin for these clans (*Tree*, p. 175).
[22] See, for example, Rowe, in Steward, *Handbook*, vol. II, pp. 253–256, or Bram, pp. 22–29 on the Inca *ayllu*, and von Hagen, pp. 68–70 on the Aztec *calpulli*.

Many of the more aggressive and expanding states contain ethnic minorities which, even today, are still only partly assimilated. For example, the Ngwato tribe of Northern Bechuanaland, with a population of 101,000, contains 10,000 Bushmen, 23,000 Kalaka, 1,000 Herero, 1,000 Rotse, and 700 Yeei, none of whom are Southern Bantu like the Ngwato, and all of whom differ from one another and from the Ngwato in language and customs.[23] Similar examples could be cited from many other parts of Africa and the New World.

Discrepancies between the boundaries of societies and ethnic groups also develop because conquest states themselves sometimes undergo a process of fission or fragmentation, leading to the division of the group into a series of minor principalities or kingdoms. At this level of societal development, central authorities frequently find it impossible to prevent schismatic movements in the more remote provinces.

Sometimes both of these tendencies, i.e., conquest and fission, are evident in a single tribal group. For example, it is reported that "towards the periphery of Zande power there are many groups which have been only partially 'Zandeized' and others which have kept their own culture and language." [24] At the same time, the Azande themselves are divided into a considerable number of petty kingdoms, not unlike those into which many European peoples were divided in the Middle Ages.

The growth of the state appears to have a number of important consequences for the communities within advanced horticultural societies. To begin with, it contributes to the growth in size of those which serve as royal capitals. Many of the residents in these communities live off the economic surplus of the land as a whole and therefore the community's growth is not limited by the resources of the immediate area. Audrey Richards reports that during the 1930s the villages in which chiefs of the Bemba lived commonly had 300 to 400 huts and in earlier times were "evidently very much larger," while other villages had only thirty to fifty huts.[25] Elsewhere in Africa, notably in Nigeria, still larger communities emerged as a result of the process of empire building. For example, as early as the fifteenth century, a Portuguese explorer reported that Gwato, which was the port town for the town of Benin, had a population of 2,000,

---

[23] I. Schapera, *Government and Politics in Tribal Societies* (London: Watts, 1956), p. 19. For a good discussion of this subject see also Schapera, *The Tswana* (London: International African Institute, 1953), pp. 34–35. See also Bram, chap. 2, on the Inca.
[24] Baxter and Butt, p. 11.
[25] See Audrey I. Richards, "The Bemba of Northeastern Rhodesia," in Elizabeth Colson and Max Gluckman (eds.), *Seven Tribes of British Central Africa* (Manchester: Manchester University Press, 1951), p. 171, and also Richards, "The Political System of the Bemba Tribe of North-Eastern Rhodesia," in M. Fortes and E. E. Evans-Pritchard (eds.), *African Political Systems* (London: Oxford University Press, 1940), p. 91.

suggesting that Benin itself was substantially larger.[26] A little more than a century later a Dutch traveler described the town of Benin in the following fashion leaving even less room for doubt about its size:

> The towne seemed to be very great, when you enter into it, you goe into a great broad street, not paved, which seemeth to be seven or eight times broader than the Warmoes street in Amsterdam; which goeth right out and never crooketh, and where I was lodged with Mattheus Cornelison, it was at least a quarter of an houres going from the gate, and yet I could not see to the end of the street, but I saw a great high tree, as farre as I could discerne, and I was told the street was much longer. Then I spake with a Netherlander, who told me he had been as far as that tree, but saw no end of the street; . . . so that it is thought that that street is a mile long [a Dutch mile was equal to about four English miles] besides the Suburbs.[27]

Even in the eighteenth century, after Benin had entered a period of decline, an English visitor reported that "The town of Benin is large and populous, and contains probably 15,000 inhabitants."[28]

Benin was but one of a number of towns which flourished as capitals of small kingdoms in southern Nigeria during the last thousand years. Just how large they were we may never know, but numerous reports suggest figures of 20,000 or more in the pre-European period. While these communities were probably the largest to develop in non-Islamic Africa south of the Sahara before modern Western technology began its work of transformation, other kingdoms were widely scattered over much of the area from the Guinea Coast to South Africa, and the capitals of these kingdoms seem often to have had populations of several thousand or more.[29]

Urban tendencies were no less developed in the advanced horticultural societies of the New World. Even in the least advanced, the chiefdoms of the Circum-Caribbean area, towns of up to 3,000 are reported.[30] Mayapán, the Maya capital, is thought to have had a population of more than 20,000, and Cortes estimated that Texcoco, one of the leading cities of pre-Columbian Mexico, had a population of 30,000.[31] Tenochtitlán, the Aztec capital, and Cuzco, the Inca capital, seem to have been even larger.

---

[26] From Duarte Pacheco Pereira, *Esmeraldo de Situ Orbis*, edited by R. Mauny and translated by G. H. T. Kimble and reprinted in Thomas Hodgkin, *Nigerian Perspectives: An Historical Anthology* (London: Oxford University Press, 1960), p. 93.

[27] From *A Description and Historical Declaration of the Golden Kingdom of Guinea*, reprinted in Hodgkin, pp. 119–120. Quoted by permission.

[28] *Ibid.*, p. 175.

[29] See, for example, Schapera's comments on the capitals of the Southern Bantu groups, *Government and Politics*, p. 15.

[30] Steward and Faron, pp. 184–185, etc.

[31] von Hagen, pp. 134 and 308.

Spanish officials reported that there were seventy to a hundred thousand houses in the former and a hundred thousand in the latter, but both reports are almost certainly greatly exaggerated. Although their exact size may never be known, sixteenth-century Europeans certainly found them both impressive.

Communities in advanced horticultural societies tend to be more permanent than those in simple horticultural societies. In part this is due to advances in agricultural technology which make it possible to utilize the same plot of ground for a longer period of time. The metal hoe, for example, helps replace exhausted soil by turning over the ground to a greater depth, reaching nutrients which the simple digging stick could not reach. Equally important, the discovery of schemes of crop rotation slows down the rate at which the soil is exhausted, permitting longer continuous use. Herskovits reports, for example, that in Dahomey it is not uncommon for fields which are worked carefully to be kept continuously in cultivation for fifteen to twenty years.[32] In Ganda, where it is reported that rather high standards of cultivation were maintained, some plots of land could be occupied permanently under a regime of crop rotation.[33] The same seems to have been true of the irrigated, terraced, and fertilized fields of certain of the advanced horticulturalists of the New World.

A second factor which made possible greater permanence of certain communities was the development of kingdoms and empires. As we have seen, the residents of the capitals of these states were at least partially freed from the necessity of supplying their material needs from the immediate area. To the extent that this was true, the drain on local resources was reduced, and the possibility of permanence increased.

In the realm of occupational specialization, differences between simple and advanced horticultural societies are even more marked. A far greater number and variety of specialists are encountered in the latter. Although, as in many other comparisons, there is some degree of overlap, the upper limits of the two types of societies are quite distinct.

Clearly the most important single factor in the growth of occupational specialization has been the growth of state power. All the larger and more powerful kingdoms required complex governmental systems with numerous officials and soldiers. For example, one reliable English observer of the late seventeenth century reported that the king of Dahomey had a thousand tax collectors alone.[34] Other kinds of officials were even more numerous.

[32] Herskovits, pp. 33–34.
[33] Fallers, p. 38.
[34] Herskovits, vol. I, p. 109.

In the largest and most centralized states it was common to find hierarchies consisting of three to five levels of officials ranging from the king at the top to the local village headman at the bottom.[35] Each of these officials, especially those at the higher levels, was surrounded by his court, which included a great variety of specialists—magicians of various types, priests, tax collectors, advisers, military men, common soldiers, wives and concubines usually by the hundreds, eunuchs to guard them, entertainers of many kinds, and artisans of unusual skill and talent. In some societies full-time craftsmen were found only at the king's court and the various tools, weapons, and other things the common people needed were made either by the people themselves or by part-time specialists.[36] This indicates again the influence which political developments have in stimulating the growth of occupational specialization.

Contrasted with politically advanced groups such as the Incas, Aztecs, Dahomeans, and Ganda are other groups such as the Plateau Tonga of Northern Rhodesia, who closely resemble the more advanced simple horticultural societies with respect to the level of occupational specialization. Among these people specialization was, till recently, limited to part-time work in a few fields of activity.[37] Similarly, among the Swazi of southeastern Africa it is reported that "a certain recognition of individual aptitude has led to a limited specialization within the general skills expected of each person. Thus a few men specialize in tanning hides, cutting shields and carving; a few women in basket-ware and pottery." [38] These are all part-time occupations. The only full-time occupation not of a religious or political character is that of smith. Among the Swazi, as among most peoples of Africa, this is a highly honored, full-time occupation.

As would be expected, the volume of trade and commerce in advanced horticultural societies is closely linked with the extent of occupational specialization. In those societies in which specialization is highly developed, there is also considerable trade. In fact, in such societies one finds the development of organized markets open for business on regularly appointed days, and supervised and regulated by public officials.

[35] Most hierarchies contained only three levels, as in the case of Dahomey (Herskovits, vol. II, pp. 23ff.) or Buganda (Fallers, pp. 61ff.). However, in describing the Kongo empire, which was destroyed in 1569, Murdock reports that it was divided into six provinces which in turn were subdivided into districts each containing a number of villages, indicating a four-level hierarchy (Murdock, *Africa*, p. 298). The Inca represent the extreme, with five levels of officials ranging upward from "foreman" to emperor (Rowe, in Steward, *Handbook*, vol. II, p. 263).

[36] Fallers, p. 43.

[37] E. Colson, "The Plateau Tonga of Northern Rhodesia," in Colson and Gluckman, p. 104.

[38] Kuper, p. 31.

There are even the beginnings of systems of currency and specialization in the merchandising of goods.[39] At the other extreme, in societies with little specialization, trade is limited, and formal markets, standardized currency, and middlemen are wholly absent.

One factor restricting trade and commerce in the advanced horticultural societies of both Africa and the New World is the primitive character of transportation. The wheel, for example, was unknown in both areas. Draft animals were also lacking. So were pack animals, except among the Incas, who used the llama. Though many African tribes had cattle, they never used them as beasts of burden. Similarly, though the horse was introduced into the Sudan and Nigeria from northern Africa prior to European contact, its use seems to have been limited entirely to military operations.

As a consequence, except in Inca society all goods which had to be moved overland were transported on the backs or heads of human porters.[40] Even though good porters were capable of carrying loads of 50 to 100 pounds for extended distances, much of their labor was expended in carrying their own supplies, appreciably reducing the net volume of goods moved.[41]

The most efficient means of transportation found in most advanced horticultural societies was the canoe. Unfortunately, navigable streams and rivers were frequently lacking.

The inefficiency of techniques for moving men and goods also had important political implications. In the first place, since tribute and taxes

[39] Along the Guinea Coast and as far east as Buganda, cowrie shells long served as a form of currency. See, for example, Michael Crowder, *The Story of Nigeria* (London: Faber, 1962), pp. 66, 186, etc., or Fallers on the Ganda, p. 49. In Africa, the development of middlemen, or merchants, seems to have developed most fully on the Guinea Coast. In reports from this area there are scattered references to women buying goods in one market to sell in another (see Herskovits, vol. I, p. 56) and to men working as merchants, though usually as agents of the king [see George Peter Murdock, *Our Primitive Contemporaries* (New York: Macmillan, 1940), p. 577]. In Buganda, in east Central Africa, it is reported that "markets within easy walking distance of each other were usually held on different days, forming a cycle, so that itinerant merchants, at the close of one market, could pack up their wares and move on to the next" (Linton, *Tree*, p. 173). Probably the greatest development of mercantile specialization occurred in the New World, where full-time merchants are reported among both the Aztecs and Mayas (von Hagen, pp. 174–175 and 268–273). Aztec records indicate that this was a very late development, dating from 1504, or less than a generation before the Spanish Conquest. It is interesting to note that Aztec merchants, like those sent out by the Dahomean kings in Africa, were accused of being warriors in disguise, sent to spy out enemy lands. There may well have been some truth in these charges.
[40] Even in Inca society, men shared the burden of transporting goods with the llama and were actually more effective. (See von Hagen, p. 554.) This is a good indication of how inefficient the llama was.
[41] The figures are from Forde, *Habitat,* p. 167.

were usually in the form of goods, and since the costs of shipping the goods varied directly with the distance covered, the net gains resulting from conquests of remote areas were likely to be limited.[42] Second, since the movement of men and goods was so difficult, kings found it extremely difficult to maintain effective control over their outlying provinces. Thus, the primitive character of transport was a major factor contributing to the recurring revolts against central authority and the frequent breakup of empires.[43]

Introduction to Distributive Systems

The outstanding feature which emerges from any comparison of simple and advanced horticultural societies is the striking development of social inequality evident in so many of the latter. In many of the advanced horticultural societies of Africa, inequality is carried to a level far beyond anything ever observed in technologically less developed societies. The contrast is so pronounced that it seems as if some kind of threshold had been crossed, opening up a whole new range of possibilities.

In some of these societies one finds individuals who are regarded virtually as gods and treated accordingly. For example, even the highest ministers of state in Dahomey had to grovel in the dust when in the king's presence, and throw dirt on their heads and bodies.[44] No one could appear in his presence with his shoulders covered, or wearing sandals, shoes, or hat. No one could sit on a stool in his presence; if they sat, they were obliged to sit on the ground. The king's wealth was enormous, as suggested by the fact of his thousand tax collectors. In theory, though not in actual practice, he was regarded as the owner of all property in the land.[45] Any woman of his realm whom he fancied, whether married or not, could be taken by him and put in his royal harem. The exact number of royal wives is unclear, chiefly because it was so great, but apparently there were hundreds, and perhaps as many as two thousand.[46] The king was even

[42] See Baxter and Butt, p. 62.

[43] The Ganda seem to have been unique among the horticultural peoples of Africa in developing good roads and this may well have contributed to the stability of their political system (see Linton, *Tree*, p. 173 or Murdock, *Africa*, p. 355). The situation was much better in the New World. Even the lesser chiefdoms of the Circum-Caribbean area built roads, and the Incas and Mayas built excellent ones. See, for example, Morley, pp. 339–341; Rowe, in Steward, *Handbook*, vol. II, pp. 229–233; Bram, pp. 36–37; and Steward and Faron, pp. 198–199. These roads may also have been a factor in the relative political stability of some of these groups.

[44] Herskovits, vol. II, p. 33. Lucy Mair reports that in Ganda it was claimed that one of the kings required his subjects to kneel on iron spikes. See *Primitive Government* (Baltimore: Penguin, 1962), p. 181; see also pp. 197–205.

[45] *Ibid.*, vol. I, p. 78.

[46] *Ibid.*, vol. II, p. 45, or Murdock, *Contemporaries*, p. 582.

permitted to contract incestuous marriages, a practice forbidden to all outside the royal family.[47] All prisoners captured in war became his slaves.[48] Through the medium of his subordinates, the king "held close control over happenings of all kinds in his domain." [49] For example, he controlled all appointments to public office, and sib-heads and even the heads of extended family groups could assume their offices only if confirmed by him. He also exercised considerable influence over the various religious groups and approved the inheritance of all property. Finally, he held in his hands the powers of life and death over his subjects, and those who provoked his displeasure, even members of the royal family, could be sold into slavery or put to death.[50]

Though the king enjoyed the greatest measure of power and privilege, his chief ministers and subordinates were also men to be reckoned with. For example, the chiefs who ruled the various provinces, while humble in the royal presence, exercised despotic power in their own jurisdictions. As one writer put it, "when outside the palace, these high potentates expect the commonalty to kneel, to kiss the ground, and to clap hands before them, as if they were kings." [51] Each maintained his own court and harem, both of which were essentially scaled-down replicas of their royal models.

At the other extreme from these exalted figures was the much more numerous class of slaves.[52] These slaves had no legal rights. The majority were herded onto the king's plantations, where they were obliged to work long and hard under the control of overseers whose duty was to get the utmost yield from the fields. Another category of slaves was even more unfortunate; their function was to serve as human sacrifices in various religious ceremonies. Every morning, for example, the king dispatched two of these unfortunates as messengers to his ancestors to express his thanks for having been permitted to awaken to a new day on earth.[53]

While Dahomey is not typical of all the advanced horticultural societies of sub-Saharan Africa, it is reasonably representative of the many societies in which there were centralized governmental systems. In most of these the rulers were regarded as divine or semidivine and were the objects of extreme acts of deference, owned immense wealth, and wielded

[47] *Ibid.*, vol. I, p. 339.
[48] *Ibid.*, vol. II, pp. 95ff.
[49] *Ibid.*, vol. II, pp. 36ff.
[50] *Ibid.*, various sections of chap. 23 and elsewhere.
[51] *Ibid.*, vol. II, pp. 29–30.
[52] *Ibid.*, vol. I, pp. 99ff.
[53] *Ibid.*, vol. I, p. 53 and vol. II, p. 100. It should be noted that generally the situation of slaves in horticultural Africa was somewhat better than that in Dahomey, though their position should not be idealized.

great power.[54] Typically they asserted and enforced far-reaching claims over the time, energies, and wealth of their subjects. Subjects were usually obliged to turn over a significant portion of all they produced and in addition were usually liable for labor and military services, the benefits of which accrued chiefly to the king.[55] Sometimes it seems that the more powerful rulers of these African kingdoms laid claim to almost the entire economic surplus of their people.

One of the striking features of the advanced horticultural societies of Africa is that wherever governmental institutions developed beyond the level of local village autonomy, they tended toward a common pattern. Meyer Fortes called attention to this almost a generation ago in his pioneering analysis of African political systems. He argued that sub-Saharan political systems can be divided into two basic types. One he called Group A, consisting of "those societies which have centralized authority, administrative machinery, and judicial institutions—in short, a government—and in which cleavages of wealth, privilege and status correspond to the distribution of power and authority." [56] The second category, Group B, contains all those tribes in which local village autonomy still survives. As Fortes put it, it consists of "those [tribes] which lack centralized authority, administrative machinery, and constituted judicial institutions—in short, government—and in which there are no sharp divisions of rank, status, or wealth." In the latter, kinship systems fulfill most of the necessary political functions.[57]

More recently George Peter Murdock undertook an ambitious ethnographic survey of all the peoples of Africa. This survey led him to a conclusion which closely parallels that of Fortes. As he put it:

[54] With respect to wealth, Max Gluckman reports that a recent Zulu chief owned 30 per cent of all the cattle in his tribe. See "The Kingdom of the Zulu in South Africa," in M. Fortes and E. E. Evans-Pritchard (eds.), *African Political Systems* (London: Oxford University Press, 1940), p. 45n. Schapera reports that in the 1930s a chief of the Kgatla owned 4,000 head at a time when few other men owned as many as several hundred (*Government and Politics*, pp. 101–102).

[55] See Schapera, *Government and Politics*, chap. 4, "The Privileges and Powers of Office," for an excellent summary of the rights of southern Bantu chiefs and kings. Oberg provides a very good summary of the powers and privileges of the kings of Ankole (in Fortes and Evans-Pritchard, pp. 128–150). See, also, Mair on East Africa. Good descriptions of other African kingdoms and chiefdoms can be found in various ethnographies.

[56] Fortes and Evans-Pritchard, p. 5.

[57] More recently several other anthropologists have suggested that Fortes's scheme of classification oversimplifies things. See, for example, Aidan Southall, *Alur Society: A Study of Processes and Types of Domination* (Cambridge: Heffer, 1956), especially chap. 9, and particularly pp. 248–249; or John Middleton and David Tait (eds.), *Tribes without Rulers: Studies in African Segmentary Systems* (London: Routledge, 1958), especially pp. 2–3. It should be noted, however, that these criticisms indicate the need for amplification of Fortes's scheme, rather than its replacement. Hence, for purposes of the present analysis, Fortes's basic distinction still seems a useful one.

Specialists steeped in the African literature commonly discern wide differences among the complex political systems of different areas. To the present writer, coming to the subject after a survey of another continent, such differences appear superficial in comparison with the extraordinary resemblances in fundamental features and even in external forms. . . . It is almost as though all of Africa south of the Sahara were permeated, as it were, by a mental blueprint of a despotic political structure, transmitted from generation to generation as a part of traditional verbal culture, and always available to be transmuted into reality whenever some individual arises with the imagination, enterprise, strength, and luck to establish, with the aid of his kinsmen, an authoritarian regime over people residing beyond the limits of his local community.[58]

Murdock then lists eighteen characteristics, most of which he says are found in all of the highly developed states of Africa, with the exception of a few East African states influenced by the Galla and neighboring Eastern Cushitic tribes of southern Ethiopia. These characteristics form the basis of a system of government which Murdock labels *African despotism:*

1. Monarchical absolutism. Each king or independent paramount chief enjoys absolute power, at least in theory.
2. Eminent domain. All land, livestock, and wild game in the state belong in theory to the monarch, providing a basis for his right to derive an income from them.
3. Divine kingship. Either the ruler himself is divine or he has unique personal access to the dominant divine powers.
4. Ritual isolation. The king is isolated from physical contact with all except a few attendants and intimates. Often he eats in private or must be fed by others, or his feet may not touch the ground, or he is concealed by curtains because his glance is considered dangerous.
5. Insignia of office. Royal status is symbolized by the possession of distinctive regalia, among which stools, drums, and animal tails are especially common.
6. Capital towns. The ruler resides in a capital town along with his attendants and ministers. Typically each new monarch founds a new capital or at least establishes a new royal residence.
7. Royal courts. The monarch maintains an elaborate court with pages, guards, entertainers, personal attendants, treasurers, and a variety of chamberlains with specialized functions.
8. Protocol. Behavior at court follows detailed rules of protocol, of which abject prostration in the presence of the monarch is a nearly universal ingredient.

[58] *Africa*, p. 37. Quoted by permission. For a similar conclusion, see Linton, *Tree*, p. 181. Southall's study of the Alur and Mair's work on East Africa suggest, however, that it may be a mistake to suppose that conquest was the only means by which the more complex political systems developed.

9. Harems. The ruler is invariably surrounded by a large number of wives and concubines.

10. Queens. At most royal courts a queen mother, a queen consort, and a queen sister, or at least two of the three, enjoy extraordinary prestige, even sometimes technically outranking the king himself. Queens are commonly endowed with independent estates and often exercise restricted political authority.

11. Territorial bureaucracy. For administrative purposes each state is divided into a territorial hierarchy of provinces, districts, and local communities with bureaucratic officials at each level responsible for maintaining order, collecting and transmitting taxes, and levying troops and *corvée* labor. Even where bureaucratic posts are hereditary rather than appointive, their occupants are firmly subordinated to the central authority.

12. Ministers. Resident at the capital as assistants to the ruler in the exercise of centralized authority are always a number of ministers of state, the most important of whom form a supreme advisory council. They are distinguished by specialized functions, e.g., a vizier or prime minister, a military commander in chief, a royal executioner, a custodian of the royal tombs, a supervisor of royal princes and princesses.

13. Duality of ministerial roles. Almost universally, the ministers combine their specialized functions at the capital with offices as provincial governors in the territorial organization.

14. Titles. Characteristic of African states is a great proliferation of titles. Although a few or many may be hereditary, there are always a large number bestowable by the monarch in return for loyal services, and competition for these is often keen.

15. Security provisions. To prevent palace revolutions a king's brothers, as the most likely usurpers, may be killed, blinded, incarcerated, or banished from the capital. To prevent revolts in the provinces, positions as governors are commonly filled, not by members of the royal lineage, but by persons of categories ineligible to succeed to the throne, e.g., commoners, elevated slaves, eunuchs, or, where succession is patrilineal, sisters' sons.

16. Electoral succession. Although the ruler often designates an heir presumptive, and may even invest him with ministerial authority, succession to the throne is almost never automatic. The decision usually rests in the hands of a committee of ministers with constitutional electoral powers, who are free to follow or ignore the late king's wishes. Not infrequently the succession shifts regularly from one to another branch of the royal lineage.

17. Anarchic interregnums. Since there is always a plurality of candidates with strong supporters, and considerable political maneuvering may be necessary before the electors can agree upon a successor, a period of several days or even weeks usually intervenes between the death of one king and the selection of the next. During this interregnum laws are relaxed and social disorder prevails, often accentuated by a resort to arms by the partisans of rival claimants.

18. Human sacrifice. In many Negro states the funeral of a king is accompanied by human sacrifices, sometimes on an extravagant scale.[59]

It is impossible to say precisely what percentage of the horticultural peoples of Africa belong to Group A societies and what percentage to Group B. On the basis of Murdock's survey, however, it appears that about 65 per cent of the population is in the former.[60]

Despite the fact that there was no cultural contact between the advanced horticultural peoples of Africa and the New World, there is a striking similarity in patterns of political organization. For the most part, Murdock's characterization of the leading African states can be applied to the leading states of the New World, such as those created by the Mayas, Aztecs, and Incas. The chief differences seem to involve secondary features, such as the ritual isolation of the monarch, the exalted status of the queen mother, queen consort, or queen sister, the threat from kinsmen, the movement of capitals, and the anarchic interregnums, all of which, though prominent in Africa, are largely missing in the New World.[61] These differences are more than offset by the striking similarities in more basic matters. In the New World, for example, the rulers of advanced states were regarded as demigods and treated as such.[62] They enjoyed immense power and privilege and their subjects were compelled to display extreme deference.[63] They had at their disposal a complex and highly developed retinue of ministers, courtiers, and officials, who saw to it that their slightest order was executed and who formed a privileged class set apart from the mass of commoners.[64] Similarities even extended to the widespread practice of human sacrifice (though the Incas seem to have been abandoning this, probably because of the difficulty in obtaining foreign victims after the Empire became so inclusive), the presence of royal harems, and the practice of electoral succession.

[59] *Ibid.,* pp. 37–39. Quoted by permission. Compare with Linton, *Tree,* especially p. 181.
[60] This figure is based on my own tabulation of Murdock's summary descriptions of over 500 tribal groups south of the Sahara. These tabulations showed that about 60 per cent of the tribal groups were in Group A and that those in Group A were slightly larger on the average than those in Group B.
[61] See, for example, von Hagen, pp. 119–124, 297–304, and 493–506, or Rowe, in Steward, *Handbook,* vol. II, pp. 257–260.
[62] See, for example, von Hagen, pp. 119–124 and 493–506.
[63] See, for example, A. L. Kroeber's statement that the Chibcha "overlords were shown every respect which native imagination could conceive. Even chiefs never looked them in the face, but turned their 'shoulders' away or bent far down in their presence. The Spanish soldiers were thought shameless because they spoke to their own commanders eye to eye." See "The Chibcha," in Steward, *Handbook,* vol. II, pp. 902-903; see also Rowe, p. 259, on the Inca emperor.
[64] See, for example, Rowe, pp. 263–264, on the Incas, or Morley, pp. 168–170, on the Mayas.

In the New World, as in Africa, there were variations in the degree of political development. Not all societies attained the level of the Incas and Aztecs, or even of the Mayas and Chibchas. This was especially true in most of the chiefdoms of the Circum-Caribbean area.[65] As in Africa, these variations in political development were closely related to variations in the nature and extent of social inequality. In fact, it appears to be a basic principle that *among societies at an advanced horticultural level of development, the separation of the political and kinship systems and the resulting development of the state are necessary preconditions for the development of marked social inequality.* As a corollary of this we may add: *in Group A societies at this level of economic development, the power, privilege, and prestige of individuals and families is primarily a function of their relationship to the state.* In short, the institutions of government provide the key to the solution of the major questions concerning distribution and stratification in societies at this level.

The Causes of Variation in Political Development and Inequality

Before proceeding in our analysis, it may be well to stop and ask why some advanced horticultural societies developed centralized governments of the type described by Fortes and Murdock and others did not. Unfortunately, this problem has not yet received the systematic attention it deserves. There are, of course, numerous references in sociological and anthropological writing to the conquest theory of the state and considerable evidence to indicate that the more highly developed political systems of sub-Saharan Africa have, in fact, largely developed in this way. Still this does not answer the question of *why* some groups embarked on a career of conquest while others did not.

Murdock, in the first quotation cited above, suggests that the crucial factor may be the presence or absence of an individual with the requisite imagination, enterprise, strength, luck, and family connections. Although one cannot doubt that this is a factor, it seems unlikely that it is the major one, since the technological basis for the development of these African states has been present in most parts of the continent for centuries. It is difficult to believe that in those areas where the less developed systems were never supplanted, no individual was ever born who possessed the necessary traits.

Our general theory suggests that *environment* should be a more fruitful variable, and available evidence supports our expectations. If one plots the location of the more complex states on a map of Africa, it quickly

[65] See Steward and Faron, chaps. 6–8.

becomes evident that none were located in the heart of the rain forests. Using Murdock's ethnographic survey, it is possible to make a systematic check of this relationship. The results, in slightly simplified form, are shown in Table 1. The correlation between these two variables, using Kendall's tau, is .19.[66] If it were possible to obtain accurate information on environmental variations among the great majority of societies outside the rain forests, the correlation would undoubtedly be higher.[67]

Table 1 Level of Political Development by Environmental Conditions in Horticultural Africa, in Percentages

ENVIRONMENTAL CONDITIONS	LEVEL OF POLITICAL DEVELOPMENT					TOTAL	NUMBER OF SOCIETIES
	MAJOR STATES AND LESSER STATES	INTER-MEDIATE OR UNCER-TAIN	PARA-MOUNT CHIEF-TAINS	INTER-MEDIATE OR UNCER-TAIN	LOCAL HEAD-MEN ONLY		
Rain forest areas	3	0	34	22	41	100	96
Other areas	35	6	22	2	36	101	416

[66] The value of the relationship shown in Table 1 is only .15, but using the further details not shown in the table, the value rises to .19. While there are certain methodological difficulties involved in constructing such a table, they are not serious enough to justify a rejection of this finding. Among the difficulties, the following deserve note. First, Murdock's data are organized in terms of tribes, i.e., cultural and linguistic units, rather than societies, i.e., socially and politically autonomous units. It does not appear, however, that this introduces any systematic bias into Table 1. Second, the data are organized in terms of tribes rather than people. If people were used, the relationship would be slightly stronger than that shown, since Group A tribes tend to be a bit larger than Group B (as shown by special tabulations I have made which are not reported here). Third, Murdock's statements about the level of political organization are not as standardized as one might desire for coding purposes. This leads to uncertainty in classification in some cases, but this only involves adjacent levels. Thus, while it is sometimes difficult to determine from Murdock whether a given tribe has paramount chiefs or only local headmen, it is always clear that they do not have a highly developed state system. Finally, while some errors may have crept into Murdock's statements, no one can survey hundreds of societies without this happening occasionally. Hence, all things considered, it seems unlikely that this table is seriously in error.

[67] For example, Murdock reports that only one of the sixty-one tribes in the Nigerian Plateau area ever developed "a genuinely complex state" (*Africa*, chap. 13). From other sources, it appears that this is a very unfavorable environment (see Buchanan and Pugh, especially chaps. 1–3). The Tallensi are another non-rain-forest people who have remained quite primitive politically. Of their environment, Fortes states "the hazards of agriculture are enormous" and food is "chronically insufficient" (see "The Political System of the Tallensi of the Northern Territories of the Gold Coast," in Fortes and Evans-Pritchard, p. 249). He reports that even in an excellent season few people produce a surplus sufficient to lay up supplies against a future disaster. Under such conditions it is not surprising to find that their political system falls into Fortes's Group B.

The virtual absence of complex political systems in the rain forests of Africa reflects the difficulties such societies encounter in transportation. A complex state presupposes the ability to move both men and goods easily and cheaply. Warriors must be able to move rapidly in order to control potentially rebellious subjects and protect the state's borders. Goods must be moved from the many scattered villages where they are produced to the capital of the state, where the political authorities reside. In the rain forests of Africa, these conditions could not usually be met by horticultural societies. It is no coincidence that the three advanced states which did develop in the rain forest area were *all* on the fringes, and none in the interior portion where the obstacles to movement were more severe.[68]

A much more important factor in the variation in political development in horticultural Africa seems to be the *level of technology*. Though all of horticultural Africa belongs in the category of *advanced* horticultural societies, there are internal variations. In a pilot survey of twenty-three societies chosen from the nine major regions of sub-Saharan Africa, a correlation of .63 (Kendall's tau) was found between the level of technological development and the level of political development.[69]

[68] The exceptions were the Edo, the Ijaw, and the Itsekiri, all on the northern fringe of the rain forest in southern Nigeria. See Murdock, *Africa*, chap. 31.

[69] The nine regions chosen are those in Murdock's "World Ethnographic Survey," pp. 675–677. Wherever possible, three societies were chosen from each region, representing high, medium, and minimal political development, as reported in col. 15 of Murdock's code. In four regions it was not possible to find one or the other of the political extremes. Where choices were possible, those societies were selected for which the most and best ethnographic reports were available. The regions and societies were as follows:

> Western Sudan: Mossi, Susu, and Tallensi
> Guinea Coast: Yoruba, Mende, and Ibo
> Nigerian Plateau: Jukun and Tiv
> Eastern Sudan: Shilluk, Azande, and Lugbara
> Upper Nile: Alur and Luo
> Equatorial Bantu: Ganda, Luba, and Fang
> Northeast Bantu: Chagga and Kikuyu
> Central Bantu: Lozi, Yao, and Ila
> Southern Bantu: Zulu and Mbundu

The review of the literature and the coding were done by Thomas Brownlee, a graduate student.

Level of technology was based on the following code:

High: many full-time craft specialties, advanced metallurgy, trade, quasi money economy
Medium: a few full-time craft specialties, some metallurgy
Low: at most one or two full-time craft specialties

Level of political development was coded as follows:

High: many specialized officials, considerable bureaucratization
Medium: some specialized officials, some bureaucratization
Low: few specialized officials, no appreciable bureaucratization

Unlike environment, however, level of technology probably stands in a reciprocal relationship with level of political development, and therefore we cannot assume that the technological factor is quite as potent as this coefficient suggests. In other words, although advances in technology undoubtedly facilitate political advances, the converse is also true to some extent. This can be seen in the case of occupational specialization, which often increases once a political elite gains control of the economic surplus and begins to use it for its own purposes.

A third factor found to be associated with the level of political development in the societies in this survey was *the nature of their social environment*. Those societies which had been most threatened by neighboring societies tended to have a higher level of political development than the others. Evidently such threats force societies to respond politically, or to risk being conquered and absorbed by aggressive neighbors. The correlation between level of external threat and level of political development, using Kendall's tau, was .36.[70]

As might be expected, these three variables were interrelated to some extent. Hence, when their combined influence was measured, it did not equal the sum of their separate effects. Nevertheless, it did produce a correlation coefficient of .71, suggesting that at least half of the variance in levels of political development can be accounted for in terms of these three variables.[71] This fact is especially important in view of the strong relationship between levels of political development and the nature of distributive systems. As Fortes pointed out, social inequality is much more pronounced in the politically advanced Group A societies than in their less developed Group B counterparts. This is clearly evident in the societies and tribes in our pilot study sample. Of the fourteen Group A societies, twelve or possibly thirteen had a high or medium degree of social inequality by horticultural African standards; of the eight Group B tribes, only two had a comparable degree of stratification.[72] *This strongly suggests that variations in the level of political development are the chief proximate cause of variations in the level of social inequality in advanced horticultural societies.* Data from the New World also appear to support this conclusion.

[70] The code used here was: (1) society constantly threatened by neighboring societies; (2) sometimes threatened; and (3) rarely or never threatened.
[71] This "multiple correlation" was based on an equal weighting of each of the independent variables. In each instance a three-level, high-medium-low, code was used with highs scored 2, mediums 1, and lows 0. Once again, Kendall's tau was used. It should also be noted that when the cases involving uncertain coding were eliminated, the value of tau rose to .78.
[72] The correlation, using Kendall's tau, was .60 for this 2 × 2 classification, and .67 for a slightly more complex 3 × 3 classification.

Government and Inequality

From the theoretical standpoint, Fortes's Group A societies are much more important than his Group B tribes. One finds in them the first clear examples of substantial social inequality and the first clear evidences of institutionalized political tyranny and despotism. From the theoretical standpoint it is vitally important to explore the inner workings of these "new" societies, which differ so radically from the hunting and gathering and simple horticultural societies examined previously. Hence, for the remainder of this chapter we shall be concerned chiefly with these most advanced horticultural societies, which account for 65 per cent of the population of horticultural Africa and about the same percentage in South and Central America.[73]

One question which inevitably arises in any analysis of African despotism, to use Murdock's term, is how this system of government is related to the governmental systems of simple horticultural societies. Were these despotic governments created *de novo* by members of advanced horticultural societies, or did they evolve out of the older, more republican forms which generally prevail in simple horticultural societies? Though this question can never be answered *definitively*, it deserves attention because the answer has important theoretical implications. Also, though we lack direct evidence relevant to this question, there is considerable circumstantial evidence which points rather consistently in one direction.

In all primitive societies some system of redistribution or reciprocity is necessary. The uncertainties of production make it essential that those who have, share with those who have not. In the simplest hunting and gathering societies the logic of this practice is inescapable, since *every* family experiences periods when it is unable to obtain the necessities of life and is obliged to turn to others. Under these circumstances, those who respond generously are rewarded by being accorded special respect, and the skilled and generous hunter often becomes the leader of his community.

In many simple horticultural societies the redistributive process becomes more institutionalized and centralized, with the village headman or tribal chief functioning as the custodian and dispenser of the group's surplus. Though he controls its collection and distribution, he does so essentially in the capacity of trustee. He is not the owner of what he distributes; it is the property of the group. In some of these societies, how-

[73] For the New World, see Steward and Faron, table 2, p. 53, omitting the hunters and gatherers.

ever, there is evidence of the beginning of a lack of clarity on this point, fostered by the tendency of such groups to view their chiefs as the primary or sole symbol of tribal unity.[74] Since he is the symbol of the group, and the group is the owner of the surplus, he is its owner, or so the "logic" seems to run. As a protection against the dangers inherent in this, simple horticultural peoples usually insist that their leaders be men noted for their generosity. In fact, at this level, generosity is virtually a prerequisite for leadership. Since the powers of the chieftainship are so limited, the people are able to exercise considerable control over the office, both through their selection of those who fill it and through their control over the incumbents' continuation in office.[75]

One of the striking features of African despotism is that kings, paramount chiefs, and other high officials are expected to be generous. In other words, the "Redistributive Ethic" is still present. This is evidenced in various ways. In describing the duties and responsibilities of the Southern Bantu chief, for example, Schapera writes that "one quality always expected of him is generosity, and should he fail in this respect he soon becomes unpopular." [76] Though he is the wealthiest man in his tribe, he cannot use his wealth solely for the satisfaction of personal needs and desires. He is obliged to provide for the support of his ministers and courtiers. He must entertain all those who come to visit him. On great public occasions he is expected to slaughter many of his cattle and provide beer and porridge for all who gather at his village. He lends cattle, supports destitute widows and orphans, sends food to sick people and newly confined mothers, and in time of famine distributes corn from his own granaries or, if this is insufficient, purchases supplies from neighboring groups. Because of such activities, the Tswana say that "the chief is the wife of the tribe," and the Zulu refer to him as "the breast of the nation." [77]

Similar reports come from many other parts of Africa. Richards reports that Bemba chiefs were expected to provide food for their officials and courtiers and to support their villagers in time of famine.[78] She adds that one of their most important political tasks was to maintain their reputation for generosity.[79] Oberg reports that the kings of the Ankole used the cattle brought to them as tribute as "a savings fund, a surplus upon

[74] See Schapera, *Government and Politics*, p. 106, for a good discussion of the symbolic function of chiefs in advanced horticultural societies.
[75] *Ibid.*, p. 140.
[76] *Ibid.*, p. 75.
[77] All this material on the Southern Bantu is taken from Schapera, *ibid.* See also V. G. J. Sheddick, *The Southern Sotho* (London: International African Institute, 1953), pp. 47–48.
[78] Richards, "The Bemba of North-Eastern Rhodesia," p. 170.
[79] Richards, "The Political System of the Bemba Tribe," p. 105.

which herdsmen in distress could draw." [80] In the case of the Azande it is reported that a chief was "expected to be generous and to entertain lavishly, to assist his needy subjects with subsistence and to acquire wives [i.e., to assist in obtaining the bride price], to hold feasts and dances, while any Zande who visited court expected a substantial free meal." [81] The report goes on to say that a stingy chief knew his subjects would show their diminishing respect by lessening their gifts to him, and that the chief's reserve was "a sort of relief store."

In the New World a similar situation prevailed. The rulers of the Incas, for example, maintained storehouses throughout the country, from which supplies could be drawn in time of famine or disaster. In addition, whenever the supplies were judged to be sufficient, the ruler ordered a general distribution, sending the products of one province to another which, because of climatic differences, could not produce them. The government also maintained large herds of llamas and alpacas, whose wool was distributed to the entire population for clothing.[82] In the case of the Aztecs, the ruler distributed much of the vast store of tribute obtained from conquered peoples immediately on receipt on a per capita basis.[83]

As these examples indicate, the Redistributive Ethic flourishes in advanced horticultural societies, just as in hunting and gathering and simple horticultural societies. In politically centralized societies, however, the king or chief is usually in firm control of the redistributive process—at least so long as he meets the essential needs of his people and maintains his reputation for generosity. Compared with the tribal chiefs of simple horticultural societies, he has much more to work with, owing to the advances in productivity. This becomes extremely important when viewed in conjunction with certain other aspects of the situation. To begin with, in nearly all of these societies *there is no clear distinction made between the personal wealth of the king or chief and the people's surplus with which he is entrusted.*[84] The public treasury and the king's personal wealth are usually mingled indiscriminately.[85] Confusion is further com-

---

[80] Oberg, "The Kingdom of Ankole in Uganda," p. 148.
[81] Baxter and Butt, p. 59.
[82] Rowe, p. 267.
[83] von Hagen, pp. 172–173.
[84] Schapera indicates that the beginning of such a distinction was made among some of the Southern Bantu, but they were clearly an exception to the general rule (*Government and Politics,* p. 102).
[85] This became especially evident when Western colonial governments replaced these African monarchies and sought to rationalize the system of public finance. See Schapera, "The Political Organization of the Ngwato of Bechuanaland Protectorate," in Fortes and Evans-Pritchard, p. 78; Richards, "The Political System of the Bemba Tribe," also in Fortes and Evans-Pritchard, p. 116; Schapera, *Government and Politics,* p. 109; or Sheddick, p. 48.

pounded because these societies rarely, if ever, differentiate between the king's role as "wife of the people," and his role as self-interested individual. This may be inevitable in a society in which the king is regarded as the visible symbol, even the physical embodiment, of the nation, but it has far-reaching consequences none the less.

Under such circumstances, one would predict that rulers, as self-seeking individuals, would seize the opportunity to use a portion of the public wealth for private purposes. This would be especially easy in an expanding economy (as during the transition from simple to advanced horticulture), since this could be done without reducing the absolute quantity of goods and services redistributed to the people. In fact, while increasing the *absolute* quantity of goods being redistributed but reducing the *relative*, a chief can enhance his reputation for generosity at the same time he retains more in both relative and absolute terms for his own personal use.

Finally, if a portion of the appropriated surplus is then used to provide a comfortable living for a staff of dependent officials and retainers, who will do his bidding while ostensibly acting on behalf of the public interest, the last serious threat to such appropriation is removed.[86] *By creating an organization of persons with a vested interest in the new system, the means for silencing possible critics is prepared.* This is especially true if the chief or king himself is able to appoint and remove such persons at will (see item 11 on Murdock's list of characteristics of African despotism). The only remaining threat to royal power comes from the officials themselves, since the common people lack the organization necessary to overthrow the king and his retainers.[87]

Another factor which provides further stability to the system in many cases is the policy of conquest and imperialism. If a society organized along the lines described successfully brings neighboring groups under its control, the surplus of the group is substantially increased, and the king is in a position to enlarge his personal following. Not only can he now draw an even greater percentage of his fellow tribesmen into his retinue, but he can share his more generous bounty with many others, strengthening their ties of allegiance as well.[88] At this stage, the dangers of popular

---

[86] For a similar point of view concerning the rise of despotic governments, see Richard Thurnwald, *Economics in Primitive Communities* (Oxford: International Institute of African Languages and Cultures, 1932), pp. 12 and 106–108, or Mair, especially pp. 108–109 and 160–165.

[87] See Schapera, *Government and Politics*, pp. 108–112; Baxter and Butt, pp. 62–63; Oberg, p. 144; or Herskovits, vol. II, chap. 25.

[88] This could lead to a substantial revitalization of the old Redistributive Ethic for his own people *at the expense of the newly conquered groups.* This is, in fact, exactly what happened in the case of both the Incas and Aztecs.

revolt from his own people are virtually eliminated, though not the dangers from envious or ambitious individuals in his own establishment.

While it is impossible to prove that African despotism developed in this manner, as a natural evolutionary outgrowth of the modest tribal governments of simple horticultural societies, both theory and the evidence of ethnographic studies point this way. Considering the many significant similarities between the governmental systems at these two levels of economic development, it seems unlikely that the despotic pattern of government was created *de novo* by some act of genius. Rather, the means of effecting the transformation appear to have lain ready at hand in the older, more primitive system.[89] Thus, if this analysis is correct, *an institution which began primarily as a functional necessity of group life became, in many advanced horticultural societies, an instrument employed primarily for self-aggrandizement and exploitation.* Thus there appears to be some truth in the theories of *both* conservatives and radicals!

The Powers of Rulers

Considering the great powers concentrated in the hands of a ruler, it is hardly surprising to find that the most important single factor influencing the status of individuals and families is their relationship to the king and his subordinates. By virtue of his massive wealth and extensive powers of appointment, the king can raise men from the humblest backgrounds to positions of immense power and privilege; conversely, he can destroy men of great wealth and power. For example, it is reported that "in Yorubaland [in southwestern Nigeria] slaves of the Oba attained great power and were much feared by his subjects." [90] On the other hand, kings often mutilated, exiled, or killed their own brothers and other close relatives whom they feared might be motivated to attempt a palace revolution.[91]

A nineteenth-century visitor to Dahomey provides a vivid illustration of the crucial importance of royal favor. This writer described an occasion

[89] For a very similar analysis, which did not come to my attention until after this was written, see Mair, *op. cit.* It should be added that in some, perhaps many, societies, the new system was established by diffusion. Clearly this happened many times. However, this still begs the critical question of how the *original* transitions were made. This is the problem with which I am concerned here. The recurrence of the pattern in the New World suggests that more than diffusion must be involved.
[90] Crowder, p. 65.
[91] See Murdock's list of characteristics of African despotisms, item 15. See also Schapera, *Government and Politics*, pp. 157ff.

on which the king suddenly called for one of his officials, the Benazon, or treasurer.

> Contrary to the usual custom in such cases—when the name of the officer is scarcely out of the king's lips ere the customary answer of "*Wae*" is made, and the person asked for is seen running to the king—the Benazon did not put in an appearance. His name was called out by the heralds, and at last a messenger was despatched to his house to make inquiries. The king then made a speech, and said that it was not a good thing for a monarch to ask for any person and find that he was not in the presence; everybody ought to wait and see if the king wanted them. In about ten minutes the delinquent treasurer made his appearance with his hands bound before him, hurried along by two of the Ajkayaho's guards. When he approached the platform he fell on his knees, and began to throw dust on his head. The king then asked where he had been. He said that he had been home preparing his house for the princess whom the king had promised him in marriage. Thereupon the king ordered him to be taken to prison, and this high dignitary was hurried off as if he were one of the rabble, and ignominiously thrown into the Ajkayaho's gaol. The law in Dahomey evidently knows no distinction of persons.[92]

Another nineteenth-century visitor to Dahomey reported that if a private citizen "brings more soil under cultivation, or in any manner advances his family to riches, without the license of the king, he not only endangers his fortune, but his own life and the lives of his family; instead of becoming a man of property and head of a family, he is condemned to slavery." [93]

Obviously kings could not exercise direct supervision over the entire population. A rough approximation of this was achieved, however, through the hierarchical organization of the government which subdivided kingdoms into several levels, the head of each unit being answerable to the head of the larger unit of which his was a part, with all ultimately answerable to the king. Thus the status of the average individual was a function of his relationship to his local village headman, who was dependent on some district or provincial chief who was in turn one of the king's ministers.[94] In this way, everyone was in a direct or indirect relationship with the king.[95] For the great majority of individuals, the crucial factor in their

[92] A. J. Skertchly, *Dahomey As It Is: Being a Narrative of Eight Months' Residence in That Country* (London: 1874), p. 375, quoted by Herskovits vol. II, p. 43. Quoted by permission. See also Mair, p. 181, who states that "the near vicinity of the powerful was obviously dangerous."

[93] F. E. Forbes, *Dahomey and the Dahomans: Being the Journals of Two Missions to the King of Dahomey, and Residence at His Capital, in the Years 1849 and 1850* (London: 1851), pp. 36-37, quoted by Herskovits, vol. I, p. 99n.

[94] As noted previously, in some cases there was still another intermediate layer. See Mair, pp. 146-151 and 173ff., for a good description of the hierarchy of territorial officials in East African societies.

[95] For example, see Rowe, pp. 263-264 on the Incas, who established what was probably the most complex hierarchical system of any advanced horticultural people.

lives was their relationship to the authority figure directly above them, whether he was the village headman or the district chief. Such men exercised a power over their subordinates almost as great as that which the king exercised over them. For example, another nineteenth-century visitor to Dahomey wrote that the governor, or viceroy, of one of the provinces of Dahomey "is at once council, jury, and judge . . . [with] unlimited powers of imprisonment and bastinado." [96] Comparable examples could be cited from most of the other politically advanced horticultural societies in both Africa and the New World. [97]

Though they enjoyed great power, neither the king nor his officials could indulge every passing fancy in their relations with their subjects. To do so would invite anarchy or revolt. As Herskovits points out in reference to the king of Dahomey, "Despite his capriciousness . . . the King was not without a realization of the importance of having the whole-hearted support of these men whom he had elevated to positions of rank." [98] This realization undoubtedly served to stabilize the situation both in Dahomey and elsewhere, since no monarch or minister could destroy valuable officials without good reason and long remain in power. [99]

Another highly privileged segment of virtually every African despotism was that made up of the king's relatives and those related to former kings. Such persons constituted the nobility and usually formed a leisure class. Rank usually varied directly with the recency of the reign of one's kin, with those related to the current monarch enjoying the highest status.

Because of the practice of polygyny, the noble class was often quite large. In fact, Herskovits wrote that in the city of Dahomey it seemed as though almost everyone were descended from royalty in either the male or female line (either line of descent entitled one to membership in the royal sib). [100] In writing of the king's court, which included only those members of the royal sib who had some special claim on the king's favor, he says that they "played an essentially parasitic role. They lived lives of pleasure, often stimulating their jaded senses by sexual excesses." [101] He

---

[96] Capt. Sir Richard F. Burton, *A Mission to Gelele, King of Dahomey* . . . (London: 1893), vol. I, p. 63, quoted by Herskovits, vol. II, p. 28.

[97] See, for example, Schapera, *Government and Politics*, p. 113.

[98] Herskovits, vol. II, p. 43.

[99] Schapera and others make it clear that African rulers were often overthrown by rivals. See Schapera, *Government and Politics*, especially pp. 157ff., and more especially p. 165 including the footnotes.

[100] Herskovits, vol. II, p. 38. Bram notes a similar rapid growth in the Inca nobility because of polygyny (p. 73).

[101] In the case of the royal princesses, there were apparently no restrictions on their sexual freedom. They could divorce their husbands at will and, married or not, take lovers as they wished. Even the incest taboo did not apply to them.

concludes that they were a heavy burden on the social and economic resources of the country, and became increasingly so as their number multiplied.

The king's close male relatives, especially his sons and brothers, usually occupied a very ambiguous position in traditional African societies. On the one hand, by virtue of their close relationship to the king, they were entitled to high honor and numerous privileges. On the other hand, they were generally regarded by everyone, including the king, as the chief threat to his position and even to his life. When revolutions occurred in these societies, as they often did, one of the king's close relatives was likely to be involved in a major way. This led to the Zulu proverb that "the king should not eat with his brothers lest they poison him," and to the Swazi saying that "nobles are the chief's killers." [102] Because of this, African kings often turned to men outside the noble class, even slaves, to fill many high public offices. In Dahomey, for example, "tradition holds strongly that no king ever appointed a prince to any position of power," for "had a brother of the king been appointed to an important post, his desire for power, thus whetted, might have tempted him to cast envious eyes on the throne itself, while his office would have given him an opportunity to gain the adherence of the king's subjects in the interest of intrigue." [103] Among the Ankole of Uganda the problem was solved by having all of the king's sons engage in a struggle to the death at the time of their father's death. The one that survived became king, free of further worries about sibling rivalry.[104] Where such traditions were lacking, African kings sometimes took matters into their own hands. The famous Zulu king, Dingane, systematically exterminated all of his family, relatives, friends, and former comrades, with the exception of his half brother Mpande, "a quiet and inoffensive youth." [105] His generosity proved a serious mistake; Mpande eventually led the revolution which overthrew Dingane and resulted in his murder.

Royal fratricide was not an inevitable feature of life in politically advanced horticultural societies, however. There was little evidence of this in the New World, though the Spanish conquest of the Inca Empire was preceded and perhaps facilitated by a bitter struggle for the throne between two sons of the deceased emperor.[106] Usually, however, the process of succession took place peacefully and the emperors relied on their

---

[102] For an excellent discussion of this subject, see Schapera, *Government and Politics,* pp. 157ff.
[103] Herskovits, vol. II, p. 39.
[104] Oberg, pp. 157–159.
[105] Schapera, *Government and Politics,* pp. 158–159.
[106] See, for example, von Hagen, pp. 581–582.

closest relatives to fill the highest offices of state.[107] Even in Africa there were numerous examples of kings employing their kinsmen and other nobles as advisers and even putting them into responsible offices, though if Murdock is correct (see item 15 in his list of characteristics), this was the less common pattern.[108] Thus this seems to be a variable feature in these societies, and not a pattern dictated by either economic or political necessity.

As a result of the exercise of royal power on behalf of kinsmen or officials, three basic classes developed in every African despotism. At the top of the system there was a small minority of powerful and privileged individuals who, by virtue of royal favor, lived off the surplus produced by others. Beneath them was a more numerous, though still small, class of officials and specialists of various kinds who either catered to the whims and fancies of the governing class or performed the lesser, but often vital, tasks of government. Finally, at the bottom were the great majority of common people, who produced the surplus on which the two more privileged classes depended.

Usually each of these classes was further divided into various subclasses. For example, as we have already seen, both the nobles and officials were differentiated into various ranks and grades. Similarly, the class of technicians and specialists and the class of producers were often subdivided into two or more levels. For example, there was usually a distinction between free men and slaves, with the latter denied many important rights enjoyed by the former. Sometimes there were further distinctions, such as the substratum in Dahomey which ranked between the slaves and free men, and was composed of persons born in Dahomey of slave or mixed parents. Such persons were compelled to live on the estate of the owner of their parent or parents, and most of what they produced went to their overlord. Unlike slaves, however, they could not be sold or separated from their parents. Even the substratum of slaves was internally divided into three basic categories which, in descending order of fortune, were (1) household slaves, (2) field slaves, and (3) slaves set apart for human sacrifices.[109]

The structures of the advanced horticultural societies of the New World were strikingly similar.[110] In each case there was a class of nobles

---

[107] See Rowe, p. 263.

[108] For examples of the use of royal relatives and nobles, see Schapera, *The Tswana,* pp. 52–53, or *Government and Politics,* especially pp. 58–59 and 112–113.

[109] Herskovits, vol. I, pp. 99–101.

[110] For good descriptions of these structures, see Morley, chap. 9 on the Maya; Steward and Faron, pp. 132–138 on the Incas, and pp. 186–188 on the Circum-Caribbean tribes; and von Hagen, pp. 119–134, or Eric Wolf, *Sons of the Shaking Earth* (Chicago: University of Chicago Press, 1959), chap. 7 on the Aztecs.

which shared the responsibilities of government with the king or chief, though in definitely subordinate roles. This class tended to be hereditary in nature, especially in the more advanced states.[111] However, even in the latter, hereditary rule was apparently relaxed during periods of rapid imperial expansion when enlargement of the ruling class was necessary.[112]

The other major class consisted of the masses of common people, whose labors supported the privileged noble class. Usually there was a slave class as well, though not many apparently were born into it.[113] As in Africa, they were frequently prisoners of war, and many were destined to be slain as human sacrifices. A secondary class found in the New World, as well as in Africa, was that made up of artisans and minor officials freed by the nobility from the responsibility of food production so that they might render more specialized services.[114] This class appeared only in the most advanced societies.

Probably the most significant structural difference between Africa and the New World was that involving the realm of religion. In most of Africa, religious and political leadership tended to be combined, with the result that there was no distinct priestly class. In the few cases where it did exist, as in Dahomey, its power and privileges were not comparable to that of the noble class. By contrast, in much of the New World the priests constituted a distinct and powerful class within society and were, in effect, on a par with the nobility. As one student of the Mayas has put it, "the great temple establishments in the ceremonial centers of the Old and New Empires . . . [were] almost as big business for those days as directing the ship of state." [115] The status of the priests, like that of the nobility, was usually hereditary.

In many, if not most, advanced horticultural societies of the despotic type, a person's status is a function not only of his *personal* relationship to political authority, but also of his *collective* relationship. Because these societies are imperialistic and expansionistic, they typically include people of diverse ethnic backgrounds. Though conquered peoples might in time be assimilated culturally, these ethnic distinctions often linger on in the forms of clan distinctions. Thus in many, if not most, of these societies distinctions are made on the basis of the ethnic or lineage group to which a man belongs.[116]

[111] See, for example, Steward and Faron, p. 187.
[112] See Rowe, p. 260, or Bram, pp. 33–44 and 71–75.
[113] See, for example, Morley, pp. 176–179 on the Mayas.
[114] See, for example, Steward and Faron, p. 138 on the Incas.
[115] Morley, p. 72.
[116] See Mair, pp. 134–137 for a number of examples from East Africa.

The Ndebele of Southern Rhodesia provide a good illustration of such a pattern of organization.[117] Since pre-European days this group has been divided into three major status groups which the natives call "tribes," but the English call "castes." In descending order of status, they are the Zansi, the Enhla, and the Lozwi. They constitute approximately 15, 25, and 60 per cent of the population respectively.

The relative status of these groups has been shown to be a function of their historic relation to the Ndebele state and monarchy. The Zansi are descended from the founders of the state, a group of Swazi tribesmen who were conquered by the great Zulu king, Shaka. After rising to a position of power in the Zulu state, they revolted and fled with many of Shaka's cattle. For a time these rebels settled in the Transvaal, where they conquered resident Sotho and Tswana natives whom they forced to work for them. In the middle 1830s the founders of this new nation came under the attack of both Boers and Zulus and were obliged to flee once more, this time to their present home in Southern Rhodesia. Many of their recently conquered Sotho and Tswana subjects accompanied them. When they arrived in Southern Rhodesia they were again obliged to overcome the natives, the Lozwi, and were aided in this by their Sotho and Tswana subjects, the ancestors of the present Enhla. The three status groups in the Ndebele nation are thus the result of these two conquests, and their relative status is a function of the historic relation of each of these groups to Mzilikazi, the first king and founder of the nation.[118]

Until British rule was established, status group membership was a matter of major importance among the Ndebele. Even today it is said to be of considerable importance, though British refusal to enforce the rules of the system led to a gradual decline. In older times, however, certain important privileges were reserved to members of one or both of the two higher status groups. Only Zansi could wear the ostrich feather headdress of a warrior, for example, and only Zansi and Enhla could wear the kilt made of twisted monkey and wildcat skins and tails. Intermarriage was forbidden, and choice political and military appointments were usually reserved for Zansi. Apparently there were some exceptions in the matter of appointments, however, which created inconsistencies in status, a phenomenon which emerges whenever more than one principle of distribution is employed.

[117] See Hughes and van Velsen, especially pp. 44–45 and 71–75, or Schapera, *Government and Politics*, p. 130.
[118] According to Schapera, *ibid.*, p. 132, status group distinctions between conquerors and conquered developed in South Africa only when the two groups were culturally distinct.

Not all societies handled the problem of assimilating aliens in the same way and a variety of patterns have developed both in Africa and the New World.[119] In most instances in which alien peoples were incorporated into a state by conquest, the conquered and their descendants, *as a group,* occupied a position inferior to the conquerors and their descendants. These group distinctions were maintained even though as individuals some of the former enjoyed greater power or privilege than some of the latter. In fact, the unique inferiority of members of these status groups of alien origin often made them attractive sources of recruitment for high officials of state, strange as this may seem. The theory underlying this practice in Africa was the same one which led Turkish rulers, for several centuries, to use the sons of Christians in the army and in other posts of major importance (as in the case of the notorious Janissaries). Because of their status group connections, such persons could never aspire to the throne, and by virtue of their abrupt elevation from slavery or other inferior status could not fail to appreciate their complete and utter dependence on royal favor. Thus they were likely to be more reliable if revolution or rebellion should occur.[120]

Sometimes the conquerors accepted selected members of the conquered groups into their own ranks. This was the practice of the Incas, and may have been a response to the special problems created by the extremely rapid expansion of their empire.[121] Since the original Inca population was so small, it could not produce nearly enough administrators and officials. Hence they accepted into their ranks those who spoke their language, as well as cooperative chiefs and rulers from other conquered groups. Together, these Incas by blood and Incas by privilege formed the dominant status group which ruled the empire.

In this connection, there is an interesting and tremendously important contrast between these advanced horticultural societies with their centralized political systems and the more primitive hunting and gathering and simple horticultural societies discussed in the last two chapters. Among the latter there are many instances of men striving to avoid appointment to political office since the rewards apparently do not compensate for the added responsibilities (much as in many offices in voluntary organizations in our society today). In advanced horticultural societies of the type with which we have been primarily concerned there is no such

[119] For a much more flexible system, see Max Gluckman, "The Lozi of Barotseland in Northwestern Rhodesia," in Colson and Gluckman, p. 6.
[120] See Karl A. Wittfogel, *Oriental Despotism: A Comparative Study of Total Power* (New Haven, Conn.: Yale University Press, 1957), pp. 360–362.
[121] See Rowe, pp. 260–261, or Bram, pp. 33–44 and 71–75.

problem: *men avidly seek political office, even at the risk of their lives, a clear indication that a marked imbalance has developed between the responsibilities and the privileges of office, especially the office of king.*[122]

Other Bases of Power

Although the primary determinant of status is the relationship of the individual or group to the king and his political apparatus, it would be a mistake to suppose that this is the only determinant, or that it operates in a simple manner. The status of an individual or family is also influenced by forces to which the king is indifferent or opposed. To ignore these other forces would give an inaccurate picture of the distributive process.

To begin with, though the king and his ministers and agents have many common interests, their interests are not identical. Hence, even though these officials may never oppose the king openly, they have ample motivation for doing so covertly from time to time. Furthermore, though the king's powers are immense, he is neither omnipotent nor omniscient. As a result, he is often the victim of ministerial deception.

A classic example of this was reported by an eighteenth-century visitor to Dahomey. In writing of the fiscal practices of the kingdom, he stated that "there is nothing so mean in the whole Kingdom, that the King hath not Toll for it; which, indeed, if all honestly paid to him, would make him very rich; but the Gentlemen Collectors so largely fleece it, that the King scarce receives one fourth part of the whole." [123] Oberg reports the same pattern in the kingdom of Ankole in Uganda; tribute collectors frequently exacted more than the king authorized and kept the surplus for their personal benefit.[124] Such practices were probably common in most of the kingdoms.

A more serious problem from the standpoint of the king was the widespread tendency on the part of governors of outlying provinces to usurp various royal powers. For example, another visitor to Dahomey wrote of the governor of the important province of Whydah that "he maintained a great number of domestics and attendants, whom he attached to his person by his liberality; and to his interest by protecting them in their villainies, and screening them from justice *in defiance of the king.*" [125] This writer added that the king was naturally eager to remove

---

[122] See, for example, Schapera, *Government and Politics*, pp. 157 and 220.
[123] William Bosman, *A New and Accurate Description of the Coast of Guinea*, 2d ed. (London: 1721), pp. 336–337, quoted by Herskovits, vol. I, p. 109.
[124] Oberg, pp. 147 and 150.
[125] Robert Norris, *Memoirs of the Reign of Bossa Ahadee, King of Dahomey . . .* (London: 1789), pp. 40–41, quoted by Herskovits, vol. II, p. 27. Emphasis added.

this minister but, fearing to attack him openly, was waiting for an opportunity to get him into his hands by some stratagem. Schapera mentions that Southern Bantu kings were usually reluctant to appoint their kinsmen as governors of outlying areas for fear that they would be encouraged to seek independence by splitting off to found their own tribes.[126] Because of the primitive character of transportation in most advanced horticultural societies, control of distant territories was bound to be less effective than of areas close to the capital.

If some men acquired special powers and privilege through fraud and in defiance of royal wishes, others advanced themselves in more acceptable ways. Though kings and chiefs often made sweeping claims against the surplus product of their peoples, a careful examination of ethnographic reports indicates that they did not claim it all. Some portion of the economic surplus was left with the producers, perhaps as an incentive to promote continued industry and effort.

There are various indications that this was the case. For one thing, if a king were to appropriate all of the surplus for himself, one would find only the minimum necessities of life in the hands of the common people, and all of the surplus in the hands of the king, his ministers, and his relatives. However, this was not usually the case. To illustrate, the provincial chiefs of the Azande usually followed the practice of appointing some local man of wealth, a commoner, to serve as the equivalent of village headmen.[127] This indicates that royal taxes and tribute did not drain off all the surplus or reduce all the common people to the same subsistence level. Even in Dahomey, where the royal family and officials of state were noted for their rapaciousness, it is clear that the common people were able, by their own efforts, to increase their wealth and share in the surplus.[128] In fact, Herskovits reports that "a constant struggle to increase patrimony, and to earn property for one's self is therefore an outstanding aspect of the Dahomean attitude toward life." Clearly this could not be such a widespread pattern if the elite monopolized the entire surplus. One could multiply such examples almost indefinitely, but these suffice to indicate that, despite the great powers of most advanced horticultural rulers, some substantial portion of the economic surplus remained in the hands of the producers.

Finally, it should be noted that in some parts of Africa, especially West Africa, and in most of the New World, a portion of the surplus was

[126] *Government and Politics,* p. 172. It was perhaps no coincidence that the one fratricidal war which developed among the Incas involved a half brother with strength in an outlying province pitted against his sibling in the national capital.
[127] Baxter and Butt, p. 50.
[128] Herskovits, vol. I, chap. 5, especially pp. 86ff.

used to maintain temples, shrines, and other religious centers, and the priestly class who controlled them. The status of priests, and the privileges which accrued to them, cannot be viewed in the same light as the status and privileges of governmental officials and other specialists in the employ of the regime. Priests normally enjoyed a considerable measure of independence since the powers they exercised were not delegated by the state and its leaders. Rather, they exercised powers believed to be of supernatural origin conferred on them directly.

In many parts of Africa these supernatural powers fell into the hands of the political leaders. How this happened we do not know. It is not unreasonable to suppose that sometimes these divine and semidivine kings had evolved from religious, rather than political, functionaries, and that in some cases the combination of priest and ruler represents the displacement of the original political authorities by religious authorities rather than the reverse. (As startling as this may seem to secularly oriented moderns, it is not such a wild hypothesis when viewed in cross-cultural perspective.)[129] Regardless of how this union of powers was effected, however, the result was the development of a role with unique power, and the elimination of a potential source of countervailing power.

In some parts of Africa, notably West Africa, and also in the New World, this union was not fully effected. In Dahomey, though the king is a priestly figure of considerable importance, he does not exercise monopolistic control over the supernatural powers and hence has important priestly competitors.[130] Apparently these persons are of middle-class origin, but by virtue of the position they occupy can be considered a part of the privileged or leisure class.[131] They are freed from all manual labor and supported by gifts and services rendered by cult adherents. Though fairly prosperous, they do not compare with the king and his chief ministers; rather, they resemble the more prosperous of the common people. In the New World the position of the priests was more favorable. As noted previously, they constituted a distinct class and were apparently the equals of the nobles.[132] In some societies the priestly offices were

---

[129] See, for example, the earlier discussions of the power of priests and shamans in simple horticultural societies in chap. 6. See also Bertrand de Jouvenal, *On Power: Its Nature and the History of Its Growth,* translated by J. F. Huntington (New York: Viking, 1949), pp. 83–84.

[130] In many other parts of Africa divine kings have "competitors" in the form of magicians and witch doctors, but such individuals are rarely organized and do not have enough power to make them serious competitors with the king. Hence they are ignored in this discussion.

[131] Herskovits, vol. I, p. 102.

[132] This was true of at least the upper ranks of the priesthood. See, for example, Morley, pp. 170–174 on the Mayas; Rowe, pp. 298–299, or Steward and Faron, pp. 128–130 on the Incas; Steward and Faron, pp. 191–194 on the Circum-Caribbean tribes; and von Hagen, pp. 159–162 on the Aztecs.

hereditary; where they were not, the sons of nobles often filled the major offices. In most instances the king or emperor was regarded as the high priest, or head of the priesthood, as well as chief of state.

In West Africa the relationship between priest and king tended to be ambivalent, much as in the case of the king's relationship to his own brothers. Rulers often viewed the priests with suspicion, and on occasion the latter joined forces with dissident members of the royal house in plotting rebellion.[133] On the other hand, they sometimes conspired with the king to exploit their followers, using their priestly influence to gain information concerning wealth which the people had kept hidden from the king's tax collectors.[134] Thus, depending on the circumstances, the priests of West Africa might be either allies or opponents of the king. In the New World, by contrast, the priestly class usually remained his faithful ally.[135]

Force, Ideology, and Utility

As the foregoing indicates, the economic surplus of the politically advanced horticultural societies of Africa and the New World was distributed in accordance with two quite distinct sets of principles. On the one hand, the king and his ministers, together with the priestly class, based their claims to a share in the surplus on *an impressive combination of force, ideology, and utility;* in other words, they offered the group essential services whose value was greatly inflated by ideology and enforced by armed might. On the other hand, those who were not a part of the elite or allied with it were forced to base their claims to rewards chiefly on the grounds of *utility.*

One of the great failures of traditional theories of distribution stems from their failure to take into account this *dual* character of the distributive process in societies where the state is highly developed. Conservative theorists generally analyze these societies as though utility were the sole, or dominant, factor governing the distribution of all power, privilege, and honor. Radical theorists usually focus on the other two factors, force and ideology. Our analysis of African despotisms and their New World counterparts indicates that both approaches are half-truths which yield but a partial view of the total process. The ethnographic record clearly indicates the need for a theoretical synthesis.

Considering the superior strength of the resources available to the elite in the struggle for the surplus, one might well ask why this group

[133] Herskovits, vol. I, pp. 175–177.
[134] *Ibid.,* p. 175.
[135] Even here there was some suggestion of a struggle between the priestly and noble classes, at least in the case of the Incas. See Steward and Faron, p. 128.

does not completely monopolize it. A careful examination of the matter suggests that several factors are responsible. To begin with, no regime is omnipotent or omniscient, nor are the common people ever wholly convinced by the more extreme formulations of official ideologies. This means that *the resources of a regime are never great enough to locate every last increment of surplus and compel its producer to hand it over.* At some point the costs of further search exceed the returns.

If this were the only principle governing the actions of heads of states, however, they would obtain more of the economic surplus than they apparently do. Other factors must also be at work, limiting their acquisitive tendencies. Evidence from Africa and elsewhere indicates that the problem of motivation is involved here and that enlightened self-interest requires the elite to respect it. If rulers appropriated all of the surplus they would destroy *incentive,* one of the two basic sanctions by which they control the actions of their subjects. This would leave only fear and, as noted in an earlier chapter, fear alone has not proven nearly so effective as when it is combined with incentive. At the least, those who rule by fear alone are denied honor and respect, and few men are willing to sacrifice them entirely, simply for the sake of slightly increasing already abundant material benefits. *By allowing the producer to retain some of his surplus, the amount being in proportion to his efficiency, the king and his ministers give him the incentive to increase production.* Even though a producer does not reap the full benefit of his greater efforts, judging by the record he gets enough to generate the desired response.

Another reason for the elite's willingness to allow the more efficient producers to keep a portion of the surplus may be the divisive effect this has among the masses. *When differences of wealth exist among the common people, it is less likely that they will unite against their rulers than if they were all reduced to the same subsistence level.* While I know of no evidence which shows that horticultural rulers ever *consciously* thought in these terms, such an arrangement may well have evolved through an unplanned process of selection. Rulers who ignored this principle were probably overthrown, while those who followed it, for whatever reason, survived, thus establishing the pattern.[136]

Finally, there is reason for thinking that *ideology functions as a two-edged sword,* in these societies as in others. On the one hand, it renders the common people vulnerable to royal demands; on the other hand, it

[136] While there were no popular revolutions in advanced horticultural societies, popular unrest manifested itself, in Africa at least, by the common people's throwing their support behind the king's rival among his own kinsmen. Thus when a king encroached on the portion of the surplus left to the common people, he probably produced this pattern of reaction.

renders the rulers vulnerable to the wishes and desires of their subjects. All official ideologies incorporate the thesis that the existing system serves the common good. Since no ideology can long survive if there is *no* substance to back up this claim, a ruler must make some delivery on the promises inherent in it. Actually, in advanced horticultural societies as elsewhere, ideologies are never merely instruments of exploitation; they are simultaneously instruments for the protection of the common people.[137] In those societies which combine political stability with economic prosperity, they play a major role in the strengthening of constitutional government and the promotion of a somewhat more egalitarian distribution of power, privilege, and honor.[138] In advanced horticultural societies, as elsewhere, ideologies have often been taken seriously by rulers and hence have redounded to the benefit of their subjects. Rulers have taken pride in being called the benefactor of their people, the breast of the nation, the father or wife of the tribe, and in striving to maintain this reputation, have often gladly yielded a portion of the surplus to their people.

The Hereditary Transmission of Power and Privilege

One of the important developments associated with the rise of advanced horticultural societies is the substantial growth in both the number and value of transferable assets or resources. This development has significant implications for status mobility, since it facilitates the transfer of power and privilege from one generation to the next. So long as the primary resources in a society are personal qualities such as strength, bravery, speaking ability, and so forth (as is the case in hunting and gathering societies and even to a considerable degree in simple horticultural societies), it is extremely difficult for fathers to pass on to their sons the benefits they have won. In fact, it is sometimes difficult for a man of advanced years to preserve these gains for himself. Such problems can be very serious, particularly in hunting and gathering societies.

By the time the level of advanced horticulture has been reached, however, the means for overcoming this problem are readily available because of three important developments: (1) the development and formalization of the concept of "property rights," (2) the development and formalization of the concept of "office," and (3) the development of

[137] Gideon Sjoberg makes this same point with respect to agrarian societies. See *The Preindustrial City* (New York: Free Press, 1960), p. 226.
[138] Here again the older theoretical traditions have been guilty of a one-sided approach to the problem with the radical tradition stressing the exploitative aspects of myth, and the conservative the protective.

"transferable forms of tangible assets." Because of their importance, each deserves consideration.

With respect to property, it will be recalled that in primitive hunting and gathering societies, individual or family rights are generally recognized only with respect to personal items and artifacts such as clothes, tools, weapons, and so forth. The land and its resources are almost always the common property of the local community, and only when a resource is appropriated and used, i.e., an animal killed for meat, a nut tree harvested regularly, does it become private property. Even then there are usually obligations incumbent upon the user to make a portion of the product available to others, especially in the case of food in short supply.

With the emergence of simple horticultural societies there is some extension and elaboration of the concept of private property, but the pattern is not radically different. Land and other key resources sometimes come to be the property of clans or, in a few instances, of individual families. Furthermore, it is a generally accepted principle in these societies that an individual has special rights in the piece of land he is currently cultivating. This is not a major consideration, however, since there is always an abundance of land. Perhaps the most important development at this level is the increasing utilization of wives as an income-producing form of property, notably in certain parts of New Guinea. This and the raising of small livestock such as pigs provide certain resources which can be used throughout the whole of a man's life. Some of these assets can even be transmitted to his heirs.

With the appearance of advanced horticultural societies, we find another important development in the area of property rights, one which provides a much more effective solution to the problem of the transmission of power and privilege from one generation to the next. This is the development of the institution of slavery. For the first time in human history, it becomes a common feature of social life for men to regard other men as a form of property and exercise enforceable claims on the products of their labor.

Slavery is vastly superior to polygyny as an institutional basis for the transmission of status between generations. The ties between master and slave are not complicated by the requirements of kinship norms. A son's relation to his inherited slaves can be as simple as his father's relation to them was. This could hardly be the case were the father's wives involved. Nor could a man inherit his own brothers and sisters, though the mores of his tribe are not likely to prevent his inheriting the offspring of his father's slaves. Finally, whereas polygyny is likely to generate internal unrest, since wives are usually taken from the limited supply within the tribe, slaves are usually obtained from foreign groups. In all these ways, slavery provides a more efficient basis for the intergenerational transmission of power and privilege, and the inheritance of power and privilege is thus much more easily accomplished in advanced horticultural societies than in simple.

Closely related to the development of slavery is the development of the rights of kings and chiefs to exact tribute from conquered peoples. While such people, unlike slaves, may be technically free, the fact that others have an enforceable claim on a considerable share of what they produce indicates that functionally their status is not so very different. Considering the tremendous numbers of people who have been brought into a tributary status in advanced horticultural societies, this development is probably far more important than the development and spread of slavery. It yields far more lucrative rewards and, as in the case of slavery, tributary rights are property rights, easily transmitted from kings to their sons.

A second development facilitating the transmission of power and privilege from one generation to the next is the expansion and elaboration of formal offices, which occurs in all of the politically advanced horticultural societies. Where offices are firmly established, the importance of personal qualifications is substantially reduced, and it becomes much easier for a son of mediocre abilities to inherit benefits won by an outstanding father. Even where some controls are exercised in the transmission of office, as where, for example, the normally eligible son is passed over owing to the lack of personal qualifications, the office nearly always remains in the same family, and it is simply another son who inherits.[139]

Third, and finally, the transmission of power and privilege is facilitated by the development of new types of tangible assets which are readily transferable. Two in particular deserve note, money and cattle. In most of Africa, one or both of these forms of wealth were present and played a major role in the economy long before the first European contacts. Money, in the form of cowrie shells, was more important in West Africa, cattle in East Africa. Both provided a medium of exchange in which considerable value was concentrated and in a readily transferable form. Unlike the products of the hunt or garden, there was no storage problem. Both cattle and shells could be kept easily until needed. These storable and transferable qualities, combined with their substantial value, greatly facilitated both the accumulation of wealth and its transfer from father to son.

[139] See, for example, Schapera, *Government and Politics,* pp. 51–52, or Rowe, pp. 257–258 on the Inca in the New World.

If we assume that men regard their children, particularly their sons, as an extension of their own ego, and if advanced horticultural societies provide more efficient means for transmitting power and privilege, a decrease in the rate of both inter- and intragenerational mobility would be expected. Judging from the ethnographic record, this is what we find. In fact, *in these societies one finds for the first time the development of fairly well defined, hereditary classes.*

This is true, of course, only in the politically advanced horticultural societies of Africa and the New World, those which Fortes classified as Group A. It is not applicable in those groups in which political organization does not extend beyond the village. This indicates again the crucial importance of political institutions in the whole distributive process, and, as the analysis developed in this chapter makes clear, the character of political institutions is not a simple function of the level of development of productive institutions and their technology. This will become even more evident when we consider the variable of constitutionalism in the final section of this chapter.

Before turning to that topic, however, we must look at the other side of the stability-mobility coin and consider briefly the nature and extent of vertical mobility in these politically advanced horticultural societies. To begin with, despite the increase in opportunities for the maintenance of status throughout a lifetime and for its transmission to one's heirs, mobility is by no means eliminated from the scene. In this chapter, we have seen numerous examples of shifts in status, sometimes of a very dramatic nature. One factor which undoubtedly stimulates vertical mobility in advanced horticultural societies is *the instability of political systems.* Sooner or later most chiefdoms, kingdoms, and empires are toppled. When this happens, a host of new positions is open to the victors. A classic case of this can be seen in the rapid expansion of the Inca Empire in the fifteenth century.[140]

To a considerable degree the rise and fall of individuals and families in advanced horticultural societies depends on the same qualities which govern the rise and fall of men in simpler societies. However, as Wittfogel noted in his study of Oriental despotism, an additional factor enters the picture wherever despotic governments hold sway. This is the quality of "total and ingenious servility." [141] Once a new regime has established itself, talent and ability alone are not enough for a man to rise at court. He must also be willing and able to be submissive, cringing, and fawning in the presence of superiors and skilled in the subtle arts of manipulation

[140] See Rowe, pp. 260–261.
[141] Wittfogel, p. 364.

and dissimulation. One who masters such skills can sometimes rise to great heights. In this respect these societies differ appreciably from simpler societies, where the cultivation of such skills yields few rewards.

Constitutionalism and Its Constraints

In our analyses of hunting and gathering and simple horticultural societies, the variable of constitutionalism played a very minor role. Tyrannical government is extremely difficult to establish and maintain in such societies; the nature of the economy makes constitutional government almost inevitable. What variation there is occurs within a very limited range and hence is not very important.

With the appearance of advanced horticultural societies, at least those in which the institutions of government become elaborated and kings and chiefs acquire large numbers of dependent retainers, the situation changes. It now becomes possible for leaders to ignore the traditions and rights of their people and to govern more by force. In effect, leaders can become rulers.

Judging from the reports of ethnographers and anthropologists, two basic generalizations may be made concerning the extent of constitutionalism in the politically advanced societies of sub-Saharan Africa. (Unfortunately, the comparable record for the New World is too sparse to justify its inclusion in these generalizations.) First, *there is considerable variation in the degree of constitutionalism among such societies.* Second, *tyrannical governments are more common than constitutional.*

With respect to the first generalization, a few simple comparisons may suffice to indicate something of the range of variation. On the one hand there are a number of societies like the Lozi of Barotseland or the Tswana of Bechuanaland. In these groups there are institutionalized restraints on kingly or chiefly powers for the protection of the rights of the common people. For example, in the case of the Lozi, it is reported that the common people "do not feel themselves in the least exploited by the king's rights; they look on the king as a father who generously gives them the means of sustenance." [142] This report goes on to say that the king does not exercise his rights rigorously, and often foregoes them when crops are poor or fishing catches small. Even more significant is the statement that once a king has given land to a member of the group, the new owner's rights are protected against all comers, "including the king himself." These rights are protected by "a well-established and defined system of law, administered by an organized judiciary and executive, who are alert to protect

[142] Max Gluckman, "The Lozi," p. 63.

this security and its premises." A crucial feature of the Lozi system of government is found in the institution of Ngambelaship.[143] Every official, including the king, shares his authority with another official, known as his Ngambela, who is in part his deputy but even more a counterbalance or check. One of the chief functions of the king's Ngambela is to represent the common people, and even though he is the second most powerful individual in the nation, he cannot be of royal blood.

The various Tswana tribes are another group which has often attained a high level of constitutional government.[144] In these tribes it has long been customary to have national assemblies at which the people may voice criticisms of their chief.[145] Though it is reported to be dangerous to criticize the chief at such assemblies (since there are likely to be subsequent reprisals), nevertheless when conditions are serious, men dare to do so. On several occasions, chiefs have been severely criticized, and this public denouncement has been the catalyst which triggered their downfall. In the early nineteenth century, for example, a Tswana chief came to be greatly disliked because he took away the people's cattle and seduced their wives. When an assembly was called to discuss whether he should be banished, the chief fled the country. Others have been assassinated as an aftermath of such assemblies. In writing of the Tswana, Schapera states, "The relative frequency of the assemblies, and the fact that all tribesmen may attend and are sometimes compelled to, helps to explain why Tswana chiefs are seldom autocratic; they are directly and often in contact with the mass of their people, and it is therefore difficult for them to remain indifferent to a publicly expressed threat of opposition."

At the other extreme there are numerous examples of ruthless tyranny and high-handed autocracy. One of the classic examples is the famous Zulu king and empire builder, Shaka, of whom it is reported that "he had literally thousands of his own subjects put to death for no apparent reason except sheer personal whim." [146] Another famous tyrant was the great Christian chief of the Ngwato, Kgama III, whose motives were ideological and idealistic rather than materialistic and selfish, but who was none the less dictatorial. Another chief once rebuked him in a letter saying, "Chief, the proverb says: 'The lion said I am strong when

---

[143] *Ibid.*, pp. 43–49.
[144] Schapera, *Government and Politics*, pp. 150–152.
[145] The Ashanti of West Africa went a step further, and the common people had their own separate organization to represent their interests. This served as a powerful check on a chief's tyrannical tendencies. See Madeline Manoukian, *Akan and Ga-adangme Peoples of the Gold Coast* (London: International African Institute, 1950), pp. 39–40.
[146] Schapera, *Government and Politics*, p. 149. See also Mair, pp. 197–205 on the rulers of Ganda.

alone; the man said, I am strong through the help of others.' If you have governed by *Absolute Monarchy*, that is through the luck that God has given you, but I deny to you that Sekoma [Kgama's heir] will ever be able to maintain a government like yours unless he relies on consulting his people and on ruling constitutionally." [147] This rebuke probably reflects the fact that Kgama ruled a part of the Tswana group which, as noted previously, had a strong tradition of constitutional government. By contrast, tyrannical rule was taken for granted in many other groups.

With respect to the second generalization, the numerical dominance of tyrannical regimes relative to constitutional ones is hardly surprising, at least not after one discovers the instability of most advanced horticultural regimes. If the primary factor in the unfolding of the political cycle and the growth of constitutional government is the absence of internal or external threats to the security of the existing regime, as hypothesized in Chapter 3, the surprising thing is that constitutional governments were *ever* established, not their relative scarcity. As we have noted, rebellions initiated by royal kinsmen were a common feature of life in most African societies. In addition, the frequent migration of whole societies together with other conditions led to a chronic state of warfare between tribes and nations. This situation almost certainly promoted authoritarian and tyrannical tendencies, and inhibited the development of constitutional government. [148] Conditions in the New World were not greatly different. [149]

At the same time, however, it is clear that other factors were at work checking and limiting the degree of tyranny. [150] To begin with, despite the elaboration and expansion of the machinery of government in many of these advanced horticultural societies, this institution is still far from a perfect instrument of political control. For one thing, the system cannot provide the ruler with very effective protection against assasination; even the great empire builder, Shaka, eventually died at an assassin's hand. In addition, the system cannot usually prevent desertion by disaffected individuals and groups and, since the power and strength of a ruler depends on the size of his following, the threat of desertion is an important check on his actions. Finally, the inevitable dependence of the chief on his advisers serves as an added check on autocratic tendencies.

These same factors arise in any attempt to explain variations in de-

---

[147] *Ibid.*, pp. 146–147.
[148] *Ibid.*, p. 146.
[149] See, for example, the history of the Aztecs who have been described as "wanderers, a landless, 'wanting' tribe who came out of the north of Mexico," frequently involved in battles (von Hagen, p. 59).
[150] For a good discussion of this subject, see Schapera, *Government and Politics*, pp. 149ff.

gree of constitutionalism. Thus, *the less the danger of rebellion or foreign attack, the greater the opportunities for assassination or desertion, and the greater a king's dependence on advisers, the greater the probability of constitutional government.* Schapera argues that the last factor is one of the most important. Furthermore, he sees the dependence of the king on his advisers as often being a function of his age and length of rule. When a new king comes to power as a very young man, he usually inherits his father's advisers and is highly dependent upon them. With the passage of time, however, he gradually gains greater knowledge and replaces these older ministers with men of his own choosing, on whom he depends less. Thus, Schapera finds it no mere coincidence that Kgama, the famous Ngwato autocrat, lived to the ripe old age of ninety-three, and apparently became increasingly autocratic with each passing year.[151]

Turning from the causes of variations in the level of constitutionalism to their *consequences*, the most important one, so far as the distributive process is concerned, is their effect on the extent of social inequality. Inequality seems to increase roughly in proportion to the degree of tyranny, at least when a materialistic, rather than an ideological, ruler is in control. The Lozi, who were cited earlier as an instance of a group with a strong constitutional government, provide a good example. According to reports, living standards were very similar throughout the group, and even the king's material possessions did not differ markedly from those of his subjects.[152] In the case of the Tswana, where constitutional government also flourished, inequality was more marked than among the Lozi, but even here there were none of the extremes found in most African societies dominated by tyrannical and materialistic rulers and elites.[153] In societies where constitutional government was reasonably well established, much more of the revenues which accrued to the king and his ministers seem to have been used for public, rather than private, purposes. Hence, a greater proportion of the total surplus found its way back into the hands of the producers, and the extremes of inequality were avoided.[154]

[151] *Ibid.,* pp. 145–146 and 148.
[152] Gluckman, "The Lozi," p. 14.
[153] Schapera, *The Tswana.*
[154] In thirteen of the fourteen Group A societies in the pilot study sample referred to earlier (see p. 162), there was a correlation of −.53 between the degree of constitutionalism and the degree of inequality which supports the conclusions arrived at separately by a nonquantitative review of the ethnographic literature. Data were lacking on the degree of constitutionalism in the fourteenth society in the sample.

8/Agrarian Societies: Part I

You have put your head inside a wolf's
mouth and taken it out again in safety.
That ought to be reward enough for you.
Aesop (from The Wolf and the Crane)

IN TRACING the early history of mankind, V. Gordon Childe has directed attention to two great social revolutions, both of which profoundly altered the character of human life.[1] The first of these resulted in the formation of the first horticultural societies. The second gave rise to the first agrarian societies.

This second revolution had its beginnings five to six thousand years ago in the fertile river valleys of the Middle East. Subsequently it spread both east and west, with the result that by the end of the fifteenth century A.D. agrarian societies were firmly established throughout most of Europe, North Africa, the Middle East, and South and East Asia. With the discovery of the New World, this form of social organization was

[1] See V. Gordon Childe, *Man Makes Himself* (London: Watts, 1936), especially chaps. 5 and 7.

brought to North and South America, though here somewhat variant forms came into being because of the peculiar circumstances of settlement.[2]

This second great social revolution of antiquity was made possible by a variety of factors, the most important of which was a series of inventions and discoveries that resulted in major advances in production, transportation, and communication. Prominent among these were the invention of the plow and two related developments which greatly enhanced the value of the plow, namely, the discovery of how to harness animal energy, and the discovery of the basic principles of metallurgy. The latter made possible the forging of iron plowshares (a great advance over their wooden predecessors). As Childe puts it:

> The plow heralded an agricultural revolution. Plowing stirs up those fertile elements in the soil that in semi-arid regions are liable to sink down beyond the reach of plant roots. With two oxen and a plow a man could cultivate in a day a far larger area than can a woman with a hoe. The plot (or garden) gives place to the field, and agriculture (from Latin *ager,* "a field") really begins. And all that means larger crops, more food, and expanding populations.[3]

Paralleling these developments were the inventions of the wheel and the sail, which greatly facilitated the movement of both men and goods. This complex of events laid the foundation for the eventual emergence of a new type of society which, though it has been given other names, I shall refer to as the agrarian society, in recognition of the distinctive character of its subsistence system.

Agrarian Societies: A Generic Type?

Despite the fact that various societies have had a common agrarian economy, many scholars deny that they constitute a distinctive social type. Such men stress the innumerable differences among them, and often point out that in the last analysis each agrarian society is a unique entity in its own right. Where, they ask, does one find any true counterpart of such distinctive institutions as the imperial Chinese examination system, the Turkish Janissary system, or the medieval Catholic Church? This point of view has been expressed so often and skillfully by able historians and area specialists that it cannot be ignored.[4]

[2] See James G. Leyburn, *Frontier Folkways* (New Haven Conn.: Yale University Press, 1935), especially chap. 11, for an excellent discussion of the consequences which ensue when advanced societies are transplanted in a primitive wilderness.

[3] Childe, *Man,* p. 100. Quoted by permission of C. A. Watts & Co., Ltd.

[4] It should be noted, however, that not all historians share this extreme view. In the last generation especially, a number of very able historians such as Marc Bloch, M. M. Postan, and Ralph Turner, to name but a few, have insisted that general patterns of fairly broad scope and fundamental historical significance do exist.

No one can deny the real and important differences among societies with agrarian economies, or even that, when viewed in their totality, each constitutes a unique entity. However, the same can be said of everything we refer to in generic terms. Terms such as "chairs," "people," "atoms," "galaxies," "cells," "sonnets," and even "historians" all refer to aggregations of units which are far from uniform. Despite this, experience has shown it intellectually rewarding, even essential, to employ concepts such as these. The basic issue involved in deciding whether or not to use generic concepts is one of balance: are the similarities among the units more significant than the differences, at least in those matters which are relevant to the problem at hand? If so, the use of the generic term is justified.[5]

For purposes of the present analysis, there seems sufficient justification for treating agrarian societies as a generic type. When viewed in the perspective of *all* human societies, the similarities clearly outweigh the differences. Once again, however, it should be said that this is not to deny the existence of internal variation or even the possibility that important subtypes exist.[5a]

There is, however, a real need to differentiate betweeen agrarian societies and one other type with which they are easily confused because of geographical proximity and long historical association. These are *maritime* societies. They include such famous groups as the Phoenicians, the Carthaginians, the Venetians, and the Dutch from the mid-fifteenth

[5] This does not mean that all criticisms of the use of general concepts are based on ignorance or prejudice. Far from it. Often criticisms have arisen because of the misuse of such terms. Sociologists and others who use them sometimes forget that identity in certain respects does not imply identity in all. Societies which are very similar in some ways may vary greatly in others. By failing to recognize this and make it clear in their writings, they convey the impression of a naive, one-sided, and grossly oversimplified view of human life.

In their defense, however, it might be said that, even when the nature of this problem is clearly understood, it is extremely difficult to present a truly accurate picture which exaggerates neither the similarities nor the differences among units. This is especially difficult when quantitative data are lacking.

[5a] In response to an earlier draft of Chaps. 8 and 9, Robert Bellah argued vigorously for the need for internal differentiation of this societal type. He suggested that it might be far more fruitful to differentiate between "simple" and "advanced" agrarian, with the watershed being the first millennium B.C. He argued that these simple agrarian societies more closely resembled the most advanced horticultural societies than they do the more advanced agrarian. He feels that the key developments were the great social and cultural inventions of the first millennium, e.g., universal religions, alphabetic writing, bureaucracy, coinage, etc. He also notes that this is roughly the same period in which iron tools became common, but feels that this is not the crucial development (a view which I do not share). I believe this division may well prove useful in the future, and the reader will probably note that most of the data cited in this chapter are drawn from societies which would qualify as "advanced" agrarian, just as most in the last chapter were drawn from the more "advanced" advanced horticultural societies. Bellah also argues for a differentiation of agrarian societies into three subtypes, city-states, bureaucratic empires, and feudal regimes, which crosscut one or both of the previous types.

century. One might regard Athenian society from the sixth century B.C. until the period of Roman rule, and perhaps also English society from the sixteenth to the early nineteenth centuries, as examples of hybrid societies, part maritime and part agrarian.

Maritime societies differed from agrarian societies in various ways. From the productive standpoint, commerce rather than agriculture was the chief source of the economic surplus. This characteristic was undoubtedly related to the further fact that, in the political and distributive spheres, merchants were much more favorably situated in maritime societies than in agrarian. Also, the governments of maritime societies were typically republican and plutocratic, while those in agrarian societies were usually monarchical.[6] From the military standpoint, maritime societies were distinctive because of their reliance on naval forces, a characteristic which had important implications for both the political and the distributive spheres. Other differences might also be cited, but these should prove sufficient to indicate the need for differentiating between the two types.[7]

Common Features of Agrarian Societies

Societies which depend on agrarian economies resemble one another in many important ways, and it is to these points of similarity that we now turn. To begin with, in matters of *technology and production* agrarian societies clearly enjoy a definite advantage over the other three types of societies we have considered. The gulf which separates them technologically is substantial, indicating that the productive potential of agrarian

---

[6] For a further discussion of this point, including a consideration of some of the exceptions, see pp. 197–198 of this chapter.

[7] The need for this distinction between agrarian and maritime societies had not occurred to me when I began work on this volume, but I was driven to it by research. Recently I discovered, while rereading Franz Oppenheimer, that he was forced to the same conclusion half a century ago. See *The State,* translated by John Gitterman (Indianapolis: Bobbs-Merrill, 1914), chap. 4.

In reading this section Robert Bellah pointed out that the distinction between maritime and agrarian societies was *economic* rather than technological, and, further, that this should be the basis of distinction elsewhere. Reflecting on this, I am inclined to agree, though with the qualification that differences in the economies of societies are normally linked with and dependent on differences in their technologies. This is clearly the case in the five major types of societies with which the volume deals. Economy and technology diverge to a significant degree chiefly in special cases when varying environmental conditions force a society to concentrate on certain aspects of technology to the neglect of others, or make this advantageous. Thus certain societies which possessed a knowledge of the basic elements of agrarian technology found it more profitable to concentrate their economic efforts in overseas trade and commerce and thus became maritime societies.

societies is, on the average, considerably greater than that of the others.[8] This difference is best indicated by the superior engineering achievements of mature, or highly developed, agrarian societies, which are unmatched in any horticultural society. These include such marvels as the great cathedrals built in medieval Europe, the massive pyramids of Egypt, the far-flung irrigation systems of the Middle East, India, and China, the roads and aqueducts of Rome, the countless palaces and temples of South and East Asia, the Great Wall of China, and even the modest ships and wheeled vehicles common to all agrarian societies except in the earliest periods.[9]

These many and varied achievements rested in part on the foundation of countless small advances in technology and science too humble, in many instances, to be noted by historians in their day. These include the development of new tools and the refinement of old,[10] the development of new skills and crafts, the cultivation of new varieties of plant life and the domestication of new kinds of animals, the harnessing of new forms of energy, and countless advances in both scientific and technical knowledge. The net effect of all these innovations was the substantial enlargement of the economic surplus. Under agrarian conditions of life, far less of the total product of man's labor was required to keep him alive and productive, and hence more was available for other purposes.

Advances in productive technology were matched by advances in *military technology*. The means of waging war were substantially more efficient in agrarian societies than in horticultural. For example, the domestication of the horse and the invention of the wheel made possible chariot warfare and cavalry warfare, both significant advances. Other

[8] I do not mean to suggest that there is no overlap with respect to productivity between some of the most primitive agrarian societies and some of the most advanced horticultural. As noted in the last chapter, there is reason to think that from the standpoint of productivity the most advanced kingdoms in pre-European Africa and the New World equaled or surpassed the societies of Western Europe of the early Middle Ages and perhaps also the earliest, and most primitive, agrarian societies in the Middle East and China. It should be recognized, however, that these comparisons involve the least developed examples of one category and the most developed of another. What we are chiefly concerned with is the overall range and distribution of cases within each category, and it is this which appears to be quite distinct.
[9] Some of the most advanced horticulturalists in the New World approached agrarian societies in some respects. The greatest achievements of the Incas, Aztecs, Mayas, Toltecs, and others, especially in the realm of massive-style architecture and engineering, approximate their counterparts in early agrarian societies. The differences are most pronounced where delicate and complex feats of engineering are involved. Thus, in even these most advanced of horticultural societies, there is nothing to compare with the great medieval cathedrals or the Taj Mahal.
[10] See, for example, the description of typical farm tools in a Chinese village as reported by Martin C. Yang, *A Chinese Village: Taitou, Shantung Province* (New York: Columbia University Press, 1945), pp. 251–257. This should be compared with corresponding descriptions for horticultural societies.

advances included the development of castles and other kinds of fortifications, protective armor, and improved weapons.

For the student of stratification and distribution, these developments in military and productive technology are vitally important for two reasons. In the first place, the advances in military technology created an important social cleavage. No longer was it possible for every man to make for himself weapons as good as those of every other man. The new technology favored those who either controlled enough manpower, e.g., slaves and serfs, to build fortifications, or possessed enough wealth to hire the specialists required to build the new equipment like chariots and armor. Thus, for the first time in history, technologically based differences in military might became a basic reality within human societies, and opportunities for exploitation were correspondingly enlarged.

Advances in technology, in the areas of both production and warfare, also made possible a substantial growth in the power of the state. This possibility was not always realized, as evidenced by Europe during the early Middle Ages, but when it was, the results could be most impressive. Compared with the governments of horticultural societies, those of agrarian societies tended to be more powerful, more efficiently organized, more permanent, capable of more impressive accomplishments, and engaged in a wider range of activities.

One measure of the power of any state is *the size of the territory it controls.* A few examples from the history of agrarian societies help point up the contrast between agrarian and horticultural societies. From the standpoint of territory, the Russian Empire surpassed all rivals. As early as the reign of Peter the Great (1689–1725) it embraced nearly six million square miles, and in the reign of Alexander II in the mid-nineteenth century, nearly eight million.[11] Its nearest rival seems to have been the Spanish Empire of the eighteenth century, which contained a land area of five million square miles.[12] In the middle of the eighth century the Arab Umayyad Empire reached the zenith of its power and controlled a territory in excess of three million square miles.[13] The Roman Empire at the height of its power held sway over a land area of two million square miles, as did the Chinese Empire from the Han dynasty on.[14] Finally, the

[11] Jerome Blum, *Lord and Peasant in Russia from the Ninth to the Nineteenth Century* (Princeton, N.J.: Princeton University Press, 1961), p. 278.
[12] This can be readily computed from a standard map of the Spanish Empire at that time and a table of current national land area.
[13] This figure is based on a map in Philip K. Hitti, *History of the Arabs* (London: Macmillan, 1960), p. 216.
[14] See Ralph Turner, *The Great Cultural Traditions* (New York: McGraw-Hill, 1941), vol. II, for maps showing the approximate boundaries of these two empires.

Ottoman Empire, at the peak of its power under Suleiman the Magnificent (1520–1566), contained more than a million and a half square miles, as did the Persian Empire in its heyday and the short-lived empire of Alexander the Great.[15] While these are admittedly extreme cases, they illustrate the potential for growth inherent in agrarian states. Furthermore, there have been scores of other agrarian states with territories ranging from a hundred thousand square miles to well over a million. By contrast, few horticultural states ever attained the lower limit of this range.[16]

Population size is another measure of the power of states and also of the capacity of their economic systems. Whereas the upper limit for advanced horticultural states has been only about four million, populations of a hundred million and more were recorded for a few agrarian states, and states with populations in the millions were the rule rather than the exception. In China, a population of more than 60 million was recorded in the census of 1578, and by 1778 it had increased to 243 million.[17] The first census in Russia, taken in 1724, indicated a total population of only 14 million, but by the time of the tenth census in 1858, this figure had increased to 74 million.[18] The population of the Roman Empire is estimated to have totaled 70 million at the beginning of the third century.[19] Again, these are extreme cases, but they reveal the contrast between the potentialities of agrarian and horticultural societies.

As these examples suggest, the great agrarian states of the past were all *conquest states,* or social units formed through the forcible subjugation of one group by another.[20] The same has probably been true of all, or virtually all, their lesser rivals. Few, if any, agrarian states ever came into

[15] For the Ottoman Empire, see Hitti, map opposite p. 712. For the Persian Empire of the classical period, see A. T. Olmstead, *History of the Persian Empire* (Chicago: University of Chicago Press, 1948), pp. xx–xxi, or Turner, p. 362. For the empire of Alexander, see W. H. McNeill, *The Rise of the West* (New York: Mentor, 1965), map on p. 363.

[16] The Inca Empire, for example, though one of the largest created by an advanced horticultural society, covered an area of only about 350,000 square miles. See Victor von Hagen, *The Ancient Sun Kingdoms of the Americas* (Cleveland: World Publishing, 1961), pp. 576–577.

[17] Wolfram Eberhard, *A History of China,* 2d ed. (Berkeley: University of California Press, 1960), p. 274. As early as A.D. 140 there may have been nearly 50 million inhabitants (p. 108).

[18] Blum, *op. cit.*

[19] *The Cambridge Ancient History* (London: Cambridge University Press, 1939), vol. XII, pp. 267–268.

[20] One scholar said of the Romans that "war must be ranked with agriculture as a major industry." See F. R. Cowell, *Cicero and the Roman Republic* (London: Penguin, 1956), p. 287. This statement could be applied to most other great agrarian states.

being simply through the peaceful political evolution and expansion of a single people or through the voluntary federation or union of separate peoples.[21]

As a consequence, agrarian states are often made up of a variety of disparate ethnic groups. Those groups which remain politically united for a number of generations frequently tend to merge culturally, as in the case of the various ethnic groups which made up the English and the Chinese populations. Sometimes the distinctions disappear entirely, but this is not inevitable, as evidenced by the enduring cultural cleavage between the Greeks and Romans, which outlived the Roman Empire, or those ethnic distinctions which have been perpetuated for centuries in India in the form of certain castes.[22]

Warfare was a chronic condition in virtually all agrarian states. A generation ago Pitirim Sorokin undertook a massive survey of the incidence and magnitude of war in the histories of eleven European countries. For the period covered by his survey, Germany had the lowest incidence of war, with wars recorded for 28 per cent of the years from 1651 to 1925; Spain had the highest incidence, with wars being reported in 67 per cent of the years from 1476 to 1925.[23] The median figure for the eleven countries was 46 per cent, reported for Russia for the period from 901 to 1925. Though this study includes a few years of the modern industrial era in some cases, there is no reason to think that this raised the totals in any way. On the contrary, it probably lowered them. Furthermore, there is good reason to believe that if Sorokin's figures err, they err on the conservative side, due to his failure to take account of minor conflicts not reported in the sources he used.[24]

When struggles with foreign enemies were lacking, *internal struggles* often developed. This was especially common in nations without an insti-

[21] A record of conquest cannot necessarily be found in the history of every agrarian state. Sometimes states appeared on the stage of history for the first time only when they had already reached a stage of stability or decline, thus creating the illusion of a nonconquest state. When a state contains more than a handful of villages, however, as is invariably the case in agrarian societies, we can strongly suspect that conquest did occur in the prehistoric and preagrarian era.

[22] Not all castes have an ethnic origin, but modern research indicates that many do. For a good study of the ways in which tribes have been transformed into castes, see F. G. Bailey, *Tribe, Caste, and Nation* (Manchester: Manchester University Press, 1960).

[23] Pitirim Sorokin, *Social and Cultural Dynamics* (New York: Bedminister Press, 1962, first published 1937), vol. III, chap. 10, especially p. 352.

[24] Compare, for example, Sorokin's figures for Russia during the Tatar era with those reported by Alexandre Eck, *Le moyen âge russe* (Paris: Maison du Livre Etranger, 1933), cited by Blum, p. 59. See, also, the statement of Marc Bloch that after the collapse of the Carolingian state, Europe lived in "the state of perpetual war." See Marc Bloch, *Feudal Society*, translated by L. A. Manyon (Chicago: University of Chicago Press, 1962), p. 160.

tutionalized pattern of succession to the throne, as in both the Roman and Mughal Empires. Of the seventy-nine Roman emperors from Augustus to Romulus Augustulus, no less than thirty-one were murdered, while six others were driven to suicide, four were forcibly deposed, and several others met uncertain ends at the hands of internal enemies.[25] In the Roman Empire, these struggles were often little more than palace coups, but in the case of the Mughals, the emperor's death usually signaled the beginning of an extended period of civil war between large and well-organized factions, each supporting rival princely claimants to the throne.[26]

The high incidence of war seems related to another characteristic of agrarian societies, namely their pronounced inclination toward *monarchical government*. As various writers have pointed out, the exigencies of war generally make it advantageous to vest ultimate authority in the hands of one man.[27] Committee rule is much less effective, especially in a large and far-flung organization. Given the frequency of war and the size of agrarian states, monarchical government becomes almost inevitable.

There have been a few exceptions to his general pattern, as illustrated by the Roman Republic and the republican governments of the Swiss cantons and certain of the early Indian and Russian states. It is noteworthy that *in all of these cases one or more of the following conditions obtained: either the state was small, or it existed when agrarianism was still relatively new in the region in which it was located, or it was located in a mountainous region*. As noted above, the advantages of monarchical rule for military purposes are positively correlated with the numerical and geographical size of a society, so that republican government may not be an insuperable handicap for small agrarian states—especially if other conditions are favorable. It also seems that republics can survive more easily in the earlier stages of agrarianism, before empire building by other states has really got underway. This is simply another way of saying that it takes time for the processes of social selection to weed out the less powerful organizations. Finally, mountainous regions seem better suited to the survival of republican governments than riverine valleys and broad plains. There are several reasons for this. To begin with,

---

[25] These figures were calculated from A. E. R. Boak, *A History of Rome to 565 A. D.*, 3d ed. (New York: Macmillan, 1943) and Harold Mattingly, *Roman Imperial Civilization* (New York: Doubleday Anchor, 1959), using Mattingly's list of emperors on pp. 351–355.
[26] For a good summary of Mughal history, see *The Cambridge History of India* (London: Cambridge University Press, 1937), vol. IV.
[27] See, for example, Herbert Spencer, *The Principles of Sociology* (New York: Appleton, 1897), vol. II, part 5, chap. 17; Pitirim Sorokin, vol. III, pp. 196–198; or Stanislaw Andrzejewski, *Military Organization and Society* (London: Routledge, 1954), pp. 92–95.

the economic surplus is usually small in such areas, and because transportation problems are acute, it is difficult to assemble in one area a quantity sufficient to support a royal retinue. Furthermore, military tactics which are successful in valleys and plains frequently prove impractical in mountainous areas, thus affording the less numerous and less centrally organized inhabitants of such areas certain advantages when they are forced to defend their own territory.[28]

The history of Roman society provides an especially interesting test case for this line of analysis, both because it is so well documented and because it is so familiar. It seems more than coincidental that the shift from the Republic to the principate was linked with the growth in size of the state, the muturation of the agrarian social order in the Mediterranean world, and the expansion of the Roman state to include vast nonmountainous territories. In short, the emergence of the principate apparently depended on the decline of those conditions favorable to republican government. Having said this, however, one must concede that on the basis of these three factors alone, the Roman Republic should have disappeared long before Augustus or even Sulla, the first violator of the republican constitution and the first practitioner of the monarchical principle. The explanation for the protracted survival of republicanism in Rome seems to be related to the unique institution of the consulship, an elective office of limited tenure but with monarchical powers.[29] This office seems to have provided the Roman state with most of the military advantages of monarchical rule while permitting the retention of most of the essential features of republican rule.

Another important characteristic of agrarian societies was the regular and widespread occurrence of *urban communities.* As indicated in the last chapter, urban or semiurban communities were found in *some* of the most advanced horticultural societies, but in *many* they were absent. Furthermore, those that were found in these societies were few in number, small in size, relatively impermanent, and otherwise deficient in most of the basic attributes of urbanism.

In agrarian societies, by contrast, there was a substantial increase in the number, size, permanence, and urban character of such communities.

---

[28] Systematic study may indicate that agrarian states located in mountainous regions are sufficiently different from those located in river valleys and plains areas to justify treating them as a totally different category, e.g., "mountain-agrarian" and "riverine-agrarian" societies. For purposes of this chapter, however, I have simply treated them as subclasses within the general class of agrarian societies, their differences being a function of the influence of mountainous conditions. The further I have pursued this subject, however, the more impressed I have become with the magnitude of the differences associated with a mountainous environment.

[29] For a good description of this unusual office, see Cowell, pp. 166–171.

It was the rare exception which lacked truly urban centers.[30] The roster of agrarian cities included such famous names as Babylon, Jerusalem, Alexandria, Rome, Constantinople, Paris, London, Baghdad, Delhi, Benares, Peking, and Edo (or Tokyo), to mention but a few. According to the best available evidence, a number of these great cities of the past attained populations of several hundred thousand. It is possible that the greatest even reached and passed the million mark for brief periods, though recent research makes this seem more doubtful than formerly.[31] But even if one accepts a half million as the upper limit for city size in agrarian societies (a figure few, if any, experts would challenge), this still represents a tremendous increase over anything in advanced horticultural societies.

Though a few capitals of great empires sometimes attained such size, the majority of urban centers were always much more modest. For example, in the late fourteenth century, London still had a population of only 30,000 to 40,000, and the next largest cities, York and Bristol, had less than 10,000.[32] In the middle of the next century Frankfort had only 8,700 inhabitants, Nuremberg 20,000, Strassburg 26,000, and Brussels 40,000.[33] In this period a town of 20,000 was considered large, and the great majority of urban centers had less than 10,000. In the mid-sixteenth century, the second largest town in England, Bristol, still had a population of only 10,500, while in seventeenth-century Sweden the second largest had only about 5,000.[34] Even as late as the beginning of the nineteenth century, when the Industrial Revolution was already under way, there were less than fifty cities in the entire world with a population of 100,000 or more.[35]

As such figures suggest, the urban segment of agrarian populations was never more than a small percentage of the total. Russian records indicate that from the late seventeenth to the late eighteenth century, the

[30] There are a few instances of agrarian societies in which urban communities were wholly or largely absent, as in parts of early medieval Europe when the breakdown in the political system led to the near disappearance of urban life. Also, in the earliest stages of the transition from horticulture to agriculture, urban settlements may sometimes have been absent or few in number and small in size. These cases, however, are by no means typical. The normal pattern in reasonably mature agrarian societies involves a multiplicity of fairly large and relatively permanent urban centers.
[31] For good discussions of this subject, see Kingsley Davis, "The Origin and Growth of Urbanization in the World," *American Journal of Sociology*, 60 (1955), pp. 429–437; J. C. Russell, "Late Ancient and Medieval Population," *Transactions of the American Philosophical Society*, 48 (1958), pp. 37–101; and Gideon Sjoberg, *The Preindustrial City* (New York: Free Press, 1960), pp. 80–85.
[32] J. C. Russell, *British Medieval Population* (Albuquerque, N. Mex.: University of New Mexico Press, 1948), p. 285.
[33] Henri Pirenne, *Economic and Social History of Medieval Europe* (New York: Harvest Books, n.d., originally published 1933), pp. 170–171.
[34] Russell, *British, ibid.*, and Eli F. Heckscher, *An Economic History of Sweden*, translated by Goram Ohlin (Cambridge, Mass.: Harvard University Press, 1954), p. 111.
[35] Davis, "Urbanization," p. 434.

urban population constituted only about 3 per cent of the total, and in 1851 still totaled less than 8 per cent.[36] In England in the late fourteenth century, towns with 3,200 or more constituted less than 5.5 per cent of the population.[37] Henri Pirenne states that in the whole of Europe, Western as well as Eastern, the urban population probably never constituted more than 10 per cent of the total between the twelfth and the fifteenth centuries.[38] More recently, Gideon Sjoberg has argued that in all the agrarian societies of the world, urban populations never constituted more than 10 per cent of the total, and in some instances accounted for less than 5 per cent.[39] Regardless of the exact figures, all authorities agree that the overwhelming majority of the population in agrarian societies were always simple peasant farmers, and city dwellers and townsfolk never more than a small minority.

Despite this fact, the residents of urban centers usually dominated agrarian societies politically, economically, religiously, and culturally. This is because both wealth and political power were normally concentrated in the cities [40]—or, to state the matter more accurately, concentrations of population developed where the holders of wealth and political power resided. Thus, though urban populations were always numerical minorities in agrarian societies, they typically exercised a decisive influence in those areas of life most readily subject to conscious human control.

Urban populations in agrarian societies were not only larger than those in advanced horticultural societies, but also more truly urban. In many ways the largest communities in horticultural Africa resembled overgrown villages more than cities, and horticultural pursuits were still a major economic activity. By contrast, in the leading urban centers of agrarian societies, agricultural pursuits, though not absent by any means, were clearly a secondary activity. The residents of these centers, therefore, were relatively free to engage in other types of activity.[41]

The cities and larger towns of agrarian societies have long been noted

[36] Blum, pp. 268 and 281.
[37] Russell, *British*, p. 305.
[38] *Op. cit.*, p. 58.
[39] *Op. cit.*, p. 83.
[40] Sjoberg calls attention to this fact while attacking the popular notion that the elite in agrarian societies resided in rural areas (*ibid.*, pp. 110–116). Although I think he overstates his case, at least as it applies to Europe, his basic argument is surely sound.
[41] It would be a mistake to suppose, however, that a complete divorce was effected. As late as the sixteenth century the weavers of Norwich were obliged to drop their work at harvest time each year, and even in London the hustings court was suspended at harvest time. Even a market town such as Leicester still supplied most of its food from adjoining fields. See S. B. Clough and C. W. Cole, *Economic History of Europe* (Boston: Heath, 1941), p. 48; W. G. Hoskins, *The Midland Peasant: The Economic and Social History of a Leicestershire Village* (London: Macmillan, 1957), p. 175; and G. G. Coulton, *Medieval Panorama* (New York: Meridian Books, 1955, first published 1938), pp. 282ff.

for *the diversity of vocations* followed by their inhabitants. Among the major occupational categories represented, the following deserve note since, collectively, they included the great majority of the urban population: officials, priests, scholars, scribes, merchants, servants, soldiers, craftsmen, laborers, and beggars. In addition, there was usually a small leisure class, whose livelihood was derived from rents, pensions, profits, or political office.

Most of these major categories included a great variety of subspecialties, so that a listing of all the many specific occupations would number in the hundreds in the larger cities. Some indication of the diversity found in larger cities is revealed by a survey made in one small neighborhood in Peking early in the present century. In this neighborhood, which had a population of only 5,200 men, no less than 163 different occupations were represented.[42] While a few of these were the result of Western industrial influences, the great majority were traditional occupations of the type found in every agrarian society. If a larger portion of the city had been surveyed, an even greater number of occupations would have been found, since in such cities there is a tendency for workers engaged in the same trade or industry to cluster together.[43]

A similar pattern is indicated by a tax roll for Paris in the year 1313. This roll lists 157 different crafts, not to mention other occupations.[44] The textile industry provides some idea of the degree of specialization achieved. "There were wool merchants, flax merchants, hemp merchants, wool combers, wool spinners, silk spinners (two kinds), weavers (seven kinds for linens, woolens, tapestries of two sorts, canvas, silks of two sorts), dyers, fullers, calenderers, shearmen, textile sellers (of several kinds), tailors (four types, and two more were added in the course of the fourteenth century), headdress makers (seven kinds, including those who worked especially with felt, fur, wool and cotton, flowers, peacock feathers, gold embroidery and pearls, and silk), girdle makers, mercers (who sold articles of dress especially for women), and secondhand clothes dealers." While this same degree of specialization could be found only in larger cities such as London, Bruges, and Florence, smaller cities often had forty or fifty different kinds of craftsmen, and even small towns had ten or twenty.[45]

[42] Sidney D. Gamble, *Peking: A Social Survey* (Garden City, N.Y.: Doubleday, 1921), pp. 326-327.
[43] Eberhard, p. 197, reports that there were 420 different guilds in nineteenth-century Peking. However, this may include guilds performing the same function in different sections of the city.
[44] Clough and Cole, p. 25.
[45] *Ibid.* See also Blum, who reports that a recent Russian scholar found as many as sixty craft specialties in some of the Kievan Russian towns of the twelfth and thirteenth centuries (p. 16), and over two hundred in the sixteenth century (p. 126).

Work units in urban centers were generally quite small by modern standards. In Cicero's day a shop employing fifty men was considered very large.[46] A pewter business which employed eighteen men was the largest mentioned in any of the medieval craft records of London, and this modest size was not reached until the mid-fifteenth century.[47]

In most agrarian societies, men engaged in the same field of economic activity were organized into local groups which modern scholars commonly call guilds.[48] Actually, these organization varied so much that it could be argued that the same term should not be applied to them all. Some were chiefly religious and fraternal organizations, others primarily political and economic in character. Some were the creations of governmental authorities concerned with problems of social control and taxation, while others were the creations of workers and merchants concerned with the promotion of their own special interests.[49] Typically, however, they served the interests of both the state and their members. For example, the Japanese historian Takekoshi says of the early *za* that "they consisted of merchants granted the monopoly right of business and were the unit of responsibility for the payment of taxes." [50]

Though superficially resembling modern labor unions, these guilds were more nearly associations of merchants and manufacturers, especially those who were politically influential. Membership was usually open to workers as well as employers, but the employers normally dominated the organization by virtue of their wealth, prestige, and power. Distinctions were made even among the employers, and control of an organization normally passed to the wealthiest.[51] In medieval Europe, and

---

[46] Cowell, p. 80.

[47] Sylvia Thrupp, *The Merchant Class of Medieval London* (Ann Arbor, Mich.: Ann Arbor Paperbacks, 1962), p. 9.

[48] There have been exceptions to this general pattern, as in Russia, where the guild system was never firmly established despite the efforts of Peter the Great and several of his successors in the eighteenth century. See Blum, p. 302. Prior to the sixteenth century the guild system seems to have been absent in China, and prior to the fifteenth century in Japan. See Eberhard, *History*, p. 197 and Yosoburo Takekoshi, *The Economic Aspects of the History of the Civilization of Japan* (New York: Macmillan, 1930), vol. I, chap. 18. In India castes seem to have performed some of the usual functions of guilds, but did not preclude them by any means. See R. C. Majumdar (ed.), *The History and Culture of the Indian People* (Bombay: Bharatiya Vidya Bhavan, 1951, 1953), vol. II, pp. 601–602, and vol. III, pp. 592–593.

[49] For examples of the former, see Russia in the eighteenth century (Blum, p. 302, or Valentine Bill, *The Forgotten Class: The Russian Bourgeoisie from the Earliest Beginnings to 1900* (New York: Frederick A. Praeger, 1959), pp. 72–73) or Rome in the third century A.D. (Boak, pp. 369–370). The medieval European guilds are good examples of the latter, which is the more common pattern, though these, too, were often used by public authorities as instruments of social control. See Sylvia Thrupp, "The Guilds," in *The Cambridge Economic History of Europe* (London: Cambridge University Press, 1963), vol. III, p. 232.

[50] *Op. cit.*, pp. 242–243.

[51] See, for example, Thrupp, *London*, pp. 23 and 29–31.

perhaps elsewhere, these organizations were more democratic in the earlier years of their existence than in the later.[52]

One of the major concerns of most guilds was to protect their members against interference by outside authorities. Thus guild officers often sought and obtained the right to settle disputes among their own members and otherwise to regulate their conduct. Sometimes, notably in medieval Europe, guildsmen collaborated in efforts to free urban communities from the control of the landed aristocracy or the crown and thereby brought into existence republican islands within the framework of the larger monarchical system.[53] It seems more than coincidental that the political dominance of merchants in medieval European towns fostered the same republican pattern found in maritime societies, where merchants were also dominant.

The tendency toward increased specialization and greater division of labor, so evident within the cities and towns of agrarian societies, also manifested itself on other levels in most of these societies. Different communities and different regions tended to specialize, to a greater or lesser degree, in particular types of economic activities. In the Roman Empire, for example, North Africa and Spain were noted as suppliers of dried figs and olive oil, Gaul, Dalmatia, Asia Minor, and Syria for their wine, Spain and Egypt for salted meats, Egypt, North Africa, Sicily, and the Black Sea region for grain, and the latter also for salted fish.[54] There was also a substantial division of labor at the community level as indicated in a passage from Cato the Elder's manual for farmers, written in the second century B.C. He wrote:

> Tunics, togas, blankets, smocks and shoes should be bought at Rome; caps, iron tools, scythes, spades, mattocks, axes, harness, ornaments and small chains at Cales and Minturnae; spades at Venafrum, carts and sledges at Suessa and in Lucania, jars and pots at Alba and at Rome; tiles at Venafrum, oil mills at Pompeii and at Rufrius's yard at Nola; nails and bars at Rome; pails, oil urns, water pitchers, wine urns, other copper vessels at Capua and at Nola; Campanian baskets, pulley-ropes and all sorts of cordage at Capua, Roman baskets at Suessa and Casium.[55]

The Roman Empire was by no means unique in this respect. Reports of similar patterns of specialization come from widely scattered societies in

[52] See James Westfall Thompson, *Economic and Social History of the Middle Ages* (New York: Appleton-Century-Crofts, 1928), pp. 790–791, or L. Halphen, "Industry and Commerce," in Arthur Tilley (ed.), *Medieval France* (London: Cambridge University Press, 1922), pp. 189ff.

[53] See, for example, Thompson, pp. 779ff.; Joan Evans, *Life in Medieval France* (London: Oxford University Press, 1925), pp. 64ff.; Coulton, chap. 24; or Thrupp, *London,* chap. 1.

[54] Turner, p. 911.

[55] Cowell, p. 79. Quoted by permission.

the agrarian world.[56] Even at the village level a measure of specialization was not uncommon, since in the agricultural off-season peasants were frequently obliged to turn to handicrafts to make ends meet, and in time certain villages developed a reputation for superior skill in the production of some particular commodity.

The development of specialization necessarily implies the development of *trade and commerce*, since specialists must exchange the products of their labors for those of others. Comparing advanced horticultural and agrarian societies, it is clear that with only a few exceptions the volume of trade and commerce is substantially greater in the latter.[57] One of the clearest indications of the growth of trade is the emergence of a distinct merchant class as a normal part of almost every agrarian society.[58] This class is found in only rudimentary form in horticultural societies, where the few middlemen interposed between producer and consumer are usually either tax collectors and other government officials, or part-time traders, as in the case of the women of Dahomey.

Though the volume of trade in agrarian societies was substantially greater than in horticultural societies, it could not begin to compare with that in industrial societies. One basic reason for this was the high cost of transporting goods, especially overland. A report from China, prepared shortly after World War II, indicates the relative costs of modern and traditional means of transportation. The cost of shipping a ton of goods per mile by various means was found to be as follows (in United States cents):[59]

Rail	2.7
Animal-drawn cart	13
Pack mule	17
Wheelbarrow	20
Pack donkey	24
Pack horse	30
Carrying by pole	48

For water transportation, the modern steamboat was able to haul goods in China at a cost of 2.4 cents per ton-mile, compared with 12 cents for the

[56] See, for example, Blum, pp. 126 and 394–395 on Russia, or Ralph Linton, *The Tree of Culture* (New York: Vintage Books, 1959), p. 231 on China.

[57] Once again the early medieval period in Europe is the chief exception to the general rule and for the reasons set forth in footnote 8, page 193.

[58] See Michael Postan, "The Trade of Medieval Europe: The North," in *The Cambridge Economic History of Europe* (London: Cambridge University Press, 1952), vol. II (1952), pp. 168ff. for an excellent discussion of the development of the merchant class in western Europe.

[59] John Lossing Buck, *Secretariat Paper No. 1: Tenth Conference of the Institute of Pacific Relations*, Stratford on Avon, 1947, reprinted in Irwin T. Sanders et al., *Societies around the World* (New York: Dryden Press, 1953), p. 65.

traditional junk. As these figures indicate, modern means of transportation have cut the costs of hauling goods 80 to 95 per cent. It is this which has made possible the massive movement of men and materials which characterizes all modern industrial societies. Lest these figures from China be thought unrepresentative, it should be noted that comparable figures from Europe are strikingly similar. For example, in 1900 the cost of transporting goods by horse-drawn vehicles is reported to have been ten times greater than moving the same goods by railroad.[60] In most agrarian states these costs were further increased by the traditional practice of collecting internal customs, i.e., tariffs charged at certain provincial boundaries.[61]

Because of these high costs, only luxury items were usually transported long distances.[62] Objects such as silks and spices were small in bulk but commanded high prices, and thus could be moved for extended distances at a profit. Bulky items of limited value were usually moved only short distances and traded in local markets. In fourteenth-century England, for example, records suggest that costs incurred in transporting heavy commodities like grain a distance of 50 miles would equal 15 per cent of the total cost, whereas the movement of wool the same distance would only be 1.5 per cent.[63] In some instances, transportation costs for foodstuffs were so great that it was more profitable for rulers and their courts to travel to the various estates where they were produced than to transport them elsewhere.[64] The English historian Coulton states that "we see sovereigns and great nobles all through the Middle Ages, travelling from one estate to another with [their] ministers and trains: eating up the year's produce in a week or few days, and then passing on to eat up a fresh estate."

Medieval Europe was not typical in this respect. Normally, in agrarian societies, the economic surplus was carried to the ruling classes and their dependents. As a result, all of the more advanced agrarian societies resembled a tree or plant with a system of feeder roots spreading over a vast area, tapping the surplus and moving it, by stages, to the ultimate consumers, the urban population. At the outer limits of this system were thousands even hundreds of thousands, of small peasant villages, each

[60] Clough and Cole, p. 445.
[61] See, for example, Michael Postan, pp. 133–140 on northern Europe; Blum, p. 127 on Russia; Harold Mattingly, p. 221 on Rome; or Majumdar, vol. II, p. 605 on India.
[62] See, for example, Clough and Cole, p. 64; or Pirenne, chap. 5.
[63] Postan, p. 152.
[64] See, for example, Sidney Painter, *The Rise of the Feudal Monarchies* (Ithaca, N.Y.: Cornell University Press, 1951), pp. 130–131; or Coulton, p. 47, who reports that this was true even of the great emperor Charlemagne. See, also, D. D. Kosambi, *An Introduction to the History of India* (Bombay: Popular Book Depot, 1956), p. 283, who reports a similar pattern in the Gupta Empire in India.

typically containing a few hundred residents.[65] These transmitted their surplus to some neighboring market town, where a portion was removed for the needs of the local population and the remainder sent on to some provincial capital. Again a portion was removed and the remainder transmitted to the national capital. Those villages in the immediate environs of provincial and national capitals dealt directly with these centers. However, regardless of whether the relationship was direct or indirect, the basic pattern was the same. On the one hand there was a steady flow of *goods* from the peasant villages to the urban centers. In return, the villages received certain *services* of a political, cultural, religious, educational, and commercial nature, together with a small number of necessary or desired commodities such as salt, tools, or other manufactured objects not produced in the villages themselves. Thus these relationships which developed between the villages and the urban centers were essentially symbiotic in character, but with definite overtones of parasitism.[66]

Because of the importance and complexity of these symbiotic relationships, those most dependent on them, the city dwellers and ruling classes, were obliged to devise ways to control and regulate them. Two inventions of profound significance emerged from these endeavors—money and writing.[67]

The invention of money certainly proved a great stimulus to trade

[65] Coulton states that the average population of European villages in the fourteenth century varied from 200 to 400 or 450 (p. 68). Another writer suggests 300 as the average for English villages of this period. See H. S. Bennett, *Life on the English Manor: A Study of Peasant Conditions, 1150–1400* (London: Cambridge University Press, 1960). Russell's data from the English Poll Tax Returns of 1377 suggest an average of only 100 in that year, but this was just after the ravages of the Black Plague. Russell estimates the pre-Plague average was about 166 (see *British*, p. 309). Blum reports systematic data from mid-nineteenth-century Russia which show that 53 per cent of Russian villages had between 51 and 300 residents, with the median apparently being about 150 (p. 506). In India today there are about 500,000 villages, and as recently as 1951, despite the influence of industrialism, villages with a population of less than 500 were the most numerous. See Ashish Bose, "The First Census of Free India," *Modern Review*, 95 (1954), p. 114. Finally, a recent study of village life in northern Thailand indicates that the average village in that area has a population of 450 to 500. See John E. de Young, *Village Life in Modern Thailand* (Berkeley, Calif.: University of California Press, 1958), p. 12.

[66] This relationship was parasitic to the extent that the military superiority of the urban-based elite forced villagers to yield more of their crops or to accept less in return for them than they would have if the two parties had bargained from a position of equal political strength. However, since villager participation was not simply a function of coercion, the relationship cannot be regarded as purely parasitic.

[67] In Mexico the invention of writing preceded the invention of the plow, and the same may also have happened in the Near East. In both instances, however, the societies involved were *highly* advanced horticultural societies, which suggests that the invention of writing is linked with this general stage of technological development. Furthermore, it should be noted that though writing is found in a handful of horticultural societies, it is found in virtually all agrarian.

and commerce, providing small, easily portable objects of high value and in universal demand.[68] No longer need a producer seek out a person desiring the specific goods he had produced, or accept as payment goods for which he had no personal use or ready customers. With the development of monetary systems, the door was opened to the emergence of the specialized role of merchant and middleman.

Besides facilitating the movement of goods and increasing the volume of trade and commerce, money also proved extremely significant from the standpoint of distribution and social control. Where money is not known, there are severe limits on capital accumulation and hence on social inequality. As one writer put it, "when wealth began to be measured in the compact and imperishable medium of silver, these limits were removed. The wealthy could store up all the silver they could amass for as long as they liked."[69] Furthermore, with the development of monetary systems, debts could be extended further and moneylending could provide yet another instrument for controlling the peasants and separating them from the surplus they produced.[70] Though this was not the intent of those who devised the first monetary systems, it proved a highly rewarding by-product for the privileged classes.

It would be a mistake to suppose, however, that money entered into the daily life of the average agrarian society with anything like the frequency evident in modern industrial societies. On the contrary, in the rural areas especially, the use of money was an infrequent experience, particularly for peasants.[71]

Writing, like money, initially developed as a response to the increasingly complex economic problems faced by the urban classes in early agrarian societies.[72] If contemporary archaeologists are correct, it had its origin in the efforts of Sumerian priests to keep an accurate set of records of the numerous business transactions in which their temples were engaged. Like money, however, it soon became an instrument of social control as well as an aid to business enterprise. In particular, it provided a means of increasing the efficiency of systems of political administration.[73] In fact, it has become the foundation of every true bureaucracy.

---

[68] For a good brief review of the origin and early diffusion of monetary systems see either Turner, pp. 263–265, or A. T. Olmstead, pp. 186–191.

[69] A. Andrewes, *The Greek Tyrants* (New York: Harper Torchbooks, 1963), p. 82.

[70] *Ibid.*

[71] See, for example, Cowell, pp. 95ff. on Roman society in the third century B.C.; Pirenne, pp. 102–106 on medieval Europe; or Takekoshi, vol. I, pp. 74 and 95 on eighth-century Japan.

[72] For an excellent discussion of the origin of writing, see Childe, *Man*, pp. 143ff. See also footnote 67 above.

[73] See Turner, p. 315.

Writing also served to widen the traditional gulf between the ruling classes and the common people by introducing a major cultural distinction between the literate minority and the illiterate majority.[74] In agrarian societies *limited literacy* was the rule, a pattern setting these societies apart from both preliterate horticultural societies and largely literate industrial ones. As a result, the cultural unity of agrarian societies was seriously weakened, and a divided cultural tradition emerged. On the one hand there was what one historian has called "the high intellectual tradition," which included the sacred literature of the dominant faith, together with the great works of philosophy and literature, standards of honor and etiquette, and all other elements which were a part of the life of the literate minority.[75] Contrasted with this was "the low intellectual tradition" of the common people, filled with practical matters of peasant technology, primitive superstition, and characterized by a highly parochial view of the world. The high intellectual tradition tended to be a common denominator uniting the privileged classes in all parts of the nation; the low intellectual tradition, by contrast, was usually a divisive force, inculcating a narrow parochialism which viewed with suspicion all that was unfamiliar.[76]

Roughly paralleling the cultural cleavage between the literate minority and the illiterate majority was a second cleavage which divided the urban minority from the rural majority.[77] The way of life in these two types of communities was so very different that those raised in one typically appeared foolish when confronted with even commonplace problems of the other. This gave rise to the often pointed humor about "country bumpkins" who could not find their way about in the city, and "city slickers" who appeared stupid in a rural setting.

Before concluding this brief characterization of agrarian societies, something must be said about *the religious situation*. This is an especially difficult subject to deal with because the differences among societies often appear to loom much larger than any similarities. Sometimes it almost seems that generalizations about religion in agrarian societies are impossible. Compare, for example, the tolerant religious pluralism of the Chi-

[74] In those occasional cases where rulers were not literate, they always employed the services of men who were.
[75] See Turner, pp. 317–323. See also Marc Bloch, chap. 5 and especially p. 77.
[76] For an excellent discussion of the interrelations between these two cultural traditions, see McKim Marriott, "Little Communities in an Indigenous Civilization," in *Village India: Studies in the Little Community* (Chicago: University of Chicago Press, 1955), pp. 171–222. Marriott emphasizes the integrating role of the higher tradition more than the divisive role of the lower.
[77] The parallel was less than perfect because there were always large numbers of illiterate workers in the cities and towns and a small number of literate teachers, officials, priests, landowners, or even prosperous peasants in the rural areas.

nese Empire during parts of its history with the rigorous attitude toward dissent displayed by the leaders of ancient Israel at certain stages, or by most of the Christian and Islamic societies of a later era. Or compare the weakness of the priestly class in China and Rome with the great strength of their counterparts in India or medieval Europe.

Nevertheless, despite such variations, certain patterns have been evident in the great majority of agrarian societies. To begin with, in virtually all of these societies religion was a matter of concern to state authorities. The nature of this concern varied considerably, ranging from cynical maneuvers by rulers seeking to capitalize on the religious commitments of their subjects, to genuine efforts to act in accordance with deeply held personal commitments. In either case, however, the concern led to efforts to harness the powers of religion in the service of the state.

Such efforts usually met with a favorable response on the part of religious leaders, or at least the leaders of the group enjoying political favor. From their standpoint, much could be gained from an alliance or merger of the powers of church and state. Such a relationship assured the group and its leaders a share in the economic surplus and the defense of their interests by the coercive powers of the state.

One of the natural consequences of such developments was the gradual weakening of family and local cults and the simultaneous strengthening of national faiths. These cults seldom disappeared, as evidenced by the survival of the cults of the saints in Catholicism and Eastern Orthodoxy and of cults of household and village godlings in Hinduism; but they were usually incorporated as subsidiary elements in the politically dominant national faith.[78]

One other feature of the religious situation which deserves special attention is the appearance of organized conflict between religious groups, sometimes on a major scale. This is virtually absent in simpler societies. The reasons it developed in agrarian societies are many and varied. In part these conflicts reflected a growing cultural pluralism and diversity which resulted in tensions between ethnic groups, between classes, between countryfolk and city people, and last but not least, between uninspired religious functionaries and their charismatic critics and rivals. Frequently several of these factors worked together to generate religious conflict.

Because of the intimate relations between church and state in agrarian societies, these conflicts usually involved the state and hence the use of coercive measures. In some instances they even led to wars of religion, as in the early history of Islam or in post-Reformation Europe. When

[78] Marriott, *op. cit.*

such conditions prevailed, a man's faith was likely to have profound consequences for his chances of enjoying the rewards of society, sometimes even life itself.

The State, the Ruler, and Social Inequality

One fact impresses itself on almost any observer of agrarian societies, especially on one who views them in a broadly comparative perspective. This is the fact of *marked social inequality*. Without exception, one finds pronounced differences in power, privilege, and honor associated with mature agrarian economies. These differences surpass those found in even the most stratified horticultural societies of Africa and the New World, and far exceed those found in simple horticultural or hunting and gathering societies.

One cannot read very far in the histories of these societies without discovering also that the very unequal distribution of power, privilege, and honor in them arises largely from the functioning of their political systems. To put it more plainly, *in these societies the institutions of government are the primary source of social inequality*.

This is what we should expect, of course, in view of our general theory of stratification and our analysis of the nature of agrarian societies. Given the nature of man and society as defined earlier, we should logically anticipate an increase in social inequality as the economic surplus expands, as military technology advances to the point where the average man can no longer equip himself as well as certain others, and as the powers of the state increase. Furthermore, we should expect that the actions of men of power, who act in the name of the state, would be the primary source of this increase in social inequality.

To understand the nature of the distributive process in agrarian societies, it is essential to understand the nature of the state as viewed by the most influential members of these societies. For them, the state was not merely an organization which defined and enforced the rules in the struggle for power and privilege. It was itself one of the objects of the struggle. In fact, because of the great powers vested in it, it was *the supreme prize* for all who coveted power, privilege, and prestige. To win control of the state was to win control of the most powerful instrument of self-aggrandizement found in agrarian societies. By the skillful exercise of the powers of state, a man or group could gain control over much of the economic surplus, and with it at his disposal, could go on to achieve honor and prestige as well. As a consequence, the one who controlled the state would usually fight to preserve his control, while others would strive either to curry his favor and thus share in his good fortune, or would seek to displace him.

For those accustomed to thinking of political institutions in functionalist terms, this view of agrarian states may seem strange and distorted. However, it is the only view which can make sense out of the most basic elements in the political histories of virtually all agrarian states.[79] In nearly every instance these histories are the record of an almost continuous series of intrigues and struggles for power both within and between states. Furthermore, these struggles were usually between individuals and groups concerned far more with their own partisan advantage than with either the principles of distributive justice or the common good, except in those cases where private advantage and the common good happened to coincide.[80] Although there have been some notable exceptions to this general pattern, they have been just that—exceptions.[81] Nor have they been strikingly frequent.

Probably the best evidence of this is found in the records of the thousands of military campaigns undertaken by the rulers of agrarian states. There is very little in the historical record to indicate that the interests of the common people were seriously considered by those responsible for these wars, or that the common people ever benefited greatly from them, even when their own nation was victorious. Most wars between agrarian states were undertaken by their rulers or ruling classes solely for personal gain or glory or to protect established interests from predatory neighbors.

Similarly, the internal struggles for power, both violent and nonviolent, which plagued most agrarian states, were seldom struggles over principles. Rather, they were struggles between opposing factions of the privileged class, each seeking its own special advantage, or, occasionally, a small segment of the common people seeking political advantage and preferment for themselves. Those involved seldom even claimed to be interested in anything other than personal or factional advantage.[82]

[79] See, for example, Albert H. Lybyer, *The Government of the Ottoman Empire in the Time of Suleiman the Magnificent* (Cambridge, Mass.: Harvard University Press, 1913), p. 147, for an excellent summary of the objectives of one agrarian state. See, also, Turner, pp. 306ff. for a more general treatment of the subject.

[80] For a good illustration of this from European history, see Painter's (*Monarchies*) description of the rise of the monarchies in England, France, and Germany.

[81] The exceptions referred to were the few agrarian political leaders who placed either distributive justice or the common good *consistently* or *usually* ahead of private advantage *in matters of real importance*. Of course, many men found they could afford to be generous in trivial matters, as long as they protected their interests in fundamental ones. Such men were not exceptions to the general pattern.

[82] Classic examples of this are found in the fratricidal struggles which regularly developed in the Mughal Empire on the death of the emperor, and in the many struggles in the Roman Empire which resulted in the assassination of nearly half the occupants of the imperial office.

When one studies the consequences of these struggles, the reason for their frequency is obvious. The capture of the machinery of government, either from without or from within, was a prize that brought fabulous wealth and immense power to the victor.

It is difficult to determine accurately the real extent of the wealth of the rulers of agrarian states of the past, but scattered reports provide clear indication of the immensity of the resources they controlled. In the last decade of the twelfth century and the first decade of the thirteenth, the English Kings Richard I and John had incomes which averaged £24,000 a year (excluding two war years).[83] This was thirty times the income of the wealthiest nobleman of the period, and, in fact, equalled three-fourths of the combined income of all 160 nobles.[84] The King's income also equalled the combined annual incomes of about 24,000 field hands, who at that time were usually paid a penny a day.[85] By the reign of Richard II, at the end of the fourteenth century, English kings averaged £135,000 a year (not counting the year 1380, when there were unusually heavy military expenses).[86] This was almost forty times the income of the richest member of the nobility, and *was equal to 85 per cent of the combined incomes of the nearly 2,200 members of the nobility and squirearchy* as reported in the tax on income in 1436.[87]

The incomes of these early English kings, as great as they were, were small in comparison with the incomes of rulers of greater states. Xerxes, the great Persian emperor of pre-Christian times, is reported to have had an annual income in gold which by current standards would be worth $35 million; Suleiman the Magnificent of Turkey, $421 million; Akbar the Great of India, $120 million; and his successor, Aurangzeb, $270 million.[88] Of course, much of the income of these men was consumed in maintaining the government, suggesting that these figures constitute what a modern businessman would call "gross income" rather than "net income." On the other hand, all of these figures are based on the current cash value of bullion, and therefore, as scholars point out, may be too low as measures of actual purchasing power. Actually, what is important is the relation between the figures involved and others in the same society, not those in

---

[83] Calculated from Sir James H. Ramsay, *A History of the Revenues of the Kings of England: 1066–1399* (Oxford: Clarendon Press, 1925), vol. I, pp. 227 and 261.
[84] Sidney Painter, *Studies in the History of the English Feudal Barony* (Baltimore: Johns Hopkins, 1943), pp. 170–171.
[85] Bennett, p. 121.
[86] Ramsay, vol. II, p. 430.
[87] H. L. Gray, "Incomes from Land in England in 1436," *English Historical Review*, 49 (1934), pp. 614 and 630.
[88] See Olmstead, p. 298 on Xerxes, and Lybyer, pp. 181 and 295, on Suleiman, Akbar, and Aurangzeb. I have adjusted the figures given by these writers of a generation ago to make allowance for recent inflation.

our society today. By this standard, the figures were in every case immense.

A few other examples will help to underline the enormity of the riches available to those in control of the machinery of state in agrarian societies. In sixteenth-century China, a eunuch, Liu Chin, managed to dominate a youthful and inexperienced emperor and turn the vast powers of the Chinese state to his own advantage for several years. In that short span of time he accumulated a fortune which, when recovered, included 240,000 bars of gold, 57,800 pieces of gold, 25,000,000 ounces of silver, three bushels of precious stones, 3,000 gold rings, and various other treasures.[89] The value of this fortune exceeded the total annual budget of the government. History also tells of an eleventh-century emperor of China whose *personal budget* was nearly twice as great as the sum provided for the salaries of all the officials living in the national capital.[90] In late fifteenth- or early sixteenth-century Spain, the king was reputed to enjoy one-third of all the revenues of the land, though the wording of the original statement suggests that what he actually received was one-third of the economic surplus.[91] In eighteenth-century Prussia, the royal estates constituted "no less than one-third of the total arable area," a figure which was matched by the royal estates in neighboring Sweden.[92] Even these figures were surpassed in mid-nineteenth-century Russia, where the crown owned almost half the European territories.[93] Prior to the emancipation of the serfs, 27.4 million men and women were state peasants, whom the czars regarded as their property to dispose of as they wished. This explains how Catherine the Great and her son Paul were able to give away to various court favorites 1,400,000 serfs in the short period from 1762 to 1801 without seriously depleting the resources of the house of Romanov.[94] In our own day the premier of Thailand, the late Marshal Sarit, accumulated an estate valued at $140,000,000 in only ten years, in an agrarian society with an annual per capita income of less than $100.[95]

Of all the great agrarian states of the past, few provided a greater economic return to their masters than the Roman state under the An-

---

[89] Eberhard, p. 261.

[90] *Ibid.*, p. 210. Though the salaries paid by the Chinese government were typically small, this comparison is still impressive.

[91] Jean Hippolyte Mariéjol, *The Spain of Ferdinand and Isabella,* translated and edited by Benjamin Keen (New Brunswick, N.J.: Rutgers University Press, 1961), p. 275.

[92] See A. Goodwin, "Prussia," in A. Goodwin (ed.), *The European Nobility in the Eighteenth Century* (London: Black, 1953), p. 86, and Heckscher, p. 126.

[93] Blum, pp. 476–477 and 492.

[94] *Ibid.*, pp. 356–357.

[95] *New York Times,* July 10, 1964, p. 2.

tonines of the second century. One historian summed up the economic situation of these men this way:

> The emperor's wealth did not consist alone in the accumulated riches of his families or predecessors or in the immense *latifundia* he inherited here and there in Africa and Asia, or in the fact that he everywhere annexed the bulk of all partial or total confiscations decreed by judges. Over and above all this, nothing prevented his replenishing his private purse from the resources of the imperial Exchequer, into which poured the taxes levied for the maintenance of his soldiers, and none dared to suggest an audit of his accounts. He could dispose at will—with no need to render account to any man—of the revenue of Egypt, which was a personal possession of the Crown, and he could plunge open hands into the booty of war. . . . Almost as great a gulf separated him from the plutocrats of Rome as yawned between them and the "middle classes." [96]

To illustrate this last fact, he points out that whereas the wealthy plutocrats often had several thousand personal slaves, the emperor had a "slave family" of 20,000.

To fully understand how these vast accumulations of wealth came into existence, one must take into account *the proprietary theory of the state* which dominated the thinking of most men of power in virtually all agrarian societies. According to this theory, the state is a piece of property which its owner may use, within broad and somewhat ill-defined limits, for his personal advantage.[97] Also, like most other forms of property, it can usually be transmitted to one's heirs. This concept of the state has been well described by Max Weber in his classic analysis of traditional authority.[98]

Guided by the proprietary theory of the state, agrarian rulers saw nothing improper or immoral in the use of what we, not they, would call "public office" for private gain. It was simply a legitimate use of what they commonly regarded, and often called, their "patrimony." For example, as one historian said of the Ptolemies of Egypt, they showed the

---

[96] Jerome Carcopino, *Daily Life in Ancient Rome: The People and the City at the Height of Empire,* translated by E. O. Lorimer (London: Routledge, 1941), p. 68. Quoted by permission.

[97] Robert Bellah argues that I have overstated the case for the proprietary theory of the state and that it was not nearly so widespread as I indicate. I believe our difference stems from reliance on different types of evidence. Clearly many scholars argued that rulers owed duties to their subjects and many rulers at least gave lip service to such principles. The evidence with which I am familiar indicates, however, that most of the practical decisions made by rulers were based on the proprietary theory, and this is why I speak of it "dominating the thinking of most men of power."

[98] See Max Weber, *The Theory of Social and Economic Organization,* translated by A. M. Henderson and Talcott Parsons (New York: Free Press, 1947), pp. 341–348, together with Max Weber, *Wirtschaft und Gesellschaft,* 2d ed. (Tübingen: Mohr, 1925), vol. II, pp. 679–723.

first emperors of Rome "how a country might be run on the lines of a profitable estate." [99] The Ptolemies were by no means unique. Wherever monarchical governments prevailed in agrarian societies (and, as noted above, they were almost universal), the proprietary theory of the state held sway. Of medieval Europe we read:

> The proprietary conception of rulership created an inextricable confusion of public and private affairs. Rights of government were a form of private ownership. "Crown lands" and "the king's estate" were synonymous. There was no differentiation between the king in his private and public capacities. A kingdom, like any estate endowed with elements of governmental authority, was the private concern of its owner. Since "state" and "estate" were identical, "the State" was indistinguishable from the prince and his hereditary personal "patrimony." [100]

William Stubbs, the English constitutional historian, once summarized the position of William the Conqueror thus: "The king of Domesday is the supreme landlord; all the land of the nation, the old folkland, has become the king's; and all private land is held mediately or immediately of him." [101] This same essential pattern is found over and over again in the most widely scattered times and places: in ancient Pharaonic Egypt, in the petty states of Kievan Russia and again after the Tatar yoke was lifted in the Russia of Ivan the Terrible and his successors, in the Ottoman Empire, and in India from the days of Alexander the Great to the Mughal Empire, to cite but a few instances.[102]

In some agrarian societies the records indicate that the king did not make formal claim to ownership of all the land. Some scholars have professed to see great significance in this and have sought to develop the thesis that these societies were basically different from those in which such claims were made. Without denying that such differences are important, it seems far more important to recognize that *all agrarian rulers*

---

[99] Mattingly, p. 137. See also Turner, vol. II, p. 620 or Michael Rostovtzeff, *The Social and Economic History of the Roman Empire*, rev. ed. (Oxford: Clarendon Press, 1957), p. 54, who says of both the Ptolemies and their contemporaries, the Seleucids of Syria, that "they identified their own fortune with that of the state, claiming for themselves the right of property over all its land and all its resources."

[100] See Hans Rosenberg, *Bureaucracy, Aristocracy and Autocracy: The Prussian Experience 1660–1815* (Cambridge, Mass.: Harvard University Press, 1958), p. 506. Quoted by permission.

[101] William Stubbs, *The Constitutional History of England*, 5th ed. (Oxford: Clarendon Press, 1891), vol. I, pp. 282–283. See also J. E. A. Jolliffe, *The Constitutional History of Medieval England* (London: Black, 1937), pp. 139ff.

[102] See, for example, Adolf Erman, *Life in Ancient Egypt*, translated by H. M. Tirard (London: Macmillan, 1894), chap. 4; Blum, pp. 74 and 169, among others on Russia; Lybyer, pp. 28, 120, and 147 on Turkey, or 292 on Mughal India; Kosambi, pp. 200, 215, and 327 or Francois Bernier, *Travels in the Mughal Empire*, quoted by A. K. N. Karin, *Changing Society in India and Pakistan* (Dacca: Oxford University Press, 1956), p. 37, on India.

enjoyed significant proprietary rights in virtually all of the land in their domains. Too often modern polemics and propaganda related to the subject of private property have obscured the fact that *property consists basically of rights, not of things,* particularly of rights to things which are in short supply.[103] If this is true, then agrarian rulers are owners, or part owners, not only of their royal estates and other lands which they lease, assign, or grant as fiefs, but also of all the lands from which they, by right, exact taxes or tribute—especially when they are free to use these revenues for private purposes. They are also, for the same reason, part owners of all the business enterprises they tax.

Our modern difficulty in grasping the true nature of such taxes stems from our tendency to think of proprietary rights as somehow indivisible. Either the peasant-farmer owns the land or the king owns it; they cannot both own it at the same time. This obtuse way of thinking plagued the British during the early years of their colonial administration in Asia and Africa. Well-intentioned officials were often responsible for gross miscarriages of justice when they attempted to systematize and codify native systems of land tenure in either-or terms.[104] This approach fails to do justice to the complexities of land tenure systems and other forms of property ownership both in modern industrial societies and in traditional agrarian. In both cases it is common to find several parties simultaneously enjoying rights to the same piece of property.

While agrarian rulers enjoyed proprietary rights in virtually all the land and businesses in their realm, differences existed in the magnitude of these rights. To begin with, a specific ruler typically enjoyed greater rights with respect to some pieces of property than with respect to others. For example, he usually enjoyed exclusive rights to the economic surplus of crown lands or royal estates, while sharing rights with others in the case of lands which they "owned." [105] In addition, certain rulers enjoyed more extensive rights over the economic surpluses of their realm than other rulers did. We shall shortly have occasion to examine these differences and the factors responsible for them, but the fact such differences

---

[103] See Robin Williams, *American Society* (New York: Knopf, 1951), p. 272, for a good statement of this.

[104] See, for example, W. H. Moreland, *The Agrarian System of Moslem India* (Allahabad: Central Book Depot, n.d.), chap. 6.

[105] A similar situation existed with respect to business enterprise. Sometimes rulers conducted lucrative businesses as royal monopolies, as did the sixteenth- and seventeenth-century czars in Russia, who at various times maintained monopolies in the sale of such things as liquor, sables, grain for export, raw silks, caviar, potash, rhubarb (much valued as a purgative), and walrus tusks (used for knife and whip handles). See Blum, p. 129. See also B. B. Misra, *The Indian Middle Classes* (London: Oxford University Press, 1961), pp. 33–34, for another example of this practice. Usually, however, they have been content to share the profits of business enterprise.

exist should never obscure the far more basic similarity stemming from the almost universal application of the proprietary theory of the state.

The exercise of proprietary rights, through the collection of taxes, tribute money, rents, and services, undoubtedly provided the chief sources of income for most agrarian rulers. However, these sources were often supplemented by others. First and foremost among these was *booty* obtained through foreign conquest. Not every agrarian ruler has been militaristic, and those who were, were not always successful. However, for those who triumphed in military ventures, the rewards were tremendous.

Sulla, the great dictator of republican Rome, provides a good illustration of the possibilities inherent in military campaigns. Though technically not a king or ruler, Sulla exercised virtually all the functions of one, including the appropriation of the fruits of victory. His greatest victories were in Greece and Asia Minor, where he defeated Mithridates, the King of Pontus. As one historian described it, when Sulla returned to Rome "his baggage trains were heavy with loot from the Greek temples, from the sale of captives and from wholesale robbery thinly disguised as an indemnity to the amount of 480,000,000 sesterces inflicted upon the unfortunate inhabitants of the Near East." [106] To appreciate the magnitude of this sum, we only need note that the pay of a common soldier in the Roman legions was but 480 sesterces a year, and a century earlier Cato the Elder had calculated that a field slave could be maintained in working condition for as little as 312 sesterces a year and a free laborer with family could subsist for as little as 1,000 per year.[107] However, Cato had the reputation of being a very careful man with a sesterce, and his calculations may therefore be a bit too low, though probably not by much. Several decades after Sulla's triumph, the wealthy orator and politician, Cicero, expressed the view that a man needed an income of 600,000 sesterces a year to live like a true gentleman, and two centuries later the less affluent poet and satirist, Juvenal, referred to 20,000 sesterces a year as the "vital minimum" necessary to live in comfort and respectability.[108] Even more meaningful than these, however, is a comparison with the total annual revenue of the Roman state itself in this same period. One scholar estimated that two decades after Sulla's victory, the total annual revenue of the Roman government totalled only 202,000,000 sesterces, or less than half of Sulla's booty.[109]

Of course, not all this was clear gain for Sulla, since he incurred many

[106] Cowell, p. 290.
[107] *Ibid.*, pp. 288, 258, and 104–106.
[108] *Ibid.*, p. 110 on Cicero, and Carcopino, p. 66 on Juvenal.
[109] Cowell, p. 386.

obligations in the course of acquiring this vast treasure. Just how great his wealth actually was will never be known, since he firmly refused to render any accounting of the funds, and no man dared challenge him. However, his contemporaries were certain that after his conquests he was, by far, the wealthiest man in all the Roman world. What Sulla did was only what hundreds of other agrarian rulers have done throughout the course of history, a few on an even grander scale.

After his return to Rome, Sulla adopted a second method which agrarian rulers often employed to increase their revenues, that is, *confiscation,* the domestic equivalent of foreign conquest. As in the case of conquest, confiscation involves the forcible appropriation of the property of others. It, too, could prove a lucrative business for powerful rulers, as Sulla clearly demonstrated. Turning on his enemies in Rome with the same vigor he had displayed against the forces of Mithridates, Sulla caused the death of no less than 2,300 members of the wealthy equestrian class and 90 members of the still wealthier senatorial class.[110] Their lands and goods all came under his control and he used them to pay off his obligations to the army that had supported him. If we assume that the average member of the equestrian order was worth 400,000 sesterces (the minimum requirement set by Augustus half a century later), confiscation must have proved even more profitable than foreign conquest.

This act of confiscation by Sulla was not exceptional in the history of agrarian societies. Many other Roman rulers employed it, including Mark Antony and Octavian during their triumvirate, Tiberius, Caligula, Nero, Domitian, Commodus, and Septimus Severus, to name but a few of those who, as one scholar put it, "excelled in this method." [111] Confiscation was also a popular instrument with the czars of Russia. Ivan the Terrible confiscated from the nobles and clergy of his realm estates which covered half the nation.[112] Two centuries later, Catherine the Great confiscated all of the vast church lands in Russia, as did Henry VIII of England and Gustavus Vasa in Sweden in the sixteenth century.[113] The first three of the Tokugawa shoguns who ruled Japan in the seventeenth century left a record which has not often been matched. During their reigns, *each* of these men confiscated from the feudal nobility roughly a third of the total arable land of the country.[114] Various English kings, among

---

[110] Boak, pp. 200–201.
[111] See, for example, Léon Homo, *Roman Political Institutions* (London: Routledge, 1929), p. 258; Cowell, p. 268; or Boak, pp. 244-246, 293, 299, 308, 328, 334, 347, etc.
[112] Blum, p. 145.
[113] *Ibid.,* p. 365; and Heckscher, p. 67.
[114] Takekoshi, vol. II, pp. 26, 227, and 305.

them William II and Henry I, employed the practice frequently, though not nearly so often nor on so grand a scale as the Tokugawa shoguns.[115]

The motives for confiscation were often political rather than economic. In the case of the shoguns, for example, their primary concern seems to have been to destroy the power of the older feudal nobility. This they accomplished by seizing the nobles' land and turning it over to their own kinsmen and followers. Of all the land they confiscated, the shoguns kept slightly less than 10 per cent as their own personal holdings. In general, it appears that *the larger the scale on which confiscations were conducted, the greater the likelihood that the political motive was dominant and the economic motive secondary.*

The Governing Class

Kings and emperors never ruled alone. A small minority always shared the responsibilities of government with them. Though it is usually difficult to identify the precise boundaries of this governing class, it seems safe to say that it rarely contained more than 2 per cent of the population, and sometimes appreciably less. For example, recent research indicates that in nineteenth-century China, the gentry or degree holders, who formed the governing class, totaled about 1.3 per cent of the population in the first half of the century and about 1.9 per cent toward the end.[116] In mid-nineteenth-century Russia the nobility constituted 1.25 per cent of that nation's population.[117] In France, on the eve of the Revolution, the nobility of all ranks and grades constituted only 0.6 per cent, despite the recent influx of many wealthy mercantile families.[118] During the last days of the Roman Republic, the governing class is estimated to have included about 1 per cent of the capital's population, which suggests that the percentage would have been even smaller had the provinces been taken into account.[119] Finally, in seventeenth-century England, peers, baronets, knights, and esquires combined constituted roughly 1 per cent of the total population.[120]

[115] See, for example, Painter, *Barony*, pp. 192–193.
[116] See Chung-li Chang's excellent study, *The Chinese Gentry: Studies in Their Role in Nineteenth-Century Chinese Society* (Seattle, Wash.: University of Washington Press, 1955), p. 164.
[117] Blum, p. 349.
[118] Louis Gottschalk, *The Era of the French Revolution* (Boston: Houghton Mifflin, 1929), p. 47.
[119] Cowell, p. 283.
[120] Calculated from G. E. Aylmer, *The King's Servants: The Civil Service of Charles I* (London: Routledge, 1961), pp. 323 and 331.

The composition of the governing class varied considerably both within and between societies. It included the highest officers of state, such as the personal advisers of the ruler, as well as those whose political influence was limited to a single, small provincial community. It included civil officials as well as military. Many were members of this class solely by virtue of appointment by the present ruler while others were members by right of inheritance, having succeeded to lands or offices which constituted their family patrimony. Some of the former were even slaves, as in the case of the Janissaries of Ottoman Turkey, or recently emancipated freedmen, as in imperial Rome. Finally, the governing class included men of foreign birth, as well as native-born.

Though these differences were important in certain respects, which we shall consider shortly, the similarities were even more important. To begin with, membership in the governing class guaranteed to every individual certain unique opportunities for self-aggrandizement. To be a part of the governing class was to possess the right, acknowledged and supported by the supreme power in the land, to share in the economic surplus produced by the peasant masses and urban artisans. This was their reward for upholding and enforcing the authority of the existing regime in general and the ruler in particular.

The rewards for such services have taken varied forms, but they have always been substantial and, in the case of the ruler's chief ministers, have usually been immense. Frequently rulers granted members of the governing class vast landed estates or the incomes from them. This practice was especially common in those politically centralized states where the rulers had largely succeeded in preventing the establishment of hereditary land rights and where, therefore, estates normally reverted to the throne on the death of the estate holder. Grants of large estates were also common during periods when the ruler had acquired vast new territories through foreign conquest or wholesale confiscation at home. Of course, unless new lands were added through foreign conquest, these grants usually involved no net gain for the governing class as a whole, only a redistribution among its members. From the standpoint of the favored individual, however, it was pure gain.

Over the centuries there have been many instances of lavish grants of this type. One of the most familiar to English-speaking peoples involved William the Conqueror, who divided nearly the whole of England among his chief lieutenants.[121] Similar practices attended most important conquests.[122] In Japan, massive acts of confiscation by the first three Toku-

---

[121] See Painter, *Monarchies*, pp. 44–50.
[122] See, for example, Mariéjol, p. 262, on Spain following the Christian reconquest of the land from the Moors.

gawa shoguns were followed by large-scale grants to several hundred favored individuals and families.[123] In Ottoman Turkey and Mughal India, large grants were common because the rulers had been able to prevent the governing class from establishing hereditary rights to much of the land. Hence, with the death of every member of the governing class, lands reverted to the throne, creating a fresh supply of land for new grants.[124]

In agrarian societies, land grants nearly always carried with them definite political responsibilities. In seventeenth-century Japan, for example, the Tokugawa shogun prepared a formal schedule of military obligations which were incumbent on all holders of feudal estates. Those who had been granted estates of 1,000 koku were required to bring to the battlefield, on demand, twenty-three men, one spare spear, one bow (with arrows), and one gun (with bullets). Those with 1,200 koku were to bring twenty-seven men, three spare spears, one bow, and one gun, those with 1,300 koku, twenty-nine men, three spare spears, one bow, and one gun. This schedule extended to the level of holders of estates with 100,000 koku, who had to furnish 170 mounted men, 350 guns, 60 bows, 150 spare spears, and 20 banners.[125] A similar pattern of variable military obligations prevailed in medieval Europe, Ottoman Turkey, Mughal India, and elsewhere.[126] In addition, those given landed estates were usually expected to provide the basic elements of civil government, notably the maintenance of law and order and the collection of taxes, on their properties.[127] In short, land grants were essentially a form of appointment to governmental office.

Appointments to office did not always take this form. For various reasons they were often divorced from feudal-style land grants, especially in technologically advanced agrarian societies where money was more plentiful. Political appointment remained a lucrative reward, however, despite the fact that the salaries were usually small. Agrarian officials were always skillful in finding alternative methods of obtaining income from their posts.

[123] Takekoshi, vol. II, pp. 26, 227, 305.
[124] On Turkey, see Lybyer, chap. 2 and also pp. 82–89, 100–103, and 114–120, or Mercia Macdermott, A History of Bulgaria (London: G. Allen, 1962), pp. 26–27. On Mughal India, see Lybyer, pp. 285–286 and 297, or Moreland, pp. 9–12 and especially 92–100 and 205–206.
[125] Takekoshi, vol. II, pp. 20–21.
[126] See, for example, Bloch, pp. 220-221, or Pierre Caron, "The Army," in Arthur Tilley (ed.), Medieval France (London: Cambridge University Press), pp. 154ff. on Europe; Lybyer, pp. 100–103, or Macdermott, p. 27 on Turkey; or Lybyer, pp. 285–287, or Moreland, pp. 92–100 on India.
[127] See, for example, Blum, pp. 428ff. on Russia; Rosenberg, p. 30 on Prussia; Bennett, chap. 8 on England; Mariéjol, p. 273 on Spain; Edith M. Link, The Emancipation of the Austrian Peasant, 1740–1798 (New York: Columbia University Press, 1949), pp. 14 and 18 on Austria; or Lybyer, p. 100 on Turkey.

A favorite source of such income in virtually every agrarian society was the sale of justice. There seem to have been few agrarian societies where his was not a common practice.[128] In imperial Rome it was so widespread at one point that Constantine the Great was driven to write, "Let the grasping hands of the officials forthwith refrain, let them refrain I say, for unless after this warning they do refrain, they will be cut off by the sword. Let not the *velum* of the judge be for sale, admission purchased, the *secretarium* infamous with rival bids, the very sight of the governor [who rendered judgment] at a price. . . . Let the depredations of him who is called *princeps of the officium* [i.e., bureau chief] be removed from the opening of a case. Let the *adjutor* of the same *princeps of the officium* [a subofficial] make no extortion from the litigants. Let the intolerable assaults of centurions and other officials demanding small sums and great be repulsed. Let the insatiable greed of those who give back the record of the case to the litigants be moderated." [129] Apparently almost every official involved in the judicial process was demanding a fee or gratuity. It is no wonder that the common people of China, faced with a similar situation, developed the saying, "To enter a court of justice is to enter a tiger's mouth." [130]

Not only was justice for sale, but so were other powers of government vested in the hands of officials. Governmental officials often refused to act unless the parties concerned were willing to make it personally advantageous to them to act. One can get some idea of the frequency of such practices from the experience of Cicero, who served for a time as proconsul in the large province of Cilicia. Unlike his predecessors, he refused bribes, a practice which left the natives, in Cicero's own words, "speechless with astonishment." [131] He wrote that it was all he could do to prevent the grateful inhabitants from erecting temples and statues in his honor. Because of his honesty, Cicero was able to accrue "only" 2,200,000 sesterces during his year as proconsul in Cilicia.[132]

---

[128] See, for example, Micah 3:7 and 7:3 on ancient Israel, or other references in Isaiah, Amos, and Psalms. On ancient Egypt, see Turner, p. 311. On the Roman Empire, see A. H. M. Jones, *Studies in Roman Government and Law* (Oxford: Blackwell, 1960), pp. 170–171; on England, see Philip Lindsay and Reg Groves, *The Peasants' Revolt, 1381* (London: Hutchinson, n.d.), p. 21; on Spain, see Mariéjol, pp. 171ff.; on ancient Persia, Olmstead, p. 129; on India, W. H. Moreland, "The Revenue System of Mughal India," in *The Cambridge History of India*, vol. 4, p. 453; on China, see Robert K. Douglas, *Society in China* (London: Innes, 1894), chap. 2, or Morton Fried, *The Fabric of Chinese Society: A Study of the Social Life of a Chinese County Seat* (New York: Frederick A. Praeger, 1953), pp. 65–66, to cite but a few of the countless references to this practice.

[129] Jones, *ibid*. Quoted by permission.

[130] Douglas, p. 104.

[131] Cowell, pp. 292–293.

[132] *Ibid*., p. 294.

Earlier in his career, Cicero had seen how lucrative the business of office holding could be. In the year 70 B.C., he served as advocate for the cities of Sicily, which charged the former Roman propraetor, Verres, with numerous crimes committed while in office.[133] In the course of the trial it was revealed that in a three-year term of office Verres had looted the province of 40,000,000 sesterces, by every use and abuse of political power imaginable. One historian described his methods in this way:

> By initiating false accusation, by rendering, or intimidating other judges to render, unjust decisions, he secured the confiscation of property, the value of which he diverted to his own pockets. He sold justice to the highest bidder. While saving himself expense by defrauding the collectors of port dues of the tax on his valuables shipped out of Sicily, he added to his profits by the sale of municipal offices and priesthoods. He entered into partnership with the *decumani* or collectors of the 10 per cent produce tax and ordered the cultivators to pay whatever the collector demanded and then, if dissatisfied, seek redress in his court, a redress which, needless to say, was never gained. He loaned public funds at usurious rates of interest and either did not pay in full or paid nothing for corn purchased from the Sicilian communities for the Roman government, while charging the state the market price. At the same time he insisted upon the cities commuting into money payments at rates far above current prices the grain allotted for the upkeep of the governor's establishment. At times the demands made upon cultivators exceeded the total of their annual crop, and in despair they fled from their holdings. To the money gained by such methods Verres added a costly treasure of works of art, which he collected from both individuals and cities by theft, seizure, and intimidation. Even the sacred ornaments of the temples were not spared.[134]

Those who opposed him are reported to have been subjected to imprisonment, torture, and execution. According to Cicero, Verres kept his jails so full and his executioner so busy that one of his lieutenants amassed a small fortune from the friends and relatives of prisoners in return for granting small favors, such as a painless execution.[135] Though his actions were technically a violation of the charter granted to Sicily by the Roman senate, the governing class of Rome was largely indifferent to his actions. As the same historian summarized the case, "The sad truth was that after all Verres was only more shameless and unscrupulous than the average provincial governor, and consequently the sympathies of the Senate were with him rather than with his victims, the provincials." [136]

Neither Cicero nor Verres appears to have been typical of the office holders in either the Roman government or other agrarian governments.

[133] For a good short summary of this trial, see Boak, pp. 210–212.
[134] *Ibid.*, p. 212. Quoted by permission.
[135] Jones, p. 154.
[136] Boak, p. 212.

Verres was greedier than most, Cicero more principled. The great majority apparently were not extortioners, as was Verres, but rather were content to limit themselves to what American politicians have sometimes called "honest graft." While not easy to define, basically the term refers to illegal gains by officials which they and others (or at least other officials) do not usually condemn on moral grounds. For example, Sir Francis Bacon apparently regarded himself as an "honest grafter": when accused of accepting bribes, he insisted that he only accepted gifts or gratuities for doing what he would have done in any case! [137]

Though extortion may have been infrequent, "honest graft" appears to have been extremely common. In describing the traditional pattern of government in the German principalities before the rise of Prussian absolutism, for example, one writer refers to "the matter-of-course confusion of public business with private enterprise." [138] On the basis of a thorough study of the income of Chinese officials in the nineteenth century, Chung-li Chang concluded that income from irregular sources, i.e., both "honest graft" and extortion, "totalled *about nineteen times as much as the regular income*" derived from salary and expense money provided by the government.[139] This is, of course, only an estimate, and it applies only to a single society in a single century. It is a highly informed estimate, however, and evidence from other societies and other centuries strongly suggests that irregular sources of income were normally much greater than regular sources.[140]

Given the highly lucrative character of public office, such positions came to be regarded as a very profitable resource. From there it was but a simple step to the conception of public office as a commodity, available for a price. The sale of office was extremely widespread in agrarian societies. In fact, there seem to have been few which totally avoided the problem, though many did so for a part of their history. Offices were openly sold at various times in England, France, Prussia, Spain, Rome, the Byzantine Empire, the Ottoman Empire, China, Japan, and undoubtedly many others.[141]

[137] Aylmer, p. 179.
[138] Rosenberg, p. 54.
[139] Chung-li Chang, *The Income of the Chinese Gentry* (Seattle, Wash.: University of Washington Press, 1962), p. 42. Italics added.
[140] Only a narrow specialist in Roman history could claim, as one has done, that the *Romans* had a peculiar talent for "illicit exactions."
[141] See, for example, Aylmer, pp. 225–239 or Cecil Woodham-Smith, *The Reason Why* (New York: McGraw-Hill, 1953), especially pp. 25–29 on England; Elinor Barber, *The Bourgeoisie in 18th Century France* (Princeton, N.J.: Princeton University Press, 1955), pp. 106–116, or R. Mousnier, *La Vénalité des offices sous Henri IV et Louis XIII* (Rouen: Éditions Maugard, 1945) in France; Rosenberg, pp. 77–80 on Prussia; Roger B. Merriman, *The Rise of the Spanish Empire* (New York: Macmillan, 1934),

The sale of office has taken many forms, and has had varied significance.[142] In some cases, the ruler himself was the seller and this was
simply another method of adding to his personal income. In other cases
the seller was a royal favorite or leading minister of state, the head of the
department or subdepartment involved, the current occupant of the office,
the former occupant's heirs or executors, or the holder of a prior claim
who was surrendering his rights. Frequently the spread of this practice
indicated inefficient administration or a weakening of royal power, but
not always. For example, Cecil Woodham-Smith developed a convincing
case for the thesis that the spread of the purchase system in the British
army after the Restoration was a deliberate device to keep top military
offices out of the hands of ambitious adventurers who might again seek to
overthrow the existing regime.[143]

Only a small minority of the governing class ever benefited directly
from important offices in the *central* government. In nineteenth-century
China, for example, only 1.6 per cent of the gentry held office in the central government at any given time.[144] One might possibly add to this
figure the 1.1 per cent of the gentry who were secretarial assistants to the
officials.[145] If allowance is made for the delays encountered in entering
office and for the turnover of men in office, it seems probable that only
5 to 10 per cent of the gentry served as officials or secretarial assistants in
the central government at any point in their career.[146] Such figures are
similar to those reported for seventeeth-century England. According to the
estimate of a scholar who has studied the problem intensively, 3 to 6 per
cent of Englishmen of the rank of gentleman or above held office in the
central government during one seventeen-year period.[147]

---

vol. III, p. 193, and vol. IV, pp. 204, 217, 324, 438-439, and 463 on Spain; Homo, p.
358, or Jones, p. 156 on Rome; Jones, pp. 169–170, or Glanville Downey, *Constantinople: In the Age of Justinian* (Norman, Okla.: University of Oklahoma Press, 1960),
p. 66 on the Byzantine Empire; Lybyer, pp. 115–116 and 179 on Ottoman Turkey;
Douglas, pp. 33–35, or Chang, *The Chinese Gentry*, pp. 5, 29–30, and 115 on China;
or Takekoshi, vol. I, p. 141 and vol. II, pp. 454–456 on Japan.

[142] For a good discussion of this point, see Alymer, p. 227.
[143] Woodham-Smith, pp. 25–29.
[144] Chang, *Income*, p. 42.
[145] *Ibid.*, p. 86.
[146] Robert Marsh's study of Chinese officials during the Ch'ing, or Manchu, Dynasty
indicates a median length of official careers as twenty-five years, but his sample of
officials includes only those who achieved sufficient fame to be recorded in standard
biographies. See *The Mandarins: The Circulation of Elites in China, 1600–1900*
(New York: Free Press, 1961), p. 165. This view is supported by Hsiao-Tung Fei's
statement that "officials did not . . . like to continue as officials for a long period.
Their purpose in entering the government was to gain immunity [from taxes] and
wealth in that order." In short, they aimed to become gentlemen landowners. See
China's Gentry (Chicago: University of Chicago Press, 1953), p. 32.
[147] Calculated from Aylmer, p. 324.

Those not fortunate enough to hold office in the central government were usually involved, officially or unofficially, in the governing process at the local level. Chung-li Chang estimated that at any given time about two-thirds of the gentry in nineteenth-century China derived a portion of their income from such activities. Furthermore, the total income from this source equaled the income from offices in the central government. Because it was divided among so many more individuals, however, the average income from this source was much less. Whereas the average income from offices in the central government was more than 5,000 taels per year, the average from local offices was only a little more than 100 taels per year. Though the latter figure was quite modest in comparison with the former, it should be noted that the average annual income of those outside the governing class was only 20 to 25 taels per family.[148]

Another major source of income for the Chinese gentry was landownership. Chang estimates that approximately one-quarter of all the arable land of China was owned by the gentry in the late nineteenth and early twentieth centuries. From this land they typically received 40 to 50 per cent of the proceeds as rent (from which they paid taxes and other expenses). The rate of return on investments in land was never terribly high, ranging from a figure of 10 per cent before taxes in the late eighteenth century to a mere 4 per cent in the late nineteenth. Because of the size of the landholdings and the number of persons involved, however, the total net income from landownership seems to have equaled the total income from offices in both the central and local governments, even in the late nineteenth century. If the total income from landownership had been divided equally among the 1,443,000 heads of gentry families in this period, it would have yielded an average income of 150 taels per year before taxes or 120 taels after taxes. Since some members of the gentry did not own landed estates, the average return for those who did was probably nearer 200 taels before taxes and 150 after.[149]

Members of the governing class often assumed special privileges denied other landowners. For example, in nineteenth-century China they evaded, or were exempted from, the payment of so many taxes that their rate was considerably less than that of commoners.[150] The economic pressures on the latter were so great that sometimes they were driven to registering their lands under the names of members of the gentry, a prac-

---

[148] Most of the information above is from Chang, *Income*, chap. 2. This is supplemented by information from pp. 42 and 327. This study is unique in the wealth of detailed, systematic documentation it provides on the distributive process in an agrarian society. This is the reason I have made such extensive use of it in this area.
[149] *Ibid.*, especially chap. 5.
[150] *Ibid.*, pp. 328–329. See also pp. 133–136.

tice which frequently resulted in the eventual loss of their land.[151] Another advantage enjoyed by the gentry was that the government would normally enforce their claims to unpaid rent, a practice not followed in the case of other landlords.[152] In short, landownership was usually much more profitable for members of the governing class than for others.

Last, but not least, certain of the Chinese gentry derived income from mercantile activities. It has sometimes been argued that members of the governing classes of agrarian societies viewed mercantile activities with contempt. On critical inspection, this turns out to be a half-truth. While it is true that petty mercantile activities were regarded as degrading, as one student of the French nobility put it, "big financial transactions are always respectable." [153] This was also the case in nineteenth-century China, where a small fraction of the governing class tended to monopolize the most lucrative forms of private enterprise. Favorite fields included the salt trade and foreign trade (both government-regulated monopolies), banking, and moneylending.[154] Less than 1 per cent of the gentry seem to have been engaged in mercantile activities, but they enjoyed such fabulous profits that the total income from this source appears to have nearly equaled the income from offices in the central government and was roughly half of the gross income from landownership. The average *net* income from this source seems to have been over 11,000 taels per year.[155]

Taking all the various sources of income together, Chang estimates that the Chinese portion of the governing class [156] of China received about 645,000,000 taels per year in the late nineteenth century, or 24 per cent of the gross national product. This averaged out to not quite 450 taels per family head, a figure which, as noted before, may be compared with an average income of 20 to 25 taels per family for the rest of the society. Within the governing class there were, of course, immense variations in income. Some, such as the chief officers of state, appear to have received 200,000 taels or more per year, while those on the lower margins of the governing class (such as members of declining families wholly dependent upon small farms) probably had little more than the national average.[157]

Owing to the paucity of systematic data, it is difficult to determine

[151] *Ibid.*, p. 134.
[152] *Ibid.*, pp. 130-131.
[153] J. McManners, "France," in A. Goodwin (ed.), *The European Nobility in the Eighteenth Century* (London: Black, 1953), p. 37.
[154] The critical reader of Chang's study may wonder whether he has made sufficient allowance for moneylending, especially as an adjunct of normal landowning. See, for example, Morton Fried, pp. 125-126.
[155] Chang, *Income*, chap. 6.
[156] He excludes the Manchu segment from his analysis.
[157] *Ibid.*, Summary Remarks, supplement 2, and chap. 1.

just how typical, or atypical, these figures for nineteenth-century China are. Obviously variations existed within and between societies, both with respect to the proportion of the total national income taken by the governing class and the methods by which it was taken. One other source to which we can turn for comparable data is G. E. Aylmer's study of the civil service under Charles I of England, in the second quarter of the seventeenth century.[158] On the basis of various evidence from the period, Aylmer concludes that the governing class (men of the rank of esquire or above), who then constituted about 1 per cent of the English population, received about 24 per cent of the total national income in the form of receipts from their estates; in addition they seem to have received at least another 6 per cent of the national income from other sources.[159] This may be compared with Chang's estimate that the Chinese portion of that country's governing class, which comprised 1.9 per cent of the population, received 24 per cent of the national income.

This latter figure probably understates the governing class's share of the national income for the nineteenth century, and probably even more for the eighteenth. First, Chang's figures exclude the Manchu segment of the governing class, while including some rather marginal Chinese. If the former were included and the latter excluded, one would probably find that the top 1.5 per cent of the population received at least 30 per cent of the national income. Second, Chang himself reports that there was a substantial decline in the return on investments in land from the late eighteenth to the late nineteenth century.[160] In the earlier period land had usually yielded a 10 per cent return while in the later period this had dropped to a mere 4 per cent. Thus, eighteenth-century figures would have been closer to the British pattern reported by Aylmer than nineteenth-century figures. On the basis of available data, it appears that *the governing classes of agrarian societies probably received at least a quarter of the national income of most agrarian states, and that the governing class and ruler together usually received not less than half.* In some instances their combined income may have approached two-thirds of the total. These conclusions are based not only on analyses of the income of the political elite, but even more on analyses of the taxes and other obligations of the common people in a large number of societies (see pp. 267–270).

---

[158] Aylmer, *op. cit.*, especially pp. 322–336.

[159] *Ibid.*, pp. 323 and 331. Evidence presented by Aylmer indicates that they received between £500,000 and £700,000 from offices in the central government, and it seems safe to assume that they had an equal income from other sources. I am also assuming that the average family in the governing class had five members at this time and that the total population of England was 4.5 million.

[160] Chang, *Income*, pp. 138–139.

As the foregoing has shown, landownership and public office clearly were the two chief sources of income for the governing class. One might suppose, therefore, that they were simply two alternative means to the same end. However, this was not the case. In general, *landownership, when divorced from public office, was valued chiefly as a means to obtain prestige and economic security, while public office was used primarily for political and economic advancement.*

If this distinction has not always been clear to modern scholars, it was to those who lived in agrarian societies. Their writings bear repeated testimony to the validity of this principle. For example, one seventeenth-century English gentleman put it this way:

> It is impossible for a mere country gentleman ever to grow rich or raise his house. He must have some vocation with his inheritance, as to be a courtier, lawyer, merchant or some other vocation. If he hath no other vocation, let him get a ship and judiciously manage her, or buy some auditor's place, or be vice-admiral in his county. By only following the plough he may keep his word and be upright, but will never increase his fortune.[161]

Similar views have been expressed by Chinese writers.[162]

In this connection it seems appropriate to make explicit one point which has been implicit in much of the foregoing. In agrarian societies, wealth could often be converted into political power and vice versa, but, unlike modern capitalistic societies, it was easier to use political power to obtain wealth than the reverse. Robert Heilbroner, the economist and economic historian, formulated the relationship quite well when he stated that *"in pre-market societies* [among which he includes agrarian societies], *wealth tends to follow power; not until the market society will power tend to follow wealth."* [163]

Before concluding this examination of the governing classes of agrarian societies, it is necessary to take note of one important variable characteristic. In some societies, as in most of early medieval Europe, this class was made up wholly or largely of the members of a feudal nobility whose power and privilege rested on their membership in a hereditary legal class. In other societies, such as the Roman, Byzantine, Ottoman, and Chinese Empires at the peak of their powers, the governing class consisted to a great degree of bureaucratic officials whose power rested on their occu-

---

[161] Sir John Oglander, quoted by H. R. Trevor-Roper, *The Gentry 1540–1640,* in *The Economic History Review Supplements,* No. 1 (n.d.), p. 26. See also, pp. 11–12 and 25–34. Quoted by permission.

[162] See, for example, Chang, *Income,* p. 127.

[163] *The Making of Economic Society* (Englewood Cliffs, N.J.: Prentice-Hall, 1962), p. 27. See also, Trevor-Roper, p. 50, or Bloch, who writes of "that age when true wealth consisted in being the master" (p. 192).

pancy of offices which were not usually inheritable and who did not constitute a legally defined class. In still other societies, both elements were present and important. In effect, therefore, one may speak of a *bureaucracy-nobility continuum* which measures the relative importance of these two elements within the governing class.

The most important determinant of the location of societies on this continuum seems to have been their degree of technological advance, especially in the areas of transportation and communication. It seems no coincidence that hereditary nobilities were generally stronger in the earlier periods in most societies. Thus they were relatively strong in early Chou China, republican Rome, and early medieval Europe, while bureaucracies tended to be stronger at later stages in these same societies, as in late Ch'ing China, imperial Rome, and absolutist Europe. *Bureaucracy, being a centralized mode of government, presupposes a certain degree of efficiency in transportation and communication, and when a society lacked this, the more decentralized, feudal mode of government was likely to develop.*

A second relevant factor or set of factors were the various forces which were capable of creating political chaos and anarchy. *Anything which weakened the orderly processes of government, tended to favor the feudal elements at the expense of the bureaucratic.* The classic illustration of this is the decline and fall of Roman government in Western Europe under the combined impact of barbarian pressures from without and crises and divisions within.

A third factor which also seems to have been involved was the power of the ruler relative to the power of the governing class. *Where rulers were strong, they were usually able to strengthen the bureaucracy at the expense of the nobility, a course which they generally favored since the bureaucrats, with their limited tenure, seemed more amenable to royal control.* Thus the strength of the bureaucratic element in the governing class tended to be correlated with the position of the society on the autocracy-oligarchy continuum to be discussed below (see page 234).

The position of a society on the bureaucracy-nobility continuum undoubtedly had consequences for many aspects of its life. Obviously it was of great importance for the ruler and for those in or near the governing class, but it is not clear that it greatly affected the lives of the common people, the peasants, the artisans, the untouchables, and the expendables. This is an important problem, however, and deserves far more careful and systematic study than it has yet received.

Rulers versus Governing Classes: Variable Patterns and Their Causes

Throughout the history of every agrarian society there has been an almost continuous struggle for power between the ruler and the governing class.[164] Though the outward form of these struggles has been highly variable, their basic character has always been the same: each party has constantly fought to maximize its own rights and prerogatives.

In such a struggle, the ruler's ultimate objective was to make the enjoyment of power and privilege by members of the governing class directly dependent upon the performance of services to the crown and the ruler's continuing favor. Practically, this meant that he sought to deny the existence of inherent or inalienable rights on the part of members of this class and attempted to establish a highly autocratic government.

Members of the governing class, for their part, constantly sought to infringe upon the rights of the ruler, with the ultimate objective of reducing him to the level of a *primus inter pares,* or first among equals. To this end, they constantly sought, as rewards for their service, *rights which would not terminate with the completion of their period of service, and rights which could not be abrogated simply at the pleasure or caprice of the ruler.*

Since land (including the peasants on it) and office were the chief economic resources in agrarian societies, the most important struggles between rulers and governing classes involved the issue of their control. One of the best available indicators of the outcomes of these contests is evidence pertaining to the relative distribution of rights to these two resources.

Even a cursory examination of agrarian societies reveals that the distribution of these rights was one of their more variable features. At one extreme, there were a few agrarian societies in which the rulers succeeded for a time in preventing the governing class from establishing anything more than minimal rights with respect to offices and land. This occurred in both Ottoman Turkey and Mughal India during the reigns of the more vigorous and intelligent rulers, such as Suleiman and Akbar.[165] Under such rulers, most of the land and offices were distributed by the ruler for

---

[164] For an excellent description of such struggles in medieval Europe, see Painter, *Monarchies.* For a more detailed picture, see Painter, *Barony.*

[165] See, for example, Lybyer on Ottoman Turkey or *The Cambridge History of India,* or Moreland on Mughal India.

lifetime tenure only, and were subject to instant confiscation should the services of the holder become unsatisfactory. In India, members of the governing class were often discouraged from living on the lands assigned them, and were instead encouraged to reside at the royal court, while managers chosen by the ruler supervised their estates and transmitted the revenues to them. Furthermore, the lands assigned them were frequently shifted about, with the result that personal attachments to estates and proprietary tendencies were held to a minimum. In short, their rights consisted of little more than the right to a salary which could be terminated at any time. On the death of an official, most of his property was subject to confiscation.[166]

One Dutch traveler of the early seventeenth century left a vivid picture of conditions then prevailing in India. He wrote:

> Immediately on the death of a lord who has enjoyed the King's *jagir*, be he great or small, without any exception—sometimes even before the breath is out of the body—the King's officers are ready on the spot, and make an inventory of the entire estate, recording everything down to the value of a single piece, even to the dresses and jewels of the ladies, provided they have not concealed them. The King takes back the whole estate absolutely for himself, except in a case where the deceased has done good service in his lifetime, when the women and children are given enough to live on, but no more. . . . And so you may see a man whom you knew with his turban cocked on one side, and nearly as unapproachable as his master, now running about with a torn coat and a pinched face; for it is rarely that such men obtain similar employment from other masters, and they go about like pictures of death in life, as I have known many of them to do.[167]

In Turkey, conditions were even worse in one respect: a major portion of the governing class, including the highest officers of state, were legally slaves of the sultan, thus underlining their total dependence on his pleasure.[168]

Needless to say, most members of the governing class were not satisfied with such one-sided arrangements and efforts were made to alter them. One of the first rights sought was lifetime possession of one's estate or, better yet, lifetime tenure plus the right to transmit it to one's heir as a family patrimony. Even in such highly centralized and autocratic states as Ottoman Turkey and Mughal India, rulers found it difficult to resist the constant pressures from the governing class. Thus, in Turkey, for example,

---

[166] See Moreland, pp. 92–100, for a good summary of this system.
[167] F. Pelsaert, *Jahangir's India*, translated by W. H. Moreland and P. Geyl and quoted by Misra, p. 47. Quoted by permission.
[168] Lybyer, pp. 47–58 and 115–117.

the hereditary principle was gradually extended until eventually there developed a noble class not too different from that in Europe.[169]

At the opposite extreme from Ottoman Turkey and Mughal India was a handful of republican states without a monarchy. As noted previously, republican government usually developed only under marginal conditions and was seldom present in major agrarian states. Thus republican governments existed in certain early states in India and Russia, in remote mountainous areas such as Switzerland, and in agrarian states in transition to an industrial order, as in contemporary Latin America. The only instance in which this type of government flourished in a major agrarian state before the Industrial Revolution was in Rome, where it survived until the last century of the pre-Christian era.

Turning from these extremes, we find some of the best examples of domination by the governing class in medieval Europe, where the rights of rulers were usually minimal. As one historian put it, "The medieval state was a loose agglomeration of territories with rights of property and sovereignty everywhere shading into one another." [170] Though the landed estates of the governing class had often been obtained in exchange for a pledge of service to the royal house, such pledges frequently became unenforceable. Lands acquired by royal grants often became virtually sovereign territories, the patrimony of some noble family. The rights of the ruler, under such circumstances, were reduced to the occasional performance of military obligations and payment of taxes by his vassals. Even these were obtained only by rulers strong enough to enforce them.[171] Even the kingly office itself was, on occasion, made elective.

Though examples can be found of both extremes, i.e., rulers dominating the governing class and vice versa, the evidence suggests that the total distribution of cases resembles a somewhat flattened type of normal curve, with the cases in the intermediate range substantially outnumbering the more extreme ones. In other words, in the modal case the powers of the ruler and of the governing class would be fairly evenly balanced, with neither dominating the other. This pattern apparently prevailed during much of Chinese, Roman, and Japanese history, and most of the postmedieval period in European societies, to cite a few of the more familiar cases. It should be noted, however, that in all of these societies there were substantial shifts over the years, with the ruler tending to dominate at certain times, and the governing class at others. Nevertheless, even these

[169] *Ibid.*, p. 120.
[170] Thompson, p. 699.
[171] There are many accounts of this period and the process by which royal rights were lost; for one of the better accounts see Bloch, especially chaps. 14 and 24. See also Painter, and Blum, chap. 2.

variations seldom reached the extremes of what might be called the "autocracy-oligarchy continuum."[172]

Ever since the days of the early Greek philosophers, political theorists have sought to understand why agrarian societies vary in this way. As a result of their efforts, it seems today that no single factor is capable of explaining either the variation itself, or the tendency toward clustering in the middle range.

One modern scholar, however, has held out against a pluralistic approach, and still insists upon what is essentially a one-factor explanation. Karl Wittfogel, author of the provocative volume, *Oriental Despotism*, seeks to revive the thesis propounded by Marx and Lenin, among others, that autocracy prevails in those areas where governments are obliged to promote large scale irrigation systems, while feudalism, a form of oligarchy, prevails where this is not necessary.[173] To make the theory fit certain inconsistent facts, Wittfogel introduces a second variable, namely diffusion, which he invokes to explain the presence of autocratic governments in countries such as Russia, Greece, Rome, and Spain, where large scale water works have been absent.[174] However, diffusion is of secondary importance, according to Wittfogel, as evidenced by the tendency of governments in these countries to regress toward the feudal pattern.

Unfortunately, as critics have pointed out, it takes more than the principle of diffusion to make this intriguing, but highly oversimplified, theory fit the facts.[175] The power of rulers in "hydraulic" Asia was not nearly so consistently autocratic, nor autocracy so absent from western Europe and Japan as Wittfogel argues.[176] For example, though Louis XIV of France probably never said, "L'état c'est moi," he could have said

---

[172] It is difficult to find, for the two ends of this continuum, labels which are not already overburdened with irrelevant or misleading connotations. The terms "autocracy" and "oligarchy" seem the best available for present purposes. As indicated, the continuum refers simply to variations in the relative power of the ruler and the governing class. The idea of such a continuum seems implicit in Weber's distinction between "sultanism" and "ständische Herrschaft," or "decentralized authority," as this has been translated into English (see *Theory*, pp. 347ff.). The distinction is also fairly similar to Wittfogel's distinction between "despotic" and "feudal" societies [see *Oriental Despotism: A Comparative Study of Total Power* (New Haven, Conn.: Yale University Press, 1957)], though he tends to minimize the idea of a continuum while blending this distinction with the bureaucracy-nobility distinction noted earlier.

[173] See especially chaps. 1 and 2 of *Oriental Despotism*.

[174] *Ibid.*, chap. 6.

[175] See, for example, Wolfram Eberhard, *Conquerors and Rulers: Social Forces in Medieval China* (Leiden: Brill, 1952), chap. 2, or Eberhard's review of *Oriental Despotism*, in *American Sociological Review*, 23 (1958), pp. 446–448.

[176] See, for example, the rights of English kings to exact relief, i.e., payments for the privilege of inheriting a fief. These payments were often set so high as to remind one of the autocratic practices of the Turkish sultans and Mughal emperors. See, for example, Painter, *Monarchies*, pp. 50–57 and 67–69, or *Barony*, pp. 56–64.

it more truthfully than most of the later emperors of the Ming dynasty in China, who were notoriously weak rulers.[177] Similarly, the early rulers of Prussia, from Frederick William, the Great Elector, to Frederick the Great, had far better claim to the title of autocrat than did the many Ottoman emperors who were forcibly deposed by elements of the governing class.[178] In fact, no less than fifteen of the thirty-five sultans in the Ottoman dynasty were forcibly deposed, compared with only six of the thirty-three kings who reigned in France from the time of Hugh Capet to Louis XVI.[179]

One further difficulty in Wittfogel's work stems from the fact that the irrigation systems of Asia have not depended on the central government nearly so much as he and others in his tradition have supposed. Wolfram Eberhard, a noted student of Chinese society, has assembled considerable evidence to show that the construction and maintenance of these systems was much more dependent on the initiative and action of local authorities than Wittfogel recognizes.[180] Recent work by other scholars points in the same direction.[181] To summarize, then, *the evidence we now possess indicates that the need for large scale irrigation systems has probably been a factor stimulating the growth of autocracy, but not the dominant factor, and perhaps not even a major one.*

Two other factors which have influenced the location of nations and dynasties on the autocracy-oligarchy scale are the size of the political units involved and the quality of transportation and communication facilities. *The larger a state becomes, and the poorer its transportation and communication facilities, the greater the opportunities for members of the governing class to infringe on royal prerogatives.*

The influence of the size of states is seen quite clearly in the many accounts of the difficulties which rulers in the far-flung Chinese and In-

[177] For example, the emperor Ying Tsung was once captured by the Mongols and held for ransom. The leaders of the various court cliques were so indifferent to his fate that the Mongols were forced to lower their ransom substantially to get him off their hands. On his return, he was made a quasi prisoner while another man ruled in his stead, and he regained the throne on the death of the other only because the opposing court factions found it impossible to agree on any other candidate. See Eberhard, *History,* pp. 259–269 on the later years of the Ming dynasty, and pp. 259–260 on Ying Tsung.

[178] See Rosenberg on Prussia and A. D. Alderson, *The Structure of the Ottoman Dynasty* (Oxford: Clarendon Press, 1956), especially chap. 10, on Turkey.

[179] These are my own computations. One might argue that the French kings survived because they were weak and therefore obliged to make concessions which placated their powerful opponents. As a general rule, however, forcible deposition was most likely to occur when rulers were weak. It has been the Bayezids, not the Suleimans, who have been deposed in most cases.

[180] Eberhard, *Rulers,* pp. 32–45.

[181] See, for example, Chang's work on the functions of the Chinese gentry in *The Chinese Gentry,* pp. 58-61 and in *Income,* pp. 48–50.

dian Empires had in maintaining effective control over the governors of the more remote provinces. Such officials often usurped many of the prerogatives of the emperor and, in some instances, even went on to challenge his right to the throne.[182]

The influence of transportation and communication facilities are evident in the histories of both China and Europe.[183] In each instance there is evidence of a long-term shift from oligarchical rule to autocratic rule (though not without significant short-term reversals). During the early Chou dynasty, for example, feudalism flourished in China, just as it did in the early medieval period in Europe. Later, with advances in methods of transportation and communication, there was a definite shift toward more autocratic forms of government in both areas.

The quality and efficiency of transportation were, to some degree at least, functions of environmental conditions. Rugged and mountainous terrain was a serious obstacle to the movement of armies, especially prior to industrialization. Hence, autocratic government was less likely to develop or flourish in such areas than in the broad flood plains, where the rapid movement of armies was normally possible. As noted previously, it seems more than coincidence that the few cases in which republican governments managed to survive the early stages of agrarianism were largely, or entirely, in mountainous areas.

The outcome of wars seems yet another factor influencing the outcome of struggles between rulers and their governing classes. *Rulers who were successful at war, and were able to annex foreign territories, could subordinate their governing classes much more effectively.* Their ability to distribute booty was a powerful instrument of control. The redistribution of land acquired by confiscation had the same effect, especially when those whose lands were confiscated had no strong ties of kinship or friendship with the new elite. Thus, confiscations would be most likely to strengthen autocratic rule at the time of the establishment of a new dynasty, when the old governing class was being wholly or partially replaced by a new one (as, for example, in the early Tokugawa period in Japan). Under other conditions, however, confiscations tended to unite the governing class against the ruler.

Losses in war, of course, had a deleterious effect on the ruler's relation to his governing class. As various writers have noted, the power of rulers depended in part on the myth of their invincibility. Once a ruler's

---

[182] See, for example, Franz Michael, *The Origin of Manchu Rule in China: Frontier and Bureaucracy as Interacting Forces in the Chinese Empire* (Baltimore: Johns Hopkins, 1942). This volume provides an excellent account of the process by which the Manchu leaders raised themselves from feudal vassals to emperors of China.
[183] Andrzejewski, pp. 79–80.

vincibility was shown, his power was weakened and his rights were more likely to be challenged. In a very real sense he lost something of his charismatic character.

Still another factor that influenced the outcome of struggles for power between rulers and their governing classes was the role of the latter in military affairs. *Where the governing class was a military elite, highly skilled in the arts of war, its powers were much greater than where it allowed other elements in the population, e.g., mercenaries, to assume military responsibilities.* It is no coincidence that the great growth in royal powers in Europe occurred during the late Middle Ages, when the governing class tended to abandon its former warlike ways.[184] A very similar pattern developed in Rome when the governing class gave up its traditional military role.

This development seems to have been the result, at least in part, of still another factor, namely *the spread of a money economy*. Where money was scarce, rulers were obliged to build their armies from vassals who pledged their services. Such armies were generally difficult to control, especially when there was rebellion in the ranks, since vassals were often reluctant to support their lord against one of their fellows. Also, since the period of service required of such vassals was usually of limited duration, e.g., forty days per year, a rebellious vassal did not need to defend himself for long. With a stout castle, he could easily defend himself for the necessary period, or until the ruler's army dissolved and went home, and thus establish quasi sovereignty. With the growth of a money economy, kings began to hire mercenaries and found that such problems were much more easily solved.[185]

The relative power of rulers and governing classes also seems to have depended on the nature of inheritance among both parties. *Where a system of primogeniture was followed by the governing class, it prevented the breakup of large estates, thus keeping intact this important basis of power.*[186] Rules governing succession to the throne were also tremendously important, since they influenced the character of the rulers themselves. *Where there was a principle of automatic succession, as in most European countries, children and other weak individuals could ascend the throne, thus providing the governing class with an excellent oppor-*

---

[184] See, for example, Mariéjol, pp. 270–271.

[185] For a good discussion of the importance of money in this area, see Painter, *Monarchies*, pp. 16–17.

[186] The importance of primogeniture has been noted by many writers. See, for example, Wittfogel, pp. 79ff.; Alan Simpson, *The Wealth of the Gentry, 1540–1660* (London: Cambridge University Press, 1961), pp. 107–108; Blum, pp. 82 and 378; Misra, pp. 44 and 50; or Mariéjol, pp. 276–277.

tunity to increase its powers.[187] On the other hand, where there was an open contest for the throne on the death of each monarch, as in the Mughal Empire, there were few weak rulers. To become ruler of the Mughal Empire a man was obliged to wade through a sea of blood, including that of his own brothers. This insured a long succession of strong rulers, who held to the barest minimum the rights of the governing class.[188] Throughout most of the Mughal period, most of the governing class held land only on assignment, which meant that they were entitled to the income from a given piece of land only so long as their services proved satisfactory to the emperor.[189]

Another factor influencing the location of states on the autocracy-oligarchy continuum was *the amount of dissension within the governing class and the skill with which the ruler exploited this for his own advantage.* One of the most important causes of division within that class was wealth. A few specific examples reveal the magnitude of these differences. In mid-nineteenth-century Russia, Count Sheremetev, the largest single landholder, owned nearly 300,000 serfs and almost 2,000,000 acres of land, while at the same time more than 40 per cent of the nobility owned twenty serfs or fewer.[190] Although the lesser nobility were far more numerous, they lacked power, as is indicated by the fact that they owned less than 3 per cent of all serfs owned by the nobility, while the top 1 per cent of this class owned 29 per cent. In what is now the Loire Department of France, in the latter half of the thirteenth century the incomes of the nobility ranged from as little as £5 per year to as much as £2,400.[191] Those in the former category maintained a style of life that was hardly distinguishable from that of the surrounding peasantry; as one historian has put it, "they were living from hand to mouth." In seventeenth-century England, the leading members of the governing class, the peers of the realm, are estimated to have had an average income from land forty times that of gentlemen and twelve times that of esquires, who together constituted the lower ranks of the governing class.[192] In fifteenth-century England, the fifty-one wealthiest barons had incomes which averaged nearly thirty times that of the lowest stratum of the governing class, the squire-archy.[193] Taking the individual extremes within this class, more than a hundred-fold difference is indicated (from £20 to £3,230).[194] A com-

---

[187] See, for example, Painter, *Monarchies*, pp. 127–129.
[188] See *The Cambridge History of India*, vol. 4.
[189] See Moreland, pp. 92–100.
[190] Blum, pp. 369–370.
[191] See Edouard Perroy's excellent study, "Social Mobility among the French *Noblesse* in the Later Middle Ages," *Past and Present*, 21 (1962), pp. 27–28.
[192] Aylmer, p. 331.
[193] Gray, p. 630.
[194] *Ibid.*, pp. 614 and 630.

parable range prevailed four centuries earlier, during the reign of William the Conqueror.[195] Chang's work on nineteenth-century China indicates that the upper gentry, who comprised about 14 per cent of the entire gentry class, had an average income ten to twelve times that of the other members of the class, and the variation between the extremes was more than a thousand-fold.[196]

In addition to these differences in wealth, members of the governing class felt the divisive effects of variations in rank, function, ethnicity, legal status, family prestige, relationship to the royal house, place of residence, e.g., court versus provinces, and military skills, to mention some of the most important. Such differences were of tremendous value to every would-be autocrat, since he, a single individual, could never maintain a position of superiority if the entire governing class were to unite against him. Thus, his only hope, when faced with opposition from members of this class, was to exploit these divisions among them, playing off the richer members against the not so rich, the old nobility against the newer elements, native elites against foreign, courtiers against provincials, and so forth. His power, therefore, was in part a function of the seriousness of these divisions and of his skill in exploiting them.[197]

Last, but by no means least, the outcome of every struggle between ruler and governing class was influenced by personality factors. A ruler who was weak, indecisive, stupid, or neglectful of affairs of state could quickly dissipate the accumulated gains of a succession of strong predecessors. On the other hand, a strong, ruthless, and intelligent ruler could often add substantially to the powers and privileges of the royal office. Personality variations counted for less in the case of the governing class, since these usually canceled out owing to the numbers of persons involved. The presence or absence of a dynamic, charismatic leader in this class, however, could well influence the outcome of its struggles with the ruler.

Sociologists are generally skeptical of the importance of personality variables in social processes. In the main this skepticism seems well founded, owing to the tendency for variations to cancel out each other when large populations are involved. Theoretically, however, it would seem that personality variables should grow in importance as the number

---

[195] Painter, *Barony*, pp. 17–18.

[196] The comparison between the upper and lower portions of the gentry class is calculated from data presented in *Income*, especially on p. 330. The comparison between the extremes is based on Chang's evidence that the top officials received an annual income of at least 180,000 taels, while many lesser gentry received well under 180 taels a year.

[197] For an example of the application of the policy of "divide and rule," see Mariéjol, pp. 264ff., on late fifteenth- and sixteenth-century Spain. See, also, Rosenberg, pp. 152ff., on Prussia.

of cases in a population declines and also as the resources at the disposal of the population aggregate increase. If this is true, *personality variables should be most important in the case of a population of one with immense resources at his disposal, as in the case of rulers of nations.* At any one point in the history of a given nation, there is no "canceling out" of the personal idiosyncrasies of the ruler. Substantial variations are possible, and these become extremely important because of the immense resources under his control.[198]

To cite the significance of personality variables is not to minimize the influence of other variables, nor to deny that the personality traits of rulers are in part the product of social forces. However, heredity also plays a role in shaping personality and, from the standpoint of the social analyst, this unpredictable factor is capable, on occasion, of upsetting the most careful predictions based on an analysis of the social factors involved.[199]

Considering the many forces apparently influencing the outcome of struggles between rulers and their governing classes, it is not surprising that total victory for either side was rare and that cases falling in the middle range of the autocracy-oligarchy continuum were more numerous than those at the extremes. This was to be expected since it would be as unlikely for all these forces to favor one party at the expense of the other as it would be for ten tosses of a coin all to come up heads.

In this connection, one further point should be noted. When conditions were favorable for the maximization of royal power and a ruler pressed his advantage, he soon discovered the law of diminishing returns. After a certain point was reached (and it was reached long before the ruler could deprive the governing class of all its rights), the gains to the ruler were more than offset by the loss of incentive on the part of the governing class. To press the governing class further would harm himself as well as them.

There is good reason to believe that this point was reached at the height of royal power in the Mughal Empire. Here the emperors became so powerful that as much as seven-eighths of the land held by the governing class was theirs only on assignments of short and uncertain tenure. European visitors to the area often commented upon the inefficiency and low productivity of Indian agriculture. In seeking an explanation for these conditions, one reported the following as typical of the attitudes of the governing class:

---

[198] For a documentation of this principle on a lower level of organization, see Gitel P. Steed, "Notes on an Approach to a Study of Personality Formation in a Hindu Village in Gujarat," in Marriott, pp. 124–143.

[199] When sociologists shift from predictions to explanations of past events, they can usually find some personally satisfying explanation for everything without resort to personality variables, but this is not altogether convincing.

Why should the neglected state of this land create uneasiness in our minds? And why should we expend our money and time to render it fruitful? We may be deprived of it in a single moment, and our exertions would benefit neither ourselves nor our children. Let us draw from the soil all the money we can, though the peasant should starve or abscond, and we should leave it, when commanded to quit, a dreary wilderness.[200]

If this observer was correct, the emperors had so monopolized proprietary rights that the governing class developed what modern landlords call a tenant mentality.

Before concluding this examination of the struggles between rulers and governing classes, we should consider briefly their effect on the rest of society. This is a very important subject, but one on which it is difficult to obtain much more than individual opinions and impressions, and scattered bits and pieces of evidence. On occasion, rulers seem to have turned to the common people as a counterforce in their struggles with a well-entrenched and united nobility.[201] Sometimes the common people turned to the ruler for protection from predatory members of the governing class.[202] Alliances between the governing classes and the masses were much less common, probably because the governing class normally had sufficient resources to control the ruler if they could only maintain a united front. The ruler, by contrast, invariably needed allies.

Despite this occasional tendency of rulers to seek support from the common people, the latter seemed to gain little from it. What gains they made were always minor, and worse yet, short-lived. It is no great exaggeration to say that *the outcomes of all the countless struggles between rulers and their governing classes had almost no effect on the living conditions of the common people, except as these struggles sometimes led to violence and destroyed their very livelihood.*

A few writers argue that the growth of royal power was contrary to the interests of the masses, since it led to despotism and thereby destroyed freedom. Karl Wittfogel and the French political journalist, Bertrand de Jouvenal, are two of the most persuasive proponents of this point of view.[203] However, their criticism of autocracy as detrimental to the in-

[200] Francois Bernier, *Travels in the Mogul Empire*, quoted by Moreland, p. 205. Quoted by permission. See also Moreland, pp. 92–100.

[201] See, for example, Aristotle, *Politics*, translated by Benjamin Jowett (New York: Modern Library, 1943), p. 238 (1310b), and Plato, *The Republic*, translated by Benjamin Jowett (New York: Modern Library, n.d.), p. 323 (565), both of whom comment upon the tendency of certain rulers, i.e., tyrants, to ally themselves with the common people in opposition to the governing class. Similarly the Roman emperors often allied themselves with the urban masses in their struggle with the senatorial class.

[202] See, for example, Lindsay and Groves, pp. 19–22 and chaps. 9 and 10. As these cases illustrate, their efforts often came to naught.

[203] For de Jouvenal, see *On Power: Its Nature and the History of Its Growth*, translated by J. F. Huntington (New York: Viking, 1949).

terests of the common people appear more relevant to the masses in today's industrial societies than to those of bygone agrarian societies. These writers are concerned with the threat of modern totalitarianism, and they claim to find its roots in agrarian autocracy. They are probably correct in their assertion that the governing classes of agrarian states, who sought to establish rights and privileges which could not be taken away at the whim of the ruler, helped to lay the foundation for modern civil liberties. However, we need to keep an historical perspective and to remember that these efforts of governing classes were motivated almost wholly by self-interest, and in their own day benefitted few besides themselves.

9/Agrarian Societies: Part II

The art of taxation consists in so plucking the goose as to get the most feathers for the least hissing.
Colbert

The Retainer Class

IN EVERY AGRARIAN SOCIETY the ruler and governing class employed or otherwise maintained a small army of officials, professional soldiers, household servants, and personal retainers, all of whom served them in a variety of more or less specialized capacities. These individuals, together with their families, constituted what might be called "the retainer class or classes." Though this is not a familiar label, it communicates better than any of the alternatives the most important characteristic of this class, namely its dependence on the political elite.

On first inspection, it may seem strange to lump such diverse occupational groups together when their specific functions were so different. However, despite such differences, their basic function was always the same—service to the political elite. In return for this, they were separated from, and elevated above, the mass of common people, and to a limited degree shared in the economic surplus. It should also be noted that in many agrarian societies the boundaries between the several specialties which formed the retainer class were not nearly so sharp or well defined as members of modern industrial societies might suppose them to have been. In societies with a "matter-of-course confusion of public business with private enterprise," there was nothing at all strange about the use of personal retainers or household servants in official capacities, whether civil or military. Also, in societies where war was an almost continuous feature of life for the governing class, the mingling of civil and military functions is hardly surprising.[1]

If the boundaries between the several segments of the retainer class were often fuzzy, so, too, was the boundary between the retainer class and the governing class. High-ranking servants of powerful members of the governing class or of the ruler often enjoyed a much greater measure of power and privilege than the lower-ranking members of the governing class. This can be seen in the case of certain of the household servants or slaves of the Roman emperors who, on occasion, exercised considerable political influence and enjoyed many privileges. For example, it is reported that a slave of Tiberius, a bachelor named Musicus, occupied "the not very elevated position of a dispensator in the *fiscus Gallicus provinciae Lugdunensis*," but nevertheless received from the emperor a household staff of sixteen consisting of a *negotiator* to manage his business affairs, a *sumptuarius* to control his household expenditure, two cooks, two footmen, a valet, two chamberlains, two butlers, three secretaries, a doctor, and a lady "whose functions are discreetly veiled." [2] Similar patterns can be observed in the Chinese Empire, especially in the case of the imperial eunuchs, who, though servants, sometimes wielded considerable power, or in medieval Europe where the serving men of powerful princes often shared in their lord's power. In a number of instances, lesser members of the governing class voluntarily entered the service of more powerful members of their own class, in the hope of thereby improving their fortunes.[3]

[1] See, for example, A. E. R. Boak, *A History of Rome to 565 A.D.*, 3d ed. (New York: Macmillan, 1943), pp. 344f. or Harold Mattingly, *Roman Imperial Civilization* (Garden City, N.Y.: Doubleday Anchor, 1959), pp. 152f. on the use of household servants in official capacities in Rome, or Adolf Erman, *Life in Ancient Egypt*, translated by H. M. Tirard (London: Macmillan, 1894), pp. 105f., on ancient Egypt. On the mingling of civil and military functions and functionaries, see A. H. M. Jones, *Studies in Roman Government and Law* (Oxford: Blackwell, 1960), pp. 161f. These examples are chiefly from the Roman Empire, where specialization was, by agrarian standards, rather highly developed. Where there was less specialization, as in medieval Europe, distinctions were even less clear.
[2] Jones, p. 160.
[3] Marc Bloch's *Feudal Society*, translated by L. A. Manyon (Chicago: University of Chicago Press, 1962), provides valuable insights into this phenomenon as it developed in western Europe. See especially part 4.

Because of the constant movement of men in both directions, it is often difficult to say exactly where one class began and the other ended.

At the other extreme, the retainer class was bounded by the peasant class, and here, too, it is sometimes difficult to define the boundary. In medieval England, for example, reeves and haywards were neither fish nor fowl, much like the modern foreman. On the one hand, they served the lord of the manor in an official capacity and sometimes derived a significant portion of their income for this. On the other hand, they were from the peasant class and usually returned to it after a relatively brief term of office. Furthermore, even while serving in these offices, they usually found it necessary to carry on their own farming activities. In short, they were marginal to both classes.[4] Similarly, within the lord's household the most menial chores were often performed by individuals who functioned at other times as mere peasants. Finally, the masses of common soldiers were recruited from the peasantry and, if they survived, returned to civilian life as peasants, with little or no sense of deprivation.

As might be expected, the character of the retainer class varied according to the character of the governing class. In societies where bureaucratic officials were more powerful, the retainer class tended to take on a bureaucratic character. By contrast, in societies where an hereditary nobility was dominant, the retainer class tended to reflect the particularistic values of that group.

It is almost impossible to obtain from the historical record reliable figures on the size of the retainer class. On both theoretical and empirical grounds, however, it seems likely that it was usually several times the size of the governing class. If governing classes averaged about 1 per cent of the total population, the retainer class probably averaged somewhere in the neighborhood of 5 per cent. Much less than this seems unlikely, in view of the many functions this class was expected to perform; much more seems unlikely because of the strain such numbers would place on the economy.[5]

[4] For good discussions of these offices and the individuals who filled them, see H. S. Bennett, *Life on the English Manor: A Study of Peasant Conditions, 1150–1400* (London: Cambridge University Press, 1960), pp. 166f., or George C. Homans, *English Villagers of the Thirteenth Century* (Cambridge, Mass.: Harvard University Press, 1942), pp. 292f.

[5] Karl A. Wittfogel, *Oriental Despotism: A Comparative Study of Total Power* (New Haven, Conn.: Yale University Press, 1957), reports that minor civil officials numbered 1.7 million in the last days of the Chinese Empire (p. 307). This indicates that they, with their families, equaled about 2 per cent of the population. If servants and soldiers were added, the total would probably not be far from 5 per cent. In nineteenth-century Russia, household servants in the homes of the rich constituted 2 to 3 per cent of the population. See Jerome Blum, *Lord and Peasant in Russia from the Ninth to the Nineteenth Century* (Princeton, N.J.: Princeton University Press, 1961), p. 460.

Collectively, the members of the retainer class were very important, especially from the standpoint of the maintenance of the distributive system. To begin with, they provided badly needed numerical support for the ruler and governing class in their efforts to maintain their essentially exploitative position in society. It seems unlikely that the military technology of these societies was advanced to the point where a minority of only 1 to 2 per cent of the population, no matter how well organized, could effectively subordinate the other 98 or 99 per cent (a ratio of 50 or 100 to 1). However, their technology may well have permitted an organized minority of 6 or 7 per cent, i.e., the governing class and its retainers, to dominate the rest of the population (a ratio of about 15 to 1), especially if the latter were unorganized.

Collectively the retainer class was also important because it performed the crucial task of mediating relations between the governing class and the common people. It was the retainers who actually performed most of the work involved in effecting the transfer of the economic surplus from the producers to the political elite. How efficiently this was done depended in large measure on their skill and diligence. Furthermore, because they were the intermediaries, the retainers deflected much of the hostility and resentment which otherwise would have been directed at the political elite. Peasants and other members of the lower orders could never be certain whether the difficulties they experienced were due to the tax collectors, petty officials, and other members of the retainer class with whom they interacted, or to those higher up. Because of their lack of contact with the governing class, the peasants were likely to give them at least some of the benefit of the doubt. By deflecting and diffusing hostility in this way, the retainer class contributed still further to the survival and stability of the highly exploitative agrarian distributive system.

Though collectively the members of this class were terribly important to their superiors, individually most of them were expendable. Except perhaps for clerks and others whose work required literacy, their skills were usually ones which could be mastered by others without too much difficulty. This greatly weakened their bargaining position with the governing class. In general, the wages paid retainers were quite modest, though there is evidence that they took advantage of every possible opportunity for "honest graft," just as their superiors did.[6] In medieval England,

[6] See, for example, Bennett, pp. 174–175 or F. R. Cowell, *Cicero and the Roman Republic* (London: Penguin, 1956), p. 64. Sometimes more than "honest graft" was involved, as shown by Francois Ganshof, "Medieval Agrarian Society in Its Prime: France, the Low Countries, and Western Germany," in *The Cambridge Economic History*, vol. I, pp. 293–294, or Erman, p. 127, on ancient Egypt.

the seneschal, chief official in the service of a wealthy lord, received a salary of about £15 a year, plus most of his living expenses and other perquisites.[7] This, together with a certain amount of "honest graft," afforded him an income equal to that of the average squire a century later.[8] A bailiff supervising a single manor was paid £4 to £6 a year plus most of his living expenses, from perfectly legitimate income alone, while a reeve, the lowest-ranking manorial official, received £1 a year or less (supplemented, of course, by income from his own land).[9] As modest as these incomes seem by modern standards, the bailiff received as much as some of the poorest gentlemen and more than was required to support a scholar comfortably, while the reeve's income was "at least double that received by plowmen or carters," and four times that of shepherds.[10] There were, of course, far more reeves than bailiffs, and far more bailiffs than seneschals.

Within the retainer class, rewards varied inversely with the ease with which the individual could be replaced. Thus, those positions which required the least ability and training commanded the fewest rewards, while those requiring considerable ability, unusual talents, or extensive training commanded more. Superficially, this seems a confirmation of the functionalists' theory of rewards, but, in effect, it is nothing of the kind, because what was rewarded was service to the elite, not service to society at large.

Members of this class, like those above them, constantly sought to maximize their rights and privileges. Various methods were used depending upon the particular subclass involved. Of all the subclasses, the most threatening to the political elite was the military. *Whenever the governing class abdicated its military responsibilities and allowed the officer corps of the army to become dominated by professional soldiers up from the ranks, they created a dangerous situation for themselves.* Unless these professionals were highly rewarded, even perhaps to the point of admission into the governing class, they were likely to use the resources at their command to seize control of the state.[11] This was the experience of the later Roman Empire, where professional soldiers, who were not a part of

[7] Bennett, p. 158.
[8] H. L. Gray, "Incomes from Land in England in 1436," *English Historical Review,* 49 (1934), p. 630.
[9] Bennett, pp. 163 and 175, or May McKisack, *The Fourteenth Century* (Oxford: Clarendon Press, 1959), p. 317.
[10] Gray, p. 630, Sidney Painter, *Studies in the History of the English Feudal Barony* (Baltimore: Johns Hopkins, 1943), p. 172, and Bennett, p. 163.
[11] On this point, see Gaetano Mosca, *The Ruling Class,* translated by Hannah Kahn (New York: McGraw-Hill, 1939), pp. 235–237, and Cecil Woodham-Smith, *The Reason Why* (New York: McGraw-Hill, 1953), pp. 25–29.

the governing class, often intervened in domestic politics, either to seize the throne for themselves or for someone of their choosing. A similar situation developed in Egypt at the time of the Mamluk seizure of power, in Turkey under the Janissaries, and in the later Abbasid Empire at Samarra.[12]

The civilian segments of the retainer class never posed such a serious threat to the political elite as a whole, though individual rulers and members of the governing class were sometimes assassinated by household servants or other retainers. Such events, though vitally important to the individuals concerned, seldom had any significant effect on the distributive system.

Significant and enduring gains by the civilian members of the retainer class were much more likely to come "a drop at a time." Through a gradual process of attrition, minor officials and servants slowly transformed special favors or opportunities into precedents, temporary advantages into permanent, and permanent advantages into hereditary. These gains were symptomatic of the difficulties encountered by a tiny governing class striving to preserve its many and far-flung interests. *Such gains by retainers were likely to be greatest during periods when the governing class was dominated by a hedonistic ethic, and least when an ethic of responsibility and duty held sway.* If Pareto and others are correct in stating that the sterner qualities prevail in the earlier generations of a regime and are gradually replaced by a less responsible attitude, then the gains of the retainer class should have been greater in the later stages of most regimes and less in the earlier stages. In fact, one might expect the appearance of a new regime to result in a sharp reversal in the usual pattern, with the retainers' gains of a century or more wiped out in a single generation.

The Merchant Class

Though the rulers and governing classes of agrarian societies generally sought to achieve complete control over the economic surplus, they seldom succeeded. Virtually always, others arose to contest their claims, and usually with some measure of success. None was more successful than the members of the merchant class, a segment of the population whose activities the political elite usually found it difficult to direct and control.

Much ink has been spilled in scholarly debates over the origins of this class, and while the issue is still not finally settled, it seems clear that the

[12] See Philip K. Hitti, *History of the Arabs* (London: Macmillan, 1960), pp. 466–467 on the Abbasid dynasty and chap. 47 on the Mamluks. See A. D. Alderson, *The Structure of the Ottoman Dynasty* (Oxford: Clarendon Press, 1956), chap. 10 on Turkey.

great majority of its earliest members came from humble backgrounds. Henri Pirenne, for example, argues that in Europe they "were originally recruited from among landless men," the younger sons of peasants who were not destined to inherit their father's land.[13] Such men were forced to choose between living out their lives in straitened circumstance as bachelors and semiservants dependent on their elder brother, or taking their chances elsewhere.[14] Given the age at which such decisions were typically made (from about fifteen to twenty-five), it is hardly surprising that large numbers took to the highways, where they sought whatever means of livelihood they could find. Although the great majority were probably reduced to beggary or worse, a few apparently discovered that the mobility of the disinherited could be turned to advantage, at least by the clever. For example, as Pirenne has noted, "in an age when local famines were continual, one had only to buy a very small quantity of grain cheaply in regions where it was abundant, to realize fabulous profits, which could then be increased by the same methods."[15] Or, a man might get his start by becoming a beachcomber, as did St. Godric of Finchale, selling items of value salvaged from the not uncommon shipwrecks.[16]

In some instances the merchant class seems to have evolved slowly from the ranks of peasants who, during slack periods, engaged in mercantile activities on a limited basis to make ends meet.[17] This pattern of activity, it will be recalled, was not uncommon in advanced horticultural societies. With the greater economic opportunities afforded by agrarian societies, some peasants took the step from part- to full-time commercial activity.

One indication of the humble origins of the merchant class is found in the low prestige accorded "mere merchants," i.e., those engaged in mercantile activity but not members of the governing class, almost everywhere in the early agrarian world. In the traditional status systems of China and Japan, merchants were ranked at or near the bottom of the social scale, and clearly below both peasant farmers and artisans.[18] Though there is reason to doubt that the merchant class was really re-

---

[13] Henri Pirenne, *Economic and Social History of Medieval Europe* (New York: Harvest Books, n.d., originally published in 1933), p. 45.
[14] See, for example, Homans, pp. 137f.
[15] Pirenne, p. 46.
[16] *Ibid.*
[17] See James Westfall Thompson, *Economic and Social History of the Middle Ages* (New York: Appleton-Century-Crofts, 1928), p. 772, or Blum, pp. 288f.
[18] See, for example, Robert Bellah, *Tokugawa Religion: The Values of Pre-industrial Japan* (New York: Free Press, 1957), pp. 24–25; Morton Fried, *The Fabric of Chinese Society: A Study of the Social Life of a Chinese County Seat* (New York: Frederick A. Praeger, 1953), p. 211; Robert K. Douglas, *Society in China* (London: Innes, 1894), pp. 139–140; or Wolfram Eberhard, *Social Mobility in Traditional China* (Leiden, Netherlands: Brill, 1962), p. 6.

garded so poorly by the majority of men,[19] it is doubtful that they would ever have been ranked in this way if their origins had not originally been rather humble.[20] In medieval Europe, merchants were not treated with the same measure of official disdain, but even there the merchant class was viewed as definitely inferior to the governing class, and so regarded itself, as evidenced by the eagerness with which its members adopted the ways of life of the governing class and sought to marry into noble families.

Whatever its origins, the merchant class aspired to better things, and in time attained them. In virtually every mature agrarian society merchants managed to acquire a considerable portion of the wealth, and in a few instances a measure of political power as well.

The reasons for their success are not altogether clear but were linked, apparently, with certain peculiar features of their role. To begin with, from a very early date merchants managed to free themselves from the direct and immediate authority of the ruler and governing class. This meant that, in the economic sphere, merchants stood in a *market* relationship with the governing class, not an *authority* relationship.[21] This made it possible for the merchant class to deal with the governing class, in part at least, on terms more favorable to themselves than to their opponents.

In authority relations, the political elite had a distinct advantage. They held nearly all the high cards, so to speak, and thus could largely dictate terms, as they did with the retainer class. By contrast, they were not nearly so well equipped in market relations. In fact, their efforts to acquire the resources needed to dominate authority relations may have weakened their position in market relations.

As has long been recognized, these two types of relations call for very different skills and resources. Control of a large body of armed retainers is tremendously helpful in authority relations, but not very useful in market relations. Conversely, familiarity with subtle variations in the

---

[19] On the basis of descriptions of these societies it is difficult to believe that these traditional prestige systems were not devices developed by the governing classes, with the assistance of scholars, to put the troublesome merchant class in "its place." In other words, they were apparently weapons used in the struggle between classes more than they were objective rating devices as some modern scholars seem to regard them.

[20] Robert Bellah suggests that the low status of merchants was due chiefly to their preoccupation with money, which "runs counter to both the upper class ethic and the religious ethic." This may well have been an added factor but I find it somewhat difficult to document an indifference to wealth on the part of the upper class—though obviously they were averse to working for it. See also Gideon Sjoberg, *The Pre-industrial City* (New York: Free Press, 1960), p. 136, and elsewhere for a view somewhat similar to Bellah's.

[21] I do not mean to suggest that the merchant class completely escaped the authority relationship: politically they were still subject to the governing class. For economic purposes, however, they were not.

quality of merchandise, skill in the manipulation of weights and measures, and knowledge of prices in other markets and the costs of moving goods between them are great assets in market relations, but of little account in authority relations. Much of the success of the merchant class depended on these differences.[22]

It is interesting to consider why members of the merchant class were able to escape the employee status when so many others were not. At this stage we can only speculate, since detailed historical evidence is still largely lacking. Probably the foremost factor responsible for the independent entrepreneurial status of merchants was the mobile character of their occupation. Given the relatively primitive character of transportation and communication, the political elite may have found that it was not worth the effort to try to maintain the same detailed supervision over the activities of merchants that they did over the activities of their retainers. Furthermore, unlike most of the members of the retainer class, the merchants were not active in the political realm, and hence posed no obvious threat. Finally, in some cases merchants were obliged to cross national boundaries as a normal part of their business. At such times, they were beyond the control of the political elite of their own country. All these factors undoubtedly helped the merchant class establish a different kind of relationship to the political elite from that of the retainer class.

Other factors may also have been involved. The nontraditional character of the role, together with the substantial financial risks involved, may have contributed to the willingness of the political elite to grant merchants a freedom denied to others.

Whatever the reasons, this development was not without benefits for both parties. The wealth which could be acquired through mercantile activity has become proverbial. The literature and other records of the great agrarian societies of the past are filled with accounts of wealthy merchants whose riches rivaled those of the political elite. For example, the Japanese historian, Takekoshi, provides a detailed list of the property of the house of Yodoya at the time it was confiscated by the fifth Tokugawa shogun. Among the items listed were the following: storehouses with contents valued at 730,000 ryo of gold, 21 solid gold hens with 10 chicks (7,300 ryo), 277 large junks (263,500 ryo), 150 gold-leaf folding screens (15,000 ryo), 10 paintings by the Emperor Kiso of China (20,000 ryo), 150,000 pounds of quicksilver (25,000 ryo), 3,500,000 ryo in gold coin, 1,500,000 kwamme of silver (14,166,000 ryo), plus numerous houses, farms, and forests, and countless other artifacts. This famly was also reported to have over 100 million ryo in outstanding loans to members of

[22] See, for example, Fried, pp. 126 and 161–162.

the governing class, though this figure is believed to be an exaggeration.[23]

Though obviously the Yodoya family was exceptional, in most agrarian societies there was an appreciable overlap between the wealth of the merchant class and that of the governing class. How great this overlap was, is difficult to say, though it is clear that leading members of the merchant class were usually much wealthier than the lesser members of the governing class.[24]

Naturally, not all merchants became rich. Many remained quite poor. This was especially true of those who served the poorer classes, as in the case of itinerant peddlers in the countryside and self-employed merchant-artisans in the cities.[24a] Thus the merchant class cannot be thought of as a single stratum forming a distinctive layer within a neatly stratified structure of superimposed classes. Rather, as Figure 1 (page 284) suggests, its members covered a considerable portion of the social scale. Nevertheless, they constituted a single class in the sense set forth in Chapter 4 since all depended ultimately on the same essential resource—their special knowledge and skills in the buying and selling of goods—and it was this which gave them a definite advantage in relations in the market place and made possible the rise of some to fame and fortune.

If the merchants benefited from their distinctive entrepreneurial status, so, too, did the political elite. Not only did they enjoy ready access to commodities which otherwise would have been rare or unobtainable, they also shared in the profits of mercantile activity through taxes placed on the merchants' goods. Besides providing an important source of revenue, taxation of this kind had the added advantage of *shifting to the merchants part of the responsibility for extracting the economic surplus from the common people.* This made it more difficult for the common people to fix the blame for their unhappy situation on the political elite and thus increased the safety and stability of the entire sociopolitical system.

The political elite was not always content with what it could obtain from merchants through taxation and often turned to other devices. For example, they sometimes resorted to confiscation of the merchants' prop-

[23] Yosoburo Takekoshi, *The Economic Aspects of the History of the Civilization of Japan* (New York: Macmillan, 1930), vol. II, pp. 252–254.
[24] See, for example, the account of the Baghdad jeweler who remained wealthy even after 16 million dinars of his property were confiscated (Hitti, p. 344). See also, Blum, p. 473; Douglas, p. 140; A. Andrewes, *The Greek Tyrants* (New York: Harper Torchbooks, 1963), p. 80; Sylvia Thrupp, *The Merchant Class of Medieval London* (Ann Arbor, Mich.: Ann Arbor Paperbacks, 1962), pp. 11 and 110f.; or Alan Simpson, *The Wealth of the Gentry 1540–1660* (London: Cambridge University Press, 1961), chap. 3. Compare such accounts with those of the poorer members of the nobility (see p. 238 above).
[24a] See, for example, Sjoberg, pp. 201–202.

erty.[25] Another practice was to borrow substantial sums and refuse repayment.[26] Still another practice was to marry noble sons to merchants' daughters, an honor for which they charged dearly.[27] Wealthy merchants were also separated from large sums, given eagerly, in exchange for titles of nobility.[28]

All of these methods proved to be effective in separating the merchant class from a portion of its gains, but only a portion. In the end, a political elite always had to weigh its desire for the merchants' wealth against its need for their services. No ruler or governing class could ever really enjoy the fruits of political power unless merchants were available to provide them with those rare and unusual commodities which elevated the life of the privileged classes above that of the common herd and caused them to be envied and admired. Thus there were always limits beyond which a political elite would not go in their efforts to appropriate the wealth of the merchant class. Like the goose which laid the golden eggs, the merchant class was protected by its intrinsic utility against all but the most short-sighted and foolish of elites.

As one would expect, merchants were not indifferent to the efforts of the elite to cut themselves in on mercantile profits. They always resisted, though the methods of resistance varied considerably. Where the ruler and governing class were extremely strong and greedy, merchants were

[25] This practice was especially common in Mughal India, where any visible accumulation of wealth by merchants invited confiscation. See B. B. Misra, *The Indian Middle Classes* (London: Oxford University Press, 1961), pp. 25–27. Also see Takekoshi, vol. II, pp. 251f. on Japan, or Painter, *Barony*, p. 186, or Sir James H. Ramsay, *A History of the Revenues of the Kings of England 1066–1399* (Oxford: Clarendon Press, 1925), vol. I, p. 58 on medieval England, where the confiscation of the property of Jewish moneylenders and merchants was a fairly common practice.

[26] This was a common practice in Tokugawa Japan. See, for example, Takekoshi, vol. II, pp. 258f., or Bellah, pp. 28–29. See, also, Blum, pp. 384–385 on Russia, or Thrupp, *Merchant Class*, pp. 53 and 259 on England.

[27] This practice was especially common in Europe, though it was adopted elsewhere. On Europe, see Elinor Barber, *The Bourgeoisie in 18th Century France* (Princeton, N.J.: Princeton University Press, 1955), pp. 100f.; Thrupp, *Merchant Class*, pp. 265–269; H. R. Trevor-Roper, "The Gentry 1540–1640," *The Economic History Review Supplements*, No. 1 (n.d.), p. 26; or Jean Hippolyte Mariéjol, *The Spain of Ferdinand and Isabella*, translated and edited by Benjamin Keen (New Brunswick, N.J.: Rutgers University Press, 1961), p. 42 (who reports intermarriages between Spanish nobles and wealthy Jewish merchants' daughters). For an earlier period, the Roman era, see Cowell, p. 340.

[28] This practice was especially common in France and China, but was practiced in many other countries as well. On France, see E. Barber, pp. 106ff., Louis Gottschalk, *The Era of the French Revolution* (Boston: Houghton, Mifflin, 1929), pp. 52–53, or J. McManners, "France," in A. Goodwin (ed.), *The European Nobility in the Eighteenth Century* (London: Black, 1953), pp. 22f. On China, see Chung-li Chang, *The Chinese Gentry* (Seattle, Wash.: University of Washington Press, 1955), pp. 102f., etc., or Robert Marsh, *The Mandarins: The Circulation of Elites in China, 1600–1900* (New York: Free Press, 1961), pp. 5, 13, 64, etc. See, also, Takekoshi, vol. II, pp. 454–456 on Japan, or Cowell, p. 237 on Rome.

forced to rely on wit and cunning, one resource in which they were likely to enjoy an advantage. In Mughal India, for example, wealthy merchants usually pretended to be poor, and buried their wealth to prevent its confiscation.[29] By contrast, in medieval Europe, where political elites were not so strong, the merchant class sometimes rose in armed rebellion and seized political rights for themselves.[30] In less extreme cases, the merchant class even bought political privileges from hard pressed rulers. For example, in the early thirteenth century the merchants of London paid King John the substantial sum of £2,000 for a charter granting them certain fundamental political rights.[31]

In short, just as rulers and governing classes constantly struggled with one another to enlarge their respective rights and privileges, so, too, the merchant class struggled with both segments of the political elite. The ultimate objective of the merchant class was to maximize the area in which market relations prevailed and minimize the area of authority relations, while the aim of the political elite was the reverse.

Little effort has been made to determine why the results of these struggles varied as they did. As noted above, the outcomes have ranged from the situation in Mughal India where merchants did not dare show their wealth for fear of confiscation, to that in late medieval Europe where merchants became, in effect, the governing class in the newly emerging urban centers. The modal pattern apparently lay between these two extremes, and was one in which merchants were able to accumulate wealth with relative freedom from the threat of confiscation (though not without numerous "gifts" to the political elite and substantial taxes), but were denied any appreciable measure of political power.

On theoretical grounds there are several hypotheses regarding the causes of these variations which suggest themselves, and are supported by a casual and unsystematic historical survey. To begin with, if wit and cunning were the basic resources of the merchant class, and control of the means of violence the basic resource of the political elite, then it follows that *any developments which increased the opportunities and need for wit and cunning, and reduced the opportunities and need for violence, should have improved the position of the merchant class.*[32] For example,

---

[29] Misra, pp. 25–26.

[30] See, for example, Thompson, p. 780; Pirenne, p. 54; or Max Weber, *The City,* translated by Dan Martindale and Gertrude Neuwirth (New York: Free Press, 1958), pp. 157f.

[31] G. G. Coulton, *Medieval Panorama* (New York: Meridian Books, 1955), p. 285. For other examples, see Thrupp, *Merchant Class,* p. 87.

[32] I hesitate to extend this generalization to include a decline in warfare between nations, since merchants often profited greatly from supplying munitions. War was a threat to the merchant class only when the habits developed in war were employed in domestic affairs.

the existence of orderly procedures governing succession to the throne, such as prevailed in most of Europe but were conspicuously lacking in Mughal India, should have strengthened the position of merchants, other things being equal. Similarly, the growth in the power of a centralized political authority and the decline of feudalism should have improved the position of the merchant class by reducing the opportunities for the profitable exercise of violence in the political life of the nation.

Using the same logic, one would predict that *anything which facilitated the growth of trade and commerce would enhance the position of the merchant class in relation to the elite*, once again if other things were equal. This follows from the fact that one of the basic resources of the merchant class was its wealth. Since wealth tended to be proportional to profits and profits proportional to the volume of business, anything which increased the volume of business was likely to increase the power of the merchant class. Thus, one would expect the position of merchants to improve after the early medieval period in Europe, owing to the reestablishment of law and order and the resulting increase in the volume of trade and commerce. One would also expect that in general the position of the merchant class would be much better in agrarian societies approaching industrialism than in those not far removed from the horticultural level. In short, technological advance within agrarian societies stimulated commerce and thereby favored the merchant class.

On the basis of the foregoing, one might suppose that merchants were the implacable enemies of political elites. Actually, the struggle between the merchant class and the political elite was more like a contest between brothers than a fight between strangers. In addition to the things which divided them and set them at enmity, there were other elements which united them and tended to hold the divisive elements in check. To begin with, the merchant class, like the elite, was a privileged class in society and hence was dependent on the power of the elite to hold the hostility of the lower classes in check. In addition, the political elite were the best customers of the merchant class. As noted earlier in the chapter, much of the trade and commerce in agrarian societies involved luxury goods which only the wealthy could afford. Finally, members of the merchant class were drawn to the political elite by admiration for their way of life. Though there were some exceptions, the great majority of merchants in agrarian societies seem to have had the consuming desire to be like the members of the governing class, to be accepted by them as equals, and eventually, if possible, to become one with them.[33]

---

[33] See, for example, E. Barber, p. 89. Of course, this usually was not possible for members of the merchant class who were members of minority status groups, such as the Jews.

For their part, members of the political elite found the merchant class indispensable. Without them, political power would not have been nearly so desirable. Furthermore, the merchant class could always be counted on to defend the fundamental principle of social inequality and most of the institutions which gave it expression. This was no small matter in societies where those who held political power were as badly outnumbered as in agrarian societies. Finally, as we have noted before, merchants played a valuable role in the important process of extracting the economic surplus from the common people. For all these reasons, then, the political elite was not anxious to destroy the merchant class. Their struggles were therefore limited struggles of the kind which develops whenever the parties involved are united by important ties of mutual dependence.

Before concluding this discussion of the merchant class, there is one important qualification which should be added. In many agrarian societies the merchant class included considerable numbers of persons from minority status groups, such as the Jews in Europe or the Parsis in India. By virtue of their membership in these groups, such individuals were usually prevented from entering the governing class through purchase or marriage, no matter how successful they might have been from an economic standpoint. Furthermore, by virtue of the barrier which set them apart and the stigma attached to them, they tended to be more vulnerable than other members of their class to forcible expropriation and other hardships.

The Priestly Class

Last but not least among the privileged elements in agrarian societies was that composed of the leaders of organized religion, the priestly class. Strictly speaking, this term refers only to those who mediate relations between God, or the gods, and men through the performance of sacrificial rites. I shall use the term more broadly, however, to include monks, ministers, rabbis, imams, and all other religious leaders whose livelihood and status in society were dependent primarily on their leadership role in the religious system.

The nature of the priestly class varied considerably from one agrarian society to another, especially where religious traditions diverged. In some societies it mediated the basic relations between God and man; in others it had little more than a teaching function. In some it controlled access to spiritual resources essential to salvation; in others it completely lacked such powers. In some it was a celibate, nonhereditary order; in others marriage was allowed for all or for certain subclasses. Where marriage was permitted, an hereditary priestly class often developed, though not invariably. In some societies the priestly class was organized into a fairly well-coordinated national hierarchy; in others this was absent, and members of the priestly class were either equal in status or differentiated only on the basis of local hierarchies. Finally, over and above all of these variations there were vitally important differences in doctrine and differences in relations between the priestly class and the rest of the population, e.g., whether it enjoyed the support of the majority or only a small minority, and whether or not it enjoyed the support of the political elite. Because of all these variations, it is extremely dangerous to generalize about the role of the priestly class. It may even be that the nature of this class was the most variable feature of importance in agrarian societies, when viewed from the standpoint of the distributive process.

When this class enjoyed the favor of the political elite, as some segment of it usually did, its opportunities for accumulating wealth were enormous. Though Ramses III, founder of the twentieth dynasty in ancient Egypt, ranks among the most generous benefactors of the priestly class, his gifts reveal the potentialities.[34] According to the record prepared at the time of his death, his gifts to the gods and to their servants, the priests, included 169 towns, 113,433 slaves, 493,386 cattle, 1,071,780 plots of ground, 2,756 images of the gods containing 1,400 pounds of gold and 2,200 pounds of silver, and a vast array of other things.

Though Ramses was unusually generous, others in all walks of life bestowed gifts on the priestly class, with the result that it was often one of the wealthiest in agrarian societies. For example, in Egypt in the century after Ramses III, in the twelfth century B.C., the priestly class owned 15 per cent of the land.[35] The same figure is reported for France in the eighteenth century.[36] In the early Islamic state, 20 per cent of all the booty won in war was claimed for the support of the priestly class.[37] In Ottoman Turkey, as much as a third of all the land was set aside as *vakf*, i.e., as a religious endowment.[38] At the time of Charles Martel, it is estimated that the Church in France owned a third of the land, and a similar figure is reported for England in the fourteenth century.[39] The Church in

---

[34] See Erman, pp. 299–305.
[35] Ralph Turner, *The Great Cultural Traditions* (New York: McGraw-Hill, 1941), p. 288.
[36] Shepard B. Clough, *The Economic Development of Western Civilization* (New York: McGraw-Hill, 1959), p. 298.
[37] Albert H. Lybyer, *The Government of the Ottoman Empire in the Time of Suleiman the Magnificent* (Cambridge, Mass.: Harvard University Press), p. 276.
[38] *Ibid.*, pp. 200–201.
[39] On France, see Coulton, p. 53. On England, see Philip Lindsay and Reg Groves, *The Peasants' Revolt, 1381* (London: Hutchinson, n.d.), p. 76. See, also, Thrupp, *Merchant Class*, p. 182, who reports that in London in the fourteenth and fifteenth centuries the Church owned a quarter or more of the land.

pre-Reformation Sweden owned 21 per cent of the land, while in sixteenth-century Russia, it owned 40 per cent or more in certain districts
(though on a national basis the figure was not nearly this high).[40] The
Primate of the Spains, the Archbishop of Toledo, is reported to have
ranked "immediately below the king in point of power, wealth, and the
extent of his dominions" in the early sixteenth century.[41] In Ceylon, Buddhist monasteries are reported to have controlled about a third of the
land.[42] It is difficult to find reliable estimates of the total wealth of the
priestly class in India, China, and Japan, but it seems clear from reports
that it was substantial, in some periods at least.[43] In addition to their great
wealth, members of the priestly class often enjoyed tax exemption, which
greatly enhanced the economic value of their property.

Though the holdings of the priestly class as a whole were often immense, all members of the class did not share equally in them. In medieval Europe, for example, there was a division between the upper clergy
and the lower clergy which duplicated the cleavage between the governing class and the peasantry. The upper clergy were usually recruited from
the governing class and lived in a style commensurate with their background, while the lower clergy, the parish priests who served the common
people, were generally recruited from the common people and lived but
little better than their kinsmen.[44] Even in the monasteries, where one
would expect class distinctions to have broken down, they often remained
very pronounced. For example, in a church council convened in Moscow
in 1503 the question was debated whether monasticism and wealth were
necessarily incompatible. The two chief protagonists at this council were
Nil Sorskii, a monk and son of a peasant, and Joseph Sanin, also a monk

[40] On Sweden, see Eli F. Heckscher, *An Economic History of Sweden,* translated by
Goram Ohlin (Cambridge, Mass.: Harvard University Press, 1954), p. 67. On Russia,
see Blum, pp. 177–178 and 188f.
[41] Mariéjol, p. 251.
[42] Max Weber, *The Religion of India,* translated by Hans Gerth and Don Martindale
(New York: Free Press, 1958), p. 257.
[43] See, for example, D. D. Kosambi, *An Introduction to the History of India* (Bombay: Popular Book Depot, 1956), pp. 291–308, or McKim Marriott (ed.), *Village
India: Studies in the Little Community* (Chicago: University of Chicago Press, 1955),
pp. 5, 11–12, 38, 41, and 212 on India; Wolfram Eberhard, *A History of China,* 2d
ed. (Berkeley, Calif.: University of California Press, 1960), pp. 134 and 188 on
China; and Takekoshi, vol. I, chap. 8 on Japan.
[44] The extent to which the ranks of the upper clergy were open to men of humble
birth varied considerably from period to period and from country to country but there
seems never to have been true equality of opportunity. For discussions of the subject,
see S. E. Gleason, *An Ecclesiastical Barony in the Middle Ages: The Bishopric of
Bayeux, 1066–1204* (Cambridge, Mass.: Harvard University Press, 1936), pp. 36f.;
E. Barber, p. 126f.; Mariéjol, pp. 162 and 254; Thompson, pp. 642, 658, and 678;
McKisack, p. 262; Homans, p. 135; or George Vernadsky, *History of Russia* (New
Haven, Conn.: Yale University Press, 1958), vol. IV, pp. 270–271.

but of upper-class origins. Nil argued that monks should "resist and avoid like deadly poison the desire to possess earthly goods." Joseph replied, "If a monastery does not own villages, how can an honorable and well-born man become a monk, and if there are no monks of noble origin, where will men be gotten who are worthy of becoming metropolitans, archbishops, bishops, or of filling other high church offices?"[45] Similar problems plagued the Western Church, where certain monastic orders were closed to anyone not of noble birth.[46] In countries where an hereditary priestly class held sway, as in India, equally great differences were evident, usually a reflection of differences in the individual's or temple's relation to the political elite.

The holdings of the upper segment of the priestly class, though often extensive, were seldom secure. The histories of agrarian societies are filled with acts of confiscation by political elites. Henry VIII was but one of the rulers of Europe who seized the far-flung properties of the Church. As early as the eighth century, Charles Martel and also the dukes of Bavaria confiscated many Church properties.[47] During the medieval period, the so-called Age of Faith, the properties and incomes of the Church were often taken by members of the governing class, and even by retainers employed by the monasteries, by either force or deceit.[48] The Protestant Reformation of the sixteenth century resulted in widespread confiscations of monastery properties throughout the whole area in which Protestantism became dominant.[49] In Russia, the fortunes of the Church varied from century to century and even from ruler to ruler, but the most extensive confiscations occurred in the eighteenth century under such rulers as Peter the Great and Catherine, who deprived the Orthodox Church of virtually all its land.[50] There are also reports of wholesale confiscations in China on several occasions. Prior to the twentieth century, the most extensive may have been one in the ninth century which drove more than a quarter of a million Buddhist monks from the monasteries and secularized millions of acres of tax-exempt monastery lands.[51]

The highly variable fortunes of the priestly class were a reflection of

[45] See Blum, pp. 194–196.
[46] Thompson, p. 680.
[47] *Ibid.*, p. 649.
[48] *Ibid.*, pp. 604 and 651ff.; Ganshof, pp. 293–294; Hans Nabholz, "Medieval Agrarian Society in Transitions," in *The Cambridge Economic History*, vol. I, pp. 527 and 537; or Philip Hughes, *A Popular History of the Catholic Church* (New York: Macmillan, 1950), p. 136.
[49] See, for example, the confiscations of Christian III in Denmark or Gustavus Vasa in Sweden.
[50] Blum, pp. 362–366.
[51] Eberhard, *History*, p. 188. For another example of large-scale confiscations, see p. 246.

its members' heavy involvement in politics, since only the political elite was capable of bestowing land and other forms of wealth in such lavish fashion, and only the political elite was capable of such massive confiscations. This involvement in politics points up the complementary character of the needs of these two classes. Each needed what the other, and only the other, could supply. For its part, the political elite badly needed the blessing of the priestly class. Only the latter could establish the legitimacy of a regime which constantly used its power to separate the common people from the major part of what they produced. The significance of this power to confer legitimacy is difficult to exaggerate. One need only recall the discussion (see pages 51 to 52) of the costliness of efforts to rule by naked force, to realize the benefits which accrued to a political elite when it could obtain the blessing of the priestly class.[52]

The priestly class also performed other functions of great value to the political elite, and sometimes also to society at large. In societies where limited literacy was the rule, the clergy were often called upon to perform those administrative tasks which required a mastery of the art of writing. Our modern term "clerk" reflects the historical association between this activity and the priestly class, or clergy. The clergy were also called upon to serve as diplomats, officials, educators, and even military leaders.[53] In some instances they played an important role in effecting the pacification, civilization, and subjugation of primitive peoples on the borders of agrarian states, thus contributing to the extension of the political influence of the elite with whom they were allied.[54]

For their part, the political elite were able to do much to assist the priestly class. Above all, they used their skills in the art of violence to defend or spread the faith. Although it is true that some faiths, such as early Christianity and Buddhism, spread to some degree without political support, and some, like later Judaism, survived for extended periods without such support, there was usually a high correlation between the measure of political support received by agrarian religions and their numerical

[52] See, for example, Kosambi, p. 291, who says of the Brahmin that he "was an essential adjunct of the state in reducing the mechanism of violence; his preaching of submission reduced the total administrative cost." See also Polybius, a Greek observer of the Roman scene in the second century B.C., who said of Roman religion that "I regard it as an instrument of government" (quoted by Cowell, p. 184). For a very good discussion of the nature of ideology and its social significance, see Homans, pp. 340f.

[53] See, for example, Thompson, p. 649; Marc Bloch, p. 350; or David M. Lang, *The Last Years of the Georgian Monarchy, 1658–1832* (New York: Columbia University Press, 1957), pp. 77–79.

[54] This happened both in India and in Europe. In India, the Brahmins played this important role on a number of occasions. See, for example, Kosambi, pp. 291f. For Russia, see Blum, p. 76. For Central Europe, see Kenneth S. Latourette, *A History of Christianity* (New York: Harper & Row, 1953), pp. 397f.

and geographical spread. Few religious leaders were able to resist the temptation to spread the "true faith" swiftly and surely with the aid of the sword, rather than to rely on the slower and less certain techniques of persuasion. The support of the political elite also proved invaluable when the established faith was challenged by heresies or new faiths, since a vigorous display of force against the dissidents was usually enough to put down the threat.

The support of the political elite proved valuable in yet another way. Few members of the priestly class did not seek to honor God with splendid temples, statues, and works of art, all of which were extremely costly. Here, again, the political elite was singularly equipped to satisfy this desire. In short, there was a natural basis for a symbiotic relationship between these two classes.

Had this been all there was to the relationship, however, there would never have been the massive confiscations noted earlier, nor the many struggles between church and state which fill the historical record. These struggles had many causes, but the underlying one was the fact of divided authority. Except in those cases where the ruler was the human, or semi-divine, head of the religious organization, priestly powers were derived from a source other than the ruler. This meant that whenever the interests of the priestly class and the ruler diverged, as sooner or later they invariably did, the problem arose as to which was the higher authority. In most cases, this could be settled only by a protracted struggle for power. Usually the secular authorities won,[54a] though not without making substantial concessions to the priestly class. Sometimes, however, the religious authorities triumphed, as in ancient Egypt, for example, where the successors of Ramses III in the twentieth dynasty were little more than figurehead rulers manipulated by the priests of Amon, and where, in the twenty-first dynasty, the priests themselves actually occupied the throne.[55] In Europe, following the Gregorian reform, various popes, notably Innocent III, were also able to command the kings and princes of their day, and until the nineteenth century, the popes continued to function as rulers over the Papal States.

It is difficult to say today what factors were responsible for the variations in the outcomes of these struggles. Obviously, *much depended on the religious beliefs of the rulers themselves.* To the degree that they accepted the claims of the priestly class at face value, they were vulner-

---

[54a] Robert Bellah adds, "This is true only in the short run. Religious organizations have been more resilient than political ones and have survived the downfall of many political regimes, often overtly or covertly contributing to their downfall" (personal communication).

[55] Erman, pp. 50 and 305.

able to its pressure. If they believed that their fate in this life or the next would be determined by their treatment of a particular religious group and its leaders, they would unhesitatingly extend themselves to accord them favors. This, of course, raises the additional question of why some rulers were pious men, subject to priestly influence, while others were not. Many factors were undoubtedly involved, but several stand out. First, piety in rulers, as in other men, was likely to depend on childhood training. Thus, to the degree that kings and princes were trained in childhood by the clergy, and more especially by politically minded clerics, to that degree they were likely to be responsive to priestly pressures in later years. Second, piety in rulers, as in other men, probably depended on the homogeneity of the religious influences to which they were exposed. Those raised in religiously homogeneous societies were likely to be more supportive of the priesthood than those raised in societies where various faiths competed.[56] Finally, rulers, like other men, were greatly influenced by individuals in whom they placed special trust, and the attitudes and beliefs of such persons were likely to be transmitted to the rulers themselves. Thus, wives, mothers, ministers, and close friends undoubtedly influenced their actions in this area.

The position of the clergy also seems to have been a function of a number of factors other than the religious beliefs of the ruler. It probably varied directly with the degree of popular support the clergy enjoyed, as well as with the extent of the ruler's need for support of the kind the priestly class could provide, whether for political struggles with the governing class at home or with foreign enemies abroad. The classic case of the latter is found in the efforts of the Roman emperors from Constantine's day on to mobilize the resources of the Christian Church behind the increasingly shaky standard of imperial rule.

In their many struggles for power, the motives of the priestly class were usually rather mixed. In part, its members were often motivated by a desire to glorify and serve God, or the gods. At the same time they were often motivated by a desire for personal power and privilege. The best proof of this is found in the many voices raised by devout men of many faiths, often members of the priestly class themselves, protesting against the materialism, power grabbing, and self-seeking of so many religious leaders.[57] It can also be seen in the spread of practices such as simony, or

[56] The great Mughal emperor, Akbar, is a classic example of a ruler who came to distrust the priestly class of his own faith as a result of exposure to other faiths.
[57] This theme recurred again and again in the Judaic-Christian tradition, from the days of such early Hebrew prophets as Amos and Micah, down to the days of Peter Waldo, St. Francis, Wyclif, Hus, Erasmus, Luther, and, in fact, to the end of the agrarian era.

the sale of priestly offices, which was a widespread evil from the early Middle Ages until the Protestant Reformation.[58]

Though it is clear that the clergy usually fell considerably short of the ideals they professed, and furthermore that they contributed to the stability and perpetuation of systems of inequality by legitimizing the rule of the political elite, this is not the whole story. On many occasions, especially in the Judaic-Christian tradition, though not there alone, the priestly class opposed tyranny and injustice and supported the needs and interests of the weaker elements in society.[58a] For example, though the Christian tradition provided an ideological undergirding for the *status quo*, it also provided an ideological basis for such revolutionary movements as the Peasants' Revolt of the fourteenth century in England, and the Levellers' movement of the seventeenth. One of the important leaders of the earlier movement was the famous priest, John Ball, who used as a text for many of his sermons the popular jingle:

> When Adam delved and Eve span
> Who was then the gentleman?

According to the monk who wrote the *Chronicon Angliae*, Ball's argument was simply,

> At the beginning we were all created equal; it is the tyranny of perverse men which has caused servitude to arise, in spite of God's law; if God had willed that there should be serfs He would have said at the beginning who should be serf and who should be lord.[59]

This argument was very similar to that adopted by Gerrard Winstanley and the Levellers, several centuries later (see page 9).

Less extreme, but therefore probably more effective, was the tradition embodied in the Western religions that God is above all a God of justice and that His awesome powers will be used to punish the unjust. One finds this, for example, in the ancient code of Hammurabi, who claimed:

[58] See, for example, Hughes, p. 85, the noted Catholic historian, who, in writing of the early medieval period, speaks of the many bishops who "bought their nomination to the see," and then made their reign "a long financial torture for the unfortunate subjects, while the prelate endeavored to recoup his initial expenses." See, also, Mercia Macdermott, *A History of Bulgaria* (London: G. Allen, 1962), pp. 51 and 52, who describes how the Ottoman sultans sold bishoprics in the Orthodox Church to the highest bidder, or W. E. D. Allen, *The History of the Georgian People* (London: Routledge, 1932), p. 272, who describes the practice of simony in the Georgian church.
[58a] See, for example, S. N. Eisenstadt, "Religious Organizations and Political Process in Centralized Empires," *The Journal of Asian Studies*, 21 (1962), p. 286.
[59] Lindsay and Groves, p. 72. Quoted by permission.

At that time Anu and Enlil named me, Hammurabi, the exalted prince, the worshipper of gods, to cause righteousness to prevail in the land, to destroy the wicked and the evil, to prevent the strong from injuring the weak, to go forth like the sun over the blackheaded people, to enlighten the land, and to further the welfare of the people.[60]

The Mosaic code presents the same essential conception of a divine concern for justice and righteousness, and the prophets of ancient Israel poured out bitter condemnations on the political elite and merchant class of their society, all in the name of Yahweh.[61] They charged the members of these privileged classes with selling justice, extortion, bribery, the use of false weights, theft, and, above all, oppression of the poor. Apparently, they gained a hearing, even in the court of the king, and, because they spoke in Yahweh's name, were extremely difficult to silence. Though technically most of the prophets were not priests, and, in fact, criticized the priestly class no less than the others, it was the priestly class which was the basic transmitter of the Mosaic tradition and its concept of Yahweh's concern for justice and righteousness.

These same elements appear in the Christian tradition, even in the most unlikely places. For example, the Russian Church at an early date began urging the humane treatment of slaves and encouraged their emancipation at their owner's death.[62] Apparently these efforts bore fruit. During the same period, the Western church went further and in the Third Lateran Council of 1179 declared that no Christian could hold a fellow Christian as a slave.[63] A century later the English Church took a firm stand in opposition to the thesis that serfs "owned nothing but their bellies" and therefore were not entitled to make a will and transmit property to their heirs. The Church fought for nearly a century to have its more liberal view established as law, despite opposition from Parliament, which argued, in a petition to the king, that such practice "is against reason." [64]

Even the doctrine of the divine right of kings was used by the priestly class to restrain rulers, at least in lands where God was felt to be concerned with justice and where the political elite possessed a measure of

[60] A. T. Olmstead, *History of the Persian Empire* (Chicago: University of Chicago Press, 1948), p. 122. Quoted by permission.
[61] See, for example, the books of Amos, Micah, and Isaiah, and also II Sam. chaps. 11 and 12, for the dramatic account of Nathan's denunciation of King David for his murder of Uriah the Hittite and subsequent marriage to Uriah's widow.
[62] Blum, pp. 52–54, and 113.
[63] Latourette, p. 558.
[64] Bennett, pp. 249–250.

piety and faith.[65] For example, during the eleventh century the clergy played a major, though by no means solitary, role in establishing the Peace of God, which brought an end to the constant depredations by the governing class. As one historian put it, "The Church created a category of a specially protected class. It asserted that a defenseless peasantry, however weak, still had rights before the law which the baronage, however violent, would be compelled to respect" on pain of excommunication.[66] The following is a typical oath imposed on the governing class by the clergy:

> I will not carry off either ox or cow or any other beast of burden; I will seize neither peasant nor merchant; I will not take from them their pence, nor oblige them to ransom themselves; I do not wish them to lose their goods because of wars carried on by their seigniors, and I will not beat them to obtain their subsistence. I will seize neither horse, mare, nor colt from the pasture; I will not destroy nor burn their houses; I will not uproot their vines or gather their grapes under pretext of war; I will not destroy mills and I will not take the flour therein, unless they are on my land, or unless I am on war service.[67]

In medieval London the clergy often warned merchants that such practices as the giving of short measure, misrepresentation of goods, and usury were sins in the sight of God. Such sermons evidently were not without influence, as indicated by the many wills and testaments which provided for the restitution of goods or money acquired dishonestly.[68] Sometimes restitution was made to specific individuals, at other times to the poor in general. The sums involved were often considerable. For example, one man left £1,800 to charity, most of it to be distributed in gifts of half a mark, i.e., nearly seven shillings apiece, to five thousand poor city householders. Though the size of this bequest was unusual, it was long customary for men of means to assign from a third to a half of their movable goods to uses that would benefit their souls. In addition to these individual acts of charity stimulated by the Church, there was also a very substantial amount of charitable work carried on by the monasteries.[69] Islam, also, has had a tradition of charity on both an individual

[65] Even in India, where ethical elements have not loomed nearly so large as in the Judaic-Christian tradition, the divine right of kings was linked by the priests with a doctrine of the divine responsibility of kings to their people. See R. C. Majumdar (ed.), *The History and Culture of the Indian People* (Bombay: Bharatiya Vidya Bhavan, 1951, 1953), vol. II, pp. 304f.

[66] Thompson, p. 668.

[67] *Ibid.* Quoted by permission.

[68] Thrupp, *Merchant Class*, pp. 174–180.

[69] See, for example, Thompson, p. 632; Coulton, pp. 266–267; or Latourette, pp. 538 and 558.

and organized basis. To support the latter, Muslims were obliged to give one-fortieth of their income either in money or in kind.[70]

The foregoing is, of course, only one side of the coin. Many members of the priestly class were grasping, mercenary, self-seeking, cruel, tyrannical, and exploitative. James Westfall Thompson best summarized the contradictory elements in the priestly class when he wrote of the medieval Catholic Church, "Democratic, yet aristocratic; charitable, yet exploitative; generous, yet mercenary; humanitarian, yet cruel; indulgent, yet severely repressive of some things; progressive, yet reactionary; radical, yet conservative—all these are qualities of the Church in the Middle Ages." [71]

To say even this, however, is to say that the Church and its leaders played a unique role among the privileged classes in agrarian societies. In a type of society in which men of power saw to it that there was a massive flow of goods and services from the many to the few, some members of the priestly class managed to slow this movement and even to stimulate a small flow in the opposite direction. *In this respect, the priestly class tended to function as the preserver of the ancient Redistributive Ethic of primitive societies, where the accumulation of goods in private hands had served as a form of communal insurance rather than as private property.* The extent to which the priestly class performed this important function varied considerably from religion to religion, and within religions from century to century and area to area. Of all the factors responsible for this variation, the most important seems to have been the actual content of a faith and the degree to which God was believed to be concerned with social justice. A second factor of importance seems to have been the power of the spiritual weapons at the command of the clergy. When they had the power to deny men salvation, as in the medieval Catholic Church, they had a singularly potent weapon at their disposal, one which no believing ruler could safely ignore.

The Peasant Class

Ultimately, the burden of supporting the state and the privileged classes fell on the shoulders of the common people, and especially on the peasant farmers who constituted a substantial majority of the population. Even taxes levied on the more prosperous segments of the population were

[70] See H. A. R. Gibb, *Mohammedanism: An Historical Survey* (New York: Mentor Books, 1955), p. 56.
[71] Thompson, p. 684.

usually shifted to the peasants and urban artisans by one means or another.[72]

One can get a good idea of the extent of the burdens imposed on the peasants by studying the numerous taxes and other obligations they owed. In Japan, during the Tokugawa period and earlier, practices varied considerably from area to area and decade to decade, with the political elite claiming anywhere from 30 to 70 per cent of the crop.[73] This spread reflected the operation of a variety of factors, but there is evidence that indicates that the lower rates prevailed when the governing class also employed a number of other methods to acquire the economic surplus, while the higher rates prevailed when reliance was placed on that single tax. For example, in the sixteenth century, Toyotomi Hideyoshi, the then effective ruler of Japan, abolished all taxes except the land tax, which he then set at two-thirds of the total crop.[74] This is probably the best indication we have of the *total* take of the political elite (both ruler and governing class) when the land tax was low, but a multiplicity of other taxes were in effect.

In China, peasants traditionally paid rents of 40 to 50 per cent of their total produce to landowners.[75] In India, both Muslim and Hindu rulers are reported to have customarily demanded from one-third to one-half of the crops in the pre-British era.[76] During the Sukodhya period in Thailand, peasants were obliged to pay one-fourth of the total yield of their land.[77] In Hammurabi's Babylon, taxes varied from one-third to one-half of the crop, while according to Hebrew tradition, Egyptian taxes during the captivity equaled one-fifth.[78] In Achaemenian Persia, taxes varied from

---

[72] See, for example, Michael Rostovtzeff, *The Social and Economic History of the Roman Empire,* rev. ed. (Oxford: Clarendon Press, 1957), p. 385, who states that in Rome under the Flavians and Antonines "as in Russia under the old regime the privileged classes knew how to escape such burdens and shift them onto the shoulders of the peasants." See, also, Eileen Power, *Medieval People* (Garden City, N.Y.: Doubleday Anchor, 1954, originally 1924), pp. 19 and 33; W. H. Moreland, "The Revenue System of the Mughul Empire," *The Cambridge History of India,* vol. 4, pp. 470–471; or William Stubbs, *The Constitutional History of England,* 5th ed. (Oxford: Clarendon Press, 1891), vol. I, p. 303. Occasionally, however, this proved impossible, as in the late Roman Empire. See Mattingly, p. 152.

[73] Takekoshi, vol. I, p. 415, and vol. II, pp. 228, 305, and 311.

[74] Takekoshi, vol. I, p. 415, and vol. III, p. 386.

[75] See Eberhard, *History,* pp. 72 and 213 or Chung-li Chang, *The Income of the Chinese Gentry* (Seattle, Wash.: University of Washington Press, 1962), pp. 132–133.

[76] See W. H. Moreland, "Revenue System," p. 453; Moreland, *The Agrarian System of Moslem India* (Allahabad: Central Book Depot, n.d.), chap. 8; or Marriott, p. 109.

[77] John E. de Young, *Village Life in Modern Thailand* (Berkeley, Calif.: University of California Press, 1958), pp. 156–157.

[78] Turner, p. 309.

20 to 30 per cent.[79] Many centuries later, in Ottoman Turkey, they varied from 10 to 50 per cent.[80] In the sixteenth and seventeenth centuries share-croppers in Russia paid from one-fifth to one-half.[81]

The lowest rate of taxation on peasant production I have been able to discover in agrarian societies was that which the Romans imposed on the provinces of Sicily and Asia in the period when they first assumed control. According to reports, they demanded only a tenth of the total yield, a figure which was actually *less* than the peasants had previously paid.[82] Some modern historians believe that the Romans deliberately set the rate low in order to win support in these newly conquered countries and thus solidify their base of power. The low rate was probably also a reflection of the impossibility of double-cropping the land, a common practice in most of agrarian Asia.

Another heavy burden laid on peasants in most agrarian societies was the *corvée*, or forced labor. Often this involved a considerable portion of their time and energy. In medieval Europe, for example, peasants were commonly obliged to work on their lord's land from one to seven days a week throughout the year, the average being about three.[83] However, usually only one member of he family was required to serve, so that the burden was not so great as it might seem, though it was still substantial. Also, recent research indicates that, in England at least, a "day's work" could often be completed in half a day.[84] Furthermore, the extent of the obligation commonly varied with the size of the holding, so that peasants with large holdings, and therefore greater resources, were the ones who had the five, six, and seven day obligations, while those with small holdings had the lesser ones.[85] Perhaps the worst feature of these obligations was the lord's right, in many cases, to shift the burden from one week to the next to suit his own convenience, and especially his tendency to demand more work in the harvest season when time was most precious.[86]

It should also be noted that in addition to his duty to his own lord, the peasant sometimes had obligations to the king or other higher authorities as well. For example, in eighteenth-century France peasants owed

[79] Olmstead, p. 76.
[80] Lybyer, p. 31.
[81] Blum, pp. 102 and 221.
[82] Boak, p. 125, or Mattingly, p. 220.
[83] See, for example, Coulton, p. 73; Homans, p. 257; Power, p. 18; Clough and Cole, p. 14; Gottschalk, p. 31; or Blum, pp. 225–227 and 444–445.
[84] Bennett, pp. 103–104.
[85] *Ibid.*
[86] *Ibid.*, pp. 106 and 110.

the king twelve days' labor a year in addition to the several days per week they owed their local lord.[87]

In some instances, forced labor became a very heavy burden. For example, in feudal Thailand adult male peasants were obliged to serve as much as a third of the year in the king's service.[88] In China, during the building of the Great Wall, peasants were sometimes kept on forced labor projects for most of their adult lives.[89] In still more extreme cases, peasants were enslaved, as in the American South or Rome, and obliged to devote all of their energies to the service of the state or individual members of the political elite.[90]

When land taxes, rents, and labor services failed to secure the whole of the economic surplus, or left the peasants time or energy to spare, still other taxes and obligations were devised. During the period of Ottoman rule in Bulgaria, for example, the Turks imposed approximately eighty different types of taxes and obligations.[91] These included one known as the "tooth tax," which was leveled on a village by the Turks after they had eaten and drunk their fill, ostensibly for the wear and tear sustained by their teeth during the meal.[92] The cruelest tax of all was the *ispendzh*, which required that every five years a certain number of the finest Christian children were taken either for slavery or for service in the Corps of Janissaries.[93]

In Christian Europe, too, the peasants were subject to a great variety of taxes and other obligations during the Middle Ages, though none like the *ispendzh*. When a man died, the lord of the manor could claim his best beast or most valuable movable possession, and the priest could often claim the second best. Often the lord took more than the single beast to which he was entitled, with the result that a third or more of a peasant's estate would be lost at his death.[94] If his daughter married off the manor, or married without the lord's permission, the father was subject to a fine. If any of his children sought to leave the manor, even for the sake of entering the priesthood, the father was subject to a fine. In eighteenth-century France, if a peasant wished to sell his land, he would often have to

---

[87] Gottschalk, p. 24.
[88] de Young, p. 156.
[89] See Max Weber, *The Religion of China*, translated by Hans Gerth (New York: Free Press, 1951), p. 52, on the building of the Great Wall. See Eberhard, *History*, pp. 235–237, on the *corvées* levied by the Mongols.
[90] See, for example, Boak, p. 127.
[91] Macdermott, p. 28.
[92] *Ibid.*, p. 48.
[93] *Ibid.*, pp. 28–29.
[94] Bennett, pp. 144–147.

pay the noble who held hereditary title to it a tax equal to as much as 25 per cent of the selling price. At various times during the year, peasants were obliged to provide the lord of the manor with special "gifts," such as eggs at Easter, honey in season, and so forth. Frequently the lord operated a mill, an oven, or a wine press, and peasants were obliged to use these facilities and, of course, to pay dearly for them. When the lord had goods to be carted to market, his peasants would often be made to perform this time-consuming chore without receiving credit as a part of their regular labor services. The Church, meanwhile, commanded a tithe of all they produced (and often a goodly portion of this passed into the hands of the landed aristocracy).[95] Finally, in certain periods in some countries, the lord claimed the right to take anything he wished from the personal property of his peasants without payment, on the theory that the peasants owned "nothing but their bellies." [96] In short, the great majority of the political elite sought to use the energies of the peasantry to the full, while depriving them of all but the basic necessities of life.[97] The only real disagreement concerned the problem of how this might best be done.

In this endeavor, the elite seem to have been highly successful. The great majority of peasant farmers throughout history had little more than the bare necessities of life. The chief exceptions occurred only in those societies where, in the words of Marc Bloch, "every free man remained a warrior, liable to be constantly called into service and distinguished from the pick of the fighting men by nothing essential in his equipment." [98]

For the vast majority, however, life was extremely primitive. For example, one student of medieval England concludes that the diet of the

---

[95] Bloch, p. 252.

[96] For good discussions of the variety of miscellaneous obligations imposed on peasants in various societies, see Bloch, pp. 248–254; Clough and Cole, pp. 14–17; Bennett, chaps. 5 and 6; Blum, pp. 103, 434, 444ff., and 453-455; Gottschalk, pp. 34–37; Lindsay and Groves, chap. 1; Allen, pp. 262ff.; and Takekoshi, vol. III, pp. 386 and 402ff. For expressions of the view that peasants owned "nothing but their bellies," see Coulton, p. 76; Homans, p. 228; Bennett, p. 249; or Blum, p. 289, who reports that this was legally true at one time in Russia.

One finds frequent references to the fact that legal documents from agrarian societies have little to say about the rights of peasants, but much about the rights of their superiors, indicating that at most times, in most of these societies, peasants had few enforceable rights. See, for example, Moreland, "Revenue System," pp. 452-453, on India.

[97] See, for example, Blum, p. 232, who says of the Russian elite, "their object was to tax the peasant to the maximum of his capacity to pay. . . . ," or Moreland, *Agrarian System*, p. 207, who writes of Mughal India that, "The direct result was to take from the peasant whatever he could be made to pay. . . ." Of course, there were exceptions, such as St. Hugh of Lincoln, who reputedly refused on one occasion to take from a peasant woman her only animal, an ox to which he was entitled by virtue of the death of the woman's husband (see Bennett, p. 147). Unfortunately, saints were as rare then as now.

[98] Bloch, p. 248. See p. 275 below for a further discussion of this subject.

average peasant consisted of little more than the following: a hunk of bread and a mug of ale in the morning; a lump of cheese and bread with perhaps an onion or two to flavor it, and more ale at noon; a thick soup or pottage followed by bread and cheese at the main meal in the evening.[99] Meat was rare, and the ale was usually thin. Household furniture consisted of a few stools, a table, and a chest to hold the best clothes and other treasured possessions.[100] Beds were uncommon and most peasants simply slept on earthen floors covered with straw. Other household possessions were apparently limited to cooking utensils.

In some cases, the lot of the peasant was not even this good. On many occasions conditions became so oppressive that it was impossible to eke out a livelihood and the peasants were forced to flee the land.[101] In China, conditions were so wretched that female infanticide was practiced on a wide scale. One nineteenth-century scholar reported that records indicated that as many as a quarter of the female infants born in some districts were killed at birth.[102] In such areas signs were sometimes posted, "Girls may not be drowned here." Though this was admittedly an extreme practice, the conditions which gave rise to it were by no means limited to China. On the contrary, the great majority of peasants who lived in the various agrarian societies of the past apparently lived at, or close to, the subsistence level.

To compound the misery created by their economic situation, the peasants were often subjected to cruel and inhumane treatment by their superiors. For example, in Russia, as in the American South, families were often split up if it served the economic interests of their masters.[103] Pretty peasant girls were often sold for immoral purposes, and peasants found it difficult to defend their wives against lustful masters.[104] Finally, peasants were subject at all times to the whims and temper of their superiors. To cite but two examples, admittedly extreme, Ivan Turgenev's mother sent two of her serfs to Siberia simply because they neglected to bow to her when she passed by while they were working, and in medieval England peasants were hanged for stealing a few eggs.[105]

From the standpoint of the political elite, all this was only natural.

[99] Bennett, p. 236.
[100] Ibid., pp. 232–233.
[101] See, for example, Bernier on Mughal India as quoted by Moreland, *Agrarian System*, p. 147, or Blum, pp. 163, 266–268, 309–310, and 552f. on Russia.
[102] Douglas, p. 354.
[103] Blum, pp. 424, 428, etc. See also Lang, p. 69, on European Georgia.
[104] Blum, pp. 426–427 and 437. See also G. M. Carstairs, "A Village in Rajasthan," in M. N. Srinivas (ed.), *India's Villages* (Calcutta: West Bengal Government Press, 1955), pp. 37–38.
[105] Blum, p. 438, and Bennett, p. 196.

In most instances they viewed the peasantry as, at best, a very different breed of people from themselves—people largely or wholly lacking in those qualities of personality which the elite prized and respected. For example, the scribes of ancient Egypt referred to the slaves as being "without heart," i.e., without understanding, and said that therefore they had to be driven with a stick like cattle.[106] Aristotle argued that "it is clear . . . that some men are by nature free, and others slaves, and that for these latter slavery is both expedient and right." [107] Aristotle also likened slaves to animals, a comparison whch recurs time and again in the writings of members of the privileged classes. In legal documents in medieval England, the children of a peasant were not called *familia,* but *sequela,* meaning "brood" or "litter." [108] In both Europe and Asia there are documents in which the peasants on an estate were listed with the livestock.[109] The same view was taken of the Negro "peasants" in the agrarian South in this country, both before the Civil War and subsequently. Given this view of the peasantry, it is hardly surprising that so civilized a man as Cato the Elder should have argued that slaves, like livestock, should be disposed of when no longer productive.[110]

As shocking as such views may be to members of modern industrial societies, they were not completely unreasonable, given the nature of the social system. To begin with, there was always a great social and cultural barrier separating the peasants from the political elite. Even in medieval Europe, when the manorial system held sway and the governing class lived on the land, there were few personal contacts between lord and peasants, modern romantic myths to the contrary notwithstanding. Nearly always at least one level of officials of the retainer class intervened, mediating the relation and reducing opportunities for direct contact to a minimum. According to Bloch, such officials were found "even on the smallest manor." [111] Furthermore, there were usually great differences in the customs and ways of life of the elite and the peasants. Often these differences resulted from the fact that the peasants were of alien stock

[106] Erman, p. 128.

[107] Aristotle, *Politics,* translated by Benjamin Jowett (New York: Modern Library, 1943), p. 60.

[108] Coulton, p. 77, or Thompson, p. 708. In a recent study of an Indian village, the author reports that a Rajput landowner dismissed a lower caste boy with the gesture used in "shooing" animals and adds that "culture encouraged a conception of [such persons] as in some way less human than others." See Henry Orenstein, *Gaon: Conflict and Cohesion in an Indian Village* (Princeton, N.J.: Princeton University Press, 1965), pp. 155–156.

[109] See, for example, Stubbs, vol. I, p. 454n.; Eberhard, *History,* p. 32; or Takekoshi, vol. I, pp. 60–63.

[110] See Boak, p. 127, or Cowell, p. 64. For an example of the application of Cato's principle in medieval Europe, see Bennett, p. 283.

[111] Bloch, p. 337. See also Homans, p. 229.

and stigmatized by their defeat in war or, worse yet, by an earlier tradition of servitude (as when one elite destroyed another and seized the latter's already degraded peasantry, thus destroying the memory of a period of independence and freedom). These differences were further compounded by the disparity in life style between an elite which had wealth and leisure at its disposal and could cultivate either the arts of war or of gracious living, and a peasantry utterly lacking in opportunities to acquire good manners, education, military skills, or even literacy. Under such conditions, the surprising thing is that some members of the privileged strata recognized the fact of their common humanity, not that the majority failed to do so.

For their part, the peasants seem to have been highly ambivalent about their status in society. On the one hand, they were aware of the great cultural chasm which separated them from their "betters," and many undoubtedly accepted without question the explanations provided by the dominant ideology. On the other hand, their physical nature created in them an intense desire for survival and, when survival was assured, a desire for a better life. In other words, like their superiors they were motivated to maximize their rewards, insofar as their situation permitted it. Thus, struggles inevitably developed between the peasantry and their masters.

Usually these struggles were nonviolent in character, at least on the peasants' side. For the most part, their efforts consisted of little more than attempts to evade taxes, rents, labor services, and other obligations, usually by concealment of a portion of the harvest, working slowly and sometimes carelessly as well, and similar devices.[112] For example, old memorial court records from England reveal fines levied on peasants for failure to come to the harvest, or for coming late, or for performing badly when they did come, for grinding meal at home rather than at the lord's mill, and for a host of other petty offenses aimed at preventing the lord of the manor from obtaining the whole of the surplus.[113]

Sometimes, however, the political elite pushed the peasants too far, and they turned from petty trickery to violence. As E. J. Hobsbawn has shown in his fascinating book, *Primitive Rebels*, young peasants, after a brush with the authorities, were often forced to become outlaws and bandits.[114] If, then, they limited their attacks to members of the privileged

---

[112] Such practices seem to have been almost universal. See, for example, Fried, pp. 104–105 on China, Moreland, *Agrarian System*, pp. 168 and 207 on India, or Bennett, pp. 100–101, 112–113, and 131ff. on England.

[113] See Bennett, especially pp. 112–113 and 131f.

[114] *Primitive Rebels*, 2d ed. (New York: Frederick A. Praeger, 1963), especially chap. 2.

classes, in the Robin Hood tradition, they could count on the support of most of their fellow peasants. In effect, their struggles with the authorities became a form of class conflict. This pattern was especially likely to develop in mountainous areas and in areas where dense forests provided necessary cover for the operation of outlaw bands; it was rare where such protection was lacking.

A still more extreme response on the part of peasants was open revolt. Though these are often forgotten or ignored, a careful reading of the histories of agrarian societies indicates that they were by no means uncommon.[115] One Chinese expert states that "There were peasant rebellions almost every year in China," while a Russian expert reports that in the short period between 1801 and 1861 there were no less than 1,467 peasant risings in various parts of the Russian Empire.[116]

Though the number of risings was impressive, the number of peasants involved usually was not. For the most part, these risings were local affairs involving at most a few hundred or a few thousand individuals. Thus it would be a mistake to suppose that the peasantry was in a constant state of revolt. Nothing could be further from the truth.

Most of these rebellions were hopeless affairs from the start. Sometimes minor victories were won in isolated local struggles, as when the peasants of Preston, England, burned the steward's house and threatened his life "until he swore not to make exactions [i.e., noncustomary ones] against their will in the future." [117] Revolts which spread had less chance of success, since they quickly encountered the organized forces of the political elite. A few, such as the famous English revolt of 1381 or the German Peasants' War of 1524–25, spread more widely and for a time seemed to threaten the existing order, but in the end were crushed. A very, very few succeeded in overthrowing the existing regime. That this did not happen often is indicated by the fact that in all the long history of China, only three succeeded prior to the twentieth century, and even this was a higher incidence than in most societies.[118]

[115] See, for example, Robert K. Reischauer, *Japan: Government-Politics* (New York: Nelson, 1939), p. 51 on Japan; Wolfram Eberhard, *Conquerors and Rulers: Social Forces in Medieval China* (Leiden, Netherlands: Brill, 1952), p. 52 on China; Cowell, pp. 43–44 and 66 on Rome; Blum, pp. 164, 267f., 365, 368, 555f., and 587 on Russia; Edith M. Link, *The Emancipation of the Austrian Peasant, 1740–1798* (New York: Columbia University Press, 1949), p. 12 on Austria-Hungary; Mariéjol, p. 273f. on Spain; Lindsay and Groves, pp. 19, 168 and, in fact, the whole book, on England; and Thompson, pp. 681f. on Western Europe generally.
[116] Eberhard, *Conquerors*, p. 52 on China, and Blum, p. 558 on Russia.
[117] Bennett, p. 170. House burnings were a common peasant tactic, and in the Ukraine before the Revolution were known as "letting out the red rooster."
[118] Eberhard, *Conquerors*, p. 52.

Even the handful of peasant revolts which succeeded in overthrowing the existing regime failed to create a new and more equitable social order. On the contrary, they produced nothing more than a change in personnel at the top with the traditional institutional structure remaining virtually unaltered. Thus, though a few individual members of the peasantry rose to riches and power by means of these revolts, the great majority gained little or nothing except insofar as the memory of such revolts survived and made the new elite somewhat more cautious than they might otherwise have been.[119]

Paradoxically, though peasant revolts seldom accomplished much for the masses, milder forms of pressure sometimes did, especially when they occurred in conjunction with other significant social developments.[120] Among these related developments, none influenced the economic and political situation of the average peasant more than changes in military tactics and technology. On the basis of both theory and research, a general proposition can be formulated to the effect that *the greater the military importance of the peasant farmer, the better his economic and political situation tended to be, and conversely, the less his military importance, the poorer his economic and political situation.* A peasantry armed and skilled in the use of weapons was a class which could not be ignored politically or exploited economically nearly as easily as one lacking military skills and equipment.

Many examples could be cited from the historical record to illustrate how changing patterns of military organization and tactics, combined with constant pressure from the peasantry, influenced their political and economic situation. In ancient Rome, the rise of the plebeians seems clearly to have been linked with changed methods of warfare.[121] In Western Europe, the growing importance and power of mounted and armored men during the Middle Ages was clearly linked with the decline of the free farmer and the growth of an oppressed class of peasant serfs.[122] In ancient China, during the Period of the Contending States, the opposite pattern appeared. Here there was a shift from wars fought between small

[119] Success was usually achieved only with the aid of a portion of the governing class, with the result that afterwards these same individuals continued in power and only a small number of peasants gained entrée into the political elite. See, for example, Eberhard, *Conquerors*, chap. 3.

[120] The explanation of this paradox seems to be that peasant revolts were most likely to occur at the very time when conditions were most hopeless. They were, in effect, a last resort, attempted when more moderate efforts had failed, and, since they occurred under the most unfavorable conditions, seldom achieved results.

[121] Stanislaw Andrzejewski, *Military Organization and Society* (London: Routledge, 1954), pp. 53–55.

[122] See, for example, Bloch.

groups of nobles in war chariots, to ones in which the charioteers were supported by relatively large armies of armed peasant infantry. During the period of this shift, there was apparently a marked decline in the landholdings of the nobility and a substantial increase in small farms owned by free peasants.[123]

Several other factors also influenced the political and economic situation of the peasant class. The most important seems to have been the demographic factor of mortality. Ironically, though revolutions seldom improved the lot of the ordinary peasant for long, *disasters sometimes did.* Plagues, widespread famines, and devastating wars sometimes had the effect of creating an acute labor shortage, thus driving up the price of peasant labor. Normally, man's reproductive capacity insured a constant oversupply of peasant labor, permitting the political elite to offer them no more than a subsistence income.

Disasters occasionally altered this. Some of the best evidence of the beneficial consequences of disasters is found in connection with the Great Plague which struck Western Europe in the middle of the fourteenth century. Shortly thereafter the records begin to be filled with reports of peasants demanding, *and receiving,* substantially higher wages than formerly.[124] Parliament was driven to try to control the rise in wages through legislation, but had little success, since landlords were much readier to pay the higher wages than to see their fields sit idle. In France, the Hundred Years' War seems to have had similar beneficial effects for the surviving members of the peasantry.[125]

On a few occasions a labor shortage was created without a major disaster. For example, in the German frontier settlements in the East during the Middle Ages the peasant settlers enjoyed personal liberty, economic independence, and opportunities for amassing a modest measure of wealth.[126] A similar situation prevailed in Russia during periods of expansion into new eastern territories.[127]

Four other factors also seem to have affected the condition of the peasantry. First, the content of the dominant religious systems apparently had some effect. As noted previously, the religions of the East, especially Hinduism and Confucianism, were compatible with extremes of exploitation in a way that Judaism and Christianity were not; the former

[123] Eberhard, *History,* pp. 52–54.
[124] See, for example, McKisack, pp. 331–340, or Lindsay and Groves, pp. 30, 34, and 63.
[125] Charles V. Langlois, "History," in Arthur Tilley (ed.), *Medieval France* (London: Cambridge University Press, 1922), pp. 150–151.
[126] Hans Rosenberg, *Bureaucracy, Aristocracy and Autocracy: The Prussian Experience 1660–1815* (Cambridge, Mass.: Harvard University Press, 1958), pp. 28–29.
[127] Blum, pp. 61 and 88.

left the peasantry more defenseless than the latter.[128] Second, the presence of the institution of slavery seems to have had an appreciable influence on the social condition of the peasant class, and, as in the case of religion, this variable was not a simple function of any one other variable. Third, inflation sometimes worked to the advantage of the peasantry, at least when their obligations were fixed in absolute, rather than relative, terms. When peasants owed their lords a fixed sum of money rather than a percentage of their crop, they stood to benefit by an inflation which slowly reduced the value of the lord's income, especially if it was so gradual as to be unnoticeable. A goodly number of economic historians contend that something of this sort occured in late medieval Europe, though there is some objection to this thesis.[129] Finally, as noted earlier (see pages 241 to 242), some maintain that the position of the peasantry tended to improve when rulers dominated the governing class, and to decline when the governing class became dominant.[130]

No discussion of the peasant class would be complete if notice were not taken of intraclass differences. Despite the heavy burdens laid on the class, not all its members were reduced to the same level. In most agrarian societies there were important intraclass dfferences in power, privilege, and honor. In thirteenth-century England, for example, there were three fairly distinct subclasses, sometimes known as franklins, husbonds, and cotters.[131] The franklins were the most prosperous and also, as one would expect, the least numerous. As their name indicates, the franklins were free men, answerable only to the royal court, not the local manorial courts, and free from the servile obligations of villeinage. Often these men owed special services of a more honorable nature, such as overseeing the work of the ordinary peasants on the lord's land. In addition, they usually paid a modest rent for their land, which was two to four times as large as that of the husbonds immediately below them. The term "husbond" referred to a householder, in contrast to the cotters, who lived in a cottage or poorer dwelling. Husbonds usually held from ten to forty acres of land and in return for this owed the lord of the manor several days' work every

[128] See pp. 263–266 above.
[129] See, for example, W. G. Hoskins, *The Midland Peasant: The Economic and Social History of a Leicestershire Village* (London: Macmillan, 1957), pp. 90, 196f.; Langlois, p. 150; Trevor-Roper, p. 13; Simpson, chap. 5. The same may also have occurred in Ottoman Turkey. See Lybyer, p. 177.
[130] For an interesting discussion of Greek views on this subject,, see Andrewes, *op. cit.* For a challenging modern statement of this thesis, see Bertrand de Juvenal, *On Power: Its Nature and the History of Its Growth*, translated by J. F. Huntington (New York: Vikings, 1949), especially chap. 9. For some evidence to support this thesis, see Lang, p. 62.
[131] For good descriptions of these three subclasses, see Homans, pp. 242ff., and Bennett, chap. 3.

week plus various other services. In contrast, cotters normally held five acres of land or less and, unlike the husbonds, owned no ox for plowing. Though their labor obligations were proportionally lighter than those of the husbonds, their land holdings were usually too small to support a family and these men were forced to work for wages for others, e.g., the lord of the manor, prosperous franklins, or even the widows of husbonds. Sometimes they became plowmen or shepherds, other times carpenters, smiths, or millers.

Such differences were found within the peasant class in most agrarian societies, and the pattern was similar in them all: the prosperous peasants were far fewer in numbers than those who lived at or near the bare subsistence level.[132] Whatever else may be said of these differences, they always served the "useful" function of dividing the peasantry, thus facilitating the efforts of the political elite to maintain its control despite its small numbers.

The Artisan Class

In the traditional status hierarchies of China and Japan, the peasant class was usually followed by the artisan class.[133] Despite the fact that there was always considerable overlap between these two classes, this pattern of ranking probably reflected not merely the prejudices of the governing class, but also certain economic realities. In most agrarian societies, the artisan class was originally recruited from the ranks of the dispossessed peasantry and their noninheriting sons and was continually replenished from these sources. Furthermore, despite the substantial overlap between the wealth and income of the peasant and artisan classes, the median income of artisans apparently was not so great as that of peasants. For example, one observer in nineteenth-century China wrote of them as living in "even a deeper state of poverty than that which afflicts agriculturalists," and went on to say that "they live perpetually on the verge of destitution."[134] Many were so poor that they were unable to marry, with the result that the sex ratio in agrarian cities was sometimes badly out of balance. For example, until fairly recent times men outnumbered women by a nearly 2-to-1 ratio in Peking.[135] Even in Europe, where the situation of the artisan was generally somewhat better, the city fathers of Bruges in

---

[132] See, for example, Blum, chap. 3 and pp. 99f., 232f., and 471f. on Russia.
[133] See, for example, Fried, p. 211 on China, or Bellah, pp. 24–25 on Japan.
[134] Douglas, p. 137.
[135] Sidney D. Gamble, *Peking: A Social Survey* (Garden City, N.Y.: Doubleday, 1921), p. 30; see also, p. 101. This extreme ratio was probably due to the greater tendency of poor males to migrate to the cities.

the mid-thirteenth century passed a law which linked artisans with thieves and counterfeiters, indicating their low status.[136]

The artisan class was never large. If the estimates reported in the last chapter are accurate (see page 200), and urban populations numbered only 5 to 10 per cent of the total population, then the artisan class could not have numbered more than 3 to 7 per cent.

The majority of artisans were probably employees of the merchant class, though there were nearly always some itinerants traveling about and seeking work where they could find it. The wages of the members of this class were largely a function of the degree of skill involved in their trade and hence of the relative supply of labor. In trades where skills were minimal, and hence the supply of labor abundant, wages were also minimal, while trades which required highly developed skills commanded higher wages. For example, in Peking at the time of World War I, the wages of artisans varied from $2.50 per month for members of the Incense and Cosmetic Workers Guild to $36 per month for members of the Gold Foil Beaters Guild.[137] This difference was probably not due to the inability of the masses of Chinese workers to acquire the skills of goldsmiths, but rather to their inability to acquire them *quickly*. Those who employed the goldsmiths, therefore, could not obtain replacements as readily as those who employed the incense and cosmetic makers, and hence were in a poorer bargaining position.

Sometimes organized groups of artisans attempted to improve their economic situation by controlling admissions to apprenticeship and thus reducing the supply of trained workers.[138] This happened, for example, in fifteenth-century London. However, it does not seem to have been a very common practice.

Artisans, like peasants, sometimes rebelled against those in authority over them. Sometimes this took the form of strikes, sometimes of riots.[139] Such reactions did not seem to occur among artisans nearly so often as among peasants, except perhaps in medieval Europe. This may be only an illusion generated by the great difference in size of the two classes, but probably not. If there was a difference, there is no obvious explanation for it on either theoretical or empirical grounds.

The struggles of the artisans differed from those of the peasants in

---

[136] Thompson, p. 792.
[137] Gamble, p. 183.
[138] Thrupp, *Merchant Class*, p. 113.
[139] See, for example, H. van Werveke, "The Rise of Towns," in *The Cambridge Economic History of Europe*, pp. 34–37; L. Halphen, "Industry and Commerce," in Arthur Tilley (ed.), *Medieval France* (London: Cambridge University Press, 1922), pp. 190–192; Thompson, p. 792; or Pirenne, pp. 187–206.

yet another way, at least in medieval Europe: *they produced some noteworthy benefits for the disadvantaged class.* For example, in the thirteenth century there was a series of struggles between the merchant class and the artisan class in the Low Countries. These culminated in a battle at Courtrai in 1302, where the Flemish artisans crushed the French forces supporting the merchant class, bringing the century-old struggle to a successful conclusion.[140] For the next two decades the artisan class exercised a decisive influence in Flemish towns and, even though a reaction set in after 1320, they continued to play an important role in municipal government for well over a century. Similar developments occurred elsewhere in Europe.

These successes of the artisan class seem to have been due to several factors. To begin with, in the Flemish towns and certain others, their guilds served as the basis of military organization for the defense of the towns.[141] Thus they were equipped to defend their rights. Furthermore, the artisans were given support by the rural population. Finally, their guilds provided the benefits of organization, an advantage denied most peasant groups. Probably no one of these factors alone would have been sufficient to achieve victory, but taken together they were.

Unclean and Degraded Classes

In some agrarian societies, especially in the Orient, there were one or more "unclean" classes. The most famous instance of this is found in the untouchables of Hindu society, but there were similar groups in other societies. In Japan there were the *hinin* (literally "nonpeople") and the Eta. In a number of societies, both in the Middle East and Europe, certain necessary but offensive occupational groups, such as the tanners, were forced to live and work more or less separate from the masses of peasants and artisans.

Sometimes these groups were formally and legally hereditary in character, as in the case of the untouchables. In other cases, the basis of the hereditary pattern was more informal and spontaneous, reflecting the tendency of "decent" folk to avoid those in unclean or degraded classes. Sometimes the degraded status of these groups reflected inferior ethnic origins, again as in the case of many of the untouchables; at other times the status reflected obnoxious or offensive characteristics of the occupation of the group. Thus, there was a certain variability in the character of this class. In every case, however, it occupied a position

[140] van Werveke, p. 35.
[141] *Ibid.*

in society which was clearly inferior to that of the masses of common people.

One other group which may be mentioned at this point, since its position in the hierarchy of power, privilege, and prestige was roughly comparable, was that made up of persons who had only their bodies and animal energies to sell and who were forced to accept occupations which quickly destroyed them. The classic case of this was the Oriental rickshaw puller, who had a very short work life.[142] One might add to this porters who competed with, or took the place of, pack animals, miners who engaged in heavy work under dangerous conditions, and the prostitutes who serviced the many lower class males too poor to marry. Sometimes such tasks were performed by slaves who had no choice in the matter, but many times "free" laborers who could find no other work gravitated into such employment. For such persons, this type of work was often a transitional step, leading to the ranks of the expendables.

The Expendables

At the bottom of the class system in every agrarian society, except perhaps for brief periods following great disasters, there was a fairly large class of expendable persons for whom the other members of society had little or no need. These included a variety of types, ranging from petty criminals and outlaws to beggars and underemployed itinerant workers, and numbered all those forced to live solely by their wits or by charity. This class, which I shall refer to as the expendables, is inevitable in any society where the possibilities for population growth are severely limited and where methods of limiting population growth fail to prevent more births than are required to satisfy the demand for labor.

This class is often ignored in analyses of agrarian societies, and when dealt with is not usually recognized as possessing the distinctive characteristics of a class, i.e., a common relationship to essential resources. Rather, its members are treated as deviant individuals—individuals who lack either the intelligence or moral character necessary to function as useful members of society. As plausible as this view may appear, it contradicts the facts. The historical record is filled with evidence which clearly indicates that despite high rates of infant mortality, the occasional practice of infanticide, the more frequent practice of celibacy, and adult mortality caused by war, famine, and disease, agrarian societies usually produced *more people than the dominant classes found it profitable to*

---

[142] In Peking in the early part of this century, the average work life of rickshaw men was only five years, according to one authority. See Gamble, p. 283.

employ.[143] As the italicized phrase indicates, the problem was not that agrarian economies could not support larger populations, but rather that they could not do so without reducing, and ultimately destroying, the privileges of the upper classes. Eventually, of course, even if the whole population were reduced to the subsistence level, the problem of excess population would have arisen again.

Hobbes's famous statement about the conditions of life for men living in a state of nature aptly describes the conditions of life for the great majority of those who had the misfortune to become members of the expendable class. For them life was usually "poor, nasty, brutish, and short," and sometimes "solitary" as well. The chief exceptions to this were men who organized in outlaw bands in areas where the government's power was weak. Such persons sometimes enjoyed a certain measure of affluence for a time, but in most cases this was short-lived since the authorities usually caught up with them.[144] Nevertheless, it seems safe to say that *illegal activity was the best hope of those who fell into this class, and for the poorest peasants as well.*[145]

Judging from accounts, the members of this class were seldom able to maintain normal marriages, and owing to infanticide, malnutrition, disease, and deprivation, seldom reproduced themselves.[146] However, such losses as accrued to this class because of high death rates were usually offset by the steady stream of new recruits forced into its ranks from the classes immediately above it. These recruits were largely the sons and

[143] See, for example, J. J. Jusserand, *English Wayfaring Life in the Middle Ages,* 3d ed., translated by L. T. Smith, (London: Benn, 1925), especially part 2, chap. 3; Homans, chap. 10; Charles J. Ribton-Turner, *A History of Vagrants and Vagrancy and Beggars and Begging* (London: Chapman & Hall, 1887); Frank Aydelotte, *Elizabethan Rogues and Vagabonds* (Oxford: Clarendon Press, 1913); Maurice Keen, *The Outlaws of Medieval Legend* (London: Routledge, 1961) chaps. 13 and 14; Hobsbawn, especially chap. 2; Pirenne, p. 45; Cowell, pp. 69 and 119 and chap. 17; Thompson, pp. 571, 649, and 715f.; McKisack, p. 204; Lindsay and Groves, p. 64; Gamble, pp. 274–275; Olmstead, p. 78; Mohinder Singh, *The Depressed Classes: Their Economic and Social Condition* (Bombay: Hind Kitabs, 1947), pp. 96–99 and 105–106; Sjoberg, pp. 246–249; Coulton, p. 375; Takekoshi, vol. III, p. 397; and Hsiao-Tung Fei, "Peasantry and Gentry," in Bendix and Lipset, p. 642.

Some recent research suggests that in the past demographers have underestimated the importance of celibacy as a method of population control. See, for example, William Petersen, "The Demographic Transition in the Netherlands," *American Sociological Review,* 25 (1960), especially pp. 341–345. While one can agree with Petersen that celibacy was sometimes a more effective restraint on population growth than has been generally recognized by modern demographers, the almost universal presence of an expendable class indicates that it was not so completely effective as he, at times, seems to suggest.

[144] Hobsbawn, p. 19.

[145] *Ibid.,* chap. 2, especially pp. 22–23.

[146] See Hobsbawn on the short duration of the careers of bandits and outlaws, who constituted the elite of the expendables (chap. 2).

daughters of poor peasants and artisans who inherited little more than the shirts on their backs and a parental blessing.[147] The best that most of them could hope for was occasional work at planting and harvest time and charity in between. Often the ranks of the expendable class were swelled by the addition of peasants who had got into trouble with the privileged classes and had turned bandits.[148] Sometimes this class was also increased by dispossessed nobles or noninheriting sons of nobles who preferred outlawry and a life of illegal violence to demeaning labor or trade in any form.[149]

It is difficult today to determine just how large the class of expendables was in the average agrarian society. However, there are some estimates and some clues. In London, for example, a count made in 1517 revealed a total of 1,000 persons classified as "deserving beggars." [150] A half century later, a report indicated that 13,000 rogues and masterless men had been apprehended during the year, though probably some individuals were arrested more than once. A decade later, in 1577, a writer stated that there were 10,000 beggars in the city, while in 1594 the figure was set at 12,000. In 1545 the total population of the borough of London was reported to be 80,000.[151] From these figures it would appear that 10 to 15 per cent of the population of London was in the expendable class. Such figures are probably too high to serve as estimates for the total society since members of the expendable class have always tended to migrate to urban centers. However, lest it be supposed that these figures are much too high, it should be noted that one careful observer of the French scene late in the seventeenth century wrote, "I have concluded with certainty that, in these recent times, close to a tenth part of the population is reduced to beggary, and actually begs." [152]

Probably the best estimate we can make of the situation in agrarian societies is that in normal times from 5 to 10 per cent of the population found itself in this depressed class, with the figure rising as high as 15 per cent on some occasions and falling almost to zero on others. These estimates seem to correspond reasonably well with the general impres-

---

[147] See, for example, Homans, chap. 10; Hoskins, pp. 75f; Fei, "Peasantry and Gentry," p. 642; or Takekoshi, vol. III, p. 397.

[148] Hobsbawn, chap. 2.

[149] See, for example, the stories of Fulk Fitzwarin, the outlawed baron of the days of King John, or the continental Raubritter (see Keen, chap. 4).

[150] This and the following figures are all from Aydelotte, p. 4.

[151] J. C. Russell, *British Medieval Population* (Albuquerque, N. Mex.: University of New Mexico Press, 1948), p. 285.

[152] Quoted by Jean Fourastié, *The Causes of Wealth*, translated by Theodore Caplow (New York: Free Press, 1960, first published 1951), p. 27.

sions historical accounts give of the frequency of beggars, criminals, and other unemployed persons. The figures would undoubtedly be much higher, of course, were it not for the very high mortality rates which prevailed in this class.

A Graphic Summary

Because of the complexity of the interrelations among the various classes in agrarian societies, it may prove helpful to attempt a graphic characterization of a "typical" agrarian society.[153] Despite its limitations, Figure

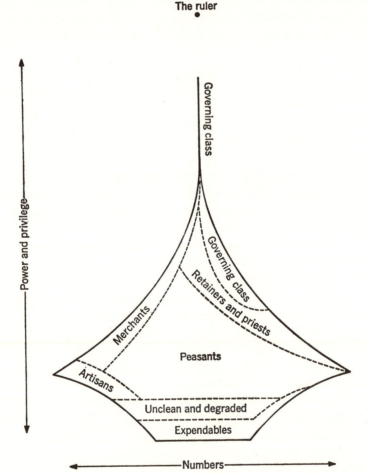

Figure 1   A graphic representation of the relationship among classes in agrarian societies.

[153] Because of the considerable variability among agrarian societies, any diagram over-simplifies reality. What I have sought to portray are the central tendencies.

1 can serve several useful purposes. First, it should help to make clear that the classes within agrarian societies cannot be thought of simply as a series of layers superimposed one on the other. On the contrary, each covers a range of the distributive spectrum, and what is more, each overlaps certain others to some degree. Second, this diagram may serve as a reminder of the inaccuracy of the familiar pyramidal view of societies, which ignores the depressed classes at the very bottom of the social order and minimizes the degree of inequality (which, incidentally, is still minimized by the diagram shown here; it would require a spire far higher and far slenderer than these pages permit to show accurately the relationship between the upper classes and the common people). Finally, this diagram may help to make clear that there is a *continuum* of power and privilege, not a series of separate and distinct strata in the geological sense of that term.

Status Groups

Because agrarian states were generally conquest states, their populations were often divided along ethnic and religious lines. This fact was usually of considerable importance from the distributive standpoint, since ethnic and religious groups often became status groups, and the ethnic and religious identification of an individual tended to become either a resource facilitating his advancement in society or an obstacle hindering it.

Usually those who belonged to the same ethnic or religious group as the ruler were favored, while members of alien, or conquered, groups were at a disadvantage. China during the Ch'ing, or Manchu, dynasty provides a good illustration of this. As one writer put it, "A Manchu would always have his bowl of rice, a small pension at least, paid to the member of the conquering group by the conquered people." [154] This, of course, was the minimum. For those with ability or special connections, far better opportunities were available, as shown in Marsh's study of mobility in China's governing class. In the early part of the Ch'ing dynasty roughly 40 per cent of all officials in the country were Manchus, and though this figure gradually declined, in the last sixty years of the dynasty 20 per cent were still Manchu.[155] As Marsh puts it, "Even this lowest proportion of Manchus in office far over-represented the actual proportion of Manchus

[154] Franz Michael, *The Origin of Manchu Rule in China: Frontier and Bureaucracy as Interacting Forces in the Chinese Empire* (Baltimore: Johns Hopkins, 1942), p. 119.
[155] Marsh, p. 48. An even more pronounced pattern of discrimination prevailed during the earlier Mongol dynasty. See Tsui Chi, *A Short History of Chinese Civilization* (New York: Putnam, 1943), p. 184.

in the Chinese population." Marsh's study further shows that they were especially overrepresented in *the highest ranking offices.* For example, he found, in the sample he studied, that 84 per cent of the Manchus achieved the highest rank, compared with only 44 per cent of the Chinese. Furthermore, these Manchu officials averaged more than twenty-one years in this rank, while the Chinese averaged less than nine.[156] These remarkable "achievements" of the Manchus occurred even though only 14 per cent of them had received the Chin-shih degree, awarded to those who passed the most difficult "qualifying" examinations. By contrast, 64 per cent of their less successful Chinese colleagues had been awarded it.[157] Furthermore, only 24 per cent of the Manchu officials in his sample had followed the "regular" career path leading through a succession of examinations, while 76 per cent of their Chinese counterparts had done so.[158] The majority of Manchu officials had relied instead on the purchase of office and other "irregular" methods. Beneath the Chinese, it should be noted, were the members of various tribal minorities who were even more subject to discrimination in the distributive realm.[159]

Similar practices are evident in many other agrarian societies. For example, in Mughal India under Akbar, the most tolerant of all the Mughal emperors, only 12 per cent of the top 415 officers of the realm, and only 23 per cent of the scholars supported by royal patronage, were Hindus, despite the fact that Hindus constituted the great majority of the population.[160] On a number of occasions, Muslim caliphs in the Middle East forbade Christians to hold public office.[161] In addition, Christians and Jews were sometimes required to wear special clothes (a practice similar to the Manchu requirement that Chinese males wear pigtails), affix wooden images of devils to their house, ride without saddles, and suffer a host of other indignities. Furthermore, the testimony of Christians and Jews against Muslims could not be accepted in a court of law. In Europe, many of the same disabilities were imposed on the Jews, and in Latin America a distinction has long been made between Europeans, mestizos, and Indians with the former groups favored in many ways.[162] In short, *access to rewards was often a function of the ethnic or religious*

---

[156] *Ibid.,* pp. 133 and 138. To simplify my presentation I have combined his figures for the sons of Chinese officials and the sons of Chinese commoners.

[157] *Ibid.,* p. 125.

[158] *Ibid.,* p. 132.

[159] Chung-li Chang, *The Chinese Gentry: Studies in Their Role in Nineteenth-Century Chinese Society* (Seattle, Wash.: University of Washington Press, 1955), p. 80.

[160] Misra, pp. 45 and 62.

[161] Hitti, pp. 234 and 353f.

[162] See, for example, Melvin Tumin, *Caste in a Peasant Society* (Princeton, N.J.: Princeton University Press, 1952).

group with which a member of an agrarian society was affiliated and its relationship to the dominant political force in the society.

In many respects the Hindu caste system can be viewed as a slightly variant and extreme form of this same basic mode of stratification.[163] The chief difference is that in the caste system the group to which the individual belongs is of overriding importance in determining his access to rewards and his opportunities for improving his situation, while in other systems of stratification the collectivity is less important (though sometimes it has been almost as important). There are, of course, other differences, but they seem generally to be of secondary importance. In fact, the more closely one examines the realities of the distributive system in traditional India, instead of Hindu religious theory, the more one is impressed by its similarities to the systems of other agrarian societies, and the less by its differences.

Sometimes, though rarely, membership in a subordinated status group has proven an asset in agrarian societies. The classic case of this occurred in Ottoman Turkey during the era of the Janissaries. When the Janissary system was functioning properly, all of the high officials of state were selected from the ranks of youths taken from Christian families, made slaves of the sultan, trained for military or civil careers, and converted to Islam.[164] High public office was virtually closed to the children of Muslims even though Turkey was a Muslim state.

The explanation for this peculiar pattern seems to lie in the struggles for power between the sultan and the Turkish elements of the governing class. By cutting the latter off from high public office, and filling these positions instead with persons recruited from a despised and conquered minority, the sultan greatly strengthened his own hand. Such officials were much more vulnerable than ones of native Turkish origin would ever have been, and thus more pliant. Furthermore, by denying admission to the corps of Janissaries to persons of Muslim parentage (including the sons of Janissaries), the sultan prevented the establishment of an hereditary nobility in the usual sense. Unfortunately for the sultans, it proved impossible to maintain such an aberrant system indefinitely, and eventually the Janissaries and other prominent Muslim families succeeded in securing the admission of their sons to this elite organization. This marked the beginning of the end of the effectiveness of the system.

The Janissary principle has been applied in varying degrees in cer-

---

[163] For an early statement of this view, see Max Weber, *From Max Weber: Essays in Sociology,* translated by H. H. Gerth and C. Wright Mills (Fair Lawn, N.J.: Oxford University Press, 1946), pp. 188–189.
[164] For an excellent description of the system, see Lybyer, chaps. 2–4.

tain other agrarian states, but never with such great success.[165] Probably the best examples are pre-Mamluk Egypt and the Muslim kingdom of Delhi. Of course, in these cases advancement was contingent on conformity to the dominant faith and the culture of the dominant ethnic group.

Another type of variable which often influenced the access of individuals to rewards in agrarian societies was their *legal status*. Three legal statuses which deserve special note were nobility, serfdom, and slavery. The former set certain individuals apart from others by providing them with advantages; the latter two by burdening them with disabilities.

The term slavery has been used to describe a number of quite distinct positions of servitude in horticultural and agrarian societies. For example, the prime ministers and other top officials of Ottoman Turkey were legally slaves of the sultan, but they wielded immense powers. Yet this same term, slave, is applied to Cato's field hands and others who were denied virtually every human satisfaction except survival.[166]

At the other extreme, nobility proves an equally variable concept. As one writer said in discussing the concept of nobility in France, "There never had been a general theory of nobility, for if the concept of the noble 'vivant noblement' was recognizable [throughout France], each province had varying customs regarding immunity from *taille* and the privileges resulting from holding a noble fief." [167] If this was true of the various provinces within France, it was even truer of the agrarian world as a whole. The concept of nobilty, like the concept of slavery or serfdom, varied considerably from area to area and society to society. The one common denominator was that nobility was always linked with certain legally assured privileges, while slavery and serfdom were always linked with certain legally enforced limitations on freedom. These distinctive benefits and handicaps were written into the legal code of the nation and enforced by the courts and other agencies of societal authority.

When these special statuses were hereditary (and they, as well as religious and ethnic statuses, usually were), the possibility of status discrepancies arose. We know from the historical record that such discrepan-

---

[165] See, for example, Rosenberg, p. 65, or Sidney Painter, *The Rise of the Feudal Monarchies* (Ithaca, N.Y.: Cornell University Press, 1951), p. 52, on its application in Europe.

[166] The concept of serfdom was equally variable. See, for example, D. Kumar, "Caste and Landlessness in South India," *Comparative Studies in Society and History*, 4, (1962), pp. 341f.

[167] C. A. J. Armstrong, "France of the Hundred Years War and the Renaissance," in J. M. Wallace-Hadrill and John McManners (eds.), *France: Government and Society* (London: Methuen, 1957), p. 94. See also Blum, p. 349, on the various types of nobility in eighteenth-century Russia.

cies were, in fact, a fairly common occurrence. On the one hand, we find ample evidence of impoverished noblemen, far poorer than many commoners; on the other hand there are numerous reports of slaves and serfs who were far wealthier than the vast majority of commoners and even than many of the less wealthy nobility. In eighteenth- and nineteenth-century Russia, for example, a number of serfs entered various fields of business and became extremely wealthy.[168] One serf paid 135,000 rubles, plus a factory, land, and serfs (which he owned) for his freedom, and still remained a wealthy man. At that same time, a member of the nobility in the province of Riazin reported that one-fourth of the 1,700 noble families in his province were so poor that "together with their peasants they form one family, eat at one table and live in one hut." [169] Similar comparisons can be found in almost every other agrarian society where statuses of nobility, serfdom, or slavery had been hereditary for generations.[170]

Where religious and ethnic statuses were important, they, too, tended to become inconsistent with economic status. Thus, certain members of subordinate religious or ethnic grous, like the Jews in Europe or the Christians and Jews in the Middle East, acquired considerable wealth, while numerous members of the dominant groups lived in poverty. One of the important problems for future research is the determination of the consequences of status inconsistency in these societies.

Vertical Mobility

Agrarian societies have often been depicted as societies in which there was very little vertical mobility. This simply was not so. Any careful examination of the historical record makes it clear that there was considerable mobility, though much of it was of a type which members of modern industrial societies, especially Americans, are likely to overlook. This may explain why agrarian societies are so often misrepresented in sociological writing.

To appreciate the extent of vertical mobility in these societies, one must pay much closer attention to *downward mobility* than is customarily done. The rate of downward mobility is not necessarily equal to the rate of upward mobility, as sometimes is assumed; hence the rate of upward mobility is not always an adequate measure of total societal mobility. It is the tendency to make these assumptions which has caused so much of

[168] Blum, pp. 472–474.
[169] *Ibid.*, p. 376.
[170] See, for example, Mariéjol, pp. 266f. on Spain; McManners, "France," p. 36 on France; Rosenberg, pp. 144f. on Prussia; Thrupp, *Merchant Class*, pp. 236f. on England; or Douglas, pp. 30–31 on China.

the confusion in discussions of mobility in agrarian societies. The fact is, unhappily, that *in the long run, in all of these societies, downward mobility was much more frequent than upward*. Failure to recognize this has led to most of the misleading assertions about the low rate of mobility in agrarian societies.

The explanation for this somewhat surprising feature is found in the simple fact of human fecundity. Mankind, unfortunately, is able to produce considerably more offspring than there are positions to be filled in agrarian societies. This is true despite the high levels of infant mortality, the occasional practices of infanticide, the more frequent practices of monasticism and prostitution (the latter of which is a rough equivalent of polyandry from the demographic standpoint), celibacy, and the influence of war, disease, and famine. Though these factors occasionally combined to create brief manpower shortages, over the long run they have not been enough to balance the constant supply of new offspring.[170a] Therefore, in societies where there are not important new frontiers, either geographical or economic, surplus manpower is usually driven downward in the class system in the direction of the expendable class, which performs the unavoidable function of redressing the demographic balance.

The influence of surplus population can be seen at every class level in agrarian societies. As we have already noted, the common people, and especially the peasants, were constantly faced with this problem. In some societies, as in China, they sought to solve it by dividing the family patrimony more or less equally among all of the sons, but this soon had the effect of reducing individual holdings to the point where they were too small to provide the necessities of life for those who occupied them. At this point, the land passed into the hands of the minority of officials, merchants, or prosperous peasants who were in the process of building estates. However, in the hands of *their* descendants the same cycle was usually repeated. This was true even of families with vast estates when there were many sons, but none especially adept in the difficult art of fortune building.[171]

Sometimes the problem was dealt with by the practice of primogeni-

---

[170a] See the second paragraph of fn. 143 for a comment on recent research on fertility limitation in the Middle Ages.

[171] See, for example, Chang, *Income,* pp. 128f. on China; Misra, p. 50 on India; or Blum, pp. 66, 68, 82f., 172, and 376f. on Russia. It should be noted that when a descendant of an estate builder proved skillful in that same way, this usually benefited only his own immediate descendants and not his brothers' and cousins' descendants. The Chinese differed somewhat in this and maintained stronger ties in the extended family, so that all benefited to some extent if any member of the extended kin group recouped the family fortune. Even in China, however, the greatest benefits went to the immediate family of the successful man.

ture or some other system of inheritance which avoided the fragmentation of the family estate. This was the usual practice in Western Europe. The chief effect of this system, however, was to speed the decline of the noninheriting sons while permitting one son to preserve his father's status. *The simple fact is that there is no way to avoid a net downward movement in societies in which all but the lowest classes produce more offspring than there are status vacancies.*

Though downward mobility was the more common form of vertical mobility in agrarian societies, *upward* mobility was not uncommon. Despite the constant downward pressures generated by demographic forces, a certain number of individuals managed to rise. Sometimes they filled new positions, e.g., in the merchant class in an era of expanding trade and commerce, sometimes positions vacated by the death of men who left no heirs, and sometimes positions vacated by individuals who lacked the skills or luck necessary to hold them. Of these three, the second and third patterns were the most common. Compared with industrial societies, the creation of new positions was relatively infrequent.

Upward mobility, whether on an inter- or intragenerational basis, was usually limited to one step in a lifetime, though, as will be noted, there were some cases of "rags to riches." Frequently a step-at-a-time advance was simply movement within a class. As indicated previously, none of the major classes was completely homogeneous; each could be subdivided into several subclasses, as in the peasant class in thirteenth-century England with its subdivisions into franklins, husbonds, and cotters. The majority of advances seem to have been the equivalent of movement from cotter to husbond, from husbond to franklin, or from franklin to the lowest rank of the governing class. As modest as such advances may seem to members of modern industrial societies, they represented no small accomplishment in agrarian societies, where the cards were normally stacked against advances of any kind. In such societies, most men counted themselves fortunate if they were able to pass on to their offspring a patrimony as great as that which they themselves had received.[172]

It is not easy to document at the present time why a few men were upwardly mobile while the majority were not. Differences in innate ability and vitality were undoubtedly important. Chance happenings, too, must surely have played a part. For example, those who escaped serious illnesses and accidents undoubtedly fared better on the average than those who did not. Fertility probably was a factor, favoring the parents of large peasant families, but handicapping their offspring. A large family meant the benefit of more free labor for the parents, but from the children's

[172] See, for example, Chang, *Income*, pp. 128f.

standpoint, it meant a smaller per capita inheritance, especially in those societies where estates were divided equally among the offspring. Finally, there is considerable evidence that sectarian religious movements which stress hard work and asceticism often contributed to the success of their adherents, especially when they constituted a minority in a population which ignored these values. The economic success of the Old Believers in Russia was but one of a number of examples of this.[173]

In most generations, a very small minority managed to make more dramatic advances. Sir Nicholas Bacon, father of Sir Francis Bacon, was born the son of a sheep reeve but rose to become one of the chief officers of state and one of the wealthiest men of his day.[174] St. Godric of Finchale was one of the noninheriting sons of a poor peasant father at the end of the eleventh century, and was forced to live by his wits. In time, however, he became a wealthy merchant doing business in the ports of England, Scotland, Flanders, and Denmark.[175] Robert Grosseteste, a famous bishop of Lincoln, England, was said to have been born a villein.[176] Savva Morozov, founder of the famous Morozov industrial empire in czarist Russia, was the son of a serf and spent his early years fishing and tending cattle, and later was hired as a weaver for food, lodging, and five rubles a year.[177] An eighteenth-century primate of the Catholic Church in Spain was the son of a Gibraltarian charcoal burner.[178] In Ottoman Turkey during the heyday of the Janissary system, virtually all of the chief officers of state were the sons of poor Christian peasants.[179] In China, the founders of at least three dynasties appear to have been of peasant origin, while a number of the later emperors of Rome were men "up from the ranks." [180] These are but a few of the thousands of whom we still have record who made dramatic advances.

As these examples suggest, such advances did not come to those who stuck to the plow and the awl. Farming and the crafts promised limited advances at best. Those who made the more dramatic advances did so by turning to occupations with which wealth and power were normally associated—commerce, the army, the Church, or civil government. In fields such as these, a handful, but only a handful, of men found an op-

---

[173] See, for example, Valentine Bill, *The Forgotten Class: The Russian Bourgeoisie from the Earliest Beginnings to 1900* (New York: Frederick A. Praeger, 1959), especially chap. 4, or Blum, pp. 301 and 310.
[174] For a fascinating analysis of Bacon's rise, see Simpson, chap. 2.
[175] Pirenne, p. 46.
[176] Homans, p. 135.
[177] Bill, p. 18.
[178] Raymond Carr, "Spain," in A. Goodwin (ed.), *The European Nobility in the Eighteenth Century* (London: Black, 1953), p. 47.
[179] Lybyer, chaps. 2–5.
[180] Eberhard, *History*, pp. 71, 203, and 239 and Homo, p. 354.

portunity to rise well above their origins. The great majority in these fields advanced little, if at all, since the positions at the top were usually defended with all the vigor, skill, and resources at their occupants' command.

An important problem, one which deserves far more systematic attention than it has yet received, is the question of the stability, or lack of it, in the composition of the upper classes. Logic and common sense suggest that they were very stable, except perhaps in times of great crises. However, there is a good bit of evidence which suggests this was not the case. For example, we know that even though the Roman nation survived well into the Christian era, the old patrician class did not. Of sixty-one patrician gentes whose existence in the early days of the Republic is historically confirmed, only twenty-four survived to the year 367 B.C., and by the early second century of the Christian era, only a single one of the original patrician families remained.[181] A recent study of the French nobility in Forez in south-central France (an area almost coextensive with the Loire department today) revealed that of 215 noble lineages in existence in the thirteenth century, 30 per cent had disappeared by the end of that century. Less than a third survived to the end of the fourteenth century, a seventh to the end of the fifteenth century, and exactly five to the French Revolution in the late eighteenth century.[182] In England few of the great families of the medieval period survived the Wars of the Roses and the proscriptions of the Tudors.[183] Even in the medieval period, the position of English noble families was far from secure.[184] In Russia, numerous princely families were destroyed by confiscation and by the practice of dividing the family patrimony equally among the male offspring.[185] Such evidence strongly indicates that the position of families in the governing class in many agrarian societies was far from secure. Those families which did not die out naturally were usually destroyed by the death of the heir in battle, by confiscation, fragmentation of the family patrimony, or stupidity or profligacy on the part of the heir.

Before concluding this brief discussion, a few comments are necessary on *variations in rates of vertical mobility*. This subject is extremely difficult to deal with in societies as complex as agrarian ones. To begin with, systematic, quantitative data of a reliable nature are largely lacking. In addition, there is no single rate of mobility in such societies, but liter-

---

[181] Homo, p. 35, and Turner, p. 921.
[182] See Edouard Perroy's fascinating study, "Social Mobility among the French *Noblesse* in the Later Middle Ages," *Past and Present*, 21 (1962), p. 31.
[183] H. J. Habakkuk, "England," in Goodwin, p. 18.
[184] Painter, *Barony*, pp. 175–176.
[185] Blum, pp. 66, 68, 82f., 172, 376f., etc.

ally several dozen different rates, e.g., the rate of movement from the peasant class to the merchant class, to the expendable class, to the retainer class, etc. For example, if one considers only the nine major classes defined in this and the preceding chapter,[186] and ignores the various subclasses, there still are 72 (9×8) rates of movement possible between classes; and, while a few of the possibilities may be unrealized in certain periods, none can safely be ignored. Finally, it is not at all certain that any one of these rates is at all typical of the rest. Thus the usual comments about *the* rate of mobility in such societies are often extremely misleading: *there is no single rate and none which can safely be used as an indicator of all the others.*

Because of this, the most that can be done in the brief space available here is to take note of a few of the forces which probably had important consequences for the more important rates of mobility. To begin with, it seems clear that autocracy, or the dominance of the ruler over the governing class, would increase the rate of movement into and out of the governing class.[187] Conversely, oligarchy would probably increase the rate of mobility into and out of the ruler's office. The explanation for this is simply that power tends to increase with tenure, and those who fear the increase of power in others, and have the means to prevent it, are likely to do so. There is one limitation on the application of this principle: when the survival or welfare of both parties in a power struggle is threatened by a third party, the original protagonists are likely to refrain from taking hostile action against each other.

Second, wars, famines, and other disasters would tend to increase the rates of upward mobility, at least when the loss of life is so great that the more privileged classes cannot replace their losses from within their own ranks. At the same time, such disasters would be likely to reduce the rates of downward mobility.

Third, the spread of practices such as infanticide, abortion, celibacy, and prostitution would reduce the rates of downward mobility. They would be less likely to affect the rates of upward mobility since they would probably not prevent the privileged classes from producing sufficient offspring to fill all the higher positions.

Fourth, the opening of new economic opportunities, especially in the area of trade and commerce, would increase the rates of upward movement into the merchant class in the short run, and into the governing class in the long run, as merchants often use their wealth to buy status. Simi-

---

[186] I am counting the ruler as a separate class, a practice consistent with modern set theory.

[187] See, for example, Misra, p. 51, or Lybyer, chaps. 5 and 6.

larly, the opening of new political opportunities, especially through the conquest of new territories, would increase the rates of movement into the governing and retainer classes of the victorious nation. On the other hand, it would lead to a significant increase in the rate of downward movement in the conquered group.

These, in brief, are a few of the more important factors contributing to variations in the rates of mobility in agrarian societies. While this list is far from complete, it may serve to communicate something of the complexity of the problem.

A Note on Distributive Justice

Before concluding this discussion of stratification in agrarian societies, a few brief comments on the subject of distributive justice are in order. On the whole, agrarian societies give the impression of gross injustice in the distributive realm. As we have seen, a small number of individuals enjoyed immense luxury, consuming in a single day goods and services sufficient to support large numbers of the common people for a year. At the same time a considerable portion of the population was denied the basic necessities of life and was marked out by the social system for a speedy demise. It does not take much imagination to conceive of a more equitable method of distribution.

However, when the demographic factor is introduced into the analysis, we suddenly discover that the problem was never so simple as it sometimes seems to those of us who live in the comfort of a modern industrial society. Despite the ravages of war, famine, plague, and other disasters, and despite the influences of infanticide, abortion, monasticism, and prostitution, those segments of the population which were at, or above, the subsistence level continued to produce more offspring than could be employed except by a steady reduction in privilege. Thus, barring an effective method of controlling fertility, which no agrarian society ever discovered, there seems to have been no alternative to the existence of a class of expendables, as harsh as such a statement may sound to modern ears. The most that could have been achieved, had the elite permitted it, was the temporary elimination of this class for the short time it would take population growth to eliminate the economic surplus.

This line of reasoning also points up an interesting feature of the economic surplus which is often overlooked. The surplus of any society is not determined solely by the means of production available to its members. *It also depends on the nature of the distributive system.* Given the same productive system and identical environments, several societies could have economic surpluses of very different size depending upon the skill and ruthlessness of the dominant classes. To the degree that the elite permitted the peasantry to retain more than they needed for survival, and to the degree that they permitted them to farm inefficiently small parcels of land, to that degree they would reduce the size of the economic surplus. This is a point which is easily overlooked in societies, such as our own, where productive techniques seem to be regarded as all-important and distributive techniques quite secondary.

One other point should be made in defense of the rulers and governing classes of agrarian societies. Though clearly these persons exploited the common people (in the sense that they used force to obtain what the common people would not have given them in free exchange), nevertheless they did perform one useful function: they maintained a fair degree of *law and order*. This was vitally important in an agrarian society, where the nature of the economy made anarchy intolerable. A single crop failure for any reason (such as delay in planting due to political strife) could mean death for thousands, and two successive failures disaster. As Robert Bellah put it, "When the Islamic ulema said, 'A hundred years of despotism are better than one day of anarchy,' they were not just apologists for the ruling class. They were often deeply opposed to the rulers and entirely alienated from them. But they knew what days of anarchy are like in such societies." [188] One is reminded here of Luther's equally ambivalent view of the German princes of his day. In short, though the rulers and governing classes of agrarian societies clearly charged more for their services than the common people were willing to pay without coercion, they did render certain services of value (one might add, of value to themselves as well as others). Hence, though their relations with the common people were highly exploitative and parasitic, they were not only exploitative and parasitic. This was probably one of the chief reasons for the durability of the agrarian state as an institution. There was really no alternative.

[188] Personal communication in response to an earlier draft of the manuscript. This paragraph was added at his suggestion.

10/Industrial Societies: Part I

*Question: What is the difference between
Capitalism and Communism?
Answer: Under Capitalism man exploits
man; under Communism it's
the other way around.
Russian saying*

DURING THE LAST TWO CENTURIES, the productive systems of many societies have undergone a profound change. In this relatively short space of time, techniques of production and patterns of economic organization which had endured for thousands of years have been replaced by new and radically different ones. These developments have laid the foundation for a new and profoundly different kind of society, the modern industrial.

Unfortunately for purposes of the present analysis, it is still not possible to observe a fully mature industrial society. As events of the last twenty years have made clear, the technological revolution of modern times is far from complete, and those who supposed otherwise a few short years ago were badly mistaken. Though it is tempting to speculate about the nature of more advanced industrial societies than any yet in existence, such efforts are likely to degenerate into social science fiction, *à la* Huxley and Orwell. Hence this and the next two chapters claim to be no more than an analysis of the distributive systems of the most advanced industrial societies *of the present time*, except for pages 432 to 433 where the intriguing, but treacherous, problems of the future are briefly examined.

Common Features of Industrial Societies

From the technological standpoint, the more advanced industrial societies of the present day differ greatly from agrarian. The raw materials used are far more diversified, the sources of energy quite different, and the tools far more complex and efficient. Differences are so great, in fact, that it is possible to mention only a few of the most significant in the compass of the present analysis.

One of the most important differences sociologically pertains to the sources of energy used in the performance of "work," i.e., activities such as pushing, pulling, lifting, cutting, and digging which have been, or theoretically could be, performed by the muscle power of men, but *not* activities such as smelting metals, cooking food, or providing heat, light, or refrigeration.[1] In agrarian societies, men and animals were the two chief sources of such energy. In a recent study it was estimated that in the United States in 1850, 65 per cent of the energy employed in work activities was supplied by men and animals, despite the fact that industrialization was already under way.[2] Another 28 per cent was supplied by the ancient triad of wind, water, and wood which have long supplemented the efforts of men and animals. Only 7 per cent was provided by any of the newer energy sources, and this entirely in the form of coal.

A century later the picture was radically altered. All of the traditional forms combined—men, animals, wind, water, and wood—supplied only 1.6 per cent of the energy used in work. All the rest was supplied by the newer forms, the fossil fuels and hydroelectric power. In fact, 65 per cent of the energy came from sources, such as petroleum, natural gas, and hydroelectric power, which were virtually unknown a century earlier. At the present time, still another new energy source is becoming significant, namely, atomic power.

Not only have energy sources changed, but the quantities consumed have multiplied. In 1850 the work output of the American nation totaled only 435 horsepower-hours per person per year, a figure probably not far

[1] This definition of work is based on J. Frederic Dewhurst and Associates, *America's Needs and Resources* (New York: Twentieth Century Fund, 1955), pp. 905–906.
[2] *Ibid.*, p. 1116.

in excess of the average for advanced agrarian societies.[3] By 1950 this had increased more than ten-fold, to a total of 4,470 horsepower-hours per person per year. Furthermore, if all forms of energy consumption are included (and not work alone), a twenty-fold increase is indicated for the century in question.

The greatly increased consumption of energy associated with the rise of industrial societies is matched by the consumption of other resources. For example, as recently as 1800 the total production of iron in all parts of the world is estimated to have equaled only 400,000 metric tons, or about 1 metric ton for every 2,000 persons.[4] By 1950 iron production totaled 132 million metric tons, or more than 1 ton for every twenty persons. In other words, on a worldwide basis there was a hundred-fold increase in the per capita consumption of iron in the period from 1800 to 1950. If the comparison were limited to the more advanced industrial societies, it would be even more dramatic. In the United States, for instance, there was 1 metric ton produced for every two persons in 1950, representing a thousand-fold increase over the worldwide figure for 1800.[5]

Equally dramatic increases are indicated in the consumption of other raw materials. As long ago as 1949, America was consuming 7,300 pounds of stone, sand, and gravel, 520 pounds of cement, 210 pounds of common salt, 130 pounds of phosphates, 89 pounds of gypsum, 71 pounds of sulphur, 23 pounds of copper, 16 pounds of zinc, 13 pounds of aluminum, and 13 pounds of chromium *per person per year*, to cite but a few of the more familiar items.[6] Consumption of most of these items is still rising, and no end to the increase is in sight.

The great increase in the consumption of raw materials is paralleled by a very substantial increase in *production*. For example, from 1849 to 1961 the per capita income of the American people rose from approximately $320 to $1,950 per year.[7] Since these figures are standardized on

[3] All figures in this paragraph are based on the Twentieth Century Fund's study of America's resources, Dewhurst, pp. 1114 and 1116, together with census data. The per capita figures are my own calculations based on these sources.

[4] Iron production figures are from W. S. Woytinsky and E. S. Woytinsky, *World Population and Production: Trends and Outlook* (New York: Twentieth Century Fund, 1953), pp. 1101 and 1117. Population figures are from A. M. Carr-Saunders, *World Population* (Oxford: Clarendon Press, 1936), p. 30, and the *Demographic Yearbook, 1953* (New York: United Nations, 1953), p. 14. Per capita iron production figures are my own calculation.

[5] Harrison Brown, *The Challenge of Man's Future* (New York: Viking Compass Books, 1956), p. 189.

[6] *Ibid.*, pp. 189–190.

[7] The former figure is from Woytinsky and Woytinsky, p. 381. The latter is calculated from data on national income, price indexes, and population provided in *Statistical Abstract of the United States, 1962* (Washington, D.C.: GPO, 1962), pp. 5, 312, and 343.

the value of the dollar in 1949, they represent a *real* increase, not merely a paper increase. Especially significant is the pattern of the trend: half the total increase was registered in the last two decades alone, indicating a rapidly accelerating rate.

As great as the difference is between the figures above, even they fail to reveal fully the magnitude of the change involved in the shift from an agrarian to an advanced industrial economy. To begin with, the United States in 1849 was by no means typical of advanced agrarian societies. Industrialization had already been under way for some decades, especially in New England. Furthermore, the population was still quite sparse, permitting much larger farms than were customary in agrarian societies, thus raising the per capita income well above what it would otherwise have been. One can get a far better idea of the traditional agrarian pattern by examining figures from nations which in the mid-twentieth century were still essentially agrarian in character. In 1948, for example, the per capita income of Mexico, as measured in American dollars, was only $106 per year; of Brazil, $112; Peru, $82; Egypt, $112; India, $75; and Thailand, $79. The Chinese figure for 1938, adjusted upward to allow for the inflation of the American dollar in the next decade, was still only about $35 per person per year.[8] Keeping in mind that all these societies had been influenced by industrialization to some degree, it seems clear that in pure agrarian societies of times past, the per capita income was almost certainly no more than $100 per year as measured by 1949 dollars, and probably less. In other words, the per capita income of the United States today is already at least *twenty times* that of the typical agrarian society of the past, and is still rising.

The technological advances responsible for this tremendous increase in productivity have also affected almost every other aspect of human existence. Some of the most direct and substantial effects have been on the economic institutions of society. To begin with, the technological revolution of the last two centuries has destroyed economic self-sufficiency. Even farmers no longer provide most of their own necessities, except in the more remote and backward regions. Exchange relationships are rapidly becoming essential for every member of these societies. This means, among other things, that money plays a much more important role in the economic life of industrial societies than in agrarian. In the latter, money did not enter into the usual daily routine of the peasant masses, while in the more advanced industrial societies, it is an integral element in the daily lives of even the poorest citizens.

[8] Woytinsky and Woytinsky, pp. 389–393.

With advances in the fields of transportation and communication, local market systems have been all but destroyed through absorption into larger and more inclusive market systems. As a consequence, the economically self-sufficient community is virtually absent in advanced industrial societies. The trend toward the enlargement of markets has, in fact, already been carried to the point where international markets now exist for most major commodities, and if it were not for political restrictions, the entire world would soon become a single market for many commodities.

As markets have grown and technology has become more complex, ever larger units of production have become a necessity. In the United States today there are a number of corporations which employ a hundred thousand or more workers and pool the capital resources of hundreds of thousands of investors. American Telephone and Telegraph is at present the largest, employing three-quarters of a million people.

This growth in the scale of organization in the economic area has facilitated another development, intensive specialization. According to the Department of Labor, there are currently more than twenty thousand different kinds of jobs in this country, most of them extremely specialized in nature.[9] This is true not only of manual work, as on the assembly line, but also of nonmanual. The general practitioner is rapidly becoming an anachronism, not only in medicine but in most other professions.

Intensive specialization is also characteristic of communities. Some specialize in the production of autos, others in textiles, recreation, education, or government. Even at the national level, there is evidence of specialization. In a world dominated by advanced industrial nations, some countries specialize in the production of machine tools, some in oil, and some in other raw materials. Were it not for the division of the world into autonomous nation-states, this tendency would be even more pronounced, since greater specialization would be more economical.

These changes in technology and in the economy have inevitably produced demographic changes. To begin with, these advances, like earlier ones, have made possible substantial increases in numbers and density at the societal level. Table 1 shows the growth in population of a number of industrial societies which were formerly advanced, and heavily populated, agrarian societies. As this table indicates, all except France at least doubled in population during the period covered, and in most instances a three-fold increase is indicated, with populations still growing.

[9] See *Dictionary of Occupational Titles*, 2d ed. (Washington: GPO, 1949), vol. I, p. xi.

Table 1　Population Growth in Selected Countries from 1800
(or Year of Earliest Record) to 1960

COUNTRY	POPULATION IN MILLIONS	
	1800 (OR FIRST YEAR OF RECORD)	1960
Belgium	4.3 (1850)	9.2
France	27.3	45.5
Germany	24.6	70.7
Italy	18.1	49.4
Japan	37.0 (1880)	93.2
Netherlands	3.1 (1850)	11.5
Spain	10.5	30.1
Sweden	2.3	7.5
U.S.S.R.	37.0	214.4
United Kingdom	16.1	52.5

Source: For earlier years, W. S. Woytinsky and E. S. Woytinsky, *World Population and Production: Trends and Outlook* (New York: Twentieth Century Fund, 1953), p. 44; for later years, *Statistical Abstract of the United States, 1962* (Washington: GPO, 1962), pp. 911–912, and *World Almanac, 1961* (New York: World-Telegram, 1961), p. 358.

Industrialization has also led to the enlargement of communities. In agrarian societies, it may be recalled, the largest communities never numbered much over a million persons, and in the 5,000 years of agrarian history, this figure was attained only a few times, and then only by the capitals of great empires. Today, by contrast, there are already approximately a hundred cities with a population of a million or more, and nearly twenty with a population of three million.[10] Greater New York has passed the ten million mark and the metropolitan communities of Greater London and Tokyo are rapidly approaching that figure.

Industrialization means not only larger cities, but also a greater proportion of the population living in urban communities. In Chapter 8 it was noted that typically 90 per cent of the population of agrarian societies lived in rural communities and only about 10 per cent in urban. In the most advanced industrial societies, these figures are just about reversed. In the United Kingdom, for example, farmers constituted only 4.5 per cent of the total population in 1955 (though that country was not agriculturally self-sufficient).[11] In the United States in 1962 only 9 per cent of the males in the labor force were in farming, and this small group con-

[10] *World Almanac, 1961* (New York: World-Telegram, 1961), pp. 103 and 397–398.
[11] J. Frederic Dewhurst and Associates, *Europe's Needs and Resources* (New York: Twentieth Century Fund, 1961), appendix 3–2, table A.

stantly produced surpluses.[12] No more than 5 per cent of the male labor force need have been engaged in agricultural activity (assuming the smallest and least efficient farmers were eliminated). Assuming another 5 per cent of the male labor force are in related occupations, e.g., farm implement distributors, teachers, ministers, etc., which necessitate rural residence, no more than 10 per cent seem to be required to live in truly rural communities, i.e., communities in which the production of food and fibers is the major economic activity.

Industrialization affects human populations in yet another way. It results in drastically lowered birth and death rates and correspondingly increased life expectancy. In most of the more advanced industrial societies, the crude death rate is 10 or less per 1,000 population per year, whereas two centuries ago "a death rate of 40 per 1,000 inhabitants was not unusual . . . [and] a rate of 25 per 1,000 was considered exceptionally low." [13] The decline in the birthrate has not been so precipitous, but it, too, has been substantial. In the traditional agrarian societies of the past, birthrates seem to have averaged well over 30 per 1,000 per year, and in many instances 40 or more.[14] In advanced industrial societies, by contrast, they presently range from about 15 to 25 per 1,000 population, with the mode around 17 or 18 per 1,000.[15]

These figures point to what has probably been the most revolutionary demographic development of modern times, namely, the development of safe and efficient techniques of limiting fertility. At the bottom of the class system in every agrarian society, the unhappy expendables testified to the perennial demographic crisis. Today, thanks to technological advances in various fields, the more advanced industrial societies are approaching the point where the birthrate largely reflects the wishes and desires of its members. This is indicated by the variability of the birthrate and its tendency to follow fluctuations in the business cycle.

Industrialization has also contributed to a number of significant developments in the political realm. In the first place, there has been a virtual elimination of the monarchical form of government, especially in the classical sense of the ruler with proprietarial and patrimonial rights. In its stead, republican governments of various types have assumed power, though in a number of instances certain monarchical trappings have been retained (as in Britain, Scandinavia, and the Low Countries). In a few other instances, individuals have assumed dictatorial powers for a time,

---

[12] *Statistical Abstract, 1962*, p. 215.
[13] Woytinsky and Woytinsky, pp. 166 and 163, and *Statistical Abstract of the United States, 1962*, pp. 913–914.
[14] Woytinsky and Woytinsky, pp. 141f.
[15] *Statistical Abstract, 1962*, pp. 913–914.

but this has never yet led to a truly stable, institutionalized system of one-man rule. At most this appears to be a possible, but less likely, alternative to the usual republican pattern.

Though obviously there are wide variations in the degree to which the members of different industrial societies share in the political process, on the average political power is much more widely diffused in industrial societies than in agrarian. This development has important consequences for the distributive process, as will become evident shortly. For the present it is enough to note that one of the concomitants of this development is the emergence of mass political parties. These are unique to industrial societies, and to societies under their influence or in process of becoming industrialized.[16]

This relative democratization of the state is linked with a second important development, the tremendous increase in the functions performed by the state. This trend is most pronounced in socialist nations, and especially in those governed by parties with a totalitarian philosophy. However, the trend is also evident in nations, such as the United States, where the philosophies of both socialism and totalitarianism have been rejected. One need only examine a list of the various departments and agencies of this country, together with their major subdivisions, to realize how many varied functions the Federal government now performs.[17] Such a list must be compared with lists from the late eighteenth and early nineteenth centuries to appreciate the magnitude of the change involved.

A third important political development has been the growth in the military power of governments. This trend was readily apparent in World Wars I and II and has become even more pronounced with the development of atomic weapons. From the standpoint of the distributive process, however, this may be less significant than a related development, the trend toward total warfare, or the involvement of the total population in the war effort. In agrarian societies wars were usually the concern of professional military men, and the majority of the population was not greatly involved. Since World War I, however, the distinction between soldier and civilian has become quite blurred.

The growth in the military power of industrial societies in the nineteenth and twentieth centuries also led to the creation of a number of European colonial empires, which for a time virtually circled the earth.

---

[16] See, for example, Maurice Duverger, *Political Parties: Their Organization and Activity in the Modern State,* translated by Barbara North and Robert North (London: Methuen, 1959), p. xxiii.

[17] See, for example, *The World Almanac, 1961,* pp. 121–123 for a list of the major divisions of the ten departments of government, and pp. 755–756 for a list of the many agencies.

This development, together with advances in the field of communications, led to the rapid spread of European culture traits throughout most of the world. Now, for the first time in human history, mankind seems to be approaching the point where all peoples could share a single basic culture (this would not, of course, preclude regional, class, age, sex and other kinds of subcultures). Whether this possibility will ever be realized is still debatable, but the technological base for its accomplishment is taking shape rapidly. The same may be said regarding the possibility of a unified government for the entire planet. From the technological standpoint, the obstacles preventing this are steadily being eliminated.

The general level of knowledge is substantially higher in industrial societies than in agrarian, especially with respect to literacy. Whereas the ability to read and write was limited to a small minority in agrarian societies, in the more advanced industrial societies it is nearly universal. In fact, in an increasing number of these societies, the majority of young people receive formal education through their middle teens, and a growing minority receives it well into the third decade of life. In the United States, for example, 92 per cent of males aged fourteen to seventeen were in school in 1961, 49 per cent of those aged eighteen and nineteen, and 20 per cent of those aged twenty to twenty-four.[18] In fact, 7 per cent of the males from twenty-five to twenty-nine, and 3 per cent of those from thirty to thirty-five, were still enrolled in schools and universities of some kind.

The great growth of educational institutions has been due in part to the need for more extensive training, but it has also reflected the declining need for child labor. Thus, in the more advanced industrial societies, educational institutions often perform a custodial function in addition to their educational function, occupying the time of young people whose labor is not needed. In the process, however, the schools isolate them from the adult population, with the result that a significant cultural cleavage is created, and adolescent members of these societies increasingly develop their own distinctive subculture. The differences between the adolescent and adult subcultures in industrial societies are often as important and as divisive as those which separated city dwellers and countryfolk in agrarian societies. As we shall see later, there is good reason to believe that the cultural cleavage which divides adolescents and adults is linked with a very important new development in distributive systems.

Before leaving the subject of educational institutions, it is necessary to take note of their changing character. In agrarian societies, educational institutions were typically adjuncts of religious institutions. This is much less often the case in industrial societies. Even where religious institutions

[18] *Statistical Abstract, 1962,* p. 114.

have managed to retain their formal control over educational institutions, formal religious instruction is seldom the chief activity. Educational institutions have come increasingly under the control of organized communities of teachers and scholars. The development of these communities and their great growth in power and influence are among the more important developments associated with the rise of industrial societies.

This trend is linked with yet another, the growing emphasis on planning in all fields of human activity. In agrarian societies, planning was at best an occasional activity. Men typically assumed that the outcomes of their activities were beyond their control, and trusted in Fate or Destiny. With the rapid increase in scientific and technical knowledge, and with the development of new techniques for storing, organizing, and reacquiring specific pieces of information, e.g., via modern methods of accounting or through the use of computers, continuous and comprehensive planning has become a practical and profitable activity for the first time in human history. Increasingly, every major organization engages in planning.

As many writers have noted, the shift from agrarian to industrial societies has also affected the family.[19] To begin with, it has meant a substantial transfer of functions to other institutions. Many activities which were once the responsibility of families have been relinquished by them. From the standpoint of the distributive process, one of the more important of these transfers has been that involving the care of the aged. Once this was the exclusive concern of the family; today it is increasingly the concern of the state. With the transfer of functions, there has been a corresponding decline in the need for large families. In industrial societies, unlike agrarian, children are liabilities from the economic standpoint, and parents have a positive incentive to limit the number of their offspring.

The rise of industrial societies has also brought greater freedom to women. With fewer children and with greatly expanded opportunities for education, they are no longer severely limited in their choice of careers. Furthermore, industrialization has generally meant increased legal rights, including the franchise. It has also meant the elimination of polygyny. In short, the last vestiges of the ancient concept of women as property are rapidly disappearing.

Finally, with respect to religious institutions, the rise of industrial societies has been associated with a significant shift in the content of religious thought. In agrarian societies, the forces shaping the destiny of men were usually thought of in personal terms, and the dominant religions

[19] See especially William J. Goode, *World Revolution and Family Patterns* (New York: Free Press, 1963).

were theistic in character.[20] In advanced industrial societies, by contrast, new religions which conceive of these forces in impersonal terms have enjoyed great growth, sometimes through persuasion, sometimes through coercion. Humanism is the classic example of the former, Communism of the latter. Both of these faiths have gained considerably at the expense of older ones, such as Christianity, Judaism, Islam, Buddhism, Hinduism, and Confucianism, which emerged in the agrarian era. While it is doubtful that the older faiths will be eliminated, they have nevertheless been altered to some degree. In various subtle ways, their theologies are undergoing a partial process of depersonalization.[21]

This shift from a personal to an impersonal theology, which is linked with the rise of industrial societies, may be, in part, a reflection of the changing character of society itself, and especially of its dominant institutions. In agrarian societies the dominant political and economic institutions were operated on a highly personal patrimonial basis; in industrial societies they are run on an impersonal bureaucratic basis. This change in the nature of the most powerful human institutions may well have contributed to the shift in men's conception of the Ultimate Power.[21a]

The rise of industrial societies seems to have affected the religious scene in yet another way. Alliances between state and church are much less common in industrial societies than in agrarian, and where such ties survive, they are usually of a tenuous nature. However, as the emergence of Communism as the state religion in a number of nations demonstrates, this trend is by no means universal.

The explanation for the decline in church-state alliances appears to be linked with the decline of patrimonial and proprietary monarchies, the rise of republican governments, and the wider diffusion of political power generally. In democratic or republican nations, governments are not so dependent on the legitimizing function that religious groups are capable of performing, because they now provide real and obvious benefits to a considerable portion of the population and thus can be justified on mundane utilitarian grounds.[22] Hence, many governments are able to dispense

[20] Hinayana Buddhism might be called an exception to this, but even there the impersonal view of the forces controlling life was largely transformed into a personal view.

[21] See, for example, the writings of Christian theologians such as Tillich and Bultmann or the recent book *Honest to God* by Bishop Robinson of the Anglican Church. One can argue, however, that these writers are not introducing something new, but merely reasserting in modern form the ancient doctrine of the transcendence of God.

[21a] I do not mean to exclude here the more obvious influence of modern science which also presents an impersonal view of power in the physical realm.

[22] See Gerhard Lenski, "Religious Pluralism in Theoretical Perspective," *Internationales Jahrbuch für Religionssoziologie* (Köln: Westdeutscher Verlag, 1965), vol. I, pp. 25–42.

with the services of their former religious allies. This trend has probably been hastened by the weakening hold of the traditional faiths on certain important segments of the population and the spread of new and competing cults such as Humanism, Freudianism, and so forth. Confronted with the growing heterogeneity of religious belief, political authorities have moved even more rapidly toward disestablishment than they might have otherwise.

Reversal of a Basic Trend

Of all the types of societies we have examined, none illustrates better than the industrial, the difficulties and limitations of a *purely* deductive and highly general approach to stratification theory. Given the vastly increased productivity of this type of society and the greatly enlarged powers of industrial states, nothing would be more logical than to predict inequalities in power and privilege even greater than those found in agrarian societies. However, even a limited survey of the contemporary scene suggests that this is not the case, and a more intensive examination confirms this impression. If anything, inequalities in power and privilege seem usually somewhat *less* pronounced in mature industrial societies than in agrarian. In short, *the appearance of mature industrial societies marks the first significant reversal in the age-old evolutionary trend toward ever increasing inequality.*

The evidence supporting these assertions takes several basic forms. To begin with, a comparison of the political systems of agrarian and industrial societies makes it clear that political power is much more concentrated in the former. In agrarian societies, the powers of government were nearly always vested in the hands of the few; the great majority were *wholly excluded* from the political process. In industrial societies this is a minority pattern, limited only to those societies in the earlier stages of industrialization and to those ruled by totalitarian parties. In the majority of industrial societies, all adult citizens not only enjoy voting privileges but, far more important, the right to organize politically to promote their own special interests or beliefs, even when these are in opposition to the interests or beliefs of those in power.[23] While this does not mean that all inequalities in political power are eliminated or the democratic millennium ushered in, it does mean a significant reduction in political inequality and a substantial diffusion of political power, both of which are readily evident when these societies are compared with agrarian. This

[23] In some countries the right of opposition is limited to those who are willing to support democratic procedures, with the result that Communist and Fascist parties are excluded by law, but even this limitation is absent in the majority of democratic nations.

can be seen most clearly in the case of the Scandinavian democracies, where Socialist Parties have been the dominant political force in recent decades, but the pattern is also evident in countries such as the United States and France, where the political influence of the lower classes has not been nearly so great. It should also be noted that even in some of those industrial societies where democracy was not permitted, as in post-Stalinist Russia or Peron's Argentina, the political elite used much of its power to promote programs designed to benefit the lower classes, a practice virtually unknown in agrarian societies.

A second indication of declining inequalities can be found in data on the distribution of income. Earlier we saw evidence which indicated that in agrarian societies the top 1 or 2 per cent of the population, usually received *not less than half* of the total income of the nation.[24] In the case of industrial societies the comparable figure is substantially less. According to official governmental reports, the top 2 per cent of the population of democratic nations receives about 10 per cent of the total personal cash income after taxes. For example, British figures for 1954 indicate that the top 2 per cent received 8.5 per cent of the total income after taxes; Swedish figures for 1950 show the top 1.8 per cent received 9.9 per cent before taxes; Danish figures for 1949 show the top 1.1 per cent received 10.3 per cent *before taxes;* United States figures for 1958 show the top 1.3 per cent received 8.1 per cent, and the top 2.3 per cent received 11.6 per cent, *before taxes.*[25]

These figures cannot, of course, be taken at face value. As a number of recent writers have pointed out, they do not include many billions of dollars of income, sometimes because of fraud and evasion by taxpayers, but more often because the tax statutes do not define certain forms of income as income.[26] For example, as Gabriel Kolko has shown, in the United States such factors have led to underreporting of cash income to the extent of more than $30 billion each year; in addition, corporate ex-

[24] *Supra,* p. 228. This figure includes the income of the ruler as well as that of the governing class.

[25] British figures are calculated from G. D. H. Cole, *The Post-War Condition of Britain* (London: Routledge, 1956), p. 223; Swedish figures are from George R. Nelson (ed.), *Freedom and Welfare: Social Patterns in the Northern Countries of Europe* (sponsored by the Ministries of Social Affairs of Denmark, Finland, Iceland, Norway, and Sweden, 1953), p. 54; Danish figures are from K. Lemberg and N. Ussing, "Redistribution of Income in Denmark," in Alan Peacock (ed.), *Income Redistribution and Social Policy* (London: Cape, 1954), p. 72; United States figures are calculated from *The World Almanac, 1961,* p. 744. All figures are from official governmental sources.

[26] See, for example, Gabriel Kolko, *Wealth and Power in America: An Analysis of Social Class and Income Distribution* (New York: Frederick A. Praeger, 1962), especially chap. 1 or Philip Stern, *The Great Treasury Raid* (New York: Random House, 1964), on the United States. See Richard M. Titmuss, *Income Distribution and Social Change* (Toronto, Canada: University of Toronto Press, 1962) on Britain.

pense account outlays are estimated to have been between $5 and $10 billion.[27] Kolko suggests that, conservatively, a third of the corporate expense account outlay represented income-in-kind for the top 10 per cent of the population, and that from a third to a half of the errors and evasions should be assigned to the same group. If one accepts these estimates (and they are not likely to be low, given Kolko's evident political sympathies), this means that the upper-income tenth received from $12 to $18 billion more in annual income than was reported in their tax returns. If, to avoid *any* danger of conservative bias, we assume that almost all of this went to the upper 2 per cent of the population, we arrive at an error estimate of $10 to $15 billion for this group. Offsetting this in part, however, is the balance of the evasions and errors estimate, totaling roughly $20 billion, which must be assigned to the remaining 98 per cent of the population. Taking the higher estimate for underreporting by the upper-income group, i.e., $15 billion, we arrive at the conclusion that, before taxes, 15.5 per cent of the personal income of the American people went to the top 2.3 per cent.

Even this figure, however, is far short of the 50 per cent estimated to be the elite's share of the gross national product in agrarian societies. This difference arises, in part, because the revenues of government are included in agrarian societies but not in industrial. On first inspection this may seem both arbitrary and unjust. Actually it is neither. In agrarian societies government functions almost entirely, as we have seen, as an instrument of, by, and for the few. In modern industrial societies, this is no longer the case. While it is true that the upper classes still benefit disproportionately from the actions of government in every industrial society, it is also true that the masses of ordinary citizens benefit to an extent undreamed of in the agrarian societies of the past, or even in those which still survive.

It is impossible to determine with any precision what percentage of the benefits of government go to the top 2 per cent of the population and what percentage to the remainder in industrial societies. However, even if one were to assume that they went *entirely* to the elite, the total would still fall short of the agrarian figure of 50 per cent. In most industrialized societies, the costs of government at all levels, from local to national, constitute only 20 to 30 per cent of the gross national product, with an average of about 25 per cent.[28] If this average figure were added to our earlier estimate that up to 15 per cent of *personal income* (which means about 12 per cent of the gross national product), goes to the upper 2 per cent,

[27] Kolko, pp. 16–23.
[28] See Dewhurst, *Europe's Needs*, p. 407. See also Dewhurst, *America's Needs*, p. 579.

then less than 40 per cent of the gross national product would go to the equivalent of the agrarian elite, i.e., the top 2 per cent. If we were to assume, more realistically, that only as much as half of the benefits of government went to the favored 2 per cent, the elite's share of the gross national product would drop to only 25 per cent.[29] Thus, while it may not be possible to determine precisely what percentage of the gross national product is enjoyed by the top 2 per cent in mature industrial societies, it is safe to conclude that the percentage is considerably less than in agrarian. In fact, it is probably no more than half so large, and quite possibly less than that.[30]

Since the foregoing estimates are all based on data from democratic nations, one may properly ask whether the situation in totalitarian states is not different. This question is not easily answered owing to the paucity of trustworthy quantitative data. However, such as we have indicates that in the Soviet Union, at least, income inequality is substantially less than in the United States. According to one recent study, the minimum Soviet wage is 300 rubles monthly, and the average from 800 to 900. By comparison, highly placed executives in Soviet industry receive from 4,500 to 7,500 rubles per month, fifteen to twenty-five times the minimum and five to ten times the average.[31] These figures are very similar to those reported by others who have studied the subject.[32] However, one other re-

[29] Critically minded readers may wonder why lower estimates of the elite's share of governmental benefits have not been used. In part this is because it is not necessary to prove the basic point. In part, however, it is because it appears that the privileged classes benefit from the actions of government to a far greater degree than we ordinarily suppose. For example, it is the wealthy owners of private property who are the chief beneficiaries of the expenditures for defense and police services. It is they, not the poor, who would be the chief losers if their country were conquered, or could not protect its interests abroad, or if internal anarchy developed. They also benefit disproportionately by highways and other governmental services which facilitate trade and commerce. They even benefit to a considerable degree from the technical education their nation provides, since this insures their industries a ready supply of skilled technicians, engineers, and scientists. By contrast, welfare expenditures, which go chiefly to the lower classes, are only a minor cost of government in comparison—despite the heated controversies they create. Thus, all things considered, it is probably not unrealistic to estimate that one-third to two-thirds of the value of all governmental services redound to the benefit of the most privileged 2 per cent.

[30] For evidence on declining inequality in France in recent centuries, see Jean Fourastié, *The Causes of Wealth*, translated by Theodore Caplow (New York: Free Press, 1960, first published 1951), chap. 1.

[31] David Granick, *The Red Executive* (Garden City, N.Y.: Doubleday Anchor, 1961), p. 92.

[32] See, for example, Nicholas DeWitt, *Education and Professional Employment in the USSR* (Washington, D.C.: National Science Foundation, 1961), especially pp. 537–545 and appendix table 6-W. DeWitt states that the Russian government reported that the average wage was 710 rubles in 1955, and estimated that this had risen to 800 rubles by 1960. He also shows that wages reported in official Soviet publications sometimes ranged up to thirteen times the average without bonuses, and that with bonuses, which were largely limited to upper income groups, wage differentials would

cent report adds that top incomes in the Soviet Union "reach a million rubles a year," or about 80,000 rubles per month.[33] This is nearly three hundred times the minimum and about a hundred times the average. As in the case of non-Communist nations, these figures omit many very tangible benefits for the rich as well as the poor. It appears, however, that these are roughly proportional to cash incomes and thus have no great effect on the ratios.

Turning to the United States, we find that one who currently earns the minimum wage for businesses engaged in interstate commerce would, if fully employed, receive about $2,500 per year. The median income reported in 1958 tax returns was about $4,000 per year.[34] The earned incomes of important executives in major industries in recent years have ranged from $50,000 to over $500,000 a year and have almost alway been supplemented appreciably by unearned income from stock and bond holdings.[35] At the upper end of the income ladder, we have definite knowledge of one officially reported income of over $28 million in 1960, and if it is true, as reported, that J. Paul Getty owns assets valued at $2 billion, and if he obtains no more than a modest 4 per cent return on his investments, he should have an income of about $80 million per year (though obviously most of this would not be classified as "income" by the government).[36] Putting all these figures together, we find that American industrial executives receive from twenty to two hundred times the income indicated by the minimum wage law, and from 12 to 125 times the median income. Ignoring estimates of Getty's income, and taking as the maximum the more modest figure of $28 million, we find that this is eleven

---

be increased 20 to 50 per cent. See also Emily Clark Brown, "The Soviet Labor Market," in Morris Bornstein and Daniel Fusfeld (eds.), *The Soviet Economy* (Homewood, Ill.: Irwin, 1962), fn. 19, pp. 201–202, who reports a range for manual workers from 450 to 2,500 rubles per month, with the latter apparently very exceptional. She reports average earnings for production workers in five large plants as ranging from 750 to 1,000 rubles per month. Margaret Dewar reports that after the reforms scheduled for 1962, there would probably be a 15 to 1 differential in income between the extremes in Soviet industry, i.e., between top managers and workers at the minimum wage. See "Labour and Wage Reforms in the USSR," in Harry G. Shaffer (ed.), *The Soviet Economy: A Collection of Western and Soviet Views* (New York: Appleton-Century-Crofts, 1963), p. 222.

[33] Klaus Mehnert, *Soviet Man and His World*, translated by Maurice Rosenbaum (New York: Frederick A. Praeger, 1961), p. 24.

[34] See *The World Almanac, 1961*, p. 744.

[35] See, for example, Mabel Newcomer, *The Big Business Executive* (New York: Columbia University Press, 1955), p. 124, or the annual reports in *United States News and World Report.*

[36] For the reported income of $28 million in 1960, see the speech of Sen. Paul Douglas, reported in *The Washington Post*, Dec. 14, 1963, p. A-4. On Getty's wealth, see Philip Stern, p. 21, or *Newsweek*, July 15, 1963, p. 48. As Stern makes clear, only half of capital gains are classified as "income" if taken during one's lifetime and none are so classified if the assets are kept until death (pp. 91–92).

thousand times the minimum and seven thousand times the average. All these ratios are substantially larger than the corresponding Soviet ratios, which suggests that income inequality is much less pronounced in the Soviet Union than in the United States, a conclusion in keeping with the unsystematic and impressionistic observations of most trained visitors to Russia. Thus, it appears that the Soviet Union provides no exception to the conclusion about the historic decline in income inequality formulated on the basis of data from democratic nations.

Causes of the Reversal

From the theoretical standpoint, the decline in political and economic inequality associated with the emergence of industrial societies is extremely important. This constitutes a reversal in a major historical trend, and the reasons for this reversal are by no means obvious. On the contrary, given the increased productivity of industrial societies and the growth in the powers of the state, one would normally predict even greater inequality than in agrarian societies. The fact that the opposite occurred indicates either that one or more of the basic postulates with which we began is in error, or that other factors are at work which were not taken into account (or, at least, not sufficiently) in our original, highly general formulation. The evidence, as I shall show, favors the latter interpretation, indicating again the serious difficulties which attend any effort to develop a general theory by purely deductive means.

Among the factors not considered in our earlier assumptions about the nature of man and society, was the relationship between technological and cultural complexity on the one hand, and administrative efficiency on the other. In modern industrial societies, technology in particular, and culture in general, are far more complex than in even the most advanced agrarian societies.[37] In fact, they are so complex that it is no longer possible for those in positions of high command to begin to understand the work of all those beneath them. In effect, there is a growing "ignorance" on the part of those in positions of command. This is not to say that those in authority in industrial societies are less intelligent or knowledgeable than their counterparts in agrarian societies, but rather that they are masters of *a smaller proportion* of what they need to know to maintain effective control over those beneath them. Thus, because of the many gaps in their knowledge, they are often compelled either to issue commands based on insufficient information, or to leave matters to the discretion of

---

[37] One of the best evidences of this is the rapid growth of vocabulary in the language of every industrial society.

their subordinates, thus opening the door to encroachments on their pre-rogatives. In the former case, authority is preserved, but at the expense of efficiency and productivity, while in the latter case a measure of authority is sacrificed to increase efficiency and productivity. In short, *the relation-ship between productivity and authority appears to be curvilinear in in-dustrial societies, at least up to the present time.*[38] Thus, unless political authorities are willing and able to sacrifice productivity, it is unlikely that they will be able to rely on the technique of command to the extent their agrarian counterparts did. However, to the degree that they delegate authority or rely on market mechanisms, they facilitate the diffusion of power and privilege.

A second factor which seems to have contributed to the reversal in the historic trend toward greater inequality is *the rapidity and magnitude of the increases in productivity.* In societies in which the gross national product and per capita income are rapidly rising, and promise to con-tinue rising, elites find themselves in the paradoxical situation in which they can maximize their *net* input of rewards by responding to pressures from below and making certain concessions. By granting the lower classes some share in the economic surplus, they can reduce worker hostility and the accompanying losses from strikes, slowdowns, and industrial sabotage. In an expanding economy, an elite can make economic concessions in *relative* terms without necessarily suffering any loss in *absolute* terms. In fact, if the concessions are not too large, and the rate of the economy's growth is great enough, relative losses can even be accompanied by *sub-stantial* absolute gains. For example, an elite would enjoy a substantially greater income if it took 40 per cent of the gross national product in a $100 billion economy, than if it stubbornly fought to maintain a 50 per

---

[38] Recent events in the Soviet Union provide a good illustration of this. The increasing reliance on market mechanisms in economic decision making represents a deliberate effort to increase efficiency and productivity while sacrificing centralized authority. This development was forced on Soviet authorities by the physical impossibility of developing an adequate, workable, and comprehensive plan for the whole Soviet econ-omy. According to reports, one Soviet economist predicted that unless there were dras-tic reforms, planning work would increase thirty-six-fold by 1980, and would require the services of the entire adult population, and this presumably would not raise the level of efficiency of the planning procedures. Another Soviet economist is reported to have argued that a sound plan must take account of all the possible interrelation-ships between products in the plan and the number of these interrelations is the square of the number of products. Since the Soviet machine industry alone now turns out 125,000 different products, a comprehensive plan for this one industry would re-quire provision for more than 15 billion interrelations. See Joseph Alsop, "Matter of Fact," *The Washington Post*, Jan. 13, 1964. While the use of modern high-speed com-puters will undoubtedly alleviate the problems of planners to a considerable degree, it is not likely that in the foreseeable future the curvilinearity in the relationship be-tween productivity and authority can be eliminated, especially in societies in which the diversity of goods and services produced is constantly increasing.

cent share and thereby held the economy at the $50 billion level. *If we assume that the majority of men would willingly make modest relative concessions for the sake of substantial absolute gains, and if we also assume that leading members of the elites in industrial societies have an awareness of the benefits they can obtain from concessions, then we can only predict they will make them.*

A willingness to make concessions may also be encouraged by the principle of marginal utility. This principle serves as a reminder that the first million dollars normally has greater value to a man than any subsequent million he may acquire. In societies with very productive economies, many members of the elite may be prepared to make some *economic* concessions in order to maximize other kinds of rewards, such as safety, respect, and leisure. In other words, after a certain level of wealth has been attained, elites may prefer to sacrifice a portion of the economic surplus in order to reduce hostility and the dangers of revolution, and to win for themselves a greater measure of respect and affection. Or, they may find it impossible to maintain tight control over political and economic organizations and at the same time enjoy the benefits of leisure, and so permit a portion of the economic surplus to pass into other hands. In short, *because elites have multiple goals, and are not concerned with maximizing material rewards alone, they may be willing to make certain economic concessions in a highly productive and expanding economy.*

Yet another factor which has played a role in reducing inequality is the development of new and highly effective methods of birth control. In the past, the natural tendency of the human race to multiply usually had the effect of offsetting whatever economic gains might otherwise have resulted from technological advance. Numbers tended to increase up to the carrying power of the economy *except as limited by the development of tyrannical political systems which diverted the "economic surplus" to the elite at the expense of further population increase.* One consequence, of course, was the large and wretched class of expendables, whose very presence served to prevent any substantial long-run improvement in the lot of the peasants and artisans with whom they constantly competed for employment.

Today the situation is rapidly changing, and promises to change even more in the future. For the first time in history, mankind has found safe, simple, and effective means of controlling population growth. In societies where these have been most widely used, the rate of population growth has been slowed to the point where real and substantial gains in per capita income have been achieved in a fairly short time, thus reducing the intensity of the competitive pressures. Now, for almost the first time in centuries, the lower classes are able to bargain for wages in markets no longer perennially glutted with labor. This development has almost certainly contributed to the decline in inequality.

Another factor that has probably contributed to the decline in inequality is the great expansion in human knowledge. In the past, the dominant class chiefly needed unskilled labor, and thanks to human fecundity, this was always plentiful. This put the vast majority of men in a poor bargaining position, and hence the price of labor was minimal. Today, in the more advanced industrial societies, the situation is radically changed. Because of the great functional utility of so much of the new knowledge, a host of occupational specialists have appeared who are not interchangeable to any great degree. This introduces into the labor market certain rigidities which favor the sellers of labor, especially in an era in which the demand for technical skills is rapidly rising. Furthermore, even if the dominant classes could obtain the necessary labor for a subsistence wage, it is doubtful that this would prove expedient. The efficiency of work requiring mental effort or alertness can be seriously reduced when those performing it are not physically fit. Two men working at 50 per cent efficiency in this situation are not the equal of one man working at top efficiency, as in work requiring brute strength alone. Moreover expensive machines and tight production schedules are vulnerable to the mistakes of inattentive workers to a degree that is not characteristic of agrarian societies. These factors all prevent the dominant classes from driving the wages of this increasingly numerous segment of the population down to the subsistence level, and prevent the system from reaching the level of economic inequality that is found in agrarian societies, both past and present.

The egalitarian trend in modern industrial societies is evident in the *political* area no less than in the economic. In many respects the trend toward greater political equality is more surprising than the corresponding economic trend, because the struggle for political power is essentially a zero-sum "game," i.e., gains by one party necessarily entail corresponding losses by opponents. The struggle for privilege, on the other hand, is a positive-sum "game," thanks to the constantly rising level of productivity. Thus in the political realm the privileged classes cannot accept losses in relative terms and still realize absolute gains.

All the reasons for the spread of democratic government are still not completely understood. Obviously, it has not been dictated by economic necessity, as shown by the vigor of a number of nondemocratic, totalitarian nations. On the other hand, the relative frequency of democratic government in industrial states and its virtual absence in agrarian, strongly indicate some connection. Specifically, this suggests that industrialization creates conditions favorable to the growth of democracy, but does not make it inevitable.

One favorable condition is the spread of literacy and the extension of education. An illiterate peasantry lacking access to mass media of information is in a poor position to participate in the political process; a literate middle and working class with many media of information available is much more favorably situated. Advances in the level of living have a similar effect. Peasants and artisans living at, or near, the subsistence level cannot afford the luxury of sustained political activity; workers in an industrial society have more leisure, energy, and money to devote to this. Still another factor favoring the growth of democracy is the modern pattern of warfare which involves the entire population to an extent unknown in agrarian societies.[39] As many observers have noted, the traditional distinction between the military and civilian segments of the population has been almost obliterated, and military men have come to regard urban centers of production as prime military targets. If Andrzejewski and other writers are correct, this trend should have an egalitarian influence, since inequality tends to be most pronounced where military activities are limited to the few.

More important than any of these, however, has been the rise and spread of *the new democratic ideology* which asserts that the state belongs to the people.[40] This ideology is not simply a reflection of changing economic conditions, though, as we have seen, it has been affected by them. Rather, the historical record indicates it had its origin in religious and philosophical developments of the seventeenth century and spread rather widely in the eighteenth century in countries which were still thoroughly agrarian in character, e.g., the United States and France. In fact, there appears to be as much justification for the thesis that this new ideology contributed to the emergence of industrial societies as for the converse.

In any case, this new ideology became an important force in the political life of industrial societies. It captured the imagination of all kinds of men, even some of the political elite, thus making the traditional monopoly of political power increasingly untenable. As the democratic

[39] See, for example, Walter Millis, *Arms and Men: A Study of American Military History* (New York: Putnam, 1956).

[40] In one sense this ideology is not at all new, as shown in Chap. 1 and also in the practices of hunting and gathering and simple horticultural peoples. In another sense, however, modern democratic beliefs can be said to derive from the work of seventeenth-century political theorists such as John Locke, who put this ancient idea in a modern form which made it a significant force first in the intellectual world and then in the political.

ideology spread, those who governed had to make substantial concessions in order to avoid massive challenges to their power—challenges which would have been costly to resist, and might even have led to their overthrow. The idea that the state should be the servant of all the people continues to be a major force in the modern era, mobilizing the egoistic impulses of the disadvantaged classes in an idealistic cause, thereby uniting morality and egoism in a manner reminiscent of their union under the banner of "the divine right of kings," but with the opposite effect.

Wherever democratic theory has become institutionalized, a dramatic new possibility has arisen: *now the many can combine against the few, and even though individually the many are weaker, in combination they may be as strong or stronger*. With this development, the door is opened to a host of revolutionary developments in the distributive realm.

The Role of Government

In industrial societies, as in agrarian, control of the machinery of government is vitally important from the standpoint of the distributive process. Those who control the government are able to determine the rules governing the competition for rewards in society, and by virtue of this power are able to influence profoundly the outcome of this competition.[40a]

It would be a mistake to suppose, however, that government plays the same role in industrial societies that it does in agrarian. Given the democratic revolution of modern times, this is impossible. To begin with, the age-old concept of the state as a piece of private property to be handed down from father to son has been completely destroyed in all of the more advanced industrial nations. This has had many far-reaching consequences. Above all, it has meant that the powers of government may no longer be used solely for the benefit of the few at the expense of the many. It also means that in the majority of the more advanced industrial societies all, or nearly all, segments of the population are permitted to organize and act politically, *even for the purpose of opposing the policies and programs of those currently in power*. Thus, the machinery of government has become the object of a never ending struggle between a variety of organized groups which, in their totality, represent the special interests of most of the population.

This typical pattern is currently evident in all the Scandinavian countries, the United Kingdom and all the English-speaking overseas members of the British Commonwealth, the Low Countries, Switzerland, West

[40a] For an excellent statement of this, see Harold Laski, *The State in Theory and Practice* (New York: Viking, 1935), p. 94.

Germany, Austria, France, Italy, the United States, and Japan.[41] In all these countries three basic conditions prevail:

1. There is universal, or virtually universal, adult suffrage.
2. The right of organized political opposition is protected by both law and custom.
3. Disadvantaged elements in the population are permitted to organize and engage in collective action on their own behalf.

While some of the nations listed above refuse to permit antidemocratic parties to participate in the political process, this is not done with the intent to destroy the principle of political opposition or the right of disadvantaged classes to organize, as partisans of the totalitarian parties often claim. The falsity of their claim is best demonstrated by the freedom these same nations accord Socialist and Labor Parties, which are committed to the principles of political democracy, even when they advocate radical changes in distributive policies.

To date, the outcomes of the struggles for power in the more advanced industrial democracies have varied considerably. To illustrate the range of variation, one need only compare the Swedish pattern with the American. In Sweden the Socialist Party, representing the special interests of the urban working class, has been the leading political force since 1932.[42] With the exception of a brief three-month period in 1936, the Socialists have either been in exclusive control of the government or formed the dominant element in a coalition government. Though some of the party's leaders have come from the middle and even the upper classes, all observers agree that it has functioned as a party of, by, and for the working class, at least in those matters where class interests are relevant.[43] This is evidenced by the fact that labor unions played the major role in the formation of the party at the end of the last century, and still continue to play a dominant role. In recent years, two-thirds of the party's dues-pay-

[41] The same pattern, or a similar one, is evident in some other countries not listed here, such as India and the Philippines. These countries cannot be called advanced industrial nations, but neither can they be called agrarian. As noted earlier, such nations require a special analysis since they are, in effect, hybrid societies. Furthermore, unlike the agrarian societies of an earlier era, they are forced to exist in a world dominated by industrial societies, a fact of profound importance for them.

[42] See especially Dankwart A. Rustow, *The Politics of Compromise: A Study of Parties and Cabinet Government in Sweden* (Princeton, N.J.: Princeton University Press, 1955), especially chap. 3. See also Nils Andrén, *Modern Swedish Government* (Stockholm: Almqvist & Wiksell, 1961), especially pp. 219–225.

[43] See, for example, Gunnar Heckscher, "Interest Groups in Sweden: Their Political Role," in Henry W. Ehrmann (ed.), *Interest Groups on Four Continents* (Pittsburgh, Pa.: University of Pittsburgh Press, 1958), pp. 162–163. See also Rustow, chaps. 2–5, Andrén, pp. 24–25, or Wilfrid Fleisher, *Sweden: The Welfare State* (New York: John Day, 1956), especially chap. 1.

ing members have been union members enrolled "collectively" by their unions, and two-thirds to three-quarters of the party's representatives in the Riksdag are persons who are, or have been, union members.[44] Furthermore, in recent years roughly 70 per cent of the working-class vote has been given to the Socialist Party, and this has constituted about three-fourths of the party's total vote.[45] But most important of all, the party's policies have been directed consistently toward the goal of advancing the interests of the working class, and have resulted in the creation of a welfare state in which social inequalities of nearly every kind have been substantially reduced.[46] However, it must be added that the continuing strength of the opposition parties, and the inability of the Socialists to obtain a decisive majority either at the polls or in the Riksdag, serve as restraining influences on the party's leaders. On the other hand, the basic principles of the welfare state have now come to be accepted by all the opposition parties, even the Conservatives.[47]

In the United States the situation is quite different. To begin with, the Republican Party, which prides itself on its defense of traditional property rights, enjoys a far greater degree of electoral success than its Swedish counterpart, the Conservative Party (even greater, in fact, than the Conservatives and Liberals combined). Though it has controlled the executive branch of the Federal government for only eight years since 1932, and the Congress for even less, its power has been substantial because of the absence of party discipline in Congress and the frequent support of Southern Democrats.[48] Also, thanks to gerrymandering of state legislatures, Republican strength was, till recently, disproportionate to its voting strength at the state level, outside of the one-party South.[49]

However, more important than the power of the Republican Party is the nature of the Democratic Party, which is the only significant alternative. Though this party has often been called the instrument of the labor

[41] On the "collective" affiliation of union members, see either Rustow, pp. 48–49 and 155, or Andrén, p. 25. On union members in the Riksdag, see Andrén, p. 57, who reports that a study of the Riksdag in 1949 showed that 37 per cent of the total membership were or had been union members. Since almost all such individuals were members of the Socialist Party, and since the Socialists constituted slightly less than half of the total membership of the Riksdag at the time, it appears that two-thirds to three-quarters of the Socialist members were or had been union members.

[45] Rustow, pp. 140–141. These figures are based on Gallup polls.

[46] See Fleisher, op. cit.; Nelson, op. cit; J. A. Lauwerys, Scandinavian Democracy (Copenhagen: Danish Institute et al., 1958), especially chaps. 1 and 5; or Göran Tegner, Social Security in Sweden (Tiden: Swedish Institute, 1956).

[47] Among others, see Andrén, p. 30, or Rustow, pp. 232f.

[48] On party discipline in the Congress, see Donald Matthews, U. S. Senators and Their World (Chapel Hill, N.C.: University of North Carolina Press, 1960), especially chap. 6.

[49] Recent Supreme Court decisions may change this, though the struggle over reapportionment is still far from ended.

unions and the representative of the working class, the relationship has never been comparable to that between the Swedish Socialist Party and the unions or working class. Though the rhetoric of the leaders of the Democratic Party and their official platforms have often had a pronounced working-class bias, the legislation enacted by the party has not reflected this with any great consistency. For example, though the Democrats have controlled the White House and Congress most of the time since 1932, it was still possible, in 1959, for fifteen persons with annual incomes ranging from $1 million to $28 million to incur *no Federal income tax obligations whatsoever,* while those with incomes of less than $1,000 per year were held liable for an average tax of $13.[50]

This situation reflects the nature of the Democratic Party and the pronounced differences between it and the Socialist Party in Sweden. As Maurice Duverger, the noted French student of political parties, observed, the Democratic Party is a nineteenth-century style party, lacking the centralized authority, party discipline, and ideological commitments which are the mark of twentieth-century type parties.[51] Instead, it tends to be a loose-knit (though enduring) federation of locally based politicians and political organizations which cooperate with one another only to the extent they deem it mutually beneficial. Each individual or local organization is free to seek support, both in votes and money, wherever it can be found. This is true even of those members of the party who are elected to Congress, a situation which forces many to enter into *quid pro quo* relationships with well-financed lobbyists representing business interests in particular and privilege in general.[52]

Compared with the Swedish Socialist Party, leadership positions in the American Democratic Party are more often "up for grabs" by anyone with money or financial backing and a reasonably attractive personality.

[50] See the statement of Sen. Paul H. Douglas of Illinois as reported in *The Washington Post,* Dec. 14, 1963, p. A-4, or his speech to the Senate of Nov. 1, 1963, on the tax obligations of millionaires. See *The World Almanac, 1961,* p. 744 on the taxes of those with incomes of less than $1,000 per year. For an excellent discussion of this subject, see Stern, especially chap. 16.

[51] Duverger, *op. cit.* See especially the Introduction.

[52] See, for example, Matthews, chap. 8; Raymond Bauer, Ithiel de Sola Pool, and Lewis Dexter, *American Business and Public Policy: The Politics of Foreign Trade* (New York: Atherton, 1963), especially chaps. 23 and 24; or V. O. Key, Jr., *Politics, Parties, and Pressure Groups,* 3d ed. (New York: Crowell, 1952), especially chap. 18. These writers generally agree that the influence of lobbyists and money in American politics has often been exaggerated, but also insist that it is far from negligible. The vulnerability of Congress is due not only to the nature of the party organizations, but also to the unwillingness of Congress to appropriate sufficient funds to provide adequate staffs for its members. For an opposing, and I believe much too optimistic, view on the influence of money in American politics, see Alexander Heard, *The Costs of Democracy: Financing American Political Campaigns* (Garden City, N.Y.: Doubleday Anchor, 1962), especially chap. 4.

As a consequence, persons from the upper-middle and upper classes tend to predominate. For example, Donald Matthews has shown in his study of the United States Senate that 58 per cent of the Democrats in that body from 1947–1957 were the sons of business and professional men, while only 5 per cent were the sons of industrial wage earners.[53] Another 33 per cent were the sons of farmers, but judging from the fact that 87 per cent of these sons attended college (and this at a time when only 15 per cent of the American population could do this), it is safe to say that most of their fathers were of upper-middle-class status or better.[54] Thus, probably no more than 10 per cent of these influential leaders of the Democratic Party were born into the working class or poor farm families, and Matthews's data indicate even fewer were still in those classes at the time of their election. Lest these figures be thought unrepresentative, one should note a statement of G. Mennen Williams, former Governor of Michigan, a state in which labor influences in the Democratic Party have been as great as anywhere in the country. In an article in the *Harvard Business Review,* Williams stated that in Michigan "people associated with business outnumbered those identified with labor in the roster of delegates and alternates to the 1956 Democratic National Convention," and that business and professional people constituted a majority of the county chairmen in that state.[55] If this is true in Michigan, one suspects that the pattern is even more pronounced in most other states, and especially in the one-party states of the South.

In view of all this, it is clear that the Democratic Party does not stand in the same relationship to the working class as does the Socialist Party of Sweden. If we add to this the fact that the Democratic Party has had to share power to a degree that the Socialists in Sweden have not, it becomes clear that the two situations differ greatly. In fact, one must conclude that *in the United States, unlike Sweden, the propertied classes and their allies still remain the dominant political force.*

Among the more advanced industrial societies with democratic regimes, the United States and Sweden appear to represent the two extremes with respect to the pattern of political control. Most other industrialized democracies stand somewhere in between. The other Scandi-

[53] Matthews, p. 21.

[54] *Ibid.,* p. 27. The remainder of the senators, 3 per cent, were sons of clerks and salesmen. The national figure is from Dewhurst, *America's Needs,* p. 380.

[55] Quoted by Heard, p. 109. That Williams saw fit to publicize these facts, and in the way he did, is indicative of the desire of even the more liberal of Democratic leaders to cultivate support among members of the privileged classes. While most of these Michigan Democrats from the ranks of business and the professions are undoubtedly liberals, few are Socialists. In Sweden, most of these men would be members of the Liberal Party, not the Socialist, given their political position.

navian countries approach the Swedish model, the chief difference being that the Socialist Parties in these countries have not achieved quite the same measure of popular support, and conversely, those parties representing the propertied classes have retained a somewhat greater measure of electoral support and political power.[56]

Britain appears to be roughly midway between the Swedish and American patterns in most respects.[57] One indicator of this is the representation of the working class in parliamentary bodies. In Sweden in 1949, 37 per cent of the members of the Riksdag were, or had been, members of workers' trade unions; in Britain in 1959, 19 per cent of the members of the House of Commons were members of the working class; in the United States in 1949, only 3 per cent of the members of the House of Representatives were recruited from the working class.[58] Britain's Socialist Party, like Sweden's, is relatively impervious to financial subversion by propertied interests. However, unlike the Swedish Socialists, the British Socialists have been unable to win elections and control the government with any great consistency. Nevertheless, they are such a serious threat that their chief rivals, the Conservatives, have been forced to accept much of their welfare program (including even the nationalization of the railroads and mines). It should also be noted, however, that the Socialists have found it expedient to give up their more extreme positions on the nationalization of industry, and that the British system of public education still lags far behind the American when judged by socialist standards.[59]

In Australia a somewhat similar pattern has developed, though the Australian Labor Party does not seem to have been quite so closely tied to the labor unions nor so strongly committed to the goal of socialism as the British Labor Party.[60] In Belgium, the Socialist Party (formerly the

[56] Duverger, p. 311; Lauwerys, chap. 3; Rustow, "Scandinavia: Working Multiparty System," in Sigmund Neumann (ed.), *Modern Political Parties: Approaches to Comparative Politics* (Chicago: University of Chicago Press, 1956), pp. 169–193.

[57] See, for example, Robert Alford, *Party and Society: The Anglo-American Democracies* (Chicago: Rand McNally, 1963), p. 15, chap. 5, etc.

[58] See Andrén, p. 57 on the Swedish Riksdag, and Alford, p. 98 on the House of Commons and the House of Representatives.

[59] See, for example, D. E. Butler and Richard Rose, *The British General Election of 1959* (London: Macmillan, 1960); Cole, chap. 29; Alford, chap. 5; Samuel H. Beer, "Great Britain: From Governing Elite to Mass Parties," in Neumann, pp. 9–57; Anthony Richmond, "The United Kingdom," in Arnold Rose (ed.), *The Institutions of Advanced Societies* (Minneapolis: University of Minnesota Press, 1958), pp. 43–130; etc., etc.

[60] See L. F. Crisp, *The Australian Federal Labour Party, 1901–1951* (London: Longmans, 1955); Louise Overacker, *The Australian Party System* (New Haven, Conn.: Yale University Press, 1952); Alford, p. 15 and chap. 7; and Gwendolen Carter, "The Commonwealth Overseas: Variations on a British Theme," in Neumann, pp. 85–89 and 92–105.

Labor Party) has shared in governmental coalitions most of the time since 1914, but the party has not yet won the support of even 40 per cent of the electorate. Furthermore, the party has been dominated by moderates committed to a pragmatic approach.[61] France and Italy stand closer yet to the American pattern, since in neither of these countries have the two major working class parties, the Socialists and Communists, ever been in really effective control of the government, as the British Socialists were from 1945 to 1950 and, more recently, since 1964. Furthermore, those parties which have been in control have been highly vulnerable to the financial blandishments of propertied interests, a fact reflected in their legislative record if not in their rhetoric.[62] Though details vary considerably among the other advanced industrial nations, most seem closer to the American pattern of governmental control than to the Swedish or even to the British. This appears true of the Federal Republic of Germany, Switzerland, Holland, Canada, Japan, and New Zealand.[63]

On the basis of the foregoing, one might conclude that the American pattern, or some slight modification of it in the British direction, represents the normal pattern for advanced industrial democracies. However, this ignores one very important fact, namely, *the shift to the left in the political spectrum*. In virtually all of the nations mentioned above, the long-term trend in governmental control has involved a strengthening of those parties, and those factions within parties, which are most responsive to the desires and demands of the common people. Sometimes this trend has manifested itself in declining support for conservative parties and growing support for liberal and socialist parties.[64] Other times it has been evident in a progressive leftward shift in the stands of the major parties. Often, as in the United States, both tendencies have been evident. This trend suggests that the modal pattern for advanced industrial democracies will eventually be somewhere substantially to the left of the present

[61] Felix Oppenheim, "Belgium: Party Cleavage and Compromise," in Neumann, pp. 155–168.

[62] For an excellent discussion of this subject, see Henry W. Ehrmann, *Organized Business in France* (Princeton, N.J.: Princeton University Press, 1957), chap. 5. See also Philip Williams, *Politics in Post-War France* (London: Longmans, 1954), especially part 4.

[63] See, for example, R. M. Chapman, W. K. Jackson, and A. V. Mitchell, *New Zealand Politics in Action* (London: Oxford University Press, 1962); Sigmund Neumann, "Germany: Changing Patterns and Lasting Problems," and Carter, *op. cit.*, in Neumann, pp. 354–394, 305–353, and 61–74 respectively; and Duverger, *op. cit.*

[64] A recent report by George Gallup documents the decline of the Republican Party in recent decades. In 1940 he found that 38 per cent of Americans called themselves Republicans, and 42 per cent Democrats (the remainder called themselves Independents). By 1950 these figures had changed to 33 and 45 per cent respectively, by 1960 to 30 and 47 per cent, and by 1964 to 25 and 53 per cent. See *The Washington Post*, Nov. 8, 1964.

American pattern, though just how far is not yet clear. In view of the difficulties, both economic and electoral, encountered by Swedish and British Socialists in their efforts to carry out the classical Socialist program, it seems unlikely that, in the next generation at least, the trend will carry the modal pattern much beyond the present British position.[65] It could, in fact, stop considerably short of that point.

Ruling Class: Fact or Myth?

With the rise and spread of political democracy, students of power have become increasingly divided over the applicability of the concept of a governing or ruling class in industrial societies. Some claim to see no great change from the past and write persuasively of the Power Elite and The Establishment; others deny their existence and write no less persuasively of Political Pluralism, Countervailing Power, and Strategic Elites.[66]

As is so often the case in controversies of this nature, there is a measure of truth in both positions. For example, if one compares traditional agrarian societies with modern industrial, it is clear that political power has become much more widely diffused in the latter, at least in the democratic nations which constitute the great majority. One cannot honestly say of the governmental institutions of any of these societies that they are of, by, and for the privileged few to anything like the degree observed in virtually all agrarian states. On the other hand, if one compares any of these societies with the egalitarian ideal, it is clear that none approaches this standard either. In all industrial societies there are substantial inequalities in political power; most political decisions are made by a small number of men, and the average citizen plays no role at all. In fact, he is often totally unaware of the decisions being made.

As noted in an earlier chapter, there is much to be gained by viewing this problem in *variable*, rather than categorical, terms. Much more is gained by asking *to what degree* the political leadership of advanced in-

[65] For evidence of the difficulties encountered by Swedish and British Socialists, see Rustow, *Compromise*, chap. 8; Fleisher, chaps. 12 and 13; or Cole, chap. 29.

[66] Among recent American writers on this subject, Floyd Hunter and C. Wright Mills have been the two most prominent spokesmen for the elitist view, while Robert Dahl, Suzanne Keller, David Riesman, and Kenneth Galbraith have been influential spokesmen for the opposing view. See especially Floyd Hunter, *Community Power Structure* (Chapel Hill, N.C.: University of North Carolina Press, 1953); C. Wright Mills, *The Power Elite* (Fair Lawn, N.J.: Oxford, 1956); Robert Dahl, *Who Governs?: Democracy and Power in an American City* (New Haven, Conn.: Yale University Press, 1961); Suzanne Keller, *Beyond the Ruling Class: Strategic Elites in Modern Society* (New York: Random House, 1963); David Riesman et al., *The Lonely Crowd* (New Haven, Conn.: Yale University Press, 1950); and Kenneth Galbraith, *American Capitalism: The Concept of Countervailing Power* (Boston: Houghton Mifflin, 1952.)

dustrial nations conforms to the theoretical ideal of a ruling class monop-
olizing power and privilege, than by asking whether or not a ruling class
exists.

Viewed in this way, it quickly becomes evident that there are varying
degrees of approximation of the elitist ideal in industrial societies. In the
Scandinavian democracies, the departure from the ideal is so marked that
continued use of traditional concepts such as "the ruling class" can only
cause confusion. In these societies, inequalities in power and privilege
seem to approach the minimum which is possible without seriously jeop-
ardizing the Socialists' chances of attaining other party and national goals.[67]
Furthermore, in these societies power and privilege have largely been
separated: those who enjoy the greatest measure of political power no
longer enjoy a corresponding measure of economic privilege, and those
who enjoy the greatest measure of economic privilege tend to be weak
politically. By contrast, in those societies where the American pattern
prevails, inequalities in power and privilege not only are much greater but
are more highly correlated with one another. The concept of a ruling
class is, therefore, somewhat more appropriate, though, as already stated,
not nearly so appropriate as in traditional agrarian societies. In totalitarian
societies of the fascist variety (a relatively uncommon type), a still better
approximation of the elitist ideal is customary, with inequalities in both
power and privilege being even greater and more highly correlated than
in democracies of the American pattern. In totalitarian societies of the
Communist variety, inequalities in power are extreme, but inequalities in
privilege are more limited, though unlike the situation in Scandinavia,
power and privilege are highly correlated. In short, *there is considerable
variability among industrial societies in this respect, but the modal pattern is quite different from that observed in traditional agrarian societies,
indicating the need for considerable caution in the use of concepts such
as "the ruling class," "the governing class," and "the political elite" in reference to industrial societies.*

If one turns from past and present patterns to current trends and
probable future patterns, the need for caution becomes even greater. In
nearly all industrial societies the long-term trend has been, and continues

[67] This statement is no more than an educated guess, but it is based on observations
of the reluctance of the Scandinavian Socialist Parties to press for complete economic
equality, despite historic ideological commitments. This seems to reflect an awareness on
the part of party leaders that the single-minded pursuit of this one goal could endanger
their chances of attaining other important goals, e.g., the party goal of retaining control
of the government or the national goal of maximizing production and productive
efficiency. The accuracy of this interpretation can be tested properly only if these
Socialist governments press for more perfect economic equality and the consequences
of their efforts are observed.

to be, one involving a reduction in both political and economic inequality. The chief exceptions to this generalization seem to be (1) the Soviet Union, where there has been a definite rise in economic inequality since 1931, and (2) the Scandinavian democracies, where there seems to be a definite slowing, and perhaps even a halting, of the drive toward economic equality.[68] Both exceptions involve societies in which economic inequality had already been greatly reduced, and there is reason to think that the halting or reversal of the general trend reflected their leaders' commitment to a plurality of partially incompatible goals and their unwillingness to jeopardize other goals solely for the sake of this one.[69] Thus, looking to the future, one is led to make two predictions. First, *the great majority of the more advanced industrial societies will move even further from the traditional elitist ideal in which a tiny minority monopolizes both power and privilege.* Second, *this trend will stop substantially short of the egalitarian ideal in which power and privilege are shared equally by all members of society.*

The Political Class System

Despite substantial movement toward the democratic ideal, political inequality is still a basic fact of life in all advanced industrial societies, and political resources are the basis of one of the more important, but neglected, class systems. Where an individual stands with respect to such resources can have a decisive influence on his chances of obtaining many of the things he desires most. Though political status is obviously more important for an individual in a totalitarian nation than in a democratic, it is not without considerable influence in both.

Since the nature of the political class system is more clearly defined in totalitarian nations, it may be well to start with them. In such nations one can readily identify at least four basic classes, each standing in a different relation to the means of political control—that is, the Party.

At the top of this hierarchy, one always finds a rather small group of *Party functionaries,* persons who serve the Party on a full-time basis and for whom Party activity is their livelihood. This class can be further differentiated into a small Party elite, which controls the decision-making process within the Party, and the great majority of lesser functionaries, whose task it is to implement the decisions of the elite. Beneath the functionaries

[68] On the Soviet Union, see Mehnert, chaps. 6–8 or Alex Inkeles, "Social Stratification and Mobility in the Soviet Union: 1940–1950," *American Sociological Review,* 15 (1950), pp. 465–479; on Sweden, see Fleisher, chaps. 12 and 13.

[69] See footnote 67 above for suggestions of the nature of other goals of the Scandinavian Socialists.

is the class made up of *Party members,* persons who hold membership in the Party without being engaged in full-time Party work. This class, too, can be subdivided into activists, who provide leadership in the lower echelons of the Party on a volunteer basis, and others, who do little more than what is necessary to maintain membership in the Party.

Still lower in the class hierarchy of totalitarian states is the class composed of persons who, though outside the Party, are not regarded by the Party as hostile to it. This *non-Party* class has always been the largest class, including, as it does, at least three types of persons: (1) those who desire membership in the Party but lack relevant qualifications, (2) those who are covertly hostile to the Party and do not seek membership on grounds of principle, and (3) those who are indifferent. Finally, beneath the non-Party class there is usually a class of persons who are officially classified as enemies of the Party. This class varies considerably in size and social situation. Its members are subject to imprisonment or even execution, but, under favorable circumstances, are allowed their freedom subject to penalties or limitations not imposed on others.

Political class systems of this type develop automatically in any industrial society where a single, authoritarian party gains control of the state. Considering the heterogeneity of a modern industrial society and the self-seeking tendencies of men, it is impossible for all to agree voluntarily on any single political program or policy. Varying responses to the programs of a totalitarian party are inevitable, and lay the foundation for the differentiation of the population into Party members, non-Party people, and Party enemies. Furthermore, the needs of the Party lead quite naturally to the differentiation of Party members into the categories described above.

The existence of this type of class system is coming to be recognized even in the Communist sphere, where the first to speak openly of it was Milovan Djilas, once Marshal Tito's chief lieutenant. In a series of essays published in the early 1950s, Djilas strongly condemned the rise of what he called "the new class." [70] He stated that the new class is "made up of those who have special privileges and economic preference because of the administrative monopoly they hold." More specifically, he identified it with the "Party bureaucracy," or those we have labeled the Party functionaries. Since the death of Stalin, criticism of the new class has emerged even in the Soviet Union, though most critics there are still quite cautious about applying the hated label "class" to the objects of their attacks. [71]

[70] See *The New Class: An Analysis of the Communist System* (New York: Frederick A. Praeger, 1959), especially pp. 37–69.
[71] See Mehnert, especially pp. 112–115, or Hugh McLean and Walter Vickery, *The Year of Protest, 1956: An Anthology of Soviet Literary Materials* (New York: Vintage Books, 1961).

Thanks to the work of these critics and of foreign scholars as well, it is now possible to form a fairly clear image of the nature of this class system and how it operates within the Soviet Union. To begin with, official Party reports show that approximately 10 million persons are currently members of the Communist Party.[72] This is about 8 per cent of the adult population. At the present time it is not altogether clear in what ways and to what extent ordinary Party members benefit from Party membership. In the past, however, there were obvious material benefits. For example, one Russian refugee interviewed after World War II described the situation this way:

> Now take the time of the famine; who lived and who didn't live? The party people lived because when everybody else had nothing to eat, the party people could go to special stores and get food.

Turning to the then current situation, he went on to say:

> Suppose I am a Communist and you are not. I will live well and you will live poorly. If I am a nonparty man and I have three children, they cannot get the education they need and they cannot get the food they need. If I am a party man, we will have plenty of money and we will get along well. Our kids can go to school.[73]

At the present time, with food and other consumer goods more plentiful, it appears that Party membership and activity are important chiefly as qualifications for occupational advancement. Apparently non-Party people cannot hope to rise to the top in most fields of endeavor.[74] It must be noted, however, that in more recent years entry into the Party has been made relatively easy for talented and ambitious persons. In fact, it seems to have become a deliberate policy to recruit such persons for the Party.[75]

The desire of Party leaders to recruit the more talented elements in the population has led to an interesting and important bias in the composition of its membership. Official Party statistics reveal that the Party includes a disproportionate number of persons in professional and managerial occupations, and is underrepresented among workers and peasants. For example, one report indicates that 73 per cent of the delegates to the Twenty-first Party Congress in 1959, and 52 per cent of all Party members, were at least secondary school graduates, even though only 16 per cent of

[72] Merle Fainsod, *How Russia Is Ruled,* rev. ed. (Cambridge, Mass.: Harvard University Press, 1963), p. 249.
[73] Alex Inkeles and Raymond Bauer, *The Soviet Citizen* (Cambridge, Mass.: Harvard University Press, 1959), pp. 324–325. See also the interview quoted on pp. 328–329. Quoted by permission.
[74] See, for example, Fainsod, pp. 215 and 234; Granick, p. 173; Inkeles and Bauer, pp. 324–329; Djilas, pp. 72–73; or DeWitt, p. 537 and 463–466.
[75] T. H. Rigsby, "Social Characteristics of the Party Membership," in Alex Inkeles and Kent Geiger (eds.), *Soviet Society* (Boston: Houghton Mifflin, 1961), p. 140.

the general population had reached this level.[76] Since educational attainments are so highly correlated with occupational status, there are similar discrepancies between the status of Party members and others in the occupational class system. For example, despite the fact that professionals and semiprofessionals constitute only 1.8 per cent of the total population, or roughly 4 per cent of the labor force, they represent more than a quarter of the Party's membership.[77] As one expert put it, "Although the integration of professionals with the Communist Party is far from complete, substantial interlocking between the two groups is in effect. . . . The degree of interlocking between the top echelons of the party and the leading administrative elite is even more extensive." [78] Recent reports from Yugoslavia reveal a similar situation there, and less systematic evidence from other Communist nations suggests that the pattern is virtually universal.[79]

Things were not always so in the Communist Party. At the time of the Russian Revolution, more than 60 per cent of the Party members were listed in Party records as being of worker origin, and another 8 per cent of peasant origin.[80] By 1956 the percentage of the former had been almost halved (to 32 per cent), and though the percentage of peasant origin had risen (to 17 per cent), together they accounted for less than half of the Party's membership.[81]

Despite its proletarian ideology, this kind of development seems almost inevitable. Merle Fainsod identified the basic factor responsible for the trend when he wrote, "As the dominating force in Soviet society, the Party can discharge its governing responsibilities effectively only by assimilating the most highly trained and educated representatives of the younger generations. In consolidating its position as a governing elite, the Party needs to incorporate the rising stratum in Soviet society—the engineers and technicians, the plant managers, the bureaucrats, and other representatives of the new technical, administrative, and cultural intelligentsia." [82] In short, *there is no alternative to at least partial coordination of the political class system with the occupational and educational class systems in totalitarian nations.*

[76] See DeWitt, pp. 533 and 534 and table 6-79. Fainsod reports somewhat lower figures for Party members, but still a substantial difference between them and the general population (see p. 281).

[77] DeWitt, pp. 533 and 535.

[78] *Ibid.,* pp. 536–537.

[79] According to a recent report to the Eighth Yugoslav Party Congress, at least half of all Party members are now office employees and "others" (presumably members of the intelligentsia). See *The Washington Post,* December 9, 1964, p. A-22.

[80] Fainsod, table 3, p. 250.

[81] *Ibid.,* p. 276.

[82] *Ibid.,* p. 282. Quoted by permission.

Though all Party members probably benefit somewhat because of their membership, the chief beneficiaries are the Party functionaries who make up "the new class" which Djilas attacked. The exact size of this class is not known, but it has recently been estimated to number from 150,000 to 750,000.[83] The powers of this class, which are immense, derive ultimately from its control of the state. This means that the entire police system and all of the armed forces are at its disposal and can be used at all times to implement its decisions.

Since the Party is organized along authoritarian, hierarchical lines, tenure and advancement within Party ranks have depended to a large degree on an individual's ability to satisfy his superiors. As a result, positions in the organization have often been quite insecure. This reached its extreme during the Stalin era. Premier Khrushchev reported in his famous address to the Twentieth Party Congress that "of the 139 members and candidates of the Party's Central Committee who were elected at the Seventeenth Congress, 98 were arrested and shot (mostly in 1937–38)" and that of the 1,966 delegates with either voting or advisory rights at the same congress, 1,108 "were arrested on charges of antirevolutionary crimes." [84] While there has been a substantial improvement in the security of Party functionaries since Stalin's death, the dangers are not completely eliminated. As one authority put it very recently,

> The life of the apparatchik remains hazardous. Though there have been no blood baths on the scale of the Great Purge since the mid-thirties, shake-ups in the apparatus are frequent, and punishment for serious missteps is severe. Even the most powerful may fall from the heights to the lowest depths with dizzying swiftness.[85]

Because of the serious risks involved, compensations have been essential. Among these, two in particular stand out. The first is the opportunity for rapid advancement, an inevitable by-product of shake-ups, dismissals, and purges. The more high ranking officials removed from office, the more openings become available for younger men of lesser rank. Furthermore, there is a multiplicative tendency involved, because a single dismissal of a high ranking official normally creates the need for a series of promotions in a multilevel organization.

The second compensation which the Party has traditionally offered is privilege on a lavish scale. This was especially true during the Stalin period, when risks were so very great.[86] However, the privileges accorded

[83] The lower estimate is by Fainsod, pp. 206–207, and the higher by Mehnert, p. 21.
[84] Fainsod, pp. 195–196.
[85] *Ibid.*, p. 207. Quoted by permission.
[86] See, for example, David J. Dallin, *The New Soviet Empire* (New Haven, Conn.: Yale University Press, 1951), chap. 9.

members of the political elite even today are comparable in many respects to those enjoyed by the property and managerial elites in capitalistic nations.[87] These include not only such material benefits as lovely homes and estates, fine clothes, good food, and servants, but also the opportunity to provide one's children with special access to elite positions.[88] This is especially important because it lays the foundation for the hereditary transmission of power and privilege from generation to generation.

Despite the lavish rewards the political elite receives, not all of them are satisfied. It is apparent from Soviet sources that the *apparatchiki* have often used their powers of office for private gain, sometimes on a very substantial scale.[89] This supports Djilas's thesis about the declining influence of the Party's egalitarian ideology in its own ranks and the growing influence of simple self-seeking.

Though the existence of a political class system is most easily seen in one-party, totalitarian nations like the Soviet Union, it can also be observed in any multiparty nation in which the nature and extent of a person's political activity affect his access to rewards. Naturally, however, there are certain differences in the structure and functioning of such systems. To begin with, a democratic party cannot dominate the state as can a totalitarian. Therefore, it is not able to use so freely the resources of the state to support party personnel. This means that the political class, i.e., the party functionaries, or professional politicians, tends to be smaller in democratic nations. Second, because of this inability to utilize freely the resources of the state, party leaders are forced to turn elsewhere. In many instances this permits wealthy individuals to "buy" their way into the inner circle of democratic parties.[90] This is most likely to occur in non-ideological, brokerage-type parties, such as exist in the United States, and least likely to occur in Socialist and Labor parties, with their strong egalitarian ideology. Third, the distinction between party members and non-party people is highly blurred in most multiparty states, with the result that large numbers of persons who regard themselves as party members or adherents, pay no dues and in no way share in party activities. Finally, there is much less likely to be a class of political outcastes in multiparty

[87] See Mehnert, especially chaps. 5 and 8, or Djilas.
[88] Mehnert, p. 108, or David Burg, "Observations of Soviet University Students," in Richard Pipes (ed.), *The Russian Intelligentsia* (New York: Columbia University Press, 1961), pp. 80–81.
[89] Fainsod, pp. 240–242. See also recent Soviet novels, such as Dudintsev's, *Not by Bread Alone*.
[90] For examples of this, see James Reichley, *The Art of Government: Reform and Organization Politics in Philadelphia* (New York: Fund for the Republic, 1959); Robert Lynd and Helen Lynd, *Middletown in Transition* (New York: Harcourt, Brace & World, 1937), especially chaps. 3 and 9; or Key, pp. 537–547, among many others.

nations, and when one does exist (as in the case of Communists in the United States), the numbers involved tend to be small and the individual is normally free to leave the class if he is willing to abandon his deviant views.[91] By contrast, in totalitarian states, escape from that class is entirely dependent upon the decision of officials of the party in power, and merely adjuring one's former beliefs cannot insure escape.

Membership in the political class often is just as rewarding in multi-party nations as in one-party nations. Though it has long been known that political activity in the former affords unusual opportunities for self-aggrandizement, the magnitude of these opportunities has not always been appreciated by those outside political circles. In a famous study of twenty American city bosses, made more than a generation ago, it was found that at least nine left estates officially valued at $1 million or more, including one valued in excess of $11 million.[92] In addition, two others were millionaires at some point in their career, and five others left estates valued at $200,000 to $800,000. Only three men never accumulated a substantial fortune, and no information was available on the finances of one. All this they achieved in an age when the dollar was worth at least twice what it is today, and despite the fact that none came from prosperous homes (six were raised in abject poverty and eight came from poor homes).[93] These men were not unique. The list could be extended considerably.[94] In recent years, the opportunities for financial gain through party politics seem to have declined considerably, though a recent study of the financial history of President Johnson indicates that it would be premature to suppose that such opportunities have ceased altogether. According to this study, President Johnson, his wife, and daughters were worth approximately $9 million in 1964, and this vast fortune "was amassed almost entirely while Mr. Johnson was in public office; mainly since he entered the Senate and began his rise to national power in 1948." [95]

[91] A notable exception to this is the case of the Negroes of the deep South at present, and much of the South in an earlier period. It is noteworthy, however, that this pattern has existed in areas lacking a true multiparty system.

[92] Harold Zink, *City Bosses in the United States: A Study of Twenty Municipal Bosses* (Durham, N.C.: Duke University Press, 1930), pp. 37–38. Some of the figures which follow are based on data presented in the individual biographies in the second section of this book.

[93] *Ibid.*, p. 9.

[94] See, for example, the career of the former Kansas City boss, Tom Pendergast, who in a single year bet $2 million on horse races and lost $600,000, and made over $300,000 on a single "deal." Over a ten-year period Pendergast failed to report over $1 million in income in his tax returns (the record fails to show how much more he reported). See William Reddig, *Tom's Town: Kansas City and the Pendergast Legend* (Philadelphia: Lippincott, 1947), pp. 278–279, and Maurice Milligan, *The Missouri Waltz* (New York: Scribner, 1948), p. 191.

[95] *New York Times*, June 10, 1964, p. 25. Later reports raised the estimate of the Johnson family fortune to $14 million.

It is often supposed that when party leaders in countries like the United States acquire great fortunes it is by illegal means. While this has sometimes been true, it overlooks the fact that those who occupy high positions in party organizations have many opportunities to get rich without ever violating the law. Boss Crump of Memphis made a fortune by channeling most of the insurance business of that city through a firm in which he had a major interest. Boss Pendergast made many thousands of dollars selling Kansas City concrete, which it bought in inordinate quantities at premium prices. Others have used inside information about city plans as a basis for "speculation" in real estate or have invested in businesses whose markets are protected by governmental agencies vulnerable to their influence. In short, there has been no lack of perfectly legal opportunities for self-aggrandizement by the political elite in the United States.

Despite the fact that both American and Soviet political elites have benefited enormously from their control of key political offices, it should not be supposed that this is a universal pattern in industrial societies. In some instances political elites have studiously avoided economic self-aggrandizement. This has been true of Socialist Party elites in both Scandinavia and Britain. Similarly, in the Conservative Party in Britain, the pattern seems to have been rare in recent years. The explanation for these differences appears to lie largely in the nature of the party organizations. In Socialist parties with their strong egalitarian ideology, strict discipline, and freedom from terror, excessive rewards are not necessary, and individuals usually have neither the desire nor the opportunity to use their political office as a means of self-aggrandizement. The same can also be true of such parties as the Conservative Party in Britain, where discipline is strict, where subelites (such as the backbenchers in Parliament) have little independence, and where the top leadership is made up largely of persons of considerable wealth who are less interested in using party office as a resource for private financial aggrandizement than as a means of protecting class and national interests.

Though membership in the political class is often highly rewarding in nontotalitarian nations, this is not true of mere party membership. Psychic rewards and the chance of moving into the ranks of the party professionals seem to be the chief benefits a party has to offer mere members.[96] This is undoubtedly one of the reasons why this class is seldom more than a small minority of the population. In the United States, for example, studies show that not more than 10 per cent of the adult popula-

[96] See, for example, Duverger, pp. 109–116, or Robert Dahl, *Who Governs?: Democracy and Power in an American City* (New Haven, Conn.: Yale University Press, 1961), pp. 97–100.

tion claims ever to have had any kind of active involvement in party organizations.[97] The situation in Europe does not seem to be very different. Duverger has shown that only a minority of the voters who support the highly organized Socialist parties at the polls are even dues paying members, e.g., less than 10 per cent in France, Germany, and Holland.[98] He also shows that the true activists are only a fraction of the dues paying minority, stating that, "In no party do they seem to exceed a half of the [dues paying] membership: when they reach a third or a quarter, the party may be considered to be active." [99]

When one examines political class systems in a comparative and historical perspective, two important trends seem to emerge. In the first place, it appears that there is a widespread trend toward *a decline in the importance of political class systems relative to other class systems, especially the occupational class system.* A declining proportion of the rewards in advanced industrial nations are distributed on the basis of the individual's status in the political system. This trend is clearly evident in the United States, where the political class has been under attack for roughly a century by major segments of the propertied, entrepreneurial, and managerial classes. Hoping to reduce the costs of government while increasing its efficiency, these groups have introduced a number of major reforms designed to reduce the powers of professional politicians.[100] One of the early reforms sought to replace the traditional patronage system, which placed vast appointive powers in the hands of party leaders, with the merit, or civil service, system. Though party leaders have found ways to get around these laws to some extent, their powers of appointment have been greatly curtailed. To cite but a single example, in New York City the proportion of exempt appointments in the classified service, i.e., not subject to civil service regulations, was reduced more than 80 per cent in the first half of the present century.[101] While this figure is probably higher than average, it reflects the general trend.

[97] See, for example, Angus Campbell, Philip Converse, Warren Miller, and Donald Stokes, *The American Voter* (New York: Wiley, 1960), pp. 90–93.
[98] Duverger, book 1, chap. 2, especially p. 95. In some countries, such as Sweden and Britain, where many union members are automatically enrolled in the Socialist Party by their union, the proportion rises to a third or more, but only because the responsibility is taken out of the individual's hands.
[99] *Ibid.*, p. 114.
[100] For a good discussion of this reform movement, see Edward Banfield and James Wilson, *City Politics* (Cambridge, Mass.: Harvard University and M. I. T. Presses, 1963), especially part 3 and the concluding chapter.
[101] Theodore J. Lowi, *At the Pleasure of the Mayor: Patronage and Power in New York, 1898–1958* (New York: Free Press, 1964), table 4.1. Lowi also reports that the percentage of nonparty appointments in the mayor's "cabinet" rose from 10 per cent in the predepression era to 30 per cent since World War II (p. 92).

A second important reform has been the rise of the council-manager form of local government and related developments, which put increasing power in the hands of professional administrators. At the present time, more than 36 per cent of American cities with a population of 5,000 or more have managers.[102] As one writer put it, "In practice, although the manager plays a public role of 'the expert' who is available only to answer questions and to administer, in fact, he or his subordinates are the principal sources of policy innovation in [council-manager] cities today." [103] Even in cities which have not adopted the council-manager plan, the same trend is evident, with the power of administrators or managers steadily increasing as the departments they manage grow in size and complexity.[104]

Similar trends exist in the Soviet Union. During the first two decades of Communist rule, Party membership and loyalty were often sufficient qualifications for appointment to important posts in industry and government.[105] As a consequence, as late as 1934, 50 per cent of the factory directors in the Soviet Union had only a primary school education. Today, Party loyalty is not enough. Higher education is the chief criterion and Party membership has become a secondary requirement. While Party membership apparently is still essential to appointment in top managerial posts, entry into the Party seems little more than a formality for occupationally qualified persons. Another indication of the weakening of the Party and the political class system can be seen in recent decisions, in the Soviet Union and other Eastern European countries, to reduce the scope of planning in their economies and to increase the scope of market forces.[106] Whatever the reasons behind these decisions, the results will almost certainly be increased power for the managerial and professional classes and further reduction in the power of Party functionaries. Finally, political status has come to count for relatively little in those countries of Western Europe where the Socialist Party is dominant, and probably for little more in others, like Britain, where a strong civil service system has become entrenched. In short, political class systems seem to be in a period of decline in most advanced industrial nations.

The reasons for this are varied, but most of them are related to the great growth in the size and complexity of economic and governmental

---

[102] See Charles Adrian, *Governing Urban America*, 2d ed. (New York: McGraw-Hill, 1961), p. 220.
[103] *Ibid.*, p. 250.
[104] See Banfield and Wilson, p. 184.
[105] See, for example, Fainsod, pp. 503–505.
[106] Various aspects of this development have been widely reported in the press in 1964. See footnote 38 above.

organizations. A considerable measure of autonomy has become essential for the managers of these organizations. What is more, the management must be technically trained. The only alternative would be the sacrifice of efficiency and productivity, and this is a price few political elites are willing or able to pay.[107]

The second trend is more debatable, since the evidence suggesting it is limited to the United States and Soviet Union. It is possible that it may not apply to all, or even most, advanced industrial societies. In these two nations, however, one can observe *a definite curvilinear trend in the correlation between status in the political class system and status in several of the other important class systems.* During the early stages of industrialization, status in the political class system was highly correlated with status in the occupational, educational, and property systems, reflecting the agrarian pattern. With the rise of mass parties and the increasing power of the working class, this relationship was weakened in all industrial societies, and especially those under Socialist or Communist control. In recent years, however, there have been definite signs of a reversal of this trend.[108] In both the United States and the Soviet Union, political status is increasingly correlated with occupational and educational status, and in the United States with property status as well. Whether the same trend exists in the democracies of Western Europe is not clear at present.

Though the reasons for this trend vary somewhat in the two countries, in both instances the recent reversal is linked with the weakening of the political system of stratification. In the United States the reversal apparently reflects the decline in the number of low-level patronage positions, which formerly gave men of humble background an opportunity to get a start in politics as a career. With the spread of civil service, traditional channels for upward mobility within the party have been reduced and the higher posts within the parties are increasingly taken by persons of means who can "afford" them. In the Soviet Union the increasing correlation between political, economic, and occupational status appears to be due to the weakening of the Party through the loss of ideological fervor and the Party's resultant desire to strengthen itself by bringing into its ranks the leading elements in the population. As a result, the correlation between political status on the one hand and occupational and educational status on the other is probably at least as high in the Soviet Union as in any non-Communist democracy.

[107] For a more extended discussion of this and related points, see pp. 313–314 of this chapter and pp. 347–361 of the next.
[108] In the case of the United States, see Dahl, chap. 4, on the rise of "the new men," or Banfield and Wilson's concluding chapter. On the U.S.S.R., see the statistics cited previously (pp. 329–330) on the changing composition of the Party.

The Property Class System

A second important resource in the majority of advanced industrial societies is the ownership of private property. This is especially true in those societies conforming to the American pattern, where wealth can be a means of obtaining both political and economic power. In societies corresponding to the Swedish pattern, and in fascist states, wealth loses much of its political utility, but retains its economic value. In Communist states, its economic value is restricted to the purchase of consumer goods and services and to the earning of modest interest payments.[109]

Where private property functions as a resource, there is, of necessity, a system of property classes. However, contrary to Marx's expectations, there has been no polarization of populations along this line. On the contrary, tables depicting the distribution of wealth for advanced industrial societies invariably reveal an unbroken gradient ranging upward by small increments from tiny holdings to great estates of massive proportions, with no clear lines of demarcation at any point. Evidence of this can be seen in Tables 2 and 3, which show recent estimates of the distribution of wealth in the United States and Britain.

Nevertheless, despite the gradient, and despite the fact that in these societies virtually everyone owns some property, there is a sense in which it is not only possible, but useful, to speak of a *propertied class*. Tables 2 and 3 clearly show that some members of British and American societies benefit from the system of private property in a way that others do not: *some own more than their proportionate, i.e., per capita, share of private property and therefore receive more than their proportionate share of the rewards of such property.* Thus, such persons have a special interest in the preservation of this historic institution. It is this segment of the population, therefore, which I shall refer to as the propertied class.

On the basis of Lampman's recent study of the distribution of wealth in the United States, it appears that roughly 25 per cent of the American population belongs to the propertied class so defined. The members of this class own approximately 80 per cent of the privately held wealth.[110] In

[109] In the U.S.S.R., for example, money deposited for six months or more earns 5 per cent interest, while demand deposits earn 3 per cent. See F. D. Holzman, "Financing Soviet Economic Development," in Bornstein and Fusfeld, p. 148.
[110] These estimates are based on the Lorenz curve shown by Robert Lampman in *The Share of Top Wealth-holders in National Wealth: 1922–1956* (Princeton, N.J.: Princeton University Press, 1962), p. 212. Almost identical results are reported by John C. Bowen in a study carried out independently of Lampman's. See *Some Aspects of Transfer Taxation in the United States* (unpublished doctoral dissertation, University of Michigan, 1958), chart 11.6 and table 6.13.

England and Wales, where there has long been a greater degree of inequality in the ownership of private property, the propertied class constituted only about 12 per cent of the population in the late 1940's, but owned approximately 85 per cent of the privately held wealth.[111]

Table 2   Estimated Distribution of Wealth in the United States, 1953

ASSETS	PERCENTAGE OF ADULT POPULATION	PERCENTAGE OF WEALTH
Less than $3,500	50.0	8.3
$3,500 to $10,000	18.4	10.2
$10,000 to $20,000	21.2	29.3
$20,000 to $30,000	5.8	13.4
$30,000 to $50,000	2.7	9.5
$50,000 to $100,000	1.0	6.2
$100,000 to $1,000,000	0.9	16.6
$1,000,000 to $10,000,000	0.04	5.2
$10,000,000 and over	0.0006	1.3
Total	100.0	100.0

Source: Calculated from Robert J. Lampman, *The Share of Top Wealth-holders in National Wealth: 1922–1956* (Princeton, N.J.: Princeton University Press, 1962), tables 34 and 99.

Table 3   Estimated Distribution of Wealth in Britain, 1946–1947

ASSETS IN POUNDS	PERCENTAGE OF POPULATION	PERCENTAGE OF WEALTH
Less than 100	60.6	4.2
100 to 999	27.8	11.6
1,000 to 4,999	8.9	21.0
5,000 to 9,999	1.4	11.4
10,000 to 24,999	0.9	16.4
25,000 to 99,999	0.4	19.2
100,000 and over	0.06	16.3
Total	100.0	100.0

Source: Kathleen M. Langley, "The Distribution of Capital in Private Hands in 1936–38 and 1946–47 (part 2)," *Bulletin of the Oxford University Institute of Statistics* (February, 1951), table XVB, p. 46. Included as table 100 in Lampman.

For some purposes it is enough simply to differentiate between those who belong to the propertied class and those who do not. For other pur-

---

[111] Lampman, pp. 212 and 216.

poses, however, further discrimination is desirable. For example, if one wishes to understand the political activities of the propertied class, it becomes necessary to differentiate between the thousands of lesser members whose holdings are relatively modest (for example, as small as $11,000 in 1953 in the United States, or £1,000 in Britain in 1946–1947), and the tiny minority whose holdings are great enough to constitute an important political and economic resource. This latter group may be called the *property elite*.

Again, there is no obvious or necessary line of demarcation, but a meaningful one might separate from the rest that segment of the propertied class whose income from property *alone* is great enough to permit a comfortable style of life. To facilitate international comparisons, I shall define the property elite as *that segment of the population whose income from property alone is at least twice the national median from all sources.*

In 1953, the year covered by Lampman's study, it appears that only two-thirds of 1 per cent of the American population were members of this elite, but this small number of people owned 20 per cent of the privately held wealth.[112] In the late 1940s, the property elite in England constituted about 1 per cent of the population and owned approximately *45 per cent* of the privately held wealth.[113] As these figures, and those for the propertied class as a whole, make clear, a relatively small minority in both countries has derived a major share of the *direct* benefits from the institution of private property.[114]

In part, this pattern of distribution is the natural result of the operation of a market economy, in which there are always certain forces at work generating inequality in both income and wealth. For example, as noted earlier, men are not born with equal endowments, and some are more favored by nature with intelligence and other economically profitable attributes. Furthermore, the factor of scarcity, i.e., the fact that the

---

[112] These estimates were arrived at in the following fashion. According to government statistics, the median *money* income for families and unrelated individuals in that year was $3,789 (see the *Statistical Abstract, 1962*, p. 332). Total income, therefore, probably equalled about $4,000, and twice this would qualify one as a member of the property elite. The rest of the calculations were made on the basis of tables 34 and 99 in Lampman's book.

[113] These figures are based on the income data reported in David Marsh, *The Changing Social Structure of England and Wales, 1871–1951* (London: Routledge, 1958), p. 219, and the property distribution indicated in Lampman, p. 214, assuming a 6 per cent average return on investments.

[114] Some would argue that all members of society benefit substantially from the existence of the system of private property, since it functions to motivate men to work harder and accumulate wealth, and thus raises the gross national product more rapidly than alternative systems. This is a very difficult thesis to prove or disprove, and to avoid becoming entangled in it, I shall discuss only the *direct* or *immediate* benefits which accrue to the owner himself by virtue of his property rights.

demand for most goods and services exceeds the supply, insures that under conditions of private ownership some will own what others cannot. Also, the fact of differential scarcity among commodities insures that what some own will inevitably prove more valuable than what others own.

While the operation of such factors is commonly recognized, many overlook the fact that *in a free market system, i.e., one free from political regulation, small inequalities tend to generate greater inequalities and great inequalities still greater ones.* In short, a free market system itself tends to foster the monopolization of wealth by the few. This is due chiefly to the influence of "fixed costs" which, to the degree they are present in an industry, provide a constant competitive advantage to larger producers, who are thereby enabled to price their products below their smaller competitors. With lower prices, they tend to win a larger share of the market, which permits them to lower their prices still further while forcing up the prices of their competitors, thus setting in motion a vicious circle which normally ends in the elimination of the smaller firms.[115] In other words, in a completely free and politically unfettered market economy, there is a natural tendency for "the rich to get richer and the poor to get poorer." In the past, inefficient systems of transportation and communication, together with the limited development of rational systems of economic organization and administration, served to check this tendency, but with modern advances in technology and social organization, these limitations are fast disappearing.

This would lead one to expect increasing concentration of wealth in non-Communist nations. The fact that this has not happened is due chiefly to the working of *political* forces which, in industrial societies no less than agrarian, appear to be the most important determinant of the distribution of wealth. In fact, it is no exaggeration to say that the action of economic forces in modern industrial societies takes place increasingly within a framework defined by law. With increasing frequency, governmental bodies determine the uses to which economic resources may be put, thus ultimately determining their value.

In democratic nations, the propertied class, and particularly its elite, is inevitably at some disadvantage in this situation owing to its lack of numbers. Since the propertied class is a creature of the market system, it will always be a minority of the population. Hence its members have a vested interest (whether recognized or not) in preventing those outside its ranks from influencing political decisions. During the earlier stages of industrialization, this was achieved by setting property requirements for

[115] For an excellent description of a classic case of this process, see Edward Higbee, *Farms and Farmers in an Urban Age* (New York: Twentieth Century Fund, 1963).

the right of franchise, so that only men of means could vote. This practice proved politically untenable, however, and was eventually eliminated. In the United States it was virtually eliminated by the 1840s, but in Europe, not until late in the nineteenth century or, in some cases, until well into the twentieth.[116] In Sweden, for example, property restrictions on the franchise were not finally eliminated until after World War I.[117]

Though it might seem that elimination of property restrictions doomed the propertied class and the institution of private property, this has not been the case. In part, this is because of the nature of modern democracy, which makes wealth an important political resource. Given the size of modern industrial states, pure democracy is impossible, and representative government inevitable. This means that constituencies are large and elections costly. Those who are elected to high public office (where the constituencies are largest) must therefore be either (1) wealthy in their own right, (2) financed by persons of wealth, or (3) financed by large, mass organizations of persons of modest means, as in the case of the Socialist and Labor Parties. So long as the third possibility can be avoided, the propertied class in general, and the property elite in particular, are readily able to translate their financial resources into political resources.[118] The possibilities of accomplishing this are further enhanced by the sheer complexity of modern governmental action, which frequently defies comprehension by anyone but the expert. The legislative process often involves a bewildering number of steps, many more or less invisible and inaccessible to the average citizen, and legislation is commonly written in the specialized language of lawyers.

As a consequence, the propertied class and its elite are often able to block legislation hostile to their interests and secure legislation of a favorable nature, provided they show enough restraint to avert a massive popular reaction. One result of this can be seen in the peculiar character of so much of the political life of modern democracies, where *the rhetoric of politicians is frequently egalitarian in character, but the legislation more often aristocratic.*[119] Thus, we have the strange situation in which the "official" tax rates in the United States in 1960 ranged up to an almost

[116] See Chilton Williamson, *American Suffrage: From Property to Democracy, 1760–1860* (Princeton, N.J.: Princeton University Press, 1960).

[117] See Rustow, *Compromise*, pp. 84–85, or Fleisher, pp. 18–19.

[118] See, for example, Ehrmann, *France*, pp. 224f., on the use of campaign contributions by the property elite in France.

[119] See, for example, Stern's report of the Democratic Congressman who said, "Ways and Means is the strangest of all the House committees—and the hardest to understand. Judging by the voting records of its members on the floor of the House, the liberals *ought* to have darn near a working majority. But their public *voting* records and their *'operating'* records in the committee, behind closed doors, are two different things." *Op. cit.*, p. 284. See also Ehrmann, *France*, chap. 5.

confiscatory 91 per cent on income of more than $200,000 per year, *while the average rate actually paid by persons with reported incomes of $5 million or more was a mere 24.6 per cent.*[120] Similarly, though the "official" rate for inheritance taxes on estates of $20 million and over was listed at 69 per cent in 1958, *actual taxes on estates of this size equalled only 15.7 per cent of their value.*[121]

In the long run, however, the relative success of the propertied class and its elites may be due as much to the nature of the resource they cherish as to their skill in political intrigue and manipulation. *Wealth, by its very nature, is almost infinitely divisible, which means that it is possible for every member of society to own some property and thereby come to identify his personal interests with those of the propertied class.* While the holdings of many are too negligible to produce this kind of identification, in most industrial societies many people outside the propertied class have holdings which are sufficient to produce either ambivalence or outright support for the system of private property. Thus in many controversies over the rights of property, the propertied class obtains considerable support from persons outside its ranks, which helps to insure the survival of the system even in societies where universal adult suffrage prevails. However, it is important to note that this support is *not unconditional.* Much of it is likely to be withdrawn if the propertied class pushes its demands to the point where the economic well-being of its nonmember supporters is undermined. Awareness of this tends to serve as a check on the self-seeking tendencies of the members of this class.

Finally, one other factor favoring the propertied class is the support it receives from the rising managerial class. This class, though small in numbers, has a tremendously important resource at its disposal and, for reasons discussed in the next chapter, usually supports the propertied class in its struggles with its opponents. The importance of this can hardly be overstated.

Despite all these factors, the net balance of forces has tended to be unfavorable to the propertied class and property elite. Thus, *in the long run there has been a slow but certain decline in their rights and powers.* In most industrial societies, this was first manifested in the broadening of the franchise. More recently, it has been evident in the passage of a constantly growing body of legislation which restricts the ways in which property may be used. More and more, "human rights" are being given priority over property rights, and common interests over private interests,

[120] This figure is from the Bureau of Internal Revenue's *Statistics of Income,* and is reproduced by Stern, p. 6.
[121] *Ibid.,* p. 254.

when these conflict. This has been accomplished by the passage of anti-trust legislation, food and drug laws, minimum wage laws, social security programs, unemployment compensation, and a host of other laws. While there are illusory aspects to some of this legislation, as in the case of certain "official" tax rates, there is also considerable substance, even in countries where the American pattern of control prevails. Even a mildly progressive tax system, i.e., one in which tax rates are higher for the wealthy than for the poor, represents a significant advance over traditional agrarian or early industrial societies where tax systems were *normally regressive*. Finally, the trend toward greater equality is manifested in the growth of *public property, public ownership,* and *public enterprise* (for example, in 1954 between a quarter and a third of Britain's total labor force was employed by the government in a civilian capacity).[122]

It is difficult to predict how far this trend will go. Some argue that it is leading inexorably to the elimination of the entire concept of private property. However, this view is not consistent with available evidence. Even in the Soviet Union the Communist Party has found it inexpedient to eliminate entirely the private ownership of property, and now permits an individual to own a house, a garden up to several acres in size, savings accounts, and personal possessions of many kinds.[123] Of even greater significance, the more utilitarian and less doctrinaire Socialist Parties of Europe are abandoning their former demands for complete nationalization of industry and accepting, even advocating, the principle of a mixed economy.[124]

In part this trend is the Socialists' response to political resistance which apparently mounts in proportion to the degree of change accomplished, which suggests that a self-limiting principle is operating. One may hypothesize that *to the degree that parties representing the working class succeed in enacting laws which bring about a more equal distribution of private property, they reduce the number of persons favoring further socialization of the economy and increase the number opposing it.* If this hypothesis is sound, it would help explain the increasing resistance which the more successful Socialist Parties have encountered in recent years.

[122] Cole, pp. 121–122. For a more detailed discussion of the general subject, see J. W. Grove, *Government and Industry in Britain* (London: Longmans, 1962).
[123] See Mehnert, especially chap. 6, or Kazimierz Grzybowski, *Soviet Legal Institution: Doctrines and Social Functions* (Ann Arbor, Mich.: University of Michigan Press, 1962), p. 148.
[124] See, for example, Kurt Shell, *The Transformation of Austrian Socialism* (New York: University Publishers, 1962), especially chaps. 6 and 7. See also Fleisher, chaps. 12 and 13, or Rostow, *Compromise,* chap. 8, on the Swedish Socialists, or Cole, chap. 29, on the British.

This does not seem to be the whole story, however, and the Socialists' modification of their program after they come into power seems to reflect a growing uncertainty about the utilitarian value of their traditional policy. To begin with, there is a growing recognition that complete ownership of property places an almost impossible administrative burden on the agencies of government. In addition, it invites the inefficiencies associated with excessive centralization. Finally, there is a growing belief that a high level of public ownership undermines certain socially necessary forms of motivation based on men's natural tendency to maximize their personal resources. Thus, it appears that while the long-run trend will probably lead to some further reduction in property rights, it is unlikely that the institution of private property will be eliminated, or even that private ownership of the means of production will disappear.

11/Industrial Societies: Part II

*'Tis a sthrange thing whin ye come to think
iv it that th' less money a man gets f'r his
wurruk, the more nicissary it is to th'
wurruld that he shud go on wurrukin'.*
Mr. Dooley

FOR MOST MEMBERS of industrial societies *the occupational class* system, the subject of the present chapter, is the chief determinant of power, privilege, and prestige. Though it is impossible to say what proportion of *all* rewards are distributed on the basis of occupational activity, approximately three-quarters or more of all *cash* income is distributed on this basis.[1] For the vast majority of individuals, those who are not members of the property elite, the figure is substantially higher.

[1] This is based on reports of national income in non-Communist nations which show that three-quarters or more of national income takes the form of employee compensation or proprietarial income. See, for example, *Statistical Abstract of the United States, 1962* (Washington: GPO, 1962), table 426, or Allan M. Cartter, *The Redistribution of Income in Postwar Britain* (New Haven, Conn.: Yale University Press, 1955), table 2.

The great importance of the occupational class system is further indicated by the fact that one of the chief rewards distributed by most other class systems is access to favored occupations. This is clearly the case with respect to the educational class system and, to a lesser degree, the class systems based on age, sex, status-group membership, political status, and even property.

The Entrepreneurial Class

During the earlier stages of industrialization, the entrepreneurial class appeared destined to be the dominant class in the new societies. Today this is no longer the case. This class has already vanished in some industrial societies and is slowly but surely declining, in both size and power, in most of the rest.

Because of the close relationship between this class and the propertied class, and because the two are easily confused, it is necessary to make clear the distinction between them. The entrepreneurial class includes *those individuals who are actively engaged in the management of business enterprises which they own.* As this definition makes clear, the entrepreneurial class is a unit within the occupational system of stratification, not within the property system. However, its position in the former is based on its resources in the latter. Nevertheless, not all members of the entrepreneurial class are members of the propertied class, nor are all members of the propertied class members of the entrepreneurial. Many small entrepreneurs do not have sufficient capital to qualify as members of the propertied class, and many members of the propertied class do not exercise active control of business enterprises. In short, despite considerable overlap, the two can easily be differentiated on both the analytical and empirical levels.

The decline of the entrepreneurial class can be shown in a number of ways, especially in the case of the United States, where it is more pronounced than in other non-Communist nations. In this country entrepreneurs dropped from 11.4 per cent of the labor force in 1870 to 6.0 per cent in 1954.[2] The 1960 census revealed still further decline: during the preceding decade, the number of self-employed proprietors in construction, manufacturing, transportation, communications, utilities, wholesale and retail trade, banking and finance, insurance and real estate, and several lesser categories declined from 2.2 to 1.7 million, or from 5.2 to 2.9

[2] Kurt Mayer, "Recent Changes in the Class Structure of the United States," in *Transactions of the Third World Congress of Sociology* (London: International Sociological Association, 1956), vol. III, p. 70.

per cent of the male labor force.[3] During the same period, the number of salaried managers in these same industries increased from 1.6 to 2.3 million.

Far more important, the entrepreneurial class has declined in terms of power. Among the first to call attention to this trend were Professors Berle and Means, who, already a generation ago, marshaled a considerable body of evidence to support the thesis that in the United States the ownership of wealth was becoming increasingly separated from the control of wealth.[4] Analyzing the nation's 200 largest companies, which controlled nearly half the country's corporate wealth, they showed that 44 per cent were controlled by their managers rather than by their owners, and that this same 44 per cent controlled 58 per cent of the assets of all these firms, indicating that the pattern was more common in the larger concerns.[5] As Berle and Means pointed out, this pattern of control was a result of the extreme fragmentation of ownership in these giant corporations, which made it exceedingly difficult for anyone other than the managers to organize a majority of the stockholders. The managers could do this chiefly because of their control of the proxy machinery and other resources of the company which they could turn to their own advantage. As Berle and Means put it, "management control, though resting on no legal foundation, appears to be comparatively secure where stock is widely scattered." [6]

Subsequent studies have not only provided support for their conclusions, but have helped clarify the basis of the growing power of the managerial elite.[7] For example, in the middle 1940s Robert Gordon conducted an important study of leadership and decision-making in large American corporations, and concluded:

> For the most part, the board of directors [which represents the owners] as a formal group has surrendered its function of active decision-making in the large corporation. "Outside" directors function, if at all, primarily as financial and business advisers. The value of advice by competent and interested directors should not be minimized. But the job of actually making

[3] U.S. *Census of Population, 1960: Occupational Characteristics,* table 25.
[4] Adolf A. Berle and Gardiner C. Means, *The Modern Corporation and Private Property* (New York: Macmillan, 1932), especially book 1.
[5] *Ibid.,* p. 94.
[6] *Ibid.,* p. 88.
[7] For interesting data on the subject of the trend itself, see Mabel Newcomer, *The Big Business Executive* (New York: Columbia University Press, 1955), table 4, p. 27. This table shows that in a sample of American corporations in 1900 only 7.3 per cent had boards of directors with half or more of the members from the firm's own management; by 1952 this figure had climbed to 33.5 per cent. See also E. S. Mason (ed.), *The Corporation in Modern Society* (Cambridge, Mass.: Harvard University Press, 1959), who writes, "Almost everyone now agrees . . . that, typically, control is in the hands of management; and that management normally selects its own replacements" (p. 4).

the decisions which are the essence of the leadership function rests primarily with the executives themselves. Those who seek to restore the board as a true decision-making body misread the problem of large-scale management organization. The withering away of the active leadership function of the board is unavoidable. It is merely a reflection of the fact that *large-scale business leadership can be performed efficiently only by a single group of working officials willing and able to devote the necessary time to the business.*[8]

As Gordon indicates, the growing power of the managerial elite is a function not only of its ability to rig elections, but also of the growing complexity of the large corporation and all that entails. The management of a large corporation has become demanding, full-time work, and those who are unwilling or unable to devote full attention to it, as is true of most owners and directors, soon find that control passes to those who can.

Census data on income provide additional insights into the relative power of entrepreneurs and managers. In those industries previously cited, in which the number of proprietors dropped while the number of managers rose, the median income for managers was $7,479 in 1959; by contrast, the median income for proprietors or entrepreneurs in those same industries was only $5,932.[9] The latter figure was even less than the national averages for professional, technical and kindred workers ($6,778), and for foremen ($6,705), and was not, in fact, much above the average for the entire census category of craftsmen, foremen, and kindred workers ($5,318).

Studies of private industry in other countries show much the same pattern, though usually not so far advanced. In Britain, for example, the percentage of employers in the male labor force dropped from 5 to 3 per cent in a single generation, from 1921 to 1951.[10] More significantly, control of the largest firms appears to be passing into the hands of managers, who at present occupy nearly half of the seats on the controlling boards of the largest companies, while leading stockholders occupy less than 20 per cent.[11] These figures are especially noteworthy in view of indications that men who are simultaneously either top managers and directors, or

[8] Robert A. Gordon, *Business Leadership in the Large Corporation* (Berkeley, Calif.: University of California Press, 1961, originally published by the Brookings Institution, 1945), pp. 145–146. Quoted by permission of the Brookings Institution (emphasis added).

[9] *U.S. Census of Population, 1960: Occupational Characteristics*, table 25.

[10] David Marsh, *The Changing Social Structure of England and Wales, 1871–1951* (London: Routledge, 1958), table 42. For statistics on the decline of the entrepreneurial class in Belgium, France, West Germany, Italy, and the Netherlands from 1950 to 1962, see Margaret Gordon, *Retraining and Labor Market Adjustment in Western Europe* (Washington: GPO, 1965), table 7, p. 23.

[11] P. Sargant Florence, *Ownership, Control, and Success of Large Companies: An Analysis of English Industrial Structure and Policy, 1936–1951* (London: Street & Maxwell, 1961), pp. 191–193.

leading shareholders and directors, are the dominant figures in policy making, and that other directors are of lesser importance.[12] The trend toward increasing fragmentation of stock ownership in this country has also occurred in Britain. In 1936 the twenty largest stockholders in each of the largest companies in England owned collectively an average of 30 per cent of the stock; by 1950 the average holdings of the twenty largest stockholders had dropped to 19 per cent.[13] This has undoubtedly been a factor in the decline of the entrepreneurial class in Britain.

More recently David Granick reported the results of a comparative study of business enterprise in four nations—Britain, France, West Germany, and Belgium. Though he found that the family-owned and managed firm is still thriving in some industries and some nations (notably West Germany), the prospects for continued family control are poor.[14] One of the major reasons he cites is the inability of the family firm to cope with the succession problem. Capable and energetic fathers do not always have capable and energetic sons, and even when they do, the presence of multiple heirs with contradictory views on company policy is often a serious handicap. In Granick's opinion, few families produce three successive generations of businessmen of a caliber capable of competing successfully with modern managerially controlled competitors. He argues that the chief reason family firms are currently as strong as they are on the Continent is because the great inflation of World War I and the early 1920s destroyed many of the firms then in existence. As a consequence, most family firms are still so new that they are managed either by the founder or his sons. According to Granick, "the real testing period of intergeneration stability [i.e., the appearance of the third generation] is only now appearing." [15]

Despite its decline, the entrepreneurial class and its elite still retain considerable power. This is more evident on the local level than the national, in small communities than in large, and in nations where the American pattern of political control prevails than where the Swedish or British patterns hold sway.[16] By virtue of their willingness and ability to provide

---

[12] *Ibid.*, pp. 79–80.
[13] *Ibid.*, table IIIC, pp. 68–69, or p. 186.
[14] David Granick, *The European Executive* (Garden City, N.Y.: Doubleday Anchor, 1964), chap. 24 and especially pp. 312–313.
[15] *Ibid.*, p. 312.
[16] See, for example, A. B. Hollingshead, *Elmtown's Youth* (New York: Wiley, 1949), especially chap. 6; Robert Lynd and Helen Lynd, *Middletown in Transition* (New York: Harcourt, Brace & World, 1937), chaps. 3 and 9; or Arthur Vidich and Joseph Bensman, *Small Town in Mass Society: Class, Power and Religion in a Rural Community* (Princeton, N.J.: Princeton University Press, 1958), chap. 5. All illustrate the power of the entrepreneurial class in small American communities. Compare these with any of the studies of Scandinavian politics at the national level.

the vitally essential financial support for candidates for public office, this elite often acquires considerable influence in the political arena.

Looking to the future, the prospects for this class do not seem especially bright. The forces which have brought about its decline up to this point show no signs of abating. Thus it would seem that in time the entrepreneurial class will be largely relegated to the marginal and interstitial areas in the economies of the more advanced nations, with the result that most of its members will be neither especially powerful nor privileged. They may, in fact, become hardly distinguishable from the clerical class or the upper strata of the working class. Most of the power and influence which members of this class still possess will probably pass to those members of the managerial class who replace them.

The decline of the entrepreneurial class does not, of course, necessarily imply the simultaneous decline of the propertied class. Nevertheless, the two are interdependent, and it would be quite surprising if the decline of the entrepreneurial class did not contribute to the weakening of the propertied class as well. In addition to the more obvious reasons for predicting this, there is an ideological factor which cannot be ignored. Historically, the propertied class has always defended property rights on the grounds that the men who possessed these rights were the men who actively managed and directed the economic affairs of society, and that these rights were no more than a proper reward for such efforts. Now, as ownership and management become increasingly separated, one of the major justifications for property rights in large industrial enterprises is obviously being destroyed. This cannot help but leave the members of the propertied class ideologically more vulnerable than in the past.

The Class of Party Functionaries

The class of party functionaries or professional politicians was discussed at length in the last chapter. This class has the unique quality of functioning *as a unit* within two class systems simultaneously. Not only does it stand in a distinctive relation to the dominant political organization or organizations in a society, it also fills a unique occupational role.

Little needs to be added to what we have already said about this class except to note that in Communist nations in particular, and in totalitarian nations in general, it performs many of the basic functions historically associated with the entrepreneurial class. In other words, it manages and directs the economic institutions of society, as well as the political. In recent years, however, this class has tended to lose these powers to the managerial class, and for some of the same reasons as the entrepreneurial class. In particular, this shift has been facilitated by the growth in the size and complexity of economic organizations, which makes control of managers by outsiders progressively more difficult. Though the leading members of the managerial class are normally Party members, their interests are not identical with those of the Party functionaries, as will become evident in the next section. Hence the shift in power is more than a shift from Tweedledum to Tweedledee.

The Managerial Class

In the constant struggle for power and privilege in modern industrial societies, no group has risen more rapidly than the members of the managerial class. As our analysis has already shown, this class has gained considerably at the expense of the propertied, entrepreneurial, and political classes, and there is every reason to think that it will make further gains at their expense in the future.

The key to this important development, as noted earlier, lies in the strategic location of the managerial class in the structure of modern, large-scale organizations. Members of this class sit at the very center of things, where all lines of communications converge. As a result, they have immediate access to critical information which they can use for their own purposes in dealing with owners, party functionaries, or elected officials legally responsible for formulating organizational policy. This situation develops whenever the attempt is made to divorce policy-making from administration, since the administrators invariably stand between the policy-makers and the organization itself, and are thereby able to filter selectively the information which passes back and forth. *The larger and more complex an organization becomes, the greater the opportunities for this, and the more valuable a top managerial position becomes as a resource in the struggle for power and privilege.*

Nowhere have the gains of the managerial class been greater than in the private sector of the American economy. In many companies, managers have achieved virtual autonomy, making the board of directors an appendage of management rather than the instrument of the stockholders it was designed to be. This has made it possible for managers to set their own terms of compensation, much in the manner of entrepreneurs, and they have rewarded themselves handsomely. The only factors limiting them appear to be (1) the availability of resources within the firm, (2) the danger of provoking a massive stockholder reaction by excesses, and (3) the danger of damaging the company's reputation in the important market for capital (a market to which most firms must periodically turn if they are to continue to expand and thus remain competitive).

These limitations are apparently not too restrictive. A study of the top officers of the 428 largest nonfinancial corporations in the United States made in 1950 revealed that more than 40 per cent of the company presidents received salaries and other cash payments in excess of $100,000 a year, and 84 per cent received more than $50,000.[17] The author of this study, Mabel Newcomer, pointed out that these figures understate the true income of these managers since they do not include certain substantial forms of remuneration, such as expense account payments for club memberships, entertainment, travel expenses for wives who are "considered to be a definite business asset," and the like, the value of stock options, and in some cases the corporation's contribution to the pension fund. Nevertheless, seventy of these men had incomes greater than that of the President of the United States (with its taxable expense account included).[18]

In another study of the same year, David Roberts examined a much larger sample of corporations. It included 939 of the 3,000 publicly owned, i.e., nonfamily, corporations which reported executive compensation and other data to the Securities and Exchange Commission, and hence included many smaller companies not in the Newcomer study. Nevertheless, the median income of the chief executives of these concerns was $68,000 per year and the middle 50 per cent of the sample received from $46,000 to $100,000 annually.[19] More recently, a series of annual surveys of executive compensation in this country produced very similar results. For example, the 1960 survey, which included 605 of the leading corporations in the country, showed that in companies with net sales of $30 million the average cash income of chief executive officers was $61,000. In firms with net sales of $100 million the average income was $88,000, and in those with net sales of $400 million the average income was $133,000.[20] The following year's survey indicated that in firms with net sales of $1 billion, the chief executives averaged $250,000, and in those with sales of $10 billion, the average was over $400,000.[21] Like those in Newcomer's study, these figures exclude stock options and other fringe benefits, which are often quite substantial.

[17] Newcomer, p. 124.
[18] *Ibid.*, pp. 123 and 127.
[19] David R. Roberts, *Executive Compensation* (New York: Free Press, 1959), p. 15.
[20] These and the following figures are from Arch Patton, "Trends in Executive Compensation," *Harvard Business Review*, 38 (September–October, 1960), p. 146.
[21] Arch Patton, "Executive Compensation in 1960," *ibid.*, 39 (September–October, 1961), p. 152.

These same surveys provide information on the incomes of other high-ranking managers. In 1962, second-ranking officers had incomes averaging 71 per cent of the chief executives', while the third and fourth men averaged 59 and 54 per cent respectively.[22]

The 1962 survey also provided, for the first time, information on executive compensation in some other countries, namely, Britain, West Germany, France, Argentina, and Australia. In all these countries the incomes of the top executives of private firms were very similar. In companies with net sales of $1 million, the average income was about $13,000, or roughly 60 per cent of the American figure; in firms with sales of $100 million, the average was about $35,000, or 40 per cent of the American figure.[23] However, there is reason to believe that fringe benefits and other perquisites are greater in most of these other countries than in the United States. These fringe benefits are extremely important as a source of income because in most cases the individual pays no tax on them. Hence, a British executive with a basic salary of $22,500 per year, and untaxed fringe benefits worth $14,000, has a total income the equivalent of $155,000 per year, because of the high rate of taxation.[24]

The size of managerial incomes have, quite naturally, provoked considerable comment, frequently of a critical nature. There have also been attempts to justify them as functional necessities demanded by the hierarchical nature of the corporation itself. For example, one sociologist recently pointed out that in a fifteen-layer organization with a $4,000 base wage and a 15 per cent increment by rank (to motivate men to seek advancement), the top salary would be over $28,000, and that, since the progressive tax system reduces the differentials between ranks, even larger salary differentials are needed.[25] He then went on to argue that the progressive tax system may necessitate a hundred-fold wage differential between the base and peak of the hierarchy. This reasoning is based on a confusion of official and actual tax rates for various levels of income. On the basis of the Federal income tax, which is the most progressive major tax in the United States, persons with incomes of less than $5,000 a year actually pay 9 per cent, while those with incomes of $20,000 to $50,000 per year pay only 22 per cent.[26] If allowance were made for the influence of regressive taxes, such as the sales tax, and other nonprogressive taxes,

[22] Arch Patton, "Executive Compensation Here and Abroad," *ibid.*, 40 (September–October, 1962), p. 152.
[23] *Ibid.*, p. 145.
[24] Roy Lewis and Rosemary Stewart, *The Managers: A New Examination of the English, German, and American Executive* (New York: Mentor Books, 1961), p. 224.
[25] Wilbert E. Moore, *The Conduct of the Corporation* (New York: Random House, 1962), p. 14.
[26] Philip Stern, *The Great Treasury Raid* (New York: Random House, 1964), p. 6.

such as property taxes, it is probable that the true tax differential between the chief executive of a fifteen-layer organization and a worker with the basic wage would not be much more than 10 percentage points, and probably less.[27] This means that an 8 to 1, not a 100 to 1, income differential would be ample, and that, consequently, an annual income of $32,000 would be sufficient to meet the functional problem of maintaining motivation.

Soviet experience, too, indicates that differentials of 100 or more to 1, such as exist in American industry, are not functionally necessary. According to one expert, the maximum differential in recent years has been only 25 to 1, and the new wage scale scheduled to go into effect in 1962 called for a maximum differential of only 15 to 1.[28] While these figures understate the true differential, since Soviet managers also enjoy substantial fringe benefits, they demonstrate that large-scale industrial organizations can function quite well without 100 to 1 differentials. (They also suggest that Soviet managers may now be rewarded at a level considerably above what is functionally necessary.)

The fantastically high salaries of managers in American industry can be explained only by their power position within the organization. As indicated earlier, their salaries and other benefits are as large as they are because no other group within the organization is able to prevent it.[29] Under the circumstances, they generally follow the practice of charging what the traffic will bear.

This may be the explanation for the variations in executive compensation from industry to industry, so long a puzzle to economists. For example, executive salaries in public utilities and railroads are substantially lower than salaries for comparable executives in industrial concerns.[30] It is probably no coincidence that both of the former are subject to much greater governmental scrutiny than the latter.

---

[27] See, for example, Gabriel Kolko, *Wealth and Power in America: An Analysis of Social Class and Income Distribution* (New York: Frederick A. Praeger, 1962), pp. 36–38.

[28] See David Granick, *The Red Executive* (Garden City, N.Y.: Doubleday Anchor, 1964), p. 92, and Margaret Dewar, "Labour and Wage Reforms in the USSR," in Harry B. Shaffer (ed.), *The Soviet Economy: A Collection of Western and Soviet Views* (New York: Appleton-Century-Crofts, 1963), p. 222. See, also, evidence from the American military system, which is more complex than any American corporation, yet has an income ceiling of less than $30,000 per year (see p. 363).

[29] See Robert Gordon, pp. 109–110 and 130. Moore also recognizes this, as shown by his statement: "Executive salaries are determined by members of the boards of directors, and executive officers are also members of the board. Good manners may prevent their voting on their own salaries, but the independence of boards and executives from external supervision or control does, I suggest, encourage all of the spurious rationalizations for what may amount to plunder or legal embezzlement" (p. 15).

[30] See Newcomer, p. 124, or Robert Gordon, p. 275.

This also suggests an explanation for the substantial disparity in income between the managerial elite in private industry and the managerial elites in nationalized industries (as in Britain or the Soviet Union) or government (as in the case of American city managers and school superintendents or the higher civil servants). While managers in nationalized industries and government are very well paid by comparison with the rank and file of citizens, their salaries and perquisites cannot compare with those received by executives in private industry. For example, the upper limit in industry in recent years exceeded $800,000, while for school superintendents and city managers the maximum was $48,000 and $30,000 respectively.[31] Again, the explanation for this disparity appears to be related to the way the salaries are set. In private industry, the managerial elite increasingly has the power to set its own wages, while in government, this power lies mostly with others.[32] This hypothesis would also explain the relatively low incomes of the Russian managerial elite.

Another benefit enjoyed by the managerial elite, and one which is often overlooked, is *job security*. Robert Gordon concluded on the basis of his extensive study that American business executives are "likely to have a high degree of security of tenure. Wholesale purges of executive ranks are rare, and top management, usually securely in control of the proxy machinery, seldom has to worry about retaining its position."[33] Robert Dahl makes the same point with respect to the tenure of school superintendents when he writes, "Once appointed, a superintendent is difficult to remove, not only because he builds up his own following among the public school interests but because he can invoke the support of national professional groups if his removal does not seem to be based on considerations of professional adequacy."[34] Thus, though the bases of

[31] *Time* magazine, June 5, 1964, p. 86n., reported that Frederick Donner of General Motors was the highest-paid executive in American industry in 1963 and received $806,000 exclusive of stock options and the like. The figures for school superintendents and city managers are from the *Municipal Year Book, 1963* (Chicago: International City Managers' Association, 1963), p. 222. Again, such figures understate the actual differences since perquisites for managers in industry are much greater than for those in government. The difference between city managers and school superintendents is probably due to the fact that school superintendents are employed by the largest cities in the country, while city managers are not (these cities still retain the traditional mayor-council form of government).

[32] It would be a mistake to suppose, however, that this power is entirely in other hands. A skillful city manager or school superintendent can often do much to raise his own salary. He can push for higher salaries for those beneath him, for example, thus narrowing the differential between his salary and theirs, inviting an upward adjustment in his own salary to restore the "proper" differential. This is but one of many avenues open to him.

[33] Robert Gordon, p. 311.

[34] Robert Dahl, *Who Governs? Democracy and Power in an American City* (New Haven, Conn.: Yale University Press, 1961), p. 151.

their tenure are different, the fact of job security is essentially the same for both kinds of managers.

Not surprisingly, there are differences in job security between the managers in Communist nations (and probably other totalitarian nations as well) and those in democratic. The former are much less secure in their posts and much more subject to demotion or dismissal, or worse yet, imprisonment or execution. A study of the subsequent assignments of plant directors whose replacement was reported in the Soviet press, indicated that 40 per cent were dismissed or given positions that clearly represented demotion.[35] Compared with Western managers, those in the Soviet Union are at a further disadvantage because it is impossible for them to accumulate large holdings of private property during their prosperous years to serve as a cushion after demotion or dismissal.[36] Though there has been a definite increase in job security for Soviet managers in the last decade, it is still not comparable to that enjoyed by their American and Western European counterparts.[37] This seems to be an inevitable by-product of totalitarian or semitotalitarian government.

This relative lack of job security, however, has not prevented the Soviet managerial class from becoming semihereditary. Judging from available evidence, it appears that managers who remain in the good graces of the Party elite can secure for their children special educational advantages which, as elsewhere, pave the road to membership in the managerial class or one of the other privileged segments of Soviet society. Khrushchev himself stated that only a third of the students at the university level were children of peasants or workers in the 1950s. A recently expatriated Soviet student reports that "only a handful of students attending the prestige institutions come from families outside the intelligentsia," and that "the greater the prestige of a university or institute, the more 'elite' are those who attend it." [38] Since the managerial class is counted among the *rukovodiashchie kadry,* or leading cadres, within the intelligentsia, it is safe to assume that its sons are well represented in the best universities and institutes.[39]

---

[35] Granick, *Red Executive*, p. 112. See also, Merle Fainsod, *How Russia Is Ruled*, rev. ed. (Cambridge, Mass.: Harvard University Press, 1963), p. 106, on the subject of managerial insecurity under Stalin.

[36] They can accumulate savings and other personal possessions, but the possibilities are much more limited than in the West, where managerial incomes are so much larger.

[37] Granick, *Red Executive*, pp. 112–114.

[38] David Burg, "Observations of Soviet University Students," in Richard Pipes (ed.), *The Russian Intelligentsia* (New York: Columbia University Press, 1953), pp. 80–81. For an earlier period, see Alex Inkeles, "Social Stratification and Mobility in the Soviet Union: 1940–1950," *American Sociological Review*, 15 (1950), pp. 472–476.

[39] See Leopold Labedz, "The Structure of the Soviet Intelligentsia," in Pipes, pp. 70–71, on the status of the managers within the intelligentsia. See, also, Inkeles, p. 466.

Early in the 1940s, James Burnham, a disillusioned ex-Marxist, published a book entitled *The Managerial Revolution* in which he advanced the thesis that the managerial class was destined to become the ruling class of the future in industrial societies.[40] He argued that in capitalist nations the managerial class was rapidly displacing the propertied class as the dominant class and, in similar fashion, was displacing the Party elite in the Soviet Union. It was only a matter of time, he believed, until the managers, particularly those in charge of production, became the new ruling class.

While many features of Burnham's analysis seem doubtful or clearly in error, he raised an important question, the question of how the managerial class and its elite are related to the other powerful classes and their elites. Are these opposed groups, locked in a life-and-death struggle for dominance, as Burnham argues? Or is the relationship of a different kind?

In recent years, a growing number of observers have expressed the view that Burnham is correct in attributing increasing power to the managers, but incorrect in claiming that they are displacing the older elites. For example, C. Wright Mills argued that the managerial elite, rather than displacing the property elite, is merging with it "into the more or less unified stratum of the corporate rich." [41]

While Mills's documentation of this assertion leaves much to be desired, there is considerable evidence, both circumstantial and direct, that indicates that those who become members of the managerial elite in private industry are almost certain to be, or become, members of the property elite as well. On logical grounds it seems clear that a man with an income in excess of $50,000 should have no great difficulty accumulating assets with a net value of $133,000 in a relatively few years.[42] In fact, with an income of this size supplemented by stock options, other fringe benefits, interest from existing holdings, and capital gains, this should be quite simple. Direct evidence clearly supports this line of reasoning. When members of the managerial elite have been obliged to reveal their net assets, it has become evident that they were also usually members of the property elite. Charles Wilson, former president of General Motors and later Secretary of Defense, and Robert McNamara, former president of the Ford Motor Company and also a Secretary of Defense, are but two cases in point. When these men entered governmental service and were

[40] (Bloomington, Ind.: Indiana University Press, 1960, first published 1941).
[41] Mills, *The Power Elite* (Fair Lawn, N.J.: Oxford University Press, 1956), p. 147.
[42] See fn. 112, page 340, for an explanation of the $133,000 figure as the minimum for membership in the property elite.

obliged to declare their assets, it was revealed that Wilson owned GM stock worth $2.5 million, while McNamara owned Ford stock worth $1.6 million and held an option to purchase additional shares at $18 below their market value, making them worth an additional $270,000.[43] Their other assets were not reported. Even so, an examination of Table 2, Chapter 10 (page 339) makes it clear that these men were not just marginal members of the property elite; they were among its more substantial members.

Additional evidence of the close relationship between the managerial and property elites is found in recent data on the social origins of the former. One of the best studies of this subject is Newcomer's, since she includes only persons who are definitely members of the managerial elite. More than a third of the executives in her sample came from "wealthy" homes,[44] and roughly half of their fathers had occupations of such a nature that membership in the property elite, as I have defined that group, was likely.[45] As these figures indicate, not only can membership in the managerial class lead to membership in the propertied class, but the converse is also possible. Both patterns, in fact, are common.

One final tie between the two classes deserves note, namely, their common concern for the preservation of the institution of private property. As the preceding discussion should have made clear, the managerial elite, or at least that portion employed by private industry, values this institution no less than the property elite. Wherever industries have been nationalized, managerial autonomy and power is reduced and salaries decline (at least relative to the industries still privately operated).[46]

Nevertheless, the union between the propertied and managerial classes is by no means complete. In the first place, not all managers, as we have seen, are employed by private industry. In addition to the higher civil servants, city managers, and school superintendents, many are employed in nationalized industries and by nonprofit organizations such as the Scandinavian cooperatives.[47] The average income of these managers is much less than that of those employed by private industry, and their opportunities for accumulating property, therefore, are not nearly so good. Furthermore, their position of power and privilege does not depend on

[43] *The New York Times,* Jan. 16, 1953, p. 8, and Dec. 26, 1960, pp. 12, 30, and 31.
[44] Newcomer, p. 63.
[45] *Ibid.,* pp. 53–54. Among those counted as "likely" are the following: head of the same corporation as son (11.6 per cent), entrepreneurs in finance (5.5), entrepreneurs in manufacturing, mining, and transportation (8.9), entrepreneurs in mercantile lines (15.8), upper-rank officials (7.3), lawyers (5.1), and physicians (2.7). These total 56.9 per cent.
[46] See, for example, Lewis and Stewart, p. 126.
[47] On the Scandinavian cooperatives, see, for example, Marquis Childs, *Sweden: The Middle Way,* rev. ed. (New Haven, Conn.: Yale University Press, 1947).

the private ownership of industry. Finally, because they are, in most cases, professional men trained for public service, they are likely to have acquired a more or less critical view of private enterprise where the profit motive takes precedence over concern for the public good. In short, because of their training and personal situation, these men are not likely to be strong advocates of private enterprise or strong supporters of the propertied class. Rather, their experience and interests tend to make them ambivalent or even hostile.

Even in private industry, there is something less than a complete identity of interests between managers and the propertied class. Whenever managers use their powers of office to wrest control of a corporation from the stockholders, they are attacking the principle of private property and the concept of property rights. Similarly, when they use their control over the board of directors to inflate their salaries and other perquisites, they are attacking the very foundation of the propertied class.

As a result, we are obliged to treat the propertied class and the managerial class as two *analytically* separate and distinct units which are capable of being united *empirically* to a greater or lesser degree. From the empirical standpoint, the problem is to ascertain the degree to which the individuals who belong to the propertied elite also belong to the managerial elite, and vice versa; but analytically, we recognize that membership in one elite does not automatically confer membership in the other. Furthermore, where dual membership is not held, we recognize that a basis for conflict exists. In the United States, and probably in most other non-Communist nations, a considerable measure of overlap obviously exists in the case of managers in private industry (though even Mills claimed only that the managerial elite and the propertied elite are merging into a "more or less unified stratum"). For managers in government and other nonprofit organizations, the overlap is much more limited, and ties between the two classes much more tenuous.[48]

In the Soviet Union a similar relation has developed between the managerial class and the Party functionaries. In his analysis of Soviet managers, David Granick asserts that industrial managers and full-time Party officials are "to a considerable extent . . . the same type of people. Members of both groups must normally be trusted party members, active politically; their incomes are similar, even their education is not too different."[49]

[48] A similar distinction may be necessary in the case of officeholders and property holders in agrarian societies. It appears, however, that even on analytical grounds the relation is closer in agrarian societies than in industrial. Unfortunately, the limitations of space preclude a detailed discussion of this subject here.
[49] *Red Executive*, p. 273.

Though Soviet managers have much in common with the Party functionaries, and, Granick reports, may even be the same individuals at different points in their careers, there is considerably less than a perfect identity of interests. On many points their interests diverge, a fact clearly recognized by the Party elite, who keep separate the offices of factory manager and Party secretary in every plant and enterprise throughout the Soviet Union. As one writer recently put it,

> The Party apparatus undertakes to differentiate its role from that of management, despite the fact that top factory executives are also Party members. Operating through its own independent hierarchy of secretaries in the factories and enterprises, the Party seeks to project a distinctive image of itself as the custodian of the nation's interests in contrast to the more narrowly oriented outlook of some industrial managers. This special mandate of the Party apparatus involves it in *both collaborative and potentially antagonistic relations* with factory management.[50]

With respect to Granick's second point, he does not claim that industrial managers and Party officials are "normally" the same individuals at different stages in their careers, only that they are "frequently" the same. Even this seems an overstatement, and Granick provides little more than scattered examples to justify it. His two tables bearing on the subject suggest that shifts from managerial positions in industry to full-time Party work or the reverse, are, at best, an infrequent career pattern.[51] According to another authority, the split between managers and Party workers begins while they are still students.[52]

In summary, it appears that in the Soviet Union, as elsewhere, the managerial class and its elite constitute a fairly distinct class within society. Many ties bind it to the politically dominant class, however, and it even has overlapping membership with the latter to some extent. Hence, it appears destined to play an ambivalent role in the many struggles for power and privilege within the Soviet Union.

The Military Class

In *The Power Elite*, C. Wright Mills described contemporary American society as subject to the domination of three closely interrelated groups,

---

[50] Fainsod, p. 516. Quoted by permission (emphasis added). See also Granick, *Red Executive*, chap. 10, and Klaus Mehnert, *Soviet Man and His World*, translated by Maurice Rosenbaum (New York: Frederick A. Praeger, 1961), chap. 7, on the antagonistic aspects of this relationship which, as they and Fainsod make clear, are often more than potential.

[51] Granick, pp. 274 and 276.

[52] Burg, pp. 83–85.

the corporate rich, the political directorate, and the warlords.[53] By including the military elite, he gave expression to a point of view which has gained considerable acceptance in the last decade. In essence, this view asserts that the military crisis of modern times has put immense power into the hands of the military, and extreme proponents of this view argue that the military threatens to become the dominant class in society.

No one would question that the military has great power in the modern world. But one may well doubt that its power *within* societies is substantially greater than in the past and that it is so pervasive as it is often made to appear.

With respect to the first point, it is undoubtedly true that the position of the military has changed in *American* society. But this is very different from saying that it has changed in the world generally or as a result of the shift from agrarian to industrial society. The military, as we have seen, was normally a powerful force in agrarian societies and, in a number of instances, the dominant force.[54] A careful review makes it clear that the historic American pattern of military subordination was very atypical and reflected the unique combination of events in American history which enabled this nation to survive and prosper without a strong military force.

So far as the second point is concerned, reports of the power of the modern military are greatly exaggerated, at least in the case of the more advanced industrial nations. While it is certainly true that the military establishments in the United States, the Soviet Union, and most other advanced industrial nations are very large and command immense budgets, it is no less true that the power of the military has been clearly *circumscribed* and subject to civilian control. This is true not only in all the great powers today, but, what is more remarkable, was true in Germany during the expansionistic Nazi era.

On several occasions the Soviet military, or certain elements in it, have made bids for greater power, but in each instance have been rebuffed. The best known example of this in recent years occurred when Marshal Zhukov was summarily dismissed as Minister of Defense in 1957.[55]

In the United States, one cannot find even so modest a challenge to

---

[53] *Op. cit.*

[54] See, for example, Andrzejewski on praetorianism, *Military Organization and Society* (London: Routledge, 1954), pp. 104–107, or John J. Johnson's fascinating study, *The Military and Society in Latin America* (Stanford, Calif.: Stanford University Press, 1964).

[55] See, for example, Wolfgang Leonhard, *The Kremlin Since Stalin*, translated by Elizabeth Wiskemann and Marian Jackson (New York: Frederick A. Praeger, 1962), pp. 255–259, or Fainsod, pp. 482–487.

civilian authority as that posed by Zhukov.[56] While no one can dispute the fact that the military budget has grown immensely, this has been largely the result of civilian desires; and while the military may have gained somewhat more autonomy in purely military matters, this has been due chiefly to the growing complexity of military technology and organization. With respect to other matters, the position of the military has not improved greatly, and may even have deteriorated to some extent, particularly in the distribution of power and privilege, outside the area of strictly military affairs. For example, a recent study reports that from 1929 to 1949 the ratio of Army officers' earnings to those of all persons employed full-time in the civilian labor force dropped from 2.98 to 2.53.[57] According to the same study, fringe benefits also suffered, particularly housing. It is said that "first lieutenants in the inter-war years had housing comparable to that assigned colonels in 1959." The lowering of the retirement age has also proven a real hardship for many officers, and the problem has been aggravated by the recent ruling forbidding them to accept employment with military contractors which would involve them in business dealings with that branch of the military with which they were formerly connected. Last, but not least, as recently as 1958 only a handful of the top officers in the military establishment received incomes of $20,-000 or more—or less than half the maximum paid school superintendents.

These facts take on special significance when it is recalled that the military has made repeated efforts in recent years to improve its economic status. Its relative failure can only be interpreted as evidence that it lacks the *relevant* kinds of power to achieve this within the framework of the present distributive system. *Apparently the power to obliterate whole nations with atomic missiles is one thing, and the power to enlarge one's share of the national income something else, and the former is not easily transformed into the latter.* The dilemma of the military serves as a useful reminder that the *magnitude* and *scope* of power are two different things, and immense power in one area cannot necessarily be converted into comparable power in other areas, at least not by legitimate means.

This raises the question of why the military, having failed to improve its position by legitimate means, has not turned to force. This is one of the truly remarkable features of the modern world: *successful military coups have been virtually nonexistent in the more advanced industrial nations.* They have, of course, been very common in agrarian societies of the past

[56] Probably the nearest thing to it would be the MacArthur incident during Truman's administration. This was the action of a single man, however, and did not receive support from any other ranking military leader.

[57] This and other information in this paragraph are based on Morris Janowitz, *The Professional Soldier* (New York: Free Press, 1960), pp. 181–187.

and in underdeveloped or industrializing nations of the modern world. However, among the more advanced industrial nations there has been only one instance of this. It occurred in Japan in the period immediately preceding World War II, and the record indicates that even this was something less than a true military coup since it was strongly supported by powerful civilian elements which continued to have a major voice in affairs of state until Japan's surrender in 1945.

The explanation for this virtual absence of military coups is by no means obvious, and the problem deserves far more study than it has received. However, it seems to be linked with the important ideological change of modern times. So long as the state was viewed as the private possession of a single family which had acquired its privileges by violence, there was no serious ideological barrier to military seizure. With the spread of the democratic theory of the state, the situation changed significantly. This new ideology tended to strengthen resistance to military coups *within the military itself.* To the degree that military leaders are recruited from civilian families and raised in the democratic tradition, they are likely to oppose military coups.

A second factor has probably been the changing nature of war itself. In modern warfare there are no longer civilians in the true sense of the word; virtually the entire population is engaged in the war effort. Even in peacetime, the boundary between civilians and the military is not so sharp as it was. More and more, officers live, and even work, "off the post," and thus become heavily subjected to civilian influences.[58] The net effect of these developments could only be to weaken the traditional self-image of the military as a group apart, with special and meritorious qualities which justify its use of force as an instrument of political action in internal affairs. If this analysis is correct, *the military may well become indistinguishable from the civil service, at least when viewed from the perspective of the distributive process.*

The Professional Class

Of all the changes linked with industrialization, none has been more important than the revolution in knowledge. Since the beginning of the Industrial Revolution two centuries ago, mankind's fund of useful knowledge has multiplied many times.

From the standpoint of the occupational class system, this development has been highly significant. To begin with, it has been responsible for the considerable growth in size, importance, and affluence of the pro-

[58] For a good discussion of these trends, see Janowitz.

fessional class. Second, it has caused education to become a much more valuable resource, and made educational institutions far more important in the distribution of power and privilege, than ever before in history. Finally, it has greatly reduced the ancient need for unskilled and semi-skilled labor, and is thereby threatening the livelihood of millions of people. Because of their importance, each of these developments deserves careful consideration.

One of the most troublesome problems associated with the professional class is that of definition. As students of the professions have long observed, it is much easier to speak of them than to define them.[59] Nevertheless, certain criteria stand out clearly. To begin with, the term always refers to an occupation which requires the mastery of a complex body of specialized knowledge and related skills which are basically intellectual in nature. Furthermore, these cannot be acquired quickly even by persons of ability: graduation from an institution of higher education is rapidly becoming a prerequisite for admission to all of the professions. Finally, though members of the professions often have considerable *influence* over others, they seldom have much formal *authority*; in this respect they differ greatly from members of the managerial class. For purposes of the present analysis, an occupation will be regarded as a profession to the degree that it measures up to these standards, and the professional class will be regarded as that segment of the population employed in those occupations.

This class has evolved out of the priestly class and certain elements of the retainer class in agrarian societies, e.g., physicians, mathematicians, astrologers, teachers, and the like. Except for the priests, their numbers were few and their influence limited. In large measure this was because their "knowledge" was so often unreliable. While individuals of this type sometimes gained the favor of a powerful ruler or member of the governing class and thereby achieved fame and fortune, the majority had little of either.

In the last two hundred years, and particularly in the last fifty, the professional class has emerged as a potent force in society. As the *reliability* of technical knowledge has increased, so has the demand for persons who have mastered it. As the sheer *volume* of such knowledge has grown, an ever increasing number and variety of specialists have been required. Finally, as a result of the trend toward greater economic equality and the rise in the standard of living, the number of persons able to pay for professional services has greatly increased. Given the simultaneous

[59] See, for example, A. M. Carr-Saunders and P. A. Wilson, *The Professions* (Oxford: Clarendon Press, 1933), Introduction; or Roy Lewis and Angus Maude, *Professional People* (London: Phoenix House, 1952), chap. 4.

operation of all three of these factors, the demand for trained professionals has grown immensely.

Precise figures on the numbers of professionals in traditional agrarian societies are difficult to obtain, but some idea of the magnitude of the change can be obtained by comparing the proportions of professionals in the labor force of nations still largely agrarian a generation ago with the proportions in the more advanced industrial nations of the present. In the former case, the percentages ranged from less than 1 per cent (in Mexico in 1940) to about 3 per cent (in Greece in 1928).[60] If the professionals whose work reflected the partial industrialization of these societies could be eliminated from the totals, the upper figure would probably be no more than 2 per cent, and perhaps less. By contrast, in the American labor force in 1960 nearly 10 per cent of all male workers were classified as professional, technical, and kindred workers, and this figure obviously does not represent the ultimate.[61] In fact, everything indicates that this figure will continue to rise for the indefinite future. In other industrial nations the figure is not yet this high, but the trend is the same.[62]

The growth in size of the professional class has been accompanied by corresponding increases in influence and income. Though the former is difficult to measure, the latter is not. Income data from all of the more advanced industrial nations show a considerable overlap between members of the professional class and members of the managerial class, and the medians are not greatly different. In the United States in 1959, for example, the median income of all men classified as professionals, technicians, and kindred workers was only 10 per cent less than for all salaried managers and officials ($6,778 versus $7,479).[63] A recent report on incomes in the Soviet Union suggests that the income differential between the professional and managerial classes is somewhat greater there, but it, too, reveals a substantial overlap. Certain leading professors and academicians, for example, have base salaries comparable to those of executives and managers of large industrial enterprises and of at least one

[60] W. S. Woytinsky and E. S. Woytinsky, *World Population and Production: Trends and Outlook* (New York: Twentieth Century Fund, 1953), pp. 356–357.
[61] In 1870 professionals constituted about 2.5 per cent of the American labor force. See Burton Clark, *Educating the Expert Society* (San Francisco, Calif.: Chandler, 1962), chart 2.2, p. 47.
[62] A recent study shows that the number of professionals and semiprofessionals in the Soviet Union increased from 520,000 in the 1920s to 6,820,000, or roughly 6 per cent of the labor force, in 1957 [see Nicholas DeWitt, *Education and Professional Employment in the USSR* (Washington, D.C.: National Science Foundation, 1961), p. 456]. The number of professional and technical workers in England and Wales increased from 420,000 in 1881 to 1,240,000, or again 6 per cent of the labor force, in 1951 (see David Marsh, pp. 126 and 145).
[63] U.S. *Census of Population, 1960: Occupational Characteristics*, table 25.

deputy minister in the national government. This same study also reports that members of the professional class are among those most likely to be rewarded with extremely lucrative prizes for outstanding achievement.[64]

To a considerable degree, the high incomes enjoyed by members of the professional class reflect the working of the law of supply and demand.[65] Compared with agrarian societies, there is, as we have seen, a much greater demand for intellectual manpower. Furthermore, the standards of performance are more demanding because the fund of reliable knowledge is so much greater than in the past. If the professions require above average ability, and if the supply of brainpower in societies is distributed in terms approximating a normal distribution curve, then any raising of standards would tend to reduce rapidly the supply of qualified persons. These factors are partly offset by the substantial improvement in educational systems, but the growing supply of trained professionals has not matched the even more rapidly growing demand in most fields. As a consequence, those who desire the services of the more skilled professions have been forced to bid high to obtain them.

This is not the whole story, however. Besides native ability, professionals must also have expensive and time-consuming experience. As a result, there is relatively little shifting about from one profession to another, and shortages in one field cannot normally be filled by recruits from another which may have an oversupply. These "natural" rigidities in supply are often supplemented by "artificial" or "man-made" rigidities. Most professions are organized in some manner, and most use their organizational structure to control the flow of recruits. In principle, this is for the purpose of controlling the quality of persons in the field; in practice, it also creates a greater shortage of labor than would otherwise exist. This can happen quite unintentionally simply because the leaders of the profession set higher standards for admission than are really necessary. In some instances, professions have deliberately taken steps to increase the price of their services. This works best in those fields where professionals are self-employed, but organized, and serve a widely scattered and unorganized clientele, as in the case of American physicians.

There are also certain rigidities on the demand side which can restrict the free operation of the market system. Sometimes a monopsonistic

[64] DeWitt, pp. 537–545, and especially table VI–81.

[65] This was nicely documented some years ago in the case of one profession when it was shown that the mean income of dentists varied inversely with their density in a state-by-state analysis in which variations in per capita income were controlled. See Milton Friedman and Simon Kuznets, *Income from Independent Professional Practice* (New York: National Bureau of Economic Research, 1945), charts 11C and 12C, pp. 165–166.

or oligopsonistic situation prevails, and professionals in a given field find that there is only a single buyer, or a few buyers, for their services. The former condition tends to prevail in the Soviet Union and other totalitarian states (though thus far it has not proven possible to coordinate wage scales completely; some measure of local autonomy has proven more efficient). The oligopsonistic situation is approximated in the United States in the case of school teachers and nurses, who often find that in a given community there are only a handful of potential buyers for their services. Under either monopsonistic or oligopsonistic conditions, the seller's position is weakened and prices tend to be depressed. This may well be the explanation for the fact that overall the relative income of professionals is not quite so good in the Soviet Union as in the United States.

No analysis of the professional class would be complete without reference to the many ties which link it to the propertied, managerial, and political classes in all advanced industrial societies. Studies of social interaction patterns show that most members of the professional class live in the same neighborhood, belong to the same clubs, attend the same churches, and associate and intermarry with members of these other powerful and privileged classes.[66] Many individuals are simultaneously members of both the professional and propertied classes, since the high incomes of so many professional men enable them to accumulate substantial holdings in property.[67] The nature of their work also facilitates entry into the political class. For example, a recent study of the United States Senate revealed that 64 per cent of its members were professional men (chiefly lawyers).[68] In the British Parliament, the figure has ranged from 52 to 54 per cent since World War II, an increase from the interwar year average of 45 per cent.[69] A similar situation exists in France and most other democratic nations, though the disproportions are not always so ex-

[66] See, for example, W. Lloyd Warner and Paul Lunt, *The Social Life of a Modern Community* (New Haven, Conn.: Yale University Press, 1941), or Hollingshead, *op. cit.*

[67] According to a survey conducted for the Federal Reserve Board, the net worth of professional men was three-quarters that of members of the managerial class. See "1953 Survey of Consumer Finances: part 4, Net Worth of Consumers, Early 1953," *Federal Reserve Bulletin* (September, 1953), p. 12. Another study of the same period (1950) suggested a somewhat lower figure, or about 60 per cent. See Horst Menderhausen, "The Patterns of Estate Tax Wealth," in Raymond Goldsmith, *A Study of Saving in the United States* (Princeton, N.J: Princeton University Press, 1956), vol. III, table W-60.

[68] Donald Matthews, *U.S. Senators and Their World* (Chapel Hill, N.C.: University of North Carolina Press, 1960), p. 32.

[69] J. F. S. Ross, *Elections and Electors: Studies in Democratic Representation* (London: Eyre & Spottiswoode, 1955), p. 440.

treme.[70] In the case of the Soviet Union, roughly 30 per cent of the members of the professional class are also Party members, and professional persons (including semiprofessionals) make up 25 per cent of the Party membership.[71] In short, though the professional class is a distinct entity with special interests of its own, nevertheless it is closely linked with the dominant classes in industrial societies and provides them with important support. We shall return to this later, in the discussion of class conflict.

The Clerical Class

Up to this point, the occupational classes examined have occupied a favored position in society, with respect to both power and privilege. Now we turn to those classes whose members are less favorably situated. It should be noted, however, that there is no sharp cleavage between the first group and the second. On the contrary, with respect to both power and privilege there is clearly an overlap, with a few of the most fortunate members of the less favored classes enjoying a greater measure of these valued rewards than many of the least successful members of the propertied, managerial, political, and professional classes.[72]

Historically, the most favored of the lesser classes in industrial societies has been the clerical class. Though its origins can be traced back to agrarian societies, its great growth in size has come about only in the last century. This growth has been one of the by-products of the rationalization and bureaucratization of modern industry and the growth in the size of organizations.

The British experience has been fairly typical. In 1851 clerical workers constituted less than 1 per cent of the total labor force; a century later they totaled 10.5 per cent.[73] In the United States the percentage rose from 0.6 per cent in 1870 to 15.2 per cent in 1962.[74] A second trend of

[70] On France, see Philip Williams, *Politics in Post-war France* (London: Longmans, 1954), p. 206, who reports that at the turn of the century, and still in mid-century, approximately half of the members of the National Assembly were professional men. For a less extreme case, see R. M. Chapman et al., *New Zealand Politics in Action* (London: Oxford University Press, 1962), p. 145, on New Zealand. Their figures show that a quarter of the candidates elected to the General Assembly in 1960 were professional men.

[71] DeWitt, pp. 534–536.

[72] The overlap involves more members of the higher classes because of the downward skewing of all distributions at the upper levels of the distributive system.

[73] David Lockwood, *The Blackcoated Worker: A Study in Class Consciousness* (London: G. Allen, 1958), p. 36.

[74] For the 1870 figures see Mayer, p. 70; for the 1962 figure see *Statistical Abstract, 1962*, table 297, p. 226.

importance involves the sex composition of this class. Nearly all clerical workers were men in the earlier period. In England in 1851, 99.9 per cent were males; by 1951 this figure had been reduced to 40.4 per cent, and probably has declined still further since then.[75] A similar trend has occurred in the United States and other advanced industrial nations.

In an earlier era, the status of clerical workers was clearly intermediate between that of the privileged classes and the masses of manual workers. Their position in the occupation hierarchy was roughly analogous to that of the *petite bourgeoisie* in the property hierarchy. Unlike the masses of manual workers, their working conditions were reasonably good; they were relatively free of physical danger, noise, smells, and grime. Holidays were more frequent and working hours shorter. Furthermore, their work brought them into frequent personal contact with members of the privileged classes and represented a genteel, respectable way of life. Last, but not least, their income was higher and their job tenure far more secure than that of the masses of workers.[76]

In more recent years the situation has changed and the gap between the clerical class and the working class has been steadily reduced. According to Lockwood, in England in the years prior to World War I, "the ordinary adult clerk was roughly on a par with the skilled worker" in terms of income, but by 1956 the position of clerks had deteriorated to the point where they were no better off than the average manual worker.[77] In the half century from 1905 to 1955 the average earnings of British manual workers increased 674 per cent, while the earnings of various types of clerks increased only between 265 and 463 per cent.[78] Trend data for the Soviet Union are not available, but current figures show that office employees in industrial enterprises typically have incomes somewhat above semiskilled workers in manufacturing and somewhat below skilled workers.[79] In the United States, in the twenty-year period from 1939 to 1959, the median income of craftsmen, foremen and kindred workers passed that of clerks and kindred workers, while that of operatives, or semiskilled workers, began to rival clerical incomes. The trends can be seen quite clearly in the following figures, which are for males only: [80]

[75] Lockwood, *op. cit.*
[76] Here, as elsewhere in this section, I have relied heavily on David Lockwood's excellent analysis of this class (*op. cit.*).
[77] Lockwood, p. 67.
[78] *Ibid.*, p. 217.
[79] DeWitt, table VI-81, p. 543.
[80] The figures for 1939 are from *Historical Statistics of the United States: Colonial Times to 1957* (Washington: GPO, 1960), p. 168; those for 1959 are from the U.S. *Census of Population, 1960*, vol. I, part 1, table 208.

	1939	1959
Clerical and kindred workers	$1,421	$4,785
Craftsmen and kindred workers	$1,309	$5,240
Operatives	$1,007	$4,299

Translated into percentage terms, using the income of clerical workers as the base, the pattern becomes even clearer:

	1939	1959
Clerical and kindred workers	100	100
Craftsmen and kindred workers	92	110
Operatives	71	90

The gap between the clerical and working classes has also been closed with respect to such things as hours, holidays, tenure, and pensions.[81]

There are several obvious reasons for this deterioration in the position of the clerical class. To begin with, the emancipation of middle-class women, which freed them to seek employment outside the home, has loosed a flood of potential clerical workers. Many fields of employment are largely closed to women because family involvements prevent them from working continuously over a period of many years. Hence, they tend to concentrate in fields where continuous employment is not essential, and clerical work is an obvious choice. Despite the fact that the demand for clerical workers has risen steadily, it has not kept pace with the supply, and as a result, wages in this field have not kept pace with those in most other fields.

A second factor which has probably contributed to the decline of the clerical class has been the growth in the size of work organizations. Fifty years ago most offices were so small that clerks were able to develop a personal relationship with their employer. In the modern corporation or governmental bureau employing thousands, clerical workers have become mere statistics in the table of organization and a charge against the profits of the business. Under the circumstances, modern managers feel little compunction in firing those whose services are no longer needed. This is a serious loss for members of the clerical class, since, prior to the 1920s, "it was generally assumed that office workers could rely on being permanently employed, providing they were efficient and their character good." [82]

Finally, the recent introduction of office machines which can do the work of scores of clerks has greatly slowed the rise in demand for clerical

[81] Lockwood, pp. 53ff.
[82] Ibid., p. 56.

labor. Adding machines, calculators, and most recently computers, not to mention typewriters, dictaphones, duplicating machines, and a variety of others, have all supplanted thousands of clerical workers.

Unlike the manual workers whom they long looked down upon, the majority of clerical workers have been reluctant to organize and restrict either the flow of new workers or machines into the field. They have therefore remained subject to the free play of market forces and in recent decades this has worked greatly to their disadvantage. These developments have led some sociologists to conclude that the historic cleavage between manual and nonmanual workers is vanishing. Instead of thinking of the occupational class system as divided into these two basic units, they argue, we should now think in terms of a three-fold division organized around a "middle mass" of "clerks, salesmen, craftsmen, foremen, small proprietors, semi-marginal or would-be professionals and technicians, managers and officials with few subordinates, and operatives with high income." [83]

Without denying the increasing convergence in income, and perhaps also in style of life, it should be noted that one fundamental difference remains, and it alone is sufficient to cast serious doubt on proposals to ignore the manual-nonmanual distinction: *members of the clerical class have much greater opportunities for upward mobility into the managerial, entrepreneurial, and professional classes.* Census data gathered in 1962 showed that 37 per cent of the men aged twenty-five to sixty-four whose first full-time job after leaving school was a clerical job had risen into the professional, entrepreneurial, or managerial classes; the same was true of only 26 per cent of those who were first employed as craftsmen.[84] The *sons* of clerical workers enjoy an even greater advantage over the *sons* of craftsmen. Forty-two per cent of the former have become members of the professional, entrepreneurial, or managerial classes, compared with only 27 per cent of the latter.[85] Similar results have been found in virtually every advanced industrial nation for which mobility data are available.[86] In view of such evidence, it is unwise to ignore the distinction between manual and nonmanual occupations, which still remains an important fact of life in the distributive systems of virtually all advanced industrial nations.

[83] See Harold Wilensky, "Orderly Careers and Social Participation: The Impact of Work History on Social Integration in the Middle Mass," *American Sociological Review*, 26 (1961), pp. 529–530.

[84] "Lifetime Occupational Mobility of Adult Males, March, 1962," U.S. Bureau of the Census, *Current Population Reports* (1964), Series P-23, No. 11, table 2.

[85] *Ibid.*, table 1.

[86] See S. M. Miller, "Comparative Social Mobility," *Current Sociology*, 9 (1960), No. 1, pp. 66–80.

The Sales Class

With the growth in the size of economic organizations, many functions which were once joined in a single occupational role have been separated and made the bases of more specialized roles. The selling function is a good example of this. In the small workshops which were characteristic of agrarian societies, the master craftsman, together with his journeymen and apprentices, did everything from purchasing raw materials to selling the finished product. Except in a few of the larger merchant houses, no person specialized merely in the sale of goods.

In modern industrial societies this is all changed. The growth in the size of businesses and the resultant surge of specialization have given rise to a considerable increase in the number of persons who earn their livelihood solely by selling. For example, in the United States the percentage of the labor force employed as salespeople rose from 2.5 per cent in 1870 to 6.5 per cent in 1962.[87] Though women are well represented in this field, they are by no means the majority, as in the clerical field: in 1960, only 32 per cent of the sales personnel in this country were women.

Official government figures show that the median income for the male members of this class has been fairly similar to that for men in clerical occupations and skilled trades. However, as can be seen from the figures below, the median income of salesmen has risen above that of clerks, while falling further behind that of craftsmen: [88]

	1939	1959
Clerical and kindred workers	$1,421	$4,785
Craftsmen and kindred workers	$1,309	$5,240
Salesmen	$1,277	$4,987

Actually, the summary figure for salesmen is very deceptive, since a more detailed breakdown of occupations reveals almost a bifurcation. On the one hand, there are a number of subcategories with median incomes substantially below the median for the field as a whole. In 1959 these included newsboys with $567, hucksters and peddlers with $2,826, and salesmen in retail establishments with $4,027 (or $272 less than the median for semiskilled workers). These three categories alone contained almost half of all salesmen. On the other hand, another set of sales occupations of roughly equal size had median incomes far above the median for the field as a whole. These included stock and bond salesmen with $7,730,

[87] Mayer, p. 70, and *Statistical Abstract, 1962*, table 297, p. 226.
[88] *Historical Statistics*, p. 168, and *U.S. Census of Population, 1960*, vol. I, part 1, table 208.

salesmen employed by manufacturing concerns with $6,835, real estate agents with $6,508, insurance agents with $6,331, and salesmen employed by wholesale establishments with $6,146. Taken together, this second group of men compares favorably in terms of income with men in the professions, whose median income in 1959 was only about 5 per cent more than the median for this favored group of salesmen.

These differences within the sales class provide a valuable clue to the nature of the forces governing their rewards. All of the high income fields are ones in which the dollar volume of sales per salesman is normally quite high, while all of the low income fields are ones in which the dollar volume is low. This means that, in the former fields, salaries and commissions, though higher in absolute terms, are usually a much smaller percentage of total costs. This, in turn, means that they can be raised more freely without greatly affecting either the price of the product or the firm's profit. Furthermore, since in a capitalist economy sales volume is vitally important to every firm, intelligent executives will do whatever they can to increase sales. If this can best be done by offering greater incentives to their salesmen, they will do it.

Table 1 illustrates the nature of some of the basic relationships involved. As this table shows, in an industry with a low dollar volume of

Table 1 Relationship between Sales Costs, Sales Volume, and Profits (Hypothetical)

SALES COST PER SALESMAN PER DAY	OTHER COSTS *	PROFIT	TOTAL VOLUME OF SALES	NUMBER OF ITEMS HAVING TO BE SOLD	SALES INCREASES REQUIRED
Industry with low dollar volume of sales per salesman:					
$15	$75	$10	$100	100	
$20	$90	$10	$120	120	20%
Industry with medium dollar volume of sales per salesman:					
$15	$885	$100	$1,000	100	
$20	$929	$100	$1,049	105	5%
Industry with high dollar volume of sales per salesman:					
$15	$8,985	$1,000	$10,000	100	
$20	$9,075	$1,000	$10,095	101	1%

* It is assumed that these vary in proportion to sales.

sales per salesman, even a slight increase in the salary or commission of the salesman necessitates a substantial increase in sales, just to maintain the original profit level. Under these circumstances, management will naturally pay the lowest wage at which it is possible to hire persons with the skills necessary to fill the role, and will probably rely on advertising and similar techniques to maintain sales. By contrast, in an industry with a high dollar volume of sales per salesman, a comparable raise in the salesman's income requires only a small increase in sales. In such industries, management is likely to find that the incentive of higher income will stimulate salesmen to work harder and that a better caliber of men can be recruited, with a resulting increase in profits. In short, in some industries it is profitable to provide salesmen with the opportunity to earn incomes well above the national average, while in others it is not.

With respect to mobility opportunities, the situation of salesmen is even better than that of clerks. The sample survey conducted by the Census Bureau in 1962 showed that 41 per cent of the men aged twenty-five to sixty-four whose first full-time job was that of salesman had risen to the professional, entrepreneurial, or managerial classes, compared with 37 per cent of those who started as clerks and 26 per cent of those who started as craftsmen. Similarly, 47 per cent of the sons of salesmen had risen to the professional, entrepreneurial, and managerial classes, compared with 42 per cent of the sons of clerks and 27 per cent of the sons of craftsmen.[89]

In Communist countries the importance of sales personnel is minimal, and while we have no data on their income, it seems safe to say that it is below the national average.[90] The governments of all the Communist states except Yugoslavia have, until recently, set quotas for both the production and distribution of goods, and except at the level of the consumer, the element of choice has been minimal.[91] Even there, however, the perennial emphasis on the production of capital goods at the expense of consumer goods has insured the sale of nearly everything produced, with no special effort necessary to stimulate sales.

The Working Class

In traditional agrarian societies the great majority of the population was concentrated in the peasant class. Though a remnant of the peasant or farm class still survives in more or less modified form in every industrial

[89] "Lifetime Occupational Mobility of Adult Males, March 1962," *op. cit.*, tables 1 and 2.

[90] It is unlikely that their income would be greater than that of office employees in industrial enterprises, and for the latter, incomes average only 88 per cent of the national average (DeWitt, p. 543).

[91] As noted previously, there are definite signs of change in this area throughout most of Eastern Europe, including the Soviet Union, since the Party elite apparently intends to give some scope to the market forces of supply and demand and to reduce the scope of planning and quotas.

society, its place as the largest occupational class was taken long ago by the working class, a descendant of the old artisan class. Actually, the members of this new class are not, for the most part, descendants of the artisans of an earlier era. Rather, most of them are the displaced descendants of peasants and farmers forced off the land both by excess fertility and by the mechanization of agriculture.

Though the working class is the largest occupational class in the more advanced industrial societies, it has seldom had the numerical preponderance the peasant class once had. With the single exception of Britain, the working class has probably never constituted more than 60 per cent of the total male labor force, and usually it has totaled less than 50 per cent. So far, the relative size of the working class has been quite variable, standing, apparently, in a curvilinear relationship to the degree of industrialization in a society. In the earlier stages of industrialization, the proportion of workers in the labor force steadily rises as the proportion of farmers and farm laborers declines. Eventually, when the farm population has been reduced to a small minority and migration from the rural areas has been reduced to a trickle, a turning point is reached, and the working class, too, begins to decline, at least in relative terms.

Census data indicate that the proportion of manual workers in the *urban* part of the population is already declining in many industrial societies. In the United States, for example, the percentage of males in manual occupations in the urban labor force dropped from 70 per cent in 1870 to 60 per cent in 1960.[92] A recent nationwide study of mobility in Sweden revealed that only 61 per cent of the males in the urban labor force were in manual occupations, as compared with 73 per cent of the previous generation.[93] The Hungarian census of 1949 indicated a similar decline between the last generation and the present; in the present generation only 72 per cent of males in the urban labor force were in manual occupations compared with 82 per cent in the previous generation.[94] Comparable trends can be observed in data from other countries, including France, Japan, Norway, and West Germany.[95]

The modern working class, like the peasantry before it, contains persons in varying circumstances. At one extreme are a handful of persons

[92] Calculated from *Historical Statistics*, p. 74, and *1960 Census of Population*, vol. I, part 1.
[93] These figures are calculated from Gosta Carlsson, *Social Mobility and Class Structure* (Lund: Gleerup, 1958), table 6.1. These figures might be distorted somewhat by differential fertility, but the effect of this would be to *reduce* (not increase) the difference between the two generations, since working class families were traditionally larger than middle class. The same applies to the Hungarian figures cited below.
[94] These figures are calculated from data reported in S. M. Miller, p. 72.
[95] Calculated from data assembled by Miller, *ibid.*

who earn wages higher than the median in the managerial or professional classes; at the other extreme are some who are unable to earn enough to support themselves and depend on welfare payments to supplement their earnings. Yet despite these differences, there is, as in the case of the peasantry, one attribute which makes it possible to treat them all as members of a single class in the occupational class system: *the resource on which each depends is a job involving a limited range of manual skills that could be performed by most other members of society after a relatively short period of training.*

As a consequence, members of the working class are always in a poor competitive position relative to the other classes we have examined. This has been especially true when they have sought to compete on an individual basis under anything approaching free market conditions, because of the traditional oversupply of manual labor. Since the number of persons seeking these jobs normally exceeds the number of jobs available (or has in the past), the buyers of labor are usually in a position to hire at, or near, the subsistence level—*at least so long as truly free market conditions prevail.*

As a matter of historical fact, the situation of most members of the working class has not been nearly so grim as this, especially in the more advanced industrial societies. Other factors have intervened to improve the situation for the majority. To begin with, in the early stages of industrialization it often took highly skilled artisans a number of years to master their trade (though there is reason to think the apprenticeship period could usually have been shortened considerably if speed of training had been a major objective). This introduced a degree of inelasticity into the supply factor in the market situation. Those who wished to employ highly skilled laborers knew that they could not find many replacements on short notice. Thus, though the supply of craftsmen in a given field might potentially be almost unlimited, at any given time it was severely limited. This gave the members of such crafts a bargaining power which enabled them to demand and obtain wages above the subsistence level. The extent to which this was possible varied according to the ease and speed with which replacements could be trained.

Since the beginning of the Industrial Revolution, a host of new machines have been created, many of which can perform intricate tasks which men once spent months or years mastering. What is more, they perform them more rapidly and efficiently. While it is difficult to find a precise measure of the trend, rigidities in the labor market due to skill level alone are apparently declining and an ever-increasing percentage of manual trades require a shorter period of time for mastery by the average worker. Hence, while in the past the factor of skill provided some measure of protection for a considerable number of workingmen, its influence is declining and may eventually almost disappear.[96]

A second factor which has modified the situation is *union organization*. Though the union movement dates from the eighteenth century, its chief successes have been in the last two generations.[97] By acting collectively in negotiations with employers on wages, hours, and working conditions, workers have managed to gain a considerable measure of control over the supply of labor. When well organized, they have been able to create a situation in which no labor is available below a certain price. To accomplish this, they have usually had to prevent the use of strikebreakers recruited from the ranks of the unemployed. In earlier times this was accomplished by direct (often violent) action by the union itself; more recently this has been accomplished by political action.

There are, of course, limits beyond which unions cannot go in their efforts. Above all, they cannot drive the price of labor so high that their employer or their industry loses its competitive position. To do so would be to destroy the goose that lays the golden eggs. To some extent this is what the United Mine Workers seem to have done to the coal industry after World War II: by driving the cost of labor so high in the mining industry they at least hastened the substitution of oil for coal. In advanced industrial nations, the opportunities for substituting new materials for traditional ones are increasing all the time. The case of the coal industry illustrates another limit on collective bargaining and union activity. As wages in an industry rise, employers are provided with increased incentive to replace men with machines, thus reducing the number of workers who benefit from union activity.

Perhaps the chief effect of union activity has been to create a major cleavage within the working class, dividing workers who are organized into unions from those who are not. For the former, union membership is a valuable resource which raises their wages considerably above the

[96] See, for example, Gerhard Bry, *Wages in Germany, 1871–1945* (Princeton, N.J.: Princeton University Press, 1960), pp. 283–286, who reports declining wage differentials among manual workers in Germany, Britain, and the United States, and attributes this *in part* to "mass production techniques with an accompanying breakdown of skilled operations into simpler jobs." However, as he makes clear, other factors are also responsible. See also J. Frederic Dewhurst and Associates, *Europe's Needs and Resources* (New York: Twentieth Century Fund, 1961), appendix 3–5, which reports declining wage differentials between skilled and unskilled workers for eleven countries in Europe.

[97] On the early unions, see, for example, G. D. H. Cole, *The Common People, 1746–1946* (London: Methuen, 1956, first published 1938), chap. 14, or Carroll Daugherty, *Labor Problems in American Industry*, 5th ed. (Boston: Houghton Mifflin, 1941), pp. 318–324.

subsistence level, improves their working conditions, and provides them with a measure of job security. For the rest, union membership is of little value except by indirect means.[98]

A third factor which, in the long run, has proven of greater importance than either skill level or union organization is *political organization*. So long as the machinery of government remained firmly in the hands of the propertied class and its allies, the very existence of labor unions remained in jeopardy. For example, the Combination Acts of 1799 and 1800 made union organization extremely dangerous; and, as recently as the 1930s, the property elite in Middletown (and many other American communities) used the machinery of local government to combat the unions.[99]

In most of the more advanced industrial nations, workers are now organized into Socialist, Labor, or Communist Parties, which either share in the governmental process or substantially influence it. In the United States there is no class-based party of this type, but the Democratic Party works with the labor unions and the working class. In Canada, even this is lacking: there the working-class vote is divided among the parties in much the same proportions as the vote of other classes.[100] In Communist countries, the Communist Party rules in the name of the working class, but as we have noted, it is no longer a workingmen's party in the same sense that the Socialist, Labor, and Communist Parties are in democratic nations.

Where the usual pattern prevails, workingmen's parties seek to restrict the free play of market forces, and to reduce their importance in the determination of wages. This is accomplished by various means. One of the first steps is often to curtail the supply of labor by legislative means, especially by limiting the employment of children. Later, efforts are made to establish the legal right of workingmen to organize and bargain collectively, a principal which introduces monopsonistic or oligopsonistic elements into the market situation. Still later, the party usually tries to establish a legal minimum for wages above the subsistence level, thus reducing the range within which employers can compete for labor. Another major feature of the program of workers' parties is the establishment of rights to

[98] There is evidence which indicates that in industries or communities in which a good part of the working class is organized, the employers of nonunion labor strive to keep their wages reasonably competitive to reduce the dangers of unionization of their employees. Also, to the extent that unions enter politics and secure minimum wage laws and the like, nonunion workers benefit. On the other hand, the practice of the union shop and closed shop prevents nonunion workers from competing for jobs for which they may even have superior qualifications.

[99] On the Combination Acts, see G. D. H. Cole and R. W. Postgate, *The British Common People, 1746–1938* (New York: Knopf, 1939), chap. 14; on Middletown (Muncie, Indiana), see Lynd and Lynd, chap. 2.

[100] Robert Alford, *Party and Society: The Anglo-American Democracies* (Chicago: Rand McNally, 1963), chap. 9.

goods and services based on citizenship alone (see pages 428 to 430). Other policies have the same intent: to minimize the influence of the basic market factors of supply and demand in the determination of individual income. To put the matter in slightly different terms, one might say that *the efforts of workingmen's parties are aimed largely at making the distribution of goods and services subject to political, rather than economic, determination.*

Finally, the situation of the working class has been modified and improved by most of those factors which have contributed to the decline in political and economic inequality. In other words, the working class has benefited by the rise and spread of the new democratic-egalitarian ideology, the rising level of productivity, the reduction in the birthrate, and the increased involvement of the total population in warfare. All have helped raise the income for most workingmen well above the subsistence level.

It is difficult to say exactly what a bare subsistence wage would be in most industrial societies today, and therefore difficult to determine how far removed the average workingman is from it. However, there are studies of the trends in *real* wages, i.e., after adjustments for changes in the cost of living from year to year, in various nations, and they shed considerable light on the problem. For example, one recent study showed that in the period from 1871 to 1958, real weekly wages in Germany more than doubled.[101] This same study indicated that real British wage rates nearly doubled between 1871 and 1944, while American wages rose more than four-fold. Since then still further increases have been recorded in both of the latter.[102] These gains were all made despite the substantial shortening of the work week, which in 1871 averaged about seventy-two hours in Germany and about sixty in the United States and Britain.[103] Data from Norway indicate a nearly two-fold increase in real wages in the brief period from 1920 to 1955,[104] while figures from Italy show a 13.6 per cent increase in the single decade 1948–1959.[105] If we assume that the average wage was already above the subsistence level in the first period in each of

[101] Bry, calculated from tables A-50 and A-54.
[102] In the United States real wages rose 10 per cent from 1944 to 1959, which means a 4.4-fold increase from 1871 to 1959. For the period from 1944 to 1959 see Harold Vatter, *The U.S. Economy in the 1950's: An Economic History* (New York: Norton, 1963), table 8–2.
[103] *Ibid.*, pp. 274–275.
[104] Calculated from Walter Galenson, *Labor in Norway* (Cambridge, Mass.: Harvard University Press, 1949), table 3 for the period from 1920 to 1938, and Mark Leiserson, *Wages and Economic Control in Norway, 1945–1957* (Cambridge, Mass.: Harvard University Press, 1959), table 4 for the years 1938 to 1955.
[105] Daniel Horowitz, *The Italian Labor Movement* (Cambridge, Mass.: Harvard University Press, 1963), pp. 275–276.

these time series, then it follows that the average income of members of the working class is now considerably above the subsistence level in all of the more advanced industrial societies.

The wages of industrial workers have risen not only in absolute terms in the modern era, but also relative to the income of the more privileged classes as well. This is indicated, for example, by income data from the United States for the period from 1939 to 1959, which show the following rates of increase in money (not real) wages for male workers: [106]

Nonmanual workers:

Professional and kindred workers	366%
Proprietors, managers, and officials	312%
Clerical and kindred workers	337%
Salesmen	391%

Manual workers:

Craftsmen, foremen, and kindred	400%
Operatives	427%
Laborers (nonfarm)	438%
Service workers	397%

Data from France for the period from 1910 to 1954 show the same pattern, only more pronounced: whereas the money income of various managerial and professional occupations increased 100- to 170-fold in this period, for various occupations in the working class it increased 200- to 350-fold.[107] In Communist countries also, income differentials between the working and nonmanual classes have been reduced compared with the pre-Communist era. The gains of the working class have come not only from increased wages, however, but also, in large measure, from the changing nature and growing importance of the resource of citizenship.

These political and economic advances have combined with certain other developments to produce one other significant change in the social situation of the working classes. In the earlier stages of industrialization, a great cultural chasm separated manual workers from the middle classes. This is now disappearing, or at least being substantially reduced. In part, this change stems from improvements in the economic situation of workers and from the mass production of consumer goods which makes it possible for persons of limited incomes to purchase commodities which are not nearly so distinguishable from their more expensive counterparts as comparable goods of a half century or century ago. In addition, the political

---

[106] These percentages are based on 1939 figures from *Historical Statistics*, p. 168, and 1959 figures from the *U.S. Census of Population, 1960*, vol. I, part 1, table 208.

[107] Jean Fourastié, *The Causes of Wealth*, translated by Theodore Caplow (New York: Free Press, 1960, first published 1951), table 3.

advances of the working class have greatly reduced antagonism toward existing political institutions, bringing the average worker's thinking more into line with that of the middle class. Most important, perhaps, the rise of free public schools and the mass media have stimulated a trend toward cultural convergence among the classes. The net effect of all these developments has been the adoption of many elements of middle class culture by the working class, and probably, as a result, some reduction in the traditional hostility of workers toward the existing social order.

The Farming Class

As the working class has grown, the agricultural segment of the population has steadily declined. In the United States, for example, farmers and farm laborers constituted 40 per cent of the labor force in 1870, only 7 per cent in 1962.[108] What is more, there is every indication that the figure will drop still further in the next generation, and by that time may equal no more than 2 or 3 per cent of the labor force.[109] The situation in Europe is very similar. According to one recent study, the percentage of farmers in the labor force in the non-Communist nations dropped from 42 per cent in 1910 to 27 per cent in 1950 and was continuing to decline throughout the rest of the decade.[110] The figure for West Germany, for example, dropped from 23 per cent in 1950 to 17 per cent in 1957, and in the Netherlands, from 16 per cent in 1950 to 11 per cent in 1958. In Britain, where the figure was the lowest in the world, farmers constituted only 4.5 per cent of the labor force in 1955. It appears that the farm population will soon constitute no more than 10 per cent of the total population in any of the more advanced industrial nations, with the possible exception of the Soviet Union.[111]

As important as the decline in numbers is the transformation in the character of rural life. Patterns associated with the urban economy are increasingly penetrating and transforming rural areas. Subsistence farming, for example, is rapidly becoming a thing of the past in all of the more

[108] The 1870 figure is from Mayer, p. 70; the 1962 figure is calculated from the *Statistical Abstract, 1962*, p. 215. For males only, the 1962 figure was 9 per cent.
[109] In the brief span of seven years from 1955 to 1962 the figure dropped 4 percentage points. Furthermore, census data show that the farm population now contains a very high percentage of elderly persons who are not likely to be replaced when they die.
[110] These and the following figures are from Dewhurst, *Europe's Needs*, appendix 3-2, table A.
[111] Dewhurst, *Europe's Needs*, p. 74. The Soviet Union, as is well known, has had great difficulties in the agricultural area, and as recently as 1955, peasants still constituted 45 per cent of the male labor force (DeWitt, tables VI-42–44). Even so, the farm population is declining in relative numbers, and within another generation the Soviet pattern will probably resemble the American and Western European.

advanced industrial nations. Farmers seldom produce for their own immediate needs anymore; instead, they produce for the market. This process has reached the point where many farmers now sell a product in its raw, unprocessed form and then buy it back in finished form on the retail market (for example, dairy farmers, who increasingly purchase milk and and other dairy products for home consumption).

But even this does not begin to communicate the radical nature of the transformation which agriculture is currently undergoing in the United States. As Edward Higbee so dramatically describes in *Farms and Farmers in an Urban Age*, agriculture is rapidly losing its distinctiveness and more and more coming to resemble other forms of industrial activity.[112] Mechanization has proceeded to the point where a single lettuce packing machine costs over $20,000, and a single diesel tractor as much as $32,000.[113] In fact, the average capital investment for workers in agriculture exceeds by one-third the average capital investment for workers in all other industries.[114] In addition, those farmers who are surviving and prospering in the increasingly intense competition find themselves caught up in a network of business relationships, governmental controls, and financial transactions no less complex than those of their urban counterparts in the business world. Those who lack skill in these traditionally nonagricultural activities are soon forced to sell out.

The chief consequence of all this is that the small independent farmer, who was once such an important element in American life, is now vanishing as rapidly and as surely as the proverbial Indian. The great majority have already been forced into the ranks of the urban working class, though the Census Bureau still generously counts many of them as farmers. In the brief period from 1940 to 1960, the farm population in the United States was cut in half, from 30.5 million to 15.6 million.[115] Of the latter, 44 per cent were small farmers whose annual net income from agriculture averaged only $217 in 1959, and who survived only because they had $2,884 in income from other sources.[116] Above them was a group whose net earnings from farming averaged $1,740 per year, but whose earnings from other sources averaged $1,816. According to Higbee, this group, which comprised 34 per cent of all American farmers, will almost certainly be squeezed out or die off soon (nearly two-thirds of them were already 45

[112] *Farms and Farmers in an Urban Age* (New York: Twentieth Century Fund, 1963).
[113] *Ibid.*, pp. 10 and 54.
[114] *Ibid.*, p. 11. In 1960 the figures were $21,300 and $15,900 respectively.
[115] *Statistical Abstract, 1962*, table 839. This decline was partly due to the revised definition of farm population introduced in 1960, but the revision itself was largely necessitated by the radical changes in the economic situation of the rural population which occurred in the previous twenty years.
[116] Higbee, pp. 45–46.

or more years of age).[117] In short, it appears that only about 22 per cent of the 15.6 million persons in the 1960 farm population have any real future in farming. The rest can hope to use their farms only for supplementary income, while turning to urban-centered manual trades for their main source of livelihood.

Some farmers have sought to fight these trends through organized action similar to that of the unions, but this has not proved very effective. In part this has been because of the magnitude of their problems. Not only has the farm population been large, it has also been widely scattered, making communication and coordination extremely difficult. The problem has also been ideological: the great majority of American farmers were raised in a tradition of extreme individualism which prejudiced them against reliance on collective action.[118]

In recent years, as the seriousness of their situation has become more evident and as the number of farmers has declined, organized efforts have been somewhat more successful. This is especially true of the cooperatives, which seem to be gaining in power and influence. In explaining their rise, Higbee states,

> Although it may seem incongruous that a farm organization should grow stronger as the number of farmers declines, the explanation is simple. The effectiveness of co-ops, just like the effectiveness of other vertically organized entrepreneurial enterprises, increases as weaklings drop out and the stronger survivors set about to build more efficient organizations. It takes farmers who are financially strong and well versed in economics to check production voluntarily in order to establish a favorable market position for collective bargaining. The technique is the same as that used by industry, organized labor, and professional societies such as the American Medical Association.[119]

Those farmers who survive the current struggle will be a very different breed from the small independent farmers of the past. They will be substantial members of the propertied class, skilled in the increasingly complex intricacies of farm management. The capital investment in land and buildings alone of the 22 per cent of farmers who seem likely to survive, already averages nearly $90,000 and is steadily rising.[120] In fact, the top third of these farmers have an investment of this kind averaging $135,000, enough to justify their inclusion in the property elite. If such figures seem startling to those accustomed to thinking in terms of the traditional family

[117] *Ibid.*, p. 52.
[118] There is good reason to believe that none of these characteristics, including the ideological, are peculiar to American farmers. Stalin's great difficulties with Russia's farmers are but one indication of the commitment to an individualistic outlook.
[119] *Ibid.*, p. 37. Quoted by permission.
[120] Calculated from Higbee, tables 1 and 13.

farm, it may be well to add that in 1959 there were 408 farms in the United States each with sales of $1,000,000 or more, and another 800 with sales of $500,000 to $1,000,000.[121] Many of these farms are operated like highly automated industries, with hired managers and full-time production workers increasing the resemblance between the new agricultural system and modern industry.

The same trends appear to be developing in European agriculture, though the relative size of the farm population there suggests that the development of agriculture is lagging about a generation behind. Nevertheless, the drift is evident. As one writer put it recently, after reviewing current developments, "All these changes are in the direction of turning the [Western European] farm into something like a factory which purchases raw materials, feeds them into machines (land and animals) and markets the product." [122] This same writer claims, however, that the family farm remains the European ideal and that the preservation of such farms is the goal of nearly all Western European governments.[123] Since the same could have been said of Americans and their government until the last few years, one may be pardoned for viewing such assertions with a measure of skepticism.

The position of the Soviet Union's farm population is more difficult to characterize than that of any other industrial nation. In some respects that nation is highly advanced and has broken radically with the agrarian past; in others, it is quite backward. The latter trait is evidenced both in the large percentage of the population it is still obliged to use in agriculture and in its low level of productivity. As recently as 1955, slightly over half of the total labor force was engaged in agricultural activities.[124] For men alone, the figure, while a bit lower, was still 45 per cent. Despite the heavier use of labor and the larger size of the nation, Soviet agricultural output was 20 per cent lower than in the United States, according to Soviet authorities themselves.[125] In addition, the conditions of life in most rural villages continue to be extremely primitive.

[121] *U.S. Census of Agriculture, 1959: Large-scale Farming in the U.S.* (Washington: U.S. Bureau of the Census, 1963), p. 8.

[122] P. Lamartine Yates, *Food, Land and Manpower in Western Europe* (London: Macmillan, 1960), p. 201. See Margaret Gordon, table 6, p. 21, for statistical evidence on the decline in size of farm population in Belgium, France, West Germany, Italy, The Netherlands, and the United Kingdom since World War II.

[123] *Ibid.*, pp. 186–188.

[124] This and the following estimate are based on DeWitt, tables VI–42–44. These figures are probably a bit too high, since they include collective farm workers engaged in administrative or clerical work and in crafts. See Lazar Volin, "The Collective Farm," in Alex Inkeles and Kent Geiger, *Soviet Society: A Book of Readings* (Boston, Mass.: Houghton Mifflin, 1961), p. 337.

[125] See, for example, B. I. Braginskii and D. Dumov, "Labor Productivity in Agriculture in the USSR and the USA," in Shaffer, p. 181.

On the other hand, the Soviet government has thoroughly destroyed the older forms of agricultural organization. Since the 1930s the overwhelming majority of peasants have been obliged to work on large collective farms with several hundred or several thousand others, at tasks assigned by farm managers and under their control. Though the mode of payment and certain other features of collective farm life are distinctive, one expert has concluded that the Soviet peasant is "becoming in most respects indistinguishable from a worker in the Soviet factory." [126] In short, *in the Soviet Union, as in other advanced industrial nations, the differences which historically separated farmers and peasants from urban workers seem to be disappearing, with the result that the farming or peasant class is in the process of being absorbed by other classes.*

The Unemployed and Slave-labor Classes

At the bottom of the occupational hierarchy in advanced industrial societies one often finds either a class of unemployed persons or a class of slave laborers. The former is more likely in democratic nations, the latter in totalitarian.[127] Both classes arise from the inability or unwillingness of societal leaders to achieve a balance between the forces of supply and demand in the labor market.

As our analysis of the expendables in agrarian societies made clear, the unemployed class has a long and dreary history. However, this has not prevented it from performing a social function of great value to the leading classes. Its presence has always served as a depressant on wages, thereby forcing peasants and workers to be much more cautious in their demands than they might otherwise have been.

The future of this class is difficult to predict. In recent years the level of unemployment has been quite low in most of the highly industrialized democracies of the western world. For example, in 1955 the unemployed numbered only about 1 per cent of the labor force in Britain, Finland, France, Iceland, Luxembourg, the Netherlands, Norway, Sweden, and Switzerland, and for the whole of non-Communist Europe, only 4.2 per cent.[128]

The highest rates of unemployment in Europe were registered, inter-

---

[126] Volin, p. 343. For a more detailed study of the Soviet peasantry, see Naum Jasny, *The Socialized Agriculture for the USSR* (Stanford, Calif.: Stanford University Press, 1949).

[127] A recent report by Soviet economist Yefim Manevich indicates substantial unemployment in various areas of the Soviet Union. See Edward Crankshaw in *The Washington Post,* July 18, 1965, p. A-22.

[128] Dewhurst, *Europe's Needs,* table 3–9. See also Margaret Gordon, table 1, p. 9, which shows a median figure of 1.1 per cent unemployed for seven of the leading nations of Western Europe in 1961 versus a median of 2.5 per cent for the same nations in 1955.

estingly enough, by four of the least industrialized nations, Greece, Italy, Portugal, and Spain. This suggests that unemployment tends to decline with increasing industrialization. It would be a serious mistake, however, to suppose that this is the only factor involved, or that unemployment rates automatically decline with advancing industrialization. A study of the historical sequence in any single country proves that increasing industrialization can be accompanied by *rising* rates of unemployment. In the United States, for example, the rate of unemployment among male workers rose from 2.8 per cent in 1953 to 7.9 per cent in 1961 despite obvious advances in industrialization. This demonstrates that the rate of unemployment is also a function of such things as war, the business cycle, and technological innovation (in this case, automation). Each of these affects the demand for labor, and thus the rate of unemployment.

Many observers of the contemporary scene have expressed serious misgivings about the influence of automation on the modern economy. These fears are not without foundation; automation obviously could lead to large-scale unemployment. However, it is not inevitable: men have it within their power to create institutional arrangements which can prevent it. The real question, then, is whether they will do so.[129]

While predictions in an area like this are always hazardous, the probability of massive unemployment comparable to that in the 1930s does not appear great. In most of the more advanced societies the working class, the group primarily threatened by a major increase in unemployment, now has the political instruments and experience it needs to defend itself. This is clearly true in countries where the Swedish, or even the British, model of political organization prevails. It is somewhat less certain in nations with the American model, although political leaders in such countries appear to be responsive to even moderate increases in the rate of unemployment. Furthermore, considering the high level of productivity and affluence which increasingly characterizes all industrial societies, the privileged classes would almost certainly make concessions in order to protect their many advantages.

One final factor suggests that the number of unemployed will not increase appreciably. The new, simple, and inexpensive means of contraception make it unlikely that the unemployed, or those threatened by unemployment, will continue to have large families as in the past (unless they are unintentionally encouraged to do so by faulty systems of welfare benefits). In short, while there may be fluctuations, and perhaps even some permanent increase of modest proportions, *there will probably be no substantial permanent increase in the rate of unemployment.*

If unemployment is the lowest status in the occupational class system

[129] See Kenneth Galbraith, *The Affluent Society* (Boston: Houghton Mifflin, 1958).

in democratic industrial nations, *slave labor* is its equivalent in totalitarian ones. A class of slave laborers is not an inevitable feature of totalitarian states, as the post-Stalin era in the Soviet Union demonstrates. On the other hand, the fact that both the Nazi and Communist regimes utilized it, suggests that it is not an accidental or incidental occurrence in such states.

It has sometimes been supposed that the development of the slave-labor class in Germany and Russia was merely a response to political dissent. However, though the labor camps in both countries seem to have been created for this purpose, their great expansion occurred largely because of the need for cheap labor.[130] The availability of political prisoners and other persons enabled these totalitarian regimes to employ large numbers of persons *at or below subsistence wages*, despite an expressed commitment to a socialistic or semisocialistic ideology.

It is still impossible to say just how large the slave-labor populations of Nazi Germany and the Soviet Union became. In both instances, however, they clearly numbered in the millions at their peak. Most estimates for Russia are about ten million at the time of Stalin's death.[131] As the Soviet novelist Alexander Solzhenitsyn made clear in his thinly fictionalized novel, *One Day in the Life of Ivan Denisovich*, for most members of this class, as for the expendables in agrarian societies, life was "poor, nasty, brutish, and short." [132]

At the present time there is no large slave-labor class designed to achieve economic goals in any advanced industrial society, and the prospects for the emergence of one do not seem great. As the Communists and other employers of slave labor have found, this type of labor is far better suited to unskilled and semiskilled work than to tasks requiring skilled labor or professional training. Persons living at the subsistence level and motivated only by fear do not usually perform well in the more demanding occupational roles. In view of the rapid technological advances which continually reduce the need for unskilled labor, it is improbable that any of the more advanced industrial nations will turn to slave labor for economic purposes. If a slave-labor class should develop in the near future, it would more likely be in Asia, Africa, or Latin America, or in countries which are only now making the painful transition to industrialism. In any industrializing society which comes under totalitarian control, a slave-labor class might well prove to be profitable for a time, at least when judged from the standpoint of the political elite.

[130] See, for example, Fainsod, pp. 432–433 and 459–460.
[131] *Ibid.*, pp. 458–460, or Inkeles and Geiger, p. 253.
[132] Translated by Max Hayward and Ronald Hingley (New York: Bantam, 1963).

12/Industrial Societies: Part III

Question: What is the ideal income?
Answer: 10 per cent more than you've got.
American saying

The Educational Class System

IN TRADITIONAL AGRARIAN SOCIETIES, educational institutions were few in number, and not of great importance from the distributive standpoint. In the main they served but two relevant functions: first, as "finishing schools" for children of the governing class, teaching them the distinctive social skills appropriate to their station in life, and second, as training institutions for boys recruited largely from the retainer class, providing them with some of the skills and knowledge they would need later in the service of their superiors.[1] In neither case, however, did they greatly disturb the

---

[1] For a classic discussion of the first function, see Thorstein Veblen, *The Theory of the Leisure Class* (New York: New Modern Library, 1934, first published 1899), chap. 14.

transmission of power and privilege from father to son along traditional, hereditary lines.[2] The competitive element was severely limited because the vast majority of boys were never given an opportunity to attend school, and were therefore condemned to illiteracy. The sons of peasants and artisans learned what they had to know by observing their father or, at best, by serving an apprenticeship with some master craftsman.

One of the major consequences of the modern revolution in knowledge has been the destruction of this ancient, aristocratic system of education. In advanced industrial societies, illiteracy and ignorance are handicaps not only for the illiterate and ignorant, but for the rest of society as well. A high level of productivity in an industrial society requires a labor force which is at least literate, and there is good reason to believe that the level of productivity of the economy is closely related to the level of education of the labor force. Hence, the privileged classes have a vested interest in providing educational opportunity for all—a situation radically different from that in agrarian societies. Furthermore, as a result of the democratization of government in most industrial societies, the masses of common people have a resource which they can use to demand educational facilities.

Evidence of the change can be found in contemporary statistics on school attendance. In the United States more than 99 per cent of all children aged seven to thirteen attend school, and more than 90 per cent of those aged fourteen to seventeen.[3] At ages eighteen and nineteen, nearly 40 per cent are still in attendance. By 1960 approximately 18 per cent of all American young people were graduating from college, and for males the figure was 24 per cent.[4] While American figures are the highest in the world, other industrial nations are moving in the same direction.[5]

Though the expansion of educational systems has meant increased competition for this valuable resource, one must not exaggerate the degree to which equality of educational opportunity has been approximated. The Wolfle study in the 1950s made it clear that the relationship between intelligence and academic success is far from perfect. It was found that a few

---

[2] Pitirim Sorokin takes a contrary position concerning the role of schools in traditional Indian and Chinese societies [see *Social Mobility* (New York: Harper & Row, 1927), pp. 191–193], but more recent research does not support his position (see chaps. 8 and 9 of this volume).

[3] *Statistical Abstract of the United States, 1962* (Washington, D.C.: GPO, 1962), p. 115.

[4] These figures are estimated from the *Statistical Abstract, 1962*, tables 18 and 168.

[5] See, for example, J. Frederic Dewhurst and Associates, *Europe's Needs and Resources* (New York: Twentieth Century Fund, 1961), table 10–9, which shows that in the sixteen nations of Western Europe, the median increase in secondary school enrollments between 1938 and 1955 was 81 per cent. During this same period the population of Western Europe increased only 16 per cent (appendix 2–1, table A).

individuals who ranked in the bottom 5 per cent in ability graduated from college, while some of those in the top tenth of 1 per cent did not graduate from high school.[6] More specifically, 69 per cent of those in the top 0.1 per cent in terms of intelligence graduated from college, compared with 49 per cent of those in the top 5 per cent, and 34 per cent in the top 20 per cent.[7] Other studies suggest the same conclusion: *there is a fairly strong positive correlation between intelligence and educational achievement, but no more than this.*[8]

While a number of factors, both social and psychological, are responsible for the imperfect correlation, differences in family background are among the most important. Parents in the professional, managerial, propertied, and political classes are able to provide their children with many advantages, not only financial, but, equally important, such things as linguistic skills, motivation, and facilities for private study. It seems no exaggeration to say that *the family is the most powerful single factor counteracting the egalitarian tendency inherent in modern educational systems.* As noted previously, this factor is apparently just as important in the Soviet Union today as in the United States.[9]

In the more advanced industrial societies, formal educational attainments are becoming an increasingly important resource. This is mainly due to the increasing bureaucratization of modern personnel practices, itself a product of the growth in the size of organizations. In the smaller organizations of an earlier era, hiring, firing, and promotions were occasional matters and likely to be handled in an informal manner. Particularistic criteria were invoked without apology: if the owner's son was promoted over the heads of more experienced men, this was taken for granted. Today, by contrast, it is expected that personnel decisions will be made on the basis of universalistic standards. This means that personnel managers are under pressure to find objective criteria which can be invoked to justify their decisions. Because educational institutions perform a selective function and because information on educational attainment is readily accessible, personnel managers feel, not without justification, that educational criteria can be used as basic criteria in decisions about hiring and promotion. Thus it has come to be that only high school graduates are considered for appointments to certain positions, and only college

---

[6] Dael Wolfle, *America's Resources of Specialized Talent* (New York: Harper & Row, 1954), table G.2.

[7] *Ibid.*, table VI.1.

[8] See, for example, Burton Clark, *Educating the Expert Society* (San Francisco, Calif.: Chandler, 1962), tables 2.1 and 2.2.

[9] See p. 332 above, or David Burg, "Observations of Soviet University Students," in Richard Pipes (ed.), *The Russian Intelligentsia* (New York: Columbia University Press, 1961), pp. 80–81.

graduates for others. As a result, *educational status has become increasingly important as a resource in the struggle for power and privilege.* It is becoming a necessary prerequisite for admission to most of the more rewarding occupations in advanced industrial societies. The day when men could rise to the top by serving an apprenticeship under an established professional man, e.g., as in the old practice of "reading the law," or by promotion up through the ranks, is rapidly becoming a thing of the past in bureaucratized industrial societies.[10]

These trends in employment practices are leading to an organizational arrangement which closely resembles the caste-like system of the military, with its sharp distinction between officers and enlisted men. Management stands in a position similar to that of the officers, being recruited from outside the organization and brought in over the heads of production workers and others with far more seniority and experience. Typically, recruits to management come directly from the ranks of current college and university graduates. Other employees, who are not required to have this level of education, are not permitted to enter the ranks of management, except perhaps in the capacity of foreman, a marginal role resembling the role of warrant officer in the army. For production workers

[10] See, for example, W. Lloyd Warner and James C. Abegglen, *Occupational Mobility in American Business and Industry, 1928–1952* (Minneapolis: University of Minnesota Press, 1955), p. 198, who show that the percentage of American business leaders with less than a college education dropped from 55 per cent at the time of the Taussig and Joslyn study in 1928, to 24 per cent in 1952, the year of their study. These figures would be even lower if the older executives were removed from the totals. For other figures on the trend, see Mabel Newcomer, *The Big Business Executive* (New York: Columbia University Press, 1955), table 24, p. 68. Warner has also shown that college education is now virtually a prerequisite for managerial posts in the Federal government. The percentages with some college education range from a low of 93 per cent in the case of career executives in the civil service, to a high of 98 per cent among military leaders and executives in the Foreign Service. See W. Lloyd Warner et al., *The American Federal Executive* (New Haven, Conn.: Yale University Press, 1963), table 33B, p. 354. Similar patterns are evident elsewhere. See, for example, Roy Lewis and Rosemary Stewart, *The Managers: A New Examination of the English, German and American Executive* (New York: Mentor Books, 1961), chap. 3, on the changing pattern of recruitment for executive positions in British industry; David Granick, *The European Executive* (Garden City, N.Y.: Doubleday Anchor, 1964), especially pp. 19–43 and 354–355, on France, Belgium, and Britain; and David Granick, *The Red Executive* (Garden City, N.Y.: Doubleday Anchor, 1961), chap. 4, or Nicholas DeWitt, *Education and Professional Employment in the USSR* (Washington, D.C.: National Science Foundation, 1961), on the Soviet Union. With respect to the Soviet Union, Granick states, "I received the impression from conversations that a college education is virtually an absolute requirement for a candidate for an industrial management post" (*Red Executive*, p. 46). A recent (1960) study of Japanese business leaders shows that 91 per cent had university training. See James Abegglen and Hiroshi Mannari, "Japanese Business Leaders: 1880–1960," unpublished manuscript prepared for the Conference on State and Economic Enterprise in Modern Japan, Association for Asian Studies, 1963, p. 47, or James Abegglen, *The Japanese Factory: Aspects of Its Social Organization* (New York: Free Press, 1958), table 1, p. 28.

in industry, as for enlisted men in the army, promotions are usually confined to their own segregated hierarchy, thus limiting severely upward mobility for those without college training.

One curious aspect of this development was uncovered by Warner and Abegglen in their study of American business leaders. They found an *inverse* relationship between the educational attainments of executives in an industry or firm and the rate of growth of that industry or firm.[11] This led them to conclude that educational requirements for managerial recruits may have been exaggerated. This conclusion, though admittedly speculative, presents a serious challenge to the functionalist thesis that society uses its rewards to attract the ablest members of society to the most demanding positions and to insure their effective performance in them. Moreover, it suggests that educational attainments are symbols not only of ability and motivation, but also of membership in a favored class whose members are more concerned with the advancement of their personal and class interests than with the well-being of either the nation or the firm.

Statistics compiled in recent years show clearly the relationship between income and education when the disturbing factor of age is controlled. For example, 1960 census returns revealed the following differences in annual income among white American males aged forty-five to fifty-four: [12]

0–7 years of education	$3,872
8 years of education	$4,722
1–3 years of high school	$5,335
4 years of high school	$5,829
1–3 years of college	$6,765
4 or more years of college	$9,233

Comparisons with earlier years show widening differentials both in absolute and relative terms. For example, whereas in 1946 high school graduates earned 26 per cent more than grammar school graduates, by 1958 this figure had jumped to 48 per cent.[13] Similarly, the differential between high school and college graduates rose from 57 per cent in 1939 to 65 per cent in 1958.[14] Though the time periods involved are much too short to be conclusive, they suggest an important trend.

[11] Warner and Abegglen, pp. 140–141.
[12] U.S. *Census of Population, 1960: Occupation by Earnings and Education* (Washington: U.S. Bureau of the Census, n.d.), table 1, p. 3. The figures shown are all median figures.
[13] Herman P. Miller, "Annual and Lifetime Income in Relation to Education: 1939–1959," *American Economic Review*, 50 (1960), p. 969.
[14] *Ibid*. The difference in the base years in the two comparisons is due to the absence of data on grammar school graduates in 1939.

One might wonder whether education itself is really of great importance, or whether it is merely a symptom of more basic factors, such as intelligence or family background. One recent study indicates that education is no mere symptom, but rather a factor of vital importance in its own right. This study involved a careful survey in 1962 of several hundred male students who enrolled at the University of Illinois in the fall of 1952 but left without graduating. Data were obtained on their current jobs, family background, intelligence (as measured by tests while at the University), and subsequent educational record. It was found that the chief determinant of the status of the jobs the men held in 1962 was their subsequent educational experience. Those who had returned to college and graduated held nearly all of the high status jobs; those who failed to return, or returned but did not graduate were concentrated in the medium and low status jobs. Family background (as measured by the student's father's occupation), and even intelligence, counted for little by comparison with formal educational attainment (as measured by graduation from college).[15]

An interesting question which has not yet received the attention it deserves is that of the degree to which educated people have actively striven to enhance the rewards of education. This is a difficult problem for scholars even to recognize: to those who are educated, it seems only natural to encourage education and reward the educated, since in the end "this cannot but redound to the general good." Unfortunately, once one begins to reflect on the matter, it becomes evident that this thesis of the educated class is very similar to that of businessmen who have long insisted that "what is good for business is good for the country." The self-serving aspects of such an ideology, when stated by others, are always obvious, but when stated by one's own group, are not. In one of the few serious treatments of this subject, Michael Young, a British sociologist, has suggested that the modern trend toward socialism and the welfare state may yet be reversed by a new movement toward "meritocracy," an elitist society dominated by the most talented and best educated.[16] Elusive though it is, and difficult to test in any conclusive fashion, this hypothesis deserves careful attention.

Before concluding this examination of the role of education in the distributive process, note must be taken of the unique role educational

[15] See Bruce Eckland, "Academic Ability, Higher Education, and Occupational Mobility," *American Sociological Review*, 30 (1965), pp. 735–746. Some of the statements above are based on data presented in an earlier version of this paper but subsequently deleted.
[16] *The Rise of Meritocracy, 1870–2033: The New Elite of Our Social Revolution* (New York: Random House, 1959).

institutions play in undergirding existing political and distributive systems by disseminating appropriate political ideologies. In totalitarian nations this is done quite openly and without apology, and the results have been most impressive. In the Soviet Union, for example, the great majority of those educated since the Revolution seem to accept without question the legitimacy of the Communist Party's monopoly of political power.[17]

In democratic nations this ideological function of educational institutions is less open and also less one-sided. Educational leaders are much more likely to maintain that their institutions are concerned merely with the inculcation of objective truths and the transmission of essential techniques. Usually they avoid partisan political conflict. Nevertheless, a careful examination of the content of the curriculum usually indicates that it is designed to develop in the student a respect for his nation's political traditions and heritage, and that this necessarily implies an acceptance of the basic political arrangements and their distributive correlates. This pattern is most evident in the lower grades and in those institutions which educate children from the lower and middle classes. By contrast, in the better universities, which disproportionately serve the children from the upper and upper-middle strata, more critical views are expressed with some frequency. Though systematic evidence on this point is lacking, it appears that the chief effect of this is to develop a "reformist mentality" in a significant minority of the leaders of the next generation. Such persons are committed to all of the *basic* elements in the political and distributive *status quo*, but accept the need for modification in *secondary* elements. The late President Kennedy or Governor Nelson Rockefeller of New York are good examples of individuals of this type. They are neither revolutionaries nor "standpatters." Their presence in the political leadership of democratic nations contributes greatly to their viability and, as a consequence, reduces the probability of revolution. Thus these developments in the educational sphere strengthen constitutionalism, with all that that implies for the operation of distributive systems.

Racial, Ethnic, and Religious Class Systems

Many, *though not all*, of the more advanced industrial nations of the modern world contain serious racial, ethnic, or religious cleavages. In Canada there is the increasingly serious division between French Catholics and "English" Protestants. West Germany is divided between Catho-

---

[17] See especially Alex Inkeles and Raymond Bauer, *The Soviet Citizen* (Cambridge, Mass.: Harvard University Press, 1959).

lics and Protestants, as is Holland, where the Protestants are further divided into liberal and conservative groups. Belgium is divided between the Dutch-speaking Flemings and French-speaking Walloons, with the former tending to be staunch Catholics and the latter convinced anti-clericals. Czechoslovakia is divided between Czechs and Slovaks. In the Soviet Union the major division has long been between the Russians and Ukranians, but there are innumerable other minorities, such as the Latvians, Lithuanians, Estonians, Jews, Armenians, Georgians, Kazakhs, and Uzbeks, to name but a few. In addition, there is the cleavage between believers and nonbelievers. In the United States there are cleavages between Negroes and whites, Jews and Gentiles, Protestants and Catholics, as well as Northerners and Southerners. Finally, even in a relatively homogeneous nation such as Britain, there are distinctions between English, Scots, and Welsh and between the native population, the recent Irish Catholic immigrants, and the still more recent colored immigrants from the West Indies and Pakistan.

So long as such groups are irrelevant to the distributive process, they cannot be considered classes or status groups. When, however, membership in them begins to have an appreciable influence on men's access to important rewards which are in short supply, then it becomes impossible to treat them otherwise. To call such groups classes does not mean that they are only classes, or even that they are identical with other kinds of classes. It does mean, however, that they are groups of people who stand in a common position with respect to some attribute which functions as a resource in the distributive process—in this case, race, ethnicity, religion, or region.

Far too little research has yet been directed at the problem of how much the groups cited above, and others like them, influence the distributive process. The greatest amount of research has been carried out in the United States, where it is clear that all four kinds of groups, racial, ethnic, religious, and regional, play a significant role in the distributive process, and thereby merit the label of class or status group, though in varying degree.

This has been especially evident in the case of the two major racial groups, which have long been referred to by many American sociologists as "castes" in recognition of their peculiar role in the system of stratification. The clearest single measure of their importance is found in census data on the incomes of whites and Negroes. In 1959, for example, the median income for white men was nearly double that for Negro men ($4,337 vs. $2,254).[18] This pattern of inequality is repeated in virtually

[18] *U.S. Census of Population, 1960*, vol. I, part 1, table 218.

every other aspect of the distributive system. With respect to education, whites had obtained 10.9 years on the average, compared with 8.2 for Negroes, and it is clear that the *quality* of education afforded the great majority of Negroes was substantially inferior.[19] With respect to housing, the ghetto pattern is so familiar as not to require discussion.[20] The same pattern of segregation prevails in formal social relationships, with Negroes denied admission to many clubs, churches, cliques, and, of course, to the great majority of white families which they might enter through marriage. Finally, though Negroes are more than 10 per cent of the total population, they constitute only 1 per cent of the United States Congress, and are also underrepresented in most other public offices.

It is true, of course, that the extent of inequality has been declining for a century, but until recently the rate of decline has been slow. Moreover, the pattern has been erratic, as exemplified by the fact that whites have occasionally crowded Negroes out of skilled trades which they were once permitted to monopolize.[21] During the 1950s, while gains were made on other fronts, inequality in incomes actually increased. In 1951, for example, the median income for white males was 1.62 times that for nonwhites; by 1959 this ratio had climbed to 1.86.[22]

Though the white population in the United States is often treated as a homogeneous group, it is, in fact, divided into four major subclasses or status groups which are engaged in a lively competition for scarce resources. These groups, which are defined by a combination of religion and region, are (1) Northern white Protestants, (2) Southern white Protestants, (3) Catholics, and (4) Jews. Though religion is a major basis of classification, this does not mean that all, or even most, of the members of the various groups are devout adherents of the faiths with which they are identified. The term as used here refers to the communal groupings with which most individuals identify themselves and are identified and which serve as the basis for primary type relations, rather than to the

[19] On years of education by race, see *Statistical Abstract, 1962*, table 148. The qualitative inferiority of Negro education, which is no longer disputed by educators, makes the often quoted statistics on the interrelations between income, education, and race rather misleading. Through no fault of his own, the average Negro high school graduate is not nearly so well educated as his white counterpart, and this is undoubtedly a part of the explanation for his lower income levels.

[20] See, for example, St. Clair Drake and Horace Cayton, *Black Metropolis: A Study of Negro Life in a Northern City* (New York: Harcourt, Brace & World, 1945), chap. 8.

[21] For example, at one time Negroes largely monopolized the barber trade in Washington, D.C., and many other cities and towns. Later, however, white barbers moved in and took over most of the white clientele.

[22] The 1951 figure is calculated from Herman P. Miller, *Income of the American People* (New York: Wiley, 1955), table 51; the 1959 figure is calculated from the *U.S. Census of Population, 1960*, vol. I, part 1, table 218.

churches or formal religious associations.[23] Thus, from the standpoint of status-group membership, the theological commitments of individuals are much less important than the group identifications which they make of themselves and others make of them.

Of these four groups, the Northern white Protestants have traditionally enjoyed the most privileged position. To put the matter in slightly different terms, membership in the Northern white Protestant group has had the greatest resource value. The status of this group has clearly been a function of the political history of the country. The initial settlement of the colonies and the founding of the nation were both actions of a largely Protestant people. As late as 1820, not more than about 1 per cent of the white population was Catholic or Jewish.[24] The Negro group, though it totaled 20 per cent of the population in the early years, presented no serious social, political, or economic challenge because the great majority of its members were illiterate, disenfranchised slaves.[25] During much of the period from 1790 to 1860 there was a bitter struggle for power between Northern and Southern Protestants, but this was settled in the Civil War with the decisive defeat of the South. After that, Northern white Protestants constituted the most powerful and most privileged status group in the nation.

The relative status of the other groups has been determined basically by their relationship to the dominant Northern white Protestant group. It was this group which determined that membership in the Catholic group was preferable to membership in the Jewish group, and membership in the Jewish group preferable to membership in the Negro group.[26] This ranking was not consciously formulated, but was rather a spontaneous by-product of normal social interaction. It was based essentially on the degree of cultural similarity of each of the minority groups to the dominant group, and reflected the relative willingness of members of the dominant group to establish primary relations with members of each of the other groups. Hence Catholics, as Christians, often from Northwest Europe and sometimes English-speaking, were regarded more highly than the non-

---

[23] For a more detailed discussion of this distinction, see Gerhard Lenski, *The Religious Factor* (Garden City, N.Y.: Doubleday, 1961), especially pp. 18–20 and 35–42. See also Will Herberg, *Protestant-Catholic-Jew* (Garden City, N.Y.: Doubleday, 1956), and Milton Gordon, *Assimilation in American Life: The Role of Race, Religion, and National Origins* (Fair Lawn, N.J.: Oxford University Press, 1964).

[24] On the much larger Catholic group, see Gerald Shaughnessy, *Has the Immigrant Kept the Faith?* (New York: Macmillan, 1925). On the Jewish group, see Bernard Weinryb, "Jewish Immigration and Accommodation to America," in Marshall Sklare (ed.), *The Jews: Social Patterns of an American Group* (New York: Free Press, 1958), p. 4.

[25] *Statistical Abstract, 1962*, table 15.

[26] Recent research suggests that the minority groups have tended to adopt the Northern white Protestant standard of values when evaluating groups other than their own, and to some extent even in evaluating their own group. To the extent that this happens, the influence of the dominant group is reinforced.

Christian Jews from Eastern Europe with their more alien ways, and the latter were regarded more highly than the nonwhite Negroes with their still more alien background. These values, rather than economic status, appear to have been the chief determinant, which explains why the Catholic group has ranked ahead of the more affluent Jewish group.

The position of status groups, like those of other classes, are not immutable. In the last generation, especially, the position of the Northern Protestants has come under heavy attack from all four of its rivals, and the group has lost considerable ground. It is difficult to measure precisely the magnitude of the gains of the "minority" groups or the losses of the historically dominant group, but a few examples are indicative. Within the last generation a considerable number of high political offices which were once regarded as the exclusive preserve of Northern white Protestants have been opened to other groups. Though Kennedy's election to the Presidency in 1960 is the most dramatic example, it is by no means an isolated one.[27] In Congress, the Republican Party, the political vehicle of the Northern white Protestants, has declined to the point where it has often been obliged to enter into an informal alliance with the Southern wing of the Democratic Party, the political vehicle of the Southern white Protestants, in order to remain influential. This has meant substantial concessions to special Southern interests, for example, the elimination of the discriminatory pattern of politically determined freight rates which for so long hampered the industrial development of the South. In the business world, the occupational advantages of membership in the Northern Protestant group have been largely eliminated as a result of the bureaucratization of industry, though some advantages probably still remain at the higher status levels where impersonal bureaucratic standards are more difficult to apply.[28] For a time, chiefly between World Wars I and

[27] In New England this trend began even earlier, thanks to the heavy early immigration of Irish Catholics. See, for example, Robert Dahl, *Who Governs?: Democracy and Power in an American City* (New Haven, Conn.: Yale University Press, 1961), pp. 32–51, on New Haven, Connecticut; Elin Anderson, *We Americans: A Study of Cleavage in an American City* (Cambridge, Mass.: Harvard University Press, 1938), chap. 10, on Burlington, Vermont; Kenneth Underwood, *Protestant and Catholic: Religious and Social Interaction in an Industrial Community* (Boston: Beacon Press, 1957), chap. 17, on Holyoke, Massachusetts; or Edward Banfield, *Big City Politics* (New York: Random House, 1965), chap. 2, on Boston.

[28] It is interesting to note that in one study of the managerial elite, the percentage of men identifying themselves as Catholics or Jews rose only from 11 to 14 per cent between 1900 and 1950 [see Mabel Newcomer, *The Big Business Executive* (New York: Columbia University Press, 1955), table 13]. It should be noted, however, that in both time periods roughly half of the men did not report their religious preference and, furthermore, the percentage of nonreporters rose from 44 to 56 per cent, which may hide an increase in men with less prestigeful preferences. Studies of lawyers also suggest that leading law firms have long been slow to hire Jews and members of other ethnic minorities. See, for example, Jack Ladinsky, "Careers of Lawyers, Law Practice, and Legal Institutions," *American Sociological Review*, 28 (1963), pp. 47–54.

II, many of the better educational institutions in the country maintained quotas restricting the number of Jewish students, a policy which chiefly benefited Northern white Protestant students because relatively few applications were received from the other status groups.[29] Finally, membership in the Northern white Protestant group has continued to provide entrée to the more exclusive social circles, a resource which can be of considerable economic and political value.

Northern white Protestants are not the only ones who have sought to make in-group membership a resource in the competition for power and privilege. Wherever possible, minority groups have done the same. Thus, when Catholics or Jews have controlled employment possibilities, they have frequently favored members of their own group. This has been especially evident in the distribution of political patronage at the municipal level, where Catholic machines have favored Catholic applicants for positions at city hall and on the police force.[30] Also, like Northern white Protestants, members of minority groups have preferred to associate with people from their own group, particularly in the more intimate primary relations, and this has constituted a significant resource, especially for such a prosperous group as the Jews.[31] Finally, minority groups have usually given their political support to members of their own group, and this, too, has frequently proven an important resource.[32] Though such actions are often condemned, at least when practiced by the majority, they represent one of the most natural of human reactions: the expression of support for those most like oneself.

Recent trends have led to a substantial reduction in the degree of inequality generated by the American system of status groups. While many factors have contributed to this, the most important of all has probably been the changing composition of the electorate which resulted from the heavy immigration of non-Protestant groups after 1880, as well as the more recent enfranchisement of the Negro. This combination of factors has reduced Northern white Protestants to the position of a statistical minority in the electorate. According to a large sample survey made by the Bureau

[29] See, for example, C. Bezalel Sherman, *The Jew within American Society* (Detroit: Wayne State Press, 1961), pp. 174–178.
[30] See, for example, Dahl, pp. 40–44, or Underwood, chap. 17 and especially fn. 29, pp. 460–461.
[31] The Jewish group in particular has tended to be exclusive in its primary relations. See, for example, Milton Gordon, pp. 178–182.
[32] See, for example, Lucy Dawidowicz and Leon Goldstein, *Politics in a Pluralistic Democracy: Studies of Voting in the 1960 Election* (New York: Institute of Human Relations Press, 1963); Samuel Lubell, *The Future of American Politics*, rev. ed. (Garden City: Doubleday Anchor, 1956); or Angus Campbell et al., *The American Voter,* (New York: Wiley, 1960), pp. 319–321.

of the Census in 1957, the adult population of this country was distributed as follows: [33]

Northern white Protestants	38 per cent
Roman Catholics	26 per cent
Southern white Protestants	20 per cent
Negro Protestants	9 per cent
Jews	3 per cent
Others and no religion	4 per cent

These demographic trends, combined with a democratic political system, have made it extremely difficult for the Northern white Protestant group to preserve its traditional advantages. Its difficulties have been compounded by the incorporation of so many elements of the democratic-egalitarian ideology into the constitutional system, and even into the personal belief systems of members of the favored group.

Viewing status group stratification in a broadly comparative perspective, it appears that the general trend in most advanced industrial societies is toward a reduction in the degree of inequality between such groups. Weber recognized this half a century ago and explained it as a result of the rising rate of economic change.[34] Though he did not say so, we may infer that he saw rapid economic changes as disruptive of established patterns of social relations, and thereby destructive of the important practice of status group segregation.

Without denying the importance of this factor, one may doubt that it is the entire story. The rise and spread of the democratic-egalitarian ideology is clearly involved, and it is not a simple function of the rising rate of economic change. Whatever the relationship between these two variables may ultimately prove to be, the ideological variable is apparently both a more immediate and a more powerful determinant of the trend. This ideology has been a potent weapon in the hands of minority groups, giving their cause the aura of legitimacy. This has had the effect of mobilizing and energizing the members of minority groups, while simultaneously introducing a strong element of uncertainty and confusion into the ranks of their opponents.

In this connection it is interesting to note again that there has been a gradual change in the character of the new ideology. In the eighteenth, nineteenth, and early twentieth centuries, attacks on inequality frequently appeared to be based on an ideological rejection of inequality per se.

---

[33] "Religion Reported by the Civilian Population of the United States: March, 1957," *Current Population Reports*, Feb. 2, 1958, Series P-20, No. 79, table 2.

[34] Max Weber, *From Max Weber: Esssays in Sociology*, translated by H. H. Gerth and C. Wright Mills (Fair Lawn, N.J.: Oxford University Press, 1946), pp. 193–194.

Today, however, attacks on inequality increasingly reflect a rejection of *ascribed* forms of power and privilege, but an acceptance of *achieved* forms. As Michael Young has observed, much of the enthusiasm which was once directed toward the creation of a socialist order in Britain now seems diverted toward the creation of a meritocracy.[35] According to the newer logic, the inheritance of power and privilege are wrong but their achievement is not, especially if based on educational achievement. Young's chief concern was with the emergence of this modified ideology in Britain, but it is evident in most other advanced industrial nations, including both the Soviet Union and the United States.[36]

Though there has apparently been a general reduction in the degree of inequality associated with status group stratification, there has not always been a corresponding decline in the salience of this form of stratification in the minds of citizens. On the contrary, the very struggle to reduce this form of inequality has often had the effect of increasing men's awareness of it. This is clearly evident in the racial struggle in the United States, where the decline in racial inequality has been paralleled by a heightened sense of racial identity. A similar situation may also prevail with respect to conflicts between religious and ethnic groups, as in the case of Canada. Despite a reduction in the degree of inequality between French Catholics and "English" Protestants, Canadians are currently exercised about this problem as they have not been for years. Feelings have grown so intense that more than an eighth of all French Canadians, and more than a quarter of their college graduates, say they favor the dissolution of the Canadian nation.[37] A small minority has emerged which is even willing to resort to terror and violence. Such evidence makes it clear that there is no necessary connection between the trend in the degree of status group inequality and the trend in the salience of status group stratification in the minds of men.

The Class System Based on Sex

Another much neglected aspect of the distributive systems of modern societies is the class system based on sex. This neglect has been due in large measure to the tendency of sociologists to treat families, rather than individuals, as the basic unit in systems of stratification.

This mode of analysis works reasonably well in agrarian societies where the power, privilege, and prestige of almost every woman was

---

[35] *Op. cit.*

[36] In the Soviet Union it takes the form of an increasing reluctance to press toward the historic goal of communism.

[37] *Maclean's*, 76 (Nov. 2, 1963), p. 14.

determined by the status of the man on whom she was dependent and her relation to him. With industrialization, the situation of women has changed rapidly, and it is no longer feasible to view them as merely dependents of some male. With industrialization the number of opportunities outside the traditional dependent roles of wife, daughter, or dependent kinswoman have been greatly increased. In short, the traditional barriers which long separated the female system of stratification from the male, and kept the former dependent on the latter, are clearly crumbling. Hence, in analyses of advanced industrial societies it is impossible to ignore, or treat as obvious, the role of sex in the distributive process.

One of the most dramatic indicators of the change which has occurred is found in the area of politics, long the private domain of men. As recently as 1900 women were permitted to vote only in New Zealand and four states in this country.[38] Today they enjoy this right in every advanced industrial nation except Switzerland. In addition, women may seek election or appointment to public office and they have often been successful, even winning, on occasion, cabinet posts and other high governmental offices. Women have also won the right to attend nearly all of the leading institutions of higher education. Virtually all occupations are now open to them, and they enjoy complete equality with respect to the rights of property. Finally, they have won more than equality in the area of divorce legislation.

Nevertheless, despite these many important victories, women still do not enjoy complete equality, and being male remains a resource of considerable value. Nowhere is this more evident than in the job market. Although women are now legally entitled to enter almost any field,[39] a variety of obstacles block their entry into the more rewarding ones. Thus, in 1960 women constituted only 6.7 per cent of the doctors, 3.5 per cent of the lawyers, and 0.9 per cent of the engineers in the United States.[40] In the Soviet Union women are somewhat better off in this respect, constituting nearly a third of the engineers and jurists and three-quarters of the doctors.[41] However, even there the evidence indicates that women are disproportionately concentrated on the margins of the professions and in the lower echelons. A similar pattern exists in the United States, where relatively few women are found in the upper brackets. In 1959, for ex-

---

[38] William J. Goode, *World Revolution and Family Patterns* (New York: Free Press, 1963), p. 55.

[39] According to Mikhail Zoshchenko, the Soviet satirist, they have even become managers of men's bathhouses, one of the last outposts of male supremacy.

[40] *U.S. Census of Population, 1960: Occupational Characteristics,* table 1.

[41] DeWitt, table VI-45. It should be noted that medicine is not so lucrative and prestigeful in the Soviet Union as in the United States.

ample, women constituted only 3 per cent of those with incomes of $10,000 or more, and only 6 per cent of those with incomes of $7,000 or more.[42] Were it not for the fact that women constitute about a third of the holders of large estates, these figures would be even smaller.[43] One should add that women have been even more conspicuous by their absence from the inner circles of the political elite.

There has been much speculation as to the reasons both for the improvement in the status of women in modern times and for their failure to attain full equality. With respect to the first, William Goode has argued that "the crucial crystallizing variable" responsible was the rise of the democratic-egalitarian ideology.[44] In his opinion, the demand for equal rights was a logical extension of this ideology, and it succeeded because of the prior spread of this newer view. Goode is highly critical of the view that the rise of a machine technology and the resulting increase in specialization and decline in occupational skills had anything to do with the improved status of women.[45] He maintains that women have always been capable of mastering the same skills as men, and that such a view is naive.

Without denying the importance of the ideological factor, one may doubt that Goode has done justice to the technological. Few serious scholars would argue today that women were incapable of mastering the necessary skills. They would argue, however, that the limited technological development of agrarian societies made it impossible for any significant number of women to be free to master such skills. To begin with, the high mortality rates prevailing in those societies made it necessary for women to bear far more children than is now necessary, just to maintain the labor force. Furthermore, the absence of laborsaving machines in the home meant that most of their time was required for the performance of necessary household tasks (recognition of this was embodied in the traditional saying that "man must work from sun to sun, but woman's work is never done"). What little time remained was frequently consumed by demands for assistance from the men at times of peak labor, as during the harvest. Added to this was the fact that most specialized skills in agrarian societies were usually acquired through an extended apprenticeship which required the apprentice to live in the master's home—a system not particularly suited to the training of young girls. In short, the problem was not that women were biologically or intellectually incapable of acquiring the more complex skills of the preindustrial era, but rather that social con-

[42] Calculated from the *Statistical Abstract, 1962*, table 451.
[43] Robert Lampman, *The Share of Top Wealth-Holders in National Wealth: 1922–1956* (Princeton, N.J.: Princeton University Press, 1962), p. 96.
[44] Goode, pp. 56ff.
[45] *Ibid.*, pp. 55–56.

ditions in agrarian societies made it extremely difficult, and often impossible, for them to do so. Therefore it appears that the modern trend toward increased rights for women is the result of both ideological and technological forces.

With respect to the question of why modern women have failed to achieve full equality, a number of factors appear responsible. To begin with, women still must bear the children, and though the number they bear is substantially reduced, pregnancy, menopause, and menstruation still prove handicaps in the intense competition for the more rewarding jobs.[46] Furthermore, the traditional family system, which is far from dead, places the burden of primary responsibility on the wife; it is she who must prepare meals, care for house, clothing, and other belongings, and do the shopping, to say nothing of raising the children, entertaining, and participating in civic activities. Though the modern housewife has many mechanical aids, the demands are still heavy and, as many have noted, the level of performance expected of her seems to rise with the introduction of each new laborsaving device. Third, because women have not been as successful as men on the average in the job world, and because there are good reasons for expecting that this will continue to be true, those who control access to such key resources as graduate fellowships or admission to industrial training programs reject women candidates more often than their performance records and other qualifications would warrant.[47] Finally, because of all this, and because women know there is a much less risky and much more promising route to rewards, most stop striving for success in the world of economics and politics, and compete instead in the marriage market and the world of the family.[48]

Despite the fact that modern feminists are often critical of this choice, they cannot ridicule it. It offers almost as many opportunities for attaining rewards as competition in the man's world, and the probabilities of success are far, far greater.[49] By an advantageous marriage, a woman may obtain half interest in a very substantial income, entrée into exclusive circles, and leisure to do most of the things she wishes. Even a woman whose marriage is less successful by economic standards is usually provided with a measure of economic security and, after the child-rearing

---

[46] It is interesting to note that those men who are most seriously involved in competition in private industry are often reluctant to take extended vacations because of the opportunities they provide their competitors and the dangers such absences involve for them.

[47] Wolfle, pp. 232–233.

[48] Perhaps the clearest manifestation of this is the relative lack of commitment to work shown by women. For evidence of this, see, for example, Goode, pp. 63–66.

[49] As noted previously, in the job world few women reach the upper rungs: most are concentrated on the less rewarding levels.

years, considerable leisure. In addition, of course, marriage yields many rich psychic rewards denied those who do not marry. Judging from the relative lack of interest shown in careers which must be pursued at the expense of marriage, it appears that the attractions of marriage more than match those of careers, in the estimation of most women. Hence, while it is not unreasonable to expect some further reduction in the degree of inequality between the sexes in the world of work, it is unlikely that it will be eliminated or greatly reduced beyond the present level.

The Class System Based on Age

A third resource generally neglected in analyses of the distributive process is age. Perhaps the chief reason for this is that most people pass through the same cycle of years. In other words, age is not a differentiating resource *in the long run*. However, this overlooks the fact that most people are so concerned with their immediate situation that their actions are largely responses to current needs and problems rather than to future prospects. Therefore, age does have consequences for the distributive process which cannot be ignored, especially in modern industrial societies.

The key fact with respect to age stratification in all advanced industrial societies is the economic, political, and general organizational dominance of the older segments of the population. The major instruments of power are largely in their hands. For example, in 1953 the median age of members of the property elite was nearly fifty-four years and, for the very wealthy, or those with estates valued at $5 million or more, it was nearly sixty-nine.[50] A similar situation prevails in politics: the median age of United States Senators from 1947 to 1957 was fifty-six years.[51] Moreover, because of the system of seniority which governs the selection of committee chairmen and assignments to key posts, the median age of the more influential members of the Senate was even higher. A study of business leaders in 1952 revealed a median age of fifty-four; another, limited to the managerial elite, found it to be sixty-one years in 1950.[52] Finally, a study of American military leaders found that their average age was approximately 54.5 years in 1950.[53]

Much the same situation prevails in other advanced industrial na-

[50] Calculated from Lampman, tables 48–49.
[51] Calculated from Donald Matthews, *U.S. Senators and Their World* (Chapel Hill, N.C.: University of North Carolina Press, 1960), fig. 1.
[52] Warner and Abegglen, p. 30, and Newcomer, p. 112.
[53] Calculated from Morris Janowitz, *The Professional Soldier* (New York: Free Press, 1960), p. 63.

tions. The median age of persons elected to the House of Commons in 1959 was fifty-one years, which means that by the time the next election was called, in 1964, the median age of the members approached fifty-six years.[54] In Sweden in 1953, the average age of members of the Upper House was fifty-seven years, and in the Lower House, fifty-two.[55] As Michels recognized half a century ago, even radical and revolutionary organizations eventually come under the domination of older men. The Soviet Union is no exception to this rule. A decade ago, the political elite of the Soviet Union could already be described as "a distinctly middle-aged group." [56] Today, thanks to the absence of extensive purges in the intervening years, this group is virtually indistinguishable in terms of age from their counterparts in non-Communist nations.

With respect to income, a similar pattern is evident, though the dominance of the older generation is not quite so pronounced. In the United States in 1959, for example, the median age of men with incomes of $15,000 or more was 49.4 years.[57] A similar situation seems to prevail elsewhere.

In one respect, however, the younger generation enjoys an advantage over the older. During the current period of rapidly expanding educational opportunities, age and educational attainment are *inversely* correlated in the adult populations of all advanced industrial nations. This affords the younger generation a distinct advantage in societies where job opportunity is so often determined by formal educational attainments. Sooner or later, however, this advantage will disappear, because a pattern of this kind cannot continue indefinitely.

In many ways relations between the generations in advanced industrial nations resemble those in agrarian societies. In one very important respect, however, they differ: *in agrarian societies, young people were largely integrated into the adult world and separated from one another, while in advanced industrial societies, owing to the spread of public education, young people tend to be cut off from the more inclusive adult world and thrown into a narrower world made up almost exclusively of their age peers.* The results of this development will be examined in detail in pages 426 to 428.

[54] Calculated from D. E. Butler and Richard Rose, *The British General Election of 1959* (London: Macmillan, 1960), p. 125.
[55] Nils Andrén, *Modern Swedish Government* (Stockholm: Almqvist & Wiksell, 1961), p. 57.
[56] Raymond Bauer, Alex Inkeles, and Clyde Kluckhohn, *How the Soviet System Works* (Cambridge, Mass.: Harvard University Press, 1956), p. 158.
[57] Calculated from *U.S. Census of Population, 1960: Occupational Characteristics*, table 31.

Class and Status Consistency

Considering the diversity of resources which affect the distribution of rewards in modern industrial societies, the question inevitably arises as to how they are interrelated. This, in turn, gives rise to questions of how discrepancies in an individual's statuses affect his actions, and how his actions affect the society of which he is a part.

Concern with these problems is a very recent development. As noted earlier, the multidimensional view of stratification itself appeared only a generation ago in the work of Weber and Sorokin. As a result, only a beginning has yet been made in exploring these problems.

With respect to the first problem—the degree of relationship between dimensions—census data, as well as data from other sources, make it clear that the rank of individuals and families in one dimension is never a simple function of rank in another. Correlations between property holdings, political status, occupational status, educational status, status-group rank, age status, and sex status are never perfect, and usually are far from it.

One of the closest relationships is that between education and occupation, but studies in the United States have produced correlation coefficients no higher than .77, and in some instances as low as .30.[58] At the other extreme there are certain relationships where the correlation is almost .00. This is clearly the case in the relationship between age and sex, and also with respect to relations between the following pairs: sex status and property holdings; age and occupational status; and finally, both age and sex on the one hand and status group rank and educational status on the other. Other relationships tend to fall in the middle range.

In a few rare instances, the correlations between resources are actually negative. This is true with respect to age and sex because women now outlive men. More important, it is true of age and educational status, where the younger generation has more years of schooling than the older generation because of rising educational standards.

The low correlations between the various types of resources indicates that there are substantial numbers of persons who find themselves confronted with inconsistent statuses of every type. As indicated in Chapter

[58] The highest coefficient comes from Warner's study of "Jonesville." See W. L. Warner et al., *Social Class in America* (Chicago: Science Research, 1949), table 13, p. 172. Godfrey Hochbaum et al. report a correlation of .65 from Minneapolis, in "Socioeconomic Variables in a Large City," *American Journal of Sociology*, 61 (1955), p. 34. Robert Angell reports a figure of .39 for Detroit and .30 from Samuel Stouffer's national survey on communism and civil liberties, in "Preferences for Moral Norms in Three Problem Areas," *ibid.*, 67 (1962), pp. 651–652.

4, on grounds of deductive logic a good case can be made for the hypothesis that discrepancies between major status dimensions can be a source of stress, first of all for the individuals affected and, through them, for the society of which they are a part. As yet there is only a limited amount of systematic research on this subject, but, such as it is, it tends to support the hypothesis. For example, data gathered in two sample surveys of Greater Detroit in the early 1950s showed that persons with discrepant statuses were more likely to support the Democratic Party and take liberal positions on issues than persons of consistent status.[59] This was especially true in cases where racial-ethnic status was inconsistent with occupational status, and was most pronounced when the inconsistencies were substantial. To a lesser degree, the same pattern prevailed when there were inconsistencies between occupational and educational statuses. In a study based on a national sample, similar results were obtained. Persons with discrepant statuses (involving occupation, education, and income) were more favorably disposed to changes in the distribution of power within American society than those with consistent statuses.[60]

The number of persons affected in this way by status discrepancies does not appear to be large, at least compared with the total population. More important than numbers, however, may be the fact that discrepant status brings into the ranks of the discontented, persons with many badly needed skills and other resources. In other words, such persons are singularly well equipped to provide the leadership and other resources which uneducated members of the working and nonpropertied classes are unable to provide for themselves. As noted previously, status discrepancy and the reactions it produces may well be a major source of the revolutionary leadership which Marx and Engels predicted (without explaining) would come from the ranks of the more privileged classes.

On the basis of limited studies like those cited above, one would hesitate to say that this hypothesis is much more than interesting speculation. However, there is also a considerable body of unsystematic evidence to support it. The role of ethnic and racial minorities in radical movements has long been noted, and it has also been observed that even the success-

[59] For an earlier examination of one of these samples, using a not completely satisfactory methodology, see Gerhard Lenski, "Status Crystallization: A Non-vertical Dimension of Social Status," *American Sociological Review*, 19 (1954). For data on both samples using a better methodology, see Gerhard Lenski, "Comment," *Public Opinion Quarterly*, 28 (1964), especially tables 2 and 3. See also Werner S. Landecker, "Class Crystallization and Class Consciousness," *American Sociological Review*, 28 (1963), pp. 219–229, which analyzes the first of these samples from a different perspective but obtains essentially similar results.
[60] Irwin Goffman, "Status Consistency and Preference for Change in Power Distribution," *American Sociological Review*, 22 (1957), pp. 275–281.

ful members of these minorities are attracted to such movements; in fact, they often provide much of the leadership.[61]

Obviously not all forms of status discrepancy generate political discontent. For example, one finds little of it among wealthy women or young members of the managerial class. One of the tasks for both theory and research in coming years is to specify the conditions under which this type of reaction occurs, and those under which some alternative reaction or none at all, is more likely.

Vertical Mobility

In industrial societies, as in the others we have examined, there are always struggles for power and privilege. Sometimes they take the form of individual struggles, sometimes they involve entire classes. Since the latter often develop as a result of frustrations arising from the former, we shall examine the individual struggles first.

One important difference which emerges from any comparison of agrarian and industrial societies is *the decline in the importance of ascribed factors in the distributive process.* Ancient hereditary distinctions between nobles, freemen, and slaves have been all but eliminated.[62] The advantages and disadvantages associated with the ascribed, or largely ascribed, qualities of race, ethnicity, and religion have also declined in importance. Finally, the ascribed status of sex has become somewhat less important. At the same time these developments have been occurring, access to educational opportunities has greatly improved and education has become increasingly important as a resource in job competition. The result of all these developments has been an increase in the proportion of rewards available on some kind of competitive basis.

Another factor which has probably increased competition and stimulated mobility is *the changing nature of the economy.* The occupational structure of agrarian societies was not conducive to a high rate of vertical

[61] See, for example, Robert Michels on the role of the Jews in the Socialist movement in Europe, *Political Parties: A Sociological Study of Oligarchical Tendencies in Modern Democracy,* translated by Eden and Cedar Paul (New York: Dover, 1959, first published 1915), pp. 258–262, or S. M. Lipset on the role of ethnic minorities in Canada's Socialist Party, in *Agrarian Socialism* (Berkeley, Calif.: University of California Press, 1950), p. 191. See also Stanislaw Ossowski, *Class Structure in the Social Consciousness,* translated by Sheila Patterson (New York: Free Press, 1963), p. 53, on the role of impoverished members of the Polish nobility in the early revolutionary movements in that country.

[62] In Britain, one of the few countries where an hereditary class of nobles survives, their rights have been so reduced and the rights of commoners so enlarged that in recent years, for the first time in history, some individuals have found it advantageous to renounce their titles. They have done so chiefly in order to obtain the right to sit in the House of Commons, which has replaced the House of Lords as the locus of political power.

mobility. Too many members of society were obliged to work at the same subsistence level. The occupational structure itself thus limited the volume of upward mobility. Only a small fraction of the population could move upward in any given generation. In modern industrial societies, by contrast, the occupational structure is much more differentiated. There is no single occupation which compels the great majority of the labor force to live at or near the subsistence level. Instead, there are great variations in both income and authority. Hence, the potential for movement is much greater.

While precise comparisons of the rates of mobility in agrarian and industrial societies are not possible, data on a number of industrial societies have become available. These show, for example, that in recent years approximately 30 per cent of the sons of fathers in nonagricultural occupations have been either upwardly or downwardly mobile across the manual-nonmanual line. On a country by country basis, the figures are strikingly uniform, as the following list indicates: [63]

United States	34 %
Sweden	32 %
Great Britain	31 %
Denmark	30 %
Norway	30 %
France	29 %
West Germany	25 %
Japan	25 %
Italy	22 %

[63] The figures for Britain, Denmark, Norway, France, and Japan are calculated from data provided by S. M. Miller, pp. 69–75; the figure for the United States is from "Lifetime Occupational Mobility of Adult Males, March, 1962," U.S. Bureau of the Census, *Current Population Reports* (1964), Series P-23, No. 11, table 1; the figure on Sweden is from Gosta Carlsson, *Social Mobility and Class Structure* (Lund: Gleerup, 1958), p. 93; the figure for Italy is from Joseph Lopreato, "Social Mobility in Italy," *American Journal of Sociology*, 71 (1965), p. 313; the figure for West Germany is the mean of two studies, one reported by S. M. Miller, p. 80, the other by Karl Martin Bolte, *Sozialer Aufstieg und Abstieg* (Stuttgart: Enke, 1959), p. 223 (the figures for the individual studies were 26 and 24 per cent). The French figure is also the average of two studies, the original figures for which were 31 and 27 per cent. I have omitted from the text the results of studies based on less than national surveys, surveys employing questionable procedures, and surveys of nations which cannot be classified as advanced industrial. It may be reported here, however, that these studies yielded the following results: Puerto Rico, 34 per cent; Belgium (average of two local studies), 33 per cent; Australia (one local study), 31 per cent; India (one local study), 27 per cent; U.S.S.R. (survey of emigrees), 26 per cent; Brazil (one local community), 25 per cent; Hungary, 25 per cent; Finland (doubtful procedures), 20 per cent; and Italy (doubtful procedures), 18 per cent. All of these figures are based on calculations from data in S. M. Miller, pp. 66–79. The median for the less industrialized nations, i.e., all of the above except Belgium, Australia, and the Soviet Union, is 25 per cent, compared with 30 per cent for the more advanced industrial nations listed in the text above.

If one employs a three-fold scheme of classification for urban occupations combining the lower levels of white collar occupations with the skilled workers whom they increasingly resemble in income, higher and less uniform rates of vertical mobility become evident, as the following figures show: [64]

United States	55 %
Sweden	48 %
Great Britain	45 %
Denmark	40 %
Japan	36 %

Though we have no comparable figures for agrarian societies of the pre-industrial era, it seems unlikely that such levels of vertical mobility were achieved, except perhaps for short periods under exceptional circumstances, e.g., following a devastating plague or the conquest and subjugation of a foreign country.

Not only does the rate of vertical mobility seem higher in industrial societies, *the nature of the movement is different.* We noted that the dominant pattern of mobility in agrarian societies was *downward.* In industrial societies the volume of upward movement is so much greater that a balance is usually achieved, and, *in most cases, the amount of upward movement exceeds the downward.* This can be seen clearly in the studies of mobility cited above. If one subtracts the number of downwardly mobile from the upwardly mobile, and divides by the number of men in urban occupations who are sons of fathers in urban occupations, one obtains the following coefficients (using a simple manual-nonmanual classification of occupations): [65]

Sweden	+.16
United States	+.15
Japan	+.09
Norway	+.07
Italy	+.07
West Germany	+.02
France	+.02
Great Britain	−.001
Denmark	−.03

[64] The figures for the United States, Sweden, Britain, Denmark, and Japan are calculated from the same bodies of data indicated in footnote 63 above. Norway is omitted because the data reported fail to divide nonmanual occupations, France because of the failure to divide the manual. West Germany is omitted because the upper level of the nonmanual group is so small that it is almost as though there were only two levels, not three.

[65] The sources used here are the same as those reported in footnote 63 above.

In six of the eight cases, the volume of upward mobility across the manual-nonmanual line exceeded the volume of downward mobility, and in the other two cases the excess of downward mobility is slight. If one shifts to a three-level mode of classification, the pattern changes only slightly.[66]

Even these figures understate the case. Evidence from Sweden, England, Japan, and the United States clearly shows that during the course of men's careers there is a net upward shift from manual to nonmanual occupations.[67] This fact is important because of the tendency in almost all of these studies to compare sons in mid-career with fathers whose careers are more advanced. If proper allowance could be made for the influence of this biasing tendency, it is likely that all of the coefficients would become positive.

The elimination of the great excess of downward mobility, characteristic of the agrarian societies of the past, has been due chiefly to two factors, both of which have been noted previously. The first has led to an increase in the rate of upward mobility, the second to a decrease in downward. The first *is the radical transformation of the occupational structure of societies brought about by the technological and organizational advances associated with modern industrialization.* With the increasing use of machines, the need for unskilled and semiskilled labor has steadily declined, relatively to the need for more highly skilled and trained personnel (including professional and other nonmanual workers). The organizational revolution had a similar effect: as organizations have grown in size and complexity, the problems of coordination have rapidly multiplied, necessitating the progressive enlargement of clerical and managerial staffs. In short, industrialization has meant a larger proportion of highly rewarded and otherwise desirable jobs.

The second factor is *the introduction and diffusion of effective methods of contraception.* For the first time in history, acceptable and effective means of controlling family size are available to the great majority of

[66] The coefficients for the five countries for which this is possible are as follows: the United States, +.16; Sweden, +.15; Japan, +.11; Denmark, −.02; and Great Britain, −.05.

[67] On Sweden, see C. Arnold Anderson, "Lifetime Inter-occupation Mobility Patterns in Sweden," *Acta Sociologica*, 1 (1960), tables 1-A and 2-A, which show a greater movement from the categories "industrial labor" and "general labor" to "urban enterprisers" and "functionaries" than in the reverse direction. On England, Japan, and the United States, see S. M. Lipset and Reinhard Bendix, *Social Mobility in Industrial Society* (Berkeley, Calif.: University of California Press, 1959), table A.1. Since the figures shown in this table are based on comparisons between present job and first job, and since first job may sometimes be only temporary, these figures probably exaggerate the magnitude of the trend. For a more realistic estimate of the magnitude of the shifts, see appendix table 1 of A. J. Jaffe and R. O. Carleton, *Occupational Mobility in the United States 1930–1960* (New York: King's Crown, 1954), which traces age cohorts through three censuses.

people. No longer are children produced in numbers so far in excess of the capacity of the economy to support them that the large-scale downward mobility characteristic of agrarian societies is inevitable. Now the production of offspring is more nearly geared to the opportunities afforded by the economy.

A third factor which may also have contributed to the redress in the balance between upward and downward mobility is *the rise of the mass media*. Movies, radio, television, magazines and newspapers, as noted earlier, have all helped the lower classes become better informed about the way of life of the more privileged classes. While the mass media often romanticize or otherwise distort what they describe, they transmit many elements quite accurately. The effect has been a considerable reduction in the cultural gulf which historically divided the classes and made upward mobility more difficult.

Industrial societies also differ from agrarian in *the means by which mobility is achieved*. As noted previously, in agrarian societies there were a number of channels through which men might move in their efforts to rise; no single institution played a dominant role in screening candidates for advancement. In industrial societies, as we have seen, every individual is exposed to an extended process of testing and screening by educational institutions, and this is apparently becoming a major determinant of subsequent life chances. Recent data from the United States indicate that slightly more occupational mobility occurs as a result of a man's performance in school than occurs because of his performance on the job. When the first full-time jobs of a large national sample of men aged twenty-five to sixty-four were compared with those of their fathers, it was found that 34 per cent had moved across the manual-nonmanual line. In comparison, when the current jobs of these same men were compared with their first jobs, only 28 per cent had been mobile in this way.[68] Similar differences were found when the occupational hierarchy was divided into three and four levels.[69]

As a result of the growing number of studies of vertical mobility, it is now possible to compare rates of mobility, both within nations over a period of time, and between nations at roughly the same time. Of the two,

[68] These figures are based on data presented in tables 2 and 3 in "Lifetime Occupational Mobility of Adult Males, March, 1962," *Current Population Report*, Series P-23, No 11.

[69] With three levels the figures were 55 and 51 per cent respectively; with four levels, 60 and 55 per cent. The three levels were constituted as follows: (1) professionals, managers, and entrepreneurs, (2) clerks, salesmen, craftsmen, and foremen, (3) operatives, service workers, and laborers except farm and mine. The four levels were constituted in the same way except that the second level was divided with clerks and salesmen constituting one level and craftsmen and foremen another.

the former has received far less attention, probably because of the difficulties involved in obtaining reliable data for earlier periods. Thus far, most of the trend data are from the United States. The studies from which these data come vary considerably in scope, methodology, and types of materials used. Nevertheless, *all show a striking stability in overall rates of mobility together with, in most cases, a gradual rise in the rate of upward mobility.*[70]

In the case of international comparisons, a certain uniformity is also evident. In fact, on the basis of their pioneering study of this subject, Lipset and Bendix concluded that "our major finding . . . is that the countries involved are comparable in their high amounts of total vertical mobility." [71] More recently S. M. Miller has criticized them for exaggerating the degree of similarity in mobility rates and patterns; but even he conceded that "there probably is more convergence in rates than most people had believed," adding that this "does not mean that the actual convergence is overwhelming." [72] Miller's main concern was to establish the fact that there are differences of a magnitude deserving attention. On this point one cannot argue with him, especially since the publication in

---

[70] It is impossible to review all the evidence behind this statement, and a few examples will have to suffice. Warner and Abegglen's follow-up of Taussig and Joslyn's earlier study of the social origins of America's business leaders shows that the sons of farmers and workingmen had 28 per cent as much chance as the average American male of being a business leader in 1928, and 32 per cent as much chance in 1952 (these figures are calculated from data supplied by Warner and Abegglen in table 7, p. 46). A study of mobility in Indianapolis showed that the percentage of farmers' and workingmen's sons entering the professional, managerial, and entrepreneurial classes increased from 8 to 10 per cent in the period from 1910 to 1940. See Natalie Rogoff, *Recent Trends in Occupational Mobility* (New York: Free Press, 1953); the figures are calculated from tables 54–59. A study of a national sample interviewed in 1952 indicated an increase in the percentage of sons of farmers and workingmen entering nonmanual occupations from 17.4 per cent among men born from 1873 to 1892 to 22.9 per cent for those born from 1923 to 1932. See Gerhard Lenski, "Trends in Inter-Generational Mobility in the United States," *American Sociological Review*, 23 (1958), table 7. More recently Jackson and Crockett compared the results of several national samples interviewed in the period from 1947 to 1957 and concluded that "no striking changes have occurred in mobility patterns and rates since World War II." A careful inspection of table 4 of their article indicates that if the proportion of nonmanual workers interviewed in the 1947 and 1957 studies had been the same, there would have been a very slight increase in the percentage of farmers' and workingmen's sons entering the ranks of nonmanual workers. See Elton Jackson and Harry Crockett, "Occupational Mobility in the United States: A Point Estimate and Trend Comparison," *ibid.*, 29 (1964), pp. 5–15. Finally, in a recent study of the social origins of Japanese business leaders from 1880 to 1960, the authors concluded that "the overall impression is one of singular stability in the proportions of leadership contributed from these several backgrounds, despite the great changes taking place in the occupational structure of the society and in the national economy and polity" (Abegglen and Mannari, p. 38). This study also shows a slight increase in the percentage of business leaders coming from humble backgrounds.

[71] *Op. cit.*, p. 27.

[72] *Op. cit.*, p. 58.

1964 of the Census Bureau's study of vertical mobility in the United States, which showed higher, and more deviant, rates than indicated by earlier, less reliable studies.[73]

Few attempts have been made thus far to account for these variations. Sometimes they are viewed as reflections of variations in the degree of industrialization and, therefore, the result of the same forces responsible for the differences between agrarian and industrial societies. (This thesis is consistent with the evidence cited earlier showing that the United States had the highest rate of mobility and Japan the lowest in the sample of industrial nations.) Closely related to this, variations are often attributed to changes in the occupational structure and the increasing proportion of more desirable occupations.[74] Since this is a direct consequence of industrialization, it, too, is linked with the historic shift from agrarian to industrial patterns of organization.

Other factors are probably also involved, but surprisingly little has been done to discover what they are. One would suppose, for example, that rates of mobility are influenced by the presence of status groups, and by their relative strength and importance. Where they are present, and especially where they exercise a powerful influence on educational and occupational opportunity, one would predict lowered rates of mobility. To take another example, it seems likely that private property would be a stabilizing force in societies because it tends to reduce intergenerational occupational mobility. If this is true, one would predict that, other things being equal, the rate of mobility would be greater in Communist than in non-Communist nations. Finally, if ability is not transmitted genetically with any great consistency, then it would seem that the rate of mobility would vary with the degree to which societies provide their youth with equality of educational opportunity. Unfortunately, however, as one begins to develop hypotheses of this type, the practical problems of testing quickly become evident. Given the limited number of cases, i.e., societies, together with the large number of relevant variables and the variety of techniques of measurement employed in the different national surveys, rigorous testing appears to be out of the question—at least for the present.

Before concluding this discussion, some comment is in order with respect to the almost totally neglected subject of *vertical mobility among women.* Most writers on mobility apparently assume either that this is unimportant, or that the topic is adequately covered by their discussions of male mobility. Clearly neither is the case.

[73] See footnote 63 above.
[74] See, for example, Jackson and Crockett, pp. 13–15, or Lenski, "Trends," p. 522.

For the great majority of women, the role of wife and mother is the major source of rewards in adult years. Unlike male occupational roles, however, this role is highly diversified, yielding rewards which vary almost as greatly as the total spectrum of male roles. This is only natural since the rewards accruing to a housewife are determined largely by her husband's role. Hence, for purposes of analysis in the field of stratification, it would be far more realistic if there were an explicit distinction between the role of *housewife married to a banker,* for example, and *housewife married to an unskilled worker.*

From the standpoint of the great majority of women who choose marriage rather than a career, the best opportunity for upward mobility occurs during the period of courtship. In the marriage market, the resources which are most relevant for women are quite different from those which are most relevant in the markets where men compete. Whereas educational success and the factors which contribute to it are crucial in the job market, they are not nearly so important for women in the marriage market. Physical appearance, on the other hand, is of considerable importance, though education, family background, interpersonal skills, and similar factors also play a role. Since physical appearance is, to a considerable degree, genetically determined (though in an era of cosmetics, foundation garments, and even cosmetic surgery this should not be exaggerated), it would seem that its relative importance introduces a certain randomizing element into the picture, thereby stimulating vertical mobility. At the present time, the evidence is too limited to say for certain whether mobility opportunities for women are greater or less than for men. However, such evidence as there is suggests the somewhat startling conclusion that they are, in fact, *somewhat greater.*[75]

Class Struggles

When opportunities for individual mobility are insufficient, men often resort to collective action as a means of obtaining the rewards they seek, thus generating class struggles. These are much more common in industrial societies than in agrarian, and probably for the reason that Marx suggested more than a century ago: these new societies provide *unparal-*

---

[75] For a summary of much of the relevant data, see Lipset and Bendix, pp. 42–46. Data from the Detroit Area Study of 1958 revealed that 30 per cent of the males, and 34 per cent of the married females, were mobile across the nonmanual versus manual and farm line on an intergenerational basis (with the status of married females being based on their fathers' and husbands' occupational status). When the children of farmers were excluded, the figures rose to 31 and 37 per cent respectively. In both instances the differential was greater with respect to upward mobility than downward. For details on the sample, see Lenski, *Factor,* pp. 12–16.

leled opportunities for communication among the less powerful and less privileged segments of society.

In classical Marxian theory, class struggles always referred to struggles which either were violent or would become violent. On the basis of the historical record, Marx saw almost no alternative. While such a view has considerable justification when based on a study of preindustrial societies, it has little justification when applied to the more advanced indus-industrial societies, it is not the only one. Class conflicts involve occupa-societies introduces the possibility of nonviolent, institutionalized struggles employing legitimate political means.

A second departure from classical Marxian theory becomes necessary because of Marx's obsessive concern with the single resource of property. While it is true that property is a major source of class conflict in most industrial societies, it is not the only one. Class conflicts involve occupational classes, political classes, racial, ethnic, religious, and even sex and age classes. Furthermore, as we shall see, class conflicts flourish even in "classless" societies, i.e., societies in which the private ownership· of the means of production has been eliminated, such as the Soviet Union. It is also important to note that these several forms of class conflict are often hopelessly entangled one with another.[76] When this happens, it frequently becomes difficult to determine which of the class systems is contributing what to the conflict.

Third, and finally, departure from Marxian theory is necessitated because class struggles are not nearly so pervasive a phenomenon in advanced industrial societies as Marxist theory would lead one to expect. Many persons respond to social inequality with an attitude of apathy and indifference. Others respond by emulating those above them, by individual striving, or by simple cooperation. To complicate matters further, all these patterns of response can be found in members of the same class, and often in the same individual. This is true not only in societies just making the transition from feudalism to capitalism, where Marx anticipated it, but even in the most advanced capitalist nations. In short, although the Marxian concept of class struggle continues to be a useful tool in stratification theory, its usefulness is greatly enhanced when one breaks with the narrow and unrealistic meaning given it in classical Marxian theory.

In modern industrial societies, class struggles involving *private property* are among the most important both because of the size of the stakes

[76] In Ralf Dahrendorf's terms one may speak of "superimposition." See *Class and Class Conflict in Industrial Society* (Stanford, Calif.: Stanford University Press, 1959), pp. 213–218.

involved and because of the frequency with which they serve as the focal point of political conflict. Struggles over the rights of property take various forms. Sometimes they take the form of illegal activities, chiefly crimes against property. While such actions are annoying to members of the propertied class, they pose a far less serious threat than certain of the legal alternatives. Two of these deserve particular attention, since both have resulted in definite gains for the nonpropertied class. These are (1) the struggles between labor and management and (2) the struggles between left- and right-wing political parties.

Though these two forms of class struggles are sometimes viewed as merely two aspects of the same thing, they are not. In the former instance the rights of property are challenged by the claims of *labor,* and more especially some specific segment of *organized labor;* in the latter instance they are challenged primarily by the claims of *citizenship.* While the groups which stand to benefit often include the same individuals, this is not invariably the case. It does not apply, for example, to *the unemployed,* nor frequently to *the unorganized,* i.e., workers who are not union members. When a particular union wins a pay raise or other new rights from an employer, only its own members benefit, at least directly. By contrast, gains won by liberal and socialist parties in the political arena usually have the effect of increasing the value of citizenship, a resource shared by the organized and unorganized, by the employed and unemployed, in fact, by all members of society.

This peculiar resource and its effects on the distributive process will be examined more closely in pages 428 to 430 of this chapter. Suffice it to say here that modern efforts to enhance its value represent one of the important consequences of the rise and spread of the democratic-egalitarian ideology.

Because of their identification with this ideology, liberal and socialist parties have been able to attract considerable support which they could not otherwise have won. Many individuals whose economic interests would normally lead them to support conservative parties have been won over by ideological appeals. This has been especially true of intellectuals, who are, by virtue of their vocation, vulnerable to such appeals. To a lesser degree, it has been true of persons who come under their influence in colleges and universities.

This has been a very important development for several reasons. To begin with, these ideological converts have often supplied much of the leadership for liberal and socialist parties. They are equipped with many of the skills essential for the complex maneuvering required by modern democratic politics—skills largely lacking or imperfectly developed in most members of the working class. Without these converts, it is possible that left-wing parties would never have achieved any victories of note; and without such victories, it is possible that the majority of workers and other members of the nonpropertied class would have turned from peaceful, legal channels of action to violent, revolutionary ones.

This development is also important because the presence of these ideological converts in positions of leadership has probably led to some alteration in the goals of liberal and socialist parties. While ideological considerations proved stronger than economic class interests for these converts, it does not follow that self-interest has been completely extinguished in them. On the contrary, in most cases it has remained alive, with the result that left-wing parties have sometimes pursued goals which were not especially advantageous to the working and nonpropertied classes. For example, the policies of these parties have sometimes been subtly, though probably unintentionally, altered to promote the rise of meritocracy rather than socialism. Though both systems support the principle of equality of opportunity, the former is not especially favorable to most of the other forms of equality endorsed by the latter.

Though the new democratic-egalitarian ideology has won many converts to liberal and socialist parties, the older, capitalist ideology remains powerful and attracts many to conservative parties. In every nation where free elections are held, large numbers of working men support conservative or middle-of-the-road parties. In Britain, for example, public opinion polls show that the Conservative Party enjoys the support of a quarter to a third of the members of the working class.[77] In the United States the Republican Party is supported by a third to a half of the working class, at least in Presidential elections.[78] In West Germany in 1955 the working class was divided into three groups of almost equal size: (1) those supporting the Socialist, (2) those supporting center and right-wing parties, and (3) those without any party preference.[78a] In the French election in 1951, 30 per cent of the working class voted for center or right-wing parties and 20 per cent failed to vote.[78b]

Further evidence of the influence of capitalist ideology is found in studies of workers' views of management, private property, and similar matters. For example, in a study of workers in Norway, a country with a

---

[77] Robert Alford, *Party and Society: The Anglo-American Democracies* (Chicago: Rand McNally, 1963), table B-1.

[78] *Ibid.*, table B-3.

[78a] Calculated on the basis of Morris Janowitz, "Social Stratification and Mobility in West Germany," in *American Journal of Sociology*, 64 (1958), table 16, p. 22.

[78b] *Sondages*, Etude des électeurs des différents partis d'après l'enquête sur les attitudes politiques des Français. Institut français d'opinion publique, 1952, No. 3.

highly popular Socialist government, the question was asked "Do you think workers and top management have common or opposing interests?" No less than 44 per cent responded by saying that they had common interests, and an additional 29 per cent expressed the belief that the two groups held some interests in common and some opposed; only 27 per cent said the interests were opposed.[79] Similar results have been obtained in studies in the United States. For example, in a study of class relations in Paterson, New Jersey, a community noted for poor labor-management relations, a sample of production workers was asked "How do classes get along? In general, are they like enemies, or like equal partners, or like leaders and followers?" Nearly half saw the relationship as paternalistic or cooperative, and only a third saw it as involving enmity (the other fifth had no opinion or gave vague responses).[80] Finally, one might cite Purcell's study of packinghouse workers in three cities, which showed that the great majority were favorable both to their union and their company.[81] This was true even of union leaders. Although undoubtedly there are companies and communities where unfavorable attitudes predominate, on the national level large numbers of workers apparently accept much of the traditional capitalist ideology.

The reasons for this are not hard to find. The schools and mass media are dominated by the propertied, entrepreneurial, and managerial classes, and while they permit a certain amount of criticism to be reported there, in the main these institutions are supportive of the system. Beyond this, however, these classes have proven willing to negotiate and make concessions, so that the conditions of life for the great majority of citizens have definitely improved. Finally, through the skillful manipulation of race, ethnicity, and religion, the propertied and managerial classes have often managed to divide the opposition and bind a portion of the working class to themselves by virtue of common status group ties. A classic example of this has been the use of race in parts of the United States, especially the South. By giving preference to white workers in hiring and promoting, thus protecting them against competition from Negro workers, managers and owners have created a major cleavage between the races within the working and nonpropertied classes, and have made effective cooperation

[79] J. A. Lauwerys, *Scandinavian Democracy* (Copenhagen: Danish Institute et al., 1958), p. 239. These figures are based on a study conducted by the Institute for Social Research in Oslo in thirty-four plants representing a sixth of that city's industrial workers employed in plants with joint consultation committees.

[80] Jerome Manis and Bernard Meltzer, "Attitudes of Textile Workers to Class Structure," *American Journal of Sociology*, 60 (1954), p. 33.

[81] Theodore Purcell, *Blue Collar Man: Patterns of Dual Allegiance in Industry* (Cambridge, Mass.: Harvard University Press, 1960), especially table 38. See also his review of other studies showing similar results, pp. 248–252.

between them virtually impossible. In fairness, however, it must be added that this cleavage could have been created only with the aid and cooperation of the white workers themselves.

Unlike the struggles of the peasants in agrarian societies, those of the working class have yielded many substantial benefits. Some rights have been won at the bargaining table, others in the political arena. As a result, the standard of living for workers has risen to the point where the vast majority live well above the subsistence level. This is especially evident when one takes into account the many benefits now derived by virtue of citizenship. The net effect of these developments has been to reduce to a minimum support for violent revolutionary action. A good illustration of this is the inability of the Communist Party to obtain any substantial following except in France and Italy. Even in those countries, the majority of those who support the Party in elections apparently have little enthusiasm for violent revolutionary action; if they did, their great numbers would insure the success of any reasonably well organized effort.

In the Soviet Union and other Communist countries where the institution of private property has largely been abolished and where political democracy is forbidden, class conflicts along economic lines are not nearly so open and active. However, it would be a mistake to suppose that the Communist system has eliminated economic class antagonisms; at best, it has only suppressed them. One indication of this can be found in the interviews conducted by Harvard University's Russian Research Center among Russian refugees at the end of World War II. While there is good reason to believe that these people differed in a number of ways from those who stayed behind, available evidence indicates that these differences were not extreme.[82] For example, almost 60 per cent of the refugees reported leaving the Soviet Union involuntarily, and the percentage of Communist Party members was twice as high in the sample as in the nation, despite the fact that admission of membership could have prevented immigration to the United States.[83] Furthermore, the refugees included individuals from all classes and groups within the population.

Some of the most interesting findings of this study emerged from responses to the following question: "Below is given a paired list of classes in Soviet society. We would like to know for each of these pairs . . . do their interests coincide with or contradict each other? Check the condition you think correct for each group." When the results were tabulated, it became clear that many respondents from all class levels saw the interests

[82] For a thorough discussion of the nature of this sample and this problem, see Inkeles and Bauer, pp. 7–10 and 25–40.
[83] *Ibid.*, pp. 31–32.

of workers and peasants as opposed to those of the intelligentsia, i.e., the professional and managerial classes, and other white-collar employees. For example, while 80 per cent of the peasants felt that their interests and those of workers coincided, only 44 per cent felt that their interests coincided with those of the intelligentsia, and only 48 per cent with those of white-collar employees. In the case of manual workers, the figures were 88, 56, and 67 per cent respectively. In the case of the intelligentsia, 89 per cent saw their interests as coinciding with those of white-collar employees, but only 69 per cent thought this true in the case of peasants, and only 72 per cent in the case of workers.[84] Similar results emerged from a series of questions in which the refugees were asked to indicate the relative harmfulness of the different classes. In a summary measure constructed from all of their answers, the intelligentsia emerged as the most harmful class in Soviet society in the opinion of workers and peasants, while the working class emerged as the most harmful in the opinion of the intelligentsia and white-collar employees.[85] While the peculiar nature of the sample makes comparisons difficult, these data indicate that economic class antagonisms are probably as strong in the Soviet Union as in non-Communist countries, despite vigorous governmental efforts to suppress them, and despite the elimination of the system of private property. Apparently these antagonism are destined to survive as long as the present occupational class system survives.

In all of the more advanced industrial nations, the key resources of property, occupation, education, and membership in the political class tend to be held by the same persons. As a result, it is often difficult, if not impossible, to disentangle one form of class struggle from the others. In the Soviet Union, for example, Party membership tends to be held by those who also have a university education and are members of the professional or managerial classes. In the United States and other non-Communist nations, membership in the professional and managerial classes is usually combined with higher education and membership in the propertied and political classes. To be sure, these relationships are far from perfect, and as suggested elsewhere, this leads to struggles among these privileged minorities, but these are of secondary importance compared to the more basic struggle between the "haves" and "have-nots."

Struggles between racial, ethnic, and religious status groups also tend to become entangled with the struggle between economic classes. As long as members of subordinate status groups are concentrated in the working and nonpropertied classes, it is difficult to determine to what extent their

[84] *Ibid.*, table 85.
[85] *Ibid.*, table 89.

struggles are economic class struggles and to what extent they are status-group struggles. However, once some of these people begin to rise in the occupational and property class systems the influence of status-group membership becomes more evident.

There is now a growing body of evidence which shows that the influence of status groups on voting behavior, one of the best indicators of class conflict, is not too much less than that of occupational class. One of the most valuable studies of this was Alford's recent one on voting behavior in four of the five English-speaking democracies. He shows the results of a series of national surveys of voter preference, cross-tabulated by occupational class and religion. The essence of his findings is summarized in Table 1. To facilitate analysis, both religion and class are divided into two categories: religion into Catholics and Protestants, class into manual and nonmanual occupations.

Table 1 Mean Difference in Party Preference by Occupational Class with Religion Held Constant, Mean Difference in Party Preference by Religion with Occupational Class Held Constant, and Percentage of Population Catholic, by Nation for Four English-speaking Democracies

NATION	MEAN DIFFERENCE BY CLASS WITH RELIGION HELD CONSTANT	MEAN DIFFERENCE BY RELIGION WITH CLASS HELD CONSTANT	PERCENTAGE OF POPULATION CATHOLIC	NO. OF SURVEYS
Britain	37	6	Under 10	3
Australia	33	16	20–25	7
United States	18	21	25	7
Canada	4	20	40	9
Mean of means	$\overline{23}$	$\overline{16}$		

Source: Calculated from Robert Alford, *Party and Society: The Anglo-American Democracies* (Chicago: Rand McNally, 1963), tables 6–3, 7–4, 8–4, and 9–5.

As this table makes clear, the pattern is quite variable in the four countries, with Britain and Canada representing the two extremes. In Britain, occupational class is a major determinant of voting behavior, and religious status group a rather minor factor; in Canada, the pattern is reversed. In three of the four countries, however, the struggle between religious status groups is important enough to serve as a major determinant of voting behavior. This table also suggests that *the importance of conflicts between religious status groups varies directly with the numerical strength of the chief minority group.*

One might suppose that differences in voting behavior between Protestants and Catholics simply reflect some basic difference in political philosophy and ideals and that they are unrelated to the distributive process. While philosophical differences are undoubtedly a factor to some extent, the evidence indicates that *this is also a distributive problem involving status groups vying for power, privilege, and prestige.* Moreover, these goals are sought for their secular value, and not merely because they are useful in the attainment of theologically based ideals.

It seems more than coincidental, for example, that in countries where Catholics have traditionally been the dominant group, as in Italy and France, they tend to support conservative parties, whereas in countries where they have been a minority group, as in Britain and the United States, they support liberal parties. This apparently contradictory pattern makes sense only if one takes into account the vested interests of dominant groups in the maintenance of the *status quo*, and the opposed interests of minorities in altering the *status quo*. It is also interesting to note that a recent study of Detroit showed that the probability of Catholics voting for the Democratic Party was highly correlated with the degree of their involvement in the Catholic subcommunity, i.e., the degree to which their close friends and relatives were also Catholic, but not at all with the frequency of their attendance at Mass.[86] On the contrary, there was a slight *negative* correlation between attendance at Mass and support for the Democratic Party. Finally, in a national survey study of the 1960 Presidential election it was found that, among Catholics a shift from Eisenhower (in 1956) to Kennedy was much more closely correlated with the individual's involvement in the Catholic community than with his involvement in the Catholic Church, as measured by attendance at Mass.[87]

Much the same pattern can be found where other status groups are involved. The dominant group tends to support the conservative party or parties, while the minority groups tend to support parties advocating political change.[88] *Thus, what has sometimes been thought to be merely a struggle between economic classes proves, on closer inspection, to be a struggle between status groups as well.* In fact, as the experience of nations such as Canada and Holland indicate, the economic class struggle

[86] Lenski, *Factor*, pp. 174–175 and 181–184.

[87] Philip Converse, "Religion and Politics: the 1960 Elections," unpublished paper of the Survey Research Center of the University of Michigan, 1961, pp. 32–33, especially table 4a.

[88] This means that in non-Communist, democratic nations, minorities tend to support Liberal, Socialist, and even Communist Parties. In Communist countries, where the Communist Party becomes in many ways a conservative party supporting the political *status quo*, minority status groups like the Ukranians are more likely to be anti-Communist than the dominant ethnic group, the Great Russians.

can sometimes even be subordinated to the struggle between status groups.

Before concluding this discussion of status-group struggles, it should be emphasized that these, no less than economic class struggles, have a potential for revolutionary violence. This can be seen in the recurring pattern of race riots in this country, in the recent terrorist activities of certain French-Canadian groups, and in the recurring struggles of the Ukranians.

Not too long ago, *sex status* was the basis for a unique kind of class struggle in most of the more advanced industrial societies. Women campaigned vigorously for equal rights with men. As a result of these efforts, women now have virtually equal rights before the law. However, they have not achieved full equality in the worlds of work and of politics, but despite this, the majority of women do not seem greatly concerned. The explanation for this apparent paradox lies in the family system which, as noted previously, makes it possible for most women to attain their goals through marriage as easily as most men can attain theirs through work and political activity. It is significant that the most serious charge militant feminists now make is that the role of housewife is intellectually stultifying, but most women seem to realize that this same charge could, with equal validity, be directed against most male occupations.[89] This probably explains why the feminist movement has lost most of its vigor: *for the vast majority of women, the battle for equality has been won.*

Of all the class struggles in modern societies, the most underrated may prove to be those between *age classes,* especially those between youth (in the sense of adolescents and young adults) and adults. The importance of this struggle is so underestimated, in fact, that its existence is typically overlooked altogether in discussions of class struggles, or confused with economic class struggles. Nevertheless, there is considerable evidence to indicate that the struggle between age classes is a distinctive class struggle in its own right and, furthermore, is one of the more serious and least tractable.

The basis for this struggle lies in the fact that the younger generation is subject to the authority of the older, while the older generation enjoys the lion's share of rewards. To be sure, this situation has always prevailed in politically stable and highly institutionalized societies. In two respects, however, the situation has changed, and these newer developments have tended to stimulate intergenerational conflict. In the first place, industrialization has meant a sharp increase in educational requirements, as well as

---

[89] See Betty Friedan, *The Feminine Mystique* (New York: Norton, 1963), for an example of the modern version of militant feminism.

declining opportunities for profitable employment by adolescents and young adults.[90] As a result, the period of economic dependence on the older generation, and hence of subordination, has been substantially lengthened. No longer can boys of twelve or fourteen earn their own livelihood and thereby secure their independence if they desire it. In the second place, because of these same developments, and especially because of the growth of mass education, adolescents and young adults are thrown into a world made up almost exclusively of their age peers, a world which few adults penetrate in more than a marginal way. Thus, opportunities for contact and communication are maximized in a class whose members have a common grievance. In short, ideal conditions for class conflict, as identified by Marx, have been created.

To complete the picture, two other elements should be added. First, because of their youth, the class with grievances is physically at the peak of vigor and vitality and relatively unencumbered by social responsibilities. Second, because of their youth, they have few opportunities to obtain redress through normal political channels; the great majority are too young to vote, and those who can, find that the major political parties are firmly in the control of a generation not especially interested in their kinds of problems. The net result is that struggles between the generations occur and, moreover, are likely to take violent and even revolutionary forms.

It is no coincidence that young people play a prominent role in the radical and revolutionary movements *on both sides of the Iron Curtain.* In non-Communist countries, Communist leaders often pride themselves on their Party's appeal to youth, thinking this demonstrates that it is the Party of the future.[91] What they fail to appreciate is that in the countries where their Party rules, the younger generation is also in the forefront of the opposition. One need only remember the role youth played in the Hungarian revolution and the Polish uprisings of 1956, or the East German riots of 1953, to appreciate the extent of the hostility. Even in Russia the problem exists, and seems to be growing more serious. Young people in general, and students in particular, are playing a prominent role in the libertarian movement, which sprang up a decade ago when the extreme repression of the Stalinist era was relaxed.[92]

---

[90] In 1962 the unemployment rate among persons aged fourteen to nineteen was 12.5 per cent, but only 5.1 per cent among persons aged twenty-five to forty-four. Calculated from *Statistical Abstract, 1962,* tables 281 and 283.

[91] See, for example, Philip Williams, *Politics in Post-war France* (London: Longmans, 1954), pp. 52–53, on the Communist Party in France.

[92] For a good discussion of this movement by a recent Russian refugee student, see Burg, pp. 89–99.

In this struggle between the generations it is often difficult to recognize the elements of self-interest which motivate both sides, because both sides tend to wage their battles in the name of abstract principles. Thus the younger generation fights for "freedom" and in opposition to "bureaucracy," while the older generation fights for "law and order" and for "leadership by men of experience." Frequently the struggle between age classes becomes hopelessly entangled with the economic class struggle in non-Communist countries, or the political class struggle in Communist nations. Under these circumstances, the only readily visible indication of the role which the struggle between the age classes is playing is the uneven representation of the generations in the two camps. However, the struggle is no less real simply because it is often obscured by clouds of misleading rhetoric and ideology.

The struggle between the generations, unlike that between the sexes, is not likely to be resolved in the near future. While certain current developments may ease the situation, others will undoubtedly exacerbate it. On the favorable side there is the trend by governmental bodies and other agencies to view higher education as a form of employment deserving support. This is especially evident in Communist countries, where student subsidies are the rule, but even in non-Communist countries there are a growing number of governmental and private fellowships and stipends. This, combined with a trend toward earlier marriage, a notoriously domesticating experience, may speed the entry of youth into the ranks of the adult class. On the other hand, the prolongation of education increases the number of those who are something less than full-fledged adults, as well as the number concentrated in segregated educational communities. Finally, as a stable element in the situation one must note the continued presence and importance of large-scale, bureaucratized organizations which, by their very nature, favor the principle of promotion by seniority, a principle which inevitably creates tensions between the generations. Thus, looking to the future, one can expect changes in the nature of the class struggles between the generations, but in all probability, the continuation of the struggle itself.

Citizenship and the Revival of the Redistributive Process

Of all the consequences of class struggles in the modern era, one stands out above the rest because of its profound importance. This is the transformation of the nature of the resource of citizenship.

To many it may seem strange to classify citizenship in the same category with property, occupation, education, and the other resources dealt with earlier. However, it is precisely that.[93] In earlier times it was easier to recognize this aspect of citizenship because then it was the valued possession of the few. In agrarian societies, only members of the governing class were citizens in anything like the modern sense of the term, except in urban centers, where the resource was sometimes shared more widely. Today, however, virtually every member of industrial societies is a citizen and, as a result, enjoys a wide range of valuable benefits.

The rights afforded by citizenship vary somewhat from one nation to the next. However, in nearly all of the more advanced industrial nations, it entitles individuals to many years of free education, to the use of public roads and highways, public sanitary facilities and water supply, parks and other recreational facilities, to police and fire protection, and to certain forms of income when he is old, disabled, or unemployed. Also, by virtue of government regulation of private enterprise in non-Communist countries, citizenship protects individuals against economic exploitation by monopolies and oligopolies, with respect to the pricing of goods as well as the determination of wage rates. Finally, in a growing number of countries, citizenship also entitles individuals to a variety of medical services and, through state subsidies, to various kinds of cultural activities at prices below cost.

Probably the chief reason we have difficulty thinking of citizenship as a resource is because it tends to put men on an equal footing, while all the others tend to generate inequality. Though this fact makes citizenship a unique kind of resource, it makes it a resource nonetheless. As was true of all the other things we have treated as resources, citizenship facilitates the acquisition of rewards or benefits.

The changing character of citizenship in modern times—its extension to all segments of the population, and the addition of many new rights—has revived an ancient function of government which had largely disappeared in agrarian societies, namely, the redistributive function. By assigning increased rights to the role of citizen, a role shared by all, and by charging the costs of these rights disproportionately to those best able to pay, the state in an industrial society effects a transfer of rewards from those who have more to those who have less. At present, economists still disagree as to the magnitude of this transfer. A few even question whether any effective redistribution of income is, indeed, accomplished. The great majority, however, believe that the redistributive function *is* being performed, and on an ever-increasing scale, though certainly not on the drastic scale suggested by official tax rates and much of the polemical

[93] See T. H. Marshall, *Citizenship and Social Class* (London: Cambridge University Press, 1950), pp. 1–85.

literature on the subject. There is also general agreement that this function is performed in varying degrees in different nations, and that it is most pronounced in countries where the Swedish pattern of political control prevails. In view of the trend toward the Swedish pattern, however, there is good reason to believe that the importance of citizenship will increase in most industrial societies in the next several decades.

Prestige Stratification

In this volume, little attempt has been made to examine the third great reward men seek, namely, honor or prestige. This was partly because the analysis of power and privilege alone required a lengthy volume, and partly because it was assumed that prestige can be understood more readily as a function of power and privilege than the other way around. While not denying that there is a certain element of feedback, the major causal flow has been assumed to move from power and privilege to prestige.

However, since so much of what has been written on stratification in modern industrial societies, and especially in the United States, has been concerned with the distribution of prestige, some discussion of this third element in the classic triad is in order. At the very least, we should take cognizance of some of the evidence which is relevant to our assumption of the substantial dependence of prestige on power and privilege.

Prestige may be attached to any kind of social unit, individual, role, or group. For present purposes, we are chiefly concerned with studies of the prestige of individuals and roles. One of the most important landmarks in the study of the latter was North and Hatt's investigation of occupational prestige in the United States, conducted shortly after World War II.[94] This study provided a nationwide evaluation and ranking of ninety occupations. Recently these evaluations were subjected to further analysis by Dudley Duncan, who found a correlation of .91 between these evaluations and a combined measure of the educational attainments and income of each of forty-five occupations which could be matched with census designations.[95] In other words, *five-sixths of the variance in occupational prestige is accounted for, statistically, by a linear combination*

[94] National Opinion Research Center, "Jobs and Occupations: A Popular Evaluation," *Opinion News*, 9 (Sept. 1, 1947), pp. 3–13, reprinted in Bendix and Lipset, pp. 411–426.
[95] See O. D. Duncan, "A Socioeconomic Index for All Occupations," in Albert J. Reiss, *Occupation and Social Status* (New York: Free Press, 1961), p. 124.

of indicators of the income and educational levels of the occupations.
If in keeping with the theoretical framework of our analysis, education
is viewed as a resource, and hence a form of power, and if income is
viewed as a measure of both power and privilege, *this means that most
of the variance in the prestige of this sample of American occupations can
be viewed as a reflection of occupational power and privilege.*

A third study suggests that this relationship is not peculiarly American. Inkeles and Rossi have shown that the American pattern of occupational prestige is very similar to those of Britain, Japan, New Zealand, the
Soviet Union, and Germany.[96] In each instance a correlation of at least .90
was found; the average was .94. While the number of occupations compared was limited, and by necessity excluded those which were not comparable, e.g., no comparisons of Party secretary or entrepreneur were
possible in the case of the United States and the U.S.S.R., and while we
have no study like Duncan's to prove how closely occupational prestige
in those countries is correlated with income and education, those pieces of
the puzzle which are available to us fit the pattern, and unsystematic evidence strongly suggests that the pattern is essentially the same.

With respect to *individual* prestige, the evidence suggests much the
same conclusion: individual prestige, too, seems largely a function of
power and privilige. For example, in an oft-cited study of one Midwest-
ern town, it was found that the prestige of individuals and families of Old
American background, when judged by other members of the community, had a correlation of .93 with a combined measure of the occupation
of the family head and the amount of his income, and .92 with a combined
measure of occupation and education.[97] More recently, in a study of an
Eastern city, Hollingshead found a correlation of .91 between judgments
of class position on the one hand and educational and occupational rank
on the other.[98] Other examples along this same line could also be cited.
In short, *with respect to individual or family prestige, as with respect to
occupational prestige, the chief determinants are variables which are normally subsumed under the categories of power and privilege.* It follows,
therefore, that even though little attention has been given in this volume
to the phenomenon of prestige, we have examined the factors which
largely determine the distribution of prestige in modern industrial societies.

[96] Alex Inkeles and Peter Rossi, "National Comparisons of Occupational Prestige,"
American Journal of Sociology, 61 (1956), pp. 329–339.
[97] Warner et al., *Social Class*, table 14.
[98] A. B. Hollingshead and Frederick Redlich, *Social Class and Mental Illness: A
Community Study* (New York: Wiley, 1958), p. 394.

Future Trends

In our analysis of modern industrial societies we have concentrated on current patterns of organization and distribution, and have deliberately avoided speculation about patterns of the more distant future. However, one cannot help being fascinated by questions about the future. Clearly industrial societies have not yet reached a stable equilibrium. In fact, the rate of change seems to be accelerating. This means that we have every reason to expect that the most advanced societies a century or two hence will differ as much from the most advanced societies of today as the latter differ from the first industrial societies of a century and half ago. In other words, the industrial societies described in this volume may prove to be only transitional forms, not stable types comparable to the types of societies described in earlier chapters.

From the standpoint of predicting future trends in the distributive process, six developments, all of which have been noted before, are particularly important. First, the new methods of contraception which are now appearing promise to give mankind a degree of control over human fertility that far surpasses anything known in the past or even the present. Second, the growth in human numbers, especially in the less developed countries, but also in the most advanced, is creating a set of conditions which may well lead to the acceptance of fertility planning at the national level. Third, technological advance is making possible fantastic increases in the production of goods and services and a drastic reduction in the need for human labor. Fourth, technological advance is also making possible substantial advances in techniques of social control. Fifth, technological advance in transportation and communication is making possible the creation of a single world state which could replace the present multistate system. Finally, technological advance in the military area has already made possible the virtual destruction of humanity.

No one today can say with certainty how these potentialities will be utilized, or how they may combine and interact with one another to produce new patterns of social organization. However, one can identify several basic possibilities. First, there is clearly the possibility of the termination of human existence in an atomic holocaust, or possibly in a biochemical war. Second, there is the possibility that such a war might lead to a permanent regression to the agrarian level with no possibility of a restoration of industrial societies.[99] Third, there is the possibility that new tech-

[99] See Harrison Brown, *The Challenge of Man's Future* (New York: Viking Compass Books, 1956), pp. 222–225, for an excellent discussion of this possibility.

niques of social control will be monopolized by a small minority who will use them for their own benefit, perhaps along the lines envisioned by George Orwell in his book, *1984*. Fourth, there is the possibility that new techniques of production, employed in conjunction with a voluntary or involuntary program of fertility control, will create an era of abundance and relative equality for all, in a single world state (or perhaps in a series of militarily stalemated national states). Finally, there is the possibility that, despite all the technological innovations, men will choose to keep the social order more or less as it is. Which course of action men will adopt no one can predict, and, since they are so radically different, detailed speculation about their nature seems better left to the writers of science fiction—at least for the present.

13/Retrospect and Prospect

Now this is not the end.
It is not even the beginning of the end.
But it is, perhaps, the end of the beginning.
Winston Churchill

HAVING COMPLETED our survey and analysis of the distributive process in a series of highly variant societal types, it is time to assess the adequacy of the basic theory developed in Chapters 2 through 4 and summarized in Figure 2, Chapter 4. Does the evidence of ethnography, history, and sociology support this theory, or does it contradict it? If supportive, are changes or additions indicated? Finally, what further work is required? These are the primary concerns of this chapter.

One other question which invites our attention at this point concerns the relation of this theory to the older theoretical traditions. To what extent has our inquiry led us to adopt the positions of the functionalists, and to what extent the positions of the conflict theorists? And, one must add, to what extent has our invesigation led us to positions which diverge from both?

The General Theory Reexamined

In the light of the evidence presented in Chapters 5 through 12, one can give an essentially affirmative answer to the basic question of the validity of the general theory presented in the introductory chapters. The most basic characteristics of distributive systems do appear to be shaped by the interaction of those *constant elements* in the human situation which we identified earlier and the *variable element of technology*. As hypothesized, the influence of these factors appears to be mediated by a series of social organizational factors whose variation is greatly influenced by prior variations in technology. It was this systematic covariation, of course, which made possible the development of the societal typology, which proved so valuable.

The high degree of support for the theory was not completely unexpected because of the manner in which the theory was constructed. Despite some appearances to the contrary, the theory presented in the early chapters was not a simple exercise in deductive logic. Rather, it represented the end product of an already extensive process of both induction and deduction. In a sense, the theory was designed to fit the facts, or at least those facts with which I was familiar when I began writing this volume. However, the theory with which I began writing was not the same that I had taught ten years previously. On the contrary, over the course of that decade I constantly shifted and modified my theoretical position to try to get a better fit between theory and data. In the process I found myself shifting from what was basically a functionalist position to what I have called a synthetic or synthesizing position. In other words, I found an increasing need to incorporate hypotheses and postulates which had little or no part in the functionalist tradition, yet without wholly abandoning the latter.

In the light of the evidence set forth in Chapters 5 through 12, it appears that the general theory corresponds reasonably well with the evidence, but the correspondence is not perfect and certain modifications and changes are necessary. To begin with, our survey of advanced horticultural and agrarian societies indicates that the relationship between technology and political organization is not so simple as anticipated. In these societies one finds significant variations in level of political development associated with apparently limited variations in technology. This suggests that we must think of the level of technological advance either as a *necessary*, but not *sufficient*, cause of political advance, or as the generator of a "threshold effect," whereby a limited advance in technology causes (or makes possible) a major advance in political organization. Perhaps both apply. In any case, it is clear that at certain levels of technological development, a considerable degree of variation in political development becomes possible. This has significant consequences for the distributive process because the level of political development is clearly a major determinant of the character of distributive systems.

A second modification which is indicated is a distinction at the analytical level between the concepts "technology" and "economy." In retrospect, it appears that these two terms were often used interchangeably in the preceding chapters. In the majority of instances this caused no great difficulty because differences in economy, i.e., the economic organization of a society, usually parallel differences in technology, i.e., the cultural means by which a society relates to its environment. Thus, a hunting and gathering technology is accompanied by a hunting and gathering economy. Difficulties arise, however, in the case of societal types standing on comparable levels of technological development, as in the case of agrarian and maritime societies. Here, the same elements of technology appear to be available to both, but certain elements are emphasized in one and neglected in the other. The reasons for this reflect, in part at least, the influence of environmental factors, though other factors are probably also at work. Economic variations which occur independently of technological variations appear to have effects on distributive systems comparable to those produced by political variations. Hence, we might more accurately portray the links in the causal chain as follows: [1]

In addition, of course, there are elements of feedback operating, which further complicates relations.

In addition to demonstrating the importance of technology and social organization in the shaping of distributive systems, our findings also demonstrate the influence of other factors, including some which were not identified in Chapters 2 through 4. Two of these stand out because of their widespread importance: (1) *variations in ideology,* and (2) *variations in the personal attributes of political leaders.*

Ideology seems to have its greatest impact in the more advanced societies. Ideological variations of great magnitude and importance for distributive systems presuppose the existence of specialists in ideology, supported by appropriate religious and political institutions. These devel-

---

[1] The symbols X, Y, and Z are included as a reminder that our theory assumes that other factors exercise an influence at each point in the causal chain.

opments seem to have their beginnings in advanced horticultural societies, while coming to full flower only in industrial societies.[2]

The importance of ideology was seen most clearly in the somewhat unexpected halting, and possible reversal, of the trend toward increasing social inequality, so pronounced in the evolution from hunting and gathering to agrarian societies. In Chapter 4 (page 85), it was predicted that the degree of inequality in distributive systems would vary directly with the size of a society's surplus. This was qualified in tentative fashion to make allowance for the possibility that persons who lacked power individually might, through organization, develop a measure of countervailing power; and it was "predicted" (not without some awareness of the facts) that this would be most likely in democratic nations with an egalitarian or socialistic ideology. Though it was not possible to develop any quantitative measure of overall inequality, the evidence which we reviewed strongly suggests that the average level of inequality in the most advanced industrial societies is no greater than that in the average advanced agrarian society, and probably less. Graphically, the evolutionary pattern appears to resemble the pattern in Figure 1. (It should be emphasized that this figure is intended as nothing more than a very approximate graphic summary.)

The influence of variations in the personal attributes of political leaders also seems to have its greatest impact in the more advanced societies,

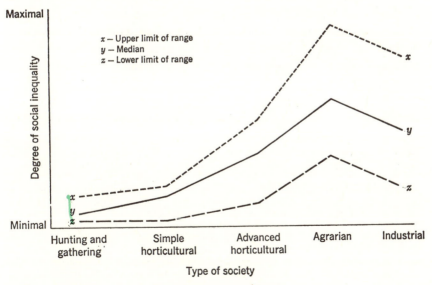

Figure 1   Degree of social inequality by type of society.

[2] One might add that they also flourish in industrializing hybrid societies.

especially when constitutionalism is at low ebb. As noted previously, personality differences do not cancel out when small numbers are involved, particularly in the case of a single individual, such as the ruler or leader of a nation. In modern industrial societies, political leaders have immense powers available to them, especially in periods of crisis and revolution. In periods of crisis, such as the great depression of the 1930s, the powers of leaders are increased through the voluntary delegation of power by others; in periods of revolution, as in Russia in 1917, the powers of leaders are increased through seizure. In either case, the ruler or leader (and often his immediate associates as well) have immense powers at their disposal. If the ruler is mad or fanatical, as in the case of Hitler and Stalin, the whole society is affected. Similarly, if he is unwell (as in the case of Wilson in his last years), indecisive, or uninformed, these attributes are likely to have serious consequences for the nation. The fact that others in the nation are healthy, decisive, or well informed will not normally cancel out the influence of such factors in the ruler or leader. Though there are obviously limits to the influence which the personal factor can exert, they are not so narrow as to make it trivial. Though the variable involved is essentially nonsociological in character, sociological theories must find a place for it.[3]

Once again it may be helpful to present in graphic form an outline of the basic elements of our general theory, but modified to take account of what has been learned from our broadly comparative survey of human societies. As a comparison of Figure 2 in Chapter 4 and Figure 2 in this chapter reveals, and as the preceding discussion indicates, a number of changes have been required, but the basic structure of the theory has not had to be altered. On the contrary, the fit between theory and data has been remarkably good on the whole.

The major differences between the figures have already been discussed, but several lesser differences also deserve note. To begin with, our

[3] One of the clearest indications of the importance of this variable in modern times can be seen in the influence of Pope John XXIII on the Roman Catholic Church. At the time of his election, no sociologist would have predicted the revolutionary character of his pontificate. All reports indicated he was a compromise candidate whose chief virtues in the eyes of his electors were his age and unspectacular record. Those who voted for him did so chiefly in the expectation that he would play the role of a harmless caretaker. By contrast, he became the most revolutionary pope of modern times. Although it is true that his revolutionary influence was only possible because of tendencies already widespread in his Church, these same forces were unable to make themselves felt to any great degree during the reigns of his predecessors. Furthermore, these same forces have found themselves checked on numerous occasions by the actions of John's successor. In short, had John not become pope, the course of Catholicism would have been very different. Much the same might be said of Germany without Hitler, etc.

The constants:

See Figure 2, Chapter 4

The variables:

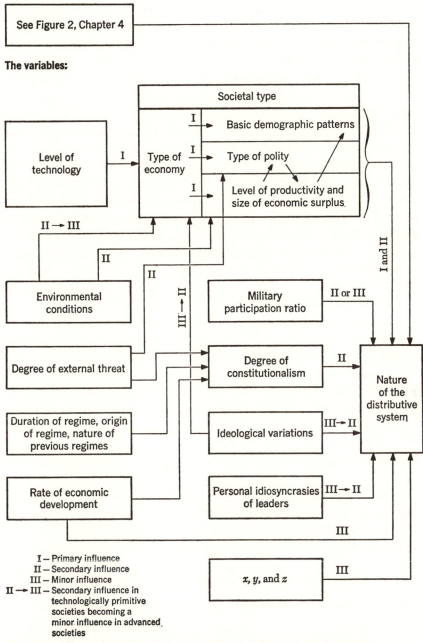

Figure 2 Diagrammatic summary of the general theory of stratification.

survey has clearly demonstrated the need for the little arrow showing feedback from the type of polity to the size of the surplus. As our analysis of agrarian societies showed, the size of the economic surplus sometimes depends on the system of social organization as well as on the level of technology. The creation and preservation of an economic surplus in agrarian societies would probably have been impossible without an authoritarian, undemocratic, and exploitative political system. Without such a polity, and without modern methods of birth control, any surplus that might have been produced would soon have been consumed by the rapid expansion of population.[4]

Two other changes involve the separation of variables out from the cluster of variables which in Figure 2 (Chapter 4) were used to predict variations in the degree of constitutionalism. The first of these is the *degree of external threat*, which we found to be linked with variations in type of polity, at least in advanced horticultural societies (see Chapter 7, page 163). The second is the *rate of economic development*, which at several points seemed linked with variations in distributive systems. Specifically, a high rate of economic development appeared to be linked with a greater willingness on the part of the dominant classes to make sacrifices in *relative* terms, i.e., in their share of the gross national product, in order to insure increases in *absolute* terms (see Chapter 10, pages 314 to 315).

These changes direct attention to what has proven a highly rewarding feature of the methodology of our analysis: *the practice of constantly alternating the processes of induction and deduction.* As noted in the introductory chapter, this is not done often enough in contemporary sociology, with the result that the fit between theory and data is often poor or unclear. By constantly comparing theory and data, and, when necessary, modifying the theory to conform to the data, cumulative growth and development are achieved. The possibility of this is further enhanced by working with an open theoretical system which permits the addition of new variables and the elimination or modification of old ones. As a consequence, a considerable number of important insights have emerged which were by no means obvious at the start of the analysis. In addition to the influences of political institutions on the size of economic surpluses, which we have already noted, one might add the discovery of the high incidence of downward mobility in agrarian societies, the clarification of

---

[4] The growth of population might possibly have been kept in check by continuous warfare. There is some evidence that this was important in horticultural societies, and perhaps early agrarian as well. In mature agrarian societies, however, the growth in the size of empires prevented this; the creation of a Pax Romana and its equivalent elsewhere was a serious hindrance.

the economic logic of "potlatch" practices in horticultural societies, and the general clarification of the importance of political institutions and their place in the causal chain shaping distributive systems. A number of other examples might be cited equally well. In short, an open theory of the type used here combines the best features of closed theories and eclecticism while avoiding their dangers and difficulties, providing, as it does, a basis for continuing growth and development.

Conservatism and Radicalism Revisited

Before turning to the problems of the future, it may be well to return briefly to the two older theoretical traditions in the field of social stratification, conservatism and radicalism. In Chapter 1 the hypothesis was developed that these traditions are gradually being supplanted by a newer one which is essentially a synthesis of both. It is only fitting, therefore, that in this final chapter we examine our theory to determine whether it is, in fact, a synthesis of the older traditions.

Probably the best method of doing this is to review the eight basic issues listed at the end of Chapter 1 which have historically divided radicals from conservatives. In reviewing them we can see to what extent the theory developed in Chapters 2 through 12 conforms to, or deviates from, the older traditions.

The first divisive issue concerns *the nature of man*. Conservatives have traditionally been distrustful of man's nature and have emphasized the need for restraining social institutions, while radicals have taken a more optimistic view. With respect to the nature of man, the position taken in the present theory leans heavily in the *conservative* direction, stressing the strongly self-seeking elements.

The second point of controversy between the two older traditions concerns the *nature of society*. Conservatives have usually emphasized the systemic nature of society, while radicals have viewed society more as a setting within which struggles take place. In this respect, our theory leans heavily in the *radical* direction, with human societies viewed as very imperfect systems.

Third, radicals and conservatives have differed on the question *of the degree to which systems of inequality are maintained by coercion*. Radicals have emphasized the importance of coercion while conservatives have argued for the importance of consensus. Here our theory tends in the *conservative* direction in the analysis of societies with little or no economic surplus, while in societies where the surplus is more substantial, it stresses the *radical's* element of coercion.

Fourth, proponents of the two traditions have differed concerning *the degree to which inequality generates conflict*. Radicals have regarded conflict as one of the chief consequences of inequality; conservatives have minimized it. Though our analysis has not been greatly concerned with consequences of inequality, it leans heavily in the *radical* direction in this respect.

Fifth, conservatives and radicals have disagreed on the question of *how rights and privileges are acquired*. Radicals have laid great stress on force, fraud, and inheritance, conservatives on hard work, delegation by others, and so forth. Our analysis has shown both kinds of factors to be involved, with the latter determining the distribution of the necessities of life, and the former having a major influence on the distribution of the surplus. However, even in the distribution of the surplus, the element of hard work is not absent, because those who serve the elites are obliged to work for what they receive and must even compete for their share of the surplus. Hence the picture is highly mixed. Futhermore, our analysis indicates that the importance of force varies greatly from one type of society to another. In the least advanced societies and in constitutionally advanced societies, force plays but a limited role. Thus, *the synthesis does not closely resemble either of the older traditions,* both of which give an oversimplified view.

Sixth, conservatives and radicals have argued the question of *the inevitability of inequality*. Conservatives have maintained that inequality is inevitable while radicals, or at least those in the egalitarian tradition, have disputed this. Here the synthesis leans strongly in the *conservative* direction, though this must be qualified by the assertion that, while inequality is apparently inevitable (given the nature of man) the degree of inequality is highly variable both within and between societal types.

Seventh, with respect to *the nature of the state and the law*, the position taken in the synthesis is a mixture of elements of both of the older traditions. In keeping with the radical tradition, the synthesis recognizes that the state and law often function as instruments of oppression and exploitation, especially in agrarian and the most advanced horticultural societies. However, even in these societies these institutions contribute something to the common good—the avoidance of anarchy, if nothing else. In certain other types of societies, notably hunting and gathering and simple horticultural, these political institutions contribute far more to the common good and far less to a privileged minority. This balance is also affected by such factors as the degree of constitutionalism, the military participation ratio, and the ideological commitments of the elite. In short, *the synthesis cannot really be identified with either of the traditional positions.*

Eighth, and finally, conservatives and radicals have tended to differ in their *conception of class*, with conservatives favoring a nominalist definition, and radicals a realist. The synthesis, by contrast, invites one to view this as essentially an empirical question, assuming, however, that the conservative or nominalist view is correct unless evidence indicates otherwise. In general, the evidence in this area supports the *conservative* position more often than the radical.

As this brief summary makes clear, the synthesis can be said to resemble both of the older traditions—and neither. On three of the eight issues, it leans heavily in the conservative direction, on two, in the radical. On the remaining three it involves a complex mixture of elements of both traditions: strongly conservative with respect to economically and technologically backward societies, and radical with respect to more advanced societies. In summary, it is *an extremely complex mixture of elements from these two older traditions, yet at the same time unique and different.*

A further point which should be noted is that the synthesis has not been achieved by some sort of misguided effort to find a compromise solution and "split the difference" between the older traditions. Nor has it been achieved by an indiscriminate selection of elements from the two traditions. This leads to eclecticism, not synthesis. Rather, our strategy has been to go back to the inevitable source of any serious social theory—the problems concerning the nature of man and society—and build systematically from that point, drawing on the accumulated insights of both traditions as they prove relevant. This has necessitated the asking of new questions and the reformulation of old ones; it has also necessitated the frequent shift from categorical to variable concepts. Though it has not been possible to deal with most of the problems in this volume in systematic, quantitative form, an effort has been made to formulate hypotheses so they are amenable to testing in quantitative terms, and data have been described in what might be called protoquantitative terms. In other words, an effort has been made to indicate the central tendency and range of variation in the relationships examined. Thus, our approach differs from the older traditions methodologically as well as substantively.

Agenda for the Future

Looking to the future, it is clear that much remains to be done. At best, only a beginning has been made. One may hope, however, that the present analysis will serve as a base on which further work can be built, and that the era of diffuse and frequently noncumulative research in the field of stratification may be drawing to a close.

If this is so, then one might well ask what the next tasks are, the tasks for the immediate future. It is to these that we now turn.

One of the first tasks obviously must be to *check and recheck* the data presented here and the conclusions based on them. Given the hundreds of generalizations, both large and small, developed in the first twelve chapters, it would be nothing short of miraculous if *all* stood up under critical scrutiny. Some will undoubtedly be disproved. If these are minor matters not linked in any essential way with the basic theory, this should cause little difficulty. On the other hand, if the general theory itself proves unsound, then this effort will have been even less than a beginning. This latter possibility seems unlikely, however, in view of the considerable body of evidence which has already been examined.

If the theory survives the critical scrutiny it will receive, then the next task will be *the sharpening of the formulation*. In its present form it is much too imprecise. Quantitative formulations of relationships have usually been impossible, and nonquantitative formulations have often been less precise than is desirable. For example, Figure 2 in this chapter differentiates between primary, secondary, and lesser influences. But what do these terms mean? Obviously they mean that *individually* the latter are less potent than the former, but is this true *collectively*? In other words, do variations in societal type alone account for more of the variance in distributive systems than all the other factors combined? The present analysis suggests that this might be the case since the differences *between* societal types generally appear greater than the differences *within* types. This could be an unintentional result of the practice of stressing central tendencies within types, but it could also be a reflection of the reality we seek to understand. This question, and many others like it, should not be left dangling indefinitely.

One aspect of stratification theory which is in special need of refinement and sharpening is the problem of the extent of *intrasocietal type* variations in distributive patterns and their causes. Too often, our analysis has been forced to gloss over such matters with little more than impressionistic judgments about central tendencies and ranges, and about the causes responsible for the variations. Intratype differences are very important from the theoretical standpoint and deserve far more careful analysis than could be given here. Some may argue that greater precision in such matters is impossible, but there is reason for optimism. Progress can be achieved even with fairly limited resources, as indicated by the pilot effort to ascertain in systematic, quantitative terms the factors responsible for the differences between Fortes's Group A and Group B advanced horticultural societies (see pages 160 to 163). There is no reason why this same mode of analysis could not be applied to most other patterns of intratype variation.

Among the areas where greater precision is needed, the following are especially worthy of note. First, there is the important problem of the extent to which *ideology* influences distributive systems and the conditions under which its influence is maximized and minimized. Second, there is the same problem with respect to the role of *altruistic behavior*. Third, there are problems concerning *the interrelations of power, privilege, and prestige*. To what extent is prestige a function of power and privilege, and to what extent is it capable of varying independently? In this volume it has been assumed that prestige is "largely" a function of power and privilege, but that is much too imprecise. As problems such as these are studied, they will lead not only to a sharpening of the present theory, but to changes and modifications as well. As stated previously, it is inconceivable that all of the many generalizations in this volume will prove valid.

Finally, the present theory needs to be *extended*. New variables, new types of societies, and new patterns of relationships must be considered. As noted previously, I have deliberately ignored certain types of societies. Some pure types such as fishing, herding, and maritime societies were not dealt with,[5] nor were hybrid types, such as the industrializing agrarian, e.g., contemporary India, and the industrializing horticultural, e.g., certain African societies. Some of these types, notably the industrializing agrarian and horticultural societies, are of tremendous importance because they constitute the underdeveloped countries of the modern world, which are experiencing such traumatic difficulties in their efforts to industrialize.

The present theory also needs to be extended by the examination of new patterns of relationships between the variables. As Figure 2 indicates, the theory in its present form takes account only of a one-way flow of influence for the most part. Though this is justified as a first approximation, there are clearly elements of *feedback* from the distributive system to other basic variables which deserve attention. V. Gordon Childe has directed our attention to one instance of this in writing of the beginnings of civilization in the Middle East five thousand years ago. In his exciting volume, *Man Makes Himself,* Childe argues that in the period prior to 2600 B.C. there was a definitely accelerating curve in the rate of invention

---

[5] One reader of the manuscript, Peter Carstens, commented that the inclusion of fishing societies would have introduced an important source of additional evidence in support of the general theory. Due to limitation of time and space, this remains a task for the future.

and technological advance. After this date, the rising trend faltered and eventually turned downward, not rising again to any appreciable degree until the Industrial Revolution.[6] In seeking to explain this strange reversal, Childe argues that one of the major reasons was the new pattern of distribution, with the virtual monopolization of the economic surplus by a tiny governing class. Under these conditions, the producers no longer had any incentive to improve the techniques of production, since all the gains were swallowed up by the political elite, and the elite were too far removed from the processes of production to be capable of invention. What is more, they now had almost unlimited reserves of labor at their disposal and therefore had no incentive to seek laborsaving inventions. Thus, the emergence of the new distributive systems associated with agrarian societies seriously weakened the forces promoting technological advance.

If one were to explore the matter carefully, he would also find evidence of feedback to some of the other independent variables in our theoretical system, and these deserve attention no less than the primary patterns of causation. One of the best examples of this is the impact of distributive systems on political institutions, especially in democratic nations, though not there alone. Another is the influence of prestige systems on power systems because, as recent research suggests, prestige systems serve to limit access to power positions.

In short, much remains to be done.

---

[6] *Man Makes Himself* (London: Watts, 1936), chap. 9.

Bibliography

Abegglen, James: *The Japanese Factory: Aspects of Its Social Organization* (New York: Free Press, 1958).

Abegglen, James, and Hiroshi Mannari: "Japanese Business Leaders: 1880–1960," unpublished manuscript prepared for the Conference on State and Economic Enterprise in Modern Japan, Association for Asian Studies, 1963.

Adrian, Charles: *Governing Urban America*, 2d ed. (New York: McGraw-Hill, 1961).

Albright, William F.: *From the Stone Age to Christianity*, 2d ed. (Garden City, N.Y.: Doubleday Anchor, 1957).

———: *The Archaeology of Palestine* (London: Penguin, 1956).

Alderson, A. D.: *The Structure of the Ottoman Dynasty* (Oxford: Clarendon Press, 1956).

Alford, Robert: *Party and Society: The Anglo-American Democracies* (Chicago: Rand McNally, 1963).

Allen, W. E. D.: *The History of the Georgian People* (London: Routledge, 1932).

Anderson, C. Arnold: "Lifetime Inter-occupation Mobility Patterns in Sweden," *Acta Sociologica*, 1 (1960), pp. 168–202.

Anderson, Elin: *We Americans: A Study of Cleavage in an American City* (Cambridge, Mass.: Harvard University Press, 1938).

Andrén, Nils: *Modern Swedish Government* (Stockholm: Almqvist & Wiksell, 1961).

Andrewes, A.: *The Greek Tyrants* (New York: Harper Torchbooks, 1963).

Andrzejewski, Stanislaw: *Military Organization and Society* (London: Routledge, 1954).

Angell, Robert C.: "Preferences for Moral Norms in Three Problem Areas," *American Journal of Sociology*, 67 (1962), pp. 650–660.

Aristotle: *Politics*, translated by Benjamin Jowett (New York: Modern Library, 1943).

Armstrong, C. A. J.: "France of the Hundred Years War and the Renaissance," in J. M. Wallace-Hadrill and John McManners (eds.), *France: Government and Society* (London: Methuen, 1957), pp. 83–104.

Aydelotte, Frank: *Elizabethan Rogues and Vagabonds* (Oxford: Clarendon Press, 1913).

Aylmer, G. E.: *The King's Servants: The Civil Service of Charles I* (London: Routledge, 1961).

Baegert, Jacob, S. J.: *Account of the Aboriginal Inhabitants of the California Peninsula*, translated and arranged by Charles Rau, *Smithsonian Institution: Annual Reports for 1863 and 1864*, reprinted in Carleton S. Coon (ed.), *A Reader in General Anthropology* (New York: Holt, 1948), pp. 61–83.

Bailey, F. G.: *Tribe, Caste, and Nation* (Manchester: Manchester University Press, 1960).

Banfield, Edward: *The Moral Basis of a Backward Society* (New York: Free Press, 1958).

———: *Big City Politics* (New York: Random House, 1965).

——— and James Wilson: *City Politics* (Cambridge, Mass.: Harvard University and M. I. T. Presses, 1963).

Barber, Bernard: *Social Stratification: A Comparative Analysis of Structure and Process* (New York: Harcourt, Brace & World, 1957).

Barber, Elinor: *The Bourgeoisie in 18th Century France* (Princeton, N.J.: Princeton University Press, 1955).

Bauer, Raymond, Alex Inkeles, and Clyde Kluckhohn: *How the Soviet System Works* (Cambridge, Mass.: Harvard University Press, 1956).

———, Ithiel de Sola Pool, and Lewis Dexter: *American Business and Public Policy: The Politics of Foreign Trade* (New York: Atherton, 1963).

Baxter, P. T. W., and Audrey Butt: *The Azande and Related Peoples* (London: International African Institute, 1953).

Beer, Samuel H.: "Great Britain: From Governing Elite to Mass Parties," in Sigmund Neumann (ed.), *Modern Political Parties: Approaches to Comparative Politics* (Chicago: University of Chicago Press, 1956), pp. 9–57.

Bellah, Robert: *Tokugawa Religion: The Values of Pre-industrial Japan* (New York: Free Press, 1957).

Bendix, Reinhard, and S. M. Lipset (eds.): *Class, Status, and Power: A Reader in Social Stratification* (New York: Free Press, 1953).

Bennett, H. S.: *Life on the English Manor: A Study of Peasant Conditions, 1150–1400* (London: Cambridge University Press, 1960).

Bergel, Egon: *Social Stratification* (New York: McGraw-Hill, 1962).

Berger, Peter: *Invitation to Sociology* (Garden City, N.Y.: Doubleday Anchor, 1963).

Berle, Adolf A., and Gardiner C. Means: *The Modern Corporation and Private Property* (New York: Macmillan, 1932).

Bierstedt, Robert: "An Analysis of Social Power," *American Sociological Review*, 15 (1950), pp. 730–738.

Bill, Valentine: *The Forgotten Class: The Russian Bourgeoisie from the Earliest Beginnings to 1900* (New York: Frederick A. Praeger, 1959).

Blau, Peter: *Exchange and Power in Society* (New York: Wiley, 1964).

Bloch, Marc: *Feudal Society*, translated by L. A. Manyon (Chicago: University of Chicago Press, 1962).

Blum, Jerome: *Lord and Peasant in Russia from the Ninth to the Nineteenth Century* (Princeton, N.J.: Princeton University Press, 1961).

Boak, A. E. R.: *A History of Rome to 565 A.D.*, 3d ed. (New York: Macmillan, 1943).

Bolte, Karl Martin: *Sozialer Aufstieg und Abstieg* (Stuttgart: Enke, 1959).

Bose, Ashish: "The First Census of Free India," *Modern Review*, 95 (1954), pp. 111–119.

Bowen, John C.: *Some Aspects of Transfer Taxation in the United States* (unpublished doctoral dissertation, University of Michigan, 1958).

Braginskii, B. I., and D. Dumov: "Labor Productivity in Agriculture in the USSR and the USA," in Harry G. Shaffer (ed.), *The Soviet Economy: A Collection of Western and Soviet Views* (New York: Appleton-Century-Crofts, 1963), pp. 176–184.

Braidwood, Robert: "The Agricultural Revolution," *Scientific American*, 203 (1960), pp. 130–148.

Bram, Joseph: *An Analysis of Incan Militarism*, Monographs of the American Ethnological Society, 4 (1941).

Bridges, Rev. Thomas: "The Canoe Indians of Tierra del Feugo," in Carleton S. Coon (ed.), *A Reader in General Anthropology* (New York: Holt, 1948), pp. 84–116.

Brown, Emily Clark: "The Soviet Labor Market," in Morris Bornstein and Daniel Fusfeld (eds.), *The Soviet Economy* (Homewood, Ill.: Irwin, 1962), pp. 195–220.

Brown, Harrison: *The Challenge of Man's Future* (New York: Viking Compass Books, 1956).

Bry, Gerhard: *Wages in Germany, 1871–1945* (Princeton, N.J.: Princeton University Press, 1960).

Buchanan, K. M. and J. C. Pugh: *Land and People in Nigeria* (London: University of London Press, 1955).

Buck, John Lossing: *Secretariat Paper No. 1: Tenth Conference of the Institute of Pacific Relations*, Stratford on Avon, 1947, reprinted in Irwin T. Sanders et al. (eds.), *Societies around the World* (New York: Dryden Press, 1953).

Burg, David: "Observations of Soviet University Students," in Richard Pipes (ed.), *The Russian Intelligentsia* (New York: Columbia University Press, 1961).

Burnham, James: *The Managerial Revolution* (Bloomington, Ind.: Indiana University Press, 1960).

Butler, D. E., and Richard Rose: *The British General Election of 1959* (London: Macmillan, 1960).

Cambridge Ancient History (London: Cambridge University Press, 1939), especially vol. 12.

Cambridge History of India (London: Cambridge University Press, 1937), especially volume 4, *The Mughal Period.*

Campbell, Angus, Philip Converse, Warren Miller, and Donald Stokes: *The American Voter* (New York: Wiley, 1960).

Carcopino, Jerome: *Daily Life in Ancient Rome: The People and the City at the Height of Empire,* translated by E. O. Lorimer (London: Routledge, 1941).

Carlsson, Gosta: *Social Mobility and Class Structure* (Lund: Gleerup, 1958).

Caron, Pierre: "The Army," in Arthur Tilley (ed.), *Medieval France* (London: Cambridge University Press), pp. 154–165.

Carr, Raymond: "Spain," in A. Goodwin (ed.), *The European Nobility in the Eighteenth Century* (London: Black, 1953), pp. 43–58.

Carr-Saunders, A. M.: *World Population* (Oxford: Clarendon Press, 1936).

———— and P. A. Wilson: *The Professions* (Oxford: Clarendon Press, 1933).

Carstairs, G. M.: "A Village in Rajasthan," in M. N. Srinivas (ed.), *India's Villages* (Calcutta: West Bengal Government Press, 1955), pp. 33–38.

Carter, Gwendolen: "The Commonwealth Overseas: Variation on a British Theme," in Sigmund Neumann (ed.), *Modern Political Parties: Approaches to Comparative Politics* (Chicago: University of Chicago Press, 1956), pp. 58–107.

Cartter, Allan M.: *The Redistribution of Income in Postwar Britain* (New Haven, Conn.: Yale University Press, 1955).

Chang, Chung-li: *The Chinese Gentry: Studies in Their Role in Nineteenth-Century Chinese Society* (Seattle, Wash.: University of Washington Press, 1955).

————: *The Income of the Chinese Gentry* (Seattle, Wash.: University of Washington Press, 1962).

Chapman, R. M., W. K. Jackson, and A. V. Mitchell: *New Zealand Politics in Action* (London: Oxford University Press, 1962).

Chi, Tsui: *A Short History of Chinese Civilization* (New York: Putnam, 1943).

Childe, V. Gordon: *Man Makes Himself* (London: Watts, 1936).

————: *New Light on the Most Ancient East,* rev. ed. (London: Routledge, 1952).

————: *Social Evolution* (London: Watts, 1951).

————: "The New Stone Age," in Harry Shapiro (ed.), *Man, Culture, and Society* (Fair Lawn, N.J.: Oxford Galaxy, 1960), pp. 94–110.

Childs, Marquis: *Sweden: The Middle Way,* rev. ed. (New Haven, Conn.: Yale University Press, 1947).

Chorley, Katharine: *Armies and the Art of Revolution* (London: Faber, 1943).

Clark, Burton: *Educating the Expert Society* (San Francisco, Calif.: Chandler, 1962).

Clough, S. B.: *The Economic Development of Western Civilization* (New York: McGraw-Hill, 1959).

———— and C. W. Cole: *Economic History of Europe* (Boston: Heath, 1941).

Cole, G. D. H.: *The Post-war Condition of Britain* (London: Routledge, 1956).

———— and R. W. Postgate: *The British Common People, 1746–1938* (New York: Knopf, 1939).

Colson, Elizabeth: "The Plateau Tonga of Northern Rhodesia," in Elizabeth Colson and Max Gluckman (eds.), *Seven Tribes of British Central Africa* (Manchester: Manchester University Press, 1951), pp. 94–163.

———— and Max Gluckman (eds.): *Seven Tribes of British Central Africa* (Manchester: Manchester University Press, 1951).

Converse, Philip: "Religion and Politics: The 1960 Elections," unpublished paper of the Survey Research Center of the University of Michigan, 1961.

Cooley, Charles Horton: *Social Organization* (New York: Scribner, 1909).

Coser, Lewis: *The Functions of Social Conflict* (New York: Free Press, 1956).

Coulton, G. G.: *Medieval Panorama* (New York: Meridian Books, 1955).

Cowell, F. R.: *Cicero and the Roman Republic* (London: Penguin, 1956).

Crisp, L. F.: *The Australian Federal Labour Party, 1901–1951* (London: Longmans, 1955).

Crowder, Michael: *The Story of Nigeria* (London: Faber, 1962).

Current Population Reports: "Lifetime Occupational Mobility of Adult Males, March, 1962," U.S. Bureau of the Census (1964), Series P-23, No. 11.

————: "Religion Reported by the Civilian Population of the United States: March, 1957," U.S. Bureau of the Census (1958), Series P-20, No. 79.

Dahl, Robert: *Who Governs?: Democracy and Power in an American City* (New Haven, Conn.: Yale University Press, 1961).

———— and Charles Lindblom: *Politics, Economics, and Welfare* (New York: Harper & Row, 1953).

Dahrendorf, Ralf: *Class and Class Conflict in Industrial Society* (Stanford, Calif.: Stanford University Press, 1959).

Dallin, David J.: *The New Soviet Empire* (New Haven, Conn.: Yale University Press, 1951).

Daugherty, Carroll: *Labor Problems in American Industry*, 5th ed. (Boston: Houghton Mifflin, 1941).

Davis, Kingsley: *Human Society* (New York: Macmillan, 1949).

————: "The Origin and Growth of Urbanization in the World," *American Journal of Sociology*, 60 (1955), pp. 429–437.

———— and Wilbert Moore: "Some Principles of Stratification," *American Sociological Review*, 10 (1945), pp. 242–249.

Dawidowicz, Lucy, and Leon Goldstein: *Politics in a Pluralist Democracy: Studies of Voting in the 1960 Election* (New York: Institute of Human Relations Press, 1963).

de Jouvenal, Bertrand: *On Power: Its Nature and the History of Its Growth*, translated by J. F. Huntington (New York: Viking, 1949).

Demographic Yearbook, 1953 (New York: United Nations, 1953).

Denig, Edwin Thompson: *Five Indian Tribes of the Upper Missouri* (Norman, Okla.: University of Oklahoma Press, 1961).

Dewar, Margaret: "Labour and Wage Reforms in the USSR," in Harry B. Shaffer (ed.), *The Soviet Economy: A Collection of Western and Soviet Views* (New York: Appleton-Century-Crofts, 1963), pp 216–225.

Dewhurst, J. Frederic, and Associates: *America's Needs and Resources* (New York: Twentieth Century Fund, 1955).

————: *Europe's Needs and Resources* (New York: Twentieth Century Fund, 1961).

DeWitt, Nicholas: *Education and Professional Employment in the USSR* (Washington, D.C.: National Science Foundation, 1961).

de Young, John E.: *Village Life in Modern Thailand* (Berkeley, Calif.: University of California Press, 1958).

Dicey, A. V.: *The Law of the Constitution* (London: Macmillan, 1885).

Dictionary of Occupational Titles, 2d ed. (Washington: GPO, 1949).

Dixon, Roland: "The Northern Maidu," in Carleton S. Coon (ed.), *A Reader in General Anthropology* (New York: Holt, 1948), pp. 263–292.

Djilas, Milovan: *The New Class: An Analysis of the Communist System* (New York: Frederick A. Praeger, 1959).

Douglas, Robert K.: *Society in China* (London: Innes, 1894).

Downey, Glanville: *Constantinople: In the Age of Justinian* (Norman, Okla.: University of Oklahoma Press, 1960).

Drake, St. Clair, and Horace Cayton: *Black Metropolis: A Study of Negro Life in a Northern City* (New York: Harcourt, Brace & World, 1945).

Drucker, Philip: *Indians of the Northwest Coast* (New York: McGraw-Hill, 1955).

Dudintsev, Vladimir: *Not by Bread Alone* (New York: Dutton, 1957).

Duncan, O. D.: "A Socioeconomic Index for All Occupations," in Albert J. Reiss, *Occupations and Social Status* (New York: Free Press, 1961), pp. 109–138.

———: "Social Organization and the Ecosystem," in Robert E. Faris (ed.), *Handbook of Modern Sociology* (Chicago: Rand McNally, 1964), pp. 36–82.

Duverger, Maurice: *Political Parties: Their Organization and Activity in the Modern State*, translated by Barbara North and Robert North (London: Methuen, 1959).

Eberhard, Wolfram: *A History of China*, 2d ed. (Berkeley, Calif.: University of California Press, 1960).

———: *Conquerors and Rulers: Social Forces in Medieval China* (Leiden, Netherlands: Brill, 1952).

———: *Social Mobility in Traditional China* (Leiden, Netherlands: Brill, 1962).

Eckland, Bruce: "Academic Ability, Higher Education, and Occupational Mobility," *American Sociological Review*, 30 (1965), pp. 735–746.

Eggan, Fred: *Social Organization of the Western Pueblos* (Chicago: University of Chicago Press, 1950).

Ehrmann, Henry W.: *Organized Business in France* (Princeton, N.J.: Princeton University Press, 1957).

Eisenstadt, S. N.: "Religious Organizations and Political Process in Centralized Empires," *The Journal of Asian Studies*, 21 (1962), pp. 271–294.

———: *The Political Systems of Empires: The Rise and Fall of the Historical Bureaucratic Societies* (New York: Free Press, 1963).

Erman, Adolf: *Life in Ancient Egypt*, translated by H. M. Tirard (London: Macmillan, 1894).

Evans, Joan: *Life in Medieval France* (London: Oxford University Press, 1925).

Ewers, John C.: "The Horse in Blackfoot Indian Culture, with Comparative Material from Other Western Tribes," Smithsonian Institution, Bureau of American Ethnology, Bulletin 159 (1955).

Fainsod, Merle: *How Russia Is Ruled,* rev. ed. (Cambridge, Mass.: Harvard University Press, 1963).

Fallers, Margaret Chave: *The Eastern Lacustrine Bantu* (London: International African Institute, 1960).

Fei, Hsiao-Tung: *China's Gentry* (Chicago: University of Chicago Press, 1953).

———: "Peasantry and Gentry: An Interpretation of Chinese Social Structure and Its Changes," *American Journal of Sociology,* 52 (1946), pp. 1–17.

Feuer, Lewis (ed.): *Karl Marx and Friedrich Engels: Basic Writings on Politics and Philosophy* (Garden City, N.Y.: Doubleday Anchor, 1959).

Fleisher, Wilfrid: *Sweden: The Welfare State* (New York: John Day, 1956).

Florence, P. Sargant: *Ownership, Control, and Success of Large Companies: An Analysis of English Industrial Structure and Policy, 1936–1951* (London: Street & Maxwell, 1961).

Forde, C. Daryll: *Habitat, Economy and Society* (London: Methuen, 1934).

———: "Primitive Economics," in Harry Shapiro (ed)., *Man, Culture, and Society* (Fair Lawn, N.J.: Oxford Galaxy, 1960), pp. 330–344.

Fortes, Meyer and E. E. Evans-Pritchard (eds.): *African Political Systems* (London: Oxford University Press, 1940).

Fourastié, Jean: *The Causes of Wealth,* translated by Theodore Caplow (New York: Free Press, 1960, first published 1951).

Fried, Morton: *The Fabric of Chinese Society: A Study of the Social Life of a Chinese County Seat* (New York: Frederick A. Praeger, 1953).

Friedan, Betty: *The Feminine Mystique* (New York: Norton, 1963).

Friedman, Milton, and Simon Kuznets: *Income from Independent Professional Practice* (New York: National Bureau of Economic Research, 1945).

Galbraith, Kenneth: *American Capitalism: The Concept of Countervailing Power* (Boston: Houghton Mifflin, 1952).

———: *The Affluent Society* (Boston: Houghton Mifflin, 1958).

Galenson, Walter: *Labor in Norway* (Cambridge, Mass.: Harvard University Press, 1949).

Gamble, Sidney D.: *Peking: A Social Survey* (Garden City, N.Y.: Doubleday, 1921).

Ganshof, Francois: "Medieval Agrarian Society in Its Prime: France, the Low Countries, and Western Germany," in *The Cambridge Economic History,* vol. I, pp. 278–322.

Gibb, H. A. R.: *Mohammedanism: An Historical Survey* (New York: Mentor Books, 1955).

Gibbs, James L. (ed.): *Peoples of Africa* (New York: Holt, 1965).

Gleason, S. E.: *An Ecclesiastical Barony in the Middle Ages: The Bishopric of Bayeux, 1066–1204* (Cambridge, Mass.: Harvard University Press, 1936).

Gluckman, Max: "The Lozi of Barotseland in Northwestern Rhodesia," in Elizabeth Colson and Max Gluckman (eds.), *Seven Tribes of British Central Africa* (Manchester: Manchester University Press, 1951), pp. 1–93.

Goffman, Irving: "Status Consistency and Preference for Change in Power Distribution," *American Sociological Review,* 22 (1957), pp. 275–281.

Goldhamer, Herbert, and Edward Shils: "Types of Power and Status," *American Journal of Sociology,* 45 (1939), pp. 171–182

Goldman, Irving: "The Zuni Indians of New Mexico," in Margaret Mead (ed.), *Cooperation and Competition among Primitive Peoples*, rev. ed. (Boston: Beacon Press, 1961), pp. 313–353.

Goldschmidt, Walter: *Man's Way: A Preface to the Understanding of Human Society* (New York: Holt, 1959).

Goode, William J.: *World Revolution and Family Patterns* (New York: Free Press, 1963).

Goodwin, A.: "Prussia," in A. Goodwin (ed.), *The European Nobility in the Eighteenth Century* (London: Black, 1953), pp. 83–101.

Gordon, Margaret: *Retraining and Labor Market Adjustment in Western Europe* (Washington: GPO, 1965).

Gordon, Milton: *Assimilation in American Life: The Role of Race, Religion, and National Origins* (Fair Lawn, N.J.: Oxford University Press, 1964).

Gordon, Robert A.: *Business Leadership in the Large Corporation* (Berkeley, Calif.: University of California Press, 1961, originally published by the Brookings Institution, 1954).

Gottschalk, Louis: *The Era of the French Revolution* (Boston: Houghton Mifflin, 1929).

Gouldner, Alvin, and R. A. Petersen: *Notes on Technology and the Moral Order* (Indianapolis, Ind.: Bobbs-Merrill, 1962).

Granick, David: *The European Executive* (Garden City, N.Y.: Doubleday Anchor, 1964).

———: *The Red Executive* (Garden City, N.Y.: Doubleday Anchor, 1961).

Gray, H. L.: "Incomes from Land in England in 1436," *English Historical Review*, 49 (1934), pp. 607–639.

Grove, J. W.: *Government and Industry in Britain* (London: Longmans, 1962).

Grzybowski, Kazimierz: *Soviet Legal Institution: Doctrines and Social Functions* (Ann Arbor, Mich.: University of Michigan Press, 1962).

Habakkuk, H. J.: "England," in A. Goodwin (ed.), *The European Nobility in the Eighteenth Century* (London: Black, 1953), pp. 1–21.

Halphen, L.: "Industry and Commerce," in Arthur Tilley (ed.), *Medieval France* (London: Cambridge University Press, 1922), pp. 179–211.

Hatcher, Mattie Austin: "Descriptions of the Tejas or Asinai Indians: 1691–1722," *Southwestern Historical Quarterly*, 30 (1927), pp. 283–304.

Heard, Alexander: *The Costs of Democracy: Financing American Political Campaigns* (Garden City, N.Y.: Doubleday Anchor, 1962).

Heckscher, Eli F.: *An Economic History of Sweden*, translated by Goram Ohlin (Cambridge, Mass.: Harvard University Press, 1954).

Heckscher, Gunnar: "Interest Groups in Sweden: Their Political Role," in Henry W. Ehrmann (ed.), *Interest Groups on Four Continents* (Pittsburgh, Pa.: University of Pittsburgh Press, 1958), pp. 154–172.

Heilbroner, Robert: *The Making of Economic Society* (Englewood Cliffs, N.J.: Prentice-Hall, 1962).

Herberg, Will: *Protestant-Catholic-Jew* (Garden City, N.Y.: Doubleday, 1956).

Herskovits, Melville: *Dahomey: An Ancient West African Kingdom* (Locust Valley, N.Y.: Augustin, 1938).

Hewes, Gordon: "The Rubric 'Fishing and Fisheries,'" *American Anthropologist,* 50 (1948), pp. 238–246.

Higbee, Edward: *Farms and Farmers in an Urban Age* (New York: Twentieth Century Fund, 1963).

Historical Statistics of the United States: Colonial Times to 1957 (Washington: GPO, 1960).

Hitti, Philip K.: *History of the Arabs* (London: Macmillan, 1960).

Hobbes, Thomas, *Leviathan* (New York: Liberal Arts, 1958).

Hobhouse, L. T., G. C. Wheeler, and M. Ginsberg: *The Material Culture and Social Institutions of the Simpler Peoples* (London: Chapman & Hall, 1930).

Hobsbawn, E. J.: *Primitive Rebels,* 2d ed. (New York: Frederick A. Praeger, 1963).

Hochbaum, Godfrey et al.: "Socioeconomic Variables in a Large City," *American Journal of Sociology,* 61 (1955), pp. 31–38.

Hodgkin, Thomas: *Nigerian Perspectives: An Historical Anthology* (London: Oxford University Press, 1960).

Hogbin, H. Ian: *Transformation Scene: The Changing Culture of a New Guinea Village* (London: Routledge, 1951).

Hollingshead A. B.: *Elmtown's Youth* (New York: Wiley, 1949).

—— and Frederick Redlich: *Social Class and Mental Illness: A Community Study* (New York: Wiley, 1958).

Holmberg, Allan: *Nomads of the Long Bow: The Siriono of Eastern Bolivia,* Smithsonian Institution, Institute of Social Anthropology, Publication No. 10 (1950).

Holzman, F. D.: "Financing Soviet Economic Development," in Morris Bernstein and Daniel Fusfeld (eds.), *The Soviet Economy* (Homewood, Ill.: Irwin, 1962), pp. 145–160.

Homans, George C. *English Villagers of the Thirteenth Century* (Cambridge, Mass.: Harvard University Press, 1942).

——: "Status among Clerical Workers," *Human Organization,* 12 (1953), pp. 5–10.

——: *Social Behavior* (New York: Harcourt, Brace & World, 1961).

Homo, Léon: *Roman Political Institutions* (London: Routledge, 1929).

Honigmann, John: *The World of Man* (New York: Harper & Row, 1959).

Hook, Sidney: *The Hero in History: A Study in Limitation and Possibility* (Boston: Beacon Press, 1955, original edition 1943).

Horowitz, Daniel: *The Italian Labor Movement* (Cambridge, Mass.: Harvard University Press, 1963).

Hoskins, W. G.: *The Midland Peasant: The Economic and Social History of a Leicestershire Village* (London: Macmillan, 1957).

Howitt, A. W.: *Native Tribes of South-east Australia* (London: Macmillan, 1904).

Hughes, A. J. B., and J. van Velsen: *The Ndebele* (London: International African Institute, 1954).

Hughes, Philip: *A Popular History of the Catholic Church* (New York: Macmillan, 1950).

Hunter, Floyd: *Community Power Structure* (Chapel Hill, N.C.: University of North Carolina Press, 1953).

Inkeles, Alex: "Social Stratification and Mobility in the Soviet Union: 1940–1950," *American Sociological Review*, 15 (1950), pp. 465–479.

—— and Raymond Bauer: *The Soviet Citizen* (Cambridge, Mass.: Harvard University Press, 1959).

—— and Kent Geiger (eds.): *Soviet Society: A Book of Readings* (Boston: Houghton Mifflin, 1961).

—— and Peter Rossi: "National Comparisons of Occupational Prestige," *American Journal of Sociology*, 61 (1956), pp. 329–339.

Jackson, Elton: "Status Consistency and Symptoms of Stress," *American Sociological Review*, 27 (1962), pp. 469–480.

—— and Peter Burke: "Status and Symptoms of Stress: Additive and Interaction Effects," *American Sociological Review*, 30 (1965), pp. 556–564.

—— and Harry Crockett: "Occupational Mobility in the United States: A Point Estimate and Trend Comparison," *American Sociological Review*, 29 (1964), pp. 5–15.

Jaffe, A. J., and R. O. Carleton: *Occupational Mobility in the United States 1930–1960* (New York: King's Crown, 1954).

Janowitz, Morris: "Social Stratification and Mobility in West Germany," *American Journal of Sociology*, 64 (1958), pp. 6–24.

——: *The Professional Soldier* (New York: Free Press, 1960).

Jasny, Naum: *The Socialized Agriculture of the USSR* (Stanford, Calif.: Stanford University Press, 1949).

John of Salisbury: *The Statesman's Book,* translated by John Dickinson (New York: Knopf, 1927).

Johnson, John J.: *The Military and Society in Latin America* (Stanford, Calif.: Stanford University Press, 1964).

Jolliffe, J. E. A.: *The Constitutional History of Medieval England* (London: Black, 1937).

Jones, A. H. M.: *Studies in Roman Government and Law* (Oxford: Blackwell, 1960).

Jusserand, J. J.: *English Wayfaring Life in the Middle Ages*, 3d ed., translated by L. T. Smith (London: Benn, 1925).

Karin, A. K. N.: *Changing Society in India and Pakistan* (Dacca: Oxford University Press, 1956).

Keen, Maurice: *The Outlaws of Medieval Legend* (Routledge, 1961).

Keller, Suzanne: *Beyond the Ruling Class: Strategic Elites in Modern Society* (New York: Random House, 1963).

Key, V. O., Jr.: *Politics, Parties, and Pressure Groups*, 3d ed. (New York: Crowell, 1952).

Kolko, Gabriel: *Wealth and Power in America: An Analysis of Social Class and Income Distribution* (New York: Frederick A Praeger, 1962).

Kosambi, D. D.: *An Introduction to the History of India* (Bombay: Popular Book Depot, 1956).

Kroeber, A. L.: *Handbook of American Indians of California*, Smithsonian Institution, Bureau of American Ethnology, Bulletin 78 (1925).

——: "Native Culture of the Southwest," University of California Publications, *American Archaeology and Ethnology*, 23 (1928), pp. 375–398.

——: "The Chibcha," in Julian Steward (ed.), *Handbook of South American*

Indians, Smithsonian Institution, Bureau of American Ethnology, Bulletin 143 (1946), vol. II, pp. 887–909.

Kumar, D.: "Caste and Landlessness in South India," *Comparative Studies in Society and History,* 4 (1962), pp. 337–363.

Kuper, Hilda: *The Swazi* (London: International African Institute, 1952).

Ladinsky, Jack: "Careers of Lawyers, Law Practice, and Legal Institutions," *American Sociological Review,* 28 (1963), pp. 47–54.

Lampman, Robert: *The Share of Top Wealth-holders in National Wealth: 1922–1956* (Princeton, N.J.: Princeton University Press, 1962).

Landecker, Werner S.: "Class Crystallization and Class Consciousness," *American Sociological Review,* 28 (1963), pp. 219–229.

Landtman, Gunnar: *The Kiwai Papuans of British New Guinea* (London: Macmillan, 1927).

———: *The Origin of the Inequality of the Social Classes* (London: Routledge, 1938).

Lang, David M.: *The Last Years of the Georgian Monarchy, 1658–1832* (New York: Columbia University Press, 1957).

Langley, Kathleen M.: "The Distribution of Capital in Private Hands in 1936–38 and 1946–47 (part 2)," *Bulletin of the Oxford University Institute of Statistics* (February, 1951).

Langlois, Charles V.: "History," in Arthur Tilley (ed.), *Medieval France* (London: Cambridge University Press, 1922), pp. 30–153.

Laski, Harold: *The State in Theory and Practice* (New York: Viking, 1935).

Lasswell, Harold: *Politics: Who Gets What, When, How* (New York: McGraw-Hill, 1936).

——— and Abraham Kaplan: *Power and Society: A Framework for Political Inquiry* (New Haven, Conn.: Yale University Press, 1950).

Latourette, Kenneth S.: *A History of Christianity* (New York: Harper & Row, 1953).

Lauwerys, J. A.: *Scandinavian Democracy* (Copenhagen: Danish Institute et al., 1958).

Laws of Manu, translated by G. Bühler, in Max Müller (ed.), *Sacred Books of the East* (Oxford: Clarendon Press, 1886), vol. 25.

Leiserson, Mark: *Wages and Economic Control in Norway, 1945–1957* (Cambridge, Mass.: Harvard University Press, 1959).

Lemberg, K., and N. Ussing: "Redistribution of Income in Denmark," in Alan Peacock (ed.), *Income Redistribution and Social Policy* (London: Cape, 1954), pp. 55–89.

Lenski, Gerhard: "Comment," *Public Opinion Quarterly,* 28 (1964), pp. 326–330.

———: "Religious Pluralism in Theoretical Perspective," in *Internationales Jahrbuch für Religionssoziologie* (Köln: Westdeutscher Verlag, 1965), vol. I, pp. 25–42.

———: "Social Participation and Status Crystallization," *American Sociological Review,* 21 (1956), pp. 458–464.

———: "Status Crystallization: A Non-vertical Dimension of Social Status," *American Sociological Review,* 19 (1954), pp. 405–413.

———: *The Religious Factor* (Garden City, N.Y.: Doubleday, 1961).

————: "Trends in Inter-generational Mobility in the United States," *American Sociological Review*, 23 (1958), pp. 514–523.

Leonhard, Wolfgang: *The Kremlin since Stalin,* translated by Elizabeth Wiskemann and Marian Jackson (New York: Frederick A. Praeger, 1962).

Lewis, Oscar: *The Effects of White Contact upon Blackfoot Culture,* Monographs of the American Ethnological Society, 6 (1942).

Lewis, Roy, and Angus Maude: *Professional People* (London: Phoenix House, 1952).

———— and Rosemary Stewart: *The Managers: A New Examination of the English, German and American Executive* (New York: Mentor Books, 1961).

Leyburn, James G.: *Frontier Folkways* (New Haven, Conn.: Yale University Press, 1936).

Lindsay, Philip, and Reg Groves: *The Peasants' Revolt, 1381* (London: Hutchinson, n.d.).

Link, Edith M.: *The Emancipation of the Austrian Peasant, 1740–1798* (New York: Columbia University Press, 1949).

Linton, Ralph: *The Tanala: A Hill Tribe of Madagascar* (Chicago: Field Museum of Natural History, 1933).

————: *The Tree of Culture* (New York: Vintage Books, 1959).

Lipset, S. M.: *Agrarian Socialism* (Berkeley, Calif.: University of California Press, 1950).

———— and Reinhard Bendix: *Social Mobility in Industrial Society* (Berkeley, Calif.: University of California Press, 1959).

Lockwood, David: *The Blackcoated Worker: A Study in Class Consciousness* (London: G. Allen, 1958).

Lopreato, Joseph: "Social Mobility in Italy," *American Journal of Sociology,* 71 (1965), pp. 311–314.

Lowi, Theodore J.: *At the Pleasure of the Mayor: Patronage and Power in New York, 1898–1958* (New York: Free Press, 1964).

Lowie, Robert: "Social and Political Organization of the Tropical Forest and Marginal Tribes," in Julian Steward (ed.), *Handbook of South American Indians,* Smithsonian Institution, Bureau of American Ethnology, Bulletin 143 (1949), vol. V, pp. 313–367.

————: *Social Organization* (New York: Holt, 1948).

Lubell, Samuel: *The Future of American Politics,* rev. ed. (Garden City, N.Y.: Doubleday Anchor, 1956).

Lybyer, Albert H.: *The Government of the Ottoman Empire in the Time of Suleiman the Magnificent* (Cambridge, Mass.: Harvard University Press, 1913).

Lynd, Robert, and Helen Lynd: *Middletown in Transition* (New York: Harcourt, Brace & World, 1937).

Macdermott, Mercia: *A History of Bulgaria* (London: G. Allen, 1962).

Mair, Lucy: *Primitive Government* (Baltimore: Penguin, 1962).

Majumdar, R. C. (ed.): *The History and Culture of the Indian People* (Bombay: Bharatiya Vidya Bhavan, 1951, 1953).

Malinowski, Bronislaw: *A Scientific Theory of Culture* (Chapel Hill, N.C.: University of North Carolina Press, 1944).

————: *Crime and Custom in Savage Society* (New York: Harcourt, Brace & World, 1926).

Malo, David: *Hawaiian Antiquities,* translated by N. B. Emerson, Bernice P. Bishop Museum, Special Publication No. 2, 1951.

Manis, Jerome, and Bernard Meltzer: "Attitudes of Textile Workers to Class Structure," *American Journal of Sociology,* 60 (1954), pp. 30–35.

Manoukian, Madeline: *Akan and Ga-adangme Peoples of the Gold Coast* (London: International African Institute, 1950).

Mariéjol, Jean Hippolyte: *The Spain of Ferdinand and Isabella,* translated and edited by Benjamin Keen (New Brunswick, N.J.: Rutgers University Press, 1961).

Marriott, McKim: "Little Communities in an Indigenous Civilization," in McKim Marriott (ed.), *Village India: Studies in the Little Community* (Chicago: University of Chicago Press, 1955), pp. 171–222.

Marsh, David: *The Changing Social Structure of England and Wales, 1871–1951* (London: Routledge, 1958).

Marsh, Robert: *The Mandarins: The Circulation of Elites in China, 1600–1900* (New York: Free Press, 1961).

Marshall, Lorna: "The Kung Bushmen of the Kalahari Desert," in James L. Gibbs (ed.), *Peoples of Africa* (New York: Holt, 1965), pp. 241–278.

Marshall, T. H.: *Citizenship and Social Class* (London: Cambridge University Press, 1950).

Mason, E. S. (ed.): *The Corporation in Modern Society* (Cambridge, Mass.: Harvard University Press, 1959).

Matthews, Donald: *U.S. Senators and Their World* (Chapel Hill, N.C.: University of North Carolina Press, 1960).

Mattingly, Harold: *Roman Imperial Civilization* (Garden City, N.Y.: Doubleday Anchor, 1959).

Mayer, Kurt: "Recent Changes in the Class Structure of the United States," in *Transactions of the Third World Congress of Sociology* (London: International Sociological Association, 1956), vol. III, pp. 66–80.

McKisack, May: *The Fourteenth Century* (Oxford: Clarendon Press, 1959).

McLean, Hugh, and Walter Vickery: *The Year of Protest, 1956: An Anthology of Soviet Literary Materials* (New York: Vintage Books, 1961).

McManners, J.: "France," in A. Goodwin (ed.), *The European Nobility in the Eighteenth Century* (London: Black, 1953), pp. 22–42.

McNeill, W. H.: *The Rise of the West* (New York: Mentor, 1965).

Mehnert, Klaus: *Soviet Man and His World,* translated by Maurice Rosenbaum (New York: Frederick A. Praeger, 1961).

Menderhausen, Horst: "The Pattern of Estate Tax Wealth," in Raymond Goldsmith, *A Study of Saving in the United States* (Princeton, N.J.: Princeton University Press, 1956), vol. III, pp. 277–381.

Merriman, Roger B.: *The Rise of the Spanish Empire* (New York: Macmillan, 1934).

Métraux, Alfred: *Native Tribes of Eastern Bolivia and Western Matto Grosso,* Smithsonian Institution, Bureau of American Ethnology, Bulletin 134 (1942).

————: "The Guaraní," in Julian Steward (ed.), *Handbook of South American*

Indians, Smithsonian Institution, Bureau of American Ethnology, Bulletin 143 (1948), vol. III, pp. 69–94.

———: "Tribes of the Eastern Slopes of the Bolivian Andes," in Julian Steward (ed.), *Handbook of South American Indians,* Smithsonian Institution, Bureau of American Ethnology, Bulletin 143 (1948), vol. III, pp. 465–506.

Michael, Franz: *The Origin of Manchu Rule in China: Frontier and Bureaucracy as Interacting Forces in the Chinese Empire* (Baltimore: Johns Hopkins, 1942).

Michels, Robert: *Political Parties: A Sociological Study of Oligarchical Tendencies in Modern Democracy,* translated by Eden and Cedar Paul (New York: Dover, 1959, first published 1915).

Middleton, John, and David Tait (eds.): *Tribes without Rulers: Studies in African Segmentary Systems* (London: Routledge, 1958).

Miller, Herman P.: *Income of the American People* (New York: Wiley, 1955).

———: "Annual and Lifetime Income in Relation to Education: 1939–1959," *American Economic Review,* 50 (1960), pp. 962–986.

Miller, S. M.: "Comparative Social Mobility," *Current Sociology,* 9 (1960), No. 1.

Milligan, Maurice: *The Missouri Waltz* (New York: Scribner, 1948).

Millis, Walter: *Arms and Men: A Study of American Military History* (New reau of American Ethnology, Bulletin 143 (1946), vol. III, pp. 465–506.

Mills, C. Wright: *The Power Elite* (Fair Lawn, N.J.: Oxford University Press, 1956).

Mishkin, Bernard: *Rank and Warfare among the Plains Indians,* Monographs of the American Ethnological Society, 3 (1940).

Misra, B. B.: *The Indian Middle Classes* (London: Oxford University Press, 1961).

Moore, Wilbert E.: *Social Change* (Englewood Cliffs, N.J.: Prentice-Hall, 1963).

———: *The Conduct of the Corporation* (New York: Random House, 1962).

Moreland, W. H.: *The Agrarian System of Moslem India* (Allahabad: Central Book Depot, n.d.).

———: "The Revenue System of the Mughul Empire," in *The Cambridge History of India,* vol. 4, pp. 449–475.

Morgan, Lewis Henry: *Ancient Society* (New York: Holt, 1877).

Morley, Sylvanus G.: *The Ancient Maya* (Stanford, Calif.: Stanford University Press, 1946).

Mosca, Gaetano: *The Ruling Class,* translated by Hannah Kahn (New York: McGraw-Hill, 1939).

Mousnier, R.: *La Vénalité des offices sous Henri IV et Louis XIII* (Rouen: Éditions Maugard, 1945).

Municipal Year Book, 1963 (Chicago: International City Managers' Association, 1963).

Murdock, George Peter: *Our Primitive Contemporaries* (New York: Macmillan, 1934).

———: *Social Structure* (New York: Macmillan, 1949).

———: "World Ethnographic Sample," *American Anthropologist,* 59 (1957), pp. 664–687.

————: *Africa: Its Peoples and Their Culture History* (New York: McGraw-Hill, 1959).

Murphy, Robert, and Buell Quain: *The Trumaí Indians of Central Brazil*, Monographs of the American Ethnographical Society, 24 (1955).

Nabholz, Hans: "Medieval Agrarian Society in Transition," in *The Cambridge Economic History*, vol. I, pp. 493–561.

National Opinion Research Center, "Jobs and Occupations: A Popular Evaluation," *Opinion News*, 9 (Sept. 1, 1947), pp. 3–13. Reprinted in Bendix and Lipset, *Class, Status, and Power*, pp. 411–426.

Nelson, George R. (ed.): *Freedom and Welfare: Social Patterns in the Northern Countries of Europe.* (Sponsored by the Ministries of Social Affairs of Denmark, Finland, Iceland, Norway, and Sweden, 1953.)

Neumann, Sigmund: "Germany: Changing Patterns and Lasting Problems," in Sigmund Neumann (ed.), *Modern Political Parties: Approaches to Comparative Politics* (Chicago: University of Chicago Press, 1956), pp. 354–394.

Newcomer, Mabel: *The Big Business Executive* (New York: Columbia University Press, 1955).

"1953 Survey of Consumer Finances: Part IV, Net Worth of Consumers, Early 1953," *U.S. Federal Reserve Bulletin* (September, 1953).

Oberg, K.: "The Kingdom of Ankole in Uganda," in M. Fortes and E. E. Evans-Pritchard (eds.), *African Political Systems* (London: Oxford University Press, 1948), pp. 121–162.

Olmstead, A. T.: *History of the Persian Empire* (Chicago: University of Chicago Press, 1948).

Oppenheim, Felix: "Belgium: Party Cleavage and Compromise," in Sigmund Neumann (ed.), *Modern Political Parties: Approaches to Comparative Politics* (Chicago: University of Chicago Press, 1956), pp. 155–168.

Oppenheimer, Franz: *The State*, translated by John Gitterman (Indianapolis: Bobbs-Merrill, 1914).

Orenstein, Henry: *Gaon: Conflict and Cohesion in an Indian Village* (Princeton, N.J.: Princeton University Press, 1965).

Ossowski, Stanislaw: *Class Structure in the Social Consciousness*, translated by Sheila Patterson (New York: Free Press, 1963).

————: "Old Notions and New Problems: Interpretations of Social Structure in Modern Society," *Transactions of the Third World Congress of Sociology*, 1956, vol. 3, pp. 18–25.

Overacker, Louise: *The Australian Party System* (New Haven, Conn.: Yale University Press, 1952).

Painter, Sidney: *Studies in the History of the English Feudal Barony* (Baltimore: Johns Hopkins, 1943).

————: *The Rise of the Feudal Monarchies* (Ithaca, N.Y.: Cornell University Press, 1951).

Pareto, Vilfredo: *The Mind and Society*, translated by A. Bongiorno and Arthur Livingston and edited by Livingston (New York: Harcourt, Brace & World, 1935).

Parsons, Talcott: "The Distribution of Power in American Society," *World Politics,* 10 (October, 1957).

———: *The Social System* (New York: Free Press, 1951).

Patton, Arch: "Executive Compensation Here and Abroad," *Harvard Business Review,* 40 (September–October, 1962), pp. 144–152.

———: "Executive Compensation in 1960," *Harvard Business Review,* 39 (September–October, 1961), pp. 144–152.

———: "Trends in Executive Compensation," *Harvard Business Review,* 38 September–October, 1960), pp. 144–154.

Perroy, Edouard: "Social Mobility among the French *Noblesse* in the Later Middle Ages," *Past and Present,* 21 (1962), pp. 25–38.

Petersen, William: "The Demographic Transition in the Netherlands," *American Sociological Review,* 25 (1960), pp. 334–347.

Pirenne, Henri: *Economic and Social History of Medieval Europe* (New York: Harvest Books, n.d., originally published in 1933).

Plato: *The Republic,* translated by Benjamin Jowett (New York: Modern Library, n.d.).

Pospisil, Leopold: "Kapauku Papuan Political Structure," in F. Ray (ed.), *Systems of Political Control and Bureaucracy in Human Societies,* Proceedings of the 1958 meetings of the American Ethnological Society, pp. 9–22.

Postan, Michael: "The Trade of Medieval Europe: The North," in *The Cambridge Economic History of Europe* (London: Cambridge University Press, 1952), vol. II (1952), pp. 119–256.

Power, Eileen: *Medieval People* (Garden City, N.Y.: Doubleday Anchor 1954, originally published 1924).

Purcell, Theodore: *Blue Collar Man: Patterns of Dual Allegiance in Industry* (Cambridge, Mass.: Harvard University Press, 1960).

Radcliffe-Brown, A. R.: *The Andaman Islanders* (New York: Free Press, 1948, originally published 1922).

Ramsey, Sir James H.: *A History of the Revenues of the Kings of England: 1066–1399* (Oxford: Clarendon Press, 1925).

Reay, Marie: *The Kuma* (Melbourne: Melbourne University Press, 1959).

Reddig, William: *Tom's Town: Kansas City and the Pendergast Legend* (Philadelphia: Lippincott, 1947).

Reichley, James: *The Art of Government: Reform and Organization Politics in Philadelphia* (New York: Fund for the Republic, 1959).

Reischauer, Robert K.: *Japan: Government-Politics* (New York: Nelson, 1939).

Revised Standard Version Bible (New York: Nelson, 1953).

Ribton-Turner, Charles J.: *A History of Vagrants and Vagrancy and Beggars and Begging* (London: Chapman & Hall, 1887).

Richards, Audrey I.: "The Bemba of Northeastern Rhodesia," in Elizabeth Colson and Max Gluckman (eds.), *Seven Tribes of British Central Africa* (Manchester: Manchester University Press, 1951), pp. 164–193.

———: "The Political System of the Bemba Tribe of North-eastern Rhodesia," in M. Fortes and E. E. Evans-Pritchard (eds.), *African Political Systems* (London: Oxford University Press, 1940), pp. 83–120.

Richmond, Anthony: "The United Kingdom," in Arnold Rose (ed.), *The Institutions of Advanced Societies* (Minneapolis: University of Minnesota Press, 1958), pp. 43–130.

Riesman, David, et al.: *The Lonely Crowd* (New Haven, Conn.: Yale University Press, 1950).

Rigsby, T. H.: "Social Characteristics of the Party Membership," in Alex Inkeles and Kent Geiger (eds.), *Soviet Society* (Boston: Houghton Mifflin, 1961).

Roberts, David R.: *Executive Compensation* (New York: Free Press, 1959).

Rogoff, Natalie: *Recent Trends in Occupational Mobility* (New York: Free Press, 1953).

Roscoe, John: *The Baganda* (London: Macmillan, 1911).

Rosenberg, Hans: *Bureaucracy, Aristocracy and Autocracy: The Prussian Experience 1660–1815* (Cambridge, Mass.: Harvard University Press, 1958).

Ross, J. F. S.: *Elections and Electors: Studies in Democratic Representation* (London: Eyre & Spottiswoode, 1955).

Rostovtzeff, Michael: *The Social and Economic History of the Roman Empire*, rev. ed. (Oxford: Clarendon Press, 1957).

Rowe, John H.: "Inca Culture at the Time of the Spanish Conquest," in Julian Steward (ed.), *Handbook of South American Indians*, Smithsonian Institution, Bureau of American Ethnology, Bulletin 143 (1946), vol. II, pp. 183–330.

Russell, J. C.: *British Medieval Population* (Albuquerque, N. Mex.: University of New Mexico Press, 1948).

————: "Late Ancient and Medieval Population," *Transactions of the American Philosophical Society*, 48 (1958), pp. 37–101.

Rustow, Dankwart A.: "Scandinavia: Working Multiparty System," in Sigmund Neumann (ed.), *Modern Political Parties: Approaches to Comparative Politics* (Chicago: University of Chicago Press, 1956), pp. 169–193.

————: *The Politics of Compromise: A Study of Parties and Cabinet Government in Sweden* (Princeton, N.J.: Princeton University Press, 1955).

Schapera, I.: *Government and Politics in Tribal Societies* (London: Watts, 1956).

————: "The Political Organization of the Ngwato of Bechuanaland Protectorate," in M. Fortes and E. E. Evans-Pritchard (eds.), *African Political Systems* (London: Oxford University Press, 1940), pp. 56–82.

————: *The Tswana* (London: International African Institute, 1953).

Seligmann, C. G.: *The Melanesians of British New Guinea* (London: Cambridge University Press, 1910).

Serrano, Antonio: "The Charrua," in Julian Steward (ed.), *Handbook of South American Indians*, Smithsonian Institution, Bureau of American Ethnology, Bulletin 143 (1946), vol. I, pp. 191–196.

Service, Elman: *Primitive Social Organization: An Evolutionary Perspective* (New York: Random House, 1962).

Shaughnessy, Gerald: *Has the Immigrant Kept the Faith?* (New York: Macmillan, 1925).

Sheddick, V. G. J.: *The Southern Sotho* (London: International African Institute, 1953).

Shell, Kurt: *The Transformation of Austrian Socialism* (New York: University Publishers, 1962).

Sherman, C. Bezalel: *The Jew within American Society* (Detroit: Wayne State Press, 1961).

Simmel, Georg: *The Sociology of Georg Simmel,* edited and translated by Kurt Wolff (New York: Free Press, 1950).

Simmons, Leo: *Sun Chief* (New Haven, Conn.: Yale University Press, 1942).

Simpson, Alan: *The Wealth of the Gentry 1540–1660* (London: Cambridge University Press, 1961).

Singh, Mohinder: *The Depressed Classes: Their Economic and Social Condition* (Bombay: Hind Kitabs, 1947).

Sjoberg, Gideon: *The Preindustrial City* (New York: Free Press, 1960).

Solzhenitsyn, Alexander: *One Day in the Life of Ivan Denisovich,* translated by Max Hayward and Ronald Hingley (New York: Bantam, 1963).

Sondages, Etude des électeurs des différents parties d'après l'enquête sur les attitudes politiques des Français. Institut français d'opinion publique, 1952, No. 3.

Sorokin, Pitirim: *Social and Cultural Dynamics* (New York: Bedminister Press, 1962).

———: *Social Mobility* (New York: Harper & Row, 1927).

———: *Society, Culture and Personality* (New York: Harper & Row, 1947).

Southall, Aiden: *Alur Society: A Study of Processes and Types of Domination* (Cambridge: Heffer, 1956).

Spencer, Baldwin, and F. J. Gillen: *The Arunta: A Study of Stone Age People* (London: Macmillan, 1927).

Spencer, Herbert: *Principles of Sociology* (New York: Appleton-Century-Crofts, 1897).

Stamp, L. Dudley: "Land Utilization and Soil Erosion in Nigeria," *Geographical Review,* 28 (1938), pp. 32–45.

Statistical Abstract of the United States, 1962 (Washington: GPO, 1962).

Steed, Gitel P.: "Notes on an Approach to a Study of Personality Formation in a Hindu Village in Gujarat," in McKim Marriott (ed.), *Village India: Studies in the Little Community* (Chicago: University of Chicago Press, 1955), pp. 102–144.

Stern, Philip: *The Great Treasury Raid* (New York: Random House, 1964).

Steward, Julian: *Basin-Plateau Aboriginal Socio-political Groups,* Smithsonian Institution, Bureau of American Ethnology, Bulletin 120 (1938).

———: "The Economic and Social Basis of Primitive Bands," in *Essays in Anthropology Presented to A. L. Kroeber* (Berkeley, Calif.: University of California Press, 1936), pp. 331–350.

———: "The Tribes of the Montaña and Bolivian East Andes," in Julian Steward (ed.), *Handbook of South American Indians,* Smithsonian Institution, Bureau of American Ethnology, Bulletin 143 (1948), vol. III, pp. 507–533.

———: *Theory of Culture Change* (Urbana, Ill.: University of Illinois Press, 1955).

———: *Handbook of South American Indians,* Smithsonian Institution, Bureau of American Ethnology, Bulletin 143 (1946–1950).

——— and Louis Faron: *Native Peoples of South America* (New York: McGraw-Hill, 1959).

Stirling, M. W.: *Historical and Ethnographical Material on the Jivaro Indians,* Smithsonian Institution, Bureau of American Ethnology, Bulletin 117 (1938).

Stubbs, William: *The Constitutional History of England,* 5th ed. (Oxford: Clarendon Press, 1891).

Sumner, William Graham: *What Social Classes Owe to Each Other* (New York: Harper & Row, 1903).

———: *Folkways* (Boston: Ginn, 1906).

——— and Albert Keller: *The Science of Society* (New Haven, Conn.: Yale University Press, 1927).

Sutherland, Edwin: *White Collar Crime* (New York: Holt, 1949).

Svalastoga, Kaare: *Prestige, Class, and Mobility* (London: Heinemann, 1959).

Swanton, John: *Source Material on the History and Ethnology of the Caddo Indians,* Smithsonian Institution, Bureau of American Ethnology, Bulletin 132 (1942).

Takekoshi, Yosoburo: *The Economic Aspects of the History of the Civilization of Japan* (New York: Macmillan, 1930).

Tawney, R. H.: *The Acquisitive Society* (New York: Harcourt, Brace and World, 1920).

Tegner, Gören: *Social Security in Sweden* (Tiden: Swedish Institute, 1956).

Thompson, James Westfall: *Economic and Social History of the Middle Ages* (New York: Appleton-Century-Crofts, 1928).

Thrupp, Sylvia: "The Guilds," in *The Cambridge Economic History of Europe* (London: Cambridge University Press, 1963), vol. III, pp. 230–280.

———: *The Merchant Class of Medieval London* (Ann Arbor, Mich.: Ann Arbor Paperbacks, 1962).

Thurnwald, Richard: *Economics in Primitive Communities* (Oxford: International Institute of African Languages and Cultures, 1932).

Titmuss, Richard M.: *Income Distribution and Social Change* (Toronto, Canada: University of Toronto Press, 1962).

Trevor-Roper, H. R.: "The Gentry 1540–1640," *The Economic History Review Supplements,* No. 1. (n.d.).

Tumin, Melvin: *Caste in a Peasant Society* (Princeton, N.J.: Princeton University Press, 1952).

Turnbull, Colin: *The Forest People* (New York: Simon and Schuster, 1961).

———: "The Lesson of the Pygmies," *Scientific American,* 208 (January, 1963), pp. 28–37.

———: "The Mbuti Pygmies of the Congo," in James L. Gibbs (ed.), *Peoples of Africa* (New York: Holt, 1965), pp. 279–318.

Turner, Ralph: *The Great Cultural Traditions* (New York: McGraw-Hill, 1941).

Underwood, Kenneth: *Protestant and Catholic: Religious and Social Interaction in an Industrial Community* (Boston: Beacon Press, 1957).

U.S. *Census of Agriculture, 1959: Large-Scale Farming in the U.S.* (Washington: U.S. Bureau of the Census, 1963).

U.S. *Census of Population, 1960: Occupation by Earnings and Education* (Washington: U.S. Bureau of the Census, n.d.).

U.S. *Census of Population, 1960: Occupational Characteristics.* (Washington: U.S. Bureau of the Census, 1962).

van den Berghe, Pierre: "Dialectic and Functionalism: Toward a Theoretical Synthesis," *American Sociological Review*, 28 (1963), pp. 695–705.

van Werveke, H.: "The Rise of Towns," in *The Cambridge Economic History of Europe* (London: Cambridge University Press, 1963), vol. 3, pp. 1–41.

Vatter, Harold: *The U.S. Economy in the 1950's: An Economic History* (New York: Norton, 1963).

Veblen, Thorstein: *The Theory of the Leisure Class* (New York: Modern Library, 1934, first published 1899).

Vernadsky, George: *History of Russia* (New Haven, Conn.: Yale University Press, 1958).

Vidich, Arthur, and Joseph Bensman: *Small Town in Mass Society: Class, Power, and Religion in a Rural Community* (Princeton, N.J.: Princeton University Press, 1958).

Volin, Lazar: "The Collective Farm," in Alex Inkeles and Kent Geiger (eds.), *Soviet Society* (Boston: Houghton Mifflin, 1961), pp. 329–349.

von Hagen, Victor: *The Ancient Sun Kingdoms of the Americas* (Cleveland: World Publishing, 1961).

Warner, W. Lloyd, et al.: *Social Class in America* (Chicago: Science Research, 1949).

———: *The American Federal Executive* (New Haven, Conn.: Yale University Press, 1963).

——— and James C. Abegglen: *Occupational Mobility in American Business and Industry, 1928–1952* (Minneapolis: University of Minnesota Press, 1955).

——— and Paul Lunt: *The Social Life of a Modern Community* (New Haven, Conn.: Yale University Press, 1941).

Weber, Max: *From Max Weber: Essays in Sociology*, translated by H. H. Gerth and C. Wright Mills (Fair Lawn, N.J.: Oxford University Press, 1946).

———: *The City*, translated by Dan Martindale and Gertrude Neuwirth (New York: Free Press, 1958).

———: *The Religion of China*, translated by Hans Gerth (New York: Free Press, 1951).

———: *The Religion of India*, translated by Hans Gerth and Don Martindale (New York: Free Press, 1958).

———: *The Theory of Social and Economic Organization*, translated by A. M. Henderson and Talcott Parsons (New York: Free Press, 1947).

———: *Wirtschaft und Gesellschaft*, 2d ed. (Tübingen: Mohr, 1925).

Weinryb, Bernard: "Jewish Immigration and Accommodation to America," in Marshall Sklare, *The Jews: Social Patterns of an American Group* (New York: Free Press, 1958).

White, Leslie: *The Science of Culture* (New York: Grove Press, 1949).

Wilensky, Harold: "Orderly Careers and Social Participation: The Impact of Work History on Social Integration in the Middle Mass," *American Sociological Review*, 26 (1961), pp. 521–539.

Williams, F. E.: *Papuans of the Trans-Fly* (Oxford: Clarendon Press, 1936).

Williams, Philip: *Politics in Post-war France* (London: Longmans, 1954).

Williams, Robin: *American Society* (New York: Knopf, 1951).

Williamson, Chilton: *American Suffrage: From Property to Democracy, 1760–1860* (Princeton, N.J.: Princeton University Press, 1960).

Winstanley, Gerrard: *Selections from His Works,* edited by Leonard Hamilton (London: Cresset Press, 1944).

Wissler, Clark: "The Influence of the Horse in the Development of Plains Culture," *American Anthropologist,* 16 (1914), pp. 1–25.

Wittfogel, Karl A.: *Oriental Despotism: A Comparative Study of Total Power* (New Haven, Conn.: Yale University Press, 1957).

Wolf, Eric: *Sons of the Shaking Earth* (Chicago: University of Chicago Press, 1959).

Wolfle, Dael: *America's Resources of Specialized Talent* (New York: Harper & Row, 1954).

Woodham-Smith, Cecil: *The Reason Why* (New York: McGraw-Hill, 1953).

World Almanac, 1961 (New York: World-Telegram, 1961).

Woytinsky, W. S., and E. S. Woytinsky: *World Population and Production: Trends and Outlook* (New York: Twentieth Century Fund, 1953).

Wrong, Dennis: "The Oversocialized View of Man," *American Sociological Review,* 26 (1961), pp. 183–193.

Yang, Martin C.: *A Chinese Village: Taitou, Shantung Province* (New York: Columbia University Press, 1945).

Yates, P. Lamartine: *Food, Land, and Manpower in Western Europe* (London: Macmillan, 1960).

Young, Michael: *The Rise of Meritocracy, 1870–2033: The New Elite of Our Social Revolution* (New York: Random House, 1959).

Zaleznik, A., et al.: *The Motivation, Productivity, and Satisfaction of Workers* (Cambridge, Mass.: Harvard University Press, 1958).

Zink, Harold: *City Bosses in the United States: A Study of Twenty Municipal Bosses* (Durham, N.C.: Duke University Press, 1930).

Author Index

Subject Index